EQUITY VALUATION

CFA® Program Curriculum

2025 • LEVEL II • VOLUME 5

WILEY

ISBN 978-1-961409-25-5 (paper)
ISBN 978-1-961409-36-1 (ebook)
August 2024

SKY120ABF36-1AE5-4CCF-92A1-F20D03D413FC_071824

Please visit our website at
www.WileyGlobalFinance.com.

CONTENTS

How to Use the CFA Program Curriculum **ix**
CFA Institute Learning Ecosystem (LES) ix
Designing Your Personal Study Program ix
Errata x
Other Feedback x

Equity Valuation

Learning Module 1 **Equity Valuation: Applications and Processes** **3**
Introduction 4
Value Definitions and Valuation Applications 4
Applications of Equity Valuation 7
Understanding the Business 10
Understanding the Business 10
Analysis of Financial Reports and Sources of Information 13
Sources of Information 15
Considerations in Using Accounting Information 17
Selecting the Appropriate Valuation Method 23
Selecting the Appropriate Valuation Model 23
Issues in Model Selection and Interpretation 27
Issues in Model Selection and Interpretation 29
The Analyst's Role and Responsibilities 30
Applying the Valuation Conclusion: The Analyst's Role and Responsibilities 31
Communicating Valuation Results 33
Contents of a Research Report 33
Format of a Research Report 35
Research Reporting Responsibilities 36
Summary *37*
References *40*
Practice Problems *41*
Solutions *47*

Learning Module 2 **Discounted Dividend Valuation** **49**
Introduction 50
Present Value Models 51
The Dividend Discount Model 58
The Expression for a Single Holding Period 59
The Expression for Multiple Holding Periods 60
The Gordon Growth Model 62
The Gordon Growth Model Equation 62
The Links among Dividend Growth, Earnings Growth, and Value Appreciation in the Gordon Growth Model 69
Share Repurchases and The Implied Dividend Growth Rate 70

The Implied Dividend Growth Rate 71
The Gordon Growth Model: Other Issues 72
Gordon Growth Model and the Price-to-Earnings Ratio 74
Estimating a Required Return Using the Gordon Growth Model 76
The Gordon Growth Model: Concluding Remarks 77
Multistage Dividend Discount Models 77
Two-Stage Dividend Discount Model 78
Valuing a Non-Dividend-Paying Company 82
The H-Model and Three-Stage Dividend Discount Models 83
Three-Stage Dividend Discount Models 85
General Modeling and Estimating a Required Return Using Any DDM 90
Estimating a Required Return Using Any DDM 92
Multistage DDM: Concluding Remarks 93
The Financial Determinants of Growth Rates 94
Sustainable Growth Rate 94
Dividend Growth Rate, Retention Rate, and ROE Analysis 96
Financial Models and Dividends 99
Summary *100*
References *104*
Practice Problems *105*
Solutions *117*

Learning Module 3 **Free Cash Flow Valuation** **125**
Introduction 126
FCFF and FCFE Valuation Approaches 127
Forecasting Free Cash Flow and Computing FCFF from Net Income 131
Computing FCFF from Net Income 131
Computing FCFF from the Cash Flow Statement 135
Additional Considerations in Computing FCFF 137
Classification of Certain Items on the Statement of Cash Flow 137
Adjustments to Derive Operating Cash Flow from Net Income 137
Adjustments to Derive Operating Cash Flow from Net Income That May Merit Additional Attention from an Analyst 138
Computing FCFE from FCFF 141
Finding FCFF and FCFE from EBITA or EBITDA 147
FCFF and FCFE on a Uses-of-Free-Cash-Flow Basis 149
Forecasting FCFF and FCFE 151
Other Issues in Free Cash Flow Analysis 155
Analyst Adjustments to CFO 155
Free Cash Flow versus Dividends and Other Earnings Components 156
Free Cash Flow and Complicated Capital Structures 159
Free Cash Flow Model Variations 161
An International Application of the Single-Stage Model 161
Sensitivity Analysis of FCFF and FCFE Valuations 163
Two-Stage Free Cash Flow Models 164
Fixed Growth Rates in Stage 1 and Stage 2 165
Declining Growth Rate in Stage 1 and Constant Growth in Stage 2 167
Three-Stage Free Cash Flow Models 172

	Integrating ESG in Free Cash Flow Models	174
	Non-operating Assets and Firm Value	177
	Summary	*177*
	References	*182*
	Practice Problems	*183*
	Solutions	*204*
Learning Module 4	**Market-Based Valuation: Price and Enterprise Value Multiples**	**223**
	Introduction	224
	Price and Enterprise Value Multiples in Valuation	225
	Price/Earnings: the Basics	228
	Price/Earnings	228
	Price/Earnings: Valuation based on Forecasted Fundamentals	240
	Justified P/E	240
	Predicted P/E Based on Cross-Sectional Regression	242
	Price/Earnings: Using the P/E in Valuation	243
	Peer-Company Multiples	246
	Industry and Sector Multiples	250
	Overall Market Multiple	250
	Own Historical P/E	253
	P/Es in Cross-Country Comparisons	255
	Using P/Es to Obtain Terminal Value in Multistage Dividend Discount Models	257
	Price/Book Value	259
	Determining Book Value	261
	Valuation Based on Forecasted Fundamentals	267
	Valuation Based on Comparables	268
	Price/Sales	269
	Determining Sales	270
	Valuation Based on Forecasted Fundamentals	271
	Valuation Based on Forecasted Fundamentals	274
	Valuation Based on Comparables	275
	Price/Cash Flow	276
	Determining Cash Flow	279
	Valuation Based on Forecasted Fundamentals	280
	Valuation Based on Comparables	281
	Price/Dividends and Dividend Yield	282
	Calculation of Dividend Yield	282
	Valuation Based on Forecasted Fundamentals	284
	Valuation Based on Comparables	284
	Enterprise Value/EBITDA	285
	Enterprise Value/EBITDA	286
	Other Enterprise Value Multiples	291
	Enterprise Value to Sales	292
	Price and Enterprise Value Multiples in a Comparable Analysis: Some Illustrative Data	293
	International Considerations when Using Multiples	293
	Momentum Valuation Indicators	295

	Valuation Indicators: Issues in Practice	301
	Averaging Multiples: The Harmonic Mean	301
	Using Multiple Valuation Indicators	303
	Summary	*307*
	References	*311*
	Practice Problems	*313*
	Solutions	*328*
Learning Module 5	**Residual Income Valuation**	**339**
	Introduction	340
	Residual Income	340
	The Residual Income Model	345
	The General Residual Income Model	348
	Fundamental Determinants of Residual Income	352
	Single-Stage and Multistage Residual Income Valuation	353
	Multistage Residual Income Valuation	354
	Relationship to Other Approaches	360
	Strengths and Weaknesses of the Residual Income Model	363
	Broad Guidelines for Using a Residual Income Model	363
	Accounting and International Considerations	364
	Violations of the Clean Surplus Relationship	365
	Accounting Considerations: Other	374
	Intangible Assets	374
	Non-recurring Items	377
	Other Aggressive Accounting Practices	377
	International Considerations	378
	Summary	*379*
	References	*382*
	Practice Problems	*383*
	Solutions	*394*
Learning Module 6	**Private Company Valuation**	**407**
	Introduction	407
	Public vs. Private Company Valuation	409
	Private Company Valuation Uses and Areas of Focus	412
	Uses of Private Company Valuation	412
	Private Company Valuation Areas of Focus	414
	Earnings Normalization and Cash Flow Estimation	416
	Earnings Normalization Issues for Private Companies	416
	Cash Flow Estimation Issues for Private Companies	421
	Private Company Discount Rates and Required Rates of Return	424
	Factors Affecting Private Company Discount Rates	425
	Required Rate of Return Models	426
	Valuation Discounts and Premiums	431
	Lack of Control Discounts	433
	Lack of Marketability Discounts	433
	Private Company Valuation Approaches	436
	Income-Based Approaches	437

Excess Earnings Method 440
Market-Based Approaches 442
GPCM 442
Private Company Valuation: Income-Based Approach 448
Private Company Valuation: Market-Based Approach 453
Practice Problems *459*
Solutions *464*

Glossary **G-1**

How to Use the CFA Program Curriculum

The CFA® Program exams measure your mastery of the core knowledge, skills, and abilities required to succeed as an investment professional. These core competencies are the basis for the Candidate Body of Knowledge (CBOK™). The CBOK consists of four components:

- A broad outline that lists the major CFA Program topic areas (www.cfainstitute.org/programs/cfa/curriculum/cbok/cbok)
- Topic area weights that indicate the relative exam weightings of the top-level topic areas (www.cfainstitute.org/en/programs/cfa/curriculum)
- Learning outcome statements (LOS) that advise candidates about the specific knowledge, skills, and abilities they should acquire from curriculum content covering a topic area: LOS are provided at the beginning of each block of related content and the specific lesson that covers them. We encourage you to review the information about the LOS on our website (www.cfainstitute.org/programs/cfa/curriculum/study-sessions), including the descriptions of LOS "command words" on the candidate resources page at www.cfainstitute.org/-/media/documents/support/programs/cfa-and-cipm-los-command-words.ashx.
- The CFA Program curriculum that candidates receive access to upon exam registration

Therefore, the key to your success on the CFA exams is studying and understanding the CBOK. You can learn more about the CBOK on our website: www.cfainstitute.org/programs/cfa/curriculum/cbok.

The curriculum, including the practice questions, is the basis for all exam questions. The curriculum is selected or developed specifically to provide candidates with the knowledge, skills, and abilities reflected in the CBOK.

CFA INSTITUTE LEARNING ECOSYSTEM (LES)

Your exam registration fee includes access to the CFA Institute Learning Ecosystem (LES). This digital learning platform provides access, even offline, to all the curriculum content and practice questions. The LES is organized as a series of learning modules consisting of short online lessons and associated practice questions. This tool is your source for all study materials, including practice questions and mock exams. The LES is the primary method by which CFA Institute delivers your curriculum experience. Here, candidates will find additional practice questions to test their knowledge. Some questions in the LES provide a unique interactive experience.

DESIGNING YOUR PERSONAL STUDY PROGRAM

An orderly, systematic approach to exam preparation is critical. You should dedicate a consistent block of time every week to reading and studying. Review the LOS both before and after you study curriculum content to ensure you can demonstrate the knowledge, skills, and abilities described by the LOS and the assigned reading. Use the LOS as a self-check to track your progress and highlight areas of weakness for later review.

Successful candidates report an average of more than 300 hours preparing for each exam. Your preparation time will vary based on your prior education and experience, and you will likely spend more time on some topics than on others.

ERRATA

The curriculum development process is rigorous and involves multiple rounds of reviews by content experts. Despite our efforts to produce a curriculum that is free of errors, in some instances, we must make corrections. Curriculum errata are periodically updated and posted by exam level and test date on the Curriculum Errata webpage (www.cfainstitute.org/en/programs/submit-errata). If you believe you have found an error in the curriculum, you can submit your concerns through our curriculum errata reporting process found at the bottom of the Curriculum Errata webpage.

OTHER FEEDBACK

Please send any comments or suggestions to info@cfainstitute.org, and we will review your feedback thoughtfully.

Equity Valuation

LEARNING MODULE

1

Equity Valuation: Applications and Processes

by Jerald E. Pinto, PhD, CFA, Elaine Henry, PhD, CFA, Thomas R. Robinson, PhD, CFA, CAIA, and John D. Stowe, PhD, CFA.

Jerald E. Pinto, PhD, CFA, is at CFA Institute (USA). Elaine Henry, PhD, CFA, is at Stevens Institute of Technology (USA). Thomas R. Robinson, PhD, CFA, CAIA, is at Robinson Global Investment Management LLC, (USA). John D. Stowe, PhD, CFA, is at Ohio University (USA).

LEARNING OUTCOMES

Mastery	*The candidate should be able to:*
☐	define valuation and intrinsic value and explain sources of perceived mispricing
☐	explain the going concern assumption and contrast a going concern value to a liquidation value
☐	describe definitions of value and justify which definition of value is most relevant to public company valuation
☐	describe applications of equity valuation
☐	describe questions that should be addressed in conducting an industry and competitive analysis
☐	contrast absolute and relative valuation models and describe examples of each type of model
☐	describe sum-of-the-parts valuation and conglomerate discounts
☐	explain broad criteria for choosing an appropriate approach for valuing a given company

1 INTRODUCTION

- ☐ define valuation and intrinsic value and explain sources of perceived mispricing
- ☐ explain the going concern assumption and contrast a going concern value to a liquidation value
- ☐ describe definitions of value and justify which definition of value is most relevant to public company valuation

Every day, thousands of participants in the investment profession—investors, portfolio managers, regulators, researchers—face a common and often perplexing question: What is the value of a particular asset? The answers to this question usually influence success or failure in achieving investment objectives. For one group of those participants—equity analysts—the question and its potential answers are particularly critical because determining the value of an ownership stake is at the heart of their professional activities and decisions. **Valuation** is the estimation of an asset's value based on variables perceived to be related to future investment returns, on comparisons with similar assets, or, when relevant, on estimates of immediate liquidation proceeds. Skill in valuation is a very important element of success in investing.

We address some basic questions: What is value? Who uses equity valuations? What is the importance of industry knowledge? How can the analyst effectively communicate his analysis? We answer these and other questions and lay a foundation for the topics that follow.

The following section defines value and describes the various uses of equity valuation. The subsequent sections examine the steps in the valuation process, including the analyst's role and responsibilities, and discuss how valuation results are communicated. They also provide some guidance on the content and format of an effective research report.

Value Definitions and Valuation Applications

Before summarizing the various applications of equity valuation tools, it is helpful to define what is meant by "value" and to understand that the meaning can vary in different contexts. The context of a valuation, including its objective, generally determines the appropriate definition of value and thus affects the analyst's selection of a valuation approach.

What Is Value?

Several perspectives on value serve as the foundation for the variety of valuation models available to the equity analyst. Intrinsic value is the necessary starting point, but other concepts of value—going-concern value, liquidation value, and fair value—are also important.

Intrinsic Value

A critical assumption in equity valuation, as applied to publicly traded securities, is that the market *price* of a security can differ from its intrinsic *value*. The **intrinsic value** of any asset is the value of the asset given a hypothetically complete understanding of the asset's investment characteristics. For any particular investor, an estimate of intrinsic value reflects his or her view of the "true" or "real" value of an asset. If one assumed that the market price of an equity security perfectly reflected its intrinsic value, "valuation" would simply require looking at the market price. Roughly, it is just such an assumption that underpins traditional efficient market theory, which suggests that an asset's market price is the best available estimate of its intrinsic value.

An important theoretical counter to the notion that market price and intrinsic value are identical can be found in the Grossman–Stiglitz paradox. If market prices, which are essentially freely obtainable, perfectly reflect a security's intrinsic value, then a rational investor would not incur the costs of obtaining and analyzing information to obtain a second estimate of the security's value. If no investor obtains and analyzes information about a security, however, then how can the market price reflect the security's intrinsic value? The **rational efficient markets formulation** (Grossman and Stiglitz 1980) recognizes that investors will not rationally incur the expenses of gathering information unless they expect to be rewarded by higher gross returns compared with the free alternative of accepting the market price. Furthermore, modern theorists recognize that when intrinsic value is difficult to determine, as is the case for common stock, and when trading costs exist, even further room exists for price to diverge from value (Lee, Myers, and Swaminathan 1999).

Thus, analysts often view market prices both with respect and with skepticism. They seek to identify mispricing, and at the same time, they often rely on price eventually converging to intrinsic value. They also recognize distinctions among the levels of **market efficiency** in different markets or tiers of markets (for example, stocks heavily followed by analysts and stocks neglected by analysts). Overall, equity valuation, when applied to market-traded securities, admits the possibility of mispricing. Throughout the discussion, then, we distinguish between the market price, P, and the intrinsic value ("value" for short), V.

For an active investment manager, valuation is an inherent part of the attempt to produce investment returns that exceed the returns commensurate with the investment's risk—that is, positive excess risk-adjusted returns. An excess risk-adjusted return is also called an **abnormal return** or **alpha**. (Return concepts will be more fully discussed later.) The active investment manager hopes to capture a positive alpha as a result of his or her efforts to estimate intrinsic value. Any departure of market price from the manager's estimate of intrinsic value is a perceived **mispricing** (i.e., a difference between the estimated intrinsic value and the market price of an asset).

These ideas can be illuminated through the following expression that identifies two possible sources of perceived mispricing:

$$V_E - P = (V - P) + (V_E - V),$$

where

V_E = estimated value

P = market price

V = intrinsic value

[Note: One can derive the above expression as $V_E - P = V_E - P + V - V = (V - P) + (V_E - V)$.]

This expression states that the difference between a valuation estimate and the prevailing market price is, by definition, equal to the sum of two components. The first component is the true mispricing—that is, the difference between the true but unobservable intrinsic value V and the observed market price P (this difference contributes to the abnormal return). The second component is the difference between the valuation estimate and the true but unobservable intrinsic value—that is, the error in the estimate of the intrinsic value.

To obtain a useful estimate of intrinsic value, an analyst must combine accurate forecasts with an appropriate valuation model. The quality of the analyst's forecasts, in particular the expectational inputs used in valuation models, is a key element in determining investment success. For active security selection to be consistently successful, the manager's expectations must differ from consensus expectations and be, on average, correct as well.

Uncertainty is constantly present in equity valuation. Confidence in one's expectations is always realistically partial. In applying any valuation approach, analysts can never be sure that they have accounted for all the sources of risk reflected in an asset's price. Because competing equity risk models will always exist, there is no obvious final resolution to this dilemma. Even if an analyst makes adequate risk adjustments, develops accurate forecasts, and employs appropriate valuation models, success is not assured. Temporal market conditions may prevent the investor from capturing the benefits of any perceived mispricing. Convergence of the market price to perceived intrinsic value may not happen within the investor's investment horizon, if at all. So, besides evidence of mispricing, some active investors look for the presence of a particular market or corporate event (**catalyst**) that will cause the marketplace to re-evaluate a company's prospects.

Going-Concern Value and Liquidation Value

A company generally has one value if it is to be immediately dissolved and another value if it will continue in operation. In estimating value, a **going-concern assumption** is the assumption that the company will continue its business activities into the foreseeable future. In other words, the company will continue to produce and sell its goods and services, use its assets in a value-maximizing way for a relevant economic time frame, and access its optimal sources of financing. The **going-concern value** of a company is its value under a going-concern assumption. Models of going-concern value are our focus.

Nevertheless, a going-concern assumption may not be appropriate for a company in financial distress. An alternative to a company's going-concern value is its value if it were dissolved and its assets sold individually, known as its **liquidation value**. For many companies, the value added by assets working together and by human capital applied to managing those assets makes estimated going-concern value greater than liquidation value (although, a persistently unprofitable business may be worth more "dead" than "alive"). Beyond the value added by assets working together or by applying managerial skill to those assets, the value of a company's assets would likely differ depending on the time frame available for liquidating them. For example, the value of nonperishable inventory that had to be immediately liquidated would typically be lower than the value of inventory that could be sold during a longer period of time (i.e., in an "orderly" fashion). Thus, such concepts as **orderly liquidation value** are sometimes distinguished.

Fair Market Value and Investment Value

For an analyst valuing public equities, intrinsic value is typically the relevant concept of value. In other contexts, however, other definitions of value are relevant. For example, a buy–sell agreement among the owners of a private business—specifying how and when the owners (e.g., shareholders or partners) can sell their ownership interest and at what price—might be primarily concerned with equitable treatment of both sellers and buyers. In that context, the relevant definition of value would likely be fair market value. **Fair market value** is the price at which an asset (or liability) would change hands between a willing buyer and a willing seller when the former is not under any compulsion to buy and the latter is not under any compulsion to sell. Furthermore, the concept of fair market value generally includes an assumption that both buyer and seller are informed of all material aspects of the underlying investment. Fair market value has often been used in valuation related to assessing taxes. In a financial reporting context—for example, in valuing an asset for the purpose of impairment testing—financial reporting standards reference **fair value**, a related (but not identical) concept and provide a specific definition: "Fair value is the amount for which an asset could be exchanged, a liability settled, or an equity instrument granted could be exchanged between knowledgeable, willing parties in an arm's length transaction."

Assuming the marketplace has confidence that the company's management is acting in the owners' best interests, market prices should tend, in the long run, to reflect fair market value. In some situations, however, an asset is worth more to a particular buyer (e.g., because of potential operating synergies). The concept of value to a specific buyer taking account of potential synergies and based on the investor's requirements and expectations is called **investment value**.

Definitions of Value: Summary

Analysts valuing an asset need to be aware of the definition or definitions of value relevant to the assignment. For the valuation of public equities, an intrinsic value definition of values is generally relevant. Intrinsic value, estimated under a going-concern assumption, is the focus of these equity valuation sections.

APPLICATIONS OF EQUITY VALUATION 2

☐ describe applications of equity valuation

Investment analysts work in a wide variety of organizations and positions. As a result, they apply the tools of equity valuation to address a range of practical problems. In particular, analysts use valuation concepts and models to accomplish the following:

- *Selecting stocks.* Stock selection is the primary use of the tools presented here. Equity analysts continually address the same question for every common stock that is either a current or prospective portfolio holding or for every stock that he or she is responsible for covering: Is this security fairly priced, overpriced, or underpriced relative to its current estimated intrinsic value and relative to the prices of comparable securities?
- *Inferring (extracting) market expectations.* Market prices reflect the expectations of investors about the future performance of companies. Analysts may ask: What expectations about a company's future performance are consistent with the current market price for that company's stock? What assumptions about the company's fundamentals would justify the current price? (**Fundamentals** are characteristics of a company related to profitability, financial strength, or risk.) These questions may be relevant to the analyst for several reasons:

  - The analyst can evaluate the reasonableness of the expectations implied by the market price by comparing the market's implied expectations to his own expectations.
  - The market's expectations for a fundamental characteristic of one company may be useful as a benchmark or comparison value of the same characteristic for another company.

  To extract or reverse-engineer a market expectation, the analyst selects a valuation model that relates value to expectations about fundamentals and is appropriate given the characteristics of the stock. Next, the analyst estimates values for all fundamentals in the model except the fundamental of interest. The analyst then solves for that value of the fundamental of interest that results in a model value equal to the current market price.

- *Evaluating corporate events.* Investment bankers, corporate analysts, and investment analysts use valuation tools to assess the impact of such corporate events as mergers, acquisitions, divestitures, spin-offs, and going-private transactions. Each of these events affects a company's future cash flows and thus the value of its equity. Furthermore, in mergers and acquisitions, the acquiring company's own common stock is often used as currency for the purchase. Investors then want to know whether the stock is fairly valued.
- *Rendering fairness opinions.* The parties to a merger may be required to seek a fairness opinion on the terms of the merger from a third party, such as an investment bank. Valuation is central to such opinions.
- *Evaluating business strategies and models.* Companies concerned with maximizing shareholder value evaluate the effect of alternative strategies on share value.
- *Communicating with analysts and shareholders.* Valuation concepts facilitate communication and discussion among company management, shareholders, and analysts on a range of corporate issues affecting company value.
- *Appraising private businesses.* Valuation of the equity of private businesses is important for transactional purposes (e.g., acquisitions of such companies or buy–sell agreements for the transfer of equity interests among owners when one of them dies or retires) and tax-reporting purposes (e.g., for the taxation of estates), among others. The absence of a market price imparts distinctive characteristics to such valuations, although the fundamental models are shared with public equity valuation. An analyst encounters these characteristics when evaluating initial public offerings, for example.
- *Share-based payment (compensation).* Share-based payments (e.g., restricted stock grants) are sometimes part of executive compensation. Estimation of their value frequently depends on using equity valuation tools.

INFERRING MARKET EXPECTATIONS

On 2 January 2019, Apple Inc. (AAPL) lowered its revenue guidance citing a variety of reasons, one of which was the weakening economies in some of its Asian markets. Apple's share price fell approximately 10%. When Biogen Inc. announced on 21 March 2019 that its experimental drug for Alzheimer's had failed in late-stage clinical trials, the company's share price dropped approximately 30%. What contributes to such large single-day price movements—changes in estimates of underlying intrinsic value, or market overreaction to negative news?

A rich stream of academic research probes overall market overreaction and underreaction based on large samples—for example, De Bondt and Thaler (1985), Abarbanell and Bernard (1992), and more recently, Bordalo et al. (2017) and Bouchaud et al. 2018). However, one classic research study addresses the topic with a case study of a single such dramatic price drop. This case study, shown in Exhibit 1, is useful for studying equity valuation.

Exhibit 1:

Cornell's (2001) case study focuses on the 21 September 2000 press release by Intel Corporation containing information about its expected revenue growth for the third quarter of 2000. The announced growth fell short of the company's prior prediction by 2 to 4 percentage points and short of analysts' projections by 3 to 7 percentage points. In response to the announcement, Intel's stock price fell nearly 30% during the following five days—from $61.50 just prior to the press release to only $43.31 five days later.

To assess whether the information in Intel's announcement was sufficient to explain such a large loss of value, Cornell (2001) estimated the value of a company's equity as the present value of expected future cash flows from operations minus the expenditures needed to maintain the company's growth. (We will discuss such *free cash flow models* in detail at a later stage.)

Using a conservatively low discount rate, Cornell estimated that Intel's price before the announcement, $61.50, was consistent with a forecasted growth rate of 20% a year for the subsequent 10 years and then 6% per year thereafter. Intel's price after the announcement, $43.31, was consistent with a decline of the 10-year growth rate to well under 15% per year. In the final year of the forecast horizon (2009), projected revenues with the lower growth rate would be $50 billion below the projected revenues based on the pre-announcement price. Because the press release did not obviously point to any changes in Intel's fundamental long-run business conditions (Intel attributed the quarterly revenue growth shortfall to a cyclical slowing of demand in Europe), Cornell's detailed analysis left him skeptical that the stock market's reaction could be explained in terms of fundamentals.

Assuming Cornell's methodology was sound, one interpretation is that investors' reaction to the press release was irrational. An alternative interpretation is that Intel's stock was overvalued prior to the press release and that the press release was "a kind of catalyst that caused movement toward a more rational price, even though the release itself did not contain sufficient long-run valuation information to justify that movement" (Cornell 2001, p. 134).

EXAMPLE 1

Knowledge Check

1. Referring to Exhibit 1 on Cornell's study of the Intel stock price reaction, explain how an analyst could evaluate the two possible interpretations.

Solution:

To evaluate whether the market reaction to Intel's announcement was an irrational reaction or a rational reduction of a previously overvalued price, one could compare the expected 20% growth implicit in the pre-announcement stock price to some benchmark—for example, the company's actual recent revenue growth, the industry's recent growth, and/or forecasts for the growth of the industry or the economy. Finding the growth rate implied in the company's stock price is an example of using a valuation model and a company's actual stock price to infer market expectations.

Note: Cornell (2001) observed that the 20% revenue growth rate implied by the pre-announcement stock price was much higher than Intel's average growth rate during the previous five years, which occurred when the company was much smaller. He concluded that Intel's stock was overvalued prior to the press release.

These examples illustrate the role of expectations in equity valuation and typical situations in which a given set of facts may be given various interpretations. These examples also illustrate that differences between market price and intrinsic value can occur suddenly, offering opportunities for astute investment managers to generate alpha.

3 UNDERSTANDING THE BUSINESS

☐ describe questions that should be addressed in conducting an industry and competitive analysis

In general, the valuation process involves the following five steps:

1. *Understanding the business.* Industry and competitive analysis, together with an analysis of financial statements and other company disclosures, provides a basis for forecasting company performance.
2. *Forecasting company performance.* Forecasts of sales, earnings, dividends, and financial position (pro forma analysis) provide the inputs for most valuation models.
3. *Selecting the appropriate valuation model.* Depending on the characteristics of the company and the context of valuation, some valuation models may be more appropriate than others.
4. *Converting forecasts to a valuation.* Beyond mechanically obtaining the "output" of valuation models, estimating value involves judgment.
5. *Applying the valuation conclusions.* Depending on the purpose, an analyst may use the valuation conclusions to make an investment recommendation about a particular stock, provide an opinion about the price of a transaction, or evaluate the economic merits of a potential strategic investment.

Most of these steps are addressed in detail later. Here, we provide an overview of each.

Understanding the Business

To forecast a company's financial performance as a basis for determining the value of an investment in the company or its securities, it is helpful to understand the economic and industry contexts in which the company operates, the company's strategy, and the company's previous financial performance. Industry and competitive analysis, together with an analysis of the company's financial reports, provides a basis for forecasting performance.

Industry and Competitive Analysis

Because similar economic and technological factors typically affect all companies in an industry, industry knowledge helps analysts understand the basic characteristics of the markets served by a company and the economics of the company. An airline industry analyst will know that labor costs and jet fuel costs are the two largest expenses of airlines and that in many markets airlines have difficulty passing through higher fuel prices by raising ticket prices. Using this knowledge, the analyst may inquire about the degree to which different airlines hedge the commodity price risk inherent in jet fuel costs. With such information in hand, the analyst is better able to evaluate risk and forecast future cash flows. In addition, the analyst would run sensitivity analyses to determine how different levels of fuel prices would affect valuation.

Various frameworks exist for industry and competitive analysis. The primary usefulness of such frameworks is that they can help ensure that an analysis gives appropriate attention to the most important economic drivers of a business. In other words, the objective is *not* to prepare some formal framework representing industry structure or corporate strategy, but rather to use a framework to organize thoughts about an industry and to better understand a company's prospects for success in competition with other companies in that industry. Further, although frameworks can provide a template, obviously the informational content added by an analyst makes the framework relevant to valuation. Ultimately, an industry and competitive analysis should highlight which aspects of a company's business present the greatest challenges and opportunities and should thus be the subject of further investigation and/or more extensive **sensitivity analysis** (an analysis to determine how changes in an assumed input would affect the outcome of an analysis). Frameworks may be useful as analysts focus on questions relevant to understanding a business.

- *How attractive are the industries in which the company operates in terms of offering prospects for sustained profitability?*

Inherent industry profitability is one important factor in determining a company's profitability. Analysts should try to understand **industry structure**—the industry's underlying economic and technical characteristics—and the trends affecting that structure. Basic economic factors—supply and demand—provide a fundamental framework for understanding an industry. Porter's (1985, 1998, 2008) five forces that characterize industry structure—explained in detail at a later stage and summarized in Exhibit 2— can help analysts assess industry profitability and prospects for companies.

Exhibit 2: Summary of Porter's Forces

Force	Features
Rivalry (intra-industry)	Lower rivalry, few competitors and/or good brand identification
Threat of new entrants	High costs to enter (& other barriers)
Threat of substitutes	Few substitutes exist, or cost to switch is high
Bargaining power of suppliers	Many suppliers exist
Bargaining power of buyers	Many customers for an industry' s product exist

Analysts must also stay current on facts and news concerning all the industries in which the company operates, including recent developments (e.g., management, technological, or financial). Particularly important to valuation are any factors likely to affect the industry's longer term profitability and growth prospects, such as demographic trends.

- *What is the company's relative competitive position within its industry, and what is its competitive strategy?*

The level and trend of the company's market share indicate its relative competitive position within an industry. In general, a company's value is higher to the extent that it can create and sustain an advantage relative to its competition. Porter identifies several generic corporate strategies for achieving above-average performance:

i. Cost leadership—being the lowest cost producer while offering products comparable to those of other companies so that products can be priced at or near the industry average
ii. Differentiation—offering unique products or services along some dimensions that are widely valued by buyers so that the company can command premium prices
iii. Focus—seeking a competitive advantage within a target segment or segments of the industry based on either cost leadership (cost focus) or differentiation (differentiation focus)

The term "business model" refers generally to how a company makes money: which customers it targets, what products or services it will sell to those customers, and how it delivers those products or services (including how it finances its activities). The term is broadly used and sometimes encompasses aspects of the generic strategies just described. For example, an airline with a generic cost leadership strategy might have a business model characterized as a low-cost carrier. Low-cost carriers offer a single class of service and use a single type of aircraft to minimize training costs and maintenance charges.

- *How well has the company executed its strategy, and what are its prospects for future execution?*

Competitive success requires both appropriate strategic choices and competent execution. Analyzing the company's financial reports provides a basis for evaluating a company's performance against its strategic objectives and for developing expectations about a company's likely future performance. A historical analysis means more than just reviewing, say, the 10-year historical record in the most recent annual report. It often means looking at the annual reports from 10 years prior, 5 years prior, and the most recent 2 years. Why? Because looking at annual reports from prior years often provides useful insights into how management has historically foreseen challenges and has adapted to changes in business conditions through time. (In general, the investor relations sections of most publicly traded companies' websites provide electronic copies of their annual reports from at least the most recent years.)

In examining financial and operational strategic execution, two caveats merit mention. First, the importance of qualitative—that is, non-numeric factors—must be considered. Such non-numeric factors include the company's ownership structure, its intellectual and physical property, the terms of its intangible assets (e.g., licenses and franchise agreements), and the potential consequences of legal disputes or other contingent liabilities. Second, it is important to avoid simply extrapolating past operating results when forecasting future performance. In general, economic and technological forces can contribute to the phenomenon of "regression toward the mean." Specifically, successful companies tend to draw more competitors into their industries and find that their ability to generate above-average profits comes under pressure. Conversely, poorly performing companies are often restructured in such a manner as to improve their long-term profitability. Thus, in many cases, analysts making long-term horizon growth forecasts for a company's earnings and profits (e.g., forecasts beyond the next 10 years) plausibly assume company convergence toward the forecasted average growth rate for the underlying economy.

ANALYSIS OF FINANCIAL REPORTS AND SOURCES OF INFORMATION

4

The aspects of a financial report that are most relevant for evaluating a company's success in implementing strategic choices vary across companies and industries. For established companies, financial ratio analysis is useful. Individual drivers of profitability for merchandising and manufacturing companies can be evaluated against the company's stated strategic objectives. For example, a manufacturing company aiming to create a sustainable competitive advantage by building strong brand recognition could be expected to have substantial expenditures for advertising but relatively higher prices for its goods. Compared with a company aiming to compete on cost, the branded company would be expected to have higher gross margins but also higher selling expenses as a percentage of sales.

EXAMPLE 2

Competitive Analysis

The following companies are among the largest publicly-traded providers of oilfield services, based on revenues in the most recent fiscal year:

- Schlumberger Ltd. (executive offices in Paris, Houston, London, and the Hague)
  - Revenue: $32.8 billion
  - Net income: $2.2 billion
- Halliburton (executive offices in Houston)
  - Revenue: $24.0 billion
  - Net income: $1.7 billion
- Baker Hughes, a GE Company (executive offices in Houston)
  - Revenue: $22.9 billion
  - Net income: $0.3 billion
- Saipem S.p.A. (executive offices in Milan)
  - Revenue (2017): €9.0 billion
  - Net income (loss) (2017): –€0.3 billion
- National Oilwell Varco Inc. (executive offices in Houston)
  - Revenue: $8.5 billion
  - Net income (loss): –$0.02 billion
- Weatherford International plc (executive offices in Baar, Switzerland)
  - Revenue: $5.7 billion
  - Net income (loss): –$2.8 billion

Note: Financial data are for fiscal 2018, except where noted.

Sources: Companies' 10-K, 20-F, or Investor Relations websites.

These companies provide tools and services—often of a very technical nature—to expedite the drilling activities of oil and gas producers and drilling companies.

1. Discuss the economic factors that may affect demand for the services provided by oilfield services companies, and explain a logical framework for analyzing and forecasting revenue for these companies.

Solution:

Because the products and services of these companies relate to oil and gas exploration and production, the levels of exploration and production activities by oil and gas producers are probably the major factors that determine the demand for their services. In turn, the prices of natural gas and crude oil are important in determining the level of exploration and production activities. Therefore, among other economic factors, an analyst should research those relating to supply and demand for natural gas and crude oil.

- Supply factors in natural gas, such as natural gas inventory levels.
- Demand factors in natural gas, including household and commercial use of natural gas and the amount of new power generation equipment being fired by natural gas.
- Supply factors in crude oil, including capacity constraints and production levels in OPEC and other oil-producing countries, as well as new discoveries of off-shore and land-based oil reserves.
- Demand factors in crude oil, such as household and commercial use of oil and the amount of new power generation equipment using oil products as its primary fuel.
- For both crude oil and natural gas, projected economic growth rates could be examined as a demand factor and depletion rates as a supply-side factor.

Note: Energy analysts should be familiar with sources for researching supply and demand information, such as the International Energy Agency (IEA), the European Petroleum Industry Association (EUROPIA), the Energy Information Administration (EIA), the American Gas Association (AGA), and the American Petroleum Institute (API).

2. Explain how comparing the level and trend in profit margin (net income/sales) and revenue per employee for the companies shown may help in evaluating whether one of these companies is the cost leader in the peer group.

Solution:

Profit margin reflects cost structure. In interpreting profit margin, however, analysts should evaluate any differences in companies' abilities to affect profit margin through power over price. A successfully executed cost leadership strategy will lower costs and raise profit margins. All else equal, we would also expect a cost leader to have relatively high sales per employee, reflecting efficient use of human resources.

With newer companies, or companies involved in creating new products or markets, nonfinancial measures may be critical to obtaining an accurate picture of corporate prospects. For example, a biotechnology company's clinical trial results or an internet company's unique visitors per day may provide information helpful for evaluating future revenue.

Sources of Information

Important perspectives on industry and competition are sometimes provided by companies themselves in regulator-mandated disclosures, regulatory filings, company press releases, investor relations materials, and contacts with analysts. Analysts can compare the information provided directly by companies to their own independent research.

Regulatory requirements concerning disclosures and filings vary internationally. In some markets, such as Canada and the United States, regulations require management to provide industry and competitive information and access to those filings is freely available (e.g., www.sedar.com for Canadian filings, www.sec.gov for US filings, and individual companies' Investor Relations websites). To take the case of the United States, in annual filings with the Securities and Exchange Commission made on Form 10-K for US companies and Form 20-F for non-US companies, companies provide industry and competitive information in the business description section and in the management discussion and analysis (MD&A). Interim filings (e.g., the quarterly SEC Form 10-Q for US companies and Form 6-K for non-US companies) provide interim financial statements but typically less-detailed coverage of industry and competition. In other jurisdictions, listed companies' financial disclosures can be found on individual companies' Investor Relations websites or centrally at government websites (e.g. Companies House in the UK at https://www.gov.uk/government/organisations/companies-house), stock exchange websites (e.g. Shenzhen Stock Exchange disclosures at http://www.szse.cn), or central banks' websites (e.g., National Bank of Belgium at https://www.nbb.be/en/central-balance-sheet-office). Required disclosures concerning industry and competitive information differ across jurisdictions.

So far as analyst–management contacts are concerned, analysts must be aware when regulations (e.g., Regulation FD in the United States) prohibit companies from disclosing material nonpublic information to analysts without also disseminating that information to the public. General management insights based on public information, however, can still be useful to analysts, and many analysts consider in-person meetings with a company's management essential to understanding a company.

The CFA Institute Code of Ethics and Standards of Professional Conduct prohibit use of material inside information, and Regulation FD (and similar regulations in other countries) is designed to prohibit companies from selectively offering such information. These ethical and legal requirements assist analysts by clarifying their main role and purpose.

Company-provided sources of information in addition to regulatory filings include press releases and investor relations materials. The press releases of most relevance to analysts are the press releases that companies issue to announce their periodic earnings. Companies typically issue these earnings press releases several weeks after the end of an accounting period and several weeks before they file their interim financial statements. Earnings press releases summarize the company's performance for the period and usually include explanations for the performance and financial statements (often abbreviated versions). Following their earnings press releases, many companies host conference calls in which they further elaborate on their reported performance and typically allocate some time to answer questions posed by analysts. On their corporate websites, many companies post audio downloads and transcripts of conference calls and presentations made in analyst conferences. The audio files and transcripts of conference calls and conference presentations provide access not only to the company's reports but also to analysts' questions and the company's answers to those questions.

Apart from company-provided sources of information, analysts also obtain information from third-party sources, such as industry organizations, regulatory agencies, and commercial providers of market intelligence.

SOURCES OF ESG INFORMATION: THE CASE OF THE US AUTO INDUSTRY

The evaluation of environmental, social, and governance (ESG) factors can help analysts identify potential business risks and practices that may produce long-term competitive advantages relative to peers. In the following example, we discuss the sources of ESG-related information that an analyst following US-domiciled automakers might consider.

The automotive industry is among the most resource-intensive manufacturing industries in the world. New vehicles are subject to multiple governmental standards concerning safety, fuel efficiency and emissions control, vehicle recycling, and theft prevention, among others. Manufacturing and assembly facilities must conform to strict standards for air emissions, water discharge, and hazardous waste management.

Because an auto company's manufacturing process and vehicles can significantly affect the environment, the industry is heavily regulated. The global nature of the automotive industry requires careful consideration of different regulatory environments within countries and regions. Regulatory bodies in the United States, such as the Environmental Protection Agency, as well as non-US regulatory bodies, such as the European Commission, the European Environment Agency, and the UK-based Environment Agency, help develop and track environmental standards and legislation.

The potential for serious injuries from manufacturing increases the importance of automobile worker safety. In addition, labor relations are also very important for US automakers because of the sizable representation of employees in labor unions. Avoiding costly lawsuits, lost production from work stoppages, and negative publicity are primary concerns for automakers.

Information relevant to analyzing ESG considerations for US automakers can be found in many sources that are common to most industries. These sources include corporate filings, press releases, investor calls and webcasts, and trade publications. Sustainability reports (often called corporate sustainability reports, or CSRs) are also relevant to analysts when examining ESG considerations. These reports address the economic, environmental, and social effects resulting from an organization's everyday activities and the organization's values and governance (see https://www.globalreporting.org/information/sustainability-reporting/Pages/default.aspx). Although there is no uniform standard for their issuance or disclosure by companies, sustainability reports can provide analysts with a better understanding of a company's sustainable business practices and whether a company's resource management supports an economically sustainable business model.

For more specific ESG-related information, analysts following US automakers may consult labor union boycott lists and disclosures from the Occupational Safety and Health Administration (OSHA) and the US Equal Employment Opportunity Commission (EEOC). As the federal agency responsible for overseeing working conditions for most private sector employers in the United States, OSHA can help analysts identify auto manufacturers that have demonstrated a history of safety violations or an improvement in workplace safety. The EEOC's litigation database helps in the investigation of any notable workplace discrimination issues that have affected individual automakers.

Several not-for-profit organizations can be valuable ESG resources to analysts of US automakers (or other industries, for that matter). The Sustainable Accounting Standards Board (SASB) sets industry-specific ESG standards and can help analysts identify ESG considerations that have a quantitative impact on companies' financial performance. The Carbon Disclosure Project collects and synthesizes self-reported environmental data that can provide for important information regarding automakers' exposure to climate change and water scarcity. Finally, Ceres, an organization committed to driving sustainability research and advocacy, can provide analysts with access to sustainability research reports for the auto industry.

CONSIDERATIONS IN USING ACCOUNTING INFORMATION

5

In evaluating a company's historical performance and developing forecasts of future performance, analysts typically rely heavily on companies' accounting information and financial disclosures. Companies' reported results vary in their persistence (i.e., sustainability). In addition, the information that companies disclose can vary substantially with respect to the *accuracy* of reported accounting results as reflections of economic performance and the *detail* in which results are disclosed.

The term **quality of earnings analysis** broadly includes the scrutiny of *all* financial statements, including the balance sheet, to evaluate both the sustainability of a company's performance and how accurately the reported information reflects economic reality. Equity analysts will generally develop better insights into a company and improve forecast accuracy by developing an ability to assess a company's quality of earnings. With regard to sustainability of performance, an analyst aims to identify aspects of reported performance that are less likely to recur. For example, earnings with significant components of nonrecurring events—such as positive litigation settlements, nonpermanent tax reductions, or gains on sales of nonoperating assets—are considered to be of lower quality than earnings derived mainly from the company's core business operations.

In addition to identifying nonrecurring events, an analyst aims to identify reporting decisions that may result in a level of reported earnings that is unlikely to continue. A good starting point for this type of quality of earnings analysis is a comparison of a company's net income with its operating cash flow. As a simple hypothetical example, consider a company that generates revenues and net income but no operating cash flow because it makes all sales on account and never collects its receivables. One systematic way to make the comparison is to decompose net income into a cash component (combining operating and investing cash flows) and an accrual component (defined as net income minus the cash component). Capital markets research shows that the cash component is more persistent than the accrual component of earnings, with the result that a company with a relatively higher amount of current accruals will have a relatively lower ROA in the future (Sloan 1996). Here, greater persistency means that compared to accruals in the current period, the cash component in the current period is more predictive of future net income. A relatively higher proportion of accruals can be interpreted as lower earnings quality.

A quality of earnings analysis for a particular company requires careful scrutiny of accounting statements, footnotes, and other relevant disclosures. Sources for studying quality of earnings analysis and accounting risk factors include Mulford and Comiskey (2005) and Schilit and Perler (2010). Examples of a few of the many available indicators of possible problems with a company's quality of earnings are provided in Exhibit 3.

Exhibit 3: Selected Quality of Earnings Indicators

Category	Observation	Potential Interpretation
Revenues and gains	Recognizing revenue early, for example: ▪ bill-and-hold sales, and ▪ recording sales of equipment or software prior to installation and acceptance by customer.	Acceleration in the recognition of revenue boosts reported income, masking a decline in operating performance.
	Classification of nonoperating income or gains as part of operations.	Income or gains may be nonrecurring and may not relate to true operating performance, possibly masking declines in operating performance.
Expenses and losses	Recognizing too much or too little reserves in the current year, such as: ▪ restructuring reserves, ▪ loan-loss or bad-debt reserves, and ▪ valuation allowances against deferred tax assets.	May boost current income at the expense of future income, or alternatively, may decrease current year's earnings to boost future years' performance.
	Deferral of expenses by capitalizing expenditures as an asset, for example: ▪ customer acquisition costs and ▪ product development costs.	May boost current income at the expense of future income. May mask problems with underlying business performance.
	Use of aggressive estimates and assumptions, such as: ▪ asset impairments, ▪ long depreciable lives, ▪ long periods of amortization, ▪ high assumed discount rate for pension liabilities, ▪ low assumed rate of compensation growth for pension liabilities, and ▪ high expected return on assets for pension.	Aggressive estimates may indicate actions taken to boost current reported income. Changes in assumptions may indicate an attempt to mask problems with underlying performance in the current period.
Balance sheet issues (may also affect earnings)	Use of off-balance sheet financing (financing that does not appear on the balance sheet), such as securitizing receivables.	Assets and/or liabilities may not be properly reflected on the balance sheet.
Operating cash flow	Characterization of an increase in a bank overdraft as operating cash flow.	Operating cash flow may be artificially inflated.

The following example illustrates the importance of accounting practices in influencing reported financial results and the need for analysts to exercise judgment when using those results in any valuation model.

EXAMPLE 3

Historical Example

Quality of Earnings Warning Signs: Aggressive Estimates

In the section of his 2007 letter to the shareholders of Berkshire Hathaway titled "Fanciful Figures—How Public Companies Juice Earnings," Warren Buffett referred to the investment return assumption (the anticipated return on a defined benefit pension plan's current and future assets):

"Decades of option-accounting nonsense have now been put to rest, but other accounting choices remain—important among these [is] the investment-return assumption a company uses in calculating pension expense. It will come as no surprise that many companies continue to choose an assumption that allows them to report less-than-solid 'earnings.' For the 363 companies in the S&P that have pension plans, this assumption in 2006 averaged 8%."

(www.berkshirehathaway.com/letters/2007ltr.pdf. See pp.18–19.)

In his explanation, Buffett assumes a 5% return on cash and bonds, which averaged 28% of US pension fund assets. Therefore, this implies that the remaining 72% of pension fund assets—predominately invested in equities—must earn a return of 9.2%, after all fees, to achieve the 8% overall return on the pension fund assets. To illustrate one perspective on an average pension fund achieving that 9.2% return, he estimates that the Dow Jones Industrial Index would need to close at about 2,000,000 on 31 December 2099 (compared to a level under 13,000 at the time of his writing) for this century's returns on that US stock index to match just the 5.3% average annual compound return achieved in the 20th century.

1. How do aggressively optimistic estimates for returns on pension assets affect pension expense?

Solution:

The amount of "expected return on plan assets" associated with the return assumption is a deduction in calculating pension expense. An aggressively optimistic estimate for the rate of return that pension assets will earn means a larger-than-warranted deduction in calculating pension expense, and subtraction will lead to understating pension expense and overstating net income. In fact, pension expense could become pension income depending on the numbers involved.

2. Where can information about a company's assumed returns on its pension assets be found?

Solution:

Information about a company's assumed return on its pension assets can be found in the footnotes to the company's financial statements.

The next examples of poor earnings quality, in which management made choices going beyond making an aggressive estimate, are reminiscent of a humorous vignette from Benjamin Graham (1936) in which the chair of a company outlines plans for return to profitability, as follows: "Contrary to expectations, no changes will be made in the company's manufacturing or selling policies. Instead, the bookkeeping system is to be entirely revamped. By adopting and further improving a number of modern accounting and financial devices, the corporation's earning power will be amazingly transformed."

EXAMPLE 4

Quality of Earnings Warning Signs: Extreme Cases

CASE A.

In 2018, the Securities and Exchange Commission (SEC) charged Tangoe Inc., a formerly publicly-traded telecommunications expense management company, with fraudulent accounting practices that had allowed the company to improperly recognize revenues. Among the violations cited by the SEC were improperly recording revenue from customers who were unlikely to pay and understating the allowance for bad debts (*Sources:* US Securities and Exchange Commission press release 2018-175, issued 4 September 2018, and the related SEC complaint.)

1. Describe the financial statement impact of the accounting violations cited by the SEC.

Solution:

On the income statement, improperly recognizing revenue from customers unlikely to pay would inflate reported revenue and—all else equal—reported earnings. On the balance sheet, the improper practices would result in inflated receivables. On the statement of cash flows, if the amount of revenues included in net income exceeds the amount of cash collected from customers—all else equal—net income will exceed operating cash flow. (In actuality, this was not the case with Tangoe, where the company had other adjustments.)

2. How would a company's Accounts Receivable turnover (or days receivable) serve as an early warning sign of the revenue accounting violations cited by the SEC?

Solution:

Improperly recognizing revenue from customers who are unlikely to pay and understating the allowance for bad debts—all else equal—would result in a lower Accounts Receivable turnover (and higher days receivable).

Note: Analysis of Tangoe's last years of publicly-reported data actually shows the following (all $ in thousands):

- Revenues increased 12% from 2013 to 2014 (from $188,914 to $212,476), while average receivables increased by 32% (from $40,701 to $50,110).
- Accounts receivable turnover decreased from 4.6x (= $188,914/$40,701) to 4.2x (= $212,476/$50,110).
- Days receivable increased from 79 days (= 365/4.6) to 87 days (= 365/4.2)

The SEC also charged the company with other revenue recognition violations, including improperly recording a loan from a business partner as revenue, counting contingency-fee receipts as revenue, and recording customers' prepayments for future services as current revenue. Violations like these would result in understating such liabilities as loans payable and unearned revenue. The company, which paid penalties to settle the SEC's charges, was delisted from the NASDAQ stock exchange in 2017 and then was subsequently purchased by a private investment firm.

CASE B.

3. Livent, Inc., was a publicly traded theatrical production company that staged a number of smash hits, such as Tony-award winning productions of Showboat and Fosse. Livent capitalized preproduction costs, including expenses for pre-opening advertising, publicity and promotion, set construction, props, costumes, and salaries and fees paid to the cast, crew, and musicians during rehearsals. The company then amortized these capitalized costs over the expected life of the theatrical production based on anticipated revenues.

   State the effect of Livent's accounting for preproduction costs on its reported earnings per share.

Solution:

Livent's accounting for preproduction costs immediately increased reported earnings per share because it deferred expenses.

4. State the effect of Livent's accounting for preproduction costs on its balance sheet.

Solution:

Instead of immediately expensing costs, Livent reported the amounts on its balance sheet as an asset. The warning signal—the deferral of expenses—can indicate aggressive accounting; preproduction costs should have been expensed immediately because of the tremendous uncertainty about revenues from theatrical productions. There was no assurance that there would be revenues against which expenses could be matched.

5. If an analyst calculated EBITDA/interest expense and debt/EBITDA based on Livent's accounting for preproduction costs without adjustment, how might the analyst be misled in assessing Livent's financial strength? (Recall that EBITDA is defined as earnings before interest, taxes, depreciation, and amortization. Such ratios as EBITDA/interest expense and debt/EBITDA indicate one aspect of a company's financial strength: debt-paying ability.)

Solution:

Livent did not deduct preproduction costs from earnings as expenses. If the amortization of capitalized preproduction costs were then added back to earnings, the EBITDA/interest and debt/EBITDA would not reflect in any way the cash outflows associated with such items as paying pre-opening salaries; but cash outflows reduce funds available to meet debt obligations. The analyst who mechanically added back amortization of preproduction costs to calculate EBITDA would be misled into overestimating Livent's financial strength. Based on a closer look at the company's accounting, the analyst would properly not add back amortization of preproduction expenses in computing EBITDA. If preproduction expenses are not added back, a very different picture of Livent's financial health would emerge.

Note: In 1996, Livent's reported debt/EBITDA was 1.7, but the ratio without adding back amortization for preproduction costs was 5.5. In 1997, debt/EBITDA was 3.7 based on a positive EBITDA of $58.3 million; however, EBITDA without the add-back was *negative* $52.6 million. In November 1998, Livent declared bankruptcy and is now defunct. The criminal trial, in Canada, concluded in 2009 with the conviction of Livent's co-founders on charges of fraud and forgery.

In general, growth in an asset account (such as accounts receivable in the Tangoe example and deferred costs in the Livent example) at a much faster rate than the growth rate of sales may indicate aggressive accounting.

Far more serious than aggressive accounting is the deliberate misstatement of financial reports (i.e., fraudulent financial reporting). In general, publicly-traded companies' annual financial statements are audited by certified, professional auditors. The official standards used by auditors can provide useful insights to analysts about a variety of risk factors that may signal possible future negative surprises. For example, both international auditing standards issued by the IAASB and US auditing standards issued by the PCAOB include examples of fraud risk indicators (IAASB 2018, PCAOB 2017). Fraud risk indicators are typically categorized as relating to incentives to commit fraud, opportunity to commit fraud, or attitude toward committing fraud. A working selection of risk factors for misreporting or misappropriation include the following:

- Excessive pressure on company personnel to make revenue or earnings targets, particularly when combined with a dominant, aggressive management team or individual.
- Management and/or directors' compensation tied to profitability or stock price (through ownership or compensation plans). Although such arrangements are usually desirable, they can be a risk factor for aggressive financial reporting.
- Economic, industry, or company-specific pressures on profitability, such as loss of market share or declining margins.
- Management pressure to meet debt covenants or earnings expectations, including "a practice by management of committing to analysts, creditors, and other third parties to achieve aggressive or unrealistic forecasts" (PCAOB, 2017).
- Existence of related-party transactions.
- Complex organizational structure, creating difficulty in determining who controls the company.
- High turnover—of management, directors, or legal counsel.
- Reported (through regulatory filings) disputes with and/or changes in auditors.
- A history of securities law violations, reporting violations, or persistent late filings.

SELECTING THE APPROPRIATE VALUATION METHOD

6

☐ contrast absolute and relative valuation models and describe examples of each type of model

The second step in the valuation process—forecasting company performance—can be viewed from two perspectives: the economic environment in which the company operates and the company's own operating and financial characteristics.

Companies do business within larger contexts of particular industries, national economies, and world trade. Viewing a company within those larger contexts, a top-down forecasting approach moves from international and national macroeconomic forecasts to industry forecasts and then to individual company and asset forecasts. For example, a revenue forecast for a major home appliance manufacturer could start with industry unit sales forecasts that are, in turn, based on GDP forecasts. Forecasted company unit sales would equal forecasted industry unit sales multiplied by the appliance manufacturer's forecasted market share. A revenue projection would be based on forecasted company unit sales and sales prices.

Alternatively, a bottom-up forecasting approach aggregates forecasts at a micro level to larger scale forecasts, under specific assumptions. For example, a clothing retailer may have several stores in operation with two new stores about to open. Using information based on the sales per square meter of the existing stores (perhaps during their initial period of operation), the analyst could forecast sales per square meter of the new stores that, added to forecasts of a similar type for existing stores, would give a sales forecast for the company as a whole. In making such a bottom-up sales forecast, the analyst would be making assumptions about selling prices and merchandise costs. Forecasts for individual retailers could be aggregated into forecasts for the group, continuing in a bottom-up fashion.

In general, analysts integrate insights from industry and competitive analysis with financial statement analysis to formulate specific forecasts of such items as a company's sales, earnings, and cash flow. Analysts generally consider qualitative as well as quantitative factors in financial forecasting and valuation. For example, an analyst might modify his or her forecasts and valuation judgments based on qualitative factors, such as the analyst's opinion about the business acumen and integrity of management and/or the transparency and quality of a company's accounting practices. Such qualitative factors are necessarily subjective.

Selecting the Appropriate Valuation Model

This section discusses the third step in the valuation process—selecting the appropriate model for the valuation task at hand. Detailed descriptions of the valuation models are presented later. Absolute valuation models and relative valuation models are the two broad types of valuation models that incorporate a going-concern assumption. Here, we describe absolute and relative valuation models in general terms and discuss a number of issues in model selection. In practice, analysts frequently use more than one approach to estimate the value of a company or its common stock (Pinto, Robinson, and Stowe 2019).

Absolute Valuation Models

An **absolute valuation model** is a model that specifies an asset's intrinsic value. Such models are used to produce an estimate of value that can be compared with the asset's market price. The most important type of absolute equity valuation models are present value models. In finance theory, present value models are considered the fundamental approach to equity valuation. The logic of such models is that the value of an asset to an investor must be related to the returns that investor expects to receive from holding that asset. Generally speaking, those returns can be referred to as the asset's cash flows, and present value models are also referred to as discounted cash flow models.

A **present value model** or **discounted cash flow model** applied to equity valuation derives the value of common stock as the present or discounted value of its expected future cash flows (such models are known as income models of valuation in private business appraisal). For common stock, one familiar type of cash flow is dividends, which are discretionary distributions to shareholders authorized by a corporation's board of directors. Dividends represent cash flows at the shareholder level in the sense that they are paid directly to shareholders. Present value models based on dividends are called **dividend discount models**. Rather than defining cash flows as dividends, analysts frequently define cash flows at the company level. Common shareholders in principle have an equity ownership claim on the balance of the cash flows generated by a company after payments have been made to claimants senior to common equity, such as bondholders and preferred stockholders (and the government as well, which takes taxes), whether such flows are distributed in the form of dividends.

The two main company-level definitions of cash flow in current use are free cash flow and residual income. Free cash flow is based on cash flow from operations but takes into account the reinvestment in fixed assets and working capital necessary for a going concern. The **free cash flow to equity model** defines cash flow net of payments to providers of debt, whereas the **free cash flow to the firm model** defines cash flows before those payments. We will define free cash flow and each model with more precision later. A residual income model is based on accrual accounting earnings in excess of the opportunity cost of generating those earnings.

Because the present value approach is the familiar technique for valuing bonds (here, the term "bonds" refers to all debt securities and loans), it is helpful to contrast the application of present value models to equity valuation with present value models as applied to bond valuation. The application of present value models to common stock typically involves greater uncertainty than is the case with bonds. That uncertainty centers on two critical inputs for present value models—the cash flows and the discount rate(s). Bond valuation discounts a stream of cash payments specified in a legal contract (the **bond indenture**). In contrast, in equity valuation an analyst must define the specific cash flow stream to be valued—dividends or free cash flow—and then forecast the amounts of those cash flows. Unlike bond valuation, no cash flow stream is contractually owed to common stockholders. Clearly, a company's total cash flows—and therefore the cash flows potentially available to common stockholders—will be affected by business, financial, technological, and other factors and are subject to greater variation than the contractual cash flow of a bond. Furthermore, the forecasts for common stock cash flows extend indefinitely into the future because common stock has no maturity date. In addition to the greater uncertainty involved in forecasting cash flows for equity valuation, significant uncertainty exists in estimating an appropriate rate at which to discount those cash flows. In contrast with bond valuation, in which a discount rate can usually be based on market interest rates and bond ratings, equity valuation typically involves a more subjective and uncertain assessment of the appropriate discount rate. Finally, in addition to the uncertainty associated with cash flows and discount rates, the equity analyst may need to address other issues, such as the value of corporate control or the value of unused assets.

The present value approach applied to stock valuation, therefore, presents a high order of complexity. Present value models are ambitious in what they attempt—an estimate of intrinsic value—and offer many challenges in application. Graham and Dodd (1934) suggested that the analyst consider stating a range of intrinsic values, and that suggestion remains valid. To that end, **sensitivity analysis** is an essential tool in applying discounted cash flow valuation. We discuss sensitivity analysis in more detail next.

Another type of absolute valuation is **asset-based valuation**, which values a company on the basis of the market value of the assets or resources it controls. For appropriate companies asset-based valuation can provide an independent estimate of value, and an analyst typically finds alternative, independent estimates of value to be useful. Exhibit 4 describes instances in which this approach to absolute valuation could be appropriate.

Exhibit 4: Asset-Based Valuation

Analysts often apply asset-based valuation to natural resource companies. For example, a crude oil producer, such as Petrobras, might be valued on the basis of the market value of its current proven reserves in barrels of oil, minus a discount for estimated extraction costs. A forest industry company, such as Weyerhaeuser, might be valued on the basis of the board meters (or board feet) of timber it controls. Today, however, fewer companies than in the past are involved only in natural resources extraction or production. For example, Occidental Petroleum features petroleum in its name but also has substantial chemical manufacturing operations. For such cases, the total company might be valued as the sum of its divisions, with the natural resource division valued on the basis of its proven resources.

Relative Valuation Models

Relative valuation models constitute the second broad type of going-concern valuation models. A **relative valuation model** estimates an asset's value relative to that of another asset. The idea underlying relative valuation is that similar assets should sell at similar prices. Relative valuation is typically implemented using price multiples (ratios of stock price to a fundamental, such as cash flow per share) or enterprise multiples (ratios of the total value of common stock and debt net of cash and short-term investments to certain of a company's operating assets to a fundamental, such as operating earnings).

Perhaps the most familiar price multiple is the price-to-earnings ratio (P/E), which is the ratio of a stock's market price to the company's earnings per share. A stock selling at a P/E that is low relative to the P/E of another closely comparable stock (in terms of anticipated earnings growth rates and risk, for example) is *relatively undervalued* (a good buy) relative to the comparison stock. For brevity, an analyst might state simply *undervalued*, but the analyst must realize that if the comparison stock is overvalued (in an absolute sense, in relation to intrinsic value), so might be the stock being called undervalued. Therefore, it is useful to maintain the distinction between *undervalued* and *relatively undervalued*. Investing to exploit perceived mispricing in either case (absolute or relative mispricing) relies on a basis of differential expectations—that is, investor expectations that differ from and are more accurate than those reflected in market prices, as discussed earlier.

The more conservative investing strategies based on relative valuation involve overweighting (underweighting) relatively undervalued (overvalued) assets, with reference to benchmark weights. The more aggressive strategies allow short selling of perceived overvalued assets. Such aggressive approaches are known as relative value investing (or relative spread investing, if using implied discount factors). A classic example is **pairs trading** that utilizes pairs of closely related stocks (e.g., two automotive stocks), buying the relatively undervalued stock and selling short the relatively overvalued stock. Regardless of which direction the overall stock market goes, the investor will be better off to the extent that the relatively undervalued stock ultimately rises more (falls less) than the relatively overvalued stock.

Frequently, relative valuation involves a group of comparison assets, such as an industry group, rather than a single comparison asset. The application of relative valuation to equity is often called the method of comparables (or just comparables) and is the subject of a later reading.

EXAMPLE 5

Relative Valuation Models

1. While researching Smithson Genomics, Inc., a (fictitious) healthcare information services company, you encounter a difference of opinions. One analyst's report claims that Smithson is at least 15% *overvalued*, based on a comparison of its P/E with the median P/E of peer companies in the healthcare information services industry and taking account of company and peer group fundamentals. A second analyst asserts that Smithson is *undervalued* by 10%, based on a comparison of Smithson's P/E with the median P/E of the Russell 3000 Index, a broad-based US equity index. Both analyses appear to be carefully executed and reported. Can both analysts be right?

Solution:

Yes. The assertions of both analysts concern *relative* valuations, and their benchmarks for comparisons differ. The first analyst compared Smithson to its peers in the healthcare information services industry and considers the company to be *relatively overvalued* compared to that group. The second analyst compared Smithson to the overall market as represented by the Russell 3000 and considers the company to be *relatively undervalued* compared to that group. If the entire healthcare information services industry is undervalued in relation to the Russell 3000, both analysts can be right because they are making relative valuations.

The investment implications of each analyst's valuation generally would depend on additional considerations, including whether the market price of the Russell 3000 fairly represents that index's intrinsic value and whether the market liquidity of an otherwise attractive investment would accommodate the intended position size. The analyst in many cases may want to supplement relative valuation with estimates of intrinsic value.

The method of comparables is characterized by a wide range of possible implementation choices; a later reading discusses various alternative price and enterprise multiples. Practitioners will often examine a number of price and enterprise multiples for the complementary information they can provide. In summary, the method of comparables does not specify intrinsic value without making the further assumption that the comparison asset is fairly valued. The method of comparables has the advantages of being simple, related to market prices, and grounded in a sound economic principle (that similar assets should sell at similar prices). Price and enterprise multiples are widely recognized by investors, so analysts can communicate the results of an absolute valuation in terms of a price or enterprise multiple.

ISSUES IN MODEL SELECTION AND INTERPRETATION 7

- ☐ describe sum-of-the-parts valuation and conglomerate discounts
- ☐ explain broad criteria for choosing an appropriate approach for valuing a given company

A variation to valuing a company as a single entity is to estimate its value as the sum of the estimated values of its various businesses considered as independent, going-concern entities. A valuation that sums the estimated values of each of the company's businesses as if each business were an independent going concern is known as a **sum-of-the-parts valuation**. (The value derived using a sum-of-the-parts valuation is sometimes called the **breakup value** or **private market value**.)

Sum-of-the-parts analysis is most useful when valuing a company with segments in different industries that have different valuation characteristics. Sum-of-the-parts analysis is also frequently used to evaluate the value that might be unlocked in a restructuring through a spin-off, split-off, tracking stock, or equity (IPO) carve-out.

Example 6 shows a case in which a sum-of-the-parts valuation could be used to gain insight into a company's future prospects. In practice, a detailed breakdown of each business segment's contribution to earnings, cash flow, and value would be needed.

EXAMPLE 6

Sum-of-the-Parts Valuation

Donaldson Company, Inc., is one of the largest and most successful filtration manufacturers in the world. Consistent with FASB guidance related to segment reporting, the company has identified two reportable segments: Engine Products and Industrial Products. Segment selection was based on the internal organizational structure, management of operations, and performance evaluation by management and the company's board of directors. 2018 10-K data (in millions of US dollars) for the segments appear in the following table.

Descriptions of the segments from the company's 2018 10-K are as follows:

The Engine Products segment sells to original equipment manufacturers (OEMs) in the construction, mining, agriculture, aerospace, defense, and truck markets and to independent distributors, OEM dealer networks, private label accounts, and large equipment fleets. Products include replacement filters for both air and liquid filtration applications, air filtration systems, liquid filtration systems for fuel, lube and hydraulic applications, and exhaust and emissions systems.

The Industrial Products segment sells to various industrial end-users, OEMs of gas-fired turbines, and OEMs and end-users requiring clean air. Products include dust, fume, and mist collectors; compressed air purification systems; gas and liquid filtration for food; beverage and industrial processes; air filtration systems for gas turbines; and specialized air and gas filtration systems for such applications as membrane-based products as well as specialized air and gas filtration systems for such applications as hard disk drives and semi-conductor manufacturing.

	Engine Products	Industrial Products	Total Company*
Fiscal 2018			
Net sales	$1,849.0	$885.2	$2,734.2
Earnings (loss) before income taxes	261.3	137.1	363.6
Assets	1,110.3	631.9	1,976.6
Capital expenditures	64.6	31.4	97.5
Fiscal 2017			
Net sales	$1,553.3	$818.6	$2,371.9
Earnings (loss) before income taxes	219.7	129.1	322.0
Assets	849.6	638.3	1,979.7
Capital expenditures	29.7	23.4	65.9
Fiscal 2016			
Net sales	$1,391.3	$829.0	$2,220.3
Earnings (loss) before income taxes	163.5	119.0	257.4
Assets	841.4	646.9	1,787.0
Capital expenditures	37.5	27.3	72.9

* *Total company results differ from the sum of the two divisions by allocated corporate and unallocated amounts.*

1. Why might an analyst use a sum-of-the-parts approach to value Donaldson?

Solution:

On the one hand, the Engine Products segment is already significantly larger than the Industrial Products segment and is growing at a much faster rate in terms of sales, income, assets, and capital expenditures. On the other hand, profit margins appear to be higher for Industrial Products. In 2018, the EBIT-to-sales ratio was 15.5% for the Industrial Products segment versus 14.1% for the Engine Products segment.

An investor presentation by Donaldson's management in May 2013 indicated that they expected Industrial Products to become 48% of the company's product portfolio by 2021. However, the recent results noted show that the Engine Products segment has become a larger and larger part of Donaldson's total business despite its lower margins. Whether or not the company will ultimately be successful in changing their product mix is fundamental to an analyst forming an opinion on Donaldson's share price.

2. How might an analyst use the provided information in an analysis and valuation?

Solution:

An analyst might use the information from Example 6 to develop separate valuations for each of the segments based on forecasts for each segment's sales and profitability. The value of the company in total would be the sum of the value of each of the segments, adjusted for corporate items—such as taxes, overhead expenses, and assets/liabilities not directly attributable to the separate operating systems.

The concept of a conglomerate discount often arises in connection with situations warranting a sum-of-the parts valuation. **Conglomerate discount** refers to the concept that the market applies a discount to the stock of a company operating in multiple, unrelated businesses compared to the stock of companies with narrower focuses. Alternative explanations for the conglomerate discount include 1) inefficiency of internal capital markets (i.e., companies' allocation of investment capital among divisions does not maximize overall shareholder value); 2) endogenous factors (i.e., poorly performing companies tend to expand by making acquisitions in unrelated businesses); and 3) research measurement errors (i.e., conglomerate discounts do not actually exist, and evidence suggesting that they do is a result of flawed measurement). Examples in which conglomerate discounts appear most observable occur when companies divest parts of the company that have limited synergies with their core businesses.

Note that a break-up value in excess of a company's unadjusted going-concern value may prompt strategic actions, such as a divestiture or spin-off.

Issues in Model Selection and Interpretation

How does one select a valuation model? The broad criteria for model selection are that the valuation model be:

- consistent with the characteristics of the company being valued;
- appropriate given the availability and quality of data; and
- consistent with the purpose of valuation, including the analyst's perspective.

Note that using more than one model can yield incremental insights.

Selection of a model consistent with the characteristics of the company being valued is facilitated by having a good understanding of the business, which is the first step in the valuation process. Part of understanding a company is understanding the nature of its assets and how it uses those assets to create value. For example, a bank is composed largely of marketable or potentially marketable assets and securities. Thus, for a bank, a relative valuation based on assets (as recognized in accounting) has more relevance than a similar exercise for a service company with few marketable assets.

In selecting a model, data availability and quality can be limiting factors. For example, a dividend discount model is the simplest discounted cash flow model; but if a company has never paid dividends and no other information exists to assess a company's future dividend policy, an analyst may have more confidence applying an apparently more complex present value model. Similar considerations also apply in selecting a specific relative valuation approach. For example, meaningful comparisons using P/Es may be hard to make for a company with highly volatile or persistently negative earnings.

Model selection can also be influenced by the purpose of the valuation or the perspective of the analyst. For example, an investor seeking a controlling equity position in a company may elect to value the company based on forecasted free cash flows rather than forecasted dividends because such flows might potentially be redirected by such an acquirer without affecting the value of the acquisition (this valuation approach will be discussed in detail in another reading). When an analyst reads valuations and research reports prepared by others, the analyst should consider how the writer's perspective (and potential biases) may have affected the choice of a particular valuation approach and/or valuation inputs. Specific guidance on model selection will be offered later when discussing present value models and price multiples.

As a final note to this introduction of model selection, it is important to emphasize that professionals frequently use multiple valuation models or factors in common stock selection. According to the *Merrill Lynch Institutional Factor Survey* (2018), respondent institutional investors report using an average of approximately 17 valuation factors in selecting stocks. (*Note:* In this report, the term "factor" covers market-based metrics, such as price multiples, as well as accounting-based metrics, such as return on equity.) There are a variety of ways in which multiple factors can be used in stock selection. One prominent way, stock screens, will be discussed in a later reading. As another example, analysts can rank each security in a given investment universe by relative attractiveness according to a particular valuation factor. The rankings for individual securities could be combined into a single composite ranking by assigning weights to the individual factors. Analysts may use a quantitative model to assign those weights.

8 THE ANALYST'S ROLE AND RESPONSIBILITIES

Converting forecasts to valuation involves more than inputting the forecast amounts to a model to obtain an estimate of the value of a company or its securities. Two important aspects of converting forecasts to valuation are sensitivity analysis and situational adjustments.

Sensitivity analysis is an analysis to determine how changes in an assumed input would affect the outcome. Some sensitivity analyses are common to most valuations. For example, a sensitivity analysis can be used to assess how a change in assumptions about a company's future growth—for example, decomposed by sales growth forecasts and margin forecasts—and/or a change in discount rates would affect the estimated value. Other sensitivity analyses depend on the context. For example, assume an analyst is aware that a competitor to the target company plans to introduce a competing product. Given uncertainty about the target company's competitive response—whether it will lower prices to retain market share, offer discounts to its distributors, increase advertising, or change a product feature—the analyst could create a baseline forecast and then analyze how different competitive responses would affect the forecasted financials and, in turn, the estimated valuation.

Situational adjustments may be required to incorporate the valuation impact of specific issues. Three such issues that could affect value estimates are control premiums, lack of marketability discounts, and illiquidity discounts. A controlling ownership position in a company (e.g., more than 50% of outstanding shares, although a far smaller percentage often affords an investor the ability to significantly influence a company) carries with it control of the board of directors and the valuable options of redeploying the company's assets or changing the company's capital structure. The value of a stock investment that would give an investor a controlling position will generally reflect a **control premium**; that is, it will be higher than a valuation produced by a generic quantitative valuation expression that did not explicitly model such a premium. A second issue generally not explicitly modeled is that investors require an extra return to compensate for lack of a public market or lack of marketability. The value of non-publicly traded stocks generally reflects a **lack of marketability discount**. Among publicly traded (i.e., marketable) stocks, the prices of shares with less depth to their markets (less liquidity) often reflect an **illiquidity discount**. An illiquidity discount would also apply if an investor wishes to sell an amount of stock that is large relative to that stock's trading volume (assuming it is not large enough to constitute a controlling ownership). The price that could be realized for that block of shares would generally be lower than the market price for a smaller amount of stock, a so-called **blockage factor**.

Applying the Valuation Conclusion: The Analyst's Role and Responsibilities

As noted earlier, the purposes of valuation and the intended consumer of the valuation vary:

- Analysts associated with investment firms' brokerage operations are perhaps the most visible group of analysts offering valuation judgments. Their research reports are widely distributed to current and prospective retail and institutional brokerage clients. The term brokerage typically means the business of acting as agents for buyers and sellers. Analysts who work at brokerage firms are known as **sell-side analysts** because brokerage firms sell investments and services to such institutions as investment management firms.
- In investment management firms, trusts and bank trust departments, and similar institutions, an analyst may report valuation judgments to a portfolio manager or to an investment committee as input to an investment decision. Such analysts are widely known as **buy-side analysts**. The analyst's valuation expertise is important not only in investment disciplines involving security selection based on detailed company analysis but also in highly quantitative investment disciplines. Quantitative analysts work in developing, testing, and updating security selection methodologies. Ranking stocks by some measure(s) of relative attractiveness (subject to a risk control discipline), as we will discuss in more detail later, forms one key part of quantitative equity investment disciplines.
- Analysts at corporations may perform some valuation tasks similar to those of analysts at money management firms (e.g., when the corporation manages in-house a sponsored pension plan). Both corporate analysts and investment bank analysts may also identify and value companies that could become acquisition targets.
- Analysts at independent vendors of financial information usually offer valuation information and opinions in publicly distributed research reports, although some focus solely on organizing and analyzing corporate information.

In conducting their valuation activities, investment analysts play a critical role in collecting, organizing, analyzing, and communicating corporate information, and in some contexts, recommending appropriate investment actions based on sound analysis. When they do those tasks well, analysts help their clients, the capital markets, and the suppliers of capital:

- Analysts help their clients achieve their investment objectives by enabling those clients to make better buy and sell decisions.
- Analysts contribute to the efficient functioning of capital markets by providing analysis that leads to informed buy and sell decisions and thus to asset prices that better reflect underlying values. When asset prices accurately reflect underlying values, capital flows more easily to its highest-value uses.
- Analysts benefit the suppliers of capital, including shareholders, when they are effective monitors of management's performance. This monitoring can serve to keep managers' actions more closely aligned with shareholders' best interests [see Jensen and Meckling (1976) for classic analysis of the costs of stockholder–manager conflicts].

WHAT ARE ANALYSTS EXPECTED TO DO?

When analysts at brokerage firms recommend a stock to the public that later performs very poorly, or when they fail to uncover negative corporate activities, they can sometimes come under public scrutiny. Industry leaders may then be asked to respond to such criticism and to comment on expectations about the role and responsibilities of analysts. One such instance occurred in the United States as a consequence of the late 2001 collapse of Enron Corporation, an energy, utility, trading, and telecommunication company. In testimony before the US Senate (excerpted below), the President and CEO of AIMR (predecessor organization of CFA Institute) offered a summary of the working conditions and responsibilities of brokerage analysts. In the following passage, **due diligence** refers to investigation and analysis in support of a recommendation; the failure to exercise due diligence may sometimes result in liability according to various securities laws. "Wall Street analysts" refers to analysts working in the US brokerage industry (sell-side analysts).

> What are Wall Street analysts expected to do? These analysts are assigned companies and industries to follow, are expected to research fully these companies and the industries in which they operate, and to forecast their future prospects. Based on this analysis, and using appropriate valuation models, they must then determine an appropriate fair price for the company's securities. After comparing this fair price to the current market price, the analyst is able to make a recommendation. If the analyst's "fair price" is significantly above the current market price, it would be expected that the stock be rated a "buy" or "market outperform."
>
> How do Wall Street analysts get their information? Through hard work and due diligence. They must study and try to comprehend the information in numerous public disclosure documents, such as the annual report to shareholders and regulatory filings . . . and gather the necessary quantitative and qualitative inputs to their valuation models.
>
> This due diligence isn't simply reading and analyzing annual reports. It also involves talking to company management, other company employees, competitors, and others, to get answers to questions that arise from their review of public documents. Talking to management must go beyond participation in regular conference calls. Not all questions can be voiced in those calls because of time constraints, for example, and because analysts, like journalists, rightly might not wish to "show their cards," and reveal the insights they have gotten through their hard work, by asking a particularly probing question in the presence of their competitors.
>
> Wall Street analysts are also expected to understand the dynamics of the industry and general economic conditions before finalizing a research report and making a recommendation. Therefore, in order for their firm to justify their continued employment, Wall Street analysts must issue research reports on their assigned companies and must make recommendations based on their reports to clients who purchase their firm's research
>
> (*Source:* Thomas A. Bowman, CFA. Testimony to the Committee on Governmental Affairs (excerpted) US Senate, 27 February 2002).

From the beginnings of the movement to organize financial analysis as a profession rather than as a commercial trade, one guiding principle has been that the analyst must hold himself accountable to both standards of competence and standards of conduct. Competence in investment analysis requires a high degree of training, experience, and discipline (as reflected in the examination and work experience requirements that are prerequisites for obtaining the CFA designation). Additionally, the investment professional is in a position of trust, requiring ethical conduct toward the public, clients, prospects, employers, employees, and fellow analysts. For CFA Institute members, this position of trust is reflected in the Code of Ethics and Standards of Professional Conduct, as well as in the Professional Conduct Statement that they submit annually. The Code and Standards guide the analyst to independent, well-researched, and well-documented analysis and are described in the following sections.

9 COMMUNICATING VALUATION RESULTS

Writing is an important part of an analyst's job. Whether for review by an investment committee or a portfolio manager in an investment management firm or for distribution to the retail or institutional clients of a brokerage firm, research reports share several common elements. In this section, we briefly discuss the content and format of an effective research report and the analyst's responsibilities for preparing a report.

Contents of a Research Report

A primary determinant of a research report's contents is what the intended readers seek to gain from reading the report. From a sell-side analyst's report, an intended reader would be interested in the investment recommendation. In evaluating how much attention and weight to give to a recommendation, the reader will look for persuasive supporting arguments. A key element supporting any recommendation is the intrinsic value of the security.

Given the importance of the estimated intrinsic value of the security, most research reports provide the reader with information about the key assumptions and expectations underlying that estimated intrinsic value. The information typically includes an update on the company's financial and operating results, a description of relevant aspects of the current macroeconomic and industry context, and an analysis and forecast for the industry and company. Because some readers of research reports are interested in background information, some reports contain detailed historical descriptive statistics about the industry and company.

A report can include specific forecasts, key valuation inputs (e.g., the estimated cost of capital), a description of the valuation model, and a discussion of qualitative factors and other considerations that affect valuation. Superior research reports also objectively address the uncertainty associated with investing in the security and/or the valuation inputs involving the greatest amount of uncertainty. By converting forecasts into estimated intrinsic value, a comparison between intrinsic value and market price provides the basis for an investment recommendation. When a research report states a target price for a stock (based on its intrinsic value) in its investment recommendation, the report should clarify the basis for computing the target, a time frame for reaching the target, and information on the uncertainty of reaching the target. An investment recommendation may be accompanied by an explanation of the underlying rationale (i.e., investment thesis), which summarizes why a particular investment offer would provide a way to profit from the analyst's outlook.

Although a well-written report cannot compensate for a poor analysis, a poorly written report can detract from the credibility of an excellent analysis. Writing an effective research report is a challenging task. In summary, an effective research report:

- contains timely information;
- is written in clear, incisive language;
- is objective and well researched, with key assumptions clearly identified;

- distinguishes clearly between facts and opinions;
- contains analysis, forecasts, valuation, and a recommendation that are internally consistent;
- presents sufficient information to allow a reader to critique the valuation;
- states the key risk factors involved in an investment in the company; and
- discloses any potential conflicts of interests faced by the analyst.

Although these general characteristics are all desirable attributes of a useful and respected report, in some situations the requirements are more specific. For example, regulations governing disclosures of conflicts and potential conflicts of interest vary across countries, so an analyst must remain up-to-date on relevant disclosure requirements. In some situations, investment recommendations are affected by policies of the firm employing an analyst; for example, a policy might require that a security's price must be *X*% below its estimated intrinsic value to be considered a "buy." Even in the absence of such a policy, an analyst needs to maintain a conceptual distinction between a "good company" and a "good investment" because returns on a common stock investment always depend on the price paid for the stock, whether the business prospects of the issuing company are good, bad, or indifferent. Exhibit 5 provides a small sample of possible research report content.

Exhibit 5: Research Reports

The following two passages are closely based on the valuation discussions of actual companies in two actual short research notes. The dates and company names used in the passages, however, are fictional.

A. At a recent multiple of 6.5, our earnings per share multiple for 2020, the shares were at a discount to our projection of 14% growth for the period ... MXI has two operating segments ... In valuing the segments separately, employing relative acquisition multiples and peer mean values, we found fair value to be above recent market value. In addition, the shares trade at a discount to book value (0.76). Based on the value indicated by these two valuation metrics, we view the shares as worth holding. However, in light of a weaker economy over the near term, dampening demand for MXI's services, our enthusiasm is tempered. [*Elsewhere in the report, MXI is evaluated as being in the firm's top category of investment attractiveness.*]

B. Although TXI outperformed the overall stock market by 20% since the start of the year, it definitely looks undervalued, as shown by its low multiples ... [*the values of the P/E and another multiple are stated*]. According to our dividend discount model valuation, we get to a valuation of €3.08, implying an upside potential of 36.8% based on current prices. The market outperform recommendation is reiterated. [*In a parenthetical expression, the current dividend, assumed dividend growth rates, and their time horizons are given. The analyst also briefly explains and calculates the discount rate. Elsewhere in the report the current price of TXI is given as €2.25.*]

Although some of the concepts mentioned in the two passages may not yet be familiar, you can begin to assess the two reporting efforts.

Passage A communicates the analysis awkwardly. The meaning of "the shares were at a discount to our projection of 14% growth for the period" is not completely clear. Presumably, the analyst is projecting the earnings growth rate for 2020 and stating that the P/E is low in relation to that expected growth rate. The analyst next discusses valuing MXI as the sum of its divisions. In describing the method as "employing relative acquisition multiples and peer mean values," the analyst does not convey a clear picture of what was done. It is probable that companies similar to each of MXI's divisions were identified; then, the mean or average value of some unidentified multiple for those comparison companies was calculated and used as the basis for valuing MXI. The writer is vague, however, on the extent of MXI's undervaluation. The analyst states that MXI's price is below its book value (an accounting measure of shareholders' investment) but draws no comparison with the average price-to-book value ratio for stocks similar to MXI, for example. (The price-to-book ratio is discussed in a later reading.) Finally, the verbal summation is feeble and hedged. Although filled with technical verbiage, Passage A does not communicate a coherent valuation of MXI.

In the second sentence of Passage B, by contrast, the analyst gives an explicit valuation of TXI and the information needed to critique it. The reader can also see that €3.08, which is elsewhere stated in the research note as the target price for TXI, implies the stated price appreciation potential for TXI [(€3.08/€2.25) – 1, approximately 37%]. In the first sentence in Passage B, the analyst gives information that might support the conclusion that TXI is undervalued, although the statement lacks strength because the analyst does not explain why the P/E is "low." Nevertheless, the verbal summary is clear. Using less space than the analyst in Passage A, the analyst in Passage B has done a better job of communicating the results of his valuation.

Format of a Research Report

Equity research reports may be logically presented in several ways. The firm in which the analyst works sometimes specifies a fixed format for consistency and quality control purposes. Without claiming superiority to other ways to organize a report, we offer Exhibit 6 as an adaptable format by which the analyst can communicate research and valuation findings in detail. (Shorter research reports and research notes obviously may employ a more compact format.)

Exhibit 6: A Format for Research Reports

Section	Purpose	Content	Comments
Table of Contents	▪ Show report's organization	▪ Consistent with narrative in sequence and language	This is typically used only in very long research reports.
Summary and Investment Conclusion	▪ Communicate the large picture ▪ Communicate major specific conclusions of the analysis ▪ Recommend an investment course of action	▪ Capsule description of the company ▪ Major recent developments ▪ Earnings projections ▪ Other major conclusions ▪ Valuation summary ▪ Investment action	An executive summary; may be called simply "Summary."
Business Summary	▪ Present the company in more detail ▪ Communicate a detailed understanding of the company's economics and current situation ▪ Provide and explain specific forecasts[a]	▪ Company description to the divisional level ▪ Industry analysis ▪ Competitive analysis ▪ Historical performance ▪ Financial forecasts	Reflects the first and second steps of the valuation process. Financial forecasts should be explained adequately and reflect quality of earnings analysis.

Section	Purpose	Content	Comments
Risks	▪ Alert readers to the risk factors in investing in the security	▪ Possible negative industry developments ▪ Possible negative regulatory and legal developments ▪ Possible negative company developments ▪ Risks in the forecasts ▪ Other risks	Readers should have enough information to determine how the analyst is defining and assessing the risks specific to investing in the security.
Valuation	▪ Communicate a clear and careful valuation	▪ Description of model(s) used ▪ Recapitulation of inputs ▪ Statement of conclusions	Readers should have enough information to critique the analysis.
Historical and Pro Forma Tables	▪ Organize and present data to support the analysis in the Business Summary		This is generally a separate section only in longer research reports. Many reports fold all or some of this information into the Business Summary section.

[a] *Actual outcomes can and generally will differ from forecasts. A discussion of key random factors and an examination of the sensitivity of outcomes to the outcomes of those factors are useful.*

Research Reporting Responsibilities

All analysts have an obligation to provide substantive and meaningful content in a clear and comprehensive report format. Analysts who are CFA Institute members, however, have an additional and overriding responsibility to adhere to the Code of Ethics and the Standards of Professional Conduct in all activities pertaining to their research reports. The CFA Institute Code of Ethics states:

> Members of CFA Institute must . . . use reasonable care and exercise independent professional judgment when conducting investment analysis, making investment recommendations, taking investment actions, and engaging in other professional activities.

Going beyond this general statement of responsibility, some specific Standards of Professional Conduct particularly relevant to an analyst writing a research report are shown in Exhibit 7.

Exhibit 7: Selected CFA Institute Standards of Professional Conduct Pertaining to Research Reports*

Standard of Professional Conduct	Responsibility
I(B)	Members and Candidates must use reasonable care and judgment to achieve and maintain independence and objectivity in their professional activities. Members and Candidates must not offer, solicit, or accept any gift, benefit, compensation, or consideration that reasonably could be expected to compromise their own or another's independence and objectivity.
I(C)	Members and Candidates must not knowingly make any misrepresentations relating to investment analysis, recommendations, actions, or other professional activities.
V(A)1	Members and Candidates must exercise diligence, independence, and thoroughness in analyzing investments, making investment recommendations, and taking investment actions.
V(A)2	Members and Candidates must have a reasonable and adequate basis, supported by appropriate research and investigation, for any investment analysis, recommendation, or action.
V(B)1	Members and Candidates must disclose to clients and prospective clients the basic format and general principles of the investment processes used to analyze investments, select securities, and construct portfolios and must promptly disclose any changes that might materially affect those processes.
V(B)2	Members and Candidates must disclose to clients and prospective clients significant limitations and risks associated with the investment process.
V(B)3	Members and Candidates must use reasonable judgment in identifying which factors are important to their investment analyses, recommendations, or actions and include those factors in communications with clients and prospective clients.
V(B)4	Members and Candidates must distinguish between fact and opinion in the presentation of investment analysis and recommendations.
V(C)	Members and Candidates must develop and maintain appropriate records to support their investment analysis, recommendations, actions, and other investment-related communications with clients and prospective clients.

* *See the most recent edition of the CFA Institute Standards of Practice Handbook (www.cfainstitute.org).*

SUMMARY

In this reading, we have discussed the scope of equity valuation, outlined the valuation process, introduced valuation concepts and models, discussed the analyst's role and responsibilities in conducting valuation, and described the elements of an effective research report in which analysts communicate their valuation analysis.

- Valuation is the estimation of an asset's value based on either variables perceived to be related to future investment returns or comparisons with closely similar assets.

- The intrinsic value of an asset is its value given a hypothetically complete understanding of the asset's investment characteristics.
- The assumption that the market price of a security can diverge from its intrinsic value—as suggested by the rational efficient markets formulation of efficient market theory—underpins active investing.
- Intrinsic value incorporates the going-concern assumption, that is, the assumption that a company will continue operating for the foreseeable future. In contrast, liquidation value is the company's value if it were dissolved and its assets sold individually.
- Fair value is the price at which an asset (or liability) would change hands if neither buyer nor seller were under compulsion to buy/sell and both were informed about material underlying facts.
- In addition to stock selection by active traders, valuation is also used for:
  - inferring (extracting) market expectations;
  - evaluating corporate events;
  - issuing fairness opinions;
  - evaluating business strategies and models; and
  - appraising private businesses.
- The valuation process has five steps:
  1. Understanding the business.
  2. Forecasting company performance.
  3. Selecting the appropriate valuation model.
  4. Converting forecasts to a valuation.
  5. Applying the analytical results in the form of recommendations and conclusions.
- Understanding the business includes evaluating industry prospects, competitive position, and corporate strategies—all of which contribute to making more accurate forecasts. Understanding the business also involves analysis of financial reports, including evaluating the quality of a company's earnings.
- In forecasting company performance, a top-down forecasting approach moves from macroeconomic forecasts to industry forecasts and then to individual company and asset forecasts. A bottom-up forecasting approach aggregates individual company forecasts to industry forecasts, which in turn may be aggregated to macroeconomic forecasts.
- Selecting the appropriate valuation approach means choosing an approach that is:
  - consistent with the characteristics of the company being valued;
  - appropriate given the availability and quality of the data; and
  - consistent with the analyst's valuation purpose and perspective.
- Two broad categories of valuation models are absolute valuation models and relative valuation models.
  - Absolute valuation models specify an asset's intrinsic value, supplying a point estimate of value that can be compared with market price. Present value models of common stock (also called discounted cash flow models) are the most important type of absolute valuation model.

- Relative valuation models specify an asset's value relative to the value of another asset. As applied to equity valuation, relative valuation is also known as the method of comparables, which involves comparison of a stock's price multiple to a benchmark price multiple. The benchmark price multiple can be based on a similar stock or on the average price multiple of some group of stocks.

- Two important aspects of converting forecasts to valuation are sensitivity analysis and situational adjustments.
  - Sensitivity analysis is an analysis to determine how changes in an assumed input would affect the outcome of an analysis.
  - Situational adjustments include control premiums (premiums for a controlling interest in the company), discounts for lack of marketability (discounts reflecting the lack of a public market for the company's shares), and illiquidity discounts (discounts reflecting the lack of a liquid market for the company's shares).
- Applying valuation conclusions depends on the purpose of the valuation.
- In performing valuations, analysts must hold themselves accountable to both standards of competence and standards of conduct.
- An effective research report:
  - contains timely information;
  - is written in clear, incisive language;
  - is objective and well researched, with key assumptions clearly identified;
  - distinguishes clearly between facts and opinions;
  - contains analysis, forecasts, valuation, and a recommendation that are internally consistent;
  - presents sufficient information that the reader can critique the valuation;
  - states the risk factors for an investment in the company; and
  - discloses any potential conflicts of interest faced by the analyst.
- Analysts have an obligation to provide substantive and meaningful content. CFA Institute members have an additional overriding responsibility to adhere to the CFA Institute Code of Ethics and relevant specific Standards of Professional Conduct.

REFERENCES

Abarbanell, Jeffery S. and Victor L. Bernard. 1992. "Tests of Analysts' Overreaction/ Underreaction to Earnings Information as an Explanation for Anomalous Stock Price Behavior." *Journal of Finance* 47 (3): 1181–207. 10.1111/j.1540-6261.1992.tb04010.x

Bordalo, Pedro, Nicola Gennaioli, Rafael La Porta, and Andrei Shleifer. 2017. "*Diagnostic Expectations and Stock Returns.*" NBER Working Paper 23863. 10.3386/w23863

Cornell, Bradford. 2001. "Is the Response of Analysts to Information Consistent with Fundamental Valuation? The Case of Intel." *Financial Management* 30 (1): 113–36. 10.2307/3666393

De Bondt, Werner F.M. and Richard Thaler. 1985. "Does the Stock Market Overreact?" *Journal of Finance* 40 (3): 793–805. 10.1111/j.1540-6261.1985.tb05004.x

Graham, Benjamin. 1936. "*U.S. Steel Announces Sweeping Modernization Scheme.*" Unpublished satire by Ben Graham, written in 1936 and given by the author to Warren Buffett in 1954. Presented in Warren Buffet's "Chairman's Letter to the Shareholders of Berkshire Hathaway Inc" (1 March 1991). www.berkshirehathaway.com/letters/1990.html.

Graham, Benjamin and David L. Dodd. 1934. *Security Analysis*. McGraw-Hill Professional Publishing.

Grossman, Sanford and Joseph Stiglitz. 1980. "On the Impossibility of Informationally Efficient Markets." *American Economic Review* 70 (3): 393–408.

International Auditing and Assurance Standards Board (IAASB). 2018. International Standard on Auditing (ISA) 240, The Auditor's Responsibility to Consider Fraud and Error in an Audit of Financial Statements. In *2018 Handbook of International Quality Control, Auditing, Review, Other Assurance, and Related Services Pronouncements*. https://www.iaasb.org/.

Jensen, Michael C. and William H. Meckling. 1976. "Theory of the Firm: Managerial Behavior, Agency Costs and Ownership Structure." *Journal of Financial Economics* 3 (4): 305–60. 10.1016/0304-405X(76)90026-X

Lee, Charles M.C., James Myers, and Bhaskaran Swaminathan. 1999. "What Is the Intrinsic Value of the Dow?" *Journal of Finance* 54 (5): 1693–741. 10.1111/0022-1082.00164

Mulford, Charles W. and Eugene F. Comiskey. 2005. *Creative Cash Flow Reporting: Uncovering Sustainable Financial Performance*. Hoboken, NJ: John Wiley & Sons.

Pinto, Jerald E., Thomas R. Robinson, and John D. Stowe. 2019. "Equity Valuation: A Survey of Professional Practice." *Review of Financial Economics* 37 (2): 219–33. 10.1002/rfe.1040

Porter, Michael E. 1985. *The Competitive Advantage: Creating and Sustaining Superior Performance*. New York: Free Press. (Republished with new introduction in 1998.)

Porter, Michael E. 2008. "The Five Competitive Forces That Shape Strategy." *Harvard Business Review* 86 (1): 78–93.

Public Company Accounting Oversight Board (PCAOB). 2017. Auditing Standard (AS) 2401: Consideration of Fraud in a Financial Statement Audit. In *Auditing Standards of the Public Company Accounting Oversight Board* (15 December). www.pcaob.org.

Schilit, Howard and Jeremy Perler. 2010. *Financial Shenanigans: How to Detect Accounting Gimmicks & Fraud in Financial Reports*, 3rd edition. New York: McGraw-Hill.

Sloan, Richard G. 1996. "Do Stock Prices Fully Reflect Information in Accruals and Cash Flows about Future Earnings?" *Accounting Review* 71 (3): 289–315.

PRACTICE PROBLEMS

The following information relates to questions 1-8

Global-Guardian Capital is a rapidly growing international investment firm. The firm's research team is responsible for identifying undervalued and overvalued publicly-traded equities that have a market capitalization greater than $500 million.

Due to the rapid growth of assets under management, Global-Guardian Capital recently hired a new analyst, Jack Richardson, to support the research process. At the new analyst orientation meeting, the director of research made the following statements about equity valuation at the firm:

Statement 1 "Analysts at Global-Guardian Capital seek to identify mispricing, relying on price eventually converging to intrinsic value. However, convergence of the market price to an analyst's estimate of intrinsic value may not happen within the portfolio manager's investment time horizon. So, besides evidence of mispricing, analysts should look for the presence of a particular market or corporate event—that is, a catalyst—that will cause the marketplace to re-evaluate the subject firm's prospects."

Statement 2 "An active investment manager attempts to capture positive alpha. But mispricing of assets is not directly observable. It is therefore important that you understand the possible sources of perceived mispricing."

Statement 3 "For its distressed securities fund, Global-Guardian Capital screens its investable universe of securities for companies in financial distress."

Statement 4 "For its core equity fund, Global-Guardian Capital selects financially sound companies that are expected to generate significant positive free cash flow from core business operations within a multiyear forecast horizon."

Statement 5 "Global-Guardian Capital's research process requires analysts to evaluate the reasonableness of the expectations implied by the market price by comparing the market's implied expectations to his or her own expectations."

After the orientation meeting, the director of research asks Richardson to evaluate three companies that are retailers of men's clothing: Diamond Co., Renaissance Clothing, and Deluxe Men's Wear.

Richardson starts his analysis by evaluating the characteristics of the men's retail clothing industry. He finds few barriers to new retail entrants, high intra-industry rivalry among retailers, low product substitution costs for customers, and a large number of wholesale clothing suppliers.

While conducting his analysis, Richardson discovers that Renaissance Clothing included three non-recurring items in their most recent earnings release: a positive litigation settlement, a one-time tax credit, and the gain on the sale of a non-operating asset.

To estimate each firm's intrinsic value, Richardson applies appropriate discount rates to each firm's estimated free cash flows over a ten-year time horizon and to the estimated value of the firm at the end of the ten-year horizon.

Michelle Lee, a junior technology analyst at Global-Guardian, asks the director of research for advice as to which valuation model to use for VEGA, a fast growing semiconductor company that is rapidly gaining market share.

The director of research states that "the valuation model selected must be consistent with the characteristics of the company being valued."

Lee tells the director of research that VEGA is not expected to be profitable for several more years. According to management guidance, when the company turns profitable, it will invest in new product development; as a result, it does not expect to initiate a dividend for an extended period of time. Lee also notes that she expects that certain larger competitors will become interested in acquiring VEGA because of its excellent growth prospects. The director of research advises Lee to consider that in her valuation.

1. Based on Statement 2, which of the following sources of perceived mispricing do active investment managers attempt to identify? The difference between:

   A. intrinsic value and market price.

   B. estimated intrinsic value and market price.

   C. intrinsic value and estimated intrinsic value.

2. With respect to Statements 3 and 4, which of the following measures of value would the distressed securities fund's analyst consider that a core equity fund analyst might ignore?

   A. Fair value

   B. Liquidation value

   C. Fair market value

3. With respect to Statement 4, which measure of value is *most* relevant for the analyst of the fund described?

   A. Liquidation value

   B. Investment value

   C. Going-concern value

4. According to Statement 5, analysts are expected to use valuation concepts and models to:

   A. value private businesses.

   B. render fairness opinions.

   C. extract market expectations.

5. Based on Richardson's industry analysis, which of the following characteristics of men's retail clothing retailing would *positively* affect its profitability? That industry's:

   A. entry costs.

B. substitution costs.

C. number of suppliers.

6. Which of the following statements about the reported earnings of Renaissance Clothing is *most accurate*? Relative to sustainable earnings, reported earnings are likely:

   A. unbiased.

   B. upward biased.

   C. downward biased.

7. Which valuation model is Richardson applying in his analysis of the retailers?

   A. Relative value

   B. Absolute value

   C. Sum-of-the-parts

8. Which valuation model would the director of research *most likely* recommend Lee use to estimate the value of VEGA?

   A. Free cash flow

   B. Dividend discount

   C. P/E relative valuation

The following information relates to questions 9-12

Bruno Santos is an equity analyst with a regional investment bank. Santos reviews the growth prospects and quality of earnings for Phoenix Enterprises, one of the companies he follows. He has developed a stock valuation model for this firm based on its forecasted fundamentals. His revenue growth rate estimate is less than that implied by the market price.

Phoenix's financial statements over the past five years show strong performance, with above average growth. Santos has decided to use a lower forecasted growth rate in his models, reflecting the effect of "regression to the mean" over time. He notes two reasons for his lower growth rate forecast:

Reason 1	Successful companies tend to draw more competition, putting their high profits under pressure.
Reason 2	Phoenix's intellectual property and franchise agreements will be weakening over time.

Santos meets with Walter Hartmann, a newly hired associate in his department. In their conversation, Hartmann states, "Security analysts forecast company performance using both top-down and bottom-up analysis. I can think of three examples:

1. A restaurant chain forecasts its sales to be its market share times forecast industry sales.
2. An electric utility company forecasts that its sales will grow proportional to increases in GDP.
3. A retail furniture company forecasts next year's sales by assuming that the sales in its newly built stores will have similar sales per square meter to that of its existing stores."

Hartmann is reviewing some possible trades for three stocks in the health care industry based on a pairs-trading strategy. Hartmann's evaluations are as follows:

- HG Health is 15% overvalued.
- Corgent Cell Sciences is 10% overvalued.
- Johnson Labs is 15% undervalued.

9. Based on Santos's revenue growth rate estimate, the shares of Phoenix are *most likely*:

   A. undervalued.

   B. fairly valued.

   C. overvalued.

10. Which of the reasons given by Santos *most likely* justifies a reduction in Phoenix's forecasted growth rate?

    A. Reason 1 only

    B. Reason 2 only

    C. Both Reason 1 and Reason 2

11. Which of Hartmann's examples of company performance forecasting *best* describes an example of bottom-up forecasting?

    A. Restaurant chain

    B. Electric utility company

    C. Retail furniture company

12. Based on his trading strategy, which of the following should Hartmann recommend?

    A. Short HG Health and Corgent Cell Sciences

    B. Buy Johnson Labs and Corgent Cell Sciences

    C. Buy Johnson Labs and short Corgent Cell Sciences

The following information relates to questions 13-16

Abby Dormier is a sell-side analyst for a small Wall Street brokerage firm; she covers publicly and actively traded companies with listed equity shares. Dormier is responsible for issuing either a buy, hold, or sell rating for the shares of Company A and Company B. The appropriate valuation model for each company was chosen based on the following characteristics of each company:

Company A is an employment services firm with no debt and has fixed assets consisting primarily of computers, servers, and commercially available software. Many of the assets are intangible, including human capital. The company has a history of occasionally paying a special cash dividend.

Company B operates in three unrelated industries with differing rates of growth: tobacco (60% of earnings), shipbuilding (30% of earnings), and aerospace consulting (10% of earnings). The company pays a regular dividend that is solely derived from the earnings produced by the tobacco division.

Dormier considers the following development in making any necessary adjustments to the models before assigning ratings:

Company B has finalized the terms to acquire 70% of the outstanding shares of Company X, an actively traded tobacco company, in an all-stock deal.

Dormier assigns ratings to each of the companies and provides a rationale for each rating. The director of research asks Dormier: "How did you arrive at these recommendations? Describe how you used a top-down approach, which is the policy at our company."

Dormier replies, "I arrived at my recommendations through my due diligence process. I have studied all of the public disclosure documents; I have participated in the company conference calls, being careful with my questions in such a public forum; and I have studied the dynamics of the underlying industries. The valuation models are robust and use an extensive set of company-specific quantitative and qualitative inputs."

13. Based on Company A's characteristics, which of the following absolute valuation models is *most* appropriate for valuing that company?

    A. Asset based

    B. Dividend discount

    C. Free cash flow to the firm

14. Based on Company B's characteristics, which of the following valuation models is *most* appropriate for valuing that company?

    A. Asset based

    B. Sum of the parts

    C. Dividend discount

15. Which of the following is *most likely* to be appropriate to consider in Company B's valuation of Company X?

    A. Blockage factor

    B. Control premium

    C. Lack of marketability discount

16. Based on Dormier's response to the director of research, Dormier's process could have been more consistent with the firm's policy by:

    A. incorporating additional micro-level inputs into her valuation models.

    B. evaluating the impact of general economic conditions on each company.

    C. asking more probing questions during publicly available company conference calls.

SOLUTIONS

1. A is correct. The difference between the true (real) but unobservable intrinsic value and the observed market price contributes to the abnormal return or alpha, which is the concern of active investment managers.

2. B is correct. The measure of value the distressed securities fund's analyst would consider that the core equity fund analyst might ignore is liquidation value. The liquidation value of a company is its value if it were dissolved and its assets sold individually.

3. C is correct. For its core equity fund, Global-Guardian Capital screens its investable universe of securities for well-capitalized companies that are expected to generate significant future free cash flow from core business operations. The concern with future free cash flows implies that going-concern value is relevant.

4. C is correct. Market prices reflect the expectations of investors about the future performance of companies. The analyst can evaluate the reasonableness of the expectations implied by the market price by comparing the market's implied expectations to his own expectations. This process assumes a valuation model, as discussed in the text.

5. C is correct. The men's retail clothing industry is characterized by a large number of wholesale clothing suppliers. When many suppliers of the products needed by industry participants exist, competition among suppliers should limit their ability to raise input prices. Thus, the large number of suppliers is a factor that should positively affect industry profitability.

6. B is correct. The effects of favorable nonrecurring events in reported earnings would tend to bias reported earnings upward relative to sustainable earnings because non-recurring items are by definition not expected to repeat. Renaissance Clothing included three non-recurring items in their most recent earnings release that all led to higher earnings for the current period: a positive litigation settlement, a one-time tax credit, and the gain on the sale of a non-operating asset.

7. B is correct. An absolute valuation model is a model that specifies an asset's intrinsic value. The most important type of absolute equity valuation models are present value models (also referred to as discounted cash flow models), and the model described by Richardson is of that type.

8. A is correct. The broad criteria for model selection are that a valuation model be consistent with the characteristics of the company being valued—that it be appropriate given the availability and quality of the data and consistent with the purpose of the valuation. VEGA currently has negative earnings, making the use of P/E relative valuation difficult if not impossible. As VEGA does not pay a dividend and is not expected to for the foreseeable future, the application of a dividend discount model is problematic. However, the lack of a dividend would not be an obstacle to free cash flow valuation. Furthermore, the director of research has advised that the possibility that competitors may seek to acquire VEGA be taken in to account in valuing VEGA. The reading states that free cash flow valuation can be appropriate in such circumstances. Thus, the director of research would be most likely to recommend free cash flow valuation.

9. C is correct. If the revenue growth rate inferred by the market price exceeds the

growth rate that the firm could reasonably expect, Santos should conclude that the market price is too high and thus that the firm is overvalued.

10. C is correct. Increased competition for successful firms can cause a regression to the mean of a company's growth rate. Expiring and weakening intellectual property and franchise agreements can also reduce potential growth.

11. C is correct. The retail furniture company forecasting sales based on sales per square meter is an example of bottom-up forecasting because it aggregates forecasts at a micro level to larger-scale forecasts.

12. C is correct. Pairs trading involves buying an undervalued stock and shorting an overvalued stock in the same industry. Hartmann should buy Johnson Labs (15% undervalued) and short Corgent Cell Sciences (10% overvalued).

13. C is correct. The free cash flow to the firm model is the most appropriate of the choices because it can be used whether the company has significant marketable assets or consistently pays a cash dividend. Much of Company A's assets are intangible, and although the company has a history of paying a dividend, it has been only occasionally and in the form of a special dividend (i.e., not a consistent cash dividend).

14. B is correct. This valuation model would be consistent with the characteristics of the company. Company B is a conglomerate operating in three unrelated industries with significantly different expected revenue growth rates. The sum-of-the-parts valuation model sums the estimated values of each of the company's businesses as if each business were an independent going concern. Sum-of-the-parts analysis is most useful when valuing a company with segments in different industries that have different valuation characteristics.

15. B is correct. A control premium may be reflected in the value of a stock investment that would give an investor a controlling position. Company B acquired 70% of the outstanding stock of Company X; more than 50% is considered a controlling ownership position.

16. B is correct. A top-down forecasting approach moves from macroeconomic forecasts to industry forecasts and then to individual company and asset forecasts. Analysts are expected to understand the general economic conditions before finalizing a research report and making a recommendation. According to Dormier's response, she did not comment on the general economic conditions—although such considerations would be consistent with the firm's policy of using a top-down approach.

LEARNING MODULE

2

Discounted Dividend Valuation

by Jerald E. Pinto, PhD, CFA, Elaine Henry, PhD, CFA, Thomas R. Robinson, PhD, CFA, CAIA, and John D. Stowe, PhD, CFA.

Jerald E. Pinto, PhD, CFA, is at CFA Institute (USA). Elaine Henry, PhD, CFA, is at Stevens Institute of Technology (USA). Thomas R. Robinson, PhD, CFA, CAIA, is at Robinson Global Investment Management LLC, (USA). John D. Stowe, PhD, CFA, is at Ohio University (USA).

LEARNING OUTCOMES

Mastery	*The candidate should be able to:*
☐	compare dividends, free cash flow, and residual income as inputs to discounted cash flow models and identify investment situations for which each measure is suitable
☐	calculate and interpret the value of a common stock using the dividend discount model (DDM) for single and multiple holding periods
☐	calculate the value of a common stock using the Gordon growth model and explain the model's underlying assumptions
☐	calculate the value of non-callable fixed-rate perpetual preferred stock
☐	describe strengths and limitations of the Gordon growth model and justify its selection to value a company's common shares
☐	calculate and interpret the implied growth rate of dividends using the Gordon growth model and current stock price
☐	calculate and interpret the present value of growth opportunities (PVGO) and the component of the leading price-to-earnings ratio (P/E) related to PVGO
☐	calculate and interpret the justified leading and trailing P/Es using the Gordon growth model
☐	estimate a required return based on any DDM, including the Gordon growth model and the H-model
☐	evaluate whether a stock is overvalued, fairly valued, or undervalued by the market based on a DDM estimate of value
☐	explain the growth phase, transition phase, and maturity phase of a business
☐	explain the assumptions and justify the selection of the two-stage DDM, the H-model, the three-stage DDM, or spreadsheet modeling to value a company's common shares

LEARNING OUTCOMES

Mastery	The candidate should be able to:
☐	describe terminal value and explain alternative approaches to determining the terminal value in a DDM
☐	calculate and interpret the value of common shares using the two-stage DDM, the H-model, and the three-stage DDM
☐	explain the use of spreadsheet modeling to forecast dividends and to value common shares
☐	calculate and interpret the sustainable growth rate of a company and demonstrate the use of DuPont analysis to estimate a company's sustainable growth rate

1 INTRODUCTION

☐	compare dividends, free cash flow, and residual income as inputs to discounted cash flow models and identify investment situations for which each measure is suitable

Common stock represents an ownership interest in a business. A business in its operations generates a stream of cash flows, and as owners of the business, common stockholders have an equity ownership claim on those future cash flows. Beginning with John Burr Williams (1938), analysts have developed this insight into a group of valuation models known as discounted cash flow (DCF) valuation models. DCF models—which view the intrinsic value of common stock as the present value of its expected future cash flows—are a fundamental tool in both investment management and investment research.

Although the principles behind discounted cash flow valuation are simple, applying the theory to equity valuation can be challenging. Four broad steps in applying DCF analysis to equity valuation are:

- choosing the class of DCF model—equivalently, selecting a specific definition of cash flow;
- forecasting the cash flows;
- choosing a discount rate methodology; and
- estimating the discount rate.

In our coverage of this topic, we take the perspective that dividends—distributions to shareholders authorized by a company's board of directors—are an appropriate definition of cash flows. The class of models based on this idea is called dividend discount models, or DDMs. The basic objective of any DDM is to value a stock. The variety of implementations corresponds to different ways to model a company's future stream of dividend payments. The steps of choosing a discount rate methodology and estimating the discount rate involve the same considerations for all DCF models, so they have been presented separately in an earlier discussion.

The sections are organized as follows: We first provide an overview of present value models. We then provide a general statement of the dividend discount model. Forecasting dividends, individually and in detail, into the indefinite future is not generally practicable, so the dividend-forecasting problem is usually simplified. One approach is to assign dividends to a stylized growth pattern. In the subsequent section, we focus on the simplest pattern—dividends growing at a constant rate forever (the constant growth or "Gordon growth" model). We then explain that for some companies, it is more appropriate to view earnings and dividends as having multiple stages of growth. We present multistage dividend discount models along with spreadsheet modeling. We lay out the determinants of dividend growth rates in the last section and conclude with a summary.

Present Value Models

Present value models as a group constitute a demanding and rigorous approach for valuing assets. In this section, we discuss the economic rationale for valuing an asset as the present value of its expected future cash flows. We also discuss alternative definitions of cash flows and present the major alternative methods for estimating the discount rate.

Valuation Based on the Present Value of Future Cash Flows

The value of an asset must be related to the benefits or returns we expect to receive from holding it. Those returns are called the asset's future cash flows (we will define *cash flow* more concretely and technically later). We also need to recognize that a given amount of money received in the future is worth less than the same amount of money received today. Money received today gives us the option of immediately spending and consuming it, so money has a time value. Therefore, when valuing an asset, before adding up the estimated future cash flows, we must **discount** each cash flow back to the present: the cash flow's value is reduced with respect to how far away it is in time. The two elements of discounted cash flow valuation—estimating the cash flows and discounting the cash flows to account for the time value of money—provide the economic rationale for discounted cash flow valuation. In the simplest case, in which the timing and amounts of future cash flows are known with certainty, if we invest an amount equal to the present value of future cash flows at the given discount rate, that investment will replicate all of the asset's cash flows (with no money left over).

For some assets, such as government debt, cash flows may be essentially known with certainty—that is, they are default risk free. The appropriate discount rate for such a risk-free cash flow is a risk-free rate of interest. For example, if an asset has a single, certain cash flow of \$100 to be received in two years, and the risk-free interest rate is 5% a year, the value of the asset is the present value of \$100 discounted at the risk-free rate, $\$100/(1.05)^2 = \$90.70$.

In contrast to risk-free debt, future cash flows for equity investments are not known with certainty—they are risky. Introducing risk makes applying the present value approach much more challenging. The most common approach to dealing with risky cash flows involves two adjustments relative to the risk-free case. First, discount the *expected* value of the cash flows, viewing the cash flows as random variables (note that the expected value of a random quantity is the mean value of its possible outcomes, in which each outcome's weight in the average is its probability of occurrence). Second, adjust the discount rate to reflect the risk of the cash flows.

The following equation expresses the concept that an asset's value is the present value of its (expected) future cash flows:

$$V_0 = \sum_{t=1}^{n} \frac{\text{CF}_t}{(1+r)^t}, \qquad (1)$$

where

V_0 = the value of the asset at time t = 0 (today)

n = number of cash flows in the life of the asset (n is set equal to ∞ for equities)

CF_t = the cash flow (or the expected cash flow, for risky cash flows) at time t

r = the discount rate or required rate of return

For simplicity, the discount rate in Equation 1 is represented as the same for all periods (i.e., a flat term structure of discount rates is assumed). The analyst has the latitude in this model, however, to apply different discount rates to different cash flows. Such action could reflect different degrees of cash flow riskiness or different risk-free rates at different time horizons. Differences in cash flow riskiness may be caused by differences in business risk, operating risk (use of fixed assets in production), or financial risk or leverage (use of debt in the capital structure). The simple expression given, however, is adequate for this discussion.

Equation 1 gives an asset's value from the perspective of today (t – 0). Likewise, an asset's value at some point in the future equals the value of all subsequent cash flows discounted back to that point in time. Example 1 illustrates these points.

EXAMPLE 1

Value as the Present Value of Future Cash Flows

An asset is expected to generate cash flows of $100 in one year, $150 in two years, and $200 in three years. The value of this asset today, using a 10% discount rate, is

$$V_0 = \frac{100}{(1.10)^1} + \frac{150}{(1.10)^2} + \frac{200}{(1.10)^3}$$
$$= 90.909 + 123.967 + 150.263 = \$365.14$$

The value at t = 0 is $365.14. The same logic is used to value an asset at a future date. The value of the asset at t = 1 is the present value, discounted back to t = 1, of all cash flows after this point. This value, V_1, is

$$V_1 = \frac{150}{(1.10)^1} + \frac{200}{(1.10)^2}$$
$$= 136.364 + 165.289 = \$301.65$$

At any point in time, the asset's value is the value of future cash flows (CF) discounted back to that point. Because V_1 represents the value of CF_2 and CF_3 at t = 1, the value of the asset at t = 0 is also the present value of CF_1 and V_1:

$$V_0 = \frac{100}{(1.10)^1} + \frac{301.653}{(1.10)^1}$$
$$= 90.909 + 274.23 = \$365.14$$

Finding V_0 as the present value of CF_1, CF_2, and CF_3 is logically equivalent to finding V_0 as the present value of CF_1 and V_1.

In the next section, we present an overview of three alternative definitions of cash flow. The selected cash flow concept defines the type of DCF model we can use: the dividend discount model, the free cash flow model, or the residual income model. We also broadly characterize the types of valuation problems for which analysts often choose a particular model. (Further details are supplied when each model is discussed individually.)

Streams of Expected Cash Flows

In present value models of stock valuation, the three most widely used definitions of returns are dividends, free cash flow, and residual income. We discuss each definition in turn.

The dividend discount model defines cash flows as dividends. The basic argument for using this definition of cash flow is that an investor who buys and holds a share of stock generally receives cash returns only in the form of dividends. In practice, analysts usually view investment value as driven by earnings. Does the definition of cash flow as dividends ignore earnings not distributed to shareholders as dividends? Reinvested earnings should provide the basis for increased future dividends. Therefore, the DDM accounts for reinvested earnings when it takes all future dividends into account. Because dividends are less volatile than earnings and other return concepts, the relative stability of dividends may make DDM values less sensitive to short-run fluctuations in underlying value than alternative DCF models. Analysts often view DDM values as reflecting long-run intrinsic value.

A stock either pays dividends or does not pay dividends. A company might not pay dividends on its stock because the company is not profitable and has no cash to distribute. Also, a company might not pay dividends for the opposite reason: because it is very profitable. For example, a company may reinvest all earnings—paying no dividends—to take advantage of profitable growth opportunities. As the company matures and faces fewer attractive investment opportunities, it may initiate dividends. Generally, mature, profitable companies tend to pay dividends and are reluctant to reduce the level of dividends (Grullon, Paye, Underwood, and Weston 2011).

Dividend policy practices have international differences and change through time, even in one market. Typically, research has shown that a lower percentage of companies in US stock markets have paid dividends than have companies in most other markets (He, Ng, Zaiats, and Zhang 2017), although the US sample may have included a disproportionate number of smaller and younger companies, which are less likely to pay dividends (Denis and Osobov 2008). Research has also shown a decline over time in the fraction of companies paying cash dividends in most developed markets such as the United States, Canada, the European Union, the United Kingdom, and Japan (Fama and French 2001; von Eije and Megginson 2008). Although trends and determinants differ across markets, in general, the decline in the proportion of companies paying dividends has been attributed to some or all of the following: a growth in the number of smaller, publicly traded companies with low profitability and high growth potential; an overall reduced propensity to pay dividends (controlling for differences in profitability and growth opportunities); or the increase usage of share repurchases as an alternative way to distribute cash to shareholders (Fama and French 2001; von Eije and Megginson 2008; Julio and Ikenberry 2004).

Analysts will frequently need to value non-dividend-paying shares. Can the DDM be applied to non-dividend-paying shares? In theory it can, as is illustrated later, but in practice it generally is not.

Predicting the timing of dividend initiation and the magnitude of future dividends without any prior dividend data or specifics about dividend policy to guide the analysis is generally not practical. For a non-dividend-paying company, analysts usually prefer a model that defines returns at the company level (as free cash flow or residual income—these concepts are defined shortly) rather than at the stockholder level (as dividends). Another consideration in the choice of models relates to ownership perspective. An investor purchasing a small ownership share lacks the ability to meaningfully influence the timing or magnitude of the distribution of the company's cash to shareholders. That perspective is the one taken in applying a dividend discount model. The only access to the company's value is through the receipt of dividends, and dividend policy is taken as a given. If dividends do not bear an understandable relation to value creation in the company, applying the DDM to value the stock is prone to error.

Generally, the definition of returns as dividends, and the DDM, is most suitable when:

- the company is dividend-paying (i.e., the analyst has a dividend record to analyze);
- the board of directors has established a dividend policy that bears an understandable and consistent relationship to the company's profitability; and
- the investor takes a non-control perspective.

Often, companies with established dividends are seasoned companies, profitable but operating outside the economy's fastest-growing subsectors. Professional analysts often apply a dividend discount model to value the common stock of such companies.

EXAMPLE 2

AB InBev and Diageo plc: Is the DDM an Appropriate Choice?

As director of equity research at a brokerage firm, you have final responsibility in the choice of valuation models. An analyst covering consumer/non-cyclicals has approached you about the use of a dividend discount model for valuing the equity of two companies: Anheuser-Busch InBev SA/NV, referred to as "AB InBev" (Euronext: ABI, NYSE: BUD), and Diageo plc (LSE: DGE, NYSE: DEO). Exhibit 1 gives 15 years of data. (In the table, EPS is earnings per share, DPS is dividends per share, and the payout ratio is DPS divided by EPS.)

Exhibit 1: BUD and DEO: The Earnings and Dividends Record

	BUD			DEO		
Year	EPS ($)	DPS ($)	Payout Ratio (%)	EPS (pence)	DPS (pence)	Payout Ratio (%)
2018	2.17	2.05	94	121.1	65.3	54
2017	3.98	4.33	109	105.5	62.2	59
2016	0.71	3.85	542	89.1	59.2	66
2015	4.96	3.95	80	94.6	56.4	60
2014	5.54	3.52	64	89.3	51.7	58
2013	8.72	2.83	32	97.4	47.4	49
2012	4.40	2.24	51	75.8	43.5	57
2011	3.58	1.55	43	74.1	40.4	55
2010	2.50	1.07	43	64.3	38.1	59
2009	2.90	0.55	19	65.0	36.1	56
2008	1.93	0.35	18	58.9	34.4	58
2007	3.06	3.67	120	55.0	32.7	59
2006	1.81	0.95	52	66.9	31.1	46
2005	1.17	0.57	49	45.2	29.6	65
2004	NA	NA	–	48.2	27.6	57

Source: Companies' websites and filings on www.sec.gov.

Answer the following questions based on the information in Exhibit 1:

1. State whether a dividend discount model is an appropriate choice for valuing AB InBev. Explain your answer.

Solution:

Based only on the data given in Exhibit 1, a DDM does not appear to be an appropriate choice for valuing AB InBev. The company's dividends have ranged from \$0.35 to \$4.33 per share, and the annual payout ratio ranged from 18% to 542%, based on reported information. (The variation of earnings, dividends, and dividend payout reflects the company's history of growth through major mergers and acquisitions. ABInBev was formed when the US company Anheuser-Busch was acquired in 2008 by the Belgian company InBev. InBev itself was originally formed by a merger of the Belgian company Interbrew with the Brazilian company AmBev. Further, in 2016 AB InBev made another major acquisition, purchasing SABMiller.)

Based on the record presented and the company's profile, it is unlikely that there will be a consistent relationship between dividends and earnings. Because dividends are unlikely to adjust to reflect changes in profitability, applying a DDM to ABInBev is probably inappropriate. Valuing ABInBev on another basis, such as a company-level definition of cash flows, appears to be more appropriate.

Valuation is a forward-looking exercise. In practice, an analyst would check for public disclosures concerning changes in dividend policy going forward. In light of the increased debt from the 2016 purchase of SABMiller, ABInBev cut its dividend in 2018 and disclosed in its annual report that paying down its debt is a priority and could "restrict the amount of dividends" it is able to pay.

2. State whether a dividend discount model is an appropriate choice for valuing Diageo. Explain your answer.

Solution:

The historical earnings of Diageo show a relatively steady, long-term upward trend, and its dividends have generally followed its growth in earnings. Earnings per share and dividends per share grew at comparable compound annual growth rates of 6.8% and 6.3% during the entire period. In most years, the payout ratio ranged between 50% and 60%. In summary, because Diageo is dividend-paying and because dividends bear an understandable and consistent relationship to earnings, using a DDM to value Diageo is appropriate.

As noted earlier, valuation is a forward-looking exercise, and an analyst would check for public disclosures concerning changes in dividend policy going forward. In its 2018 annual report, Diageo disclosed that it continues to target dividend cover (defined as EPS/DPS) of between 1.8 times and 2.2 times, which implies a payout ratio of between 45% and 56%.

A second definition of returns is free cash flow. The term *cash flow* has been given many meanings in different contexts. Earlier in our coverage the term was used informally, referring to returns to ownership (equity). We now want to give it a more technical meaning, related to accounting usage. Over a given period, a company can add to cash (or use up cash) by selling goods and services. This money is cash flow from operations (for that period). Cash flow from operations is the critical cash flow concept addressing a business's underlying economics. Companies can also generate (or use up) cash in two other ways. First, a company affects cash through buying and selling assets, including investment and disinvestment in plant and equipment. Second, a company can add to or reduce cash through its financing activities. Financing includes debt and equity. For example, issuing bonds increases cash, and buying back stock decreases cash (all else equal).

Internationally, accounting definitions may not be fully consistent with the presented concepts in distinguishing between types of sources and uses of cash. Although the implementation details are not the focus here, an example can be given. US generally accepted accounting principles include a financing item, net interest payments, in cash flow from operating activities. So, careful analysts working with US accounting data often add back after-tax net interest payments to cash flow from operating activities when calculating cash flow from operations. Under International Accounting Standards, companies may or may not include interest expense as an operating cash flow.

Assets supporting current sales may need replacement because of obsolescence or wear and tear, and the company may need new assets to take advantage of profitable growth opportunities. The concept of free cash flow responds to the reality that, for a going concern, some of the cash flow from operations is not "free" but rather needs to be committed to reinvestment and new investment in assets. **Free cash flow to the firm** (FCFF) is cash flow from operations minus capital expenditures. Capital expenditures—reinvestment in new assets, including working capital—are needed to maintain the company as a going concern, so only that part of cash flow from operations remaining after such reinvestment is "free." (This definition is conceptual; free cash flow concepts will be defined in detail later.) FCFF is the part of the cash flow generated by the company's operations that can be withdrawn by bondholders and stockholders without economically impairing the company. Conceptually, the value of common equity is the present value of expected future FCFF—the total value of the company—minus the market value of outstanding debt.

Another approach to valuing equity works with free cash flow to equity. **Free cash flow to equity** (FCFE) is cash flow from operations minus capital expenditures, or FCFF, from which we net all payments to debtholders (interest and principal repayments net of new debt issues). Debt has a claim on the cash of the company that must be satisfied before any money can be paid to stockholders, so money paid on debt is not available to common stockholders. Conceptually, common equity can be valued as the present value of expected FCFE. FCFF is a predebt free cash flow concept; FCFE is a postdebt free cash flow concept. The FCFE model is the baseline free cash flow valuation model for equity, but the FCFF model may be easier to apply in several cases, such as when the company's leverage (debt in its capital structure) is expected to change significantly over time.

Valuation using a free cash flow concept is popular in current investment practice. Free cash flow (FCFF or FCFE) can be calculated for any company. The record of free cash flows can also be examined even for a non-dividend-paying company. FCFE can be viewed as measuring what a company can afford to pay out in dividends. Even for dividend-paying companies, a free cash flow model valuation may be preferred when dividends exceed or fall short of FCFE by significant amounts. FCFE also represents cash flow that can be redeployed outside the company without affecting the company's capital investments. A controlling equity interest can bring about such redeployment. As a result, free cash flow valuation is appropriate for investors who want to take a control perspective. (Even a small shareholder may want to take such a perspective when potential exists for the company to be acquired, because the stock price should reflect the price an acquirer would pay.)

Just as there are cases in which an analyst would find it impractical to apply the DDM, applying the free cash flow approach is a problem in some cases. Some companies have intense capital demands and, as a result, have negative expected free cash flows far into the future. As one example, a retailer may be constantly constructing new outlets and be far from saturating even its domestic market. Even if the retailer is currently very profitable, free cash flow may be negative indefinitely because of the level of capital expenditures. The present value of a series of negative free cash flows is a negative number: The use of a free cash flow model may entail a long forecast horizon to capture the point at which expected free cash flow turns positive. The uncertainty associated with distant forecasts may be considerable. In such cases, the analyst may have more confidence using another approach, such as residual income valuation.

Generally, defining returns as free cash flow and using the FCFE (and FCFF) models are most suitable when:

- the company is not dividend-paying;
- the company is dividend-paying but dividends significantly exceed or fall short of free cash flow to equity;
- the company's free cash flows align with the company's profitability within a forecast horizon with which the analyst is comfortable; and
- the investor takes a control perspective.

The third and final definition of returns that we will discuss in this overview is residual income. Conceptually, **residual income** for a given period is the earnings for that period in excess of the investors' required return on beginning-of-period investment (common stockholders' equity). Suppose shareholders' initial investment is $200 million, and the required rate of return on the stock is 8%. The required rate of return is investors' **opportunity cost** for investing in the stock: the highest expected return available from other equally risky investments, which is the return that investors forgo when investing in the stock. The company earns $18 million in the course of a year. How much value has the company added for shareholders?

A return of 0.08 × $200 million = $16 million just meets the amount investors could have earned in an equivalent-risk investment (by the definition of opportunity cost). Only the residual or excess amount of $18 million − $16 million = $2 million represents value added, or an economic gain, to shareholders. So, $2 million is the company's residual income for the period. The residual income approach attempts to match profits to the period in which they are earned (but not necessarily realized as cash). In contrast to accounting net income (which has the same matching objective in principle), however, residual income attempts to measure the value added in excess of opportunity costs.

The residual income model states that a stock's value is book value per share plus the present value of expected future residual earnings. (**Book value per share** is common stockholders' equity divided by the number of common shares outstanding.) In contrast to the dividend and free cash flow models, the residual income model introduces a stock concept, book value per share, into the present value expression. Nevertheless, the residual income model can be viewed as a restatement of the dividend discount model, using a company-level return concept. Dividends are paid out of earnings and are related to earnings and book value (BV) through a simple expression:

BV of equity at t

= BV of equity at $(t-1)$ + Earnings for the period $(t-1)$ to t − Dividends paid at t

Please note that the foregoing expression is valid assuming that any items that go through the balance sheet (affecting book value) first go through the income statement (reflected in earnings), apart from ownership transactions.

The residual income model is a useful addition to an analyst's toolbox. Because the record of residual income can always be calculated, a residual income model can be used for both dividend-paying and non-dividend-paying stocks. Analysts may choose a residual income approach for companies with negative expected free cash flows within their comfortable forecast horizon. In such cases, a residual income valuation often brings the recognition of value closer to the present as compared with a free cash flow valuation, producing higher value estimates.

The residual income model has an attractive focus on profitability in relation to opportunity costs. Executive compensation schemes are sometimes based on a residual income concept. Knowledgeable application of the residual income model requires a detailed knowledge of accrual accounting; consequently, in cases for which the dividend discount model is suitable, analysts may prefer it as the simpler choice. Management sometimes exercises its discretion within allowable accounting practices to distort the accuracy of its financials as a reflection of economic performance. If the quality of accounting disclosure is good, the analyst may be able to calculate residual income by making appropriate adjustments (to reported net income and book value, in particular). In some cases, the degree of distortion and the quality of accounting disclosure can be such that the application of the residual income model is error-prone.

Generally, the definition of returns as residual income, and the residual income model, is most suitable when:

- the company is not paying dividends, as an alternative to a free cash flow model, or
- the company's expected free cash flows are negative within the analyst's comfortable forecast horizon.

In summary, the three most widely used definitions of returns to investors are dividends, free cash flow, and residual income. Although claims are often made that one cash flow definition is inherently superior to the rest—often following changing fashions in investment practice—a more flexible viewpoint is practical. The analyst may find that one model is more suitable to a particular valuation problem. The analyst may also develop more expertise in applying one type of model. In practice, skill in application—in particular, the quality of forecasts—is frequently decisive for the usefulness of the analyst's work.

In the next section, we present the general form of the dividend discount model as a prelude to discussing the particular implementations of the model that are suitable for different sets of attributes of the company being valued.

2 THE DIVIDEND DISCOUNT MODEL

☐ calculate and interpret the value of a common stock using the dividend discount model (DDM) for single and multiple holding periods

Investment analysts use a wide range of models and techniques to estimate the value of common stock, including present value models. In a survey of CFA Institute members with job responsibility for equity analysis, nearly 80% of respondents reported using a discounted cash flow approach (Stowe, Pinto, and Robinson 2018). Earlier we discussed three common definitions of cash flow for use in present value analysis: dividends, free cash flow, and residual income. In this section, we develop the most general form of the dividend discount model.

The DDM is the simplest and oldest present value approach to valuing stock. Recent survey data shows that among the analysts using a discounted cash flow approach to equity valuation, about 35.1% employ a dividend discount model (Stowe, Pinto, and Robinson 2018). Besides its continuing significant position in practice, the DDM has an important place in both academic and practitioner equity research. The DDM is, for these reasons, a basic tool in equity valuation.

The Expression for a Single Holding Period

From the perspective of a shareholder who buys and holds a share of stock, the cash flows he will obtain are the dividends paid on it and the market price of the share when he sells it. The future selling price should in turn reflect expectations about dividends subsequent to the sale. In this section, we will show how this argument leads to the most general form of the dividend discount model. In addition, the general expression developed for a finite holding period corresponds to one practical approach to DDM valuation. In that approach, the analyst forecasts dividends over a finite horizon, as well as the terminal sales price.

If an investor wishes to buy a share of stock and hold it for one year, the value of that share of stock today is the present value of the expected dividend to be received on the stock plus the present value of the expected selling price in one year:

$$V_0 = \frac{D_1}{(1+r)^1} + \frac{P_1}{(1+r)^1} = \frac{D_1 + P_1}{(1+r)^1} \qquad (2)$$

where

V_0 = the value of a share of stock today, at $t = 0$

P_1 = the expected price per share at $t = 1$

D_1 = the expected dividend per share for Year 1, assumed to be paid at the end of the year at $t = 1$

r = the required rate of return on the stock

Equation 2 applies, to a single holding period, the principle that an asset's value is the present value of its future cash flows. In this case, the expected cash flows are the dividend in one year (for simplicity, assumed to be received as one payment at the end of the year) and the price of the stock in one year. Note that throughout the discussion of the DDM, we assume that dividends for a period are paid in one sum at the end of the period.

EXAMPLE 3

DDM Value with a Single Holding Period

Suppose that you expect Carrefour SA (CA: EN Paris) to pay a €0.46 dividend next year. You expect the price of Carrefour stock to be €23.00 in one year. The required rate of return for Carrefour stock is 8%. What is your estimate of the value of Carrefour stock?

Discounting the expected dividend of €0.46 and the expected sales price of €23.00 at the required return on equity of 8%, we obtain

$$V_0 = \frac{D_1 + P_1}{(1+r)^1} = \frac{0.46 + 23.00}{(1+0.08)^1} = \frac{23.46}{1.08} = 21.72.$$

The Expression for Multiple Holding Periods

If an investor plans to hold a stock for two years, the value of the stock is the present value of the expected dividend in Year 1, plus the present value of the expected dividend in Year 2, plus the present value of the expected selling price at the end of Year 2.

$$V_0 = \frac{D_1}{(1+r)^1} + \frac{D_2}{(1+r)^2} + \frac{P_2}{(1+r)^2} = \frac{D_1}{(1+r)^1} + \frac{D_2 + P_2}{(1+r)^2} \quad (3)$$

The expression for the DDM value of a share of stock for any finite holding period is a straightforward extension of the expressions for one-year and two-year holding periods. For an n-period model, the value of a stock is the present value of the expected dividends for the n periods plus the present value of the expected price in n periods (at $t = n$).

$$V_0 = \frac{D_1}{(1+r)^1} + \cdots + \frac{D_n}{(1+r)^n} + \frac{P_n}{(1+r)^n} \quad (4)$$

If we use summation notation to represent the present value of the first n expected dividends, the general expression for an n-period holding period or investment horizon can be written as

$$V_0 = \sum_{t=1}^{n} \frac{D_t}{(1+r)^t} + \frac{P_n}{(1+r)^n}. \quad (5)$$

Equation 5 is significant in DDM application because analysts may make individual forecasts of dividends over some finite horizon (often two to five years) and then estimate the terminal price, P_n, based on one of a number of approaches. (We will discuss valuation using a finite forecasting horizon later.) Example 4 reviews the mechanics of this calculation.

EXAMPLE 4

Finding the Stock Price for a Five-Year Forecast Horizon

For the next five years, the annual dividends of a stock are expected to be \$2.00, \$2.10, \$2.20, \$3.50, and \$3.75. In addition, the stock price is expected to be \$40.00 in five years. If the required return on equity is 10%, what is the value of this stock?

The present values of the expected future cash flows can be written out as

$$V_0 = \frac{2.00}{(1.10)^1} + \frac{2.10}{(1.10)^2} + \frac{2.20}{(1.10)^3} + \frac{3.50}{(1.10)^4} + \frac{3.75}{(1.10)^5} + \frac{40.00}{(1.10)^5}.$$

Calculating and summing these present values gives a stock value of V_0 = 1.818 + 1.736 + 1.653 + 2.391 + 2.328 + 24.837 = \$34.76.

The five dividends have a total present value of \$9.926 and the terminal stock value has a present value of \$24.837, for a total stock value of \$34.76.

With a finite holding period, whether one, two, five, or some other number of years, the dividend discount model finds the value of stock as the sum of 1) the present values of the expected dividends during the holding period and 2) the present value of the expected stock price at the end of the holding period. As the holding period is increased by one year, we have an extra expected dividend term. In the limit (i.e., if the holding period extends into the indefinite future), the stock's value is the present value of all expected future dividends.

$$V_0 = \frac{D_1}{(1+r)^1} + \ldots + \frac{D_n}{(1+r)^n} + \ldots \quad (6)$$

This value can be expressed with summation notation as

$$V_0 = \sum_{t=1}^{\infty} \frac{D_t}{(1+r)^t}. \tag{7}$$

Equation 7 is the general form of the dividend discount model, first presented by John Burr Williams (1938). Even from the perspective of an investor with a finite investment horizon, the value of stock depends on all future dividends. For that investor, stock value today depends *directly* on the dividends the investor expects to receive before the stock is sold and *indirectly* on the expected dividends after the stock is sold, because those future dividends determine the expected selling price.

Equation 7, by expressing the value of stock as the present value of expected dividends into the indefinite future, presents a daunting forecasting challenge. In practice, of course, analysts cannot make detailed, individual forecasts of an infinite number of dividends. To use the DDM, the forecasting problem must be simplified. Two broad approaches exist, each of which has several variations:

1. Future dividends can be forecast by assigning the stream of future dividends to one of several stylized growth patterns. The most commonly used patterns are:

   - constant growth forever (the Gordon growth model);
   - two distinct stages of growth (the two-stage growth model and the H-model); and
   - three distinct stages of growth (the three-stage growth model).

   The DDM value of the stock is then found by discounting the dividend streams back to the present. We present the Gordon growth model, the two-stage H-model, and three-stage growth models later.

2. A finite number of dividends can be forecast individually up to a terminal point, by using pro forma financial statement analysis, for example. Typically, such forecasts extend from 3 to 10 years into the future. Although some analysts apply the same horizon to all companies under analysis, the horizon selected often depends on the perceived predictability (sometimes called the **visibility**) of the company's earnings. We can then forecast either:

   - the remaining dividends from the terminal point forward by assigning those dividends to a stylized growth pattern, or
   - the share price at the terminal point of our dividend forecasts (**terminal share price**), by using some method (such as taking a multiple of forecasted book value or earnings per share as of that point, based on one of several methods for estimating such multiples).

   The stock's DDM value is then found by discounting the dividends (and forecasted price, if any) back to the present.

Spreadsheets are particularly convenient tools for implementing a DDM with individual dividend forecasts but are useful in all cases. We address spreadsheet modeling at a later stage.

Whether analysts are using dividends or some other definition of cash flow, they generally use one of the foregoing forecasting approaches when valuing stock. The challenge in practice is to choose an appropriate model for a stock's future dividends and to develop quality inputs to that model.

3 THE GORDON GROWTH MODEL

- [ ] calculate the value of a common stock using the Gordon growth model and explain the model's underlying assumptions
- [ ] calculate the value of non-callable fixed-rate perpetual preferred stock
- [ ] describe strengths and limitations of the Gordon growth model and justify its selection to value a company's common shares

The Gordon growth model, developed by Gordon and Shapiro (1956) and Gordon (1962), assumes that dividends grow indefinitely at a constant rate. This assumption, applied to the general dividend discount model (Equation 7), leads to a simple and elegant valuation formula that has been influential in investment practice. This section explores the development of the Gordon growth model and illustrates its uses.

The Gordon Growth Model Equation

The simplest pattern that can be assumed in forecasting future dividends is growth at a constant rate. In mathematical terms, this assumption can be stated as

$$D_t = D_{t-1}(1 + g),$$

where g is the expected constant growth rate in dividends and D_t is the expected dividend payable at time t. Suppose, for example, that the most recent dividend, D_0, was €10. Then, if a 5% dividend growth rate is forecast, the expected dividend at $t = 1$ is $D_1 = D_0(1 + g) = €10 \times 1.05 = €10.5$. For any time t, D_t also equals the $t = 0$ dividend, compounded at g for t periods:

$$D_t = D_0(1 + g)^t \tag{8}$$

To continue the example, at the end of five years the expected dividend is $D_5 = D_0(1 + g)^5 = €10 \times (1.05)^5 = €10 \times 1.276282 = €12.76$. If $D_0(1 + g)^t$ is substituted into Equation 7 for D_t, it gives the Gordon growth model. If all of the terms are written out, they are

$$V_0 = \frac{D_0(1+g)}{(1+r)} + \frac{D_0(1+g)^2}{(1+r)^2} + \ldots + \frac{D_0(1+g)^n}{(1+r)^n} + \ldots \tag{9}$$

Equation 9 is a geometric series; that is, each term in the expression is equal to the previous term times a constant, which in this case is $(1 + g)/(1 + r)$. This equation can be simplified algebraically into a much more compact equation:

$$V_0 = \frac{D_0(1+g)}{r-g}, \text{ or } V_0 = \frac{D_1}{r-g} \tag{10}$$

The simplification involves the expression for the sum of an infinite geometric progression with the first term equal to a and the growth factor equal to m with $|m| < 1$ [i.e., the sum of $a + am + am^2 + \ldots$ is $a/(1 - m)$]. Setting $a = D_1/(1 + r)$ and $m = (1 + g)/(1 + r)$ gives the Gordon growth model.

Both equations are equivalent because $D_1 = D_0(1 + g)$. In Equation 10, it must be specified that the required return on equity must be greater than the expected growth rate: $r > g$. If $r = g$ or $r < g$, Equation 10 as a compact formula for value assuming constant growth is not valid. If $r = g$, dividends grow at the same rate at which they are discounted, so the value of the stock (as the undiscounted sum of all expected future dividends) is infinite. If $r < g$, dividends grow faster than they are discounted, so the value of the stock is infinite. Of course, infinite values do not make economic sense; so constant growth with $r = g$ or $r < g$ does not make sense.

To illustrate the calculation, suppose that an annual dividend of €5 has just been paid (D_0 = €5). The expected long-term growth rate is 5% and the required return on equity is 8%. The Gordon growth model value per share is $D_0(1 + g)/(r - g)$ = (€5 × 1.05)/(0.08 − 0.05) = €5.25/0.03 = €175. When calculating the model value, be careful to use D_1 and not D_0 in the numerator.

The Gordon growth model (Equation 10) is one of the most widely recognized equations in the field of security analysis. Because the model is based on indefinitely extending future dividends, the model's required rate of return and growth rate should reflect long-term expectations. Further, model values are very sensitive to both the required rate of return, r, and the expected dividend growth rate, g. In this model and other valuation models, it is helpful to perform a sensitivity analysis on the inputs, particularly when an analyst is not confident about the proper values.

Earlier we stated that analysts typically apply DDMs to dividend-paying stocks when dividends bear an understandable and consistent relation to the company's profitability. The same qualifications hold for the Gordon growth model. In addition, the Gordon growth model form of the DDM is most appropriate for companies with earnings expected to grow at a rate comparable to or lower than the economy's nominal growth rate. Businesses growing at much higher rates than the economy often grow at lower rates in maturity, and the horizon in using the Gordon growth model is the entire future stream of dividends.

To determine whether the company's growth rate qualifies it as a candidate for the Gordon growth model, an estimate of the economy's nominal growth rate is needed. This growth rate is usually measured by the growth in **gross domestic product**, a money measure of the goods and services produced within a country's borders. National government agencies as well as the World Bank (www.worldbank.org) publish GDP data, which are also available from several secondary sources. Exhibit 2 shows the real GDP growth record for a number of major developed markets.

Exhibit 2: Average Annual Real GDP Growth Rates: 1988–2017

	Period		
Country	**1988–1997**	**1998–2007**	**2008–2017**
Australia	3.2%	3.5%	2.6%
Canada	2.1	3.2	1.6
Denmark	2.0	2.0	0.8
France	2.2	2.4	0.8
Germany	2.6	1.7	1.3
Italy	1.9	1.5	-0.5
Japan	2.8	1.0	0.5
Netherlands	3.1	2.8	0.9
Sweden	1.4	3.5	1.6
Switzerland	1.5	2.4	1.4
United Kingdom	2.4	2.9	1.1
United States	3.1	3.1	1.5

Source: OECD.

Based on historical and/or forward-looking information, nominal GDP growth can be estimated as the sum of the estimated real growth rate in GDP plus the expected long-run inflation rate. For example, using 10 years of historical data through 2018, one estimate of the underlying real growth rate of the Canadian economy is 1.6%. Adjusting for the Bank of Canada's inflation target of 2% as the expected inflation rate gives an estimate of the Canadian economy's nominal annual growth rate of 1.6% + 2% = 3.6%. Publicly traded companies constitute varying amounts of the total corporate sector but always less than 100%. As a result, the overall growth rate of the public corporate sector can diverge from the nominal GDP growth rate during a long horizon; furthermore, within the public corporate sector, some subsectors may experience persistent growth rate differentials. Nevertheless, an earnings growth rate far above the nominal GDP growth rate is not sustainable in perpetuity.

When forecasting an earnings growth rate far above the economy's nominal growth rate, analysts should use a multistage DDM in which the final-stage growth rate reflects a growth rate that is more plausible relative to the economy's nominal growth rate, rather than using the Gordon growth model.

EXAMPLE 5

Valuation Using the Gordon Growth Model (1)

Joel Williams follows Sonoco Products Company (NYSE: SON), a manufacturer of paper and plastic packaging for both consumer and industrial use. Sonoco appears to have a dividend policy of recognizing sustainable increases in the level of earnings with increases in dividends, typically keeping the dividend payout ratio within a range of 40% to 60%. Williams also notes the following:

- Sonoco's most recent quarterly dividend, declared 13 February 2019, was \$0.41, consistent with a current annual dividend of 4 × \$0.41 = \$1.64 per year.
- His forecasted dividend growth rate is 4.5% per year.
- With a beta (β_i) of 0.95, given an equity risk premium (expected excess return of equities over the risk-free rate, $E(R_M) - R_F$) of 4.5% and a risk-free rate (R_F) of 3%, Sonoco's required return on equity is $r = R_F + \beta_i[E(R_M) - R_F] = 3.0 + 0.95(4.5) = 7.3\%$, using the capital asset pricing model.

Williams believes the Gordon growth model may be an appropriate model for valuing Sonoco.

1. Calculate the Gordon growth model value for Sonoco stock.

Solution:

Using Equation 10,

$$V_0 = \frac{D_0(1+g)}{r-g} = \frac{\$1.64 \times 1.045}{0.073 - 0.045} = \frac{\$1.7138}{0.028} = \$61.21.$$

2. The current market price of Sonoco stock is $59.55. Using your answer to Question 1, judge whether Sonoco stock is fairly valued, undervalued, or overvalued.

Solution:

The market price of $59.55 is $1.66, or approximately 2.7% less than the Gordon growth model intrinsic value estimate of $61.21. Sonoco appears to be slightly undervalued based on the Gordon growth model estimate.

The next example illustrates a Gordon growth model valuation introducing some problems the analyst might face in practice. The example refers to adjusted beta; the most common calculation adjusts raw historical beta toward the overall mean value of one for beta.

EXAMPLE 6

Valuation Using the Gordon Growth Model (2)

As an analyst for a US domestic equity–income mutual fund, Robert Kim is evaluating Middlesex Water Company (NASDAQ: MSEX), a publicly traded water utility, for possible inclusion in the approved list of investments. Kim is conducting the analysis in early 2019.

Not all countries have traded water utility stocks. In the United States, most of the population gets its water from government entities; however, a group of investor-owned water utilities also supplies water to the public. With a market capitalization of about $880 million as of early 2019, MSEX is among the 10 largest publicly traded US water utilities. MSEX's historical base is the Middlesex System, serving residential, industrial, and commercial customers in a well-developed area of central New Jersey. Through various subsidiaries, MSEX also provides water and wastewater collection and treatment services to areas of southern New Jersey and Delaware.

MSEX's return on equity averaged 8.5% over the past 10 years with relatively little variation, and its profit margins are above industry averages. When MSEX's credit rating was upgraded in 2015, the reasons cited by Standard & Poor's included the company's "improving management of regulatory risk that is expected to result in less volatile profitability measures, moderately improved cash flow measures and the ability to consistently earn closer to its authorized returns" (according to MSEX's Form 8-K filed with the SEC on 24 August 2015). Because MSEX obtains most of its revenue from the regulated business of providing an important staple, water, to a relatively stable population, Kim feels confident in forecasting future earnings and dividend growth. MSEX appears to have a policy of maintaining an average dividend payout ratio between 60% and 70%. Other facts and forecasts include the following:

- MSEX's per-share dividends for 2018 (D_0) were $0.911.
- Kim forecasts a long-term earnings growth rate of 4.5% per year.
- MSEX's raw beta and adjusted beta are, respectively, 0.70 and 0.80 based on 60 monthly returns. The R^2 associated with beta, however, is under 20%.
- Kim estimates that MSEX's pretax cost of debt is 4.8% based on Standard & Poor's issuer rating of A for MSEX and on the current corporate yield curve.
- Kim's estimate of MSEX's required return on equity is 6.8%.

- MSEX's current market price is $43.20.

1. Calculate the Gordon growth model estimate of value for MSEX using Kim's required return on equity estimate.

Solution:

From Equation 10,

$$V_0 = \frac{D_0(1+g)}{r-g} = \frac{\$0.911\,(1.045)}{0.068 - 0.045} = \$41.39.$$

2. State whether MSEX appears to be overvalued, fairly valued, or undervalued based on the Gordon growth model estimate of value.

Solution:

Because the Gordon growth model estimate of $41.39 differs from the market price of $43.20 by a relatively small amount (less than 5%), MSEX appears to be fairly valued.

3. Justify the selection of the Gordon growth model for valuing MSEX.

Solution:

The Gordon growth model, which assumes that dividends grow at a stable rate in perpetuity, is a realistic model for MSEX for the following reasons:

- MSEX profitability is stable as reflected in its return on equity. This stability reflects predictable demand and regulated prices for its product, water.
- Dividends bear an understandable and consistent relationship to earnings, as evidenced by the company's policy of predictable dividend payout ratios.
- Although the company's earnings growth has been higher in recent years, the forecasted earnings growth rate of 4.5% a year seems both attainable and reasonable compared with the historical long-term nominal annual GDP growth for the United States (approximately 4.3% over the 20-year period 1998–2018, based on data from the US Bureau of Economic Analysis).
- The earnings growth forecast for the company does not include a period of forecasted very high or very low growth.

4. Calculate the CAPM estimate of the required return on equity for MSEX under the assumption that beta reverts to the mean. (Assume an equity risk premium of 4.5% and a risk-free rate of 3% as of the price quotation date.)

Solution:

The assumption of reversion to the mean is characteristic of adjusted historical beta. The required return on equity as given by the CAPM assuming a risk-free rate of 3% and an equity risk premium of 4.5% is given by the following: 3% + 0.80(4.5%) = 6.6% using adjusted beta, which assumes reversion to the mean of 1.0.

5. Calculate the Gordon growth estimate of value using A) the required return on equity from your answer to Question 4, and B) a bond-yield-plus-risk-premium approach with a risk premium of 2.5%.

Solution:

A. The Gordon growth value of MSEX using a required return on equity of 6.6% is

$$V_0 = \frac{D_0(1+g)}{r-g} = \frac{\$0.911 \times 1.045}{0.066 - 0.045} = \$45.33.$$

$$V_0 = \frac{D_0(1+g)}{r-g} = \frac{\$0.911(1.045)}{0.066 - 0.045} = \$45.33$$

B. The bond-yield-plus-risk-premium estimate of the required return on equity is 4.8% + 2.5% = 7.3%. The Gordon growth value of MSEX using a required return on equity of 7.3% is

$$V_0 = \frac{D_0(1+g)}{r-g} = \frac{\$0.911(1.045)}{0.073 - 0.045} = \$34.00.$$

6. Evaluate the effect of uncertainty in MSEX's required return on equity on the valuation conclusion in Question 2.

Solution:

Using the CAPM estimate of the required return on equity (Question 5A), MSEX appears to be fairly valued; although the estimated value of $45.33 exceeds the current market price, the difference is only around 5%. Further, according to the facts given concerning R^2, beta explains less than 20% of the variation in MSEX's returns. Using a bond-yield-plus-risk-premium approach, MSEX appears to be significantly overvalued ($34.00 is more than 20% lower than the market price of $43.20). No specific evidence, however, supports the particular value of the risk premium selected in the bond-yield-plus-risk-premium approach. In this case, because of the uncertainty in the required return on equity estimate, one has less confidence that MSEX is overvalued. Given the results of the other two approaches, the analyst may view MSEX as relatively fairly valued.

As mentioned earlier, an analyst needs to be aware that Gordon growth model values can be very sensitive to small changes in the values of the required rate of return and expected dividend growth rate. Example 7 illustrates a format for a sensitivity analysis.

EXAMPLE 7

Valuation Using the Gordon Growth Model (3)

In Example 6, the Gordon growth model value for MSEX was estimated as $41.39 based on a current dividend of $0.911, an expected dividend growth rate of 4.5%, and a required return on equity of 6.8%. What if the estimates of r and g each vary by 25 bps? How sensitive is the model value to changes in the estimates of r and g? Exhibit 3 provides information on this sensitivity.

Exhibit 3: Estimated Price Given Uncertain Inputs

	g = 4.25%	g = 4.50%	g = 4.75%
r = 6.55%	$41.29	$46.44	$53.02
r = 6.80%	$37.24	**$41.39**	$46.55
r = 7.05%	$33.92	$37.33	$41.49

A point of interest following from the mathematics of the Gordon growth model is that when the spread between r and g is the widest (r = 7.05% and g = 4.25%), the Gordon growth model value is the smallest ($33.92), and when the spread is the narrowest (r = 6.55% and g = 4.75%), the model value is the largest ($53.02). As the spread goes to zero, in fact, the model value increases without bound. The largest value in Exhibit 3, $53.02, is more than 55% larger than the smallest value, $33.92. Two-thirds of the values in Exhibit 3 are lower than MSEX's current market price of $43.20. All but two of the estimates, however, are within 10% of the current price, which supports the conclusion that MSEX is relatively fairly valued or slightly overvalued. In summary, the best estimate of the value of MSEX given the assumptions is $41.39, bolded in Exhibit 3, but the estimate is quite sensitive to rather small changes in inputs.

Example 6 and Example 7 illustrate the application of the Gordon growth model to a utility, a traditional source for such illustrations because of the stability afforded by providing an essential service in a regulated environment. Before applying any valuation model, however, analysts need to know much more about a company than industry membership. For example, if a utility company undertook an aggressive growth-by-acquisition strategy, then its expected growth in income and dividends could potentially diverge significantly from other companies in the industry. Furthermore, many utility holding companies in the United States have major, unregulated business subsidiaries so the traditional picture of steady and slow growth often does not hold.

In addition to individual stocks, analysts have often used the Gordon growth model to value broad equity market indexes, especially in developed markets. Because the value of publicly traded issues typically represents a large fraction of the overall corporate sector in developed markets, such indexes reflect average economic growth rates. Furthermore, in such economies, a sustainable trend value of growth may be identifiable.

The Gordon growth model can also be used to value the non-callable form of a traditional type of preferred stock, **fixed-rate perpetual preferred stock** (stock with a specified dividend rate that has a claim on earnings senior to the claim of common stock, and no maturity date). Perpetual preferred stock has been used particularly by financial institutions such as banks to obtain permanent equity capital while diluting the interests of common equity. Generally, such issues have been callable by the issuer after a certain period, so valuation must take account of the issuer's call option. Valuation of the non-callable form, however, is straightforward.

If the dividend on such preferred stock is D, because payments extend into the indefinite future a **perpetuity** (a stream of level payments extending to infinity) exists in the constant amount of D. With g = 0, which is true because dividends are fixed for such preferred stock, the Gordon growth model becomes

$$V_0 = \frac{D}{r}. \quad (11)$$

The discount rate, r, capitalizes the amount D, and for that reason is often called a **capitalization rate** in this expression and any other expression for the value of a perpetuity.

EXAMPLE 8

Valuing Noncallable Fixed-Rate Perpetual Preferred Stock

1. Kansas City Southern Preferred 4% (KSU-P), issued 2 January 1963, has a par value of $25 per share. Thus, a share pays 0.04($25) = $1.00 in annual dividends. The required return on this security is estimated at 5.5%. Estimate the value of this issue.

Solution:

According to the model in Equation 11, KSU-P preferred stock is worth D/r = 1.00/0.055 = $18.18.

A perpetual preferred stock has a level dividend, thus a dividend growth rate of zero. Another case is a declining dividend—a negative growth rate. The Gordon growth model also accommodates this possibility, as illustrated in Example 9.

EXAMPLE 9

Gordon Growth Model with Negative Growth

1. Afton Mines is a profitable company that is expected to pay a $4.25 dividend next year. Because it is depleting its mining properties, the best estimate is that dividends will decline forever at a rate of 4%. The required rate of return on Afton stock is 9%. What is the value of Afton shares?

Solution:

For Afton, the value of the stock is

$$V_0 = \frac{4.25}{[0.09 - (-0.04)]}$$
$$= \frac{4.25}{0.13} = \$32.69$$

The negative growth results in a $32.69 valuation for the stock.

The Links among Dividend Growth, Earnings Growth, and Value Appreciation in the Gordon Growth Model

The Gordon growth model implies a set of relationships for the growth rates of dividends, earnings, and stock value. With dividends growing at a constant rate g, stock value also grows at g as well. The current stock value is $V_0 = D_1/(r - g)$. Multiplying both sides by $(1 + g)$ gives $V_0(1 + g) = D_1(1 + g)/(r - g)$, which is $V_1 = D_2/(r - g)$. So, both dividends and value have grown at a rate of g (holding r constant). Given a constant payout ratio—a constant, proportional relationship between earnings and dividends—dividends and earnings grow at g.

To summarize, g in the Gordon growth model is the rate of value or capital appreciation (sometimes also called the capital gains yield). Some textbooks state that g is the rate of price appreciation. If prices are efficient (price equals value), price is indeed expected to grow at a rate of g. If there is mispricing (price is different from value), however, the actual rate of capital appreciation depends on the nature of the mispricing and how fast it is corrected, if at all. This topic is discussed in the coverage of return concepts.

Another characteristic of the constant growth model is that the components of total return (dividend yield and capital gains yield) will also stay constant through time, given that price tracks value exactly. The dividend yield, which is D_1/P_0 at $t = 0$, will stay unchanged because both the dividend and the price are expected to grow at the same rate, leaving the dividend yield unchanged through time. For example, consider a stock selling for €50.00 with a **forward dividend yield** (a dividend yield based on the anticipated dividend during the next 12 months) of 2% based on an expected dividend of €1. The estimate of g is 5.50% per year. The dividend yield of 2%, the capital gains yield of 5.50%, and the total return of 7.50% are expected to be the same at $t = 0$ and at any future point in time.

4 SHARE REPURCHASES AND THE IMPLIED DIVIDEND GROWTH RATE

- ☐ calculate the value of a common stock using the Gordon growth model and explain the model's underlying assumptions
- ☐ calculate and interpret the implied growth rate of dividends using the Gordon growth model and current stock price

An issue of increasing importance in many developed markets is share repurchases. Companies can distribute free cash flow to shareholders in the form of share repurchases (also called buybacks) as well as dividends. In the United States, more than half of dividend-paying companies have also been making regular share repurchases (Skinner 2008). Clearly, analysts using DDMs need to understand share repurchases. Share repurchases and cash dividends have several distinctive features:

- Share repurchases involve a reduction in the number of shares outstanding, all else equal. Selling shareholders see their relative ownership position reduced compared with non-selling shareholders.
- Whereas many corporations with established cash dividends are reluctant to reduce or omit cash dividends, corporations generally do not view themselves as committed to maintaining share repurchases at any specified level.
- Cash dividends tend to be more predictable in money terms and more predictable as to timing (Wagner 2007). Although evidence from the United States suggests that, for companies with active repurchase programs, the amount of repurchases during two-year intervals bears a relationship to earnings, companies appear to be opportunistic in timing exactly when to repurchase (Skinner 2008). Thus, share repurchases are generally harder to forecast than the cash dividends of companies with an identifiable dividend policy.
- As a baseline case, share repurchases are neutral in their effect on the wealth of ongoing shareholders if the repurchases are accomplished at market prices.

The analyst could account for share repurchases directly by forecasting the total earnings, total distributions to shareholders (via either cash dividends or share repurchases), and shares outstanding. Experience and familiarity with such models is much less than for DDMs. Focusing on cash dividends, however, DDMs supply accurate valuations consistent with such an approach if the analyst takes account of the effect of expected repurchases on the per-share growth rates of dividends. Correctly applied, the DDM is a valid approach to common stock valuation even when the company being analyzed engages in share repurchases.

The Implied Dividend Growth Rate

Because the dividend growth rate affects the estimated value of a stock using the Gordon growth model, differences between estimated values of a stock and its actual market value might be explained by different growth rate assumptions. Given price, the expected next-period dividend, and an estimate of the required rate of return, the dividend growth rate reflected in price can be inferred assuming the Gordon growth model. (Actually, it is possible to infer the market-price-implied dividend growth based on other DDMs as well.) An analyst can then judge whether the implied dividend growth rate is reasonable, high, or low, based on what she knows about the company. In effect, the calculation of the implied dividend growth rate provides an alternative perspective on the stock's valuation (fairly valued, overvalued, or undervalued). Example 10 shows how the Gordon growth model can be used to infer the market's implied growth rate for a stock.

EXAMPLE 10

The Growth Rate Implied by the Current Stock Price

Suppose a company has a beta of 1.1. The risk-free rate is 5.6%, and the equity risk premium is 6%. The current dividend of $2.00 is expected to grow at 5% indefinitely. The price of the stock is $40.

1. Estimate the value of the company's stock.

Solution:

The required rate of return is 5.6% + 1.1(6%) = 12.2%. The value of one share, using the Gordon growth model, is

$$\begin{aligned} V_0 &= \frac{D_0(1+g)}{r-g} \\ &= \frac{2.00(1.05)}{0.122-0.05} \\ &= \frac{2.10}{0.072} = \$29.17 \end{aligned}$$

2. Determine the constant dividend growth rate that would be required to justify the market price of $40.

Solution:

The valuation estimate of the model ($29.17) is less than the market value of $40.00, and thus the market price must be forecasting a growth rate above the assumed 5%. Assuming that the model and the required return assumption are appropriate, the growth rate in dividends required to justify the $40 stock price can be calculated by substituting all known values into the Gordon growth model equation except for *g*:

$$40 = \frac{2.00(1+g)}{0.122-g}$$

$$4.88 - 40g = 2 + 2g$$

$$42g = 2.88$$

$$g = 0.0686$$

An expected dividend growth rate of 6.86% is required for the stock price to be correctly valued at the market price of $40.

5 THE GORDON GROWTH MODEL: OTHER ISSUES

- ☐ calculate and interpret the present value of growth opportunities (PVGO) and the component of the leading price-to-earnings ratio (P/E) related to PVGO
- ☐ calculate and interpret the justified leading and trailing P/Es using the Gordon growth model
- ☐ describe strengths and limitations of the Gordon growth model and justify its selection to value a company's common shares
- ☐ estimate a required return based on any DDM, including the Gordon growth model and the H-model
- ☐ evaluate whether a stock is overvalued, fairly valued, or undervalued by the market based on a DDM estimate of value

The value of a stock can be analyzed as the sum of 1) the value of the company without earnings reinvestment and 2) the **present value of growth opportunities** (PVGO). PVGO, also known as the **value of growth**, sums the expected value today of opportunities to profitably reinvest future earnings. More technically, PVGO can be defined as the forecasted total net present value of future projects. In this section, we illustrate this decomposition and discuss how it may be interpreted to gain insight into the market's view of a company's business and prospects.

Earnings growth may increase, leave unchanged, or reduce shareholder wealth depending on whether the growth results from earning returns in excess of, equal to, or less than the opportunity cost of funds. Consider a company with a required return on equity of 10% that has earned €1 per share. The company is deciding whether to pay out current earnings as a dividend or to reinvest them at 10% and distribute the ending value as a dividend in one year. If it reinvests, the present value of investment is €1.10/1.10 = €1.00, equaling its cost, so the decision to reinvest has a net present value (NPV) of zero. If the company were able to earn more than 10% by exploiting a profitable growth opportunity, reinvesting would have a positive NPV, increasing shareholder wealth. Suppose the company could reinvest earnings at 25% for one year: The per-share NPV of the growth opportunity would be €1.25/1.10 – €1 ≈ €0.14. Note that any reinvestment at a positive rate below 10%, although increasing EPS, is not in shareholders' interests. Increases in shareholder wealth occur only when reinvested earnings earn more than the opportunity cost of funds—that is, when investments are in positive NPV projects (condition of profitability as return on equity [ROE] > *r*, with ROE calculated with the market value of equity rather than the book value of equity in the denominator). Thus, investors actively assess whether and to what degree companies will have opportunities to invest in profitable projects. In principle, companies without prospects for investing in positive NPV projects should distribute most or all earnings to shareholders as dividends so the shareholders can redirect capital to more attractive areas.

A company without positive expected NPV projects is defined as a **no-growth company** (a term for a company without opportunities for *profitable* growth). Such companies should distribute all their earnings in dividends because earnings cannot be reinvested profitably and will be flat in perpetuity, assuming a constant ROE. This flatness occurs because earnings equal ROE × Equity, and equity is constant because retained earnings are not added to it. If assets are in place to support the growth in earnings for the next year (t = 1) compared with the prior year (t = 0), E_1 is the appropriate measure of earnings to use in estimating the no-growth value per share. E_1 is t = 1 earnings, which is the constant level of earnings or the average earnings of a no-growth company if return on equity is viewed as varying about its average level. The **no-growth value per share** is defined as E_1/r, which is the present value of a perpetuity in the amount of E_1 where the capitalization rate, r, is the required rate of return on the company's equity. E_1/r can also be interpreted as the per-share value of assets in place because of the assumption that the company is making no new investments because none are profitable. For any company, the actual value per share is the sum of the no-growth value per share and the present value of growth opportunities:

$$V_0 = \frac{E_1}{r} + \text{PVGO} \quad (12)$$

If prices reflect value ($P_0 = V_0$), P_0 less E_1/r gives the market's estimate of the company's value of growth, PVGO. Referring back to Example 6, suppose that MSEX is expected to have average EPS of \$1.52 if it distributed all earnings as dividends. Its required return of 6.8% and a current price of \$43.20 gives

$$\$43.20 = (\$1.52/0.068) + \text{PVGO}$$

$$= \$22.42 + \text{PVGO}$$

and PVGO = \$43.20 – \$22.42 = \$20.78. So, 48% (\$20.78/\$43.20 = 0.48) of the company's value, as reflected in the market price, is attributable to the value of growth.

Exhibit 4 presents selected data from early 2019 for three companies: Alphabet, Inc. (NASDAQ: GOOGL), McDonald's Corporation (NYSE: MCD), and Macy's, Inc. (NYSE: M). The data indicate that the value of growth represented about 53% of the market value of technology company Alphabet (the parent company of Google) and a much smaller percentage of McDonald's market value and Macy's market value. The negative value for Macy's PVGO could be explained in several ways: It could reflect the expected continued challenges that traditional retailers face from online competition, or it might indicate that the estimated no-growth value per share was too high because the earnings estimate was too high and/or the required return on equity estimate was too low.

Exhibit 4: Estimated PVGO as a Percentage of Price

Company	β	r	E_1	Price	E_1/r	PVGO	PVGO/Price
Alphabet, Inc.	1.16	8.2%	\$47.49	\$1,236.34	\$579.14	\$657.20	53.16%
McDonald's Corp	0.52	5.3%	\$8.23	\$194.12	\$155.28	\$38.84	20.01%
Macy's Inc.	0.45	5.0%	\$3.09	\$25.11	\$61.80	(\$36.69)	n.m.

Source: NASDAQ for earnings estimate and S&P equity research for beta.
Note: The required rate of return is estimated using the CAPM with 3.0% for the risk-free rate of return

and 4.5% for the equity risk premium.

What determines PVGO? One determinant is the value of a company's options to invest, captured by the word "opportunities." In addition, the flexibility to adapt investments to new circumstances and information is valuable. Thus, a second determinant of PVGO is the value of the company's options to time the start, adjust the scale, or even abandon future projects. This element is the value of the company's **real options** (options to modify projects, in this context). Companies that have good business opportunities and/or a high level of managerial flexibility in responding to changes in the marketplace should tend to have higher values of PVGO than companies that do not have such advantages. This perspective on what contributes to PVGO can provide additional understanding of the results in Exhibit 4.

As an additional aid to an analyst, Equation 12 can be restated in terms of the familiar P/E based on forecasted earnings:

$$\frac{V_0}{E_1} \text{ or } \frac{P_0}{E_1} \text{ or P/E} = \frac{1}{r} + \frac{\text{PVGO}}{E_1} \tag{13}$$

The first term, $1/r$, is the value of the P/E for a no-growth company. The second term is the component of the P/E value that relates to growth opportunities. For MSEX, the P/E is \$43.20/\$1.52 = 28.4. The no-growth P/E is 1/0.068 = 14.7 and is the multiple at which the company should sell if it has no growth opportunities. The growth component of \$20.78/\$1.52 = 13.67 reflects anticipated growth opportunities.

As analysts, the distinction between no-growth and growth values is of interest because the value of growth and the value of assets in place generally have different risk characteristics (as the interpretation of PVGO as incorporating the real options suggests).

Gordon Growth Model and the Price-to-Earnings Ratio

The price-to-earnings ratio is perhaps the most widely recognized valuation indicator, familiar to readers of newspaper financial tables and institutional research reports. Using the Gordon growth model, one can develop an expression for P/E in terms of the fundamentals. This expression has two uses:

- When used with forecasts of the inputs to the model, the analyst obtains a **justified (fundamental) P/E**—the P/E that is fair, warranted, or justified on the basis of fundamentals (given that the valuation model is appropriate). The analyst can then state his view of value in terms not of the Gordon growth model value but of the justified P/E. Because P/E is so widely recognized, this method may be an effective way to communicate the analysis.
- The analyst may also use the expression for P/E to weigh whether the forecasts of earnings growth built into the current stock price are reasonable. What expected earnings growth rate is implied by the actual market P/E? Is that growth rate plausible?

The expression for P/E can be stated in terms of the current (or trailing) P/E (today's market price per share divided by trailing 12 months' earnings per share) or in terms of the leading (or forward) P/E (today's market price per share divided by a forecast of the next 12 months' earnings per share, or sometimes the next fiscal year's earnings per share).

Leading and trailing justified P/E expressions can be developed from the Gordon growth model. Assuming that the model can be applied for a particular stock's valuation, the dividend payout ratio is considered fixed. Define b as the retention rate, the fraction of earnings reinvested in the company rather than paid out in dividends. The dividend payout ratio is then, by definition, $(1 - b)$ = Dividend per share/Earnings per share = D_t/E_t. If $P_0 = D_1/(r - g)$ is divided by next year's earnings per share, E_1, we have

$$\frac{P_0}{E_1} = \frac{D_1/E_1}{r-g} = \frac{1-b}{r-g}. \tag{14}$$

This calculation represents a leading P/E, which is current price divided by next year's earnings. Alternatively, if $P_0 = D_0(1 + g)/(r - g)$ is divided by the current-year's earnings per share, E_0, the result is

$$\frac{P_0}{E_0} = \frac{D_0(1+g)/E_0}{r-g} = \frac{(1-b)(1+g)}{r-g}. \tag{15}$$

This expression is for trailing P/E, which is current price divided by trailing (current year) earnings.

EXAMPLE 11

The Justified P/E Based on the Gordon Growth Model

Harry Trice wants to use the Gordon growth model to find a justified P/E for the French company L'Oréal SA (EN Paris: OR), a global cosmetics manufacturer. Trice has assembled the following information:

- Current stock price = €242.70.
- Trailing annual earnings per share = €7.08.
- Current level of annual dividends = €3.85.
- Dividend growth rate = 4.25%.
- Risk-free rate = 2.0%.
- Equity risk premium = 5.0%.
- Beta versus the CAC index = 0.72.

1. Calculate the justified trailing and leading P/Es based on the Gordon growth model.

Solution:

For L'Oréal, the required rate of return using the CAPM is

$$r_i = 2.0\% + 0.72(5.0\%)$$

$$= 5.6\%$$

The dividend payout ratio is

$$(1 - b) = D_0/E_0$$

$$= 3.85/7.08$$

$$= 0.54$$

The justified leading P/E (based on next year's earnings) is

$$\frac{P_0}{E_1} = \frac{1-b}{r-g} = \frac{0.5438}{0.056 - 0.0425} = 40.28.$$

$$\frac{P_0}{E_1} = \frac{1-b}{r-g} = \frac{0.5438}{0.056 - 0.0425} = 40.28$$

The justified trailing P/E (based on trailing earnings) is

$$\frac{P_0}{E_0} = \frac{(1-b)(1+g)}{r-g} = \frac{0.5438(1.0425)}{0.056 - 0.0425} = 42.00.$$

2. Based on the justified trailing P/E and the actual P/E, judge whether L'Oréal is fairly valued, overvalued, or undervalued.

Solution:

Based on a current price of €242.70 and trailing earnings of €7.08, the trailing P/E is €242.70/€7.08 = 34.3. Because the actual P/E of 34.3 is smaller than the justified trailing P/E of 42.0, the conclusion is that L'Oréal appears to be undervalued. The apparent mispricing can also be expressed in terms of price using the Gordon growth model. Using Trice's assumptions, the Gordon growth model assigns a value of 3.85(1.0425)/(0.05 – 0.0425) = €297.31, which is above the current market price of €242.70.

We will later present multistage DDMs. Expressions for the P/E can be developed in terms of the variables of multistage DDMs, but the usefulness of these expressions is not commensurate with their complexity. For multistage models, the simple way to calculate a justified leading P/E is to divide the model value directly by the first year's expected earnings. In all cases, the P/E is explained in terms of the required return on equity, expected dividend growth rate(s), and the dividend payout ratio(s). All else equal, higher prices are associated with higher anticipated dividend growth rates.

Estimating a Required Return Using the Gordon Growth Model

Under the assumption of efficient prices, the Gordon growth model has been used to estimate a stock's required rate of return, or equivalently, the market-price-implied expected return. The Gordon growth model solved for r is

$$r = \frac{D_0(1+g)}{P_0} + g = \frac{D_1}{P_0} + g. \tag{16}$$

As explained in the coverage of return concepts, r in Equation 16 is technically an internal rate of return (IRR). The rate r is composed of two parts: the dividend yield (D_1/P_0) and the capital gains (or appreciation) yield (g).

EXAMPLE 12

Finding the Expected Rate of Return with the Gordon Growth Model

Bob Inguigiatto, CFA, has been given the task of developing mean return estimates for a list of stocks as preparation for a portfolio optimization. On his list is NextEra Energy, Inc. (NYSE: NEE). On analysis, he decides that it is appropriate to model NextEra Energy using the Gordon growth model, and he takes prices as reflecting value. The company paid dividends of $4.44 in 2018 and in February 2019 announced an increase in quarterly dividends from $1.11 to $1.25, implying an annual dividend of $5.00. The current stock price is $169.83. The growth rate of dividends per share has averaged around 11.0% per year, based on the past five years. NextEra's recent earnings growth has been affected by non-recurring items, but based on his analysis, Inguigiatto has decided to use 5.50% as his best estimate of the long-term earnings and dividend growth rate. Next year's projected dividend, D_1, is $5.00(1.055) = $5.275. Using the Gordon growth model, NextEra Energy's expected rate of return is

$$\begin{aligned} r &= \frac{D_1}{P_0} + g \\ &= \frac{5.275}{169.83} + 0.055 \\ &= 0.0311 + 0.055 \\ &= 0.0860 = 8.60\% \end{aligned}$$

The expected rate of return can be broken into two components: the dividend yield (D_1/P_0 = 3.11%) and the capital gains yield (g = 5.50%).

The Gordon Growth Model: Concluding Remarks

The Gordon growth model is the simplest practical implementation of discounted dividend valuation. The Gordon growth model is appropriate for valuing the equity of dividend-paying companies when its key assumption of a stable future dividend and earnings growth rate is expected to be satisfied. Broad equity market indexes of developed markets frequently satisfy the conditions of the model fairly well. As a result, analysts have used it to judge whether an equity market is fairly valued or not and for estimating the equity risk premium associated with the current market level. In the multistage models discussed in the next section, the Gordon growth model has often been used to model the last growth stage, when a previously high-growth company matures and the growth rate drops to a long-term sustainable level. In any case in which the model is applied, the analyst must be aware that the model's output is typically sensitive to small changes in the assumed growth rate and required rate of return.

The Gordon growth model is a single-stage DDM because all future periods are grouped into one stage characterized by a single growth rate. For many or even the majority of companies, however, future growth can be expected to consist of multiple stages. Multistage DDMs are the subject of the next section.

MULTISTAGE DIVIDEND DISCOUNT MODELS 6

- ☐ explain the growth phase, transition phase, and maturity phase of a business
- ☐ explain the assumptions and justify the selection of the two-stage DDM, the H-model, the three-stage DDM, or spreadsheet modeling to value a company's common shares
- ☐ describe terminal value and explain alternative approaches to determining the terminal value in a DDM
- ☐ calculate and interpret the value of common shares using the two-stage DDM, the H-model, and the three-stage DDM
- ☐ evaluate whether a stock is overvalued, fairly valued, or undervalued by the market based on a DDM estimate of value

Earlier we noted that the basic expression for the DDM (Equation 7) is too general for investment analysts to use in practice because one cannot forecast individually more than a relatively small number of dividends. The strongest simplifying assumption—a stable dividend growth rate from now into the indefinite future, leading to the Gordon growth model—is unrealistic for many or even most companies. For many publicly traded companies, practitioners have typically assumed that growth falls into three stages (see Sharpe, Alexander, and Bailey 1999):

- **Growth phase.** A company in its growth phase typically enjoys rapidly expanding markets, high profit margins, and an abnormally high growth rate in earnings per share (**supernormal growth**). Companies in this phase often have negative free cash flow to equity because the company invests heavily in expanding operations. Given high prospective returns on equity, the dividend payout ratios of growth-phase companies are often low or even zero. As the company's markets mature or as unusual growth opportunities attract competitors, earnings growth rates eventually decline.

- **Transition phase.** In this phase, which is a transition to maturity, earnings growth slows as competition puts pressure on prices and profit margins or as sales growth slows because of market saturation. In this phase, earnings growth rates may be above average but declining toward the growth rate for the overall economy. Capital requirements typically decline in this phase, often resulting in positive free cash flow and increasing dividend payout ratios (or the initiation of dividends).
- **Mature phase.** In maturity, the company reaches an equilibrium in which investment opportunities on average just earn their opportunity cost of capital. Return on equity approaches the required return on equity, and earnings growth, the dividend payout ratio, and the return on equity stabilize at levels that can be sustained long term. The dividend and earnings growth rate of this phase is called the **mature growth rate**. This phase, in fact, reflects the stage in which a company can properly be valued using the Gordon growth model, and that model is one tool for valuing this phase of a current high-growth company's future.

A company may attempt and succeed in restarting the growth phase by changing its strategic focuses and business mix. Technological advances may alter a company's growth prospects for better or worse with surprising rapidity. Nevertheless, this growth-phase picture of a company is a useful approximation. The growth-phase concept provides the intuition for multistage discounted cash flow (DCF) models of all types, including multistage dividend discount models. Multistage models are a staple valuation discipline of investment management firms using DCF valuation models.

A survey of CFA Institute members with job responsibility for equity analysis indicates that, among respondents using a dividend discount model, two-stage and multistage models are used more often than the single-stage model (Stowe, Pinto, and Robinson 2018). Among analysts using a dividend discount model, 55% use a two-stage model, 11% use an H-model (a type of two-stage model), and 50% use a model with more than two stages (Stowe, Pinto, and Robinson 2018). (Because analysts often use more than one model, the response percentages add up to more than 100%).

In the following sections, we present three popular multistage DDMs: the two-stage DDM, the H-model, and the three-stage DDM. Keep in mind that all these models represent stylized patterns of growth; they are attempting to identify the pattern that most accurately approximates an analyst's view of the company's future growth.

Two-Stage Dividend Discount Model

Two common versions of the two-stage DDM exist. Both versions assume constant growth at a mature growth rate (for example, 7%) in Stage 2. In the first version ("the general two-stage model"), the whole of Stage 1 represents a period of abnormal growth—for example, growth at 15%. The transition to mature growth in Stage 2 is generally abrupt.

In the second version, called the H-model, the dividend growth rate is assumed to decline from an abnormal rate to the mature growth rate during the course of Stage 1. For example, the growth rate could begin at 15% and decline continuously in Stage 1 until it reaches 7%. The second model will be presented after the general two-stage model.

The first two-stage DDM provides for a high growth rate for the initial period, followed by a sustainable and usually lower growth rate thereafter. The two-stage DDM is based on the multiple-period model

$$V_0 = \sum_{t=1}^{n} \frac{D_t}{(1+r)^t} + \frac{V_n}{(1+r)^n}, \tag{17}$$

where V_n is used as an estimate of P_n. The two-stage model assumes that the first n dividends grow at an extraordinary short-term rate, g_S:

$$D_t = D_0\left(1+g_S\right)^t$$

After time n, the annual dividend growth rate changes to a normal long-term rate, g_L. The dividend at time n + 1 is $D_{n+1} = D_n(1 + g_L) = D_0(1 + g_S)^n(1 + g_L)$, and this dividend continues to grow at g_L. Using D_{n+1}, an analyst can use the Gordon growth model to find V_n:

$$V_n = \frac{D_0\left(1+g_S\right)^n\left(1+g_L\right)}{r-g_L} \tag{18}$$

To find the value at $t = 0$, V_0, simply find the present value of the first n dividends and the present value of the projected value at time n.

$$V_0 = \sum_{t=1}^{n} \frac{D_0\left(1+g_S\right)^t}{(1+r)^t} + \frac{D_0\left(1+g_S\right)^n\left(1+g_L\right)}{(1+r)^n\left(r-g_L\right)} \tag{19}$$

EXAMPLE 13

Valuing a Stock Using the Two-Stage Dividend Discount Model

1. Carl Zeiss Meditec AG (AFX:GR), 65% owned by the Carl Zeiss Group, provides screening, diagnostic, and therapeutic systems for the treatment of ophthalmologic (vision) problems. Reviewing the issue as of early 2019, when it is trading for €80.55, Hans Mattern, a buy-side analyst covering Meditec, forecasts that the current dividend of €0.55 will grow by 9% per year during the next 10 years. Thereafter, Mattern believes that the growth rate will decline to 5% and remain at that level indefinitely.

   Mattern estimates Meditec's required return on equity as 5.88% based on a beta of 0.90 against the equity market benchmark DAX, a 1.2% risk-free rate, and his equity risk premium estimate of 5.2%.

   Exhibit 5 shows the calculations of the first 10 dividends and their present values discounted at 5.88%. The terminal stock value at $t = 10$ is

$$V_{10} = \frac{D_0\left(1+g_S\right)^n\left(1+g_L\right)}{r-g_L}$$

$$= \frac{0.55(1.09)^{10}(1.05)}{0.0588-0.05}$$

$$= 155.358$$

   The terminal stock value and its present value are also given.

Exhibit 5: Carl Zeiss Meditec AG

Time	Value	Calculation	D_t or V_t	Present Values $D_t/(1.0588)^t$ or $V_t/(1.0588)^t$
1	D_1	$= 0.55 \times (1 + 0.09)^1$	€0.600	€0.5662
2	D_2	$= 0.55 \times (1 + 0.09)^2$	0.653	0.5829
3	D_3	$= 0.55 \times (1 + 0.09)^3$	0.712	0.6001
4	D_4	$= 0.55 \times (1 + 0.09)^4$	0.776	0.6178
5	D_5	$= 0.55 \times (1 + 0.09)^5$	0.846	0.6360
6	D_6	$= 0.55 \times (1 + 0.09)^6$	0.922	0.6547
7	D_7	$= 0.55 \times (1 + 0.09)^7$	1.005	0.6740
8	D_8	$= 0.55 \times (1 + 0.09)^8$	1.096	0.6938
9	D_9	$= 0.55 \times (1 + 0.09)^9$	1.195	0.7143
10	D_{10}	$= 0.55 \times (1 + 0.09)^{10}$	1.302	0.7353
10	V_{10}	$= [0.55 \times (1 + 0.09)^{10} \times 1.05]/(0.0588 - 0.05)$	155.358	87.7395
Total				€94.2145

In this two-stage model, the dividends are forecast during the first stage and then their present values are calculated. The Gordon growth model is used to derive the terminal value (the value of the dividends in the second stage as of the beginning of that stage). As shown in Exhibit 5, the terminal value is $V_{10} = D_{11}/(r - g_L)$. Ignoring rounding errors, the Period 11 dividend is €1.3671 (= $D_{10} \times 1.05$ = €1.302 × 1.05). By using the standard Gordon growth model, V_{10} = €155.36 = €1.3671/(0.0588 – 0.05). The present value of the terminal value is €87.74 = €155.36/1.0588^{10}. The total estimated value of Meditec is €94.21 using this model. Notice that approximately 93% of this value, €87.74, is the present value of V_{10}, and the balance, €94.21 – €87.74 = €6.47, is the present value of the first 10 dividends. If we recall the discussion of the sensitivity of the Gordon growth model to changes in the inputs, we can calculate an interval for the intrinsic value of Meditec by varying the mature growth rate through the range of plausible values.

The two-stage DDM is useful because many scenarios exist in which a company can achieve a supernormal growth rate for a few years, after which time the growth rate falls to a more sustainable level. For example, a company may achieve supernormal growth through possession of a patent, first-mover advantage, or another factor that provides a temporary lead in a specific marketplace. Subsequently, earnings will most likely descend to a level that is more consistent with competition and growth in the overall economy. Accordingly, that is why in the two-stage model, extraordinary growth is often forecast for a few years and normal growth is forecast thereafter. A possible limitation of the two-stage model is that the transition between the initial abnormal growth period and the final steady-state growth period is abrupt.

The accurate estimation of V_n, the **terminal value of the stock** (also known as its **continuing value**) is an important part of the correct use of DDMs. In practice, analysts estimate the terminal value either by applying a multiple to a projected terminal value of a fundamental, such as earnings per share or book value per share, or they estimate V_n using the Gordon growth model. In our coverage of market multiples, we will discuss using price–earnings multiples in this context.

In the examples, a single discount rate, *r*, is used for all phases, reflecting both a desire for simplicity and lack of a clear objective basis for adjusting the discount rate for different phases. Some analysts, however, use different discount rates for different growth phases.

The following example values P&G (Procter & Gamble Company) by combining the dividend discount model and a P/E valuation model.

EXAMPLE 14

Combining a DDM and P/E Model to Value a Stock

1. An analyst is reviewing the valuation of Procter & Gamble Company known as "P&G" (NYSE: PG) as of the beginning of 2019 when P&G was selling for \$96.47. In the previous year, P&G paid a \$2.79 dividend that the analyst expects to grow at a rate of 4% annually for the next four years. At the end of Year 4, the analyst expects the dividend to equal 60% of earnings per share and the trailing P/E for P&G to be 22. If the required return on P&G common stock is 6.5%, calculate the per-share value of P&G common stock.

Exhibit 6 summarizes the relevant calculations. When the dividends are growing at 4%, the expected dividends and the present value of each (discounted at 6.5%) are shown. The terminal stock price, V_4, deserves some explanation. As shown in the table, the Year 4 dividend is $\$2.79(1.04)^4$ = \$3.2639. Because dividends at that time are assumed to be 60% of earnings, the EPS projection for Year 4 is $EPS_4 = D_4/0.60$ = \$3.2639/0.60 = \$5.4398. With a trailing P/E of 22.0, the value of P&G at the end of Year 4 would be 22.0(\$5.4398) = \$119.6765. Discounted at 6.5% for four years, the present value of V_4 is \$93.0273.

Exhibit 6: Value of Procter & Gamble Common Stock

Time	Value	Calculation	D_t or V_t	Present Values $D_t/(1.065)^t$ or $V_t/(1.065)^t$
1	D_1	$\$2.79(1.04)^1$	\$2.9016	\$2.7245
2	D_2	$\$2.79\ (1.04)^2$	3.0177	2.6606
3	D_3	$\$2.79\ (1.04)^3$	3.1384	2.5981
4	D_4	$\$2.79\ (1.04)^4$	3.2639	2.5371
4	V_4	$22 \times [2.79\ (1.04)^4/0.60]$ $= 22 \times (3.2639/0.60)$ $= 22 \times 5.4398$	119.6765	93.0273
Total				\$103.5476

The present values of the dividends for Years 1 through 4 sum to \$10.52. The present value of the terminal value of \$119.68 is \$93.03. The estimated total value of P&G's common stock is the sum of these, or \$103.55 per share.

Valuing a Non-Dividend-Paying Company

The fact that a stock is currently paying no dividends does not mean that the principles of the dividend discount model do not apply. Even though D_0 and/or D_1 may be zero, and the company may not begin paying dividends for some time, the present value of future dividends may still capture the value of the company. Of course, if a company pays no dividends and will never be able to distribute cash to shareholders, the stock is worthless.

To value a non-dividend-paying company using a DDM, generally an analyst can use a multistage DDM model in which the first-stage dividend equals zero. Example 15 illustrates the approach.

EXAMPLE 15

Valuing a Non-Dividend-Paying Stock

1. Assume that a company is currently paying no dividend and will not pay one for several years. If the company begins paying a dividend of \$1.00 five years from now, and the dividend is expected to grow at 5% thereafter, this future dividend stream can be discounted back to find the value of the company. This company's required rate of return is 11%. Because the expression

$$V_n = \frac{D_{n+1}}{r - g}$$

values a stock at period n using the next period's dividend, the $t = 5$ dividend is used to find the value at $t = 4$:

$$V_4 = \frac{D_5}{r - g} = \frac{1.00}{0.11 - 0.05} = \$16.67$$

To find the value of the stock today, simply discount V_4 back for four years:

$$V_0 = \frac{V_4}{(1 + r)^4} = \frac{16.67}{(1.11)^4} = \$10.98$$

The value of this stock, even though it will not pay a dividend until Year 5, is \$10.98.

If a company is not paying a dividend but is very profitable, an analyst might be willing to forecast its future dividends. Of course, for non-dividend-paying, unprofitable companies, such a forecast would be very difficult. Furthermore, as discussed previously, it is usually difficult for the analyst to estimate the timing of the initiation of dividends and the dividend policy that will then be established by the company. Thus, the analyst may prefer a free cash flow or residual income model for valuing such companies.

THE H-MODEL AND THREE-STAGE DIVIDEND DISCOUNT MODELS

7

- ☐ explain the assumptions and justify the selection of the two-stage DDM, the H-model, the three-stage DDM, or spreadsheet modeling to value a company's common shares
- ☐ describe terminal value and explain alternative approaches to determining the terminal value in a DDM
- ☐ calculate and interpret the value of common shares using the two-stage DDM, the H-model, and the three-stage DDM
- ☐ evaluate whether a stock is overvalued, fairly valued, or undervalued by the market based on a DDM estimate of value

The basic two-stage model assumes a constant, extraordinary rate for the supernormal growth period that is followed by a constant, normal growth rate thereafter. The difference in growth rates may be substantial. For instance, in Example 13, the assumed growth rate for Carl Zeiss Meditec was 9% annually for 10 years, followed by a drop to 5% growth in Year 11 and thereafter. In some cases, a smoother transition to the mature phase growth rate would be more realistic. Fuller and Hsia (1984) developed a variant of the two-stage model in which growth begins at a high rate and declines linearly throughout the supernormal growth period until it reaches a normal rate at the end. The value of the dividend stream in the H-model is

$$V_0 = \frac{D_0(1+g_L)}{r-g_L} + \frac{D_0 H(g_S - g_L)}{r-g_L} \tag{20}$$

or

$$V_0 = \frac{D_0(1+g_L) + D_0 H(g_S - g_L)}{r-g_L},$$

where

V_0 = value per share at $t = 0$

D_0 = current dividend

r = required rate of return on equity

H = half-life in years of the high-growth period (i.e., high-growth period = $2H$ years)

g_S = initial short-term dividend growth rate

g_L = normal long-term dividend growth rate after Year $2H$

The first term on the right-hand side of Equation 20 is the present value of the company's dividend stream if it were to grow at g_L forever. The second term is an approximation of the extra value (assuming $g_S > g_L$) accruing to the stock because of its supernormal growth for Years 1 through $2H$ (see Fuller and Hsia 1984 for technical details). Logically, the longer the supernormal growth period (i.e., the larger the value of H, which is one-half the length of the supernormal growth period) and the larger the extra growth rate in the supernormal growth period (measured by g_S minus g_L), the higher the share value, all else equal.

We can provide some intuition on the expression. On average, the expected excess growth rate in the supernormal period will be $(g_S - g_L)/2$. Through $2H$ periods, a total excess amount of dividends (compared with the level given g_L) of $2HD0(g_S - g_L)/2 = D0H(g_S - g_L)$ is expected. This term is the H-model upward adjustment to the first dividend term, reflecting the extra expected dividends as growth declines from g_S to g_L during the first period. Note, however, that the timing of the individual dividends in the first period is not reflected by individually discounting them; the expression is thus an approximation.

To illustrate the expression, if the analyst in Example 13 had forecast a linear decline of the growth rate from 9% to 5% over the next 10 years, his estimate of value of Meditec using the H-model would have been €78.13 (rather than €94.21 as in Example 13):

$$V_0 = \frac{D_0(1+g_L) + D_0 H(g_S - g_L)}{r - g_L}$$

$$= \frac{0.55(1.05) + 0.55(5)(0.09 - 0.05)}{0.0588 - 0.05}$$

$$= 78.13$$

Note that an H of 5 corresponds to the 10-year high-growth period of Example 13. Example 16 provides another illustration of the H-model.

EXAMPLE 16

Valuing a Stock with the H-Model

An analyst has decided to use the H-model to estimate the value of a company and has gathered the following facts and forecasts:

- The share price is €41.70.
- The current dividend is €1.77.
- The initial dividend growth rate is 7%, declining linearly during a 10-year period to a final and perpetual growth rate of 4%.
- The analyst estimates the company's required rate of return on equity as 8.0%.

1. Using the H-model and the information given, estimate the company's per-share value.

Solution:

Using the H-model expression gives

$$V_0 = \frac{D_0(1+g_L) + D_0 H(g_S - g_L)}{r - g_L}$$

$$= \frac{1.77(1.04) + 1.77(5)(0.07 - 0.04)}{0.08 - 0.04}$$

$$= \frac{1.84 + 0.27}{0.04}$$

$$= 52.75$$

2. Estimate the value of the company's shares if its normal growth period began immediately.

Solution:

If the company experienced normal growth starting now, its estimated value would be the first component of the H-model estimate, €46 (=1.84/0.04). The faster initial growth assumption adds €6.75 (=0.27/0.04) to its value, resulting in an estimated value of €52.75 per share.

3. Evaluate whether the company's shares appear to be fairly valued, overvalued, or undervalued.

Solution:

€52.75 is approximately 26% higher than the company's current market price of €41.70. Thus the company appears to be undervalued.

The H-model is an approximation model that estimates the valuation that would result from discounting all of the future dividends individually. In many circumstances, this approximation is very close. For a long extraordinary growth period (a high H) or for a large difference in growth rates (the difference between g_S and g_L), however, the analyst might abandon the approximation model for the more exact model. Fortunately, the many tedious calculations of the exact model are made fairly easy using a spreadsheet program.

Three-Stage Dividend Discount Models

There are two popular versions of the three-stage DDM, distinguished by the modeling of the second stage. In the first version ("the general three-stage model"), the company is assumed to have three distinct stages of growth and the growth rate of the second stage is typically constant. For example, Stage 1 could assume 20% growth for three years, Stage 2 could have 10% growth for four years, and Stage 3 could have 5% growth thereafter. In the second version, the growth rate in the middle (second) stage is assumed to decline linearly to the mature growth rate: essentially, the second and third stages are treated as an H-model.

The following example shows how the first type of the three-stage model can be used to value a stock.

EXAMPLE 17

The Three-Stage DDM with Three Distinct Stages

1. An analyst is analyzing a technology company and makes the following estimates:

   - the current required return on equity for the company is 9%; and
   - dividends will grow at 14% for the next two years, 12% for the following five years, and 6.75% thereafter.

   The company pays a dividend of $3.30 per year, and its stock currently trades at $194.98. Based only on the information given, estimate the value of the company's stock using a three-stage DDM approach.

Solution:

Exhibit 7 gives the calculations.

Exhibit 7: Estimated Value Using a Three-Stage DDM

Time	Value	Calculation	D_t or V_t	Present Values $D_t/(1.09)^t$ or $V_t/(1.09)^t$
1	D_1	3.30(1.14)	$3.7620	$3.4514
2	D_2	$3.30(1.14)^2$	4.2887	3.6097
3	D_3	$3.30(1.14)^2(1.12)$	4.8033	3.7090
4	D_4	$3.30(1.14)^2(1.12)^2$	5.3797	3.8111
5	D_5	$3.30(1.14)^2(1.12)^3$	6.0253	3.9160
6	D_6	$3.30(1.14)^2(1.12)^4$	6.7483	4.0238
7	D_7	$3.30(1.14)^2(1.12)^5$	7.5581	4.1346
7	V_7	$3.30(1.14)^2(1.12)^5(1.0675)/(0.09 - 0.0675)$	$358.5908	196.161
Total				$222.8171

Given these assumptions, the three-stage model indicates that a fair price should be $222.82, more than 14% above the current market price. Characteristically, the present value of the terminal value of $196.16 constitutes the overwhelming portion (here, about 88%) of total estimated value.

A second version of the three-stage DDM has a middle stage similar to the first stage in the H-model. In the first stage, dividends grow at a high, constant (supernormal) rate for the whole period. In the second stage, dividends decline linearly as they do in the H-model. Finally, in Stage 3, dividends grow at a sustainable, constant growth rate. The process of using this model involves four steps:

- Gather the required inputs:
  - the current dividend;
  - estimates of the lengths of the first, second, and third stages and the expected growth rate during each stage; and
  - an estimate of the required return on equity.
- Compute the expected dividends in the first stage and find the sum of their present values.
- Apply the H-model expression to the second and third stages to obtain an estimate of their value as of the beginning of the second stage. Then find the present value of this H-value as of today ($t = 0$).
- Sum the values obtained in the second and third steps.

In the first step, analysts often investigate the company more deeply, making explicit, individual earnings and dividend forecasts for the near future (often 3, 5, or 10 years), rather than applying a growth rate to the current level of dividends.

EXAMPLE 18

The Three-Stage DDM with Declining Growth Rates in Stage 2

Elsie Bouvier is evaluating Rhinestone Energy (a hypothetical company) for possible inclusion in a small-cap, growth-oriented portfolio. The company is a diversified energy company involved in oil and gas exploration as well as natural gas distribution. In light of Rhinestone Energy's aggressive program of purchasing oil and gas producing properties, Bouvier expects above-average growth for the next five years. She establishes the following facts and forecasts:

- The current market price is $56.18.
- The current dividend is $0.56.
- Bouvier forecasts an initial five-year period of 11% per year earnings and dividend growth.
- Bouvier anticipates that Rhinestone Energy can grow 6.5% per year as a mature company and allows 10 years for the transition to the mature growth period.
- To estimate the required return on equity using the CAPM, Bouvier uses an adjusted beta of 1.2 based on two years of weekly observations, an estimated equity risk premium of 4.2%, and a risk-free rate based on long bond yields of 3%.
- Bouvier considers any security trading within a band of ±20% of her estimate of intrinsic value to be within a "fair value range."

1. Estimate the required return on Rhinestone Energy's equity using the CAPM. (Use only one decimal place in stating the result.)

Solution:

The required return on equity is $r = 3\% + 1.2(4.2\%) = 8\%$.

2. Estimate the value of Rhinestone Energy's common stock using a three-stage dividend discount model with a linearly declining dividend growth rate in Stage 2.

Solution:

The first step is to compute the five dividends in Stage 1 and find their present values at 8%. The dividends in Stages 2 and 3 can be valued with the H-model, which estimates their value at the beginning of Stage 2. This value is then discounted back to find the dividends' present value at $t = 0$.

The calculation of the five dividends in Stage 1 and their present values are given in Exhibit 8. The H-model for calculating the value of the Stage 2 and Stage 3 dividends at the beginning of Stage 2 ($t = 5$) is

$$V_5 = \frac{D_5(1+g_L)}{r-g_L} + \frac{D_5 H(g_S - g_L)}{r-g_L},$$

where

$D_5 = D_0(1 + g_S)^5 = 0.56(1.11)^5 = \$0.9436$

$g_S = 11.0\%$

$g_L = 6.5\%$

$r = 8.0\%$

$H = 5$ (the second stage lasts $2H = 10$ years)

Substituting these values into the equation for the H-model gives V_5 as follows:

$$V_5 = \frac{0.9436(1.065)}{0.08-0.065} + \frac{0.9436(5)(0.11-0.065)}{0.08-0.065}$$
$$= 66.9979 + 14.1545$$
$$= \$81.1524$$

The present value of V_5 is $\$81.1524/(1.08)^5 = \$55.2310$.

Exhibit 8: Rhinestone Energy

Time	D_t or V_t	Explanation of D_t or V_t	Value of D_t or V_t	PV at 8%
1	D_1	$0.56(1.11)^1$	\$0.6216	\$0.5756
2	D_2	$0.56(1.11)^2$	0.6900	0.5915
3	D_3	$0.56(1.11)^3$	0.7659	0.6080
4	D_4	$0.56(1.11)^4$	0.8501	0.6249
5	D_5	$0.56(1.11)^5$	0.9436	0.6422
5	V_5	H-model explained earlier	\$81.1524	55.2310
Total				\$58.2731

According to the three-stage DDM model, the total value of Rhinestone Energy is \$58.27.

3. Calculate the percentages of the total value represented by the first stage and by the second and third stages considered as one group.

Solution:

The sum of the first five present value amounts in the last column of Exhibit 8 is \$3.0422. Thus, the first stage represents \$3.0422/\$58.2731 = 5.2% of total value. The second and third stages together represent 100% – 5.2% = 94.8% of total value (check: \$55.2310/\$58.2731 = 94.8%).

4. Judge whether Rhinestone Energy's stock is undervalued or overvalued according to Bouvier's perspective.

Solution:

The band Bouvier is looking at is \$58.27 ± 0.20(\$58.27), which runs from \$58.27 + \$11.65 = \$69.92 on the upside to \$58.27 – \$11.65 = \$46.62 on the downside. Because the current price of \$56.18 is between \$46.62 and \$69.92, Bouvier would consider Rhinestone Energy to be fairly valued.

5. Some analysts are forecasting essentially flat EPS and dividends in the second year. Estimate the value of Rhinestone Energy's stock under the assumptions that EPS is flat in the second year and that 11% growth resumes in the third year.

Solution:

The estimated value becomes \$52.56 with no growth in Year 2 as shown in Exhibit 9. The value of the second and third stages is given by

$$V_5 = \frac{0.8501(1.065)}{0.08 - 0.065} + \frac{0.8501(5)(0.11 - 0.065)}{0.08 - 0.065} = \$73.1103.$$

Exhibit 9: Rhinestone Energy with No Growth in Year 2

Time	D_t or V_t	Explanation of D_t or V_t	Value of D_t or V_t	PV at 8%
1	D_1	$0.56(1.11)^1$	\$0.6216	\$0.5756
2	D_2	No growth in Year 2	0.6216	0.5329
3	D_3	$0.56(1.11)^2$	0.6900	0.5477
4	D_4	$0.56(1.11)^3$	0.7659	0.5629
5	D_5	$0.56(1.11)^4$	0.8501	0.5786
5	V_5	H-model explained earlier	\$73.1103	49.7576
Total				\$52.5553

In Problem 5 of Example 18, the analyst examined the consequences of 11% growth in Year 1 and no growth in Year 2, with 11% growth resuming in Years 3, 4, and 5. In the first stage, analysts may forecast earnings and dividends individually for a certain number of years.

The three-stage DDM with declining growth in Stage 2 has been widely used among companies using a DDM approach to valuation. An example is the DDM adopted by Bloomberg L.P., a financial services company that provides "Bloomberg terminals" to professional investors and analysts. The Bloomberg DDM is a model that provides an estimated value for any stock that the user selects. The DDM is a three-stage model with declining growth in Stage 2. The model uses earnings estimates for assumed Stage 1 and the cost of capital for Stage 3 growth rates, and then it assumes that the Stage 2 rate is a linearly declining rate between the Stage 1 and Stage 3 rates. The model also makes estimates of the required rate of return and the lengths of the three stages, assigning higher-growth companies shorter growth periods (i.e., first stages) and longer transition periods, and slower-growth companies longer growth periods and shorter transition periods. Fixing the total length of the growth and transition phases together at 17 years, the growth stage/transition stage durations for Bloomberg's four growth classifications are 3 years/14 years for "explosive growth" equities, 5 years/12 years for "high growth" equities, 7 years/10 years for "average growth" equities, and 9 years/8 years for "slow/mature growth" equities. Analysts, by tailoring stage specifications to their understanding of the specific company being valued, should be able to improve on the accuracy of valuations compared with a fixed specification.

8 GENERAL MODELING AND ESTIMATING A REQUIRED RETURN USING ANY DDM

- ☐ explain the use of spreadsheet modeling to forecast dividends and to value common shares
- ☐ estimate a required return based on any DDM, including the Gordon growth model and the H-model

DDMs, such as the Gordon growth model and the multistage models presented earlier, assume stylized patterns of dividend growth. An analyst can use *any* assumed dividend pattern, however, to create a spreadsheet to value the stock and to test sensitivity of the value to growth and return assumptions. The following example presents the results of a valuation incorporating dividends that are estimated to change substantially over the forecast period.

EXAMPLE 19

Finding the Value of a Stock with Varying Dividend Assumptions

1. Yang Co. is expected to pay a \$21.00 dividend next year. An analyst estimates that the dividend will decline by 10% annually for the following three years (i.e., the "growth rate" will equal −10%). In Year 5, Yang is expected to sell off assets worth \$100 per share. The Year 5 dividend, which includes a distribution of some of the proceeds of the asset sale, is expected to be \$60. In Year 6, the dividend is expected to decrease to \$40 and to be maintained at \$40 for one additional year. The dividend is then expected to grow by 5% annually thereafter. If the required rate of return is 12%, what is the value of one share of Yang?

Solution:

The value is shown in Exhibit 10. Each dividend, its present value discounted at 12%, and an explanation are included in the table. The final row treats the dividends from t = 8 forward as a Gordon growth model because after Year 7, the dividend grows at a constant 5% annually. V_7 is the value of these dividends at t = 7.

Exhibit 10: Value of Yang Co. Stock

Year	D_t or V_t	Value of D_t or V_t	Present Value at 12%	Explanation of D_t or V_t
1	D_1	\$21.00	\$18.75	Dividend set at \$21
2	D_2	18.90	15.07	Previous dividend × 0.90
3	D_3	17.01	12.11	Previous dividend × 0.90
4	D_4	15.31	9.73	Previous dividend × 0.90
5	D_5	60.00	34.05	Set at \$60
6	D_6	40.00	20.27	Set at \$40

Year	D_t or V_t	Value of D_t or V_t	Present Value at 12%	Explanation of D_t or V_t
7	D_7	40.00	18.09	Set at $40
7	V_7	600.00	271.41	$V_7 = D_8/(r - g)$ $V_7 = (40.00 \times 1.05)/(0.12 - 0.05)$
Total			$399.48	

As the table in Example 19 shows, the total present value of Yang Co.'s dividends is $399.48. In this example, the terminal value of the company (V_n) at the end of the first stage is found using the Gordon growth model and a mature growth rate of 5%.

Several alternative approaches to estimating g are available in this context:

- Use the formula g = (b in the mature phase) × (ROE in the mature phase). We will discuss the expression $g = b \times$ ROE later. Analysts estimate mature-phase ROE in several ways, such as the following:
  - The DuPont decomposition of ROE based on forecasts for the components of the DuPont expression.
  - Setting ROE = r, the required rate of return on equity, based on the assumption that in the mature phase companies can do no more than earn investors' opportunity cost of capital.
  - Setting ROE in the mature phase equal to the median industry ROE.
- The analyst may estimate the growth rate, g, with other models by relating the mature growth rate to macroeconomic, including industry, growth projections.

When the analyst uses the sustainable growth expression, the earnings retention ratio, b, may be empirically based. For example, Bloomberg L.P.'s model has been assuming that $b = 0.55$ in the mature phase, equivalent to a dividend payout ratio of 45%, a long-run average payout ratio for mature dividend-paying companies in the United States. In addition, sometimes analysts project the dividend payout ratio for the company individually.

EXAMPLE 20

A Sustainable Growth Rate Calculation

1. An analyst is estimating the dividend growth rate of a company to incorporate in the final stage of a multistage dividend discount model. Assume the company's payout ratio is 25% and its ROE is equal to its estimated required return on equity of 9%. An estimate of the sustainable growth rate can be derived using the expression

   g = (b in the mature phase) × (ROE in the mature phase)

   = 0.75(9%) = 6.75%.

   The analyst's estimate of the company's sustainable dividend growth rate is 6.75%.

Estimating a Required Return Using Any DDM

We have focused on finding the value of a security using assumptions for dividends, required rates of return, and expected growth rates. Given current price and all inputs to a DDM except for the required return, an IRR can be calculated. Such an IRR has been used as a required return estimate (although reusing it in a DDM is not appropriate because it risks circularity). This IRR can also be interpreted as the expected return on the issue implied by the market price—essentially, an efficient market expected return. In the following discussion, keep in mind that if price does not equal intrinsic value, the expected return will need to be adjusted to reflect the additional component of return that accrues when the mispricing is corrected, as discussed earlier.

In some cases, finding the IRR is very easy. In the Gordon growth model, $r = D_1/P_0 + g$. The required return estimate is the dividend yield plus the expected dividend growth rate. For a security with a current price of \$10, an expected dividend of \$0.50, and expected growth of 8%, the required return estimate is 13%.

For the H-model, the expected rate of return can be derived as

$$r = \left(\frac{D_0}{P_0}\right)\left[(1 + g_L) + H(g_S - g_L)\right] + g_L. \quad (21)$$

When the short- and long-term growth rates are the same, this model reduces to the Gordon growth model. For a security with a current dividend of \$1, a current price of \$20, and an expected short-term growth rate of 10% declining over 10 years ($H = 5$) to 6%, the expected rate of return would be

$$r = \left(\frac{\$1}{\$20}\right)[(1 + 0.06) + 5(0.10 - 0.06)] + 0.06 = 12.3\%.$$

For multistage models and spreadsheet models, finding a single equation for the rate of return can be more difficult. The process generally used is similar to that of finding the IRR for a series of varying cash flows. Using a computer or trial and error, the analyst must find the rate of return such that the present value of future expected dividends equals the current stock price.

EXAMPLE 21

Finding the Expected Rate of Return for Varying Expected Dividends

1. An analyst expects Johnson & Johnson's (NYSE: JNJ)) dividend of \$3.60 for 2019 to grow by 7.0% for six years and then grow by 5% into perpetuity. A recent price for JNJ as of early 2019 is \$136.61. What is the IRR on an investment in JNJ's stock?

In estimating the expected rate of return with a two-stage model, using trial and error is one approach. Having a good initial approximation is helpful. In this case, the expected rate of return formula from the Gordon growth model and JNJ's long-term growth rate can be used to find a first approximation: $r = (\$3.60 \times 1.07)/\$136.61 + 0.05 = 7.8\%$. Because the estimated growth rate for the first six years is higher than the long-term growth rate of 5%, the implied estimated rate of return must be above 7.8%. Exhibit 11 shows the value estimate of JNJ's shares for two discount rates, 8% and 8.5%.

Exhibit 11: Estimation of Required Return: Johnson & Johnson

Time	D_t	Present Value of D_t and V_6 at r = 8%	Present Value of D_t and V_6 at r = 8.5%
1	\$3.8520	\$3.5667	\$3.5502
2	\$4.1216	\$3.5336	\$3.5011
3	\$4.4101	\$3.5009	\$3.4527
4	\$4.7188	\$3.4685	\$3.4050
5	\$5.0491	\$3.4363	\$3.3579
6	\$5.4025	\$3.4045	\$3.3114
7	\$5.6726		
Subtotal 1	(t = 1 to 6)	\$20.91	\$20.58
Subtotal 2	(t = 7 to ∞)	\$119.16	\$99.34
Total		\$140.07	\$119.92
Market Price		\$136.61	\$136.61

In the exhibit, the amount labeled "Subtotal 1" is the present value of the expected dividends for Years 1 through 6. The amount labeled "Subtotal 2" is the present value of the terminal value, $V_6/(1 + r)^6 = [D_7/(r - g)]/(1 + r)^6$. For r = 8%, that present value is $[5.6726/(0.08 - 0.05)]/(1.08)^6$ = \$119.16. The present value for other values of r is found similarly.

Using 8.0% as the discount rate, the value estimate for JNJ is \$140.07, which is about 2.5% larger than JNJ's market price of \$136.61. This fact indicates that the IRR is greater than 8%. With an 8.5% discount rate, the present value of \$119.92 is significantly less than the market price. Thus, the IRR is slightly more than 8%. The IRR can be determined to be 8.08% using a spreadsheet. For example, using the Goal Seek function of Excel: In the "set cell" parameter, enter the reference for the cell that contains the Total present value; in the "by changing" parameter, enter the current price as an amount; and in the "by changing cell" parameter, enter the reference for the cell that contains the discount rate.

Multistage DDM: Concluding Remarks

Multistage dividend discount models can accommodate a variety of patterns of future streams of expected dividends.

In general, multistage DDMs make stylized assumptions about growth based on a lifecycle view of business. The first stage of a multistage DDM frequently incorporates analysts' individual earnings and dividend forecasts for the next two to five years (sometimes longer). The final stage is often modeled using the Gordon growth model based on an assumption of the company's long-run sustainable growth rate. In the case of the H-model, the transition to the mature growth phase happens smoothly during the first stage. In the case of the standard two-stage model, the growth rate typically transitions immediately to mature growth rate in the second period. In three-stage models, the middle stage is a stage of transition. Using a spreadsheet, an analyst can model an almost limitless variety of cash flow patterns.

Multistage DDMs have several limitations. Often, the present value of the terminal stage represents more than three-quarters of the total value of shares. Terminal value can be very sensitive to the growth and required return assumptions. Furthermore, technological innovation can make the lifecycle model a crude representation.

9 THE FINANCIAL DETERMINANTS OF GROWTH RATES

☐ calculate and interpret the sustainable growth rate of a company and demonstrate the use of DuPont analysis to estimate a company's sustainable growth rate

In a number of examples earlier, we have implicitly used the relationship that the dividend growth rate (g) equals the earning retention ratio (b) multiplied by the return on equity (ROE). In this section, we explain this relationship and show how it can be combined with a method of analyzing return on equity, called DuPont analysis, as a simple tool for forecasting dividend growth rates.

Sustainable Growth Rate

We define the **sustainable growth rate** as the rate of dividend (and earnings) growth that can be sustained for a given level of return on equity, assuming that the capital structure is constant through time and that additional common stock is not issued. The reason for studying this concept is that it can help in estimating either 1) the stable growth rate in a Gordon growth model valuation or 2) the mature growth rate in a multistage DDM in which the Gordon growth formula is used to find the terminal value of the stock.

The expression to calculate the sustainable growth rate is

$$g = b \times \text{ROE}, \tag{22}$$

where

g = dividend growth rate

b = earnings retention rate (1 – Dividend payout ratio)

ROE = return on equity

More precisely, in Equation 22 the retention rate should be multiplied by the rate of return expected to be earned on new investment. Analysts commonly assume that the rate of return is well approximated by the return on equity, as shown in Equation 22; however, whether that is actually the case should be investigated by the analyst on a case-by-case basis.

Example 22 illustrates the fact that growth in shareholders' equity is driven by reinvested earnings alone (no new issues of equity and debt growing at the rate g). Note that in scenarios in which debt is growing at g, the capital structure is constant. If the capital structure is not constant, ROE will not be constant in general because ROE depends on leverage.

EXAMPLE 22

Example Showing $g = b \times \text{ROE}$

Suppose that a company's ROE is 25% and its retention rate is 60%. According to the expression for the sustainable growth rate, the dividends should grow at $g = b \times \text{ROE} = 0.60 \times 25\% = 15\%$.

To demonstrate the working of the expression, suppose that, in the year just ended, a company began with shareholders' equity of $1,000,000, earned $250,000 net income, and paid dividends of $100,000. The company begins the next year with $1,000,000 + 0.60($250,000) = $1,000,000 + $150,000 = $1,150,000 of shareholders' equity. No additions to equity are made from the sale of additional shares.

If the company again earns 25% on equity, net income will be 0.25 × $1,150,000 = $287,500, which is a $287,500 − $250,000 = $37,500 or a $37,500/$250,000 = 0.15% increase from the prior year level. The company retains 60% of earnings, 60% × $287,500 = $172,500, and pays out the other 40%, 40% × $287,500 = $115,000 as dividends. Dividends for the company grew from $100,000 to $115,000, which is exactly a 15% growth rate. With the company continuing to earn 25% each year on the 60% of earnings that is reinvested in the company, dividends would continue to grow at 15%.

Equation 22 implies that the higher the return on equity, the higher the dividend growth rate, all else constant. That relation appears to be reliable. Another implication of the expression is that the lower (higher) the earnings retention ratio, the lower (higher) the growth rate in dividends, holding all else constant; this relationship has been called *the dividend displacement of earnings*. Of course, all else may not be equal—the return on reinvested earnings may not be constant at different levels of investment, or companies with changing future growth prospects may change their dividend policy. Furthermore, research has shown that dividend-paying companies had higher future growth rates during the period studied, indicating that caution is appropriate in assuming that dividends displace earnings (Arnott and Asness 2003; ap Gwilym, Seaton, Suddason, and Thomas 2006; Zhou and Ruland 2006).

A practical logic for defining *sustainable* in terms of growth through internally generated funds (retained earnings) is that external equity (secondary issues of stock) is considerably more costly than internal equity (reinvested earnings), for several reasons including the investment banker fees associated with secondary equity issues. In general, continuous issuance of new stock is not a practical funding alternative for companies. Growth of capital through issuance of new debt, however, can sometimes be sustained for considerable periods. Further, if a company manages its capital structure to a target percentage of debt to total capital (debt and common stock), it will need to issue debt to maintain that percentage as equity grows through reinvested earnings. (This approach is one of a variety of observed capital structure policies.) In addition, the earnings retention ratio nearly always shows year-to-year variation in actual companies. For example, earnings may have transitory components that management does not want to reflect in dividends. The analyst may thus observe actual dividend growth rates straying from the growth rates predicted by Equation 22 because of these effects, even when her input estimates are unbiased. Nevertheless, the equation can be useful as a simple expression for approximating the average rate at which dividends can grow over a long horizon.

Dividend Growth Rate, Retention Rate, and ROE Analysis

Thus far we have seen that a company's sustainable growth, as defined earlier, is a function of its ability to generate return on equity (which depends on investment opportunities) and its retention rate. We now expand this model by examining what drives ROE. Remember that ROE is the return (net income) generated on the equity invested in the company:

$$\text{ROE} = \frac{\text{Net income}}{\text{Shareholders' equity}} \tag{23}$$

If a company has a ROE of 15%, it generates $15 of net income for every $100 invested in stockholders' equity. For purposes of analyzing ROE, it can be related to several other financial ratios. For example, ROE can be related to return on assets (ROA) and the extent of financial leverage (equity multiplier):

$$\text{ROE} = \frac{\text{Net income}}{\text{Total assets}} \times \frac{\text{Total assets}}{\text{Shareholders' equity}} \tag{24}$$

Therefore, a company can increase its ROE either by increasing ROA or through the use of leverage (assuming the company can borrow at a rate lower than it earns on its assets).

This model can be expanded further by breaking ROA into two components, profit margin and turnover (efficiency):

$$\text{ROE} = \frac{\text{Net income}}{\text{Sales}} \times \frac{\text{Sales}}{\text{Total assets}} \times \frac{\text{Total assets}}{\text{Shareholders' equity}} \tag{25}$$

The first term is the company's profit margin. A higher profit margin will result in a higher ROE. The second term measures total asset turnover, which is the company's efficiency. A turnover of one indicates that a company generates $1 in sales for every $1 invested in assets. A higher turnover will result in higher ROE. The last term is the equity multiplier, which measures the extent of leverage, as noted earlier. This relationship is widely known as the DuPont model or analysis of ROE. Although ROE can be analyzed further using a five-way analysis, the three-way analysis will provide insight into the determinants of ROE that are pertinent to our understanding of the growth rate. By combining Equation 22 and Equation 25, we can see that the dividend growth rate is equal to the retention rate multiplied by ROE:

$$g = \frac{\text{Net income} - \text{Dividends}}{\text{Net income}} \times \frac{\text{Net income}}{\text{Sales}} \times \frac{\text{Sales}}{\text{Total assets}} \times \frac{\text{Total assets}}{\text{Shareholders' equity}} \tag{26}$$

This expansion of the sustainable growth expression has been called the PRAT model. Growth is a function of profit margin (P), retention rate (R), asset turnover (A), and financial leverage (T). The profit margin and asset turnover determine ROA. The other two factors, the retention rate and financial leverage, reflect the company's financial policies. So, the growth rate in dividends can be viewed as determined by the company's ROA and financial policies. Analysts may use Equation 26 to forecast a company's dividend growth rate in the mature growth phase.

Theoretically, the sustainable growth rate expression and this expansion of it based on the DuPont decomposition of ROE hold exactly only when ROE is calculated using beginning-of-period shareholders' equity, as illustrated in Example 22. Such calculation assumes that retained earnings are not available for reinvestment until the end of the period. Analysts and financial databases more frequently prefer to use average total assets in calculating ROE and, practically, DuPont analysis is frequently performed using that definition. The following example illustrates the logic behind this equation.

EXAMPLE 23

ROA, Financial Policies, and the Dividend Growth Rate

Baggai Enterprises (a fictional company) has an ROA of 10%, retains 30% of earnings, and has an equity multiplier of 1.25. Mondale Enterprises also has an ROA of 10%, but it retains two-thirds of earnings and has an equity multiplier of 2.00.

1. What are the sustainable dividend growth rates for (A) Baggai Enterprises and (B) Mondale Enterprises?

Solution:

A. Baggai's dividend growth rate should be $g = 0.30 \times 10\% \times 1.25 = 3.75\%$.

B. Mondale's dividend growth rate should be $g = (2/3) \times 10\% \times 2.00 = 13.33\%$.

2. Identify the drivers of the difference in the sustainable growth rates of Baggai Enterprises and Mondale Enterprises.

Solution:

Because Mondale has the higher retention rate and higher financial leverage, its dividend growth rate is much higher.

If growth is being forecast for the next five years, an analyst should use the expectations of the four factors driving growth during this five-year period. If growth is being forecast into perpetuity, an analyst should use very long-term forecasts for these variables.

To illustrate the calculation and implications of the sustainable growth rate using the expression for ROE given by the DuPont formula, assume the growth rate is $g = b \times \text{ROE} = 0.60\ (15\%) = 9\%$. The ROE of 15% was based on a profit margin of 5%, an asset turnover of 2.0, and an equity multiplier of 1.5. Given fixed ratios of sales-to-assets and assets-to-equity, sales, assets, and debt will also be growing at 9%. Because dividends are fixed at 40% of income, dividends will grow at the same rate as income, or 9%. If the company increased dividends faster than 9%, this growth rate would not be sustainable using internally generated funds. Earning retentions would be reduced, and the company would be unable to finance the assets required for sales growth without external financing.

An analyst should be careful in projecting historical financial ratios into the future when using this analysis. Although a company may have grown at 25% a year for the last five years, this rate of growth is probably not sustainable indefinitely. Abnormally high ROEs, which may have driven that growth, are unlikely to persist indefinitely because of competitive forces and possibly other reasons, such as adverse changes in technology or demand. In the following example, an above-average terminal growth rate is plausibly forecasted because the company has positioned itself in businesses that may have relatively high margins on an ongoing basis.

EXAMPLE 24

Forecasting Growth with the PRAT Formula

1. An analyst is estimating a mature-phase growth rate for International Business Machines (NYSE: IBM) to use in her multistage dividend discount model. The company's ROE for 2018 was around 52%, and over the past 10

years, IBM's retention rate has averaged around 62%. Applying the formula for sustainable growth rate that was described previously [namely, g = (b in the mature phase) × (ROE in the mature phase] would yield an unrealistic long-term growth rate, particularly given the decline in the company's sales and earnings over the past several years. Further, IBM's annual investment in property, plant, and equipment has also declined—from $3.7 billion in 2014 to $3.4 billion in 2018.

The analyst therefore decides to estimate the company's growth rate using the DuPont decomposition and PRAT formula. A decomposition of IBM's ROE for the past 10 years is shown in Exhibit 12. In addition, the exhibit shows a benchmark based on the median values of ROE components for a group of firms with the same two-digit SIC code as IBM.

Exhibit 12: ROE Decomposition for IBM

Year	ROE	Profit Margin	Asset Turnover	Financial Leverage
2018	52.0%	11.0%	0.65	7.35
2017	32.7%	7.3%	0.63	7.12
2016	65.1%	14.9%	0.68	6.44
2015	92.5%	16.1%	0.74	7.75
2014	101.3%	13.0%	0.79	9.90
2013	72.3%	16.5%	0.79	5.54
2012	88.0%	15.9%	0.88	6.32
2011	78.7%	14.8%	0.92	5.78
2010	64.4%	14.9%	0.88	4.92
2009	59.3%	14.0%	0.88	4.82

Benchmark Average

ROE	Profit Margin	Asset Turnover	Financial Leverage
13.5%	10.5%	0.62	2.07

IBM's ROE is much higher than the benchmark average, primarily because of much higher financial leverage. Its profit margin and asset turnover do not differ significantly from the benchmark average.

Suppose the analyst believes that IBM's profit margin and asset turnover will be roughly the same as the benchmark average. The analyst also believes that capital investment will continue to decline in IBM's maturity stage, and cash flow that was previously used for investment will be used to retire debt and pay dividends. The analyst forecasts a financial leverage ratio of 2.0, similar to the industry benchmark. The analyst also sees the dividend payout ratio continuing its recent rise and ultimately reaching a level of 50%.

Based on a profit margin of 10.5%, an asset turnover ratio of 0.62, and financial leverage of 2.0, a forecast of ROE in the maturity phase is (10.5%)(0.62)

(2.0) = 13.0%. Therefore, based on this analysis, the estimate of the sustainable growth rate for IBM would be g = (0.50)(13.0%) = 6.5%.

FINANCIAL MODELS AND DIVIDENDS

10

☐ explain the use of spreadsheet modeling to forecast dividends and to value common shares

Analysts can also forecast dividends by building more-complex models of the company's total operating and financial environment. The company's ability to pay dividends in the future can be predicted using one of these models. The following example shows the dividends that a highly profitable and rapidly growing company can pay when its growth rates and profit margins decline because of increasing competition over time.

EXAMPLE 25

A Model for Forecasting Dividends Using More-Detailed Assumptions

1. An analyst is preparing a forecast of dividends for Hoshino Distributors (a fictional company) for the next five years. He uses a model with the following assumptions:

    - Sales are $100 million in Year 1. They grow by 20% in Year 2, 15% in Year 3, and 10% in Years 4 and 5.
    - Operating profits (earnings before interest and taxes, or EBIT) are 20% of sales in Years 1 and 2, 18% of sales in Year 3, and 16% of sales in Years 4 and 5.
    - Interest expenses are 10% of total debt for the current year.
    - The income tax rate is 40%.
    - Hoshino pays out 20% of earnings in dividends in Years 1 and 2, 30% in Year 3, 40% in Year 4, and 50% in Year 5.
    - Retained earnings are added to equity in the next year.
    - Total assets are 80% of the current year's sales in all years.
    - In Year 1, debt is $40 million and shareholders' equity is $40 million. Debt equals total assets minus shareholders' equity. Shareholders' equity will equal the previous year's shareholders' equity plus the addition to retained earnings from the previous year.
    - Hoshino has 4 million shares outstanding.
    - The required return on equity is 15%.
    - The value of the company at the end of Year 5 is expected to be 10.0 times earnings.

    The analyst wants to estimate the current value per share of Hoshino. Exhibit 13 adheres to the foregoing modeling assumptions. Total dividends and earnings are found at the bottom of the income statement.

Exhibit 13: Hoshino Distributors Pro Forma Financial Statements (in millions)

	Year 1	Year 2	Year 3	Year 4	Year 5
Income statement					
Sales	$100.00	$120.00	$138.00	$151.80	$166.98
EBIT	20.00	24.00	24.84	24.29	26.72
Interest	4.00	4.83	5.35	5.64	6.18
EBT	16.00	19.17	19.49	18.65	20.54
Taxes	6.40	7.67	7.80	7.46	8.22
Net income	9.60	11.50	11.69	11.19	12.32
Dividends	1.92	2.30	3.51	4.48	6.16
Balance sheet					
Total assets	$80.00	$96.00	$110.40	$121.44	$133.58
Total debt	40.00	48.32	53.52	56.38	61.81
Equity	40.00	47.68	56.88	65.06	71.77

Dividing the total dividends by the number of outstanding shares gives the dividend per share for each year shown in the following table. The present value of each dividend, discounted at 15%, is also shown.

	Year 1	Year 2	Year 3	Year 4	Year 5	Total
DPS	$0.480	$0.575	$0.877	$1.120	$1.540	$4.59
PV	0.417	0.435	0.577	0.640	0.766	2.84

The earnings per share in Year 5 are $12.32 million divided by 4 million shares, or $3.08 per share. Given a P/E of 10, the market price in Year 5 is predicted to be $30.80. Discounted at 15%, the required return on equity by assumption, the present value of this price is $15.31. Adding the present values of the five dividends, which sum to $2.84, gives a total stock value today of $18.15 per share.

SUMMARY

We have provided an overview of DCF models of valuation, discussed the estimation of a stock's required rate of return, and presented in detail the dividend discount model.

- In DCF models, the value of any asset is the present value of its (expected) future cash flows

$$V_0 = \sum_{t=1}^{n} \frac{CF_t}{(1+r)^t},$$

where V_0 is the value of the asset as of $t = 0$ (today), CF_t is the (expected) cash flow at time t, and r is the discount rate or required rate of return. For infinitely lived assets such as common stocks, n runs to infinity.

- Several alternative streams of expected cash flows can be used to value equities, including dividends, free cash flow, and residual income. A discounted dividend approach is most suitable for dividend-paying stocks in which the company has a discernible dividend policy that has an understandable relationship to the company's profitability and the investor has a non-control (minority ownership) perspective.
- The free cash flow approach (FCFF or FCFE) might be appropriate when the company does not pay dividends, dividends differ substantially from FCFE, free cash flows align with profitability, or the investor takes a control (majority ownership) perspective.
- The residual income approach can be useful when the company does not pay dividends (as an alternative to a FCF approach) or free cash flow is negative.
- The DDM with a single holding period gives stock value as

$$V_0 = \frac{D_1}{(1+r)^1} + \frac{P_1}{(1+r)^1} = \frac{D_1 + P_1}{(1+r)^1},$$

where D_1 is the expected dividend at Time 1 and V_0 is the stock's (expected) value at Time 0. Assuming that V_0 is equal to today's market price, P_0, the expected holding-period return is

$$r = \frac{D_1 + P_1}{P_0} - 1 = \frac{D_1}{P_0} + \frac{P_1 - P_0}{P_0}.$$

- The expression for the DDM for any given finite holding period n and the general expression for the DDM are, respectively,

$$V_0 = \sum_{t=1}^{n} \frac{D_t}{(1+r)^t} + \frac{P_n}{(1+r)^n} \text{ and } V_0 = \sum_{t=1}^{\infty} \frac{D_t}{(1+r)^t}.$$

- There are two main approaches to the problem of forecasting dividends. First, an analyst can assign the entire stream of expected future dividends to one of several stylized growth patterns. Second, an analyst can forecast a finite number of dividends individually up to a terminal point and value the remaining dividends either by assigning them to a stylized growth pattern or by forecasting share price as of the terminal point of the dividend forecasts.
- The Gordon growth model assumes that dividends grow at a constant rate g forever, so that $D_t = D_{t-1}(1 + g)$. The dividend stream in the Gordon growth model has a value of

$$V_0 = \frac{D_0(1+g)}{r-g}, \text{ or } V_0 = \frac{D_1}{r-g} \text{ where } r > g.$$

- The value of non-callable fixed-rate perpetual preferred stock is $V_0 = D/r$, where D is the stock's (constant) annual dividend.
- Assuming that price equals value, the Gordon growth model estimate of a stock's expected rate of return is

$$r = \frac{D_0(1+g)}{P_0} + g = \frac{D_1}{P_0} + g.$$

- Given an estimate of the next-period dividend and the stock's required rate of return, the Gordon growth model can be used to estimate the dividend growth rate implied by the current market price (making a constant growth rate assumption).

- The present value of growth opportunities is the part of a stock's total value, V_0, that comes from profitable future growth opportunities in contrast to the value associated with assets already in place. The relationship is $V_0 = E_1/r + \text{PVGO}$, where E_1/r is defined as the no-growth value per share.
- The leading price-to-earnings ratio (P_0/E_1) and the trailing price-to-earnings ratio (P_0/E_0) can be expressed in terms of the Gordon growth model as, respectively,

$$\frac{P_0}{E_1} = \frac{D_1/E_1}{r-g} = \frac{1-b}{r-g} \text{ and } \frac{P_0}{E_0} = \frac{D_0(1+g)/E_0}{r-g} = \frac{(1-b)(1+g)}{r-g}.$$

  The foregoing expressions give a stock's justified price-to-earnings ratio based on forecasts of fundamentals (given that the Gordon growth model is appropriate).
- The Gordon growth model may be useful for valuing broad-based equity indexes and the stock of businesses with earnings that are expected to grow at a stable rate comparable to or lower than the economy's nominal growth rate.
- Gordon growth model values are very sensitive to the assumed growth rate and required rate of return.
- For many companies, growth falls into phases. In the growth phase, a company enjoys an abnormally high growth rate in earnings per share, called supernormal growth. In the transition phase, earnings growth slows. In the mature phase, the company reaches an equilibrium in which such factors as earnings growth and the return on equity stabilize at levels that can be sustained long term. Analysts often apply multistage DCF models to value the stock of a company with multistage growth prospects.
- The two-stage dividend discount model assumes different growth rates in Stage 1 and Stage 2:

$$V_0 = \sum_{t=1}^{n} \frac{D_0(1+g_S)^t}{(1+r)^t} + \frac{D_0(1+g_S)^n(1+g_L)}{(1+r)^n(r-g_L)},$$

  where g_S is the expected dividend growth rate in the first period and g_L is the expected growth rate in the second period.
- The terminal stock value, V_n, is sometimes found with the Gordon growth model or with some other method, such as applying a P/E multiplier to forecasted EPS as of the terminal date.
- The H-model assumes that the dividend growth rate declines linearly from a high supernormal rate to the normal growth rate during Stage 1 and then grows at a constant normal growth rate thereafter:

$$V_0 = \frac{D_0(1+g_L)}{r-g_L} + \frac{D_0 H(g_S-g_L)}{r-g_L} = \frac{D_0(1+g_L) + D_0 H(g_S-g_L)}{r-g_L}.$$

- There are two basic three-stage models. In one version, the growth rate in the middle stage is constant. In the second version, the growth rate declines linearly in Stage 2 and becomes constant and normal in Stage 3.
- In addition to valuing equities, the IRR of a DDM, assuming assets are correctly priced in the marketplace, has been used to estimate required returns. For simpler models (such as the one-period model, the Gordon growth model, and the H-model), well-known formulas may be used to calculate

these rates of return. For many dividend streams, however, the rate of return must be found by trial and error, producing a discount rate that equates the present value of the forecasted dividend stream to the current market price.

- Multistage DDM models can accommodate a wide variety of patterns of expected dividends. Even though such models may use stylized assumptions about growth, they can provide useful approximations.
- Dividend growth rates can be obtained from analyst forecasts, statistical forecasting models, or company fundamentals. The sustainable growth rate depends on the ROE and the earnings retention rate, b: $g = b \times \text{ROE}$. This expression can be expanded further, using the DuPont formula, as

$$g = \frac{\text{Net income} - \text{Dividends}}{\text{Net income}} \times \frac{\text{Net income}}{\text{Sales}} \times \frac{\text{Sales}}{\text{Total assets}} \times \frac{\text{Total assets}}{\text{Shareholders' equity}}.$$

REFERENCES

Arnott, Robert D. and Clifford S. Asness. 2003. "Surprise! Higher Dividends = Higher Earnings Growth." *Financial Analysts Journal* 59 (1): 70–87. 10.2469/faj.v59.n1.2504

Denis, David J. and Igor Osobov. 2008. "Why Do Firms Pay Dividends? International Evidence on the Determinants of Dividend Policy." *Journal of Financial Economics* 89 (1): 62–82. 10.1016/j.jfineco.2007.06.006

Fama, Eugene F. and Kenneth R. French. 2001. "Disappearing Dividends: Changing Firm Characteristics or Lower Propensity to Pay?" *Journal of Financial Economics* 60 (1): 3–43. 10.1016/S0304-405X(01)00038-1

Fuller, Russell J. and Chi-Cheng Hsia. 1984. "A Simplified Common Stock Valuation Model." *Financial Analysts Journal* 40 (5): 49–56. 10.2469/faj.v40.n5.49

Gordon, Myron J. 1962. *The Investment, Financing, and Valuation of the Corporation*. Homeward, IL: Richard D. Irwin.

Gordon, Myron J. and Eli Shapiro. 1956. "Capital Equipment Analysis: The Required Rate of Profit." *Management Science* 3 (1): 102–10. 10.1287/mnsc.3.1.102

Grullon, Gustavo, Bradley Paye, Shane Underwood, and James P. Weston. 2011. "Has the Propensity to Pay Out Declined?" *Journal of Financial and Quantitative Analysis* 46 (1): 1–24. 10.1017/S0022109010000633

Gwilym, Owain, James Seaton, Karina Suddason, and Stephen Thomas. 2006. "International Evidence on the Payout Ratio, Earnings, Dividends, and Returns." *Financial Analysts Journal* 62 (1): 36–53. 10.2469/faj.v62.n1.4057

He, Wen, Lilian Ng, Nataliya Zaiats, and Bohui Zhang. 2017. "Dividend Policy and Earnings Management across Countries." *Journal of Corporate Finance* 42:267–86. 10.1016/j.jcorpfin.2016.11.014

Julio, Brandon and David L. Ikenberry. 2004. "Reappearing Dividends." *Journal of Applied Corporate Finance* 16 (4): 89–100. 10.1111/j.1745-6622.2004.tb00676.x

Skinner, Douglas J. 2008. "The Evolving Relation between Earnings, Dividends, and Stock Repurchases." *Journal of Financial Economics* 87 (3): 582–609. 10.1016/j.jfineco.2007.05.003

Stowe, J., J Pinto, and T. Robinson. Equity Valuation: A Survey of Professional Practice", October 2018, Review of Financial Economics.

von Eije, J. Henk and William L. Megginson. 2008. "Dividends and Share Repurchases in the European Union." *Journal of Financial Economics* 89:347–74. 10.1016/j.jfineco.2007.11.002

Williams, John Burr. 1938. *The Theory of Investment Value*. Cambridge, MA: Harvard University Press.

Zhou, Ping and William Ruland. 2006. "Dividend Payout and Future Earnings Growth." *Financial Analysts Journal* 62 (3): 58–69. 10.2469/faj.v62.n3.4157

PRACTICE PROBLEMS

The following information relates to questions 1-6

Brian Dobson, an analyst at UK-based globally diversified equity mutual fund, has been assigned the task of estimating a fair value of the common stock of Charmed Energy. Dobson is aware of several approaches that could be used for this purpose. After carefully considering the characteristics of the company and its competitors, he believes Charmed will have extraordinary growth for the next few years and normal growth thereafter. So, he has concluded that a two-stage DDM is the most appropriate for valuing the stock.

Charmed pays semi-annual dividends. The total dividends during 2016, 2017, and 2018 have been C$0.114, C$0.15, and C$0.175, respectively. These imply a growth rate of 32% in 2017 and 17% in 2018. Dobson believes that the growth rate will be 14% in the next year. He has estimated that the first stage will include the next eight years.

Dobson is using the CAPM to estimate the required return on equity for Charmed. He has estimated that the company's beta, as measured against the S&P/TSX Composite Index (formerly TSE 300 Composite Index), is 0.84. The Canadian risk-free rate, as measured by the annual yield on the 10-year government bond, is 4.1%. The equity risk premium for the Canadian market is estimated at 5.5%. Based on these data, Dobson has estimated that the required return on Charmed Energy's stock is 0.041 + 0.84(0.055) = 0.0872, or 8.72%. Dobson is doing the analysis in January 2019, and the stock price at that time is C$17.

Dobson realizes that even within the two-stage DDM, there could be some variations in the approach. He would like to explore how these variations affect the stock's valuation. Specifically, he wants to estimate the value of the stock for each of the following approaches separately.

i. The dividend growth rate will be 14% throughout the first stage of eight years. The dividend growth rate thereafter will be 7%.

ii. Instead of using the estimated stable growth rate of 7% in the second stage, Dobson wants to use his estimate that eight years later, Charmed Energy's stock will be worth 17 times its earnings per share (trailing P/E of 17). He expects that the earnings retention ratio at that time will be 0.70.

iii. In contrast to the first approach, in which the growth rate declines abruptly from 14% in the eighth year to 7% in the ninth, the growth rate would decline linearly from 14% in the first year to 7% in the ninth.

1. What is the terminal value of the stock based on the first approach?

   A. C$17.65.

   B. C$31.06.

   C. C$33.09.

2. In the first approach, what proportion of the stock's total value is represented by

the value of second stage?

A. 0.10.

B. 0.52.

C. 0.90.

3. What is the stock's terminal value based on the second approach (earnings multiple)?

   A. C$12.12.

   B. C$28.29.

   C. C$33.09.

4. What is the stock's current value based on the second approach?

   A. C$16.24.

   B. C$17.65.

   C. C$28.29.

5. Based on the third approach (the H-model), the stock is:

   A. undervalued.

   B. fairly valued.

   C. overvalued.

6. Dobson is wondering what the consequences would be if the duration of the first stage was assumed to be 11 years instead of 8, with all the other assumptions and estimates remaining the same. Considering this change, which of the following is true?

   A. In the second approach, the proportion of the total value of the stock represented by the second stage would not change.

   B. The total value estimated using the third approach would increase.

   C. Using this new assumption and the first approach will lead Dobson to conclude that the stock is overvalued.

The following information relates to questions 7-15

Gianna Peters is an investment analyst who focuses on dividend-paying stocks. Peters uses a DCF approach to stock selection. She is meeting with her staff to evaluate portfolio holdings based on a bottom-up screening of stocks listed in the United States and Canada. Peters and her staff begin by reviewing the characteristics of the following portfolio candidates.

Company ABC

A Canadian company in the consumer staples sector with a required rate of return of 7.35%. Recent media reports suggest that ABC might be a takeover candidate. Peters and her team estimate that if the incumbent Canadian prime minister's party retains its power, the company's current annual dividend of C$0.65 per share will grow 12% a year for the next four years and then stabilize at a 3.5% growth rate a year indefinitely. If a new government takes office in Canada, however, then the team estimates that ABC will likely not experience the elevated 12% short-run growth because of new regulatory and tax changes, and instead it will grow by 3.5% indefinitely.

Company XYZ

A mid-sized US company in the utilities sector with a required rate of return of 10%. Peters and her team believe that because of a recent restructuring, the company is unlikely to pay dividends for the next three years. The team expects XYZ to pay an annual dividend of US$1.72 per share beginning four years from now, however. Thereafter, the dividend is expected to grow indefinitely at 4% even though the current price implies a growth rate of 6% during this same period.

Company JZY

A large US company in the telecom sector with a required rate of return of 8%. The stock is currently trading at US$32.76 per share with an implied earnings growth rate of 5.3%. Peters believes that because JZY is mature and has a stable capital structure, the company will grow at its sustainable growth rate. Over the past 10 years, the company's return on equity (ROE) has averaged 8.17% and its payout ratio has averaged 40%. Recently, the company paid an annual dividend of US$0.84 per share.

Peters asks a newly hired analyst, Kurt Thomas, to comment on the evaluation approach for these three stocks. Thomas makes the following statements:

1. A free cash flow valuation model would not be appropriate to evaluate Company ABC if the firm becomes a takeover candidate.
2. A dividend discount model cannot be applied to Company XYZ if dividends are suspended for a few years.
3. A dividend discount model is suitable for evaluating the stock of Company JZY because of the historically consistent payout ratio.

Peters then asks the team to examine the growth opportunities of three Canadian stocks currently held in the portfolio. These stocks are listed in Exhibit 1. Peters believes that the stocks are fairly valued.

Exhibit 1: Selected Stock Characteristics

Stock	Required Rate of Return	Next Year's Forecasted EPS (C$)	Current Price per Share (C$)
ABTD	10.5%	7.30	80.00
BKKQ	8.0%	2.12	39.00
CPMN	12.0%	1.90	27.39

7. Which of the following statements made by Thomas is *correct*?

A. Statement 1

B. Statement 2

C. Statement 3

8. Assuming the incumbent government retains office in Canada, Peters and her team estimate that the current value of Company ABC stock would be *closest* to:

   A. C$22.18.

   B. C$23.60.

   C. C$25.30.

9. Assuming a new government takes office in Canada, Peters and her team estimate that the current intrinsic value of Company ABC would be *closest* to:

   A. C$9.15.

   B. C$16.88.

   C. C$17.47.

10. Assume that a new government takes office in Canada. If Peters and her team use the Gordon growth model and assume that Company ABC stock is fairly valued, then which of the following would *most likely* be true?

    A. The total return of ABC stock will be 10.85%.

    B. The dividend yield of ABC stock will be 3.85%.

    C. The stock price of ABC will grow at 7.35% annually.

11. If the team uses the dividend discount model, the current intrinsic value of Company XYZ stock would be *closest to*:

    A. US$19.58.

    B. US$20.36.

    C. US$21.54.

12. The dividend growth rate implied in the stock price of Company XYZ suggests that XYZ's stock price is *most likely*:

    A. undervalued.

    B. fairly valued.

    C. overvalued.

13. Based on the relationship between the implied growth rate and the sustainable growth rate, Peters' team should conclude that Company JZY's stock price is *most likely*:

    A. undervalued.

    B. fairly valued.

    C. overvalued.

14. Based on Exhibit 1, the stock with the largest present value of growth opportunities (PVGO) is:

    A. ABTD.

B. BKKQ.

C. CPMN.

15. Based on Exhibit 1, the growth component of the leading P/E is largest for:

A. ABTD.

B. BKKQ.

C. CPMN.

The following information relates to questions 16-21

Jacob Daniel is the chief investment officer at a US pension fund sponsor, and Steven Rae is an analyst for the pension fund who follows consumer/non-cyclical stocks. At the beginning of 20X9, Daniel asks Rae to value the equity of Tasty Foods Company for its possible inclusion in the list of approved investments. Tasty Foods Company is involved in the production of frozen foods that are sold under its own brand name to retailers.

Rae is considering whether a dividend discount model would be appropriate for valuing Tasty Foods. He has compiled the information in the following table for the company's EPS and DPS during the last five years. The quarterly dividends paid by the company have been added to arrive at the annual dividends. Rae has also computed the dividend payout ratio for each year as DPS/EPS and the growth rates in EPS and DPS.

Year	EPS ($)	DPS ($)	Payout Ratio	Growth in EPS (%)	Growth in DPS (%)
20X8	2.12	0.59	0.278	2.9	3.5
20X7	2.06	0.57	0.277	2.5	5.6
20X6	2.01	0.54	0.269	6.3	5.9
20X5	1.89	0.51	0.270	6.2	6.3
20X4	1.78	0.48	0.270		

Rae notes that the company's EPS has been increasing at an average rate of 4.48% per year. The dividend payout ratio has remained fairly stable, and dividends have increased at an average rate of 5.30%. In view of a history of dividend payments by the company and the understandable relationship dividend policy bears to the company's earnings, Rae concludes that the DDM is appropriate to value the equity of Tasty Foods. Further, he expects the company's moderate growth rate to persist and decides to use the Gordon growth model.

Rae uses the CAPM to compute the return on equity. He uses the annual yield of 4% on the 10-year Treasury bond as the risk-free return. He estimates the expected US equity risk premium, with the S&P 500 Index used as a proxy for the market, to be 6.5% per year. The estimated beta of Tasty Foods against the S&P 500 Index is 1.10. Accordingly, Rae's estimate for the required return on equity for Tasty Foods is 0.04 + 1.10(0.065) = 0.1115, or 11.15%.

Using the past growth rate in dividends of 5.30% as his estimate of the future growth rate in dividends, Rae computes the value of Tasty Foods stock. He shows his analysis to Alex Renteria, his colleague at the pension fund who specializes in the frozen foods industry. Renteria concurs with the valuation approach used by Rae but disagrees with the future growth rate he used. Renteria believes that the stock's current price of $8.42 is the fair value of the stock.

16. Which of the following is *closest* to Rae's estimate of the stock's value?

    A. $10.08.

    B. $10.54.

    C. $10.62.

17. What is the stock's justified trailing P/E based on the stock's value estimated by Rae?

    A. 5.01.

    B. 5.24.

    C. 5.27.

18. Rae considers a security trading within a band of ±10% of his estimate of intrinsic value to be within a "fair value range." By that criterion, the stock of Tasty Foods is:

    A. undervalued.

    B. fairly valued.

    C. overvalued.

19. The beta of Tasty Foods stock of 1.10 that Rae used in computing the required return on equity was based on monthly returns for the last 10 years. If Rae uses daily returns for the last five years, the beta estimate is 1.25. If a beta of 1.25 is used, what would be Rae's estimate of the value of Tasty Foods stock?

    A. $8.64.

    B. $9.10.

    C. $20.13.

20. Renteria has suggested that the market price of Tasty Foods stock is its fair value. What is the implied growth rate of dividends given the stock's market price? Use the required return on equity based on a beta of 1.10.

    A. 3.87%.

    B. 5.30%.

    C. 12.1%.

21. If Renteria is correct that the current price of Tasty Foods stock is its fair value, what is the expected capital gains yield on the stock?

    A. 3.87%.

    B. 4.25%.

    C. 5.30%.

The following information relates to questions 22-28

BJL Financial provides clients with professional investment management services that are tailored to the specific needs of each client. The firm's portfolio manager, Angelique Kwaza, has called a meeting with the senior analyst, Samira Khan, to discuss the quarterly rebalancing of three client portfolios. The valuation model used in the analyses is the discounted dividend model.

- Client 1 has a portfolio with significant exposure to dividend-paying stocks.
- Client 2 is interested in including preferred stock in the portfolio.
- Client 3 has a growth-oriented equity-only portfolio.

Khan has identified two utilities (ABC and XYZ) for possible inclusion in Client 1's portfolio, as shown in Exhibit 1. She uses a discount rate of 7% for both common stocks.

Exhibit 1: Candidate Stocks for Client 1

Stock	Company Description
ABC	▪ ABC is a publicly traded utility with an expected constant growth rate for earnings and dividends of 3.5%. ▪ The most recent year's dividend payout is 70%. The expected dividend payout in future years is 60%. ▪ The common stock price is $14.49 per share.
XYZ	▪ XYZ is a publicly traded utility with several unregulated business subsidiaries. ▪ The company generates 3% growth in dividends and has an annual dividend payout of 80%. No changes in dividend growth or payout are expected. ▪ The common stock price is $10 per share. ▪ The current year earnings are $0.45 per share, and next year's earnings are expected to be $0.50 per share.

Kwaza asks Khan to investigate the most appropriate models for valuing utility companies. She tells Khan about the following points mentioned in various research reports on the utilities sector.

Report 1: A resurgence in domestic manufacturing activity will generate long-term growth in earnings and dividends that exceeds the cost of equity.

Report 2: Share repurchases are expected to increase. The report expresses confidence in the forecasts regarding the magnitude and timing of these repurchases.

Report 3: The report forecasts earnings growth of 4.5%. The key growth drivers are increases in population and business creation associated with stable GDP growth of 2.75%.

For Client 2's portfolio, Khan has identified the non-callable perpetual preferred stocks of Standard Company and Main Company.

- The Standard Company's preferred stock pays 2.75% on a par value of $100. Khan believes it to be fairly valued at a market price of $49.60.

- The perpetual preferred stock of Main Company has a par value of $50 per share and pays an annual dividend of 5.5%. Khan estimates a capitalization rate at 6%. The current market price of Main Company preferred stock is $42.

Finally, Khan has identified three stocks, shown in Exhibit 2, as likely candidates for Client 3's portfolio.

Exhibit 2: Candidate Stocks for Client 3

Stock	Company Description
BIOK	▪ BIOK is a profitable biotech firm that currently pays an annual dividend of $1.20 per share. ▪ The current annual dividend growth rate is 15%. ▪ Patent protection runs out in eight years, after which dividend growth will likely decline at a steady rate over three years before stabilizing at a mature growth rate.
CCAX	▪ CCAX builds communication software for state and federal prisons and detention facilities. ▪ The company is expected to hold its cash dividends steady at $0.56 per share for six years as it builds out facilities and acquires properties. ▪ Dividends are expected to grow at the nominal GDP growth rate after the next six years.
HLTV	▪ HLTV is a health care equipment and services firm that is expected to maintain a stable dividend payout ratio. ▪ Earnings are forecast to grow over the next two years by 27% annually. ▪ After that, earnings will likely grow by 12% annually for another 10 years before stabilizing at a mature growth rate.

22. Based on the Gordon growth model, the justified leading P/E for ABC stock is *closest* to:

    A. 17.1.

    B. 17.7.

    C. 20.0.

23. Based on its justified leading P/E and the Gordon growth model, XYZ stock is:

    A. undervalued.

    B. fairly valued.

    C. overvalued.

24. Which sector report *best* describes a situation in which the Gordon growth model could be used to value utility stocks?

    A. Report 1

    B. Report 2

    C. Report 3

25. Based on Khan's estimate of the capitalization rate, Main Company's preferred stock is:

    A. undervalued.

    B. fairly valued.

    C. overvalued.

26. The capitalization rate of the preferred stock of Standard Company is *closest* to:

    A. 2.75%.

    B. 4.96%.

    C. 5.54%.

27. Based on Exhibit 2, which stock can most appropriately be valued using a three-stage DDM with the second and third stages being treated as an H-model?

    A. BIOK

    B. CCAX

    C. HLTV

28. Which of the following models is *most* appropriate for valuing HLTV?

    A. H-model

    B. Three-stage DDM

    C. Gordon growth model

The following information relates to questions 29-38

June Withers is analyzing four stocks in the processed food industry as of 31 December 2019. All stocks pay a dividend at the end of each year.

Ukon Corporation

Withers estimates a required rate of return for Ukon Corporation of 8% and notes that the dividend for 2019 was EUR 2.315 per share. Her first valuation approach is a basic two-stage DDM, with dividends growing at a rate of 5% from 2020 through 2023, after which time dividends will grow at a sustainable rate of 3%. Her second valuation approach is the H-model, assuming that dividend growth of 5% in 2020 declines linearly during the years 2021 through 2023 to the 3% growth rate after 2023. Exhibit 1 summarizes Withers's dividend growth assumptions.

Exhibit 1: Ukon Corporation Dividend Growth Assumptions, by Model

Model	Period	Rate
Two-stage DDM	2020 through 2023	5%
	Beginning 2024	3%
H-model	2020	5%
	2021 through 2023	Declining linearly to 3.5%
	Beginning 2024	3%

Venus Company

Withers has assembled the data on Venus Company in Exhibit 2. After analyzing competitive pressures and financial conditions in the industry, she predicts that Venus Company will lose market share because of new entrants but will stabilize within a few years. The required rate of return for Venus Company is 8%. Beginning with a per-share dividend of USD3.15 in 2019, she develops two scenarios regarding Venus Company's dividend growth. The scenarios, shown in Exhibit 2, are summarized as follows:

- In Scenario 1, the growth rate will fall in a linear manner over the years 2020 through 2023 from 8% to 4%. Using the H-model, Withers calculates a value of USD58.79 per share of Venus Company stock.
- In Scenario 2, the growth rate falls from 8% in 2019 to 6% in 2020 and 2021, to 5% in 2022 and 2023, and then to a sustainable rate of 3% for 2024 and beyond.

Exhibit 2: Venus Company Dividend Growth Scenarios

Scenario	Period	Rate
Scenario 1	2020 through 2023	Declining linearly to 4%
	Beginning 2024	Remaining stable at 4%
Scenario 2	2020 and 2021	6%
	2022 and 2023	5%
	Beginning 2024	Remaining stable at 3%

Wakuni Corporation

Withers evaluates Wakuni Corporation and uses recent financial data from Exhibit 3 to calculate a sustainable growth based on the DuPont model. In addition to this estimate, she performs a sensitivity analysis on the sustainable growth rate whereby the dividend payout ranges from 0% to 10% and the return on equity ranges from 8% to 12%.

Exhibit 3: Selected Data for Wakuni Corporation (JPY billions)

Net income	43,923
Sales	423,474
Total assets, average during year	486,203

Shareholders' equity, beginning of year	397,925
Dividends paid	1,518

Xavier Corporation

In her analysis of the stock of Xavier Corporation, Withers observes that it has a dividend of USD2 per share and a stock price of USD52. Two analyst interns have offered estimates of the company's required rate of return and dividend growth rate, as shown in Exhibit 4.

Exhibit 4: Xavier Corporation Required Rate of Return and Dividend Growth Rates (Estimates)

	Intern 1	Intern 2
Required rate of return	8.3%	7.8%
Growth rate, first four years	5.0%	4.8%
Growth rate, beyond first four years	3.6%	4.0%

29. Based on Exhibit 1, when Withers applies the first valuation approach to Ukon Corporation, the estimated value of the stock at the end of the first stage represents the:

    A. present value of the dividends beyond year 2023.

    B. present value of the dividends for years 2020 through 2023.

    C. sum of the present value of the dividends for 2020 through 2023 and the present value of dividends beyond year 2023.

30. Using her first valuation approach and Exhibit 1, Withers's forecast of the per share stock value of Ukon Corporation at the end of 2019 should be *closest to*:

    A. EUR48.

    B. EUR50.

    C. EUR51.

31. Using Withers's assumptions for the H-model and the basic two-stage dividend discount model, the forecasted Ukon stock price at the end of the year 2023 for the H-model should be:

    A. lower than the basic two-stage model.

    B. the same as the basic two-stage model.

    C. higher than the basic two-stage model.

32. Under her Scenario 1 and based on Exhibit 2, the required rate of return that Withers used for Venus Company stock valuation is *closest* to:

    A. 8.0%.

    B. 9.6%.

C. 10.0%.

33. Under Scenario 2 and based on Exhibit 2, Withers estimates that the value of the Venus Company stock to be *closest* to:

A. USD69.73.

B. USD71.03.

C. USD72.98.

34. Using the data in Exhibit 3, Withers can estimate the sustainable growth of the Wakuni Corporation as being *closest* to:

A. 10.66%.

B. 11.04%.

C. 14.05%.

35. Withers's sensitivity analysis of Wakuni Corporation should produce a range of sustainable growth estimates between:

A. 0.0% and 1.2%.

B. 7.2% and 12.0%.

C. 8.0% and 13.3%.

36. Based on Exhibit 4 and Intern 1's analysis, Xavier Corporation's sustainable dividend payout ratio is *closest* to:

A. 43.4%.

B. 44.6%.

C. 56.6%.

37. Based on Exhibit 4, Intern 2 should conclude that the Xavier stock is:

A. underpriced.

B. fairly priced.

C. overpriced.

38. Based on Exhibit 4 and Intern 1's estimate of the required rate of return and the dividend growth rate for the first four years, the growth rate beyond the first four years consistent with the current price of USD52 is *closest* to:

A. 3.80%.

B. 4.17%.

C. 4.23%.

SOLUTIONS

1. B is correct. The following table provides the calculations needed to compute the value of the stock using the first approach, including the calculations for the terminal value V_8. As the table shows, the terminal value V_8 = C$31.0550.

Time	Value	Calculation	D_t or V_t	Present Values $D_t/(1.0872)^t$ or $V_t/(1.0872)^t$
1	D_1	C$0.175(1.14)	C$0.1995	C$0.1835
2	D_2	$0.175(1.14)^2$	0.2274	0.1924
3	D_3	$0.175(1.14)^3$	0.2593	0.2018
4	D_4	$0.175(1.14)^4$	0.2956	0.2116
5	D_5	$0.175(1.14)^5$	0.3369	0.2218
6	D_6	$0.175(1.14)^6$	0.3841	0.2326
7	D_7	$0.175(1.14)^7$	0.4379	0.2439
8	D_8	$0.175(1.14)^8$	0.4992	0.2557
8	V_8	$0.175(1.14)^8(1.07)/(0.0872 - 0.07)$	31.0550	15.9095
Total				C$17.6528

2. C is correct. As shown in the foregoing table, the value of the second stage = PV of V_8 = C$15.9095. The total value is C$17.6528. As a proportion, the second stage represents 15.9095/17.6528 = 0.90 of the total value.

3. B is correct.

   $V_8/E_8 = 17$

   $D_8/E_8 = 1 - 0.70 = 0.30$

   From the table with the calculation details for the solution to Problem 22, D_8 = C$0.4992. So, 0.4992/ E_8 = 0.30, which means that E_8 = 0.4992/0.30 = 1.6640.

   $V_8/E_8 = 17$ implies that $V_8/1.6640 = 17$, which gives $V_8 = 17(1.6640)$

   = C$28.2880.

4. A is correct. As computed earlier, V_8 = 17(1.6640) = C$28.2880.

   PV of $V_8 = 28.2880/1.0872^8 = 14.4919$

   From the table with the calculation details for the solution to Problem 22,

   Sum of PV of D_1 through D_8 = 1.7433

   So, the value of stock V_0 = 14.4919 + 1.7433 = C$16.2352.

5. C is correct. Using the H-model,

$$V_0 = \frac{D_0(1+g_L) + D_0 H(g_S - g_L)}{r - g_L},$$

where

$D_0 = 0.175$

$r = 0.0872$

$H = 4$

$g_S = 0.14$

$g_L = 0.07$

$$V_0 = \frac{0.175(1.07) + 0.175(4)(0.14 - 0.07)}{0.0872 - 0.07} = 13.7355.$$

The market price is C$17, which is greater than C$13.7355. So, the stock is overvalued in the market.

6. B is correct. If the extraordinary growth rate of 14% is expected to continue for a longer duration, the stock's value would increase. Choice A is false because given that the first stage is longer (11 years instead of 8), the terminal value is being calculated at a later point in time. So, its present value would be smaller. Moreover, the first stage has more years and contributes more to the total value. Overall, the proportion contributed by the second stage would be smaller. Choice C is false because the intrinsic value of the stock would be higher and the appropriate conclusion would be that the stock would be undervalued to a greater extent based on the first approach.

7. C is correct. A dividend discount model is especially useful when dividend policy bears an understandable and consistent relationship to the company's profitability. The relatively consistent dividend payout ratio suggests Company JZY would be a suitable candidate for a dividend discount model.

8. B is correct. The value of ABC stock can be computed as follows:
   Given: Dividend (D_0) = C$0.65, Return ($r$) = 7.35%, Short-term growth (g_S) = 12% for 4 years, Long-term growth (g_L) = 3.5% thereafter.
   Then:

   $D_1 = D_0(1 + g_S)^1 = 0.65(1.12) = \text{C\$}0.7280$

   $D_2 = D_0(1 + g_S)^2 = 0.65(1.12)^2 = \text{C\$}0.8154$

   $D_3 = D_0(1 + g_S)^3 = 0.65(1.12)^3 = \text{C\$}0.9132$

   $D_4 = D_0(1 + g_S)^4 = 0.65(1.12)^4 = \text{C\$}1.0228$

   $P_4 = [D_4(1 + g_L)]/(r - g_L) = [D_4(1.035)]/(0.0735 - 0.035) = \text{C\$}27.4960.$

   $V_0 = D_1/(1 + r)^1 + \ldots. + D_4/(1 + r)^4 + P_4/(1 + r)^4.$

   $V_0 = [0.7280/(1.0735)^1] + [0.8154/(1.0735)^2] + [0.9132/(1.0735)^3] + [1.0228/(1.0735)^4] + [27.4960/(1.0735)^4]$

   $= \text{C\$}23.5984$ (rounded to C$23.60).

9. C is correct. The value of ABC would be calculated using the Gordon growth model as follows:

   $V_0 = [D_0(1 + g)]/(r - g) = [0.65(1.035)]/(0.0735 - 0.035) = \text{C\$}17.47.$

10. B is correct. In the Gordon growth model, Total return = Dividend yield + Capital gains yield (i.e., constant growth rate). When a stock is fairly valued, the expected total return will equal the required return or discount rate (i.e., 7.35%). In the case of ABC, the total return is 7.35% and the capital gains yield is 3.5%. Therefore, the dividend yield is 7.35% – 3.5% = 3.85%.

11. C is correct. The current value of XYZ stock would be calculated as follows:

    $V_0 = [P_3/(1 + r)^3]$, where $P_3 = D_4/(r - g)$.

    Given $D_4 = 1.72$, $r = 10\%$, and $g = 4\%$,

    $V_0 = [1.72/(0.10 - 0.04)]/(1.10)^3 = \text{US\$}21.54$.

12. C is correct. The dividend growth rate implied in the stock price of XYZ (i.e., 6%) is greater than the growth rate assumed by the analyst (i.e., 4%), suggesting that XYZ is overvalued.

13. C is correct. The sustainable growth rate of JZY stock = g = Retention ratio × ROE = 0.60 × 0.0817 = 4.9%. JZY stock's implied growth rate of 5.3% is higher than the sustainable growth rate of 4.9%. Consequently, the stock is overvalued—that is, the intrinsic value of the stock will be less than its current market price.

    The current intrinsic value of JZY stock is as follows:

    $V_0 = [D_0(1 + g)]/(r - g)$

    $= [0.84\ (1.0490)]/(0.08 - 0.0490)$

    $= \text{US\$}28.42 < \text{US\$}32.76$

14. B is correct. BKKQ has the largest PVGO, calculated as follows:

    PVGO (ABTD) = $P_0 - E_1/r$ = 80.00 – [7.30/0.105] = C$10.48

    PVGO (BKKQ) = $P_0 - E_1/r$ = 39.00 – [2.12/0.08] = C$12.50

    PVGO (CPMN) = $P_0 - E_1/r$ = 27.39 – [1.90/0.12] = C$11.56

    where P_0 is the current price per share, E_1 is the forecasted earnings per share, and r is the required rate of return.

15. C is correct. The leading P/E is calculated as follows:

    $P_0/E_1 = [1/r] + [\text{PVGO}/E_1]$,

    where $1/r$ captures the no-growth component of P/E and PVGO/E_1 captures the growth component of the P/E.

    PVGO is computed as follows:

    PVGO (ABTD) = $P_0 - E_1/r$ = 80.00 – [7.30/0.105] = C$10.48

    PVGO (BKKQ) = $P_0 - E_1/r$ = 39.00 – [2.12/0.08] = C$12.50

    PVGO (CPMN) = $P_0 - E_1/r$ = 27.39 – [1.90/0.12] = C$11.56

    where P_0 is the current price per share, E_1 is the forecasted earnings per share, and r is the required rate of return.

    The growth component of the P/E for each stock [PVGO/E_1] is as follows:

    ABTD: 10.48/7.30 = 1.44×

    BKKQ: 12.50/2.12 = 5.90×

CPMN: 11.56/1.90 = 6.08×

16. C is correct. Using the Gordon growth model,

$$V_0 = \frac{D_1}{r-g} = \frac{0.59(1+0.0530)}{0.1115-0.0530} = \$10.62.$$

17. A is correct. The justified trailing P/E or P_0/E_0 is V_0/E_0, where V_0 is the fair value based on the stock's fundamentals. The fair value V_0 computed earlier is \$10.62 and E_0 is \$2.12. So, the justified trailing P/E is 10.62/2.12 = 5.01.

18. A is correct. Rae's estimate of the intrinsic value is \$10.62. So, the band Rae is looking at is \$10.62 ± 0.10(\$10.62), which runs from \$10.62 + \$1.06 = \$11.68 on the upside to \$10.62 – \$1.06 = \$9.56 on the downside. Because \$8.42 is less than \$9.56, Rae would consider Tasty Foods to be undervalued.

19. B is correct. Using a beta of 1.25, Rae's estimate for the required return on equity for Tasty Foods is 0.04 + 1.25(0.065) = 0.1213, or 12.13%. The estimated value of the stock is

$$V_0 = \frac{D_1}{r-g} = \frac{0.59 \times (1+0.0530)}{0.1213-0.0530} = \$9.10.$$

20. A is correct. The price of the stock is \$8.42. If this price is also the fair value of the stock,

$$\begin{aligned} V_0 &= 8.42 = \frac{D_1}{r-g} = \frac{0.59 \times (1+g)}{0.1115-g} \\ 0.9388 - 8.42g &= 0.59 + 0.59g \\ 9.01g &= 0.3488 \\ g &= 0.0387 \text{ or } 3.87\text{percent} \end{aligned}$$

21. A is correct. If the stock is fairly priced in the market as per the Gordon growth model, the stock price is expected to increase at *g*, the expected growth rate in dividends. The implied growth rate in dividends, if price is the fair value, is 3.87%. Therefore, the expected capital gains yield is 3.87%.

22. A is correct. The justified leading P/E is calculated as

$$\frac{P_0}{E_1} = \frac{(1-b)}{(r-g)},$$

where b is the retention ratio, $1 - b$ is the dividend payout ratio, r is the discount rate, and g is the long-term growth rate.

ABC's dividend payout rate, $1 - b$, is given as 0.60. For Company ABC, the justified leading P/E is

$$\frac{P_0}{E_1} = \frac{(1-b)}{(r-g)} = \frac{(0.60)}{(0.07-0.035)} \approx 17.1.$$

23. B is correct. The justified leading P/E is calculated as

$$\frac{P_0}{E_1} = \frac{(1-b)}{(r-g)},$$

where b is the retention ratio, $1 - b$ is the dividend payout ratio, r is the discount rate, and g is the long-term growth rate.

The justified leading P/E is

$$\frac{P_0}{E_1} = \frac{0.8}{(0.07 - 0.03)} = 20.$$

XYZ's actual leading P/E is

$$\frac{P_0}{E_1} = \frac{\$10}{\$0.50} = 20.$$

Because the justified leading P/E equals the actual leading P/E, the stock is fairly valued.

24. B is correct because the Gordon growth model can accurately value companies that are repurchasing shares when the analyst can appropriately adjust the dividend growth rate for the impact of share repurchases.

25. A is correct. The value of a share of Main Company's preferred stock is

$$V_0 = \frac{D}{r} = \frac{\$50 \times 0.055}{0.06} = \frac{\$2.75}{0.06} = \$45.83.$$

The current price of a share of Main Company's preferred stock is \$42, so the stock is currently undervalued.

26. C is correct. The value of non-callable fixed-rate perpetual preferred stock is calculated as

$$V_0 = \frac{D}{r} \rightarrow r = \frac{D}{V_0},$$

where D is the constant dividend per share and r is the discount rate. The discount rate of a perpetuity is often called the capitalization rate.
For Standard Company, the dividend is D = 2.75% × \$100 = \$2.75.
Therefore,

$$r = \frac{\$2.75}{\$49.60} = 5.54\%.$$

27. A is correct because the dividend growth is declining linearly during the second stage of a three-stage DDM used to value BIOK. As noted in the text, a three-stage valuation clearly has an H-model process in the second and third stages. In contrast, abrupt—rather than linearly declining—dividend growth rates are implied for CCAX and HLTV.

28. B is correct because HLTV is forecast to have three growth stages: the growth phase (2 years at 27%), the transition phase (10 years at 12%), and the mature phase. Because the earnings growth has three stages and the dividend payout ratio is stable, a three-stage DDM is appropriate.

29. A is correct because the estimated value of the stock at the end of the first stage of a basic two-stage DDM (terminal value) is the present value of all dividends beyond the first stage. The first stage is 2020 through 2023, and the second stage begins in 2024, so the terminal value (that is, the value of the stock at the end of 2023) is the present value of future dividends beyond 2023.

30. C is correct based on Withers's assumptions applied to the dividend valuation model.
The stock value as of the end of 2019 equals the present value of all future dividends in 2020 through 2022 plus the present value of the terminal value at the end of 2022. The forecasted stock value equals EUR51.254:

Year	Dividend	Terminal Value	D_t or V_t	Present Value of D_t or V_t
2020	2.315(1.05) = 2.431		2.431	2.251
2021	2.431(1.05) = 2.553		2.553	2.189
2022	2.553(1.05) = 2.681		2.681	2.128
2023	2.681(1.05) = 2.815	57.980	60.795	44.686
2024	2.815(1.03) = 2.899			
Total				51.254

The terminal value at the end of 2023 is calculated using the dividend in the first year beyond the first stage, divided by the difference between the required rate of return and the growth rate in the second stage.

$$\text{Terminal value at end of 2023} = \frac{2.815(1.03)}{(0.08 - 0.03)} = 57.980$$

31. A is correct. During the first stage, the basic two-stage model has higher (i.e., 5%) growth than the H-model, in which growth is declining linearly from 5.0% to 3.5%. Higher growth rates result in higher forecasted dividends and stock prices at the beginning of the sustained growth phase. Because the long-term dividend growth rates are the same for both models, the difference in forecasted stock price arises from growth rate differences in the first stage.

    Therefore, the dividend at the end of the first stage will be lower for the H-model than for the basic two-stage DDM, and the terminal value will be lower in the H-model than in the two-stage model. Specifically, the 2023 dividends will be 2.734 (i.e., 2.315 × 1.05 × 1.045 × 1.04 × 1.035) for the H-model versus 2.815 [i.e., 2.315 × $(1.05)^4$] for the basic two-stage DDM.

32. C is correct, based on Exhibit 2 and the H-model.

    Estimate the required rate of return using Equation 21:

    $$r = \frac{D_0}{P_0}\left[(1 + g_L) + H(g_S - g_L)\right] + g_L$$

    Substitute the following:

    $D_0 = 3.15$

    $g_S = 8\%$

    $g_L = 4\%$

    $H = 4 \div 2 = 2$

    The model thus produces

    $$r = \frac{3.15}{58.79}[(1 + 0.04) + 2(0.08 - 0.04)] + 0.04$$

    $$= (0.053581 \times 1.12) + 0.04$$

    $$= 0.060010 + 0.04 = 0.10001 \approx 10\%.$$

33. B is correct based on the present value of forecasted dividends. The dividend at the end of 2019, based on case material, is USD3.15 per share.

Year	Dividend per Share, Prior Year	Growth Rate during Year	Dividend per Share, Current Year	Terminal Value	D_t or V_t	Present Value of D_t or V_t
2020	3.150	6%	3.339		3.339	3.092
2021	3.339	6%	3.539		3.539	3.034
2022	3.539	5%	3.716		3.716	2.950
2023	3.716	5%	3.902	80.381	84.283	61.951
					Total	71.027

$$\text{Terminal value at the end of 2023} = \frac{3.902\,(1.03)}{(0.08-0.03)} = 80.381$$

34. A is correct, based on the use of average total assets and beginning-of-year shareholders' equity.

$$g = \frac{\text{Net income} - \text{Dividends}}{\text{Net income}} \times \frac{\text{Net income}}{\text{Sales}} \times \frac{\text{Sales}}{\text{Total assets}} \times \frac{\text{Total assets}}{\text{Shareholders' equity}}$$

To calculate sustainable growth,

$$g = \frac{43,923 - 1,518}{43,923} \times \frac{43,923}{423,474} \times \frac{423,474}{486,203} \times \frac{486,203}{397,925}$$

$$= 96.544\% \times 10.372\% \times 87.100\% \times 122.200\%$$

$$= 10.658\%$$

35. B is correct because the sustainable growth is the product of the return on equity and the retention ratio. If the payout ratio ranges from 0% to 10%, the percentage of earnings retained by the firm ranges from 100% to 90%.

Sensitivity: Sustainable Growth Rates

Return on Equity	Retention Ratio	
	90%	100%
8%	7.2%	8.0%
12%	10.8%	12.0%

36. C is correct because it is based on the sustainable growth rate and the required rate of return:

$$\text{Sustainable growth rate} = (b \text{ in mature phase}) \times (\text{Return on equity})$$

$$= (1 - \text{Dividend payout}) \times (\text{Return on equity})$$

$$0.036 = (1 - \text{Dividend payout}) \times 0.083$$

Solving for the dividend payout ratio, the dividend payout = 56.627% ≈ 56.6%.

37. A is correct. Intern 2 values Xavier stock at USD56.372 per share, which is higher than the current price of USD52.

$D_1 = 2.000 \times (1.048)^1 = 2.096$

$D_2 = 2.000 \times (1.048)^2 = 2.197$

$$D_3 = 2.000 \times (1.048)^3 = 2.302$$

$$D_4 = 2.000 \times (1.048)^4 = 2.413$$

$$D_5 = 2.000 \times (1.048)^4 \times 1.04 = 2.510$$

$$\text{Value per share} = \frac{2.096}{(1+0.078)^1} + \frac{2.197}{(1+0.078)^2} + \frac{2.302}{(1+0.078)^3} + \frac{2.413 + \frac{2.510}{(0.078-0.04)}}{(1+0.078)^4}$$
$$= \text{USD}56.372$$

38. B is correct. The candidate can arrive at the answer one of two ways. The first way is to use Equation 19 and solve for g_L:

$$P_0 = \left[\sum_{t=1}^{n} \frac{D_0(1+g_S)^t}{(1+r)^t}\right] + \left[\frac{D_0(1+g_S)^n(1+g_L)}{(1+r)^n(r-g_L)}\right]$$

Insert the known values:

$$\text{USD}52 = \sum_{t=1}^{4} \frac{2(1+0.05)^t}{(1+0.083)^t} + \frac{2(1+0.05)^4(1+g_L)}{(1+0.083)^4(0.083-g_L)}$$

$$= 7.4089 + \frac{2.431(1+g_L)}{1.37567(0.083-g_L)}$$

Solve for g_L:

$g_L = 4.172\%$.

Check:

$$7.4089 + \frac{2.431(1+0.04127)}{1.3757(0.083-0.04172)} = 7.4089 + 44.5830 \approx 52.00$$

The second way is to use Equation 19 and substitute the different choices to determine the value that produces a value of USD52 per share:

$$\text{USD}52 = \sum_{t=1}^{4} \frac{2(1+0.05)^t}{(1+0.083)^t} + \frac{2(1+0.05)^4(1+0.0417)}{(1+0.083)^4(0.083-0.0417)}$$

LEARNING MODULE

3

Free Cash Flow Valuation

by Jerald E. Pinto, PhD, CFA, Elaine Henry, PhD, CFA, Thomas R. Robinson, PhD, CFA, CAIA, and John D. Stowe, PhD, CFA.

Jerald E. Pinto, PhD, CFA, is at CFA Institute (USA). Elaine Henry, PhD, CFA, is at Stevens Institute of Technology (USA). Thomas R. Robinson, PhD, CFA, CAIA, Robinson Global Investment Management LLC, (USA). John D. Stowe, PhD, CFA, is at Ohio University (USA).

LEARNING OUTCOMES

Mastery	*The candidate should be able to:*
☐	compare the free cash flow to the firm (FCFF) and free cash flow to equity (FCFE) approaches to valuation
☐	explain the ownership perspective implicit in the FCFE approach
☐	explain the appropriate adjustments to net income, earnings before interest and taxes (EBIT), earnings before interest, taxes, depreciation, and amortization (EBITDA), and cash flow from operations (CFO) to calculate FCFF and FCFE
☐	calculate FCFF and FCFE
☐	describe approaches for forecasting FCFF and FCFE
☐	explain how dividends, share repurchases, share issues, and changes in leverage may affect future FCFF and FCFE
☐	compare the FCFE model and dividend discount models
☐	evaluate the use of net income and EBITDA as proxies for cash flow in valuation
☐	explain the use of sensitivity analysis in FCFF and FCFE valuations
☐	explain the single-stage (stable-growth), two-stage, and three-stage FCFF and FCFE models and justify the selection of the appropriate model given a company's characteristics
☐	estimate a company's value using the appropriate free cash flow model(s)
☐	describe approaches for calculating the terminal value in a multistage valuation model; and
☐	evaluate whether a stock is overvalued, fairly valued, or undervalued based on a free cash flow valuation model

1 INTRODUCTION

- [ ] compare the free cash flow to the firm (FCFF) and free cash flow to equity (FCFE) approaches to valuation
- [ ] explain the ownership perspective implicit in the FCFE approach

Discounted cash flow (DCF) valuation views the intrinsic value of a security as the present value of its expected future cash flows. When applied to dividends, the DCF model is the discounted dividend approach or dividend discount model (DDM). Our coverage extends DCF analysis to value a company and its equity securities by valuing free cash flow to the firm (FCFF) and free cash flow to equity (FCFE). Whereas dividends are the cash flows actually paid to stockholders, free cash flows are the cash flows *available* for distribution to shareholders.

Unlike dividends, FCFF and FCFE are not readily available data. Analysts need to compute these quantities from available financial information, which requires a clear understanding of free cash flows and the ability to interpret and use the information correctly. Forecasting future free cash flows is a rich and demanding exercise. The analyst's understanding of a company's financial statements, its operations, its financing, and its industry can pay real "dividends" as he or she addresses that task. Many analysts consider free cash flow models to be more useful than DDMs in practice. Free cash flows provide an economically sound basis for valuation.

A study of professional analysts substantiates the importance of free cash flow valuation (Pinto, Robinson, Stowe 2019). When valuing individual equities, 92.8% of analysts use market multiples and 78.8% use a discounted cash flow approach. When using discounted cash flow analysis, 20.5% of analysts use a residual income approach, 35.1% use a dividend discount model, and 86.9% use a discounted free cash flow model. Of those using discounted free cash flow models, FCFF models are used roughly twice as frequently as FCFE models. Analysts often use more than one method to value equities, and it is clear that free cash flow analysis is in near universal use.

Analysts like to use free cash flow as the return (either FCFF or FCFE) whenever one or more of the following conditions is present:

- The company does not pay dividends.
- The company pays dividends, but the dividends paid differ significantly from the company's capacity to pay dividends.
- Free cash flows align with profitability within a reasonable forecast period with which the analyst is comfortable.
- The investor takes a "control" perspective. With control comes discretion over the uses of free cash flow. If an investor can take control of the company (or expects another investor to do so), dividends may be changed substantially; for example, they may be set at a level approximating the company's capacity to pay dividends. Such an investor can also apply free cash flows to uses such as servicing the debt incurred in an acquisition.

Common equity can be valued directly by finding the present value of FCFE or indirectly by first using an FCFF model to estimate the value of the firm and then subtracting the value of non-common-stock capital (usually debt) to arrive at an estimate of the value of equity. The purpose of the coverage in the subsequent sections is to develop the background required to use the FCFF or FCFE approaches to value a company's equity.

In the next section, we define the concepts of free cash flow to the firm and free cash flow to equity and then present the two valuation models based on discounting of FCFF and FCFE. We also explore the constant-growth models for valuing FCFF and FCFE, which are special cases of the general models. The subsequent sections turn to the vital task of calculating and forecasting FCFF and FCFE. They also explain multistage free cash flow valuation models and present some of the issues associated with their application. Analysts usually value operating assets and non-operating assets separately and then combine them to find the total value of the firm, an approach described in the last section on this topic.

FCFF and FCFE Valuation Approaches

The purpose of this section is to provide a conceptual understanding of free cash flows and the valuation models based on them. A detailed accounting treatment of free cash flows and more-complicated valuation models follow in subsequent sections.

Defining Free Cash Flow

Free cash flow to the firm is the cash flow available to the company's suppliers of capital after all operating expenses (including taxes) have been paid and necessary investments in working capital (e.g., inventory) and fixed capital (e.g., equipment) have been made. FCFF is the cash flow from operations minus capital expenditures. A company's suppliers of capital include common stockholders, bondholders, and, sometimes, preferred stockholders. The equations analysts use to calculate FCFF depend on the accounting information available.

Free cash flow to equity is the cash flow available to the company's holders of common equity after all operating expenses, interest, and principal payments have been paid and necessary investments in working and fixed capital have been made. FCFE is the cash flow from operations minus capital expenditures minus payments to (plus receipts from) debtholders.

The way in which free cash flow is related to a company's net income, cash flow from operations, and measures such as EBITDA (earnings before interest, taxes, depreciation, and amortization) is important: The analyst must understand the relationship between a company's reported accounting data and free cash flow in order to forecast free cash flow and its expected growth. Although a company reports cash flow from operations (CFO) on the statement of cash flows, CFO is *not* free cash flow. Net income and CFO data can be used, however, in determining a company's free cash flow.

The advantage of FCFF and FCFE over other cash-flow concepts is that they can be used directly in a DCF framework to value the firm or to value equity. Other cash flow– or earnings-related measures, such as CFO, net income, EBIT, and EBITDA, do not have this property because they either double-count or omit cash flows in some way. For example, EBIT and EBITDA are before-tax measures, and the cash flows available to investors (in the firm or in the equity of the firm) must be after tax. From the stockholders' perspective, EBITDA and similar measures do not account for differing capital structures (the after-tax interest expenses or preferred dividends) or for the funds that bondholders supply to finance investments in operating assets. Moreover, these measures do not account for the reinvestment of cash flows that the company makes in capital assets and working capital to maintain or maximize the long-run value of the firm.

Using free cash flow in valuation is more challenging than using dividends because in forecasting free cash flow, the analyst must integrate the cash flows from the company's operations with those from its investing and financing activities. Because FCFF is the after-tax cash flow going to all suppliers of capital to the firm, the value of the firm is estimated by discounting FCFF at the weighted average cost of capital

(WACC). An estimate of the value of equity is then found by subtracting the value of debt from the estimated value of the firm. The value of equity can also be estimated directly by discounting FCFE at the required rate of return for equity (because FCFE is the cash flow going to common stockholders, the required rate of return on equity is the appropriate risk-adjusted rate for discounting FCFE).

The two free cash flow approaches for valuing equity, FCFF and FCFE, theoretically should yield the same estimates if all inputs reflect identical assumptions. An analyst may prefer to use one approach rather than the other, however, because of the characteristics of the company being valued. For example, if the company's capital structure is relatively stable, using FCFE to value equity is more direct and simpler than using FCFF. The FCFF model is often chosen, however, in two other cases:

- *A levered company with negative FCFE.* In this case, working with FCFF to value the company's equity might be easiest. The analyst would discount FCFF to find the present value of operating assets, adding the value of excess cash ("excess" in relation to operating needs) and marketable securities and of any other significant non-operating assets to get total firm value. He or she would then subtract the market value of debt to obtain an estimate of the intrinsic value of equity.
- *A levered company with a changing capital structure.* First, if historical data are used to forecast free cash flow growth rates, FCFF growth might reflect fundamentals more clearly than does FCFE growth, which reflects fluctuating amounts of net borrowing. Second, in a forward-looking context, the required return on equity might be expected to be more sensitive to changes in financial leverage than changes in the WACC, making the use of a constant discount rate difficult to justify.

Specialized DCF approaches are also available to facilitate the equity valuation when the capital structure is expected to change. The **adjusted present value** (APV) approach is one example of such models. In the APV approach, firm value is calculated as the sum of (1) the value of the company under the assumption that debt is not used (i.e., unlevered firm value) and (2) the net present value of any effects of debt on firm value (such as any tax benefits of using debt and any costs of financial distress). In this approach, the analyst estimates unlevered company value by discounting FCFF (under the assumption of no debt) at the unlevered cost of equity (the cost of equity given that the firm does not use debt). For more info, see Luehrman (1997), who explained APV in a capital budgeting context.

In the following section, we present the general form of the FCFF valuation model and the FCFE valuation model.

Present Value of Free Cash Flow

The two distinct approaches to using free cash flow for valuation are the FCFF valuation approach and the FCFE valuation approach. The general expressions for these valuation models are similar to the expression for the general dividend discount model. In the DDM, the value of a share of stock equals the present value of forecasted dividends from Time 1 through infinity discounted at the required rate of return for equity.

Present Value of FCFF

The FCFF valuation approach estimates the value of the firm as the present value of future FCFF discounted at the weighted average cost of capital:

$$\text{Firm value} = \sum_{t=1}^{\infty}\frac{\text{FCFF}_t}{(1+\text{WACC})^t}. \quad (1)$$

Because FCFF is the cash flow available to all suppliers of capital, using WACC to discount FCFF gives the total value of all of the firm's capital. The value of equity is the value of the firm minus the market value of its debt:

$$\text{Equity value} = \text{Firm value} - \text{Market value of debt}. \quad (2)$$

Dividing the total value of equity by the number of outstanding shares gives the value per share.

The cost of capital is the required rate of return that investors should demand for a cash flow stream like that generated by the company being analyzed. WACC depends on the riskiness of these cash flows. The calculation and interpretation of WACC were discussed earlier under the topic of return concepts; that is, WACC is the weighted average of the after (corporate) tax required rates of return for debt and equity, where the weights are the proportions of the firm's total market value from each source, debt and equity. As an alternative, analysts may use the weights of debt and equity in the firm's target capital structure when those weights are known and differ from market value weights. The formula for WACC is

$$\text{WACC} = \frac{\text{MV(Debt)}}{\text{MV(Debt)} + \text{MV(Equity)}} r_d (1 - \text{Tax rate}) + \frac{\text{MV(Equity)}}{\text{MV(Debt)} + \text{MV(Equity)}} r. \quad (3)$$

MV(Debt) and MV(Equity) are the current market values of debt and equity, not their book or accounting values, and the ratios of MV(Debt) and MV(Equity) to the total market value of debt plus equity define the weights in the WACC formula. The quantities $r_d(1 - \text{Tax rate})$ and r are, respectively, the after-tax cost of debt and the after-tax cost of equity (in the case of equity, one could just write "cost of equity" because net income, the income belonging to equity, is after tax). In Equation 3, the tax rate is in principle the marginal corporate income tax rate.

Present Value of FCFE

The value of equity can also be found by discounting FCFE at the required rate of return on equity, r:

$$\text{Equity value} = \sum_{t=1}^{\infty} \frac{\text{FCFE}_t}{(1 + r)^t}. \quad (4)$$

Because FCFE is the cash flow remaining for equity holders after all other claims have been satisfied, discounting FCFE by r (the required rate of return on equity) gives the value of the firm's equity. Dividing the total value of equity by the number of outstanding shares gives the value per share.

Single-Stage (Constant-Growth) FCFF and FCFE Models

In the DDM approach, the Gordon (constant- or stable-growth) model makes the assumption that dividends grow at a constant rate. The assumption that free cash flows grow at a constant rate leads to a single-stage (stable-growth) FCFF or FCFE model.

Constant-Growth FCFF Valuation Model

Assume that FCFF grows at a constant rate, g, such that FCFF in any period is equal to FCFF in the previous period multiplied by $(1 + g)$:

$$\text{FCFF}_t = \text{FCFF}_{t-1}(1 + g).$$

If FCFF grows at a constant rate,

$$\text{Firm value} = \frac{\text{FCFF}_1}{\text{WACC} - g} = \frac{\text{FCFF}_0(1 + g)}{\text{WACC} - g}. \quad (5)$$

Subtracting the market value of debt from the firm value gives the value of equity.

EXAMPLE 1

Using the Constant-Growth FCFF Valuation Model

Cagiati Enterprises has FCFF of 700 million Swiss francs (CHF) and FCFE of CHF620 million. Cagiati's before-tax cost of debt is 5.7%, and its required rate of return for equity is 11.8%. The company expects a target capital structure consisting of 20% debt financing and 80% equity financing. The tax rate is 33.33%, and FCFF is expected to grow forever at 5.0%. Cagiati Enterprises has debt outstanding with a market value of CHF2.2 billion and has 200 million outstanding common shares.

1. What is Cagiati's weighted average cost of capital?

Solution:

From Equation 3, WACC is calculated as follows:

$$\text{WACC} = 0.20(5.7\%)(1 - 0.3333) + 0.80(11.8\%) = 10.2\%.$$

2. What is the value of Cagiati's equity using the FCFF valuation approach?

Solution:

The firm value of Cagiati Enterprises is the present value of FCFF discounted by using WACC. For FCFF growing at a constant 5% rate, the result is

$$\text{Firm value} = \frac{\text{FCFF}_1}{\text{WACC} - g} = \frac{\text{FCFF}_0(1+g)}{\text{WACC} - g} = \frac{700(1.05)}{0.102 - 0.05}$$

$$= \frac{735}{0.052} = \text{CHF}14,134.6 \text{ million.}$$

The value of equity is the value of the firm minus the value of debt:

$$\text{Equity value} = 14,134.6 - 2,200 = \text{CHF}11,934.6 \text{ million.}$$

3. What is the value per share using this FCFF approach?

Solution:

Dividing CHF11,934.6 million by the number of outstanding shares gives the estimated value per share, V_0:

$$V_0 = \text{CHF}11,934.6 \text{ million}/200 \text{ million shares}$$

$$= \text{CHF}59.67 \text{ per share.}$$

Constant-Growth FCFE Valuation Model

The constant-growth FCFE valuation model assumes that FCFE grows at constant rate g. FCFE in any period is equal to FCFE in the preceding period multiplied by $(1 + g)$:

$$\text{FCFE}_t = \text{FCFE}_{t-1}(1 + g).$$

The value of equity if FCFE is growing at a constant rate is

$$\text{Equity value} = \frac{\text{FCFE}_1}{r - g} = \frac{\text{FCFE}_0(1+g)}{r - g}. \quad (6)$$

The discount rate is r, the required rate of return on equity. Note that the growth rate of FCFF and the growth rate of FCFE need not be and frequently are not the same.

In this section, we presented the basic ideas underlying free cash flow valuation and the simplest implementation, single-stage free cash flow models. The next section examines the precise definition of free cash flow and introduces the issues involved in forecasting free cash flow.

FORECASTING FREE CASH FLOW AND COMPUTING FCFF FROM NET INCOME

2

- ☐ explain the appropriate adjustments to net income, earnings before interest and taxes (EBIT), earnings before interest, taxes, depreciation, and amortization (EBITDA), and cash flow from operations (CFO) to calculate FCFF and FCFE
- ☐ calculate FCFF and FCFE
- ☐ describe approaches for forecasting FCFF and FCFE

Estimating FCFF or FCFE requires a complete understanding of the company and its financial statements. To provide a context for the estimation of FCFF and FCFE, we first discuss the calculation of free cash flows, including the relationship between free cash flow and accounting measures of income. We then describe approaches to forecasting free cash flow. For most of this section, we assume that the company has two sources of capital: debt and common stock. We then incorporate preferred stock as a third source of capital.

Computing FCFF from Net Income

FCFF is the cash flow available to the company's suppliers of capital after all operating expenses (including taxes) have been paid and operating investments have been made. The company's suppliers of capital include bondholders and common shareholders (plus, occasionally, holders of preferred stock, which we ignore until later). Keeping in mind that a noncash charge is a charge or expense that does not involve the outlay of cash, we can write the expression for FCFF as follows:

FCFF = Net income available to common shareholders (NI)
Plus: Net noncash charges (NCC)
Plus: Interest expense × (1 − Tax rate)
Less: Investment in fixed capital (FCInv)
Less: Investment in working capital (WCInv).

This equation can be written more compactly as

$$\text{FCFF} = \text{NI} + \text{NCC} + \text{Int}(1 - \text{Tax rate}) - \text{FCInv} - \text{WCInv}. \quad (7)$$

Consider each component of FCFF. The starting point in Equation 7 is net income available to common shareholders—usually, but not always, the bottom line in an income statement. It represents income after depreciation, amortization, interest expense, income taxes, and the payment of dividends to preferred shareholders (but not payment of dividends to common shareholders).

To derive cash flow from net income, it is necessary to make adjustments for any items that involved decreases and increases in net income but did not involve cash inflows or outflows. These items are referred to as noncash charges (NCC). If noncash decreases in net income exceed the increases, as is usually the case, the total adjustment is positive. If noncash increases exceed noncash decreases, the total adjustment is negative. The most common noncash charge is depreciation expense. The depreciation expense reduces net income but is not a cash outflow. Depreciation expense is thus one (the most common) noncash charge that must be added back in computing FCFF. In the case of intangible assets, there is a similar noncash charge, amortization expense, which must be added back. Other noncash charges vary from company to company and are discussed later.

After-tax interest expense must be added back to net income to arrive at FCFF. This step is required because interest expense net of the related tax savings was deducted in arriving at net income, but interest is a cash flow available to one of the company's capital providers (i.e., the company's creditors). In many countries, interest is tax deductible (reduces taxes) for the company (borrower) and taxable for the recipient (lender). As we explain later, when we discount FCFF, we use an after-tax cost of capital. For consistency, we thus compute FCFF by using the after-tax interest paid. Note that we could compute WACC on a pretax basis and compute FCFF by adding back interest paid with no tax adjustment. Whichever approach is adopted, the analyst must use mutually consistent definitions of FCFF and WACC.

Similar to the treatment of after-tax interest expense, dividends on preferred stock that are deducted in arriving at net income available to common shareholders must be added back to derive FCFF. The reason for the add-back is that preferred stock dividends are also a cash flow available to one of the company's capital providers and thus constitute part of overall FCFF.

Investments in fixed capital represent the outflows of cash to purchase the fixed capital necessary to support the company's current and future operations. These investments are capital expenditures for long-term assets, such as the property, plant, and equipment (PP&E) necessary to support the company's operations. Necessary capital expenditures may also include intangible assets, such as trademarks. In the case of a cash acquisition of another company instead of a direct acquisition of PP&E, the cash purchase amount can also be treated as a capital expenditure that reduces the company's free cash flow (note that this treatment is conservative because it reduces FCFF). In the case of large acquisitions (and all noncash acquisitions), analysts must take care in evaluating the impact on future free cash flow. If a company receives cash in disposing of any of its fixed capital, the analyst must deduct this cash in calculating investment in fixed capital. For example, suppose a company sells equipment for $100,000. This cash inflow would reduce the company's cash outflows for investments in fixed capital.

The company's statement of cash flows is an excellent source of information on capital expenditures as well as on sales of fixed capital. Analysts should be aware that some companies acquire fixed capital without using cash—for example, through an exchange for stock or debt. Such acquisitions do not appear in a company's statement of cash flows but, if material, must be disclosed in the footnotes. Although noncash exchanges do not affect historical FCFF, if the capital expenditures are necessary and may be made in cash in the future, the analyst should use this information in forecasting future FCFF.

Finally, the adjustment for net increases in working capital represents the net investment in current assets (such as accounts receivable) less current liabilities (such as accounts payable). Analysts can find this information by examining either the company's balance sheet or its statement of cash flows.

Although working capital is often defined as current assets minus current liabilities, working capital for cash flow and valuation purposes is defined to exclude cash and short-term debt (which includes notes payable and the current portion of long-term debt). When finding the net increase in working capital for the purpose of calculating free cash flow, we define working capital to exclude cash and cash equivalents as well as notes payable and the current portion of long-term debt. Cash and cash equivalents are excluded because a change in cash is what we are trying to explain. Notes payable and the current portion of long-term debt are excluded because they are liabilities with explicit interest costs that make them financing items rather than operating items.

Example 2 shows the adjustments to net income required to find FCFF.

EXAMPLE 2

Calculating FCFF from Net Income

1. Cane Distribution, Inc., incorporated on 31 December 2017 with initial capital infusions of $224,000 of debt and $336,000 of common stock, acts as a distributor of industrial goods. The company managers immediately invested the initial capital in fixed capital of $500,000 and working capital of $60,000. Working capital initially consisted solely of inventory. The fixed capital consisted of nondepreciable property of $50,000 and depreciable property of $450,000. The depreciable property has a 10-year useful life with no salvage value. Exhibit 1, Exhibit 2, and Exhibit 3 provide Cane's financial statements for the three years following incorporation. Starting with net income, calculate Cane's FCFF for each year.

Exhibit 1: Cane Distribution, Inc., Income Statement (in Thousands)

	Years Ending 31 December		
	2018	**2019**	**2020**
Earnings before interest, taxes, depreciation, and amortization (EBITDA)	$200.00	$220.00	$242.00
Depreciation expense	45.00	49.50	54.45
Operating income	155.00	170.50	187.55
Interest expense (at 7%)	15.68	17.25	18.97
Income before taxes	139.32	153.25	168.58
Income taxes (at 30%)	41.80	45.97	50.58
Net income	$97.52	$107.28	$118.00

Exhibit 2: Cane Distribution, Inc., Balance Sheet (in Thousands)

	Years Ending 31 December			
	2017	**2018**	**2019**	**2020**
Cash	$0.00	$108.92	$228.74	$360.54
Accounts receivable	0.00	100.00	110.00	121.00
Inventory	60.00	66.00	72.60	79.86
Current assets	60.00	274.92	411.34	561.40
Fixed assets	500.00	500.00	550.00	605.00
Less: Accumulated depreciation	0.00	45.00	94.50	148.95
Total assets	$560.00	$729.92	$866.84	$1,017.45
Accounts payable	$0.00	$50.00	$55.00	$60.50
Current portion of long-term debt	0.00	0.00	0.00	0.00
Current liabilities	0.00	50.00	55.00	60.50
Long-term debt	224.00	246.40	271.04	298.14

	Years Ending 31 December			
	2017	2018	2019	2020
Common stock	336.00	336.00	336.00	336.00
Retained earnings	0.00	97.52	204.80	322.80
Total liabilities and equity	$560.00	$729.92	$866.84	$1,017.45

Exhibit 3: Cane Distribution, Inc., Working Capital (in Thousands)

	Years Ending 31 December			
	2017	2018	2019	2020
Current assets excluding cash				
Accounts receivable	$0.00	$100.00	$110.00	$121.00
Inventory	60.00	66.00	72.60	79.86
Total current assets excluding cash	60.00	166.00	182.60	200.86
Current liabilities excluding short-term debt				
Accounts payable	0.00	50.00	55.00	60.50
Working capital	$60.00	$116.00	$127.60	$140.36
Increase in working capital		$56.00	$11.60	$12.76

Solution:

Following the logic in Equation 7, we calculate FCFF from net income as follows: We add noncash charges (here, depreciation) and after-tax interest expense to net income and then subtract the investment in fixed capital and the investment in working capital. The format for presenting the solution follows the convention that parentheses around a number indicate subtraction. The calculation follows (in thousands):

	Years Ending 31 December		
	2018	2019	2020
Net income	$97.52	$107.28	$118.00
Noncash charges − Depreciation	45.00	49.50	54.45
Interest expense × (1 − Tax rate)	10.98	12.08	13.28
Investment in fixed capital	(0.00)	(50.00)	(55.00)
Investment in working capital	(56.00)	(11.60)	(12.76)
Free cash flow to the firm	$97.50	$107.26	$117.97

COMPUTING FCFF FROM THE CASH FLOW STATEMENT

3

- ☐ explain the appropriate adjustments to net income, earnings before interest and taxes (EBIT), earnings before interest, taxes, depreciation, and amortization (EBITDA), and cash flow from operations (CFO) to calculate FCFF and FCFE
- ☐ calculate FCFF and FCFE
- ☐ describe approaches for forecasting FCFF and FCFE

FCFF is the cash flow that is available to all providers of capital (debt and equity). Analysts frequently use cash flow from operations, taken from the statement of cash flows, as a starting point to compute free cash flow because CFO incorporates adjustments for noncash expenses (such as depreciation and amortization) as well as for net investments in working capital.

In most cases, companies include interest paid as part of operating cash flow. Under US generally accepted accounting principles (GAAP), companies must include interest paid in operating cash flow. Under International Financial Reporting Standards (IFRS), companies may include interest paid in either financing or operating. According to Gordon, Henry, Jorgensen, and Linthicum (2017), most IFRS-reporting European firms choose to classify interest paid within the operating cash flow section of the statement of cash flows. This will be discussed later. Assuming that interest paid is included in operating cash flow, FCFF can be estimated as follows:

Free cash flow to the firm = Cash flow from operations
Plus: Interest expense × (1 − Tax rate)
Less: Investment in fixed capital,

or

$$\text{FCFF} = \text{CFO} + \text{Int}(1 - \text{Tax rate}) - \text{FCInv}. \quad (8)$$

To reiterate, as with the calculation shown as Equation 7, the after-tax interest expense is added back because it was previously taken out of net income but must be included in FCFF because it is a component of the total cash flows available to all suppliers of the firm's capital. In comparison with Equation 7, neither depreciation nor the investment in working capital appears in Equation 8 because both are already included in CFO. Example 3 illustrates the use of CFO to calculate FCFF. In this example, the operating section of the statement of cash flows begins with net income and presents each adjustment required to derive operating cash flow. This presentation, known as the "indirect" method because it derives operating cash flows indirectly from net income via adjustments, is the most common presentation of the statement of cash flows.

EXAMPLE 3

Calculating FCFF from CFO

1. Use the information from the statement of cash flows given in Exhibit 4 to calculate FCFF for the three years 2018–2020. The tax rate (as given in Exhibit 1) is 30%.

Exhibit 4: Cane Distribution, Inc., Statement of Cash Flows: Indirect Method (in Thousands)

	Years Ending 31 December		
	2018	**2019**	**2020**
Cash flow from operations			
Net income	$97.52	$107.28	$118.00
Plus: Depreciation	45.00	49.50	54.45
Increase in accounts receivable	(100.00)	(10.00)	(11.00)
Increase in inventory	(6.00)	(6.60)	(7.26)
Increase in accounts payable	50.00	5.00	5.50
Cash flow from operations	86.52	145.18	159.69
Cash flow from investing activities			
Purchases of PP&E	0.00	(50.00)	(55.00)
Cash flow from financing activities			
Borrowing (repayment)	22.40	24.64	27.10
Total cash flow	108.92	119.82	131.80
Beginning cash	0.00	108.92	228.74
Ending cash	$108.92	$228.74	$360.54
Notes:			
Cash paid for interest	($15.68)	($17.25)	($18.97)
Cash paid for taxes	($41.80)	($45.98)	($50.57)

Solution:

As shown in Equation 8, FCFF equals CFO plus after-tax interest expense minus the investment in fixed capital:

	Years Ending 31 December		
	2018	**2019**	**2020**
Cash flow from operations	$86.52	$145.18	$159.69
Interest expense × (1 – Tax rate)	10.98	12.08	13.28
Investment in fixed capital	(0.00)	(50.00)	(55.00)
Free cash flow to the firm	$97.50	$107.26	$117.97

ADDITIONAL CONSIDERATIONS IN COMPUTING FCFF

4

- ☐ calculate FCFF and FCFE
- ☐ describe approaches for forecasting FCFF and FCFE

Whether an analyst selects net income or cash flow from operations as a starting point in calculating free cash flows, some situations warrant a closer examination. In this section, we first describe classification of certain items on the statement of cash flows that merit attention when deriving free cash flow using cash flow from operations as a starting point. We then review the common adjustments for noncash charges made in deriving cash flow from net income and highlight several areas that merit additional attention from an analyst.

Classification of Certain Items on the Statement of Cash Flow

As noted above, IFRSallow the company to classify interest paid as either an operating or financing activity. Furthermore, IFRS allow dividends paid to be classified as either an operating or financing activity. In contrast, under US GAAP, interest paid to providers of debt capital must be classified as part of cash flow from operations (as are interest income and dividend income), but payment of dividends to providers of equity capital is classified as a financing activity.

Exhibit 5 summarizes IFRS and US GAAP treatment of interest and dividends.

Exhibit 5: IFRS vs. US GAAP Treatment of Interest and Dividends

	IFRS	US GAAP
Interest received	Operating or investing	Operating
Interest paid	Operating or financing	Operating
Dividends received	Operating or investing	Operating
Dividends paid	Operating or financing	Financing

To estimate FCFF by starting with CFO, it is necessary to examine the classification of these items. For example, if the after-tax interest expense was taken out of net income and out of CFO, which is required under US GAAP and allowed under IFRS, then after-tax interest must be added back to get FCFF. However, if interest paid was not classified as an operating cash outflow (i.e., it was classified as a financing cash outflow as allowed under IFRS), then it is not necessary to add interest when operating cash flow is the starting point for calculating FCFF.

Adjustments to Derive Operating Cash Flow from Net Income

The operating cash flow section of the statement of cash flows provides detail on the adjustments made in deriving operating cash flow from net income. Exhibit 6 summarizes the common adjustments (other than changes in working capital) to derive operating cash flow from net income and indicates whether each item is added to or subtracted from net income in arriving at FCFF.

Exhibit 6: Noncash Items and FCFF

Noncash Item	Adjustment to NI to Arrive at FCFF
Depreciation expense	Added back
Amortization expense and impairment of intangibles	Added back
Restructuring charges (expense)	Added back
Restructuring charges (income resulting from reversal)	Subtracted
Amortization of long-term bond discounts	Added back
Amortization of long-term bond premiums	Subtracted
Losses on non-operating activity	Added back
Gains on non-operating activity	Subtracted
Deferred taxes	Added back but calls for special attention

An adjustment to reported net income is required for any item that was treated as an expense in calculating net income on the income statement but did not result in an equivalent cash outflow in the reporting period. For example, both depreciation and amortization expenses reduce net income, but neither involves a cash outflow in the period. Therefore, to derive operating cash flow or FCFF from net income, it is necessary to add back these amounts to net income.

Adjustments to eliminate the amount of gains and losses are made for two reasons in general. First, such transactions are typically not operating activities (e.g., a sale of fixed assets, which is an investing activity), and thus the effects must be removed from the operating section of the statement of cash flows. Second, the amount of gain or loss reported in the income statement is not necessarily equivalent to the amount of cash involved in the transaction. For example, if a company sells a piece of equipment with a book value of €60,000 for €100,000, it reports the €40,000 gain as part of net income. The €40,000 gain, however, is not equivalent to the transaction's cash flow and, therefore, must be subtracted to derive operating cash flow from net income. Further, the €100,000 *is* a cash flow, and that amount will appear as a component of the company's cash flow for investing activity. Alternatively, if the company had sold the equipment with a book value of €60,000 for €40,000 and thus reported a loss of €20,000 as part of net income, that amount would be added back in deriving operating cash flow and FCFF.

Adjustments to Derive Operating Cash Flow from Net Income That May Merit Additional Attention from an Analyst

The item "deferred taxes" in Exhibit 6 requires special attention because deferred taxes result from differences in the timing of reporting income and expenses in the company's financial statements and the company's tax return. The income tax expense deducted in arriving at net income for financial reporting purposes is not the same as the amount of cash taxes paid. Over time, these differences between book income and taxable income should offset each other and have no impact on aggregate cash flows. Generally, if the analyst's purpose is forecasting and, therefore, identifying the persistent components of FCFF, then the analyst should not add back deferred tax changes that are expected to reverse in the near future. In some circumstances, however, a company may be able to consistently defer taxes until a much later date. If a company is growing and has the ability to indefinitely defer its tax liability, adding back deferred taxes to net income is warranted. Nevertheless, an acquirer must be aware that these taxes may be payable at some time in the future.

Similarly, companies often record expenses (e.g., restructuring charges) for financial reporting purposes that are not deductible for tax purposes or record revenues that are taxable in the current period but not yet recognized for financial reporting purposes. In these cases, taxable income exceeds financial statement income, so cash outflows for current tax payments are greater than the taxes reported in the income statement. This situation results in a deferred tax *asset* and a necessary adjustment to subtract that amount in deriving operating cash flow from net income. If, however, the deferred tax asset is expected to reverse in the near future, to avoid underestimating future cash flows, the analyst should not subtract the deferred tax asset in a cash flow forecast. If the company is expected to have these charges on a continual basis, however, a subtraction that will lower the forecast of future cash flows is warranted.

A second area that may warrant an analyst's attention to the adjustments made in derivation of operating cash flow from net income pertains to employee share-based compensation (stock options). Under both IFRS and US GAAP, companies must record in the income statement an expense for options provided to employees. The granting and expensing of options themselves do not result in a cash outflow and are thus a noncash charge; however, the granting of options has long-term cash flow implications. When the employee exercises the option, the company receives some cash related to the exercise price of the option at the strike price. This cash flow is considered a financing cash flow. Also, in some cases, a company receives a tax benefit from issuing options, which could increase operating cash flow but not net income. Both IFRS and US GAAP require that a portion of the tax effect be recorded as a financing cash flow rather than an operating cash flow in the statement of cash flows. Analysts should review the statement of cash flows and footnotes to determine the impact of options on operating cash flows. If these cash flows are not expected to persist in the future, analysts should not include them in their forecasts of cash flows. Analysts should also consider the impact of stock options on the number of shares outstanding. When computing equity value, analysts may want to use the number of shares *expected* to be outstanding (based on the exercise of employee stock options) rather than the number currently outstanding.

Finally, an analyst may benefit from a careful examination of adjustments in developing expectations about the sustainability of free cash flow. When any financial forecast is developed by using historical amounts as a baseline, it is necessary to ensure that the baseline amounts are not distorted by non-recurring items. Similarly, when a forecast of free cash flows is developed using historical amounts of FCFF or FCFE as a baseline, it is necessary to ensure that the baseline amounts are not distorted by non-recurring items. Example 4 is a historical case that is adapted to illustrate issues that an analyst may face when forecasting free cash flows. Specifically, the example illustrates that when forecasting cash flows for valuation purposes, analysts should consider the sustainability of historical working capital effects on free cash flow.

EXAMPLE 4

Sustainability of Working Capital Effects on Free Cash Flow

Duplico Holdings PLC has operations in Ireland, the United Kingdom, Continental Europe, and Morocco. The operating activities section of its statement of cash flows and a portion of the investing activities section are presented in Exhibit 7. The statement of cash flows was prepared in accordance with IFRS.

Exhibit 7: Duplico Holdings PLC Excerpt from Statement of Cash Flows (Euros in Millions)

	Year Ended 31 March		
	2022	**2021**	**2020**
Operating activities			
Profit before tax	633.0	420.9	341.0
Adjustments to reconcile profits before tax to net cash provided by operating activities			
Depreciation	309.2	277.7	235.4
Increase in inventories	(0.1)	(0.2)	(0.4)
Increase in trade receivables	(0.9)	(6.3)	(2.5)
Decrease (increase) in other current assets	34.5	(20.9)	11.6
Increase (decrease) in trade payables	30.4	(3.2)	21.3
Increase in accrued expenses	11.6	135.0	189.7
Increase (decrease) in other creditors	19.7	(10.0)	30.1
Increase (decrease) in maintenance provisions	6.6	(7.9)	30.7
Gain on disposal of property, plant, and equipment	(10.4)	—	(2.0)
Loss on impairment of available-for-sale financial asset	—	—	13.5
Decrease (increase) in interest receivable	—	1.6	(1.2)
Increase (decrease) in interest payable	1.1	2.3	(0.5)
Retirement costs	(0.1)	(0.1)	(0.1)
Share-based payments	(0.7)	3.3	4.9
Income tax paid	(13.6)	(5.9)	—
Net cash provided by operating activities	1,020.3	786.3	871.5
Investing activities			
Capital expenditure (purchase of property, plant, and equipment)	(317.6)	(897.2)	(997.8)

Analysts predict that as Duplico grows in the coming years, depreciation expense will increase substantially. Based on the information given, address the following:

1. Contrast reported depreciation expense to reported capital expenditures, and describe the implications of future growth in depreciation expense (all else being equal) for future net income and future cash from operating activities.

Solution:

In the 2020–22 period, the amount of depreciation expense relative to the amount of capital expenditures changed significantly. For example, in 2022, capital expenditures of €317.6 million were just slightly more than the €309.2 million depreciation expense. In 2020, capital expenditures of €997.8 million were over 4 times more than depreciation charges of €235.4 million. The rate of growth in depreciation expense will be highly dependent on future capital expenditures.

In calculating net income, depreciation is a deduction. Therefore, as depreciation expense increases in the coming years, net income will decrease. Specifically, net income will be reduced by (Depreciation expense) × (1 – Tax rate). In calculating CFO, however, depreciation is added back in full to net income. The difference between depreciation expense—the amount added back to net income to calculate CFO—and the amount by which net income is reduced by depreciation expense is (Tax rate) × (Depreciation expense), which represents a positive increment to CFO. Thus, the projected increase in depreciation expense is a negative for future net income but a positive for future CFO. (At worst, if the company operates at a loss, depreciation is neutral for CFO.)

2. Explain the effects on free cash flow to equity of changes in 2022 in working capital accounts, such as inventory, accounts receivable, and accounts payable, and comment on the long-term sustainability of such changes.

Solution:

In 2022, the increases in inventory and accounts receivable ("trade receivables") resulted in negative adjustments to net income (i.e., the changes reduced cash flow relative to net income). The adjustments are negative because increases in these accounts are a use of cash. On the current liabilities side, the increase in trade payables, accrued expenses, and "other creditors" are added back to net income and are sources of cash because such increases represent increased amounts for which cash payments have yet to be made. Because CFO is a component of FCFE, the items that had a positive (negative) effect on CFO also have a positive (negative) effect on FCFE.

Although not the case here, declining balances for assets, such as inventory, or for liabilities, such as accounts payable, are not sustainable indefinitely. In the extreme case, the balance declines to zero and no further reduction is possible. Given the growth in its net income and the expansion of PP&E evidenced by capital expenditures, Duplico appears to be growing and investors should expect its working capital requirements to grow accordingly.

COMPUTING FCFE FROM FCFF 5

- ☐ explain the ownership perspective implicit in the FCFE approach
- ☐ calculate FCFF and FCFE
- ☐ describe approaches for forecasting FCFF and FCFE

FCFE is cash flow available to equity holders only. To find FCFE, therefore, we must reduce FCFF by the after-tax value of interest paid to debtholders and add net borrowing (which is debt issued less debt repaid over the period for which one is calculating free cash flow):

$$\begin{aligned} &\text{Free cash flow to equity} = \text{Free cash flow to the firm} \\ &\text{Less: Interest expense} \times (1 - \text{Tax rate}) \\ &\text{Plus: Net borrowing,} \end{aligned}$$

or

$$\text{FCFE} = \text{FCFF} - \text{Int}(1 - \text{Tax rate}) + \text{Net borrowing.} \quad (9)$$

As Equation 9 shows, FCFE is found by starting from FCFF, subtracting after-tax interest expenses, and adding net new borrowing. The analyst can also find FCFF from FCFE by making the opposite adjustments—by adding after-tax interest expenses and subtracting net borrowing: FCFF = FCFE + Int(1 – Tax rate) – Net borrowing.

Exhibit 8 uses the values for FCFF for Cane Distribution calculated in Example 3 to show the calculation of FCFE when starting with FCFF. To calculate FCFE in this manner, we subtract after-tax interest expense from FCFF and then add net borrowing (equal to new debt borrowing minus debt repayment).

Exhibit 8: Calculating FCFE from FCFF

	Years Ending 31 December		
	2018	**2019**	**2020**
Free cash flow to the firm	97.50	107.26	117.97
Interest paid × (1 – Tax rate)	(10.98)	(12.08)	(13.28)
New debt borrowing	22.40	24.64	27.10
Debt repayment	(0)	(0)	(0)
Free cash flow to equity	108.92	119.82	131.79

To reiterate, FCFE is the cash flow available to common stockholders—the cash flow remaining after all operating expenses (including taxes) have been paid, capital investments have been made, and other transactions with other suppliers of capital have been carried out. The company's other capital suppliers include creditors, such as bondholders, and preferred stockholders. The cash flows (net of taxes) that arise from transactions with creditors and preferred stockholders are deducted from FCFF to arrive at FCFE.

FCFE is the amount that the company can afford to pay out as dividends. In actuality, for various reasons companies often pay out substantially more or substantially less than FCFE, so FCFE often differs from dividends paid. One reason for this difference is that the dividend decision is a discretionary decision of the board of directors. Most corporations "manage" their dividends; they prefer to raise them gradually over time, partly because they do not want to cut dividends. Many companies raise dividends slowly even when their earnings are increasing rapidly, and companies often maintain their current dividends even when their profitability has declined. Consequently, earnings are much more volatile than dividends.

In Equations 7 and 8, we showed the calculation of FCFF starting with, respectively, net income and cash flow from operations. As Equation 9 showed, FCFE = FCFF – Int(1 – Tax rate) + Net borrowing. By subtracting after-tax interest expense and adding net borrowing to Equations 7 and 8, we have equations to calculate FCFE starting with, respectively, net income and CFO:

$$\text{FCFE} = \text{NI} + \text{NCC} - \text{FCInv} - \text{WCInv} + \text{Net borrowing}. \quad (10)$$

$$\text{FCFE} = \text{CFO} - \text{FCInv} + \text{Net borrowing}. \quad (11)$$

Example 5 illustrates how to adjust net income or CFO to find FCFF and FCFE.

EXAMPLE 5

Adjusting Net Income or CFO to Find FCFF and FCFE

The balance sheet, income statement, and statement of cash flows for the Pitts Corporation are shown in Exhibit 9. Note that the statement of cash flows follows a convention according to which the positive numbers of $400 million and $85 million for "cash *used for* investing activities" and "cash *used for* financing activities," respectively, indicate outflows and thus amounts to be *subtracted*. Analysts will also encounter a convention in which the value "(400)" for "cash provided by (used for) investing activities" would be used to indicate a subtraction of $400.

Exhibit 9: Financial Statements for Pitts Corporation (in Millions, Except for Per-Share Data)

	Year Ended 31 December	
Balance Sheet	**2019**	**2020**
Assets		
Current assets		
Cash and equivalents	$190	$200
Accounts receivable	560	600
Inventory	410	440
Total current assets	1,160	1,240
Gross fixed assets	2,200	2,600
Accumulated depreciation	(900)	(1,200)
Net fixed assets	1,300	1,400
Total assets	$2,460	$2,640

Liabilities and shareholders' equity Current liabilities		
Accounts payable	$285	$300
Notes payable	200	250
Accrued taxes and expenses	140	150
Total current liabilities	625	700
Long-term debt	865	890
Common stock	100	100
Additional paid-in capital	200	200
Retained earnings	670	750
Total shareholders' equity	970	1,050
Total liabilities and shareholders' equity	$2,460	$2,640

Statement of Income Year Ended 31 December	**2020**
Total revenues	$3,000
Operating costs and expenses	2,200
EBITDA	800

Statement of Income Year Ended 31 December	2020
Depreciation	300
Operating income (EBIT)	500
Interest expense	100
Income before tax	400
Taxes (at 40%)	160
Net income	$ 240
Dividends	*$ 160*
Change in retained earnings (calculated as net income minus dividends)	*$ 80*
Earnings per share (EPS)	$0.48
Dividends per share	$0.32

Statement of Cash Flows Year Ended 31 December	2020
Operating activities	
Net income	$240
Adjustments	
Depreciation	300
Changes in working capital	
Accounts receivable	(40)
Inventories	(30)
Accounts payable	15
Accrued taxes and expenses	10
Cash provided by operating activities	$495
Investing activities	
Purchases of fixed assets	400
Cash used for investing activities	$400
Financing activities	
Notes payable	(50)
Long-term financing issuances	(25)
Common stock dividends	160
Cash used for financing activities	$85
Cash and equivalents increase (decrease)	10
Cash and equivalents at beginning of year	190
Cash and equivalents at end of year	$200
Supplemental cash flow disclosures	
Interest paid	$100
Income taxes paid	$160

Note that the Pitts Corporation had net income of $240 million in 2020. Show the calculations required to do each of the following:

1. Calculate FCFF starting with the net income figure.

Solution:

The analyst can use Equation 7 to find FCFF from net income (amounts are in millions):

Net income available to common shareholders	$240
Plus: Net noncash charges	300
Plus: Interest expense × (1 – Tax rate)	60
Less: Investment in fixed capital	400
Less: Investment in working capital	45
Free cash flow to the firm	$155

In the format shown and throughout the solutions, "Less: . . . *x*" is interpreted as "subtract *x*."
This equation can also be written as

$$\text{FCFF} = \text{NI} + \text{NCC} + \text{Int}(1 - \text{Tax rate}) - \text{FCInv} - \text{WCInv}$$

$$= 240 + 300 + 60 - 400 - 45 = \$155 \text{ million.}$$

Some of these items need explanation. Capital spending is $400 million, which is the increase in gross fixed assets shown on the balance sheet and in capital expenditures shown as an investing activity in the statement of cash flows. The increase in working capital is $45 million, which is the increase in accounts receivable of $40 million ($600 million – $560 million) plus the increase in inventories of $30 million ($440 million – $410 million) minus the increase in accounts payable of $15 million ($300 million – $285 million) minus the increase in accrued taxes and expenses of $10 million ($150 million – $140 million). When finding the increase in working capital, we ignore cash because the change in cash is what we are calculating. We also ignore short-term debt, such as notes payable, because such debt is part of the capital provided to the company and is not considered an operating item. The after-tax interest cost is the interest expense times (1 – Tax rate): $100 million × (1 – 0.40) = $60 million. The values of the remaining items in Equation 7 can be taken directly from the financial statements.

2. Calculate FCFE starting from the FCFF calculated in Part 1.

Solution:

Finding FCFE from FCFF can be done with Equation 9:

Free cash flow to the firm	$155
Less: Interest expense × (1 – Tax rate)	60
Plus: Net borrowing	75
Free cash flow to equity	$170

Or it can be done by using the equation

$$\text{FCFE} = \text{FCFF} - \text{Int}(1 - \text{Tax rate}) + \text{Net borrowing}$$

$$= 155 - 60 + 75 = \$170 \text{ million.}$$

3. Calculate FCFE starting with the net income figure.

Solution:

The analyst can use Equation 10 to find FCFE from NI.

Net income available to common shareholders	$240
Plus: Net noncash charges	300
Less: Investment in fixed capital	400
Less: Investment in working capital	45
Plus: Net borrowing	75
Free cash flow to equity	$170

Or the analyst can use the equation

FCFE = NI + NCC − FCInv − WCInv + Net borrowing

= 240 + 300 − 400 − 45 + 75 = $170 million.

Because notes payable increased by $50 million ($250 million – $200 million) and long-term debt increased by $25 million ($890 million – $865 million), net borrowing is $75 million.

4. Calculate FCFF starting with CFO.

Solution:

Equation 8 can be used to find FCFF from CFO:

Cash flow from operations	$495
Plus: Interest expense × (1 – Tax rate)	60
Less: Investment in fixed capital	400
Free cash flow to the firm	$155

Or

FCFF = CFO + Int(1 − Tax rate) − FCInv

= 495 + 60 − 400 = $155 million.

5. Calculate FCFE starting with CFO.

Solution:

Equation 11 can be used to find FCFE from CFO:

Cash flow from operations	$495
Less: Investment in fixed capital	400
Plus: Net borrowing	75
Free cash flow to equity	$170

Or

FCFE = CFO − FCInv + Net borrowing

= 495 − 400 + 75 = $170 million.

FCFE is usually less than FCFF. In this example, however, FCFE ($170 million) exceeds FCFF ($155 million) because external borrowing was large during this year.

FINDING FCFF AND FCFE FROM EBITA OR EBITDA

6

- ☐ explain the appropriate adjustments to net income, earnings before interest and taxes (EBIT), earnings before interest, taxes, depreciation, and amortization (EBITDA), and cash flow from operations (CFO) to calculate FCFF and FCFE
- ☐ calculate FCFF and FCFE

FCFF and FCFE are most frequently calculated from a starting basis of net income or CFO (as shown earlier). Two other starting points are EBIT and EBITDA from the income statement.

To show the relationship between EBIT and FCFF, we start with Equation 7 and assume that the only noncash charge (NCC) is depreciation (Dep):

$$\text{FCFF} = \text{NI} + \text{Dep} + \text{Int}(1 - \text{Tax rate}) - \text{FCInv} - \text{WCInv}.$$

Net income (NI) can be expressed as

$$\text{NI} = (\text{EBIT} - \text{Int})(1 - \text{Tax rate}) = \text{EBIT}(1 - \text{Tax rate}) - \text{Int}(1 - \text{Tax rate}).$$

Substituting this equation for NI in Equation 7, we have

$$\text{FCFF} = \text{EBIT}(1 - \text{Tax rate}) + \text{Dep} - \text{FCInv} - \text{WCInv}. \quad (12)$$

To get FCFF from EBIT, we multiply EBIT by (1 − Tax rate), add back depreciation, and then subtract the investments in fixed capital and working capital.

The relationship between FCFF and EBITDA can also be easily shown. Net income can be expressed as

$$\text{NI} = (\text{EBITDA} - \text{Dep} - \text{Int})(1 - \text{Tax rate})$$

$$= \text{EBITDA}(1 - \text{Tax rate}) - \text{Dep}(1 - \text{Tax rate}) - \text{Int}(1 - \text{Tax rate}).$$

Substituting this equation for NI in Equation 7 results in

$$\text{FCFF} = \text{EBITDA}(1 - \text{Tax rate}) + \text{Dep}(\text{Tax rate}) - \text{FCInv} - \text{WCInv}. \quad (13)$$

FCFF equals EBITDA times (1 − Tax rate) plus depreciation times the tax rate minus investments in fixed capital and working capital. In comparing Equation 12 and Equation 13, note the difference in how depreciation is handled.

Many adjustments for noncash charges that are required to calculate FCFF when starting from net income are not required when starting from EBIT or EBITDA. In the calculation of net income, many noncash charges are made after computing EBIT or EBITDA, so they do not need to be added back when calculating FCFF based on EBIT or EBITDA. Another important consideration is that some noncash charges, such as depreciation, are tax deductible. A noncash charge that affects taxes must be accounted for.

In summary, in calculating FCFF from EBIT or EBITDA, whether an adjustment for a noncash charge is needed depends on where in the income statement the charge has been deducted; furthermore, the form of any needed adjustment depends on whether the noncash charge is a tax-deductible expense.

We can also calculate FCFE (instead of FCFF) from EBIT or EBITDA. An easy way to obtain FCFE based on EBIT or EBITDA is to use Equation 12 (the expression for FCFF in terms of EBIT) or Equation 13 (the expression for FCFF in terms of EBITDA), respectively, and then subtract Int(1 – Tax rate) and add net borrowing because FCFE is related to FCFF as follows (see Equation 9):

$$\text{FCFE} = \text{FCFF} - \text{Int}(1 - \text{Tax rate}) + \text{Net borrowing}.$$

Example 6 uses the Pitts Corporation financial statements to find FCFF and FCFE from EBIT and EBITDA.

EXAMPLE 6

Adjusting EBIT and EBITDA to Find FCFF and FCFE

The Pitts Corporation (financial statements provided in Example 5) had EBIT of $500 million and EBITDA of $800 million in 2020. Show the adjustments that would be required to find FCFF and FCFE:

1. Starting from EBIT.

Solution:

To get FCFF from EBIT using Equation 12, we carry out the following (in millions):

EBIT(1 – Tax rate) = 500(1 – 0.40)	$300
Plus: Net noncash charges	300
Less: Net investment in fixed capital	400
Less: Net increase in working capital	45
Free cash flow to the firm	$155

Or

$$\begin{aligned}\text{FCFF} &= \text{EBIT}(1 - \text{Tax rate}) + \text{Dep} - \text{FCInv} - \text{WCInv}\\ &= 500(1 - 0.40) + 300 - 400 - 45 = \$155 \text{ million.}\end{aligned}$$

To obtain FCFE, make the appropriate adjustments to FCFF:

$$\begin{aligned}\text{FCFE} &= \text{FCFF} - \text{Int}(1 - \text{Tax rate}) + \text{Net borrowing}\\ &= 155 - 100(1 - 0.40) + 75 = \$170 \text{ million.}\end{aligned}$$

2. Starting from EBITDA.

Solution:

To obtain FCFF from EBITDA using Equation 13, we do the following (in millions):

EBITDA(1 – Tax rate) = $800(1 – 0.40)	$480
Plus: Dep(Tax rate) = $300(0.40)	120
Less: Net investment in fixed capital	400

Less: Net increase in working capital	45
Free cash flow to the firm	$155

Or

$$\begin{aligned}\text{FCFF} &= \text{EBITDA}(1 - \text{Tax rate}) + \text{Dep}(\text{Tax rate}) - \text{FCInv} - \text{WCInv}\\ &= 800(1 - 0.40) + 300(0.40) - 400 - 45 = \$155 \text{ million.}\end{aligned}$$

Again, to obtain FCFE, make the appropriate adjustments to FCFF:

$$\begin{aligned}\text{FCFE} &= \text{FCFF} - \text{Int}(1 - \text{Tax rate}) + \text{Net borrowing}\\ &= 155 - 100(1 - 0.40) + 75 = \$170 \text{ million.}\end{aligned}$$

FCFF AND FCFE ON A USES-OF-FREE-CASH-FLOW BASIS 7

- ☐ calculate FCFF and FCFE
- ☐ explain how dividends, share repurchases, share issues, and changes in leverage may affect future FCFF and FCFE

Prior sections illustrated the calculation of FCFF and FCFE from various income or cash flow starting points (e.g., net income or cash flow from operations). Those approaches to calculating free cash flow can be characterized as showing the *sources* of free cash flow. An alternative perspective examines the *uses* of free cash flow. In the context of calculating FCFF and FCFE, analyzing free cash flow on a uses basis serves as a consistency check on the sources calculation and may reveal information relevant to understanding a company's capital structure policy or cash position.

In general, a firm has the following alternative uses of positive FCFF: (1) retain the cash and thus increase the firm's balances of cash and marketable securities; (2) use the cash for payments to providers of debt capital (i.e., interest payments and principal payments in excess of new borrowings); and (3) use the cash for payments to providers of equity capital (i.e., dividend payments and/or share repurchases in excess of new share issuances). Similarly, a firm has the following general alternatives for covering negative free cash flows: draw down cash balances, borrow additional cash, or issue equity.

The effects on the company's capital structure of its transactions with capital providers should be noted. For a simple example, assume that free cash flows are zero and that the company makes no change to its cash balances. Obtaining cash via net new borrowings and using the cash for dividends or net share repurchases will increase the company's leverage, whereas obtaining cash from net new share issuances and using that cash to make principal payments in excess of new borrowings will reduce leverage.

We calculate uses of FCFF as follows:

Uses of FCFF =

Increases (or minus decreases) in cash balances

Plus: Net payments to providers of debt capital, which are calculated as:

- Plus: Interest expense × (1 – Tax rate).

- Plus: Repayment of principal in excess of new borrowing (or minus new borrowing in excess of debt repayment if new borrowing is greater).

Plus: Payments to providers of equity capital, which are calculated as:

- Plus: Cash dividends.
- Plus: Share repurchases in excess of share issuance (or minus new share issuance in excess of share repurchases if share issuance is greater).

Uses of FCFF must equal sources of FCFF as previously calculated.

Free cash flows to equity reflect free cash flows to the firm net of the cash used for payments to providers of debt capital. Accordingly, we can calculate FCFE as follows: Uses of FCFE =

Increases (or decreases) in cash balances

Plus: Payments to providers of equity capital, which are calculated as:

- Plus: Cash dividends.
- Plus: Share repurchases in excess of share issuance (or minus new share issuance in excess of share repurchases if share issuance is greater).

Again, the uses of FCFE must equal the sources of FCFE (calculated previously).

To illustrate the equivalence of sources and uses of FCFF and FCFE for the Pitts Corporation, whose financial statements are given in Exhibit 9 in Example 5, note the following for 2020:

- The increase in the balance of cash and equivalents was \$10, calculated as \$200 – \$190.
- After-tax interest expense was \$60, calculated as Interest expense × (1 – Tax rate) = \$100 × (1 – 0.40).
- Net borrowing was \$75, calculated as increase in borrowing minus repayment of debt = \$50 (increase in notes payable) + \$25 (increase in long-term debt).
- Cash dividends totaled \$160.
- Share repurchases and issuance both equaled \$0.

FCFF, previously calculated, was \$155. Pitts Corporation used the FCFF as follows (note that payments of principal to providers of debt capital in excess of new borrowings are a use of free cash flow. Here, the corporation did not use its free cash flow to repay debt; rather, it borrowed new debt, which increased the cash flows available to be used for providers of equity capital):

Increase in balance of cash and cash equivalents		\$10
Plus:	After-tax interest payments to providers of debt capital	\$60
Minus:	New borrowing	(\$75)
Plus:	Payments of dividends to providers of equity capital	\$160
Plus:	Share repurchases in excess of share issuances (or minus new share issuance in excess of share repurchases)	\$0
Total uses of FCFF		\$155

FCFE, previously calculated, was \$170. Pitts Corporation used the FCFE as follows:

Increase in balance of cash and cash equivalents		\$10
Plus:	Payments of dividends to providers of equity capital	\$160

Plus:	Share repurchases in excess of share issuances (or minus new share issuance in excess of share repurchases)	$0
Total uses of FCFE		$170

In summary, an analysis of the uses of free cash flows shows that Pitts Corporation was using free cash flows to manage its capital structure by increasing debt. The additional debt was not needed to cover capital expenditures; the statement of cash flows showed that the company's operating cash flows of $495 were more than adequate to cover its capital expenditures of $400. Instead, the additional debt was used, in part, to make dividend payments to the company's shareholders.

8 FORECASTING FCFF AND FCFE

☐ describe approaches for forecasting FCFF and FCFE

Computing FCFF and FCFE from historical accounting data is relatively straightforward. In some cases, these data are used directly to extrapolate free cash flow growth in a single-stage free cash flow valuation model. On other occasions, however, the analyst may expect that the future free cash flows will not bear a simple relationship to the past. The analyst who wishes to forecast future FCFF or FCFE directly for such a company must forecast the individual components of free cash flow. This section extends our previous presentation on *computing* FCFF and FCFE to the more complex task of *forecasting* FCFF and FCFE.

One method for forecasting free cash flow involves applying some constant growth rate to a current level of free cash flow (possibly adjusted, if necessary, to eliminate non-recurring components). The simplest basis for specifying the future growth rate is to assume that a historical growth rate will also apply to the future. This approach is appropriate if a company's free cash flow has tended to grow at a constant rate and if historical relationships between free cash flow and fundamental factors are expected to continue. Example 7 asks that the reader apply this approach to the Pitts Corporation based on 2020 FCFF of $155 million as calculated in Examples 5 and 6.

EXAMPLE 7

Constant Growth in FCFF

Use Pitts Corporation data to compute its FCFF for the next three years. Assume that growth in FCFF remains at the historical levels of 15% a year. The answer is as follows (in millions):

	2020 Actual	2021 Estimate	2022 Estimate	2023 Estimate
FCFF	155.00	178.25	204.99	235.74

A more complex approach is to forecast the components of free cash flow. This approach is able to capture the complex relationships among the components. One popular method is to forecast the individual components of free cash flow—EBIT(1 – Tax rate), net noncash charges, investment in fixed capital, and investment in working capital. EBIT can be forecasted directly or by forecasting sales and the company's EBIT margin based on an analysis of historical data and the current and expected economic environment. Similarly, analysts can base forecasts of capital needs on historical relationships between increases in sales and investments in fixed and working capital.

In this discussion, we illustrate a simple sales-based forecasting method for FCFF and FCFE based on the following major assumption:

> Investment in fixed capital in excess of depreciation (FCInv − Dep) and investment in working capital (WCInv) both bear a constant relationship to forecast increases in the size of the company as measured by increases in sales.

In addition, for FCFE forecasting, we assume that the capital structure represented by the debt ratio (DR)—debt as a percentage of debt plus equity—is constant. Under that assumption, DR indicates the percentage of the investment in fixed capital in excess of depreciation (also called "net new investment in fixed capital") and in working capital that will be financed by debt. This method involves a simplification because it considers depreciation as the only noncash charge, so the method does not work well when that approximation is not a good assumption.

If depreciation reflects the annual cost for maintaining the existing capital stock, the difference between fixed capital investment and depreciation—incremental FCInv—should be related to the capital expenditures required for growth. In this case, the following inputs are needed:

- forecasts of sales growth rates;
- forecasts of the after-tax operating margin (for FCFF forecasting) or profit margin (for FCFE forecasting);
- an estimate of the relationship of incremental FCInv to sales increases;
- an estimate of the relationship of WCInv to sales increases; and
- an estimate of DR.

In the case of FCFF forecasting, FCFF is calculated by forecasting EBIT(1 − Tax rate) and subtracting incremental fixed capital expenditures and incremental working capital expenditures. To estimate FCInv and WCInv, we multiply their past proportion to sales increases by the forecasted sales increases. Incremental fixed capital expenditures as a proportion of sales increases are computed as follows:

$$\frac{\text{Capital expenditures} - \text{Depreciation expense}}{\text{Increase in sales}}.$$

Similarly, incremental working capital expenditures as a proportion of sales increases are

$$\frac{\text{Increase in working capital}}{\text{Increase in sales}}.$$

When depreciation is the only significant net noncash charge, this method yields the same results as the previous equations for estimating FCFF or FCFE. Rather than adding back all depreciation and subtracting all capital expenditures when starting with EBIT(1 − Tax rate), this approach simply subtracts the net capital expenditures in excess of depreciation.

Although the recognition may not be obvious, this approach recognizes that capital expenditures have two components: those expenditures necessary to maintain existing capacity (fixed capital replacement) and those incremental expenditures necessary for growth. In forecasting, the expenditures to maintain capacity are likely to be related to the current level of sales and the expenditures for growth are likely to be related to the forecast of sales growth.

When forecasting FCFE, analysts often make an assumption that the financing of the company involves a "target" debt ratio. In this case, they assume that a specified percentage of the sum of (1) net new investment in fixed capital (new fixed capital minus depreciation expense) and (2) the increase in working capital is financed based on a target DR. This assumption leads to a simplification of FCFE calculations. If we assume that depreciation is the only noncash charge, Equation 10, which is FCFE = NI + NCC – FCInv – WCInv + Net borrowing, becomes

$$\text{FCFE} = \text{NI} - (\text{FCInv} - \text{Dep}) - \text{WCInv} + \text{Net borrowing}. \quad (14)$$

Note that FCInv – Dep represents the incremental fixed capital expenditure net of depreciation. By assuming a target DR, we eliminated the need to forecast net borrowing and can use the expression

$$\text{Net borrowing} = \text{DR}(\text{FCInv} - \text{Dep}) + \text{DR}(\text{WCInv}).$$

By using this expression, we do not need to forecast debt issuance and repayment on an annual basis to estimate net borrowing. Equation 14 then becomes

$$\text{FCFE} = \text{NI} - (\text{FCInv} - \text{Dep}) - \text{WCInv} + (\text{DR})(\text{FCInv} - \text{Dep}) + (\text{DR})(\text{WCInv})$$

or

$$\text{FCFE} = \text{NI} - (1 - \text{DR})(\text{FCInv} - \text{Dep}) - (1 - \text{DR})(\text{WCInv}). \quad (15)$$

Equation 15 says that FCFE equals NI minus the amount of fixed capital expenditure (net of depreciation) and working capital investment that is financed by equity. Again, for Equation 15, we have assumed that the only noncash charge is depreciation.

Example 8 and Example 9 illustrate this sales-based method for forecasting free cash flow to the firm.

EXAMPLE 8

Free Cash Flow Tied to Sales

Carla Espinosa is an analyst following Pitts Corporation at the end of 2020. From the data in Example 5, she can see that the company's sales for 2020 were $3,000 million, and she assumes that sales grew by $300 million from 2019 to 2020. Espinosa expects Pitts Corporation's sales to increase by 10% a year thereafter. Pitts Corporation is a fairly stable company, so Espinosa expects it to maintain its historical EBIT margin and proportions of incremental investments in fixed and working capital. Pitts Corporation's EBIT for 2020 is $500 million, its EBIT margin is 16.67% (500/3,000), and its tax rate is 40%.

Note from Pitts Corporation's 2020 statement of cash flows (Exhibit 9) the amount for "purchases of fixed assets" (i.e., capital expenditures) of $400 million and depreciation of $300 million. Thus, incremental fixed capital investment in 2020 was

$$\frac{\text{Capital expenditures} - \text{Depreciation expense}}{\text{Increase in sales}}$$

$$= \frac{400 - 300}{300} = 33.33\%.$$

Incremental working capital investment in the past year was

$$\frac{\text{Increase in working capital}}{\text{Increase in sales}} = \frac{45}{300} = 15\%.$$

So, for every $100 increase in sales, Pitts Corporation invests $33.33 in new equipment in addition to replacement of depreciated equipment and $15 in working capital. Espinosa forecasts FCFF for 2013 as follows (dollars in millions):

Sales	$3,300	Up 10%
EBIT	550	16.67% of sales
EBIT(1 – Tax rate)	330	Adjusted for 40% tax rate
Incremental FC	(100)	33.33% of sales increase
Incremental WC	(45)	15% of sales increase
FCFF	$185	

This model can be used to forecast multiple periods and is flexible enough to allow varying sales growth rates, EBIT margins, tax rates, and rates of incremental capital increases.

EXAMPLE 9

Free Cash Flow Growth Tied to Sales Growth

Continuing her work, Espinosa decides to forecast FCFF for the next five years. She is concerned that Pitts Corporation will not be able to maintain its historical EBIT margin and that the EBIT margin will decline from the current 16.67% to 14.5% in the next five years. Exhibit 10 summarizes her forecasts.

Exhibit 10: Free Cash Flow Growth for Pitts Corporation (Dollars in Millions)

	Year 1	Year 2	Year 3	Year 4	Year 5
Sales growth	10.00%	10.00%	10.00%	10.00%	10.00%
EBIT margin	16.67%	16.00%	15.50%	15.00%	14.50%
Tax rate	40.00%	40.00%	40.00%	40.00%	40.00%
Incremental FC investment	33.33%	33.33%	33.33%	33.33%	33.33%
Incremental WC investment	15.00%	15.00%	15.00%	15.00%	15.00%
Prior-year sales	$3,000.00				
Sales forecast	$3,300.00	$3,630.00	$3,993.00	$4,392.30	$4,831.53
EBIT forecast	550.00	580.80	618.92	658.85	700.57
EBIT(1 – Tax rate)	330.00	348.48	371.35	395.31	420.34
Incremental FC	(100.00)	(110.00)	(121.00)	(133.10)	(146.41)
Incremental WC	(45.00)	(49.50)	(54.45)	(59.90)	(65.88)
FCFF	$185.00	$188.98	$195.90	$202.31	$208.05

The model need not begin with sales; it could start with net income, cash flow from operations, or EBITDA.

A similar model can be designed for FCFE, as shown in Example 10. In the case of FCFE, the analyst should begin with net income and must also forecast any net new borrowing or net preferred stock issue.

EXAMPLE 10

Finding FCFE from Sales Forecasts

Espinosa decides to forecast FCFE for the year 2021. She uses the same expectations derived in Example 8. Additionally, she expects the following:

- the net profit margin will remain at 8% (= 240/3,000), and
- the company will finance incremental fixed and working capital investments with 50% debt—the target DR.

Espinosa's forecast for 2021 is as follows (dollars in millions):

Sales	$3,300	Up 10%
NI	264	8.0% of sales
Incremental FC	(100)	33.33% of sales increase
Incremental WC	(45)	15% of sales increase
Net borrowing	72.50	(100 FCInv + 45 WCInv) × 50%
FCFE	$191.50	

When the company being analyzed has significant noncash charges other than depreciation expense, the approach we have just illustrated will result in a less accurate estimate of FCFE than one obtained by forecasting all the individual components of FCFE. In some cases, the analyst will have specific forecasts of planned components, such as capital expenditures. In other cases, the analyst will study historical relationships, such as previous capital expenditures and sales levels, to develop a forecast.

OTHER ISSUES IN FREE CASH FLOW ANALYSIS 9

- ☐ compare the FCFE model and dividend discount models
- ☐ explain how dividends, share repurchases, share issues, and changes in leverage may affect future FCFF and FCFE
- ☐ evaluate the use of net income and EBITDA as proxies for cash flow in valuation

We have already presented a number of practical issues that arise in using free cash flow valuation models. Other issues relate to analyst adjustments to CFO, the relationship between free cash flow and dividends, and valuation with complicated financial structures.

Analyst Adjustments to CFO

Although many corporate financial statements are straightforward, some are not transparent (i.e., the quality of the reported numbers and of disclosures is not high). Sometimes, difficulties in analysis arise either because of lack of transparency or because the companies and their transactions are more complicated than the Pitts Corporation example we just provided.

For instance, in many corporate financial statements, the changes in balance sheet items (the increase in an asset or the decrease in a liability) differ from the changes reported in the statement of cash flows. Financial statements in which the changes in the balance sheet working capital accounts do not equal the working capital amounts reported on the statement of cash flows are described as lacking "articulation." Research on financial statement non-articulation (which is not an uncommon occurrence) identifies several reasons for these differences (Casey, Gao, Kirschenheiter, Li, and Pandit 2016; Huefner, Ketz, and Largay 1989; Bahnson, Miller, and Budge 1996; Wilkins and Loudder 2000; Hribar and Collins 2002; and Shi and Zhang 2011). Two of the factors that can cause discrepancies between changes in balance sheet accounts and the changes reported in the statement of cash flows include (1) acquisitions or divestitures (and related discontinued operations) and (2) the presence of nondomestic subsidiaries. For example, an increase in an inventory account may result from purchases from suppliers (which is an operating activity) or from an acquisition or merger with another company that has inventory on its balance sheet (which is an investing activity). Discrepancies may also occur from currency translations of the earnings of nondomestic subsidiaries.

Particularly for companies with major acquisition or divestiture activity where the CFO figure from the statement of cash flows may be distorted by cash flows related to financing and/or investing activities, an analyst may need to use greater detail in forecasting. For example, the analyst may need to adjust the amount of CFO that is used as the starting point for free cash flow calculations. Alternatively, instead of (or in addition to) developing a cash flow forecast by extrapolating from reported OCF, an analyst might forecast individual components and pay careful attention to the relation between sales forecast and forecast of specific working capital items.

Free Cash Flow versus Dividends and Other Earnings Components

Many analysts have a strong preference for free cash flow valuation models over dividend discount models. Although one type of model may have no theoretical advantage over another type, legitimate reasons to prefer one model can arise in the process of applying free cash flow models versus DDMs. First, many corporations pay no, or very low, cash dividends. Using a DDM to value these companies is difficult because they require forecasts about when dividends will be initiated, the level of dividends at initiation, and the growth rate or rates from that point forward. Second, dividend payments are at the discretion of the corporation's board of directors. Therefore, they may imperfectly signal the company's long-run profitability. Some corporations clearly pay dividends that are substantially less than their free cash flow, and others pay dividends that are substantially more. Finally, as mentioned earlier, dividends are the cash flow actually going to shareholders whereas free cash flow to equity is the cash flow available to be distributed to shareholders without impairing the company's value. If a company is being analyzed because it is a target for takeover, free cash flow is the appropriate cash flow measure; once the company is taken over, the new owners will have discretion over how free cash flow is used (including its distribution in the form of dividends).

We have defined FCFF and FCFE and presented alternative (equivalent) ways to calculate both. So, the reader should have a good idea of what is included in FCFF or FCFE but may wonder why some cash flows are not included. Specifically, what role do dividends, share repurchases, share issuance, or changes in leverage have on FCFF and FCFE? The simple answer is not much. Recall the formulas for FCFF and FCFE:

$$\text{FCFF} = \text{NI} + \text{NCC} + \text{Int}(1 - \text{Tax rate}) - \text{FCInv} - \text{WCInv},$$

and

FCFE = NI + NCC − FCInv − WCInv + Net borrowing.

Notice that dividends and share repurchases and issuance are absent from the formulas. The reason is that FCFF and FCFE are the cash flows *available* to investors or to stockholders; dividends and share repurchases are *uses* of these cash flows. So, the simple answer is that transactions between the company and its shareholders (through cash dividends, share repurchases, and share issuances) do not affect free cash flow. Leverage changes, such as the use of more debt financing, have some impact because they increase the interest tax shield (reduce corporate taxes because of the tax deductibility of interest) and reduce the cash flow available to equity. In the long run, the investing and financing decisions made today will affect future cash flows.

If all the inputs were known and mutually consistent, a DDM and an FCFE model would result in identical valuations for a stock. One possibility would be that FCFE equals cash dividends each year. Then, both cash flow streams would be discounted at the required return for equity and would have the same present value.

Generally, however, FCFE and dividends will differ, but the same economic forces that lead to low (high) dividends lead to low (high) FCFE. For example, a rapidly growing company with superior investment opportunities will retain a high proportion of earnings and pay low dividends. This same company will have high investments in fixed capital and working capital and have a low FCFE (which is clear from the expression FCFE = NI + NCC − FCInv − WCInv + Net borrowing). Conversely, a mature company that is investing relatively little might have high dividends and high FCFE. Despite this tendency, however, FCFE and dividends will usually differ.

FCFF and FCFE, as defined here, are measures of cash flow designed for valuation of the firm or its equity. Other definitions of free cash flow frequently appear in textbooks, articles, and vendor-supplied databases of financial information on public companies. In many cases, these other definitions of free cash flow are not designed for valuation purposes and thus should not be used for valuation. Using numbers supplied by others without knowing exactly how they are defined increases the likelihood of making errors in valuation. As consumers and producers of research, analysts should understand (if consumers) or make clear (if producers) the definition of free cash flow being used.

Because using free cash flow analysis requires considerable care and understanding, some practitioners erroneously use earnings components such as NI, EBIT, EBITDA, or CFO in a discounted cash flow valuation. Such mistakes may lead the practitioner to systematically overstate or understate the value of a stock. Shortcuts can be costly.

A common shortcut is to use EBITDA as a proxy for the cash flow to the firm. Equation 13 clearly shows the differences between EBITDA and FCFF:

FCFF = EBITDA(1 − Tax rate) + Dep(Tax rate) − FCInv − WCInv.

Depreciation charges as a percentage of EBITDA differ substantially for different companies and industries, as does the depreciation tax shield (the depreciation charge times the tax rate). Although FCFF captures this difference, EBITDA does not. EBITDA also does not account for the investments a company makes in fixed capital or working capital. Hence, EBITDA is a poor measure of the cash flow available to the company's investors. Using EBITDA (instead of free cash flow) in a DCF model has another important aspect as well: EBITDA is a before-tax measure, so the discount rate applied to EBITDA would be a before-tax rate. The WACC used to discount FCFF is an after-tax cost of capital.

EBITDA is a poor proxy for free cash flow to the firm because it does not account for the depreciation tax shield and the investment in fixed capital and working capital, but it is an even poorer proxy for free cash flow to equity. From a stockholder's perspective, additional defects of EBITDA include its failure to account for the after-tax interest costs or cash flows from new borrowing or debt repayments. Example 11 shows the mistakes sometimes made in discussions of cash flows.

EXAMPLE 11

The Mistakes of Using Net Income for FCFE and EBITDA for FCFF

1. A recent job applicant made some interesting comments about FCFE and FCFF: "I don't like the definitions for FCFE and FCFF because they are unnecessarily complicated and confusing. The best measure of FCFE, the funds available to pay dividends, is simply net income. You take the net income number straight from the income statement and don't need to make any further adjustments. Similarly, the best measure of FCFF, the funds available to the company's suppliers of capital, is EBITDA. You can take EBITDA straight from the income statement, and you don't need to consider using anything else."

   How would you respond to the job applicant's definition of (1) FCFE and (2) FCFF?

Solution:

The FCFE is the cash generated by the business's operations less the amount it must reinvest in additional assets plus the amounts it is borrowing. Equation 10, which starts with net income to find FCFE, shows these items:

Free cash flow to equity	=	Net income available to common shareholders
		Plus: Net noncash charges
		Less: Investment in fixed capital
		Less: Investment in working capital
		Plus: Net borrowing

Net income does not include several cash flows. So, net income tells only part of the overall story. Investments in fixed or working capital reduce the cash available to stockholders, as do loan repayments. New borrowing increases the cash available. FCFE, however, includes the cash generated from operating the business and also accounts for the investing and financing activities of the company. Of course, a special case exists in which net income and FCFE are the same. This case occurs when new investments exactly equal depreciation and the company is not investing in working capital or engaging in any net borrowing.

Solution:

Assuming that EBITDA equals FCFF introduces several possible mistakes. Equation 13 highlights these mistakes:

Free cash flow to the firm	=	EBITDA(1 – Tax rate)
		Plus: Depreciation(Tax rate)
		Less: Investment in fixed capital
		Less: Investment in working capital

The applicant is ignoring taxes, which obviously reduce the cash available to the company's suppliers of capital, and is also ignoring depreciation and the investments in fixed capital and working capital.

Free Cash Flow and Complicated Capital Structures

For the most part, the discussion of FCFF and FCFE so far has assumed the company has a simple capital structure with two sources of capital—namely, debt and equity. Including preferred stock as a third source of capital requires the analyst to add terms to the equations for FCFF and FCFE to account for the dividends paid on preferred stock and for the issuance or repurchase of preferred shares. Instead of including those terms in all of the equations, we chose to leave preferred stock out because only a few corporations use preferred stock. For companies that do have preferred stock, however, the effects of the preferred stock can be incorporated in the valuation models.

For example, in Equation 7, which calculates FCFF starting with net income available to common shareholders, preferred dividends paid would be added to the cash flows to obtain FCFF. In Equation 10, which calculates FCFE starting with net income available to common shareholders, if preferred dividends were already subtracted when arriving at net income, no further adjustment for preferred dividends would be required. Issuing (redeeming) preferred stock increases (decreases) the cash flow available to common stockholders, however, so this term would have to be added in. The existence of preferred stock in the capital structure has many of the same effects as the existence of debt, except that unlike interest payments on debt, preferred stock dividends paid are not tax deductible.

Example 12 shows how to calculate WACC, FCFF, and FCFE when the company has preferred stock.

EXAMPLE 12

FCFF Valuation with Preferred Stock in the Capital Structure

Welch Corporation uses bond, preferred stock, and common stock financing. The market value of each of these sources of financing and the before-tax required rates of return for each are given in Exhibit 11:

Exhibit 11: Welch Corporation Capital Structure (Dollars in Millions)

	Market Value ($)	Required Return (%)
Bonds	400	8.0
Preferred stock	100	8.0
Common stock	500	12.0
Total	1,000	

Other financial information (dollars in millions):

- Net income available to common shareholders = $110.
- Interest expenses = $32.
- Preferred dividends = $8.
- Depreciation = $40.
- Investment in fixed capital = $70.
- Investment in working capital = $20.
- Net borrowing = $25.
- Tax rate = 30%.
- Stable growth rate of FCFF = 4.0%.
- Stable growth rate of FCFE = 5.4%.

1. Calculate Welch Corporation's WACC.

Solution:

Based on the weights and after-tax costs of each source of capital, the WACC is

$$\text{WACC} = \frac{400}{1,000}8\%(1-0.30) + \frac{100}{1,000}8\% + \frac{500}{1,000}12\% = 9.04\%.$$

2. Calculate the current value of FCFF.

Solution:

If the company did not issue preferred stock, FCFF would be

FCFF = NI + NCC + Int(1 – Tax rate) – FCInv – WCInv.

If preferred stock dividends have been paid (and net income is income available to common shareholders), the preferred dividends must be added back just as after-tax interest expenses are. The modified equation (including preferred dividends) for FCFF is

FCFF = NI + NCC + Int(1 – Tax rate) + Preferred dividends – FCInv – WCInv.

For Welch Corporation, FCFF is

FCFF = 110 + 40 + 32(1 – 0.30) + 8 – 70 – 20 = \$90.4 million.

3. Based on forecasted Year 1 FCFF, what is the total value of Welch Corporation and the value of its equity?

Solution:

The total value of the firm is

$$\text{Firm value} = \frac{\text{FCFF1}}{\text{WACC} - g} = \frac{90.4(1.04)}{0.0904 - 0.04}$$

$$= \frac{94.016}{0.0504} = \$1,865.40 \text{ million.}$$

The value of (common) equity is the total value of the company minus the value of debt and preferred stock:

Equity = 1,865.40 – 400 – 100 = \$1,365.40 million.

4. Calculate the current value of FCFE.

Solution:

With no preferred stock, FCFE is

FCFE = NI + NCC – FCInv – WCInv + Net borrowing.

If the company has preferred stock, the FCFE equation is essentially the same. Net borrowing in this case is the total of new debt borrowing and net issuances of new preferred stock. For Welch Corporation, FCFE is

FCFE = 110 + 40 – 70 – 20 + 25 = \$85 million.

5. Based on forecasted Year 1 FCFE, what is the value of equity?

Solution:

Valuing FCFE, which is growing at 5.4%, produces a value of equity of

$$\text{Equity} = \frac{\text{FCFE}_1}{r-g} = \frac{85(1.054)}{0.12-0.054} = \frac{89.59}{0.066} = \$1,357.42 \text{ million.}$$

Paying cash dividends on common stock does not affect FCFF or FCFE, which are the amounts of cash *available* to all investors or to common stockholders. It is simply a use of the available cash. Share repurchases of common stock also do not affect FCFF or FCFE. Share repurchases are, in many respects, a substitute for cash dividends. Similarly, issuing shares of common stock does not affect FCFF or FCFE.

Changing leverage (changing the amount of debt financing in the company's capital structure), however, does have some effects on FCFE particularly. An increase in leverage will not affect FCFF (although it might affect the calculations used to arrive at FCFF). An increase in leverage affects FCFE in two ways. In the year the debt is issued, it increases the FCFE by the amount of debt issued. After the debt is issued, FCFE is then reduced by the after-tax interest expense.

In this section, we have discussed the concepts of FCFF and FCFE and their estimation. The next section presents additional valuation models that use forecasts of FCFF or FCFE to value the firm or its equity. These free cash flow models are similar in structure to dividend discount models, although the analyst must face the reality that estimating free cash flows is more time-consuming than estimating dividends.

FREE CASH FLOW MODEL VARIATIONS

10

☐ explain the use of sensitivity analysis in FCFF and FCFE valuations

This section presents several extensions of the free cash flow models presented earlier. In many cases, especially when inflation rates are volatile, analysts will value real cash flows instead of nominal values. As with dividend discount models, free cash flow models are sensitive to the data inputs, so analysts routinely perform sensitivity analyses of their valuations.

Earlier, we presented the single-stage free cash flow model, which has a constant growth rate. In the following, we use the single-stage model to address selected valuation issues; we then present multistage free cash flow models.

An International Application of the Single-Stage Model

Valuation by using real (inflation-adjusted) values instead of nominal values has much appeal when inflation rates are high and volatile. Many analysts use this adaptation for both domestic and nondomestic stocks, but the use of real values is especially helpful for valuing international stocks. Special challenges to valuing equities from multiple countries include (1) incorporating economic factors—such as interest rates, inflation rates, and growth rates—that differ among countries and (2) dealing with varied accounting standards. Furthermore, performing analyses in multiple countries challenges the analyst—particularly a team of analysts—to use *consistent* assumptions for all countries.

Several securities firms have adapted the single-stage FCFE model to address some of the challenges of international valuation. They choose to analyze companies by using real cash flows and real discount rates instead of nominal values. To estimate real discount rates, they use a modification of the build-up method mentioned earlier under the topic of return concepts. Starting with a "country return," which is a real required rate of return for stocks from a particular country, they then make adjustments to the country return for the stock's industry, size, and leverage:

Country return (real)	x.xx%
+/– Industry adjustment	x.xx%
+/– Size adjustment	x.xx%
+/– Leverage adjustment	x.xx%
Required rate of return (real)	x.xx%

The adjustments in the model should have sound economic justification. They should reflect factors expected to affect the relative risk and return associated with an investment.

The securities firms making these adjustments predict the growth rate of FCFE also in real terms. The firms supply their analysts with estimates of the real economic growth rate for each country, and each analyst chooses a real growth rate for the stock being analyzed that is benchmarked against the real country growth rate. This approach is particularly useful for countries with high or variable inflation rates.

The value of the stock is found with an equation essentially like Equation 6 except that all variables in the equation are stated in real terms:

$$V_0 = \frac{\text{FCFE}_0\left(1 + g_{\text{real}}\right)}{r_{\text{real}} - g_{\text{real}}}.$$

Whenever real discount rates and real growth rates can be estimated more reliably than nominal discount rates and nominal growth rates, this method is worth using. Example 13 shows how this procedure can be applied.

EXAMPLE 13

Using Real Cash Flows and Discount Rates for International Stocks

Mukamba Ventures is a consumer staples company headquartered in Kinshasa, Democratic Republic of the Congo. Although the company's cash flows have been volatile, an analyst has estimated a per-share normalized FCFE of 1,400 Congolese francs (CDF) for the year just ended. The real country return for the Democratic Republic of the Congo is 7.30%; adjustments to the country return for Mukamba Ventures are an industry adjustment of +0.80%, a size adjustment of –0.33%, and a leverage adjustment of –0.12%. The long-term real growth rate for the Democratic Republic of the Congo is estimated to be 3.0%, and the real growth rate of Mukamba Ventures is expected to be about 0.5% below the country rate. The real required rate of return for Mukamba Ventures is calculated as follows:

Country return (real)	7.30%
Industry adjustment	+ 0.80%
Size adjustment	– 0.33%
Leverage adjustment	– 0.12%
Required rate of return	7.65%

The real growth rate of FCFE is expected to be 2.5% (3.0% – 0.5%), so the value of one share is

$$V_0 = \frac{\text{FCFE}_0(1 + g_{real})}{r_{real} - g_{real}} = \frac{1,400(1.025)}{0.0765 - 0.025} = \frac{1,435}{0.0515} = \text{CDF}27,864.$$

Sensitivity Analysis of FCFF and FCFE Valuations

In large measure, growth in FCFF and in FCFE depends on a company's future profitability. Sales growth and changes in net profit margins dictate future net profits. Sales growth and profit margins depend on the growth phase of the company and the profitability of the industry. A highly profitable company in a growing industry can enjoy years of profit growth. Eventually, however, its profit margins are likely to be eroded by increased competition; sales growth is also likely to abate because of fewer opportunities for expansion of market size and market share. Growth rates and the duration of growth are difficult to forecast.

The base-year values for the FCFF and FCFE growth models are also critical. Given the same required rates of return and growth rates, the value of the firm or the value of equity will increase or decrease proportionately with the initial value of FCFF or FCFE used.

To examine how sensitive the final valuation is to changes in each of a valuation model's input variables, analysts can perform a sensitivity analysis. Some input variables have a much larger impact on stock valuation than others. Example 14 shows the sensitivity of the valuation of Petroleo Brasileiro to four input variables.

EXAMPLE 14

Sensitivity Analysis of an FCFE Valuation

1. Antonio Sousa is valuing the equity of Petroleo Brasileiro, commonly known as Petrobras, by using the single-stage (constant-growth) FCFE model. Estimated FCFE per share for the year just ended is 2.59 Brazilian reals (BRL). Sousa's best estimates of input values for the analysis are as follows:

   - The FCFE growth rate is 7.0%.
   - The risk-free rate is 8.9%.
   - The equity risk premium is 5.3%.
   - Beta is 1.4.

   Using the capital asset pricing model (CAPM), Sousa estimates that the required rate of return for Petrobras is

   $$r = E(R_i) = R_F + \beta_i[E(R_M) - R_F] = 8.9\% + 1.4(5.3\%) = 16.32\%.$$

   The estimated value per share is

   $$V_0 = \frac{\text{FCFE}_0(1+g)}{r-g} = \frac{2.59(1.07)}{0.1632 - 0.07} = \text{BRL}29.73.$$

   Exhibit 12 shows Sousa's base case and the highest and lowest reasonable alternative estimates. The column "Valuation with Low Estimate" gives the estimated value of Petrobras based on the low estimate for the variable on the same row of the first column and the base-case estimates for the remaining three variables. "Valuation with High Estimate" gives a similar estimated value based on the high estimate for the variable at issue.

Exhibit 12: Sensitivity Analysis for Petrobras Valuation

Variable	Base-Case Estimate	Low Estimate	High Estimate	Valuation with Low Estimate	Valuation with High Estimate
Beta	1.4	1.2	1.6	BRL33.55	BRL26.70
Risk-free rate	8.9%	7.9%	9.9%	BRL33.31	BRL26.85
Equity risk premium	5.3%	4.3%	6.3%	BRL34.99	BRL25.85
FCFE growth rate	7.0%	5.0%	9.0%	BRL24.02	BRL38.57

As Exhibit 12 shows, the value of Petrobras is very sensitive to the inputs. The value is negatively related to changes in the beta, the risk-free rate, and the equity risk premium and positively related to changes in the FCFE growth rate. Of the four variables considered, the stock valuation is most sensitive to the range of estimates for the FCFE growth rate (a range from BRL24.02 to BRL38.57. The ranges of the estimates for the other three variables, while still large, are less than the range for changes in the FCFE growth rate. Of course, the variables to which a stock price is most sensitive vary from case to case. A sensitivity analysis gives the analyst a guide as to which variables are most critical to the final valuation.

11 TWO-STAGE FREE CASH FLOW MODELS

- ☐ explain the single-stage (stable-growth), two-stage, and three-stage FCFF and FCFE models and justify the selection of the appropriate model given a company's characteristics
- ☐ estimate a company's value using the appropriate free cash flow model(s)
- ☐ describe approaches for calculating the terminal value in a multistage valuation model; and

Several two-stage and multistage models exist for valuing free cash flow streams, just as several such models are available for valuing dividend streams. The free cash flow models are much more complex than the dividend discount models because to find FCFF or FCFE, the analyst usually incorporates sales, profitability, investments, financing costs, and new financing.

In two-stage free cash flow models, the growth rate in the second stage is a long-run sustainable growth rate. For a declining industry, the second-stage growth rate could be slightly below the GDP growth rate. For an industry that is expected to grow in the future faster than the overall economy, the second-stage growth rate could be slightly greater than the GDP growth rate.

The two most popular versions of the two-stage FCFF and FCFE models are distinguished by the pattern of the growth rates in Stage 1. In one version, the growth rate is constant in Stage 1 before dropping to the long-run sustainable rate in Stage 2. In the other version, the growth rate declines in Stage 1 to reach the sustainable rate at the beginning of Stage 2. This second type of model is like the H-model for discounted dividend valuation, in which dividend growth rates decline in Stage 1 and are constant in Stage 2.

Unlike multistage DDMs, in which the growth rates are consistently dividend growth rates, in free cash flow models, the "growth rate" may refer to different variables (which variables should be stated or should be clear from the context). The growth rate could be the growth rate for FCFF or FCFE, the growth rate for income (either net income or operating income), or the growth rate for sales. If the growth rate is for net income, the changes in FCFF or FCFE also depend on investments in operating assets and the financing of these investments. When the growth rate in income declines, such as between Stage 1 and Stage 2, investments in operating assets probably decline at the same time. If the growth rate is for sales, changes in net profit margins as well as investments in operating assets and financing policies will determine FCFF and FCFE.

A general expression for the two-stage FCFF valuation model is

$$\text{Firm value} = \sum_{t=1}^{n} \frac{\text{FCFF}_t}{(1+\text{WACC})^t} + \frac{\text{FCFF}_{n+1}}{(\text{WACC}-g)} \frac{1}{(1+\text{WACC})^n}. \quad (16)$$

The summation gives the present value of the first n years of FCFF. The terminal value of the FCFF from Year $n + 1$ forward is $\text{FCFF}_{n+1}/(\text{WACC} - g)$, which is discounted at the WACC for n periods to obtain its present value. Subtracting the value of outstanding debt gives the value of equity. The value per share is then found by dividing the total value of equity by the number of outstanding shares.

The general expression for the two-stage FCFE valuation model is

$$\text{Equity value} = \sum_{t=1}^{n} \frac{\text{FCFE}_t}{(1+r)^t} + \left(\frac{\text{FCFE}_{n+1}}{r-g}\right) \left[\frac{1}{(1+r)^n}\right]. \quad (17)$$

In this case, the summation is the present value of the first n years of FCFE and the terminal value of $\text{FCFE}_{n+1}/(r - g)$ is discounted at the required rate of return on equity for n years. The value per share is found by dividing the total value of equity by the number of outstanding shares.

In Equation 17, the terminal value of the stock at $t = n$, TV_n, is found by using the constant-growth FCFE model. In this case, $\text{TV}_n = \text{FCFE}_{n+1}/(r - g)$. (Of course, the analyst might choose to estimate terminal value another way, such as by using a P/E multiplied by the company's forecasted EPS.) The terminal value estimation is critical for a simple reason: The present value of the terminal value is often a substantial portion of the total value of the stock. For example, in Equation 17, when the analyst is calculating the total present value of the first n cash flows (FCFE) and the present value of the terminal value, the present value of the terminal value is often substantial. In the examples that follow, the terminal value usually represents a substantial part of total estimated value. The same is true in practice.

Fixed Growth Rates in Stage 1 and Stage 2

The simplest two-stage FCFF or FCFE growth model has a constant growth rate in each stage. Example 15 finds the value of a firm that has a 20% sales growth rate in Stage 1 and a 6% sales growth rate in Stage 2.

EXAMPLE 15

A Two-Stage FCFE Valuation Model with a Constant Growth Rate in Each Stage

1. Uwe Henschel is doing a valuation of TechnoSchaft on the basis of the following information:

   - Year 0 sales per share = €25.
   - Sales growth rate = 20% annually for three years and 6% annually thereafter.
   - Net profit margin = 10% forever.
   - Net investment in fixed capital (net of depreciation) = 50% of the sales increase.
   - Annual increase in working capital = 20% of the sales increase.
   - Debt financing = 40% of the net investments in capital equipment and working capital.
   - TechnoSchaft beta = 1.20; the risk-free rate of return = 7%; the equity risk premium = 4.5%.

   The required rate of return for equity is

   $$r = E(R_i) = R_F + \beta_i[E(R_M) - R_F] = 7\% + 1.2(4.5\%) = 12.4\%.$$

   Exhibit 13 shows the calculations for FCFE.

Exhibit 13: FCFE Estimates for TechnoSchaft (in Euros)

	Year					
	1	2	3	4	5	6
Sales growth rate	20%	20%	20%	6%	6%	6%
Sales per share	30.000	36.000	43.200	45.792	48.540	51.452
Net profit margin	10%	10%	10%	10%	10%	10%
EPS	3.000	3.600	4.320	4.579	4.854	5.145
Net FCInv per share	2.500	3.000	3.600	1.296	1.374	1.456
WCInv per share	1.000	1.200	1.440	0.518	0.550	0.582
Debt financing per share	1.400	1.680	2.016	0.726	0.769	0.815
FCFE per share	0.900	1.080	1.296	3.491	3.700	3.922
Growth rate of FCFE		20%	20%	169%	6%	6%

In Exhibit 13, sales are shown to grow at 20% annually for the first three years and then at 6% thereafter. Profits, which are 10% of sales, grow at the same rates. The net investments in fixed capital and working capital are, respectively, 50% of the increase in sales and 20% of the increase in sales. New debt financing equals 40% of the total increase in net fixed capital and working capital. FCFE is EPS minus the net investment in fixed capital per share minus the investment in working capital per share plus the debt financing per share.

Notice that FCFE grows by 20% annually for the first three years (i.e., between $t = 0$ and $t = 3$). Then, between Year 3 and Year 4, when the sales growth rate drops from 20% to 6%, FCFE increases substantially. In fact, FCFE increases by 169% from Year 3 to Year 4. This large increase in FCFE occurs because profits grow at 6% but the investments in capital equipment and working capital (and the increase in debt financing) drop substantially from the previous year. In Years 5 and 6 in Exhibit 13, sales, profit, investments, financing, and FCFE are all shown to grow at 6%.

The stock value is the present value of the first three years' FCFE plus the present value of the terminal value of the FCFE from Years 4 and later. The terminal value is

$$TV_3 = \frac{FCFE_4}{r-g} = \frac{3.491}{0.124-0.06} = €54.55.$$

The present values are

$$V_0 = \frac{0.900}{1.124} + \frac{1.080}{(1.124)^2} + \frac{1.296}{(1.124)^3} + \frac{54.55}{(1.124)^3}$$
$$= 0.801 + 0.855 + 0.913 + 38.415 = €40.98.$$

The estimated value of this stock is €40.98 per share.

As mentioned previously, the terminal value may account for a large portion of the value of a stock. In the case of TechnoSchaft, the present value of the terminal value is €38.415 out of a total value of €40.98. The present value (PV) of the terminal value is almost 94% of the total value of TechnoSchaft stock.

Declining Growth Rate in Stage 1 and Constant Growth in Stage 2

Growth rates usually do not drop precipitously as they do between the stages in the two-stage model just described, but growth rates can decline over time for many reasons. Sometimes, a small company has a high growth rate that is not sustainable as its market share increases. A highly profitable company may attract competition that makes it harder for the company to sustain its high profit margins.

In this section, we present two examples of the two-stage model with declining growth rates in Stage 1. In the first example, the growth rate of EPS declines during Stage 1. As a company's profitability declines and the company is no longer generating high returns, the company will usually reduce its net new investment in operating assets. The debt financing accompanying the new investments will also decline. Many highly profitable, growing companies have negative or low free cash flows. Later, when growth in profits slows, investments will tend to slow and the company will experience positive cash flows. Of course, the negative cash flows incurred in the high-growth stage help determine the cash flows that occur in future years.

Example 16 models FCFE per share as a function of EPS that declines constantly during Stage 1. Because of declining earnings growth rates, the company in the example also reduces its new investments over time. The value of the company depends on these free cash flows, which are substantial after the high-growth (and high-profitability) period has largely elapsed.

EXAMPLE 16

A Two-Stage FCFE Valuation Model with Declining Net Income Growth in Stage 1

1. Vishal Noronha needs to prepare a valuation of Sindhuh Enterprises. Noronha has assembled the following information for his analysis. It is now the first day of 2020.

- EPS for 2019 is $2.40.
- For the next five years, the growth rate in EPS is given in the following table. After 2024, the growth rate will be 7%.

	2020	2021	2022	2023	2024
Growth rate for EPS	30%	18%	12%	9%	7%

- Net investments in fixed capital (net of depreciation) for the next five years are given in the following table. After 2024, capital expenditures are expected to grow at 7% annually.

	2020	2021	2022	2023	2024
Net capital expenditure per share	$3.00	$2.50	$2.00	$1.50	$1.00

- The investment in working capital each year will equal 50% of the net investment in capital items.
- 30% of the net investment in fixed capital and investment in working capital will be financed with new debt financing.
- Current market conditions dictate a risk-free rate of 6.0%, an equity risk premium of 4.0%, and a beta of 1.10 for Sindhuh Enterprises.
- What is the per-share value of Sindhuh Enterprises on the first day of 2020?
- What should be the trailing P/E on the first day of 2020 and the first day of 2024?

Solution:

The required return for Sindhuh should be

$$r = E(R_i) = R_F + \beta_i\left[E(R_M) - R_F\right] = 6\% + 1.1(4\%) = 10.4\%.$$

The FCFEs for the company for years 2020 through 2024 are given in Exhibit 14.

Exhibit 14: FCFE Estimates for Sindhuh Enterprises (Per-Share Data in US Dollars)

	Year				
	2020	2021	2022	2023	2024
Growth rate for EPS	30%	18%	12%	9%	7%
EPS	3.120	3.682	4.123	4.494	4.809
Net FCInv per share	3.000	2.500	2.000	1.500	1.000

	Year				
	2020	2021	2022	2023	2024
WCInv per share	1.500	1.250	1.000	0.750	0.500
Debt financing per share[a]	1.350	1.125	0.900	0.675	0.450
FCFE per share[b]	–0.030	1.057	2.023	2.919	3.759
PV of FCFE discounted at 10.4%	–0.027	0.867	1.504	1.965	

[a] *30% of (Net FCInv + WCInv).*
[b] *EPS – Net FCInv per share – WCInv per share + Debt financing per share.*

Earnings are $2.40 in 2019. Earnings increase each year by the growth rate given in the table. Net capital expenditures (capital expenditures minus depreciation) are the amounts that Noronha assumed. The increase in working capital each year is 50% of the increase in net capital expenditures. Debt financing is 30% of the total outlays for net capital expenditures and working capital each year. The FCFE each year is net income minus net capital expenditures minus increase in working capital plus new debt financing. Finally, for years 2020 through 2023, the present value of FCFE is found by discounting FCFE by the 10.4% required rate of return for equity.
After 2024, FCFE will grow by a constant 7% annually, so the constant-growth FCFE valuation model can be used to value this cash flow stream. At the end of 2023, the value of the future FCFE is

$$V_{2023} = \frac{\text{FCFE}_{2024}}{r - g} = \frac{3.759}{0.104 - 0.07} = \$110.56 \text{ per share.}$$

To find the present value of V_{2023} as of the end of 2019, V_{2019}, we discount V_{2023} at 10.4% for four years:

$$\text{PV} = 110.56/(1.104)^4 = \$74.425 \text{ per share.}$$

The total present value of the company is the present value of the first four years' FCFE plus the present value of the terminal value, or

$$V_{2019} = -0.027 + 0.867 + 1.504 + 1.965 + 74.42 = \$78.73 \text{ per share.}$$

Solution:

Using the estimated $78.73 stock value, we find that the trailing P/E at the beginning of 2020 is

$$\text{P/E} = 78.73/2.40 = 32.8.$$

At the beginning of 2024, the expected stock value is $110.56, and the previous year's EPS is $4.494, so the trailing P/E at this time would be

$$\text{P/E} = 110.56/4.494 = 24.6.$$

After its high-growth phase has ended, the P/E for the company declines substantially.

The FCFE in Example 16 was based on forecasts of future EPS. Analysts often model a company by forecasting future sales and then estimating the profits, investments, and financing associated with those sales levels. For large companies, analysts may estimate the sales, profitability, investments, and financing for each division or large subsidiary. Then, they aggregate the free cash flows for all of the divisions or subsidiaries to get the free cash flow for the company as a whole.

Example 17 is a two-stage FCFE model with declining sales growth rates in Stage 1, with profits, investments, and financing keyed to sales. In Stage 1, the growth rate of sales and the profit margin on sales both decline as the company matures and faces more competition and slower growth.

EXAMPLE 17

A Two-Stage FCFE Valuation Model with Declining Sales Growth Rates

Medina Werks, a manufacturing company headquartered in Canada, has a competitive advantage that will probably deteriorate over time. Analyst Flavio Torino expects this deterioration to be reflected in declining sales growth rates as well as declining profit margins. To value the company, Torino has accumulated the following information:

- Current sales are C$600 million. Over the next six years, the annual sales growth rate and the net profit margin are projected to be as follows:

	Year 1 (%)	Year 2 (%)	Year 3 (%)	Year 4 (%)	Year 5 (%)	Year 6 (%)
Sales growth rate	20	16	12	10	8	7
Net profit margin	14	13	12	11	10.5	10

  Beginning in Year 6, the 7% sales growth rate and 10% net profit margin should persist indefinitely.

- Capital expenditures (net of depreciation) in the amount of 60% of the sales increase will be required each year.
- Investments in working capital equal to 25% of the sales increase will also be required each year.
- Debt financing will be used to fund 40% of the investments in net capital items and working capital.
- The beta for Medina Werks is 1.10; the risk-free rate of return is 6.0%; the equity risk premium is 4.5%.
- The company has 70 million outstanding shares.

1. What is the estimated total market value of equity?

Solution:

The required return for Medina is

$$r = E(R_i) = R_F + \beta_i [E(R_M) - R_F] = 6\% + 1.10(4.5\%) = 10.95\%.$$

The annual sales and net profit can be readily found as shown in Exhibit 15.

Exhibit 15: FCFE Estimates for Medina Werks (C$ in Millions)

	Year					
	1	2	3	4	5	6
Sales growth rate	20%	16%	12%	10%	8%	7%
Net profit margin	14%	13%	12%	11%	10.50%	10%
Sales	720.000	835.200	935.424	1,028.966	1,111.284	1,189.074
Net profit	100.800	108.576	112.251	113.186	116.685	118.907
Net FCInv	72.000	69.120	60.134	56.125	49.390	46.674
WCInv	30.000	28.800	25.056	23.386	20.579	19.447
Debt financing	40.800	39.168	34.076	31.804	27.988	26.449
FCFE	39.600	49.824	61.137	65.480	74.703	79.235
PV of FCFE at 10.95%	35.692	40.475	44.763	43.211	44.433	

As can be seen, sales are expected to increase each year by a declining sales growth rate. Net profit each year is the year's net profit margin times the year's sales. Capital investment (net of depreciation) equals 60% of the sales increase from the previous year. The investment in working capital is 25% of the sales increase from the previous year. The debt financing each year is equal to 40% of the total net investment in capital items and working capital for that year. FCFE is net income minus the net capital investment minus the working capital investment plus the debt financing. The present value of each year's FCFE is found by discounting FCFE at the required rate of return for equity, 10.95%.

In Year 6 and beyond, Torino predicts sales to increase at 7% annually. Net income will be 10% of sales, so net profit will also grow at a 7% annual rate. Because they are pegged to the 7% sales increase, the investments in capital items and working capital and debt financing will also grow at the same 7% rate. The amounts in Year 6 for net income, investment in capital items, investment in working capital, debt financing, and FCFE will grow at 7%. The terminal value of FCFE in Year 6 and beyond is

$$TV_5 = \frac{FCFE_6}{r-g} = \frac{79.235}{0.1095-0.07} = \text{C\$2,005.95 million.}$$

The present value of this amount is

$$\text{PV of } TV_5 = \frac{2,005.95}{(1.1095)^5} = \text{C\$1,193.12 million.}$$

The estimated total market value of the firm is the present value of FCFE for Years 1 through 5 plus the present value of the terminal value:

$$MV = 35.692 + 40.475 + 44.763 + 43.211 + 44.433 + 1,193.12$$

$$= \text{C\$1,401.69 million.}$$

2. What is the estimated value per share?

Solution:

Dividing C$1,401.69 million by the 70 million outstanding shares gives the estimated value per share of C$20.02.

12 THREE-STAGE FREE CASH FLOW MODELS

- ☐ explain the single-stage (stable-growth), two-stage, and three-stage FCFF and FCFE models and justify the selection of the appropriate model given a company's characteristics
- ☐ estimate a company's value using the appropriate free cash flow model(s)
- ☐ describe approaches for calculating the terminal value in a multistage valuation model; and

Three-stage models are a straightforward extension of the two-stage models. One common version of a three-stage model is to assume a constant growth rate in each of the three stages. The growth rates could be for sales, profits, and investments in fixed and working capital; external financing could be a function of the level of sales or changes in sales. A simpler model would apply the growth rate to FCFF or FCFE.

A second common model is a three-stage model with constant growth rates in Stages 1 and 3 and a declining growth rate in Stage 2. Again, the growth rates could be applied to sales or to FCFF or FCFE. Although future FCFF and FCFE are unlikely to follow the assumptions of either of these three-stage growth models, analysts often find such models to be useful approximations.

Example 18 is a three-stage FCFF valuation model with declining growth rates in Stage 2. The model directly forecasts FCFF instead of deriving FCFF from a more complicated model that estimates cash flow from operations and investments in fixed and working capital.

EXAMPLE 18

A Three-Stage FCFF Valuation Model with Declining Growth in Stage 2

Charles Jones is evaluating Reliant Home Furnishings by using a three-stage growth model. He has accumulated the following information:

- Current FCFF = $745 million.
- Outstanding shares = 309.39 million.
- Equity beta = 0.90; risk-free rate = 5.04%; equity risk premium = 5.5%.
- Cost of debt = 7.1%.
- Marginal tax rate = 34%.
- Capital structure = 20% debt, 80% equity.
- Long-term debt = $1.518 billion.
- Growth rate of FCFF =
    - 8.8% annually in Stage 1, Years 1–4.
    - 7.4% in Year 5, 6.0% in Year 6, 4.6% in Year 7.
    - 3.2% in Year 8 and thereafter.

From the information that Jones has accumulated, estimate the following:

1. WACC.

Solution:

The required return for equity is

$$r = E(R_i) = R_F + \beta_i [E(R_M) - R_F] = 5.04\% + 0.9(5.5\%) = 9.99\%.$$

WACC is

WACC = 0.20(7.1%)(1 – 0.34) + 0.80(9.99%) = 8.93%.

2. Total value of the firm.

Solution:

Exhibit 16 displays the projected FCFF for the next eight years and the present value of each FCFF discounted at 8.93%:

Exhibit 16: Forecasted FCFF for Reliant Home Furnishings

	Year							
	1	2	3	4	5	6	7	8
Growth rate	8.80%	8.80%	8.80%	8.80%	7.40%	6.00%	4.60%	3.20%
FCFF	811	882	959	1,044	1,121	1,188	1,243	1,283
PV at 8.93%	744	743	742	741	731	711	683	

The terminal value at the end of Year 7 is

$$TV_7 = \frac{FCFF_8}{WACC - g} = \frac{1,283}{0.0893 - 0.032} = \$22,391 \text{ million.}$$

The present value of this amount discounted at 8.93% for seven years is

$$\text{PV of } TV_7 = \frac{22,391}{(1.0893)^7} = \$12,304 \text{ million.}$$

The total present value of the first seven years of FCFF is $5,097 million. The total value of the firm is 12,304 + 5,097 = $17,401 million.

3. Total value of equity.

Solution:

The value of equity is the value of the firm minus the market value of debt:

17,401 – 1,518 = $15,883 million.

4. Value per share.

Solution:

Dividing the equity value by the number of shares yields the value per share:

$15,883 million/309.39 million = $51.34.

13 INTEGRATING ESG IN FREE CASH FLOW MODELS

- ☐ explain the single-stage (stable-growth), two-stage, and three-stage FCFF and FCFE models and justify the selection of the appropriate model given a company's characteristics
- ☐ estimate a company's value using the appropriate free cash flow model(s)
- ☐ describe approaches for calculating the terminal value in a multistage valuation model; and
- ☐ evaluate whether a stock is overvalued, fairly valued, or undervalued based on a free cash flow valuation model

Integrating environmental, social, and governance (ESG) considerations in valuation models can have a material impact on valuation. ESG factors may be either quantitative or qualitative. Quantitative ESG-related information, such as the effect of a projected environmental fine on cash flows, is more straightforward to integrate in valuation models. By contrast, qualitative ESG-related information is more challenging to integrate. One approach to address this challenge is to adjust the cost of equity by adding a risk premium in a valuation model. This approach can estimate the effect of ESG-related issues that are deemed material by an analyst but are difficult to quantify. When making an adjustment to the cost of equity by adding a risk premium, the analyst relies on his or her judgment to determine what value constitutes a reasonable adjustment. Example 19 provides a case study of how an analyst may develop a multistage (three-stage, in this case) FCFF valuation model that integrates ESG considerations.

EXAMPLE 19

Integrating ESG in a Three-Stage FCFF Model

American Copper Mining Company (ACMC) is a large US-based company. Copper has many uses in manufacturing, building, and other industries. The mining of copper is resource-intensive and is highly regulated.

ACMC recently announced that it is acquiring a new copper mine in a very dry region of Latin America. After the announcement, the market welcomed the news, and ACMC's share price rose to its current level of US$110 per share. The company expects the new mine to have a useful life of approximately 15 years.

Jane Dodd is a research analyst who follows ACMC and has a "hold" rating on its shares. She is preparing a new report to determine whether ACMC's acquisition of the new copper mine changes her fundamental assessment of the company. Overall, Dodd believes that the evaluation of ESG considerations can provide critical insights into the feasibility, economics, and valuation of mining companies and mining projects.

Dodd begins her analysis by evaluating the current political, labor, and environmental situation for ACMC's new mine. She has identified three primary ESG considerations that, in her opinion, may have the greatest effects on the value of the new mine and the company:

1. Local government issues
2. Labor issues
3. Water-related issues

Dodd then assesses how each of these ESG considerations may affect ACMC's operations and cash flow.

1. *Local government issues*: To operate the new mine, ACMC must obtain a mining license from the local government in the region where the mine is located. Before obtaining the mining license, ACMC is required to submit a comprehensive rehabilitation plan indicating how the new mine's natural habitat will be restored. Dodd notices that in its other mining sites, ACMC has struggled to produce comprehensive rehabilitation plans that have been approved by government authorities in a timely manner. She concludes that ACMC is overly optimistic about the time required to get approval for the mining license. She expects that rather than three years, as management anticipates, it will likely take five years before the mine can begin operating.
2. *Labor issues*: ACMC's compensation of its employees is slightly lower than its competitors in the region of the new mine. In addition, unlike many of its competitors, ACMC does not tie executive compensation to worker safety. Some competitors in the region have experienced labor strikes (and thus production interruptions) because their employees' wages are not adjusted for inflation. Because of ACMC's compensation policies, Dodd is concerned about the potential for labor unrest and subsequent reputational risk for the company.
3. *Water-related issues*: Because a large volume of water is used for mining operations, water-related costs are typically among the largest expenditures for mining companies. Given that the development of the new mine is located in a very dry region of Latin America, Dodd believes that ACMC has significantly underestimated the required capital expenditures necessary to build water wells.

Valuation Analysis

After identifying and assessing these ESG considerations, Dodd proceeds to value ACMC's share price using a three-stage FCFF model. The three stages are as follows:

- Stage 1: the period prior to expected operation of the new mine (2020–2024)
- Stage 2: the period during expected operation of the new mine (2025–2039)
- Stage 3: the period subsequent to the expected closing of the mine (2040 and onward)

Dodd makes the following assumptions in her model.

Revenues

ACMC's total revenues during 2020 were $1 billion. Dodd expects total revenues (i.e., excluding those of the new mine) to increase 2% annually through 2024 and then remain constant during 2025–2039, when the new mine operates. When the new mine begins operations under Dodd's assumption (in 2025), Dodd expects the mine to add US$400 million to ACMC's revenues in its first year. Dodd also expects that these additional revenues from the new mine will increase by 10% annually for the next six years (2026 through 2031) and then remain constant for the remaining life of the mine (2032 through 2039). Dodd assumes that once the new mine closes in 2039, the company's total revenues will grow by 1% in perpetuity. The following is a summary of revenues for the three stages:

Stage 1 (prior to expected operation of mine):

Years 2020–2024: annual total revenue growth of 2%

Stage 2 (during expected operation of new mine):

2025: constant growth of revenues excluding the new mine; additional revenue of US$400 million from new mine

2026–2039: constant growth of revenues excluding new mine during years 2026–2039); 10% annual growth of revenue from new mine during years 2026–2031; constant growth of revenues from new mine during years 2032–2039

Stage 3 (after expected closing of new mine):

2040 and beyond: annual total revenue growth of 1%

Dodd also makes the following financial assumptions for ACMC:

EBITDA:	30% of total revenues for all three stages
Taxes:	25%
Investment in fixed capital (not including water-related investments):	50% of EBITDA for all three stages
Depreciation:	40% of capital expenditures for all three stages
Investment in working capital:	10% of total revenue for all three stages
Required return (pretax) on ACMC debt:	5%
Risk-free rate:	3%
ACMC equity beta:	1.2
Equity risk premium:	5%
Debt ratio:	50%

In addition to these "traditional" financial assumptions, Dodd also reflects ESG considerations in her analysis.

Water-related investment in fixed capital

10% of non-water-related capital expenditures, which are added to the capital expenditures noted previously.

ESG equity risk premium adjustment

Dodd concludes that the potential for labor issues discussed earlier exposes ACMC to higher financial and reputational risk compared to its peers. Dodd further believes that the ESG considerations she has identified are not recognized fully in the market price of ACMC shares. As a result, Dodd estimates that a 75 basis point premium should be added to ACMC's cost of equity.

Dodd calculates the WACC as follows:

Cost of debt = (5%)(1 – 25%) = 3.75%.

Cost of equity = 3% + (1.2)(5%) + 0.75% ESG equity risk premium adjustment = 9.75%.

WACC = (0.5)(3.75%) + (0.5)(9.75%) = 6.75%.

Exhibit 17 presents the results of Dodd's model for valuing ACMC's equity. Dodd's analysis suggests that the fair value for ACMC's equity is $97 per share. By integrating ESG considerations in a traditional valuation framework, Dodd's estimate of the fair value of ACMC's shares decreased. Given that the stock is trading at US$110, she issues a "sell" recommendation for ACMC's shares.

The next section discusses an important technical issue, the treatment of non-operating assets in valuation.

NON-OPERATING ASSETS AND FIRM VALUE

14

- [ ] estimate a company's value using the appropriate free cash flow model(s)

Free cash flow valuation focuses on the value of assets that generate or are needed to generate operating cash flows. If a company has significant non-operating assets, such as excess cash (excess in relation to what is needed for generating operating cash flows), excess marketable securities, or land held for investment, then analysts often calculate the value of the firm as the value of its operating assets (e.g., as estimated by FCFF valuation) plus the value of its non-operating assets:

$$\text{Value of firm} = \text{Value of operating assets} + \text{Value of nonoperating assets.} \tag{18}$$

In general, if any company asset is excluded from the set of assets being considered in projecting a company's future cash flows, the analyst should add that omitted asset's estimated value to the cash flow–based value estimate. Some companies have substantial noncurrent investments in stocks and bonds that are not operating subsidiaries but, rather, financial investments. These investments should be reflected at their current market value. Those securities reported at book values on the basis of accounting conventions should be revalued to market values.

SUMMARY

Discounted cash flow models are widely used by analysts to value companies.

- Free cash flow to the firm (FCFF) and free cash flow to equity (FCFE) are the cash flows available to, respectively, all of the investors in the company and to common stockholders.
- Analysts like to use free cash flow (either FCFF or FCFE) as the return
    - if the company is not paying dividends;
    - if the company pays dividends but the dividends paid differ significantly from the company's capacity to pay dividends;
    - if free cash flows align with profitability within a reasonable forecast period with which the analyst is comfortable; or
    - if the investor takes a control perspective.

Exhibit 17: Estimating Fair Value of ACMC Shares (in Millions of US Dollars, Except for Per-Share Items)

						Expected Operation of New Mine								Expected Closing of Mine	
	2020	2021	2022	2023	2024	2025	2026	2027	...	2030	2031	...	2034	2035	2036
Total revenues	1,000	1,020	1,040	1,061	1,082	1,482	1,522	1,566	...	1,727	1,791	...	1,791	1,791	1,809
Revenues from new mine only						400.0	440.0	484.0		644.2	708.6		708.6	708.6	
EBITDA	300.0	306.0	312.1	318.4	324.7	444.7	456.7	469.9	...	518.0	537.3	...	537.3	537.3	542.7
EBITDA(1 – Tax rate)	225.0	229.5	234.1	238.8	243.5	333.5	342.5	352.4		388.5	403.0		403.0	403.0	407.0
Depreciation(Tax rate)	15.0	15.3	15.6	15.9	16.2	22.2	22.8	23.5	...	25.9	26.9	...	26.9	26.9	27.1
Investment in fixed capital, or FCInv	(150.0)	(153.0)	(156.1)	(159.2)	(162.4)	(222.4)	(228.4)	(235.0)	...	(259.0)	(268.7)	...	(268.7)	(268.7)	(271.3)
Investment in working capital, or WCInv*	(2.0)	(2.0)	(2.0)	(2.1)	(2.1)	(40.0)	(4.0)	(4.4)		(5.9)	(6.4)		0.0	0.0	(1.8)
Additional FCInv (water-related)	—	—	—	—	—	(22.2)	(22.8)	(23.5)	...	(25.9)	(26.9)	...	(26.9)	(26.9)	
FCFF	**88.0**	**89.8**	**91.6**	**93.4**	**95.3**	**71.2**	**110.2**	**113.1**	...	**123.6**	**127.9**	...	**134.3**	**134.3**	**161.0**
PV of FCFF up to 2039 (@ WACC of 6.75%)	82.5	78.8	75.3	71.9	68.7	48.1	69.7	67.1	...	60.3	58.4	...	38.8	36.4	
PV of FCFF Years 2016–2035	1,178														
PV of perpetual FCFF 2036 onward	758														
Total PV of future FCFF	**1,936**														
Market value of debt (50% debt ratio)	968														
Fair value of equity	968														
Fair value per share (10 million shares outstanding)	97														

Supplemental items:

					Expected Operation of New Mine								Expected Closing of Mine	
Depreciation	60.0	61.2	62.4	63.7	65.0	89.0	91.4	94.0	103.6	107.5	...	107.5	107.5	63.7
Working capital	100.0	102.0	104.0	106.1	108.2	148.2	152.2	156.6	172.7	179.1	...	179.1	179.1	180.9

Note: The 2020 investment in working capital (WCInv) reflects the change in working capital from 2019 to 2020. For simplicity, Dodd uses the same change in WCInv for 2020 as in 2021.

- The FCFF valuation approach estimates the value of the firm as the present value of future FCFF discounted at the weighted average cost of capital:

$$\text{Firm value} = \sum_{t=1}^{\infty} \frac{\text{FCFF}_t}{(1+\text{WACC})^t}.$$

The value of equity is the value of the firm minus the value of the firm's debt:

Equity value = Firm value – Market value of debt.

Dividing the total value of equity by the number of outstanding shares gives the value per share.

The WACC formula is

$$\text{WACC} = \frac{\text{MV(Debt)}}{\text{MV(Debt)} + \text{MV(Equity)}} r_d (1 - \text{Tax rate}) + \frac{\text{MV(Equity)}}{\text{MV(Debt)} + \text{MV(Equity)}} r.$$

- The value of the firm if FCFF is growing at a constant rate is

$$\text{Firm value} = \frac{\text{FCFF}_1}{\text{WACC} - g} = \frac{\text{FCFF}_0(1+g)}{\text{WACC} - g}.$$

- With the FCFE valuation approach, the value of equity can be found by discounting FCFE at the required rate of return on equity, r:

$$\text{Equity value} = \sum_{t=1}^{\infty} \frac{\text{FCFE}_t}{(1+r)^t}.$$

Dividing the total value of equity by the number of outstanding shares gives the value per share.

- The value of equity if FCFE is growing at a constant rate is

$$\text{Equity value} = \frac{\text{FCFE}_1}{r - g} = \frac{\text{FCFE}_0(1+g)}{r - g}.$$

- FCFF and FCFE are frequently calculated by starting with net income:

FCFF = NI + NCC + Int(1 – Tax rate) – FCInv – WCInv.

FCFE = NI + NCC – FCInv – WCInv + Net borrowing.

- FCFF and FCFE are related to each other as follows:

FCFE = FCFF – Int(1 – Tax rate) + Net borrowing.

- FCFF and FCFE can be calculated by starting from cash flow from operations:

FCFF = CFO + Int(1 – Tax rate) – FCInv.

FCFE = CFO – FCInv + Net borrowing.

- FCFF can also be calculated from EBIT or EBITDA:

FCFF = EBIT(1 – Tax rate) + Dep – FCInv – WCInv.

FCFF = EBITDA(1 – Tax rate) + Dep(Tax rate) – FCInv – WCInv.

FCFE can then be found by using FCFE = FCFF – Int(1 – Tax rate) + Net borrowing.

- Finding CFO, FCFF, and FCFE may require careful interpretation of corporate financial statements. In some cases, the necessary information may not be transparent.
- Earnings components such as net income, EBIT, EBITDA, and CFO should not be used as cash flow measures to value a firm. These earnings components either double-count or ignore parts of the cash flow stream.
- FCFF or FCFE valuation expressions can be easily adapted to accommodate complicated capital structures, such as those that include preferred stock.
- A general expression for the two-stage FCFF valuation model is

$$\text{Firm value} = \sum_{t=1}^{n} \frac{\text{FCFF}_t}{(1 + \text{WACC})^t} + \frac{\text{FCFF}_{n+1}}{(\text{WACC} - g)} \frac{1}{(1 + \text{WACC})^n}.$$

- A general expression for the two-stage FCFE valuation model is

$$\text{Equity value} = \sum_{t=1}^{n} \frac{\text{FCFE}_t}{(1 + r)^t} + \left(\frac{\text{FCFE}_{n+1}}{r - g}\right) \left[\frac{1}{(1 + r)^n}\right].$$

- One common two-stage model assumes a constant growth rate in each stage, and a second common model assumes declining growth in Stage 1 followed by a long-run sustainable growth rate in Stage 2.
- To forecast FCFF and FCFE, analysts build a variety of models of varying complexity. A common approach is to forecast sales, with profitability, investments, and financing derived from changes in sales.
- Three-stage models are often considered to be good approximations for cash flow streams that, in reality, fluctuate from year to year.
- Non-operating assets, such as excess cash and marketable securities, noncurrent investment securities, and nonperforming assets, are usually segregated from the company's operating assets. They are valued separately and then added to the value of the company's operating assets to find total firm value.

REFERENCES

Bahnson, P., P. B. Miller, and B. P. Budge. 1996. "Nonarticulation in Cash Flow Statements and Implications for Education, Research and Practice." *Accounting Horizons* 10 (4): 1–15.

Casey, Ryan J., Feng Gao, Michael T. Kirschenheiter, Siyi Li, and Shailendra Pandit. 2016. "Do Compustat Financial Statement Data Articulate?" *Journal of Financial Reporting* 1 (1): 37–59. 10.2308/jfir-51329

Gordon, Elizabeth A., Elaine Henry, Bjorn N. Jorgensen, and Cheryl L. Linthicum. 2017. "Flexibility in Cash-Flow Classification under IFRS: Determinants and Consequences." *Review of Accounting Studies* 22 (2): 839–72. 10.1007/s11142-017-9387-1

Hribar, P. and D. W. Collins. 2002. "Errors in Estimating Accruals: Implications for Empirical Research." *Journal of Accounting Research* 40 (1): 105–34. 10.1111/1475-679X.00041

Huefner, R. J., J. E. Ketz, and J. A. Largay. 1989. "Foreign Currency Translation and the Cash Flow Statement." *Accounting Horizons* 3 (2): 66–75.

Luehrman, T. A. 1997. "Using APV (Adjusted Present Value): A Better Tool for Valuing Operations." *Harvard Business Review* 75 (3): 145–46, 148, 150–54.

Pinto, Jerald E., Thomas R. Robinson, and John D. Stowe. 2019. "Equity Valuation: A Survey of Professional Practice." *Review of Financial Economics* 37 (2): 219–33. 10.1002/rfe.1040

Shi, Linna and Huai Zhang. 2011. "On Alternative Measures of Accruals." *Accounting Horizons* 25 (4): 811–36. 10.2308/acch-50050

Wilkins, M. S. and M. L. Loudder. 2000. "Articulation in Cash Flow Statements: A Resource for Financial Accounting Courses." *Journal of Accounting Education* 18:115–26. 10.1016/S0748-5751(00)00007-5

PRACTICE PROBLEMS

The following information relates to questions 1-2

Shimotsuke Co. LTD. has FCFF of 1.7 billion Japanese yen (JPY) and FCFE of JPY1.3 billion. Shimotsuke Co.'s WACC is 11%, and its required rate of return for equity is 13%. FCFF is expected to grow forever at 7%, and FCFE is expected to grow forever at 7.5%. Shimotsuke Co. has debt outstanding of JPY15 billion.

1. What is the total value of Shimotsuke Co.'s equity using the FCFF valuation approach?

2. What is the total value of Shimotsuke Co.'s equity using the FCFE valuation approach?

The following information relates to questions 3-6

Elina Kuznetsova is planning to value BCC Corporation, a provider of a variety of industrial metals and minerals. Kuznetsova uses a single-stage FCFF approach. The financial information Kuznetsova has assembled for her valuation is as follows:

- The company has 1,852 million shares outstanding.
- The market value of its debt is $3.192 billion.
- The FCFF is currently $1.1559 billion.
- The equity beta is 0.90; the equity risk premium is 5.5%; the risk-free rate is 5.5%.
- The before-tax cost of debt is 7.0%.
- The tax rate is 40%.
- To calculate WACC, he will assume the company is financed 25% with debt.
- The FCFF growth rate is 4%.

Using Kuznetsova's information, calculate the following:

3. WACC.

4. Value of the firm.

5. Total market value of equity.

6. Value per share.

The following information relates to questions 7-13

Yandie Izzo manages a dividend growth strategy for a large asset management firm. Izzo meets with her investment team to discuss potential investments in three companies: Company A, Company B, and Company C. Statements of cash flow for the three companies are presented in Exhibit 1.

Exhibit 1: Statements of Cash Flow, Most Recent Fiscal Year End (Amounts in Millions of Dollars)

	Company A	Company B	Company C
Cash Flow from Operating Activities			
Net Income	4,844	1,212	15,409
Adjustments			
Depreciation	500	288	3,746
Other noncash expenses	1,000	—	—
Changes in working capital			
(Increase) Decrease accounts receivable	(452)	(150)	(536)
(Increase) Decrease inventories	—	(200)	(803)
Increase (Decrease) accounts payable	(210)	100	(3)
Increase (Decrease) other current liabilities	540	14	350
Net cash from operating activities	6,222	1,264	18,163
Cash Flow from Investing Activities			
(Purchase) Sale of fixed assets	2,379	(1,000)	(3,463)
Net cash from investing activities	2,379	(1,000)	(3,463)
Cash Flow from Financing Activities			
Increase (Decrease) notes payable	25	3000	1,238
Increase (Decrease) long-term debt	(1,500)	(1,000)	(1,379)
Payment of common stock dividends	(1,000)	(237)	(15,000)
Net cash from financing activities	(2,475)	1,763	(15,141)
Net change in cash and cash equivalents	6,126	2,027	(441)
Cash and equivalents at beginning of year	50	100	3,000
Cash and equivalents at end of year	6,176	2,127	2,559
Supplemental Cash Flow Disclosures			
Interest	(353)	(50)	(552)
Income taxes	(1,605)	(648)	(3,787)

Izzo's team first discusses key characteristics of Company A. The company has a history of paying modest dividends relative to FCFE, has a stable capital structure, and is owned by a controlling investor.

The team also considers the impact of Company A's three noncash transactions in the most recent year on its FCFE, including the following:

Transaction 1: A $900 million loss on a sale of equipment

Transaction 2: An impairment of intangibles of $400 million

Transaction 3: A $300 million reversal of a previously recorded restructuring charge

In addition, Company A's annual report indicates that the firm expects to incur additional noncash charges related to restructuring over the next few years.

To value the three companies' shares, one team member suggests valuing the companies' shares using net income as a proxy for FCFE. Another team member proposes forecasting FCFE using a sales-based methodology based on the following equation:

FCFE = NI – (1 – DR)(FCInv – Dep) – (1 – DR)(WCInv).

Izzo's team ultimately decides to use actual free cash flow to value the three companies' shares. Selected data and assumptions are provided in Exhibit 2.

Exhibit 2: Supplemental Data and Valuation Assumptions

	Company A	Company B	Company C
Tax rate	35%	35%	30%
Beta	1.00	0.90	1.10
Before-tax cost of debt	6%	7%	6%
Target debt ratio	50%	30%	40%
Market data:			
Risk-free rate: 3%			
Market risk premium: 7%			

The team calculates the intrinsic value of Company B using a two-stage FCFE model. FCFE growth rates for the first four years are estimated at 10%, 9%, 8%, and 7%, respectively, before declining to a constant 6% starting in the fifth year.

To calculate the intrinsic value of Company C's equity, the team uses the FCFF approach assuming a single-stage model where FCFF is expected to grow at 5% indefinitely.

7. Based on Company A's key characteristics, which discounted cash flow model would *most likely* be used by the investment team to value Company A's shares?

   A. DDM

   B. FCFE

   C. FCFF

8. Which noncash transaction should be subtracted from net income in arriving at Company A's FCFE?

   A. Transaction 1

   B. Transaction 2

   C. Transaction 3

9. Based on Exhibit 1, Company A's FCFE for the most recent year is *closest* to:

   A. $5,318 million.

   B. $6,126 million.

C. $7,126 million.

10. Based on Exhibit 1, using net income as a proxy for Company B's FCFE would result in an intrinsic value that is:

A. lower than the intrinsic value if actual FCFE were used.

B. equal to the intrinsic value if actual FCFE were used.

C. higher than the intrinsic value if actual FCFE were used.

11. Based on Exhibit 1, using the proposed sales-based methodology to forecast FCFE would produce an inaccurate FCFE projection for which company?

A. Company A

B. Company B

C. Company C

12. Based on Exhibit 1 and Exhibit 2 and the proposed two-stage FCFE model, the intrinsic value of Company B's equity is *closest* to:

A. $70,602 million.

B. $73,588 million.

C. $79,596 million.

13. Based on Exhibit 1 and Exhibit 2 and the proposed single-stage FCFF model, the intrinsic value of Company C's equity is *closest* to:

A. $277,907 million.

B. $295,876 million.

C. $306,595 million.

The following information relates to questions 14-15

The term "free cash flow" is frequently applied to cash flows that differ from the definition for FCFF that should be used to value a firm. Two such definitions of free cash flow are given below. Compare these two definitions for free cash flow with the technically correct definition of FCFF used in our coverage of the topic.

14. FCF = Net income + Depreciation and amortization – Cash dividends – Capital expenditures.

15. FCF = Cash flow from operations (from the statement of cash flows) – Capital expenditures.

The following information relates to questions 16-18

LaForge Systems, Inc., has net income of $285 million for the year 2020.

LaForge Systems, Inc., Balance Sheet (in Millions)

Years Ended 31 December	2019	2020
Assets		
Current assets		
Cash and equivalents	$210	$248
Accounts receivable	474	513
Inventory	520	564
Total current assets	1,204	1,325
Gross fixed assets	2,501	2,850
Accumulated depreciation	(604)	(784)
Net fixed assets	1,897	2,066
Total assets	$3,101	$3,391
Liabilities and shareholders' equity		
Current liabilities		
Accounts payable	$295	$317
Notes payable	300	310
Accrued taxes and expenses	76	99
Total current liabilities	671	726
Long-term debt	1,010	1,050
Common stock	50	50
Additional paid-in capital	300	300
Retained earnings	1,070	1,265
Total shareholders' equity	1,420	1,615
Total liabilities and shareholders' equity	$3,101	$3,391

Statement of Income In Millions, except Per-Share Data	31 December 2020
Total revenues	$2,215
Operating costs and expenses	1,430
EBITDA	785
Depreciation	180
EBIT	605
Interest expense	130
Income before tax	475
Taxes (at 40%)	190
Net income	285
Dividends	90

Statement of Income In Millions, except Per-Share Data	31 December 2020
Addition to retained earnings	195

Statement of Cash Flows In Millions	31 December 2020
Operating activities	
Net income	$285
Adjustments	
Depreciation	180
Changes in working capital	
Accounts receivable	(39)
Inventories	(44)
Accounts payable	22
Accrued taxes and expenses	23
Cash provided by operating activities	$427
Investing activities	
Purchases of fixed assets	349
Cash used for investing activities	$349
Financing activities	
Notes payable	$(10)
Long-term financing issuances	(40)
Common stock dividends	90
Cash used for financing activities	$40
Cash and equivalents increase (decrease)	38
Cash and equivalents at beginning of year	210
Cash and equivalents at end of year	$248
Supplemental cash flow disclosures	
Interest paid	$130
Income taxes paid	$190

Note: The statement of cash flows shows the use of a convention by which the positive numbers of $349 and $40 for cash used for investing activities and cash used for financing activities, respectively, are understood to be subtractions, because "cash used" is an outflow.

Using information from the company's financial statements given here, show the adjustments to net income that would be required to find:

16. FCFF.

17. FCFE.

18. In addition, show the adjustments to FCFF that would result in FCFE.

The following information relates to questions 19-20

Do Pham is evaluating Phaneuf Accelerateur by using the FCFF and FCFE valuation approaches. Pham has collected the following information (currency in euros):

- Phaneuf has net income of €250 million, depreciation of €90 million, capital expenditures of €170 million, and an increase in working capital of €40 million.
- Phaneuf will finance 40% of the increase in net fixed assets (capital expenditures less depreciation) and 40% of the increase in working capital with debt financing.
- Interest expenses are €150 million. The current market value of Phaneuf's outstanding debt is €1,800 million.
- FCFF is expected to grow at 6.0% indefinitely, and FCFE is expected to grow at 7.0%.
- The tax rate is 30%.
- Phaneuf is financed with 40% debt and 60% equity. The before-tax cost of debt is 9%, and the before-tax cost of equity is 13%.
- Phaneuf has 10 million outstanding shares.

19. Using the FCFF valuation approach, estimate the total value of the firm, the total market value of equity, and the per-share value of equity.

20. Using the FCFE valuation approach, estimate the total market value of equity and the per-share value of equity.

The following information relates to questions 21-22

LaForge Systems, Inc., Balance Sheet (in Millions)

Years Ended 31 December	2019	2020
Assets		
Current assets		
Cash and equivalents	$210	$248
Accounts receivable	474	513
Inventory	520	564
Total current assets	1,204	1,325
Gross fixed assets	2,501	2,850
Accumulated depreciation	(604)	(784)
Net fixed assets	1,897	2,066
Total assets	$3,101	$3,391

Years Ended 31 December	2019	2020
Liabilities and shareholders' equity		
Current liabilities		
Accounts payable	$295	$317
Notes payable	300	310
Accrued taxes and expenses	76	99
Total current liabilities	671	726
Long-term debt	1,010	1,050
Common stock	50	50
Additional paid-in capital	300	300
Retained earnings	1,070	1,265
Total shareholders' equity	1,420	1,615
Total liabilities and shareholders' equity	$3,101	$3,391

Statement of Income In Millions, except Per-Share Data	31 December 2020
Total revenues	$2,215
Operating costs and expenses	1,430
EBITDA	785
Depreciation	180
EBIT	605
Interest expense	130
Income before tax	475
Taxes (at 40%)	190
Net income	285
Dividends	90
Addition to retained earnings	195

Statement of Cash Flows In Millions	31 December 2020
Operating activities	
Net income	$285
Adjustments	
Depreciation	180
Changes in working capital	
Accounts receivable	(39)
Inventories	(44)
Accounts payable	22
Accrued taxes and expenses	23
Cash provided by operating activities	$427
Investing activities	
Purchases of fixed assets	349

Statement of Cash Flows In Millions	31 December 2020
Cash used for investing activities	$349
Financing activities	
Notes payable	$(10)
Long-term financing issuances	(40)
Common stock dividends	90
Cash used for financing activities	$40
Cash and equivalents increase (decrease)	38
Cash and equivalents at beginning of year	210
Cash and equivalents at end of year	$248
Supplemental cash flow disclosures	
Interest paid	$130
Income taxes paid	$190

Note: The statement of cash flows shows the use of a convention by which the positive numbers of $349 and $40 for cash used for investing activities and cash used for financing activities, respectively, are understood to be subtractions, because "cash used" is an outflow.

For LaForge Systems, whose financial statements are given in Problem 2, show the adjustments from the current levels of CFO (which is $427 million), EBIT ($605 million), and EBITDA ($785 million) to find:

21. FCFF.

22. FCFE.

The following information relates to questions 23-28

Ryan Leigh is preparing a presentation that analyzes the valuation of the common stock of two companies under consideration as additions to his firm's recommended list, Emerald Corporation and Holt Corporation. Leigh has prepared preliminary valuations of both companies using an FCFE model and is also preparing a value estimate for Emerald using a dividend discount model. Holt's 2019 and 2020 financial statements, contained in Exhibit 1 and Exhibit 2, are prepared in accordance with US GAAP.

Exhibit 1: Holt Corporation Consolidated Balance Sheets (US$ Millions)

	As of 31 December	
	2020	2019
Assets		
Current assets		
Cash and cash equivalents	$ 372	$ 315
Accounts receivable	770	711

Inventories		846		780
Total current assets		1,988		1,806
Gross fixed assets	4,275		3,752	
Less: Accumulated depreciation	1,176	3,099	906	2,846
Total assets		$5,087		$4,652
Liabilities and shareholders' equity				
Current liabilities				
Accounts payable		$ 476		$ 443
Accrued taxes and expenses		149		114
Notes payable		465		450
Total current liabilities		1,090		1,007
Long-term debt		1,575		1,515
Common stock		525		525
Retained earnings		1,897		1,605
Total liabilities and shareholders' equity		$5,087		$4,652

Exhibit 2: Holt Corporation Consolidated Income Statement for the Year Ended 31 December 2020 (US$ Millions)

Total revenues	$3,323
Cost of goods sold	1,287
Selling, general, and administrative expenses	858
Earnings before interest, taxes, depreciation, and amortization (EBITDA)	1,178
Depreciation expense	270
Operating income	908
Interest expense	195
Pretax income	713
Income tax (at 32%)	228
Net income	$ 485

Leigh presents his valuations of the common stock of Emerald and Holt to his supervisor, Alice Smith. Smith has the following questions and comments:

1. "I estimate that Emerald's long-term expected dividend payout rate is 20% and its return on equity is 10% over the long term."
2. "Why did you use an FCFE model to value Holt's common stock? Can you use a DDM instead?"
3. "How did Holt's FCFE for 2008 compare with its FCFF for the same year? I recommend you use an FCFF model to value Holt's common stock instead of using an FCFE model because Holt has had a history of leverage changes in the past."
4. "In the last three years, about 5% of Holt's growth in FCFE has come from decreases in inventory."

Leigh responds to each of Smith's points as follows:

1. "I will use your estimates and calculate Emerald's long-term, sustainable dividend growth rate."

2. "There are two reasons why I used the FCFE model to value Holt's common stock instead of using a DDM. The first reason is that Holt's dividends have differed significantly from its capacity to pay dividends. The second reason is that Holt is a takeover target and once the company is taken over, the new owners will have discretion over the uses of free cash flow."
3. "I will calculate Holt's FCFF for 2020 and estimate the value of Holt's common stock using an FCFF model."
4. "Holt is a growing company. In forecasting either Holt's FCFE or FCFF growth rates, I will not consider decreases in inventory to be a long-term source of growth."

23. Which of the following long-term FCFE growth rates is *most* consistent with the facts and stated policies of Emerald?

    A. 5% or lower

    B. 2% or higher

    C. 8% or higher

24. Do the reasons provided by Leigh support his use of the FCFE model to value Holt's common stock instead of using a DDM?

    A. Yes

    B. No, because Holt's dividend situation argues in favor of using the DDM

    C. No, because FCFE is not appropriate for investors taking a control perspective

25. Holt's FCFF (in millions) for 2020 is *closest* to:

    A. \$308.

    B. \$370.

    C. \$422.

26. Holt's FCFE (in millions) for 2020 is *closest* to:

    A. \$175.

    B. \$250.

    C. \$364.

27. Leigh's comment about not considering decreases in inventory to be a source of long-term growth in free cash flow for Holt is:

    A. inconsistent with a forecasting perspective.

    B. mistaken because decreases in inventory are a use rather than a source of cash.

    C. consistent with a forecasting perspective because inventory reduction has a limit, particularly for a growing firm.

28. Smith's recommendation to use an FCFF model to value Holt is:
    - **A.** logical, given the prospect of Holt changing capital structure.
    - **B.** not logical because an FCFF model is used only to value the total firm.
    - **C.** not logical because FCFE represents a more direct approach to free cash flow valuation.

---

29. Indicate the effect on this period's FCFF and FCFE of a change in each of the items listed here. Assume a $100 increase in each case and a 40% tax rate.
    - **A.** Net income.
    - **B.** Cash operating expenses.
    - **C.** Depreciation.
    - **D.** Interest expense.
    - **E.** EBIT.
    - **F.** Accounts receivable.
    - **G.** Accounts payable.
    - **H.** Property, plant, and equipment.
    - **I.** Notes payable.
    - **J.** Cash dividends paid.
    - **K.** Proceeds from issuing new common shares.
    - **L.** Common shares repurchased.

The following information relates to questions 30-32

The management of Telluride, an international diversified conglomerate, believes that the recent strong performance of its wholly owned medical supply subsidiary, Sundanci, has gone unnoticed. To realize Sundanci's full value, Telluride has announced that it will divest Sundanci in a tax-free spin-off.

Sue Carroll is director of research at Kesson and Associates. In developing an investment recommendation for Sundanci, Carroll has gathered the information shown in Exhibit 1 and Exhibit 2.

Exhibit 1: Sundanci Actual 2019 and 2020 Financial Statements for Fiscal Years Ending 31 May (Dollars in Millions except Per-Share Data)

Income Statement	2019	2020
Revenue	$474	$598
Depreciation	20	23
Other operating costs	368	460
Income before taxes	86	115
Taxes	26	35

Income Statement	2019	2020
Net income	60	80
Dividends	18	24
EPS	$0.714	$0.952
Dividends per share	$0.214	$0.286
Common shares outstanding	84.0	84.0

Balance Sheet	2019	2020
Current assets (includes $5 cash in 2019 and 2020)	$201	$326
Net property, plant, and equipment	474	489
Total assets	675	815
Current liabilities (all non-interest-bearing)	57	141
Long-term debt	0	0
Total liabilities	57	141
Shareholders' equity	618	674
Total liabilities and equity	675	815
Capital expenditures	34	38

Exhibit 2: Selected Financial Information

Required rate of return on equity	14%
Industry growth rate	13%
Industry P/E	26

Abbey Naylor has been directed by Carroll to determine the value of Sundanci's stock by using the FCFE model. Naylor believes that Sundanci's FCFE will grow at 27% for two years and at 13% thereafter. Capital expenditures, depreciation, and working capital are all expected to increase proportionately with FCFE.

30. Calculate the amount of FCFE per share for 2020 by using the data from Exhibit 1.

31. Calculate the current value of a share of Sundanci stock based on the two-stage FCFE model.

32. Describe limitations that the two-stage DDM and FCFE models have in common.

The following information relates to questions 33-38

Gurmeet Singh, an equity portfolio manager at a wealth management company, meets with junior research analyst Cindy Ho to discuss potential investments in three companies: Sienna Limited, Colanari Manufacturing, and Bern Pharmaceutical.

Singh and Ho review key financial data from Sienna's most recent annual report, which are presented in Exhibit 1 and Exhibit 2, to assess the company's ability to generate free cash flow.

Exhibit 1: Selected Data from Sienna Limited's Statement of Income for the Year Ended 31 December 2019 (Amounts in Millions of Euros)

EBITDA	4,000
Depreciation expense	800
Operating income (EBIT)	3,200
Interest expense	440
Tax rate	35%

Exhibit 2: Sienna Limited's Statement of Cash Flows for the Year Ended 31 December 2019 (Amounts in Millions of Euros)

Cash flow from operations	
Net income	1,794
Plus: Depreciation	800
Increase in accounts receivable	(2,000)
Increase in inventory	(200)
Increase in accounts payable	1,000
Cash flow from operations	1,394
Cash flow from investing activities	
Purchases of PP&E	(1,000)
Cash flow from financing activities	
Borrowing (repayment)	500
Total cash flow	894

Singh and Ho also discuss the impact of dividends, share repurchases, and leverage on Sienna's free cash flow. Ho tells Singh the following:

Statement 1 Changes in leverage do not impact free cash flow to equity.

Statement 2 Transactions between the company and its shareholders, such as the payment of dividends or share repurchases, do affect free cash flow.

Singh and Ho next analyze Colanari. Last year, Colanari had FCFF of €140 million. Singh instructs Ho to perform an FCFF sensitivity analysis of Colanari's firm value using the three sets of estimates presented in Exhibit 3. In her analysis, Ho assumes a tax rate of 35% and a stable capital structure of 30% debt and 70% equity.

Exhibit 3: Sensitivity Analysis for Colanari Valuation

Variable	Base-Case Estimate	Low Estimate	High Estimate
FCFF growth rate	4.6%	4.2%	5.0%
Before-tax cost of debt	4.9%	3.9%	5.9%
Cost of equity	11.0%	10.0%	12.0%

Finally, Singh and Ho analyze Bern. Selected financial information on Bern is presented in Exhibit 4.

Exhibit 4: Selected Financial Data on Bern Pharmaceutical

	Market Value	Required Return
Debt	€15,400 million	6.0%
Preferred stock	€4,000 million	5.5%
Common stock	€18,100 million	11.0%
FCFF, most recent year	€3,226 million	
Corporate tax rate	26.9%	

Singh notes that Bern has two new drugs that are currently in clinical trials awaiting regulatory approval. In addition to its operating assets, Bern owns a parcel of land from a decommissioned manufacturing facility with a current market value of €50 million that is being held for investment. Singh and Ho elect to value Bern under two scenarios:

Scenario 1 Value Bern assuming the two new drugs receive regulatory approval. In this scenario, FCFF is forecast to grow at 4.5% into perpetuity.

Scenario 2 Value Bern assuming the two new drugs do not receive regulatory approval. In this scenario, FCFF is forecast using a stable growth in FCFF of 1.5% for the next three years and then 0.75% thereafter into perpetuity.

33. Based on Exhibit 1 and Exhibit 2, Sienna's FCFF in 2019 is:

A. €680 million.

B. €1,200 million.

C. €3,080 million.

34. Based on Exhibit 1 and Exhibit 2, Sienna's FCFE in 2019 is:

A. €894 million.

B. €1,466 million.

C. €2,894 million.

35. Which of Ho's statements regarding free cash flow is (are) correct?

A. Statement 1 only

B. Statement 2 only

C. Neither Statement 1 nor Statement 2

36. Based on Exhibit 3, Ho's FCFF sensitivity analysis should conclude that Colanari's value is *most* sensitive to the:

A. FCFF growth rate.

B. before-tax cost of debt.

C. required rate of return for equity.

37. Based on Exhibit 4, Bern's firm value under Scenario 1 is *closest* to:

A. €100,951.3 million.

B. €105,349.1 million.

C. €105,399.1 million.

38. Based on Exhibit 4, Singh and Ho should conclude that under Scenario 2, shares of Bern are:

A. undervalued.

B. fairly valued.

C. overvalued.

---

39. PHB Company currently sells for £32.50 per share. In an attempt to determine whether PHB is fairly priced, an analyst has assembled the following information:

- The before-tax required rates of return on PHB debt, preferred stock, and common stock are, respectively, 7.0%, 6.8%, and 11.0%.
- The company's target capital structure is 30% debt, 15% preferred stock, and 55% common stock.
- The market value of the company's debt is £145 million, and its preferred stock is valued at £65 million.
- PHB's FCFF for the year just ended is £28 million. FCFF is expected to grow at a constant rate of 4% for the foreseeable future.
- The tax rate is 35%.
- PHB has 8 million outstanding common shares.

What is PHB's estimated value per share? Is PHB's stock underpriced?

The following information relates to questions 40-41

An aggressive financial planner who claims to have a superior method for picking undervalued stocks is trying to steal one of your clients. The planner claims that the best way to find the value of a stock is to divide EBITDA by the risk-free bond rate. The planner is urging your client to invest in NewMarket, Inc. The planner says that NewMarket's EBITDA of $1,580 million divided by the long-term government bond rate of 7% gives a total value of $22,571.4 million. With 318 million outstanding shares, NewMarket's value per share found by using this method is $70.98. Shares of NewMarket currently trade for $36.50.

40. Provide your client with an alternative estimate of NewMarket's value per share based on a two-stage FCFE valuation approach. Use the following assumptions:

- Net income is currently $600 million. Net income will grow by 20% annually for the next three years.
- The net investment in operating assets (capital expenditures less depreciation plus investment in working capital) will be $1,150 million next year and grow at 15% for the following two years.
- 40% of the net investment in operating assets will be financed with net new debt financing.
- NewMarket's beta is 1.3; the risk-free bond rate is 7%; the equity risk premium is 4%.
- After three years, the growth rate of net income will be 8% and the net investment in operating assets (capital expenditures minus depreciation plus increase in working capital) each year will drop to 30% of net income.
- Debt is, and will continue to be, 40% of total assets.
- NewMarket has 318 million shares outstanding.

41. Criticize the valuation approach that the aggressive financial planner used.

The following information relates to questions 42-44

John Jones is head of the research department of Peninsular Research and is estimating the value of Mackinac Inc. The company has released its June 2019 financial statements, shown in Exhibit 1, Exhibit 2, and Exhibit 3.

Exhibit 1: Mackinac Inc. Annual Income Statement 30 June 2019 (in Thousands, except Per-Share Data)

Sales	$250,000
Cost of goods sold	125,000
Gross operating profit	125,000
Selling, general, and administrative expenses	50,000
EBITDA	75,000

Depreciation and amortization	10,500
EBIT	64,500
Interest expense	11,000
Pretax income	53,500
Income taxes	16,050
Net income	$37,450
Shares outstanding	13,000
EPS	$2.88

Exhibit 2: Mackinac Inc. Balance Sheet 30 June 2019 (in Thousands)

Current Assets			
Cash and equivalents		$20,000	
Receivables		40,000	
Inventories		29,000	
Other current assets		23,000	
Total current assets			$112,000
Noncurrent Assets			
Property, plant, and equipment	$145,000		
Less: Accumulated depreciation	43,000		
Net property, plant, and equipment		102,000	
Investments		70,000	
Other noncurrent assets		36,000	
Total noncurrent assets			208,000
Total assets			$320,000
Current Liabilities			
Accounts payable		$41,000	
Short-term debt		12,000	
Other current liabilities		17,000	
Total current liabilities			$ 70,000
Noncurrent Liabilities			
Long-term debt		100,000	
Total noncurrent liabilities			100,000
Total liabilities			170,000
Shareholders' Equity			
Common equity		40,000	
Retained earnings		110,000	
Total equity			150,000
Total liabilities and equity			$320,000

Exhibit 3: Mackinac Inc. Statement of Cash Flows 30 June 2019 (in Thousands)

Cash Flow from Operating Activities		
Net income		$37,450
Depreciation and amortization		10,500
Change in Working Capital		
(Increase) decrease in receivables	($5,000)	
(Increase) decrease in inventories	(8,000)	
Increase (decrease) in payables	6,000	
Increase (decrease) in other current liabilities	1,500	
Net change in working capital		(5,500)
Net cash from operating activities		$42,450
Cash Flow from Investing Activities		
Purchase of property, plant, and equipment	($15,000)	
Net cash from investing activities		($15,000)
Cash Flow from Financing Activities		
Change in debt outstanding	$4,000	
Payment of cash dividends	(22,470)	
Net cash from financing activities		(18,470)
Net change in cash and cash equivalents		$8,980
Cash at beginning of period		11,020
Cash at end of period		$20,000

Mackinac has announced that it has finalized an agreement to handle North American production of a successful product currently marketed by a company headquartered outside North America. Jones decides to value Mackinac by using the DDM and FCFE models. After reviewing Mackinac's financial statements and forecasts related to the new production agreement, Jones concludes the following:

- Mackinac's earnings and FCFE are expected to grow 17% a year over the next three years before stabilizing at an annual growth rate of 9%.
- Mackinac will maintain the current payout ratio.
- Mackinac's beta is 1.25.
- The government bond yield is 6%, and the market equity risk premium is 5%.

42. Calculate the value of a share of Mackinac's common stock by using the two-stage DDM.

43. Calculate the value of a share of Mackinac's common stock by using the two-stage FCFE model.

44. Jones is discussing with a corporate client the possibility of that client acquiring a 70% interest in Mackinac. Discuss whether the DDM or FCFE model is more appropriate for this client's valuation purposes.

The following information relates to questions 45-46

James Smith is valuing McInish Corporation and performing a sensitivity analysis on his valuation. He uses a single-stage FCFE growth model. The base-case values for each of the parameters in the model are given, together with possible low and high estimates for each variable, in the following table.

Variable	Base-Case Value	Low Estimate	High Estimate
Normalized $FCFE_0$	£0.88	£0.70	£1.14
Risk-free rate	5.08%	5.00%	5.20%
Equity risk premium	5.50%	4.50%	6.50%
Beta	0.70	0.60	0.80
FCFE growth rate	6.40%	4.00%	7.00%

45. Use the base-case values to estimate the current value of McInish Corporation.

46. Calculate the range of stock prices that would occur if the base-case value for $FCFE_0$ were replaced by the low estimate and the high estimate for $FCFE_0$. Similarly, using the base-case values for all other variables, calculate the range of stock prices caused by using the low and high values for beta, the risk-free rate, the equity risk premium, and the growth rate. Based on these ranges, rank the sensitivity of the stock price to each of the five variables.

The following information relates to questions 47-48

KMobile Telecom is an Asian mobile network operator headquartered in Seoul, South Korea. Sol Kim has estimated the normalized FCFE per share for KMobile to be 1,300 Korean won (KRW) for the year just ended. The real country return for South Korea is 6.50%. To estimate the required return for KMobile, Kim makes the following adjustments to the real country return: an industry adjustment of +0.60%, a size adjustment of –0.10%, and a leverage adjustment of +0.25%. The long-term real growth rate for South Korea is estimated to be 3.5%, and Kim expects the real growth rate of KMobile to track the country rate.

47. What is the real required rate of return for KMobile Telecom?

48. Using the single-stage FCFE valuation model and real values for the discount rate and FCFE growth rate, estimate the value of one share of KMobile.

49. Hugo Dubois is evaluating NYL Manufacturing Company, Ltd. In 2020, when Dubois is performing his analysis, the company is unprofitable. Furthermore, NYL pays no dividends on its common shares. Dubois decides to value NYL Manufacturing by using his forecasts of FCFE. Dubois gathers the following facts and assumptions:

- The company has 17.0 billion shares outstanding.
- Sales will be €5.5 billion in 2021, increasing at 28% annually for the next four years (through 2025).

- Net income will be 32% of sales.
- Investment in fixed assets will be 35% of sales; investment in working capital will be 6% of sales; depreciation will be 9% of sales.
- 20% of the net investment in assets will be financed with debt.
- Interest expenses will be only 2% of sales.
- The tax rate will be 10%. NYL Manufacturing's beta is 2.1; the risk-free government bond rate is 6.4%; the equity risk premium is 5.0%.
- At the end of 2025, Dubois projects NYL terminal stock value at 18 times earnings.

What is the value of one ordinary share of NYL Manufacturing Company?

50. Bron has EPS of $3.00 in 2019 and expects EPS to increase by 21% in 2020. EPS are expected to grow at a decreasing rate for the following five years, as shown in the following table.

	2020	2021	2022	2023	2024	2025
Growth rate for EPS	21%	18%	15%	12%	9%	6%
Net capital expenditures per share	$5.00	$5.00	$4.50	$4.00	$3.50	$1.50

In 2025, the growth rate will be 6%, and it is expected to stay at that rate thereafter. Net capital expenditures (capital expenditures minus depreciation) will be $5.00 per share in 2019 and then follow the pattern predicted in the table. In 2025, net capital expenditures are expected to be $1.50, and they will then grow at 6% annually. The investment in working capital parallels the increase in net capital expenditures and is predicted to equal 25% of net capital expenditures each year. In 2025, investment in working capital will be $0.375, and it is predicted to grow at 6% thereafter. Bron will use debt financing to fund 40% of net capital expenditures and 40% of the investment in working capital. The required rate of return for Bron is 12%.

Estimate the value of a Bron share using a two-stage FCFE valuation approach.

51. Minsuh Park is preparing a valuation of QuickChange Auto Centers, Inc. Park has decided to use a three-stage FCFE valuation model and the following estimates. The FCFE per share for the current year is $0.75. The FCFE is expected to grow at 10% for next year, then at 26% annually for the following three years, and then at 6% in Year 5 and thereafter. QuickChange's estimated beta is 2.00, and Park believes that current market conditions dictate a 4.5% risk-free rate of return and a 5.0% equity risk premium. Given Park's assumptions and approach, estimate the value of a share of QuickChange.

52. Astrid Nilsson has valued the operating assets of Gothenburg Extrusion AB at 720 million Swedish kronor (SEK). The company also has short-term cash and securities with a market value of SEK60 million that are not needed for Gothenburg's operations. The noncurrent investments have a book value of SEK30 million and a market value of SEK45 million. The company also has an overfunded pension plan, with plan assets of SEK210 million and plan liabilities of SEK170 million. Gothenburg Extrusion has SEK215 million of notes and bonds outstanding and 100 million outstanding shares. What is the value per share of Gothenburg Extrusion stock?

SOLUTIONS

1. The firm value is the present value of FCFF discounted at the WACC, or

$$\text{Firm value} = \frac{\text{FCFF}_1}{\text{WACC} - g} = \frac{\text{FCFF}_0(1+g)}{\text{WACC} - g} = \frac{1.7(1.07)}{0.11 - 0.07}$$
$$= \frac{1.819}{0.04} = \text{JPY45.475 billion.}$$

The market value of equity is the value of the firm minus the value of debt:

Equity = 45.475 – 15 = JPY30.475 billion.

2. Using the FCFE valuation approach, we find the present value of FCFE discounted at the required rate of return on equity to be

$$\text{PV} = \frac{\text{FCFE}_1}{r-g} = \frac{\text{FCFE}_0(1+g)}{r-g} = \frac{1.3(1.075)}{0.13 - 0.075} = \frac{1.3975}{0.055}$$
$$= \text{JPY25.409 billion.}$$

The value of equity using this approach is JPY25.409 billion.

3. The required return on equity is

$$r = E(R_i) = R_F + \beta_i\left[E(R_M) - R_F\right] = 5.5\% + 0.90(5.5\%) = 10.45\%.$$

The weighted-average cost of capital is

WACC = 0.25(7.0%)(1 – 0.40) + 0.75(10.45%) = 8.89%.

4.

$$\text{Firm value} = \frac{\text{FCFF}_0(1+g)}{\text{WACC} - g}.$$

$$\text{Firm value} = \frac{1.1559(1.04)}{0.0889 - 0.04} = \$24.583.$$

5. Equity value = Firm value – Market value of debt.
Equity value = 24.583 – 3.192 = $21.391 billion.

6. Value per share = Equity value/Number of shares.
Value per share = $21.391 billion/1.852 billion = $11.55.

7. B is correct. Company A has a history of paying modest dividends relative to FCFE. An FCFF or FCFE model provides a better estimate of value over a DDM model when dividends paid differ significantly from the company's capacity to pay dividends. Also, Company A has a controlling investor; with control comes discretion over the uses of free cash flow. Therefore, there is the possibility that the controlling shareholder could change the dividend policy. Finally, Company A has a stable capital structure; using FCFE is a more direct and simpler method to value a company's equity than using FCFF when a company's capital structure is stable.

8. C is correct. The applicable noncash adjustments to net income in arriving at FCFE are as follows:

Noncash Item	Adjustment to Net Income	Amount (millions)
Transaction 1: Loss on sale of equipment	Added back	+900
Transaction 2: Impairment of intangibles	Added back	+400
Transaction 3: Reversal of restructuring charge	Subtracted	–300

In the case of Transaction 1, a loss reduces net income and thus must be added back in arriving at FCFE. Similarly, an impairment of intangibles (Transaction 2) reduces net income and thus must be added back in arriving at FCFE. Transaction 3 (reversal of a restructuring charge) would increase net income and thus must be subtracted in arriving at FCFE.

9. C is correct. FCFE for Company A for the most recent year is calculated as follows:

Net income	$4,844
Plus: Net noncash charges	1,500
Less: Investment in working capital	122
Plus: Proceeds from sale of fixed capital	2,379
Less: Net borrowing repayment	1,475
FCFE (millions)	$7,126

Net noncash charges are found by adding depreciation to other noncash expenses:

\$500 million + \$1,000 million = \$1,500 million.

Investment in working capital is calculated by netting the increase in accounts receivable, the decrease in accounts payable, and the increase in other current liabilities:

–\$452 million – \$210 million + \$540 million = –\$122 million (outflow).

Net borrowing repayment is calculated by netting the increase in notes payable and the decrease in long-term debt:

\$25 million – \$1,500 million = –\$1,475 million (outflow).

10. A is correct. FCFE is significantly higher than net income for Company B:

Net income = \$1,212 million.

FCFE for Company B is calculated as follows:

Net income	$1,212
Plus: Net noncash charges	288
Less: Investment in WC	236
Less: Investment in fixed assets	1,000
Plus: Net borrowing	2,000
FCFE (millions)	$2,264

Investment in working capital is calculated by adding the increase in accounts receivable, the increase in inventories, the increase in accounts payable, and the increase in other current liabilities: –\$150 million – \$200 million + \$100 million + \$14 million = –\$236 million. Net borrowing is calculated by adding the increase in notes payable to the decrease in long-term debt: \$3,000 million – \$1,000 million = \$2,000 million.

Therefore, using net income of \$1,212 million as a proxy for FCFE (\$2,264 million) for Company B would result in a much lower valuation estimate than if actual FCFE were used.

11. A is correct. In addition to significant noncash charges other than depreciation in the most recent year, the annual report indicates that Company A expects to recognize additional noncash charges related to restructuring over the next few years. The given equation for forecasting assumes that the only noncash charge is depreciation. When the company being analyzed has significant noncash charges other than depreciation expense, this sales-based methodology will result in a less accurate estimate of FCFE than one obtained by forecasting all the individual components of FCFE.

12. C is correct.

FCFE for the most recent year for Company B is calculated as follows:

Net income	\$1,212
Plus: Net noncash charges	288
Less: Investment in WC	236
Less: Investment in fixed assets	1,000
Plus: Net borrowing	2,000
FCFE (millions)	\$2,264

The required rate of return on equity for Company B is

$r = E(R_i) = R_F + \beta_i[E(R_M) - R_F] = 3\% + 0.90(7\%) = 9.3\%.$

The most recent FCFE grows for the next four years at annual growth rates of 10%, 9%, 8%, and 7%, respectively, and then 6% thereafter:

t	g	Calculation	FCFE (millions)
1	10%	\$2,264.00 × 1.10	\$2,490.40
2	9%	\$2,490.40 × 1.09	\$2,714.54
3	8%	\$2,714.54 × 1.08	\$2,931.70
4	7%	\$2,931.70 × 1.07	\$3,136.92
5	6%	\$3,136.92 × 1.06	\$3,325.13

The present value of FCFE for the first four years is calculated as follows:

$$\text{PV} = \frac{2,490.40}{1.093^1} + \frac{2,714.54}{1.093^2} + \frac{2,931.70}{1.093^3} + \frac{3,136.92}{1.093^4}.$$

PV = 2,278.50 + 2,272.25 + 2,245.22 + 2.197.97 = 8,993.94.

The present value of the terminal value is calculated as follows:

$$\text{PV of TV}_4 = \frac{3,325.13}{(0.093 - 0.06)(1.093)^4} = 70,601.58.$$

So, the estimated total market value of the equity is 8,993.94 + 70,601.58 = 79,595.52 ≈ \$79,596 million.

13. C is correct. Company C's firm value is calculated as follows:

The required rate of return on equity for Company C is

$r = E(R_i) = R_F + \beta_i[E(R_M) - R_F] = 3\% + 1.1(7\%) = 10.7\%.$

$$\text{WACC} = \frac{\text{MV (Debt)}}{\text{MV (Debt)} + \text{MV (Equity)}} r_d (1 - \text{Tax rate}) + \frac{\text{MV (Equity)}}{\text{MV (Debt)} + \text{MV (Equity)}} r_e.$$

WACC = 0.40(6%)(1 – 0.30) + 0.60(10.7%) = 1.68% + 6.42% = 8.10%.

FCFF for the most recent year for Company C is calculated as follows:

Net income	$15,409.00
Plus: Net noncash charges	3,746.00
Less: Investment in working capital	992.00
Less: Investment in fixed capital	3,463.00
Plus: Interest expense × (1 – Tax rate)	386.40
FCFF (in millions)	$15,086.40

Investment in working capital is found by adding the increase in accounts receivable, the increase in inventories, the decrease in accounts payable, and the increase in other current liabilities: –$536 million – $803 million – $3 million + $350 million = –$992 million.

FCFF is expected to grow at 5.0% indefinitely. Thus,

$$\text{Firm value} = \frac{\text{FCFF}_1}{\text{WACC} - g} = \frac{\text{FCFF}_0(1 + g)}{\text{WACC} - g} = \frac{15{,}086.4(1.05)}{0.081 - 0.05} = \$510{,}990.97 \text{ million.}$$

The value of equity is the value of the firm minus the value of debt. The value of debt is found by multiplying the target debt ratio by the total firm value:

Debt value = 0.40($510,990.97) = $204,396.39.

Therefore, equity value = $510,990.97 – $204,396.39 = $306,594.58 million.

14. FCF = Net income + Depreciation and amortization – Cash dividends – Capital expenditures. This definition of free cash flow is sometimes used to determine how much "discretionary" cash flow the management has at its disposal. Management discretion concerning dividends is limited by investor expectations that dividends will be maintained. Comparing this definition with Equation 7, FCFF = NI + NCC + Int(1 – Tax rate) – FCInv – WCInv, we find that FCFF includes a reduction for investments in working capital and the addition of after-tax interest expense. Common stock dividends are not subtracted from FCFF because dividends represent a distribution of the cash available to investors. (If a company pays preferred dividends and they were previously taken out when net income available to common shareholders was calculated, they are added back in Equation 7 to include them in FCFF.)

15. FCF = Cash flow from operations (from the statement of cash flows) – Capital expenditures. Comparing this definition of free cash flow with Equation 8, FCFF = CFO + Int(1 – Tax rate) – FCInv, highlights the relationship of CFO to FCFF: The primary point is that when Equation 8 is used, after-tax interest is added back to CFO to arrive at the cash flow to all investors. Then FCInv is subtracted to arrive at the amount of that cash flow that is "free" in the sense of available for distribution to those investors after taking care of capital investment needs. If preferred dividends were subtracted to obtain net income (in CFO), they would also have to be added back in. This definition is commonly used to approximate FCFF, but it generally understates the actual FCFF by the amount of after-tax interest expense.

16. Free cash flow to the firm, found with Equation 7, is

$$\text{FCFF} = \text{NI} + \text{NCC} + \text{Int}(1 - \text{Tax rate}) - \text{FCInv} - \text{WCInv}.$$
$$\text{FCFF} = 285 + 180 + 130(1 - 0.40) - 349 - (39 + 44 - 22 - 23).$$
$$\text{FCFF} = 285 + 180 + 78 - 349 - 38 = \$156 \text{ million}.$$

17. Free cash flow to equity, found with Equation 10, is

$$\text{FCFE} = \text{NI} + \text{NCC} - \text{FCInv} - \text{WFCInv} + \text{Net borrowing}.$$
$$\text{FCFE} = 285 + 180 - 349 - (39 + 44 - 22 - 23) + (10 + 40).$$
$$\text{FCFE} = 285 + 180 - 349 - 38 + 50 = \$128 \text{ million}.$$

18. To find FCFE from FCFF, one uses the relationship in Equation 9:

$$\text{FCFE} = \text{FCFF} - \text{Int}(1 - \text{Tax rate}) + \text{Net borrowing}.$$
$$\text{FCFE} = 156 - 130(1 - 0.40) + (10 + 40).$$
$$\text{FCFE} = 156 - 78 + 50 = \$128 \text{ million}.$$

19. The FCFF is (in euros)

$$\text{FCFF} = \text{NI} + \text{NCC} + \text{Int}(1 - \text{Tax rate}) - \text{FCInv} - \text{WCInv}.$$
$$\text{FCFF} = 250 + 90 + 150(1 - 0.30) - 170 - 40.$$
$$\text{FCFF} = 250 + 90 + 105 - 170 - 40 = 235 \text{ million}.$$

The weighted-average cost of capital is

WACC = 9%(1 – 0.30)(0.40) + 13%(0.60) = 10.32%.

The value of the firm (in euros) is

$$\text{Firm value} = \frac{\text{FCFF}_1}{\text{WACC} - g} = \frac{\text{FCFF}_0(1+g)}{\text{WACC} - g} = \frac{235(1.06)}{0.1032 - 0.06}$$
$$= \frac{249.1}{0.0432} = 5,766.20 \text{ million}.$$

The total value of equity is the total firm value minus the value of debt: Equity = €5,766.20 million – €1,800 million = €3,966.20 million. Dividing by the number of shares gives the per-share estimate of V_0 = €3,966.20 million/10 million = €396.62 per share.

20. The free cash flow to equity is

$$\text{FCFE} = \text{NI} + \text{NCC} - \text{FCInv} - \text{WCInv} + \text{Net borrowing}.$$
$$\text{FCFE} = 250 + 90 - 170 - 40 + 0.40(170 - 90 + 40).$$
$$\text{FCFE} = 250 + 90 - 170 - 40 + 48 = €178 \text{ million}.$$

Because the company is borrowing 40% of the increase in net capital expenditures (170 – 90) and working capital (40), net borrowing is €48 million.

The total value of equity is the FCFE discounted at the required rate of return of equity:

$$\text{Equity value} = \frac{\text{FCFE}_1}{r - g} = \frac{\text{FCFE}_0(1+g)}{r - g} = \frac{178(1.07)}{0.13 - 0.07}$$
$$= \frac{190.46}{0.06} = €3,174.33 \text{ million}.$$

The value per share is V_0 = €3,174.33 million/10 million = €317.43 per share.

21. To find FCFF from CFO, EBIT, or EBITDA, the analyst can use Equations 8, 12, and 13.

To find FCFF from CFO:

$$\text{FCFF} = \text{CFO} + \text{Int}(1 - \text{Tax rate}) - \text{FCInv}.$$
$$\text{FCFF} = 427 + 130(1 - 0.40) - 349 = 427 + 78 - 349 = \$156 \text{ million}.$$

To find FCFF from EBIT:

$$\text{FCFF} = \text{EBIT}(1 - \text{Tax rate}) + \text{Dep} - \text{FCInv} - \text{WCInv}.$$
$$\text{FCFF} = 605(1 - 0.40) + 180 - 349 - 38.$$
$$\text{FCFF} = 363 + 180 - 349 - 38 = \$156 \text{ million}.$$

Finally, to obtain FCFF from EBITDA:

$$\text{FCFF} = \text{EBITDA}(1 - \text{Tax rate}) + \text{Dep}(\text{Tax rate}) - \text{FCInv} - \text{WCInv}.$$
$$\text{FCFF} = 785(1 - 0.40) + 180(0.40) - 349 - 38.$$
$$\text{FCFF} = 471 + 72 - 349 - 38 = \$156 \text{ million}.$$

22. The simplest approach is to calculate FCFF from CFO, EBIT, or EBITDA as was done in Part A and then to find FCFE by making the appropriate adjustments to FCFF:

$$\text{FCFE} = \text{FCFF} - \text{Int}(1 - \text{Tax rate}) + \text{Net borrowing}.$$
$$\text{FCFE} = 156 - 130(1 - 0.40) + 50 = 156 - 78 + 50 = \$128 \text{ million}.$$

The analyst can also find FCFE by using CFO, EBIT, or EBITDA directly. Starting with CFO and using Equation 11, FCFE is found to be

$$\text{FCFE} = \text{CFO} - \text{FCInv} + \text{Net borrowing}.$$
$$\text{FCFE} = 427 - 349 + 50 = \$128 \text{ million}.$$

Starting with EBIT, on the basis of Equations 9 and 12, FCFE is

$$\text{FCFE} = \text{EBIT}(1 - \text{Tax rate}) + \text{Dep} - \text{Int}(1 - \text{Tax rate}) - \text{FCInv} - \text{WCInv} + \text{Net borrowing}.$$
$$\text{FCFE} = 605(1 - 0.40) + 180 - 130(1 - 0.40) - 349 - 38 + 50.$$
$$\text{FCFE} = 363 + 180 - 78 - 349 - 38 + 50 = \$128 \text{ million}.$$

Finally, starting with EBITDA, on the basis of Equations 9 and 13, FCFE is

$$\text{FCFE} = \text{EBITDA}(1 - \text{Tax rate}) + \text{Dep}(\text{Tax rate}) - \text{Int}(1 - \text{Tax rate}) - \text{FCInv} - \text{WCInv} + \text{Net borrowing}.$$
$$\text{FCFE} = 785(1 - 0.40) + 180(0.40) - 130(1 - 0.40) - 349 - 38 + 50.$$
$$\text{FCFE} = 471 + 72 - 78 - 349 - 38 + 50 = \$128 \text{ million}.$$

23. C is correct. The sustainable growth rate is return on equity (ROE) multiplied by the retention ratio. ROE is 10%, and the retention ratio is 1 – Payout ratio, or 1.0 – 0.2 = 0.8. The sustainable growth rate is 0.8 × 10% = 8%. FCFE growth should be at least 8% per year in the long term.

24. A is correct. Justifications for choosing the FCFE model over the DDM include the following:

- The company pays dividends, but its dividends differ significantly from the company's capacity to pay dividends (the first reason given by Leigh).
- The investor takes a control perspective (the second reason given by Leigh).

25. A is correct. FCFF = NI + NCC + Interest expense(1 – Tax rate) – FCInv – WC-Inv. In this case:

NI = \$485 million

NCC = Depreciation expense = \$270 million

Interest expense(1 – Tax rate) = 195(1 – 0.32) = \$132.6 million

FCInv = Net purchase of fixed assets = Increase in gross fixed assets
= 4,275 – 3,752 = \$523 million

WCInv = Increase in accounts receivable + Increase in inventory – Increase in accounts payable – Increase in accrued liabilities

= (770 – 711) + (846 – 780) – (476 – 443) – (149 – 114)

= \$57 million

FCFF = 485 + 270 + 132.6 – 523 – 57 = 307.6, or \$308 million

26. B is correct. FCFE = NI + NCC – FCInv – WCInv + Net borrowing. In this case:

NI = \$485 million.

NCC = Depreciation expense = \$270 million.

FCInv = Net purchase of fixed assets = Increase in gross fixed assets

= 4,275 – 3,752 = \$523 million.

WCInv = Increase in accounts receivable + Increase in inventory – Increase in accounts payable – Increase in accrued liabilities

= (770 – 711) + (846 – 780) – (476 – 443) – (149 – 114)

= \$57 million.

Net borrowing = Increase in notes payable + Increase in long-term debt

= (465 – 450) + (1,575 – 1,515) = \$75 million.

FCFE = 485 + 270 – 523 – 57 + 75 = \$250 million.

An alternative calculation is

FCFE = FCFF – Int(1 – Tax rate) + Net borrowing.

FCFE = 307.6 – 195(1 – 0.32) + (15 +60) = \$250 million.

27. C is correct. Inventory cannot be reduced below zero. Furthermore, sales growth tends to increase inventory.

28. A is correct. The FCFF model is often selected when the capital structure is expected to change because FCFF estimation may be easier than FCFE estimation in the presence of changing financial leverage.

29.

For a \$100 increase in:	**Change in FCFF (in US Dollars)**	**Change in FCFE (in US Dollars)**
A. Net income	+100	+100
B. Cash operating expenses	–60	–60
C. Depreciation	+40	+40
D. Interest expense	0	–60
E. EBIT	+60	+60
F. Accounts receivable	–100	–100
G. Accounts payable	+100	+100
H. Property, plant, and equipment	–100	–100
I. Notes payable	0	+100
J. Cash dividends paid	0	0
K. Proceeds from issuing new common shares	0	0
L. Common shares repurchased	0	0

30. FCFE is defined as the cash flow remaining after the company meets all financial obligations, including debt payment, and covers all capital expenditure and working capital needs. Sundanci's FCFE for the year 2020 is calculated as follows:

Net income	= $80 million
Plus: Depreciation expense	= 23
Less: Capital expenditures	= 38
Less: Investment in WC	= 41
Equals: FCFE	= $24 million

Thus, FCFE per share equals ($24 million)/(84 million shares) = $0.286.

31. The FCFE model requires forecasts of FCFE for the high-growth years (2021 and 2022) plus a forecast for the first year of stable growth (2023) to allow for an estimate of the terminal value in 2022 based on constant perpetual growth. Because all of the components of FCFE are expected to grow at the same rate, the values can be obtained by projecting the FCFE at the common rate. (Alternatively, the components of FCFE can be projected and aggregated for each year.)

The following table provides the process for estimating Sundanci's current value on a per-share basis.

Free Cash Flow to Equity

Base assumptions:	
Shares outstanding (millions)	84
Required return on equity, r	14%

		Actual 2020	Projected 2021	Projected 2022	Projected 2023
			g = 27%	g = 27%	g = 13%
	Total	Per share			
Earnings after tax	$80	$0.952	$1.2090	$1.5355	$1.7351
Plus: Depreciation expense	$23	$0.274	$0.3480	$0.4419	$0.4994
Less: Capital expenditures	$38	$0.452	$0.5740	$0.7290	$0.8238
Less: Increase in net working capital	$41	$0.488	$0.6198	$0.7871	$0.8894
Equals: FCFE	$24	$0.286	$0.3632	$0.4613	$0.5213
Terminal value[a]				$52.1300	
Total cash flows to equity[b]			$0.3632	$52.5913	
Discounted value[c]			$0.3186	$40.4673	
Current value per share[d]	$40.7859				

[a] *Projected 2022 terminal value = Projected 2023 FCFE/(r – g).*
[b] *Projected 2022 total cash flows to equity = Projected 2022 FCFE + Projected 2022 terminal value.*
[c] *Discounted values obtained by using r = 14%.*
[d] *Current value per share = Discounted value 2021 + Discounted value 2022.*

32. The following limitations of the DDM *are* addressed by the FCFE model: The DDM uses a strict definition of cash flow to equity; that is, cash flows to equity are the dividends on the common stock. The FCFE model expands the definition of cash flow to include the balance of residual cash flows after all financial obligations and investment needs have been met. Thus, the FCFE model explicitly recognizes the company's investment and financing policies as well as its dividend policy. In instances of a change of corporate control, and thus the possibility

of changing dividend policy, the FCFE model provides a better estimate of value.

Both two-stage valuation models allow for two distinct phases of growth—an initial finite period when the growth is abnormal followed by a stable growth period that is expected to last forever. These two-stage models share the same limitations with respect to the growth assumptions:

First, the analyst must confront the difficulty of defining the duration of the extraordinary growth period. A long period of high growth will produce a higher valuation, and the analyst may be tempted to assume an unrealistically long period of extraordinary growth.

Second, the analyst must realize that assuming a sudden shift from high growth to lower, stable growth is unrealistic. The transformation is more likely to occur gradually over time.

Third, because value is quite sensitive to the steady-state growth assumption, overestimating or underestimating this rate can lead to large errors in value.

The two models also share other limitations—notably, difficulties in accurately estimating required rates of return.

33. A is correct. Sienna's FCFF in 2019 is calculated as

FCFF = EBIT(1 – Tax rate) + Dep – FCInv – WCInv.

FCInv = Purchases of PP&E = 1,000 (outflow).

WCInv = Increase in accounts receivable (outflow) + Increase in inventory (outflow) + Increase in accounts payable (inflow).

WCInv = –2,000 (outflow) + –200 (outflow) + 1,000 (inflow) = –1,200 (outflow).

FCFF = 3,200(1 – 0.35) + 800 – 1,000 –1,200.

FCFF = €680 million.

FCFF can also be computed from CFO:

FCFF = CFO + Int(1 – Tax rate) – FCInv.

FCFF = 1,394 + 440(1 – 0.35) – 1,000.

FCFF = €680 million.

34. A is correct. Sienna's FCFE in 2019 is calculated as

FCFE = CFO – FCInv + Net borrowing

= 1,394 – 1,000 + 500

= €894 million.

Alternatively, FCFE may be calculated as

FCFE = FCFF – Int(1 – Tax rate) + Net borrowing.

= 680 – 440(1 – 0.35) + 500

= €894 million.

35. C is correct. Transactions between the company and its shareholders (through cash dividends, share repurchases, and share issuances) do not affect free cash flow. However, leverage changes, such as the use of more debt financing, have

some impact on free cash flow because they increase the interest tax shield (reduce corporate taxes because of the tax deductibility of interest) and reduce the cash flow available to equity.

36. C is correct. Colanari's valuation is most sensitive to the cost of equity (r_e) because the range of estimated values is larger than the valuation ranges estimated from the sensitivity analysis of both the FCFF growth rate (GFCFF) and the before-tax cost of debt (r_d).

Variable	Base Case	Low Estimate	High Estimate	Valuation with Low Estimate (€ millions)	Valuation with High Estimate (€ millions)	Range (€ millions)
GFCFF	4.6%	4.2%	5.0%	3,274.16	4,021.34	747.18
r_d	4.9%	3.9%	5.9%	3,793.29	3,445.24	348.05
r_e	11.0%	10.0%	12.0%	4,364.18	3,079.38	1,284.80

WACC = $[w_d \times r_d(1 - \text{Tax rate})] + (w_e \times r_e)$.

Firm value = $\text{FCFF}_0(1 + g)/(\text{WACC} - g)$.

Cost of equity sensitivity

Using the base case estimates for the FCFF growth rate and the before-tax cost of debt and using the low estimate for the cost of equity (r_e) of 10.0%, the valuation estimate is

WACC = $[(0.30)(0.049)(1 - 0.35)] + (0.70)(0.10) = 7.96\%$.

Firm value = 140 million$(1 + 0.046)/(0.0796 - 0.046)$ = €4,364.18 million.

Using the base case estimates for the FCFF growth rate and the before-tax cost of debt and using the high estimate for the cost of equity (r_e) of 12.0%, the valuation estimate is

WACC = $[(0.30)(0.049)(1 - 0.35)] + (0.70)(0.120) = 9.36\%$.

Firm value = 140 million$(1 + 0.046)/(0.0936 - 0.046)$ = €3,079.38 million.

Therefore, the range in valuation estimates from using the highest and lowest estimates of the cost of equity is €1,284.80 million.

FCFF growth rate sensitivity

Using the base case estimates for the cost of equity and the before-tax cost of debt and using the low estimate for the FCFF growth rate (GFCFF) of 4.2%, the valuation estimate is

WACC = $[(0.30)(0.049)(1 - 0.35)] + (0.70)(0.11) = 8.66\%$.

Firm value = 140 million$(1 + 0.042)/(0.0866 - 0.042)$ = €3,274.16 million.

Using the base case estimates for the cost of equity and the before-tax cost of debt and using the high estimate for the FCFF growth rate (GFCFF) of 5.0%, the valuation estimate is

WACC = $[(0.30)(0.049)(1 - 0.35)] + (0.70)(0.11) = 8.66\%$.

Firm value = 140 million$(1 + 0.05)/(0.0866 - 0.05)$ = €4,021.34 million.

Therefore, the range in valuation estimates from using the highest and lowest estimates of the FCFF growth rate is €747.18 million.

Before-tax cost of debt sensitivity

Using the base case estimates for the FCFF growth rate and the cost of equity and using the low estimate for the before-tax cost of debt (r_d) of 3.9%, the valuation estimate is

WACC = [(0.30)(0.039)(1 – 0.35)] + (0.70)(0.11) = 8.46%.

Firm value = 140 million(1 + 0.046)/(0.0846 – 0.046) = €3,793.29 million.

Using the base case estimates for the FCFF growth rate and the cost of equity and using the high estimate for the before-tax cost of debt (r_d) of 5.9%, the valuation estimate is

WACC = [(0.30)(0.059)(1 – 0.35)] + (0.70)(0.11) = 8.85%.

Firm value = 140 million(1 + 0.046)/(0.0885 – 0.046) = €3,445.24 million.

Therefore, the range in valuation estimates from using the highest and lowest estimates of the before-tax cost of debt is €348.05 million.

37. C is correct. Based on Scenario 1, where Bern receives regulatory approval for its new drugs, the growth rate in FCFF for Bern will be constant at 4.5%. Therefore, a constant-growth valuation model can be used to calculate firm value.

    Bern's weighted average cost of capital is calculated as

    WACC = $[w_d \times r_d(1 - \text{Tax rate})] + (w_p \times r_p) + (w_e \times r_e)$.

    The total market value of the firm is the sum of the debt, preferred stock, and common stock market values: 15,400 + 4,000 + 18,100 = 37,500.

    WACC = [(15,400/37,500)(0.060)(1 – 0.269] + (4,000/37,500)(0.055) + (18,100/37,500)(0.11)

    = 7.70%.

    Value of operating assets = $\text{FCFF}_0(1 + g)/(\text{WACC} - g)$.

    Value of operating assets = 3,226 million(1 + 0.045)/(0.0770 – 0.045)

    = €105,349.06 million.

    Total value of the company

    = Value of operating assets + Value of non-operating assets.

    Total value of the company = 105,349.06 million + 50 million

    = €105,399.06 million.

38. A is correct.

    The total market value of the firm is the sum of the debt, preferred stock, and common stock market values: 15,400 + 4,000 + 18,100 = 37,500 million.

    WACC = $[w_d \times r_d(1 - \text{Tax rate})] + (w_p \times r_p) + (w_e \times r_e)$

    = [(15,400/37,500)(0.060)(1 – 0.269] + (4,000/37,500)(0.055) + (18,100/37,500)(0.11)

    = 7.70%.

    Under the assumption that Bern has a low growth rate because it did not receive regulatory approval for its new drugs, the value of Bern can be analyzed using a two-stage valuation model.

$$\text{Company value} = \sum_{t=1}^{n} \frac{\text{FCFF}_t}{(1+\text{WACC})^t} + \frac{\text{FCFF}_{n+1}}{(\text{WACC}-g)} \frac{1}{(1+\text{WACC})^n}.$$

Year	0	1	2	3	4
g		1.50%	1.50%	1.50%	0.75%
FCFF_n (€ millions)	3,226	3,274.39	3,323.51	3,373.36	3,398.66
Present Value Factor		0.928529	0.862167	0.800547	
Present Value (€ millions)		3,040.37	2,865.42	2,700.53	

The terminal value at the end of Year 3 is $\text{TV}_3 = \text{FCFF}_4/(\text{WACC} - g_4)$.

TV_3 = 3,398.66/(0.0770 – 0.0075) = €48,901.58 million.

The total value of operating assets

= (3,040.37 + 2,865.42 + 2,700.53) + 48,901.58/(1 + 0.0770)^3

= 8,606.32 + 39,144.95

= €47,751.27 million.

Value of Bern's common stock

= Value of operating assets + Value of non-operating assets – Market value of debt – Preferred stock

= 47,751.27 + 50.00 – 15,400 – 4,000

= €28,401.27 million.

Since the current market value of Bern's common stock (€18,100 million) is less than the estimated value (€28,401.27 million), the shares are undervalued.

39. The WACC for PHB Company is

$$\text{WACC} = 0.30(7.0\%)(1-0.35) + 0.15(6.8\%) + 0.55(11.0\%) = 8.435\%.$$

The firm value is

$$\text{Firm value} = \frac{\text{FCFF}_0(1+g)}{\text{WACC}-g}.$$

$$\text{Firm value} = \frac{28(1.04)}{0.08435-0.04}$$

$$= \frac{29.12}{0.04435}$$

= £656.60 million.

The value of equity is the firm value minus the value of debt minus the value of preferred stock: Equity = 656.60 – 145 – 65 = £446.60 million. Dividing this amount by the number of shares gives the estimated value per share of £446.60 million/8 million shares = £55.82.

The estimated value for the stock is greater than the market price of £32.50, so the stock appears to be undervalued.

40. Using the CAPM, the required rate of return for NewMarket is

$$r = E(R_i) = R_F + \beta_i[E(R_M) - R_F] = 7\% + 1.3(4\%) = 12.2\%.$$

To estimate FCFE, we use Equation 15:

$$\text{FCFE} = \text{Net income} - (1 - \text{DR})(\text{FCInv} - \text{Depreciation}) - (1 - \text{DR})(\text{WCInv}),$$

which can be written

$$\text{FCFE} = \text{Net income} - (1 - \text{DR})(\text{FCInv} - \text{Depreciation} + \text{WCInv})$$
$$= \text{Net income} - (1 - \text{DR})(\text{Net investment in operating assets}).$$

The following table shows that net income grows at 20% annually for Years 1, 2, and 3 and then grows at 8% for Year 4. The net investment in operating assets is $1,150 million in Year 1 and grows at 15% annually for Years 2 and 3. Debt financing is 40% of this investment. FCFE is NI – Net investment in operating assets + New debt financing. Finally, the present value of FCFE for Years 1, 2, and 3 is found by discounting at 12.2%.

	Year			
(in $ Millions)	**1**	**2**	**3**	**4**
Net income	720.00	864.00	1,036.80	1,119.74
Net investment in operating assets	1,150.00	1,322.50	1,520.88	335.92
New debt financing	460.00	529.00	608.35	134.37
FCFE	30.00	70.50	124.27	918.19
PV of FCFE discounted at 12.2%	26.74	56.00	87.98	

In Year 4, net income is 8% larger than in Year 3. In Year 4, the investment in operating assets is 30% of net income and debt financing is 40% of this investment. The FCFE in Year 4 is $918.19 million. The value of FCFE after Year 3 is found by using the constant-growth model:

$$V_3 = \frac{\text{FCFE}_4}{r - g} = \frac{918.19}{0.122 - 0.08} = \$21,861.67 \text{ million.}$$

The present value of V_3 discounted at 12.2% is $15,477.64 million. The total value of equity, the present value of the first three years' FCFE plus the present value of V_3, is $15,648.36 million. Dividing this amount by the number of outstanding shares (318 million) gives a value per share of $49.21. For the first three years, NewMarket has a small FCFE because of the large investments it is making during the high-growth phase. In the normal-growth phase, FCFE is much larger because the investments required are much smaller.

41. The planner's estimate of the share value of $70.98 is much higher than the FCFE model estimate of $49.21 for several reasons. First, taxes and interest expenses have a prior claim to the company's cash flow and should be taken out of the cash flows used in estimating the value of equity because these amounts are not available to equity holders. The planner did not do this.

    Second, EBITDA does not account for the company's reinvestments in operating assets. So, EBITDA overstates the funds available to stockholders if reinvestment needs exceed depreciation charges, which is the case for growing companies such as NewMarket.

    Third, EBITDA does not account for the company's capital structure. Using EBITDA to represent a benefit to stockholders (as opposed to stockholders and bondholders combined) is a mistake.

    Finally, dividing EBITDA by the bond rate is a major error. The risk-free bond rate is an inappropriate discount rate for risky equity cash flows; the proper measure is the required rate of return on the company's equity. Dividing by a fixed rate also assumes, erroneously, that the cash flow stream is a fixed perpetuity. EBITDA cannot be a perpetual stream because if it were distributed, the stream would eventually decline to zero (lacking capital investments). NewMarket is actually a growing company, so assuming it to be a nongrowing perpetuity is a mistake.

42. When a two-stage DDM is used, the value of a share of Mackinac, dividends per share (DPS), is calculated as follows:

DPS_0 = Cash dividends/Shares outstanding = \$22,470/13,000 = \$1.7285.

$DPS_1 = DPS_0 \times 1.17 = \$2.0223.$

$DPS_2 = DPS_0 \times 1.17^2 = \$2.3661.$

$DPS_3 = DPS_0 \times 1.17^3 = \$2.7683.$

$DPS_4 = DPS_0 \times 1.17^3 \times 1.09 = \$3.0175.$

When the CAPM is used, the required return on equity, r, is

$$r = \text{Government bond rate} + (\text{Beta} \times \text{Equity risk premium}) = 0.06 + (1.25 \times 0.05) = 0.1225\text{, or } 12.25\%.$$

$$\text{Value per share} = DPS_1/(1+r) + DPS_2/(1+r)^2 + DPS_3/(1+r)^3 + \left[DPS_4/\left(r - g_{stable}\right)\right]/(1+r)^3.$$

$$\text{Value per share} = \$2.0223/1.1225 + \$2.3661/1.1225^2 + \$2.7683/1.1225^3 + [\$3.0175/(0.1225 - 0.09)]/1.1225^3$$
$$= \$1.8016 + \$1.8778 + \$1.9573 + \$65.6450$$
$$= \$71.28.$$

43. When the two-stage FCFE model is used, the value of a share of Mackinac is calculated as follows (in $ thousands except per-share data):

Net income = \$37,450.
Depreciation = \$10,500.
Capital expenditures = \$15,000.
Change in working capital = \$5,500.
New debt issuance − Principal repayments = Change in debt outstanding = \$4,000

$FCFE_0$ = Net income + Depreciation − Capital expenditures− Change in working capital − Principal repayments + New debt issues.

$FCFE_0 = \$37,450 + \$10,500 - \$15,000 - \$5,500 + \$4,000 = \$31,450.$

$FCFE_0 pershare = \$31,450/13,000 = \$2.4192.$

$FCFE_1 = FCFE_0 \times 1.17 = \$2.8305.$

$FCFE_2 = FCFE_0 \times 1.17^2 = \$3.3117.$

$FCFE_3 = FCFE_0 \times 1.17^3 = \$3.8747.$

$FCFE_4 = FCFE_0 \times 1.17^3 \times 1.09 = \$4.2234.$

From the answer to A, r = 12.25%.

$$\text{Value per share} = FCFE_1/(1+r) + FCFE_2/(1+r)^2 + FCFE_3/(1+r)^3 + \left[FCFE_4/\left(r - g_{stable}\right)\right]/(1+r)^3.$$

$$\begin{aligned}\text{Value per share} &= \$2.8305/1.1225 + \$3.3117/1.1225^2 \\ &\quad + \$3.8747/1.1225^3 \\ &\quad + [\$4.2234/(0.1225 - 0.09)]/1.1225^3 \\ &= \$2.5216 + \$2.6283 + \$2.7395 + \$91.8798 \\ &= \$99.77.\end{aligned}$$

44. The FCFE model is best for valuing companies for takeovers or in situations that have a reasonable chance of a change in corporate control. Because controlling stockholders can change the dividend policy, they are interested in estimating the maximum residual cash flow after meeting all financial obligations and investment needs. The DDM is based on the premise that the only cash flows received by stockholders are dividends. FCFE uses a more expansive definition to measure what a company can afford to pay out as dividends.

45. The required rate of return for McInish found with the CAPM is

$$r = E(R_i) = R_F + \beta_i[E(R_M) - R_F] = 5.08\% + 0.70(5.50\%) = 8.93\%.$$

The value per share is

$$V_0 = \frac{\text{FCFE}_0(1+g)}{r-g} = \frac{0.88(1.064)}{0.0893 - 0.064} = \$37.01.$$

46. The following table shows the calculated price for McInish based on the base-case values for all values except the variable being changed from the base-case value.

Variable	Estimated Price with Low Value (£)	Estimated Price with High Value (£)	Range (Rank) (£)
Normalized FCFE_0	29.44	47.94	18.50 (3)
Risk-free rate	38.22	35.33	2.89 (5)
Equity risk premium	51.17	28.99	22.18 (2)
Beta	47.29	30.40	16.89 (4)
FCFE growth rate	18.56	48.79	30.23 (1)

As the table shows, the value of McInish is most sensitive to the changes in the FCFE growth rate, with the price moving over a wide range. McInish's stock price is least sensitive to alternative values of the risk-free rate. Alternative values of beta, the equity risk premium, or the initial FCFE value also have a large impact on the value of the stock, although the effects of these variables are smaller than the effect of the growth rate.

47. The real required rate of return for KMobile is

Country return (real)	6.50%
Industry adjustment	+0.60%
Size adjustment	–0.10%
Leverage adjustment	+0.25%
Required rate of return	7.25%

48. The real growth rate of FCFE is expected to be the same as the country rate of 3.5%. The value of one share is

$$V_0 = \frac{\text{FCFE}_0(1+g_{real})}{r_{real}-g_{real}} = \frac{1,300(1.035)}{0.0725-0.035} = \text{KRW}35,880.$$

49. The required rate of return found with the CAPM is

$$r = E(R_i) = R_F + \beta_i[E(R_M) - R_F] = 6.4\% + 2.1(5.0\%) = 16.9\%.$$

The following table shows the values of sales, net income, capital expenditures less depreciation, and investments in working capital. FCFE equals net income less the investments financed with equity:

$$\text{FCFE} = \text{Net income} - (1-\text{DR})(\text{Capital expenditures} - \text{Depreciation}) - (1-\text{DR})(\text{Investment in working capital}),$$

where DR is the debt ratio (debt financing as a percentage of debt and equity). Because 20% of net new investments are financed with debt, 80% of the investments are financed with equity, which reduces FCFE by 80% of (Capital expenditures – Depreciation) and 80% of the investment in working capital.

(All Data in Billions of Euros)	2021	2022	2023	2024	2025
Sales (growing at 28%)	5.500	7.040	9.011	11.534	14.764
Net income = 32% of sales	1.760	2.253	2.884	3.691	4.724
FCInv – Dep = (35% – 9%) × Sales	1.430	1.830	2.343	2.999	3.839
WCInv = (6% of Sales)	0.330	0.422	0.541	0.692	0.886
0.80 × (FCInv – Dep + WCInv)	1.408	1.802	2.307	2.953	3.780
FCFE = NI – 0.80 × (FCInv – Dep + WCInv)	0.352	0.451	0.577	0.738	0.945
PV of FCFE discounted at 16.9%	0.301	0.330	0.361	0.395	0.433
Terminal stock value		85.032			
PV of terminal value discounted at 16.9%		38.950			
PV of FCFE (first five years)		1.820			
Total value of equity		40.770			

The terminal stock value is 18.0 times the earnings in 2025, or 18 × 4.724 = €85.03 billion. The present value of the terminal value (€38.95 billion) plus the present value of the first five years' FCFE (€1.82 billion) is €40.77 billion. Because NYL Manufacturing has 17 billion outstanding shares, the value per ordinary share is €2.398.

50. The following table develops the information to calculate FCFE per share (amounts are in US dollars).

	2020	2021	2022	2023	2024	2025
Growth rate for EPS	21%	18%	15%	12%	9%	6%
EPS	3.630	4.283	4.926	5.517	6.014	6.374
Net capital expenditure per share	5.000	5.000	4.500	4.000	3.500	1.500
Investment in WC per share	1.250	1.250	1.125	1.000	0.875	0.375
New debt financing = 40% of (Capital expenditure + WCInv)	2.500	2.500	2.250	2.000	1.750	0.750

	2020	2021	2022	2023	2024	2025
FCFE = NI – Net capital expenditure – WCInv + New debt financing	–0.120	0.533	1.551	2.517	3.389	5.249
PV of FCFE discounted at 12%	–0.107	0.425	1.104	1.600	1.923	

Earnings per share for 2019 are $3.00, and the EPS estimates for 2020 through 2025 in the table are found by increasing the previous year's EPS by that year's growth rate. The net capital expenditures each year were specified by the analyst. The increase in working capital per share is equal to 25% of net capital expenditures. Finally, debt financing is 40% of that year's total net capital expenditures and investment in working capital. For example, in 2020, the per-share amount for net capital expenditures plus investment in working capital is $5.00 + $1.25 = $6.25. Debt financing is 40% of $6.25, or $2.50. Debt financing for 2021 through 2025 is found in the same way.

FCFE equals net income minus net capital expenditures minus investment in working capital plus new debt financing. Notice that FCFE is negative in 2020 because of large capital investments and investments in working capital. As these investments decline relative to net income, FCFE becomes positive and substantial.

The present values of FCFE from 2020 through 2024 are given in the bottom row of the table. These five present values sum to $4.944 per share. Because FCFE from 2025 onward will grow at a constant 6%, the constant-growth model can be used to value these cash flows.

$$V_{2024} = \frac{\text{FCFE}_{2025}}{r - g} = \frac{5.249}{0.12 - 0.06} = \$87.483.$$

The present value of this stream is $\$87.483/(1.12)^5 = \$49.640$. The value per share is the present value of the first five FCFEs (2020–2024) plus the present value of the FCFE after 2024, or $4.944 + $ 49.640 = $54.58.

51. The required return for QuickChange, found by using the CAPM, is $r = E(R_i) = R_F + \beta_i[E(R_M) - R_F] = 4.5\% + 2.0(5.0\%) = 14.5\%$. The estimated future values of FCFE per share are given in the following exhibit (amounts in US dollars):

Year *t*	Variable	Calculation	Value in Year *t*	Present Value at 14.5%
1	FCFE_1	0.75(1.10)	0.825	0.721
2	FCFE_2	0.75(1.10)(1.26)	1.040	0.793
3	FCFE_3	$0.75(1.10)(1.26)^2$	1.310	0.873
4	FCFE_4	$0.75(1.10)(1.26)^3$	1.650	0.960
4	TV_4	$\text{FCFE}_5/(r - g)$ $= 0.75(1.10)(1.26)^3(1.06)/(0.145 - 0.06)$ $= 1.749/0.085.$	20.580	11.974
0	Total value =	PV of FCFE for Years 1–4 + PV of terminal value		15.32

The FCFE grows at 10% for Year 1 and then at 26% for Years 2–4. These calculated values for FCFE are shown in the exhibit. The present values of the FCFE for the first four years discounted at the required rate of return are given in the last column of the table. After Year 4, FCFE will grow at 6% forever, so the constant-growth FCFE model is used to find the terminal value at Time 4, which is $\text{TV}_4 = \text{FCFE}_5/(r - g)$. TV_4 is discounted at the required return for four periods to find its present value, as shown in the table. Finally, the total value of the stock, $15.32, is the sum of the present values of the first four years' FCFE per share plus the present value of the terminal value per share.

52. The total value of non-operating assets is

SEK60	million short-term securities
SEK45	million market value of noncurrent assets
SEK40	million pension fund surplus
SEK145	million non-operating assets

The total value of the firm is the value of the operating assets plus the value of the non-operating assets, or SEK720 million plus SEK145 million = SEK865 million. The equity value is the value of the firm minus the value of debt, or SEK865 million − SEK215 million = SEK650 million. The value per share is SEK650 million/100 million shares = SEK6.50 per share.

LEARNING MODULE

4

Market-Based Valuation: Price and Enterprise Value Multiples

by Jerald E. Pinto, PhD, CFA, Elaine Henry, PhD, CFA, Thomas R. Robinson, PhD, CFA, CAIA, and John D. Stowe, PhD, CFA.

Jerald E. Pinto, PhD, CFA, is at CFA Institute (USA). Elaine Henry, PhD, CFA, is at Stevens Institute of Technology (USA). Thomas R. Robinson, PhD, CFA, CAIA, Robinson Global Investment Management LLC, (USA). John D. Stowe, PhD, CFA, is at Ohio University (USA).

LEARNING OUTCOMES

Mastery	*The candidate should be able to:*
☐	contrast the method of comparables and the method based on forecasted fundamentals as approaches to using price multiples in valuation and explain economic rationales for each approach
☐	calculate and interpret a justified price multiple
☐	describe rationales for and possible drawbacks to using alternative price multiples and dividend yield in valuation
☐	calculate and interpret alternative price multiples and dividend yield
☐	calculate and interpret underlying earnings, explain methods of normalizing earnings per share (EPS), and calculate normalized EPS
☐	explain and justify the use of earnings yield (E/P)
☐	describe fundamental factors that influence alternative price multiples and dividend yield
☐	calculate and interpret a predicted P/E, given a cross-sectional regression on fundamentals, and explain limitations to the cross-sectional regression methodology
☐	calculate and interpret the justified price-to-earnings ratio (P/E), price-to-book ratio (P/B), and price-to-sales ratio (P/S) for a stock, based on forecasted fundamentals
☐	calculate and interpret the P/E-to-growth (PEG) ratio and explain its use in relative valuation
☐	calculate and explain the use of price multiples in determining terminal value in a multistage discounted cash flow (DCF) model
☐	evaluate whether a stock is overvalued, fairly valued, or undervalued based on comparisons of multiples

LEARNING OUTCOMES

Mastery	The candidate should be able to:
☐	evaluate a stock by the method of comparables and explain the importance of fundamentals in using the method of comparables
☐	explain alternative definitions of cash flow used in price and enterprise value (EV) multiples and describe limitations of each definition
☐	calculate and interpret EV multiples and evaluate the use of EV/EBITDA
☐	explain sources of differences in cross-border valuation comparisons
☐	describe momentum indicators and their use in valuation
☐	explain the use of the arithmetic mean, the harmonic mean, the weighted harmonic mean, and the median to describe the central tendency of a group of multiples

1 INTRODUCTION

☐	contrast the method of comparables and the method based on forecasted fundamentals as approaches to using price multiples in valuation and explain economic rationales for each approach

Among the most familiar and widely used valuation tools are price and enterprise value multiples. **Price multiples** are ratios of a stock's market price to some measure of fundamental value per share. **Enterprise value multiples**, by contrast, relate the total market value of all sources of a company's capital to a measure of fundamental value for the entire company.

The intuition behind price multiples is that investors evaluate the price of a share of stock—judge whether it is fairly valued, overvalued, or undervalued—by considering what a share buys in terms of per share earnings, net assets, cash flow, or some other measure of value (stated on a per share basis). The intuition behind enterprise value multiples is similar; investors evaluate the market value of an entire enterprise relative to the amount of earnings before interest, taxes, depreciation, and amortization (EBITDA), sales, or operating cash flow it generates. As valuation indicators (measures or indicators of value), multiples have the appealing qualities of simplicity in use and ease in communication. A multiple summarizes in a single number the relationship between the market value of a company's stock (or of its total capital) and some fundamental quantity, such as earnings, sales, or **book value** (owners' equity based on accounting values).

Among the questions we will study for answers that will help in making correct use of multiples as valuation tools are the following:

- What accounting issues affect particular price and enterprise value multiples, and how can analysts address them?
- How do price multiples relate to fundamentals, such as earnings growth rates, and how can analysts use this information when making valuation comparisons among stocks?

- For which types of valuation problems is a particular price or enterprise value multiple appropriate or inappropriate?
- What challenges arise in applying price and enterprise value multiples internationally?

Multiples may be viewed as valuation indicators relating to individual securities. Another type of valuation indicator used in security selection is **momentum indicators**. They typically relate either price or a fundamental (such as earnings) to the time series of its own past values or, in some cases, to its expected value. The logic behind the use of momentum indicators is that such indicators may provide information on future patterns of returns over some time horizon. Because the purpose of momentum indicators is to identify potentially rewarding investment opportunities, they can be viewed as a class of valuation indicators with a focus that is different from and complementary to the focus of price and enterprise value multiples.

We first put the use of price and enterprise value multiples in an economic context and present certain themes common to the use of any price or enterprise value multiple. We then present price multiples. The treatment of each multiple follows a common format: usage considerations, the relationship of the multiple to investors' expectations about fundamentals, and using the multiple in valuation based on comparables. The subsequent sections present enterprise value multiples, international considerations in using multiples, and treatment of momentum indicators. We then discuss several practical issues that arise in using valuation indicators.

Price and Enterprise Value Multiples in Valuation

In practice, two methods underpin analysts' use of price and enterprise value multiples: the method of comparables and the method based on forecasted fundamentals. Each of these methods relates to a definite economic rationale. In this section, we introduce the two methods and their associated economic rationales.

The Method of Comparables

The **method of comparables** refers to the valuation of an asset based on multiples of comparable (similar) assets—that is, valuation based on multiples benchmarked to the multiples of similar assets. The similar assets may be referred to as the **comparables**, the **comps**, or the **guideline assets** (or in the case of equity valuation, **guideline companies**). For example, multiplying a benchmark value of the price-to-earnings (P/E) multiple by an estimate of a company's earnings per share (EPS) provides a quick estimate of the value of the company's stock that can be compared with the stock's market price. Equivalently, comparing a stock's actual price multiple with a relevant benchmark multiple should lead the analyst to the same conclusion on whether the stock is relatively fairly valued, relatively undervalued, or relatively overvalued.

The idea behind price multiples is that a stock's price cannot be evaluated in isolation. Rather, it needs to be evaluated in relation to what it buys in terms of earnings, net assets, or some other measure of value. Obtained by dividing price by a measure of value per share, a price multiple gives the price to purchase one unit of value in whatever way value is measured. For example, a P/E of 20 means that it takes 20 units of currency (for example, €20) to buy one unit of earnings (for example, €1 of earnings). This scaling of price per share by value per share also makes possible comparisons among various stocks. For example, an investor pays more for a unit of earnings for a stock with a P/E of 25 than for another stock with a P/E of 20. Applying the method of comparables, the analyst would reason that if the securities are otherwise closely similar (if they have similar risk, profit margins, and growth prospects, for example), the security with the P/E of 20 is undervalued relative to the one with the P/E of 25.

The word *relative* is necessary. An asset may be undervalued relative to a comparison asset or group of assets, and an analyst may thus expect the asset to outperform the comparison asset or assets on a relative basis. If the comparison asset or assets themselves are not efficiently priced, however, the stock may not be undervalued: It could be fairly valued or even overvalued (on an absolute basis, i.e., in relation to its intrinsic value). Example 1 presents the method of comparables in its simplest application.

EXAMPLE 1

The Method of Comparables at Its Simplest

Company A's EPS is $1.50. Its closest competitor, Company B, is trading at a P/E of 22. Assume the companies have a similar operating and financial profile.

1. If Company A's stock is trading at $37.50, what does that indicate about its value relative to Company B?

Solution:

If Company A's stock is trading at $37.50, its P/E will be 25 ($37.50 divided by $1.50). If the companies are similar, this P/E would indicate that Company A is overvalued relative to Company B.

2. If we assume that Company A's stock should trade at about the same P/E as Company B's stock, what will we estimate as an appropriate price for Company A's stock?

Solution:

If we assume that Company A's stock should trade at about the same P/E as Company B's stock, we will estimate that an appropriate price for Company A's stock is $33 ($1.50 times 22).

The method of comparables applies also to enterprise value multiples. In this application, we would evaluate the market value of an entire company in relation to some measure of value relevant to all providers of capital, not only providers of equity capital. For example, multiplying a benchmark multiple of enterprise value (EV) to earnings before interest, taxes, depreciation, and amortization (EBITDA) times an estimate of a company's EBITDA provides a quick estimate of the value of the entire company. Similarly, comparing a company's actual enterprise value multiple with a relevant benchmark multiple allows an assessment of whether the company is relatively fairly valued, relatively undervalued, or relatively overvalued.

Many choices for the benchmark value of a multiple have appeared in valuation methodologies, including the multiple of a closely matched individual stock and the average or median value of the multiple for the stock's industry peer group. The economic rationale underlying the method of comparables is the **law of one price**—the economic principle that two identical assets should sell at the same price. The method of comparables is perhaps the most widely used approach for analysts *reporting* valuation judgments on the basis of price multiples. For this reason, the use of multiples in valuation is sometimes viewed solely as a type of relative-valuation approach; however, multiples can also be derived from, and expressed in terms of, fundamentals, as discussed in the next section.

The Method Based on Forecasted Fundamentals

The **method based on forecasted fundamentals** refers to the use of multiples that are derived from forecasted fundamentals—characteristics of a business related to profitability, growth, or financial strength. For brevity, we sometimes use the phrase "based on fundamentals" in describing multiples derived using this approach. Fundamentals drive cash flows, and we can relate multiples to company fundamentals through a discounted cash flow (DCF) model. Algebraic expressions of price multiples in terms of fundamentals facilitate an examination of how valuation differences among stocks relate to different expectations for those fundamentals.

One process for relating multiples to forecasted fundamentals begins with a valuation based on a DCF model. Recall that DCF models estimate the intrinsic value of a firm or its equity as the present value of expected cash flows and that fundamentals drive cash flows. Multiples are stated with respect to a single value of a fundamental, but any price or enterprise value multiple relates to the entire future stream of expected cash flows through its DCF value.

We can illustrate this concept by first taking the present value of the stream of expected future cash flows and then expressing the result relative to a forecasted fundamental. For example, if the DCF value of a UK stock is £10.20 and its forecasted EPS is £1.2, the forward P/E multiple consistent with the DCF value is £10.20/£1.2 = 8.5. (The term **forward P/E** refers to a P/E calculated on the basis of a forecast of EPS and is discussed in further detail later in this reading.) This exercise of relating a valuation to a price multiple applies to any definition of price multiple and any DCF model or residual income model.

In summary, we can approach valuation by using multiples from two perspectives. First, we can use the method of comparables, which involves comparing an asset's multiple to a standard of comparison. Similar assets should sell at similar prices. Second, we can use the method based on forecasted fundamentals, which involves forecasting the company's fundamentals rather than making comparisons with other companies. The price multiple of an asset should be related to its expected future cash flows. We can also incorporate the insights from the method based on forecasted fundamentals in explaining valuation differences based on comparables, because we seldom (if ever) find exact comparables. In the sections covering each multiple, we will present the method based on forecasted fundamentals first so we can refer to it when using the method of comparables.

Using either method, how can an analyst communicate a view about the value of a stock? Of course, the analyst simply can offer a qualitative judgment about whether the stock appears to be fairly valued, overvalued, or undervalued (and offer specific reasons for the view). The analyst may also be more precise by communicating a **justified price multiple** for the stock. The justified price multiple is the estimated **fair value** of that multiple, which can be justified on the basis of the method of comparables or the method of forecasted fundamentals.

For an example of a justified multiple based on the method of comparables, suppose we use the price-to-book (P/B) multiple in a valuation and find that the median P/B for the company's peer group, which would be the standard of comparison, is 2.2. Note that we are using the median rather than the mean value of the peer group's multiple to avoid distortions from outliers—an important issue when dealing with peer groups that often consist of a small number of companies. The stock's justified P/B based on the method of comparables is 2.2 (without making any adjustments for differences in fundamentals). We can compare the justified P/B with the actual P/B based on market price to form an opinion about value. If the justified P/B is larger (smaller) than the actual P/B, the stock may be undervalued (overvalued). We can also, on the assumption that the comparison assets are fairly priced, translate the justified

P/B based on comparables into an estimate of absolute fair value of the stock. If the current book value per share is \$23, then the fair value of the stock is 2.2 × \$23 = \$50.60, which can be compared with its market price.

For an example of a justified multiple based on fundamentals, suppose that we are using a residual income model and estimate that the value of the stock is \$46. Then, the justified P/B based on forecasted fundamentals is \$46/\$23 = 2.0, which we can again compare with the actual value of the stock's P/B. We can also state our estimate of the stock's absolute fair value as 2 × \$23 = \$46. (Note that the analyst could report valuation judgments related to a DCF model in terms of the DCF value directly; price multiples are a familiar form, however, in which to state valuations.) Furthermore, we can incorporate the insights from the method based on fundamentals to explain differences from results based on comparables.

In the next section, we begin a discussion of specific price and enterprise value multiples used in valuation.

2 PRICE/EARNINGS: THE BASICS

- [ ] calculate and interpret a justified price multiple
- [ ] describe rationales for and possible drawbacks to using alternative price multiples and dividend yield in valuation
- [ ] calculate and interpret alternative price multiples and dividend yield
- [ ] calculate and interpret underlying earnings, explain methods of normalizing earnings per share (EPS), and calculate normalized EPS
- [ ] explain and justify the use of earnings yield (E/P)

In this section, we first discuss the most familiar price multiple, the price-to-earnings ratio. In the context of that discussion, we introduce a variety of practical issues that have counterparts for most other multiples. These issues include analyst adjustments to the denominator of the ratio for accuracy and comparability and the use of inverse price multiples. Then, we discuss four other major price multiples from the same practical perspective.

Price/Earnings

In the first edition of *Security Analysis* (Graham and Dodd 1934, p. 351), Benjamin Graham and David L. Dodd described common stock valuation based on P/Es as the standard method of that era, and the P/E is still the most familiar valuation measure today.

We begin our discussion with rationales offered by analysts for the use of P/E and with the possible drawbacks of its use. We then define the two chief variations of the P/E: the trailing P/E and the forward P/E (also called the "leading P/E"). The multiple's numerator, market price, is (as in other multiples) definitely determinable; it presents no special problems of interpretation. But the denominator, EPS, is based on the complex rules of accrual accounting and presents significant interpretation issues. We discuss those issues and the adjustments analysts can make to obtain more-meaningful P/Es. Finally, we conclude the section by examining how analysts use P/Es to value a stock using the method of forecasted fundamentals and the method of comparables. As mentioned earlier, we discuss fundamentals first so that we can draw insights from that discussion when using comparables.

Several rationales support the use of P/E multiples in valuation:

- Earning power is a chief driver of investment value, and EPS, the denominator in the P/E ratio, is perhaps the chief focus of security analysts' attention. Surveys show that P/E ranks first among price multiples used in market-based valuation (2007 survey of CFA Institute members; for more details, see Pinto, Robinson, and Stowe 2018) and that it is the most popular valuation metric when making investment decisions (2012 BofA Merrill Lynch Institutional Factor Survey).
- The P/E ratio is widely recognized and used by investors.
- Differences in stocks' P/Es may be related to differences in long-run average returns on investments in those stocks, according to empirical research (Chan and Lakonishok 2004).

Potential drawbacks to using P/Es derive from the characteristics of EPS:

- EPS can be zero, negative, or insignificantly small relative to price, and P/E does not make economic sense with a zero, negative, or insignificantly small denominator.
- The ongoing or recurring components of earnings that are most important in determining intrinsic value can be practically difficult to distinguish from transient components.
- The application of accounting standards requires corporate managers to choose among acceptable alternatives and to use estimates in reporting. In making such choices and estimates, managers may distort EPS as an accurate reflection of economic performance. Such distortions may affect the comparability of P/Es among companies.

Methods to address these potential drawbacks will be discussed later in the reading. In the next section, we discuss alternative definitions of P/E based on alternative specifications of earnings.

Alternative Definitions of P/E

In calculating a P/E, the numerator most commonly used is the current price of the common stock, which is generally easily obtained and unambiguous for publicly traded companies. Selecting the appropriate EPS figure to be used in the denominator is not as straightforward. The following two issues must be considered:

- the time horizon over which earnings are measured, which results in alternative definitions of P/E, and
- adjustments to accounting earnings that the analyst may make so that P/Es for various companies can be compared.

Common alternative definitions of P/E are trailing P/E and forward P/E.

- A stock's **trailing P/E** (sometimes referred to as a current P/E) is its current market price divided by the most recent four quarters' EPS. In such calculations, EPS is sometimes referred to as "trailing 12-month (TTM) EPS." Note, however, that the Value Line Investment Survey uses "current P/E" to mean a P/E based on EPS for the most recent six months plus the projected EPS for the coming six months. That calculation blends historical and forward-looking elements.

- The **forward P/E** (also called the **leading P/E** or **prospective P/E**) is a stock's current price divided by next year's expected earnings. Trailing P/E is the P/E usually presented first in stock profiles that appear in financial databases, but most databases also provide the forward P/E. In practice, the forward P/E has a number of important variations that depend on how "next year" is defined, as we discuss later.

Other names and time-horizon definitions for P/E exist. For example, Thomson First Call (part of Refinitiv) provides various P/Es, including ratios that have as the denominator a stock's trailing 12-month EPS, last reported annual EPS, and EPS forecasted for one year to three years ahead. Another example is Value Line's company reports which display a median P/E, which is a rounded average of the four middle values of the range of annual average P/Es over the past 10 years.

In using the P/E, an analyst should apply the same definition to all companies and time periods under examination. Otherwise, the P/Es are not comparable, for a given company over time or for various companies at a specific point in time. One reason is that the differences in P/Es calculated by different methods may be systematic (as opposed to random). For example, for companies with rising earnings, the forward P/E will be smaller than the trailing P/E because the denominator in the forward P/E calculation will be larger.

Valuation is a forward-looking process, so analysts usually focus on the forward P/E when earnings forecasts are available. For large public companies, an analyst can develop earnings forecasts and/or obtain consensus earnings forecasts from a commercial database. When earnings are not readily predictable, however, a trailing P/E (or another valuation metric) may be more appropriate than a forward P/E. Furthermore, logic sometimes indicates that a particular definition of the P/E is not relevant. For example, a major acquisition or divestiture or a significant change in financial leverage may change a company's operating or financial risk so much that the trailing P/E based on past EPS is not informative about the future and thus not relevant to a valuation. In such a case, the forward P/E is the appropriate measure. In the following sections, we address issues that arise in calculating trailing and forward P/Es.

Trailing P/Es and forward P/Es are based on a single year's EPS. If that number is negative or viewed as unrepresentative of a company's earning power, however, an analyst may base the P/E calculation on a longer-run expected average EPS value. P/Es based on such normalized EPS data may be called **normalized P/Es**. Because the denominators in normalized P/Es are typically based on historical information, they are covered in the next section on calculating the trailing P/E.

Calculating the Trailing P/E

When using trailing earnings to calculate a P/E, the analyst must take care in determining the EPS to be used in the denominator. The analyst must consider the following:

- potential **dilution** of EPS (a reduction in proportional ownership interest as a result of the issuance of new shares.);
- transitory, nonrecurring components of earnings that are company specific;
- transitory components of earnings ascribable to cyclicality (business or industry cyclicality); and
- differences in accounting methods (when different companies' stocks are being compared).

Among the considerations mentioned, potential dilution of EPS generally makes the least demands on analysts' accounting expertise because companies are themselves required to present both basic EPS and diluted EPS. **Basic earnings per share** data reflect total earnings divided by the weighted average number of shares actually outstanding during the period. **Diluted earnings per share** reflects division by the number of shares that would be outstanding if holders of securities such as executive stock options, equity warrants, and convertible bonds exercised their options to obtain common stock. The diluted EPS measure also reflects the effect of such conversion on the numerator, earnings. For example, conversion of a convertible bond affects both the numerator (earnings) and the denominator (number of shares) in the EPS calculation. Because companies present both EPS numbers, the analyst does not need to make the computation. Companies also typically report details of the EPS computation in a footnote to the financial statements. Example 2, illustrating the first bullet point, shows the typical case in which the P/E based on diluted EPS is higher than the P/E based on basic EPS.

EXAMPLE 2

Basic versus Diluted EPS

For the fiscal year ended 30 September 2018, Siemens AG (SIE-DE) reported basic EPS of €7.12 and diluted EPS of €7.01. Based on a closing stock price of €95.94 on 29 March 2019, the trailing P/E for Siemens is 13.47 if basic EPS is used and 13.69 if diluted EPS is used.

When comparing companies, analysts generally prefer to use diluted EPS so that the EPS of companies with differing amounts of dilutive securities are on a comparable basis. The other bulleted considerations frequently lead to analyst adjustments to reported earnings numbers and are discussed in order below.

Analyst Adjustments for Nonrecurring Items

Items in earnings that are not expected to recur in the future are generally removed by analysts because valuation concentrates on future cash flows. The analyst's focus is on estimating **underlying earnings** (other names for this concept include **persistent earnings**, **continuing earnings**, and **core earnings**)—that is, earnings that exclude nonrecurring items. An increase in underlying earnings reflects an increase in earnings that the analyst expects to persist into the future. Companies may disclose adjusted earnings, which may be called non-IFRS earnings (because they differ, as a result of adjustments, from earnings as reportable under International Financial Reporting Standards), non-GAAP earnings (because they differ, as a result of adjustments, from earnings as reportable under US generally accepted accounting principles), pro forma earnings, adjusted earnings, or, as in Example 3, core earnings. All of these terms indicate that the earnings number differs in some way from that presented in conformity with accounting standards. Example 3 shows the calculation of EPS and P/E before and after analyst adjustments for nonrecurring items.

EXAMPLE 3

Calculating Trailing 12-Month EPS and Adjusting EPS for Nonrecurring Items

You are calculating a trailing P/E for Evergreen PLC as of 31 May 20X9, when the share price closed at £50.11 in London. In its first quarter of 20X9, ended 31 March, Evergreen reported basic and diluted EPS according to IFRS of £0.81, which included £0.34 of restructuring costs and £0.26 of amortization of intangibles arising from acquisitions. Adjusting for all of these items, Evergreen reported "core EPS" of £1.41 for the first quarter of 20X9, compared with core EPS of £1.81 for the first quarter of 20X8. Because the core EPS differed from the EPS calculated under IFRS, the company provided a reconciliation of the two EPS figures.

Other data for Evergreen as of 31 March 20X9 are given below. The trailing 12-month diluted EPS for 31 March 20X9 includes one quarter in 20X9 and three quarters in 20X8.

Measure	Full Year 20X8 (a)	Less 1st Quarter 20X8 (b)	Three Quarters of 20X8 (c = a – b)	Plus 1st Quarter 20X9 (d)	Trailing 12-Month EPS (e = c + d)
Reported diluted EPS	£4.98	£1.27	£3.71	£0.81	£4.52
Core EPS	£6.41	£1.81	£4.60	£1.41	£6.01
EPS excluding 20X8 legal provisions	£5.07	£1.28	£3.79	£0.81	£4.60

Based on the table and information about Evergreen, address the following:

Suppose you expect the amortization charges to continue for some years and note that, although Evergreen excluded restructuring charges from its core earnings calculation, Evergreen has reported restructuring charges in previous years. After reviewing all relevant data, you conclude that, in this instance, only the legal provision related to a previously disclosed legal matter should be viewed as clearly nonrecurring.

1. Based on the company's reported EPS, determine the trailing P/E of Evergreen as of 31 March 20X9.

Solution:

Based on reported EPS and without any adjustments for nonrecurring items, the trailing P/E is £50.11/£4.52 = 11.1.

2. Determine the trailing P/E of Evergreen as of 31 March 20X9 using core earnings as determined by Evergreen.

Solution:

Using the company's reported core earnings, you find that the trailing EPS would be £6.01 and the trailing P/E would be £50.11/£6.01 = 8.3.

3. Determine the trailing P/E based on your adjustment to EPS.

Solution:

The trailing EPS excluding only what you consider to be nonrecurring items is £4.60, and the trailing P/E on that basis is £50.11/£4.60 = 10.9.

Example 3 makes several important points:

- By any of its various names, underlying earnings, or core earnings, is a non-IFRS concept without prescribed rules for its calculation.
- An analyst's calculation of underlying earnings may well differ from that of the company supplying the earnings numbers. Company-reported core earnings may not be comparable among companies because of differing bases of calculation. Analysts should thus always carefully examine the calculation and, generally, should not rely on such company-reported core earnings numbers.
- In general, the P/E that an analyst uses in valuation should reflect the analyst's judgment about the company's underlying earnings and should be calculated on a consistent basis among all stocks under review.

The identification of nonrecurring items often requires detailed work—in particular, examination of the income statement, the footnotes to the income statement, and the management discussion and analysis section. The analyst cannot rely on income statement classifications alone to identify nonrecurring components of earnings. Nonrecurring items (for example, gains and losses from the sale of assets, asset **write-downs**, goodwill impairment, provisions for future losses, and changes in **accounting estimates**) often appear in the income from continuing operations portion of a business's income statement. An analyst may decide not to exclude income/loss from discontinued operations when assets released from discontinued operations are redirected back into the company's earnings base. An analyst who takes income statement classifications at face value may draw incorrect conclusions in a valuation.

This discussion does not exhaust the analysis that may be necessary to distinguish earnings components that are expected to persist into the future from those that are not. For example, earnings may be decomposed into cash flow and accrual components (where the accrual component of earnings is the difference between a cash measure of earnings and a measure of earnings under the relevant set of accounting standards). Some research indicates that the cash flow component of earnings should receive a greater weight than the accrual component of earnings in valuation, and analysts may attempt to reflect that conclusion in the earnings used in calculating P/Es.

Analyst Adjustments for Business-Cycle Influences

In addition to company-specific effects, such as restructuring costs, transitory effects on earnings can come from business-cycle or industry-cycle influences. These effects are somewhat different from company-specific effects. Because business cycles repeat, business-cycle effects, although transitory, can be expected to recur in subsequent cycles.

Because of cyclical effects, the most recent four quarters of earnings may not accurately reflect the average or long-term earning power of the business, particularly for **cyclical businesses**—those with high sensitivity to business- or industry-cycle influences, such as automobile and steel manufacturers. Trailing EPS for such stocks is often depressed or negative at the bottom of a cycle and unusually high at the top of a cycle. Empirically, P/Es for cyclical companies are often highly volatile over a cycle even without any change in business prospects: High P/Es on depressed EPS at the bottom of the cycle and low P/Es on unusually high EPS at the top of the cycle reflect the countercyclical property of P/Es known as the **Molodovsky effect**, named after Nicholas Molodovsky, who wrote on this subject in the 1950s and referred to using average earnings as a simple starting point for understanding a company's underlying earnings power. Analysts address this problem by normalizing EPS—that is, estimating the level of EPS that the business could be expected to achieve under mid-cyclical conditions (**normalized EPS** or **normal EPS**). Please note that we are using the term "normalized earnings" to refer to earnings adjusted for the effects of a business cycle. Some sources use the term "normalized earnings" also to refer to earnings adjusted for nonrecurring items.

Two of several available methods to calculate normalized EPS are as follows:

- The method of *historical average EPS*, in which normalized EPS is calculated as average EPS over the most recent full cycle
- The method of *average return on equity*, in which normalized EPS is calculated as the average return on equity (ROE) from the most recent full cycle, multiplied by current book value per share

The first method is one of several possible statistical approaches to the problem of cyclical earnings; however, this method does not account for changes in a business's size. The second alternative, by using recent book value per share, reflects more accurately the effect on EPS of growth or shrinkage in the company's size. For that reason, the method of average ROE is sometimes preferred. When reported current book value does not adequately reflect company size in relation to past values (because of items such as large write-downs), the analyst can make appropriate accounting adjustments. The analyst can also estimate normalized earnings by multiplying total assets by an estimate of the long-run return on total assets or by multiplying shareholders' equity by an estimate of the long-run return on total shareholders' equity. These methods are particularly useful for a period in which a cyclical company has reported a loss.

Example 4 illustrates this concept. The example uses data for an **American Depositary Receipt** (ADR) but is applicable to any equity security. An ADR is intended to facilitate US investment in non-US companies. It is a negotiable certificate issued by a depositary bank that represents ownership in a non-US company's deposited equity (i.e., equity held in custody by the depositary bank in the company's home market). One ADR may represent one, more than one, or less than one deposited share. The number of or fraction of deposited securities represented by one ADR is referred to as the "ADR ratio."

EXAMPLE 4

Normalizing EPS for Business-Cycle Effects

You are researching the valuation of Zenlandia Chemical Company, a large (fictitious) manufacturer of specialty chemicals. Your research is for a US investor who is interested in the company's ADRs rather than the company's shares listed on the Zenlandia Stock Exchange. On 5 July 2021, the closing price of the US-listed ADR was $18.21. The chemical industry is notably cyclical, so you decide to normalize earnings as part of your analysis. You believe that data from 2014 reasonably capture the beginning of the most recent business cycle, and you want to evaluate a normalized P/E. Exhibit 1 supplies data on EPS (based on Zenlandia GAAP) for one ADR, book value per share (BVPS) for one ADR, and the company's ROE.

Exhibit 1: Zenlandia Chemical Company (Currency in US Dollars)

Measure	2014	2015	2016	2017	2018	2019	2020
EPS (ADR)	$0.74	$0.63	$0.61	$0.54	$1.07	$0.88	$1.08
BVPS (ADR)	$3.00	$2.93	$2.85	$2.99	$3.80	$4.03	$4.82
ROE	24.7%	21.5%	21.4%	18.1%	28.2%	21.8%	22.4%

Note: This example involves a single company. When the analyst compares multiple companies on the basis of P/Es based on normalized EPS and uses this normalization approach, the analyst should be sure that the ROEs are being calculated consistently by the subject companies. In this example, ROE for each year is being calculated by using ending BVPS and, essentially, trailing earnings are being normalized.

Using the data in Exhibit 1:

1. Calculate a normalized EPS by the method of historical average EPS and then calculate the P/E based on that estimate of normalized EPS.

Solution:

Averaging EPS over the 2014–20 period, you would find it to be ($0.74 + $0.63 + $0.61 + $0.54 + $1.07 + $0.88 + $1.08)/7 = $0.79. Thus, according to the method of historical average EPS, normalized EPS is $0.79. The P/E based on this estimate is $18.21/$0.79 = 23.1.

2. Calculate a normalized EPS by the method of average ROE and the P/E based on that estimate of normalized EPS.

Solution:

Average ROE over the 2014–20 period is (24.7% + 21.5% + 21.4% + 18.1% + 28.2% + 21.8% + 22.4%)/7 = 22.6%. Based on the current BVPS of $4.82, the method of average ROE gives 0.226 × $4.82 = $1.09 as normalized EPS. The P/E based on this estimate is $18.21/$1.09 = 16.7.

3. Explain the source of the differences in the normalized EPS calculated by the two methods, and contrast the impact on the estimate of a normalized P/E.

Solution:

From 2014 to 2020, BVPS increased from $3.00 to $4.82, an increase of about 61%. The estimate of normalized EPS of $1.09 from the average ROE method reflects the use of information on the current size of the company better than does the $0.79 calculated from the historical average EPS method. Because of that difference, the company appears more conservatively valued (as indicated by a lower P/E) when the method based on average ROE is used.

Analyst Adjustments for Comparability with Other Companies

Analysts adjust EPS for differences in accounting methods between the company and companies it is being compared with so that the P/Es will be comparable. For example, if an analyst is comparing a company that uses the last-in, first-out (LIFO) method of inventory accounting as permitted by US GAAP (but not by IFRS) with another company that uses the first-in, first-out (FIFO) method, the analyst should adjust earnings to provide comparability in all ratio and valuation analyses. In general, any adjustment made to a company's reported financials for purposes of financial statement analysis should be incorporated into an analysis of P/E and other multiples.

Dealing with Extremely Low, Zero, or Negative Earnings

Having addressed the challenges that arise in calculating P/E because of nonrecurring items and business-cycle influences and for comparability among companies, we present in this section the methods analysts have developed for dealing with extremely low, zero, or negative earnings.

Stock selection disciplines that use P/Es or other price multiples often involve ranking stocks from highest value of the multiple to lowest value of the multiple. The security with the lowest positive P/E has the lowest purchase cost per currency unit of earnings among the securities ranked. Zero earnings and negative earnings pose a problem if the analyst wishes to use P/E as the valuation metric. Because division by zero is undefined, P/Es cannot be calculated for zero earnings.

A P/E can technically be calculated in the case of negative earnings. Negative earnings, however, result in a negative P/E. A negative-P/E security will rank below the lowest positive-P/E security, but because earnings are negative, the negative-P/E security is actually the most costly in terms of earnings purchased. Thus, negative P/Es are not meaningful.

In some cases, an analyst might handle negative EPS by using normalized EPS instead. Also, when trailing EPS is negative, the year-ahead EPS and thus the forward P/E may be positive. An argument in favor of either of these approaches based on positive earnings is that if a company is appropriately treated as a going concern, losses cannot be the usual operating result.

If the analyst is interested in a ranking, however, one solution (applicable to any ratio involving a quantity that can be negative or zero) is the use of an **inverse price ratio**—that is, the reciprocal of the original ratio, which places price in the denominator. The use of inverse price multiples addresses the issue of consistent ranking because price is never negative. In the case of the P/E, the inverse price ratio is earnings to price (E/P), known as the **earnings yield**. Ranked by earnings yield from highest to lowest, the securities are correctly ranked from cheapest to most costly in terms of the amount of earnings one unit of currency buys. Earnings yield can be based on normalized EPS, expected next-year EPS, or trailing EPS. In these cases also, earnings yield provides a consistent ranking.

Exhibit 2 illustrates these points for a group of automobile companies, one of which has a negative EPS. When reporting a P/E based on negative earnings, analysts should report such P/Es as "NM" (not meaningful).

Exhibit 2: P/E and E/P for Five Automobile Companies (as of 28 June 2019; in US Dollars)

Company	Current Price	Diluted EPS (TTM)	P/E (TTM)	E/P (%)
Ford Motor Co. (F)	10.28	0.78	13.2	7.59
Honda Motor Co.	25.85	3.12	8.3	12.06
Fiat Chrysler	13.88	2.32	6.0	16.71
General Motors	38.57	6.29	11.72	8.53
Tesla Inc.	224.45	–7.72	NM	–2.51

Source: Yahoo! Finance.

In addition to zero and negative earnings, extremely low earnings can pose problems when using P/Es—particularly for evaluating the distribution of P/Es of a group of stocks under review. In this case, again, inverse price ratios can be useful. The P/E of a stock with extremely low earnings may, nevertheless, be extremely high because an earnings rebound is anticipated. An extremely high P/E—an outlier P/E—can overwhelm the effect of the other P/Es in the calculation of the mean P/E. Although the use of median P/Es and other techniques can mitigate the problem of skewness caused by outliers, the distribution of inverse price ratios is inherently less susceptible to outlier-induced skewness.

As mentioned, earnings yield is but one example of an inverse price ratio—that is, the reciprocal of a price ratio. Exhibit 3 summarizes inverse price ratios for all the price ratios we discuss in this reading.

Exhibit 3: Summary of Price and Inverse Price Ratios

Price Ratio	Inverse Price Ratio	Comments
Price to earnings (P/E)	Earnings yield (E/P)	Both forms commonly used.
Price to book (P/B)	Book to market (B/P)*	Book value is less commonly negative than EPS. Book to market is favored in research but not common in practitioner usage.
Price to sales (P/S)	Sales to price (S/P)	S/P is rarely used except when all other ratios are being stated in the form of inverse price ratios; sales is not zero or negative in practice for going concerns.

Price Ratio	Inverse Price Ratio	Comments
Price to cash flow (P/CF)	Cash flow yield (CF/P)	Both forms are commonly used.
Price to dividends (P/D)	Dividend yield (D/P)	Dividend yield is much more commonly used because P/D is not calculable for non-dividend-paying stocks, but both D/P and P/D are used in discussing index valuation.

"Book to market" is probably more common usage than "book to price." Book to market is variously abbreviated B/M, BV/MV (for "book value" and "market value"), or B/P.
Note: B, S, CF, and D are in per-share terms.

Forward P/E

The forward P/E is a major and logical alternative to the trailing P/E because valuation is naturally forward looking. In the definition of forward P/E, analysts have interpreted "next year's expected earnings" as expected EPS for

- the next four quarters,
- the next 12 months, or
- the next fiscal year.

In this section, unless otherwise stated, we use the first definition of forward P/E (i.e., the next four quarters), which is closest to how cash flows are dated in our discussion of DCF valuation. To illustrate the calculation, suppose the current market price of a stock is $15 as of 1 March 2020 and the most recently reported quarterly EPS (for the quarter ended 31 December 2019) is $0.22. Our forecasts of EPS are as follows:

- $0.15 for the quarter ending 31 March 2020,
- $0.18 for the quarter ending 30 June 2020,
- $0.18 for the quarter ending 30 September 2020, and
- $0.24 for the quarter ending 31 December 2020.

The sum of the forecasts for the next four quarters is $0.15 + $0.18 + $0.18 + $0.24 = $0.75, and the forward P/E for this stock is $15/$0.75 = 20.0.

Another important concept related to the forward P/E is the next 12-month (NTM) P/E, which corresponds in a forward-looking sense to the TTM P/E concept of trailing P/E. A stock's **NTM P/E** is its current market price divided by an estimated next 12-month EPS, which typically combines the annual EPS estimates from two fiscal years, weighted to reflect the relative proximity of the fiscal year. For example, assume that in late August 2020, an analyst is looking at Microsoft Corporation. Microsoft has a June 30 fiscal year end, so at the time of the analyst's scrutiny, there were 10 months remaining until the end of the company's 2021 fiscal year (i.e., September 2020 through June 2021, inclusive). The estimated next 12-month EPS for Microsoft would be calculated as [(10/12) × FY21E EPS] + [(2/12) × FY22E EPS]. NTM P/E is useful because it facilitates comparison of companies with different fiscal year ends without the need to use quarterly estimates, which for many companies are not available.

Applying the fiscal year concept, Thomson First Call reports a stock's "forward P/E" in two ways: first, based on the mean of analysts' *current fiscal year* (FY1 = Fiscal Year 1) forecasts, for which analysts may have actual EPS in hand for some quarters, and second, based on analysts' *following fiscal year* (FY2 = Fiscal Year 2) forecasts, which must be based entirely on forecasts. For Thomson First Call, "forward P/E" contrasts with "current P/E," which is based on the last reported annual EPS.

Clearly, analysts must be consistent in the definition of forward P/E when comparing stocks. Example 5 and Example 6 illustrate two ways of calculating forward P/E.

EXAMPLE 5

Calculating a Forward P/E (1)

A market price for the common stock of IBM in late June 2019 was $137.90. IBM's fiscal year coincides with the calendar year. At that time, the consensus EPS forecast of the 22 analysts covering IBM was $13.91 for 2019 (FY1), and the consensus EPS forecast of 20 analysts covering IBM was $14.17 for 2020 (FY2).

1. Calculate IBM's forward P/E based on the fiscal year consensus forecasted EPS for FY1.

Solution:

IBM's forward P/E is $137.90/$13.91 = 9.9 based on FY1 forecasted EPS. Note that this EPS number includes the reported first quarter earnings and a forecast of the three remaining quarters as of late June 2019.

2. Calculate IBM's forward P/E based on a fiscal year definition and the FY2 consensus forecasted EPS.

Solution:

IBM's forward P/E is $137.90/$14.17 = 9.7 based on FY2 forecasted EPS.

In Example 5, the company's EPS was expected to increase by slightly less than 2%, so the forward P/Es based on the two different EPS specifications differed from one another somewhat but not significantly. Example 6 presents the calculation of forward P/Es for a company with volatile earnings.

EXAMPLE 6

Calculating a Forward P/E (2)

In this example, we use alternative definitions of "forward" to compute forward P/Es. Exhibit 4 presents actual and forecasted EPS for Selene Gaming Corp. (Selene), which owns and operates gaming entertainment properties.

Exhibit 4: Quarterly EPS for Selene (in US Dollars; Excluding Nonrecurring Items and Discontinued Operations)

Year	31 March	30 June	30 September	31 December	Annual Estimate
2020	0.10	0.00	E(0.10)	E(0.50)	(0.50)
2021	E0.70	E0.80	E0.30	E(0.30)	1.50

Source: The Value Line Investment Survey.

On 9 August 2020, Selene closed at $12.20. Selene's fiscal year ends on 31 December. As of 9 August 2020, solve the following problems by using the information in Exhibit 4:

1. Calculate Selene's forward P/E based on the next four quarters of forecasted EPS.

Solution:

We sum forecasted EPS as follows:

3Q:2020 EPS (estimate)	(\$0.10)
4Q:2020 EPS (estimate)	(\$0.50)
1Q:2021 EPS (estimate)	\$0.70
2Q:2021 EPS (estimate)	\$0.80
Sum	\$0.90

The forward P/E by this definition is \$12.20/\$0.90 = 13.6.

2. Calculate Selene's NTM P/E.

Solution:

As of 9 August 2020, approximately five months remained in FY2020. Therefore, the estimated next 12-month EPS for Selene would be based on annual estimates in the last column of Exhibit 4: [(5/12) × FY20E EPS] + [(7/12) × FY21E EPS] = (5/12)(−0.50) + (7/12)(1.50) = 0.67. The NTM P/E would be \$12.20/\$0.67 = 18.2.

3. Calculate Selene's forward P/E based on a fiscal year definition and current fiscal year (2020) forecasted EPS.

Solution:

We sum EPS as follows:

1Q:2020 EPS (actual)	\$0.10
2Q:2020 EPS (actual)	\$0.00
3Q:2020 EPS (estimate)	(\$0.10)
4Q:2020 EPS (estimate)	(\$0.50)
Sum	(\$0.50)

The forward P/E is \$12.20/(\$0.50) = −24.4, which is not meaningful.

4. Calculate Selene's forward P/E based on a fiscal year definition and next fiscal year (2021) forecasted EPS.

Solution:

We sum EPS as follows:

1Q:2021 EPS (estimate)	\$0.70
2Q:2021 EPS (estimate)	\$0.80
3Q:2021 EPS (estimate)	\$0.30
4Q:2021 EPS (estimate)	(\$0.30)
Sum	\$1.50

The forward P/E by this definition is \$12.20/\$1.50 = 8.1.

As illustrated in Example 6, for companies with volatile earnings, forward P/Es and thus valuations based on forward P/Es can vary dramatically depending on the definition of earnings. The analyst would probably be justified in normalizing EPS for Selene. The gaming industry is highly sensitive to discretionary spending; thus, Selene's earnings are strongly procyclical.

Having explored the issues involved in calculating P/Es, we turn to using them in valuation.

3 PRICE/EARNINGS: VALUATION BASED ON FORECASTED FUNDAMENTALS

- ☐ describe fundamental factors that influence alternative price multiples and dividend yield
- ☐ calculate and interpret a predicted P/E, given a cross-sectional regression on fundamentals, and explain limitations to the cross-sectional regression methodology

The analyst who understands DCF valuation models can use them not only in developing an estimate of the justified P/E for a stock but also to gain insight into possible sources of valuation differences when the method of comparables is used. Linking P/Es to a DCF model helps us address what value the market should place on a dollar of EPS when we are given a particular set of expectations about the company's profitability, growth, and cost of capital.

Justified P/E

The simplest of all DCF models is the Gordon (constant) growth form of the dividend discount model (DDM). Presentations of discounted dividend valuation commonly show that the P/E of a share can be related to the value of a stock as calculated in the Gordon growth model through the expressions

$$\frac{P_0}{E_1} = \frac{D_1/E_1}{r-g} = \frac{1-b}{r-g} \quad (1)$$

for the forward P/E and

$$\frac{P_0}{E_0} = \frac{D_0(1+g)/E_0}{r-g} = \frac{(1-b)(1+g)}{r-g} \quad (2)$$

for the trailing P/E, where

P = price

E = earnings

D = dividends

r = required rate of return

g = dividend growth rate

b = retention rate

Under the assumption of constant dividend growth, the first expression gives the justified forward P/E and the second gives the justified trailing P/E. Note that both expressions state P/E as a function of two fundamentals: the stock's required rate of return, r, which reflects its risk, and the expected (stable) dividend growth rate, g. The dividend payout ratio, $1 - b$, also enters into the expressions.

A particular value of the P/E is associated with a set of forecasts of the fundamentals and the dividend payout ratio. This value is the stock's **justified (fundamental) P/E** based on forecasted fundamentals (that is, the P/E justified by fundamentals). All else being equal, the higher the expected dividend growth rate or the lower the stock's required rate of return, the higher the stock's intrinsic value and the higher its justified P/E.

This intuition carries over to more-complex DCF models. Using any DCF model, all else being equal, justified P/E is

- inversely related to the stock's required rate of return and
- positively related to the growth rate(s) of future expected cash flows, however defined.

We illustrate the calculation of a justified forward P/E in Example 7.

EXAMPLE 7

Forward P/E Based on Fundamental Forecasts (1)

BP p.l.c. (London: BP) is one of the world's largest integrated oil producers. The company has continued to deal with litigation concerns surrounding its role in a 2010 drilling rig accident. Jan Unger, an energy analyst, forecasts a long-term earnings retention rate, *b*, for BP of 40% and a long-term growth rate of 3.5%. Given the significant legal uncertainties still facing BP shareholders, Unger estimates a required rate of return of 7.6%. Based on Unger's forecasts of fundamentals and Equation 1, BP's justified forward P/E is

$$\frac{P_0}{E_1} = \frac{1-b}{r-g} = \frac{1-0.40}{0.076-0.035} = 14.6.$$

When using a complex DCF model to value the stock (e.g., a model with varying growth rates and varying assumptions about dividends), the analyst may not be able to express the P/E as a function of fundamental, constant variables. In such cases, the analyst can still calculate a justified P/E by dividing the value per share (that results from a DCF model) by estimated EPS, as illustrated in Example 8. Approaches similar to this one can be used to develop other justified multiples.

EXAMPLE 8

Forward P/E Based on Fundamental Forecasts (2)

Toyota Motor Corporation is one of the world's largest vehicle manufacturers. The company's most recent fiscal year ended on 31 March 2019. In late June 2019, you are valuing Toyota stock, which closed at ¥6,688 on the previous day. You have used a free cash flow to equity (FCFE) model to value the company stock and have obtained a value of ¥6,980 for the stock. For ease of communication, you want to express your valuation in terms of a forward P/E based on your forecasted fiscal year 2020 EPS of ¥720. Toyota's fiscal year 2020 is from 1 April 2019 through 31 March 2020.

1. What is Toyota's justified P/E based on forecasted fundamentals?

Solution:

Value of the stock derived from FCFE = ¥6,980.

Forecasted 2020 EPS = ¥720.
¥6,980/¥720 = 9.7 is the justified forward P/E.

2. Based on a comparison of the current price of ¥6,688 with your estimated intrinsic value of ¥6,980, the stock appears to be undervalued by approximately 4%. Use your answer to Part 1 to state this evaluation in terms of P/Es.

Solution:

The justified P/E of 9.7 is about 4% higher than the forward P/E based on current market price, ¥6,688/¥720 = 9.3.

The next section illustrates another, but less commonly used, approach to relating price multiples to fundamentals.

Predicted P/E Based on Cross-Sectional Regression

A predicted P/E, which is conceptually similar to a justified P/E, can be estimated from cross-sectional regressions of P/E on the fundamentals believed to drive security valuation. Kisor and Whitbeck (1963) and Malkiel and Cragg (1970) pioneered this approach. Their studies measured P/Es for a group of stocks and the characteristics thought to determine P/E: growth rate in earnings, payout ratio, and a measure of volatility, such as standard deviation of earnings changes or beta. An analyst can conduct such cross-sectional regressions by using any set of explanatory variables considered to determine investment value; the analyst must bear in mind, however, potential distortions that can be introduced by multicollinearity among independent variables. Example 9 illustrates the prediction of P/E using cross-sectional regression.

EXAMPLE 9

Predicted P/E Based on a Cross-Sectional Regression

You are valuing a food company with a beta of 0.9, a dividend payout ratio of 0.45, and an earnings growth rate of 0.08. The estimated regression for a group of other stocks in the same industry is

$$\text{Predicted P/E} = 12.12 + (2.25 \times \text{DPR}) - (0.20 \times \text{Beta}) + (14.43 \times \text{EGR}),$$

where DPR is the dividend payout ratio and EGR is the five-year earnings growth rate.

1. Based on this cross-sectional regression, what is the predicted P/E for the food company?

Solution:

Predicted P/E = 12.12 + (2.25 × 0.45) – (0.20 × 0.9) + (14.43 × 0.08) = 14.1. The predicted P/E is 14.1.

2. If the stock's actual trailing P/E is 18, is the stock fairly valued, overvalued, or undervalued?

Solution:

Because the predicted P/E of 14.1 is less than the actual P/E of 18, the stock appears to be overvalued. That is, it is selling at a higher multiple than is justified by its fundamentals.

A cross-sectional regression summarizes a large amount of data in a single equation and can provide a useful additional perspective on a valuation. It is not frequently used as a main tool, however, because it is subject to at least three limitations:

- The method captures valuation relationships only for the specific stock (or sample of stocks) over a particular time period. The predictive power of the regression for a different stock and different time period is not known.
- The regression coefficients and explanatory power of the regressions tend to change substantially over a number of years. The relationships between P/E and fundamentals may thus change over time. Empirical evidence suggests that the relationships between P/Es and such characteristics as earnings growth, dividend payout, and beta are not stable over time (Damodaran 2012). Furthermore, because distributions of multiples change over time, the predictive power of results from a regression at any point in time can be expected to diminish with the passage of time (Damodaran 2012).
- Because regressions based on this method are prone to the problem of multicollinearity (correlation within linear combinations of the independent variables), interpreting individual regression coefficients is difficult.

Overall, rather than examining the relationship between a stock's P/E multiple and economic variables, the bulk of capital market research examines the relationship between companies' stock prices (and returns on the stock) and explanatory variables, one of which is often earnings (or unexpected earnings). A classic example of such research is the Fama and French (1992) study showing that, used alone, a number of factors explained cross-sectional stock returns in the 1963–90 period; the factors were E/P, size, leverage, and the book-to-market multiples. When these variables were used in combination, however, size and book to market had explanatory power that absorbed the roles of the other variables in explaining cross-sectional stock returns. Research building on that study eventually resulted in the Fama–French three-factor model (with the factors of size, book to market, and beta). Another classic academic study providing evidence that accounting variables appear to have predictive power for stock returns is Lakonishok, Shleifer, and Vishny (1994), which also provided evidence that value strategies—buying stocks with low prices relative to earnings, book value, cash flow, and sales growth—produced superior five-year buy-and-hold returns in the 1968–90 period without involving greater fundamental risk than a strategy of buying growth stocks.

PRICE/EARNINGS: USING THE P/E IN VALUATION 4

- ☐ calculate and interpret the justified price-to-earnings ratio (P/E), price-to-book ratio (P/B), and price-to-sales ratio (P/S) for a stock, based on forecasted fundamentals
- ☐ calculate and interpret the P/E-to-growth (PEG) ratio and explain its use in relative valuation
- ☐ calculate and explain the use of price multiples in determining terminal value in a multistage discounted cash flow (DCF) model
- ☐ evaluate whether a stock is overvalued, fairly valued, or undervalued based on comparisons of multiples

The most common application of the P/E approach to valuation is to estimate the value of a company's stock by applying a benchmark multiple to the company's actual or forecasted earnings. An essentially equivalent approach is to compare a stock's actual price multiple with a benchmark value of the multiple. This section explores these comparisons for P/Es. Using any multiple in the method of comparables involves the following steps:

- Select and calculate the price multiple that will be used in the comparison.
- Select the comparison asset or assets and calculate the value of the multiple for the comparison asset(s). For a group of comparison assets, calculate a median or mean value of the multiple for the assets. The result in either case is the **benchmark value of the multiple**.
- Use the benchmark value of the multiple, possibly subjectively adjusted for differences in fundamentals, to estimate the value of a company's stock. (Equivalently, compare the subject stock's actual multiple with the benchmark value.)
- When feasible, assess whether differences between the estimated value of the company's stock and the current price of the company's stock are explained by differences in the fundamental determinants of the price multiple and modify conclusions about relative valuation accordingly. (An essentially equivalent approach is to assess whether differences between a company's actual multiple and the benchmark value of the multiple can be explained by differences in fundamentals.)

These bullet points provide the structure for this reading's presentation of the method of comparables. The first price multiple that will be used in the comparison is the P/E. Practitioners' choices for the comparison assets and the benchmark value of the P/E derived from these assets include the following:

- the average or median value of the P/E for the company's peer group of companies within an industry, including an average past value of the P/E for the stock relative to this peer group;
- the average or median value of the P/E for the company's industry or sector, including an average past value of the P/E for the stock relative to the industry or sector;
- the P/E for a representative equity index, including an average past value of the P/E for the stock relative to the equity index; and
- an average past value of the P/E for the stock.

To illustrate the first bullet point, the company's P/E (say, 15) may be compared to the median P/E for the peer companies currently (say, 10), or the ratio 15/10 = 1.5 may be compared to its average past value. The P/E of the most closely matched individual stock can also be used as a benchmark; because of averaging, however, using a group of stocks or an equity index is typically expected to generate less valuation error than using a single stock. We later illustrate a comparison with a single closely matched individual stock.

Economists and investment analysts have long attempted to group companies by similarities and differences in their business operations. A country's economy overall is typically grouped most broadly into **economic sectors** or large industry groupings. These groupings differ depending on the source of the financial information, and an analyst should be aware of differences among data sources. Classifications often attempt to group companies by what they supply (e.g., energy, consumer goods), by demand characteristics (e.g., consumer discretionary), or by financial market or economic "theme" (e.g., consumer cyclical, consumer noncyclical).

Two classification systems that are widely used in equity analysis are the Global Industry Classification System (GICS) sponsored by Standard & Poor's and MSCI and the Industrial Classification Benchmark (ICB). Many other classification schemes developed by commercial and governmental organizations and by academics are also in use.

The GICS structure assigns each company to one of 158 subindustries, an industry (69 in total), an industry group (24 in total), and an economic sector (11 in total: consumer discretionary, consumer staples, energy, financials, health care, industrials, information technology, materials, real estate, telecommunication services, and utilities). The assignment is made by a judgment as to the company's principal business activity, which is based primarily on sales. Because a company is classified on the basis of one business activity, a given company appears in just one group at each level of the classification. A classification ("industrial conglomerates") is available under the capital goods sector of industrials for companies that cannot be assigned to a principal business activity.

The ICB, like GICS, has four levels, but the terminology of ICB uses "sector" and "industry" in nearly opposite senses. The ICB is managed by FTSE Russell. At the bottom of the four levels are 173 subsectors, each of which belongs to one of 45 sectors; each sector belongs to one of 20 supersectors; and each supersector belongs to one of 11 industries at the highest level of classification. (The numbers in the groups were changed effective 1 July 2019; changes are made to the classification from time to time. See www.ftserussell.com/data/industry-classification-benchmark-icbwww.icbenchmark.com for updates.) The industries are technology, telecommunications, health care, financials, real estate, consumer discretionary, consumer staples, industrials, basic materials, energy, and utilities.

For these classification systems, analysts often choose the narrowest grouping (i.e., subindustry for GICS and subsector for ICB) as an appropriate starting point for comparison asset identification. To narrow the list of comparables in the subsector, an analyst might use information on company size (as measured by revenue or market value of equity) and information on the specific markets served.

Analysts should be aware that, although different organizations often group companies in a broadly similar fashion, sometimes they differ sharply. The lists of peer companies or competitors given by each of these organizations can be, as a result, quite distinct.

The comparable companies—selected by using any of the choices described previously—provide the basis for calculating a benchmark value of the multiple. In analyzing differences between the subject company's multiple and the benchmark value of the multiple, financial ratio analysis serves as a useful tool. Financial ratios can point out

- a company's ability to meet short-term financial obligations (liquidity ratios);
- the efficiency with which assets are being used to generate sales (asset turnover ratios);
- the use of debt in financing the business (leverage ratios);
- the degree to which fixed charges, such as interest on debt, are being met by earnings or cash flow (coverage ratios); and
- profitability (profitability ratios).

With this understanding of terms in hand, we turn to using the method of comparables. We begin with cross-sectional P/Es derived from industry peer groups and move to P/Es derived from comparison assets that are progressively less closely matched to the stock. We then turn to using historical P/Es—that is, P/Es derived from the company's own history. Finally, we sketch how both fundamentals- and comparables-driven models for P/Es can be used to calculate the terminal value in a multistage DCF valuation.

Peer-Company Multiples

Companies operating in the same industry as the subject company (i.e., its peer group) are frequently used as comparison assets. The advantage of using a peer group is that the constituent companies are typically similar in their business mix to the company being analyzed. This approach is consistent with the idea underlying the method of comparables—that similar assets should sell at similar prices. The subject stock's P/E is compared with the median or mean P/E for the peer group to arrive at a relative valuation. Equivalently, multiplying the benchmark P/E by the company's EPS provides an estimate of the stock's value that can be compared with the stock's market price. The value estimated in this way represents an estimate of intrinsic value if the comparison assets are efficiently (fairly) priced.

In practice, analysts often find that the stock being valued has some significant differences from the median or mean fundamental characteristics of the comparison assets. In applying the method of comparables, analysts usually attempt to judge whether differences from the benchmark value of the multiple can be explained by differences in the fundamental factors believed to influence the multiple. The following relationships for P/E hold, all else being equal:

- If the subject stock has higher-than-average (or higher-than-median) expected earnings growth, a higher P/E than the benchmark P/E is justified.
- If the subject stock has higher-than-average (or higher-than-median) risk (operating or financial), a lower P/E than the benchmark P/E is justified.

Another perspective on these two points is that for a group of stocks with comparable relative valuations, the stock with the greatest expected growth rate (or the lowest risk) is, all else equal, the most attractively valued. Example 10 illustrates a simple comparison of a company with its peer group.

EXAMPLE 10

A Simple Peer-Group Comparison

As a telecommunication industry analyst at a brokerage firm, you are valuing Verizon Communications, Inc., a telecommunication company. The valuation metric that you have selected is the trailing P/E. You are evaluating the P/E using the median trailing P/E of peer-group companies as the benchmark value. According to GICS, Verizon is in the telecommunication services sector and, within it, the integrated telecommunication services subindustry. Exhibit 5 presents the relevant data.

Exhibit 5: Trailing P/Es of Telecommunication Services Companies

Company	Trailing P/E
AT&T	13.20
Comcast Corporation	16.23
CenturyLink	NMF
China Telecom	13.14
Charter Communications Corp.	70.67
Verizon Communications	15.03

Company	Trailing P/E
Windstream Holdings	19.01
Mean*	24.55
Median	15.03

**Mean, six firms excluding CenturyLink.*

NMF = not meaningful.

Based on the data in Exhibit 5, address the following:

1. Given the definition of the benchmark stated above, determine the most appropriate benchmark value of the P/E for Verizon.

Solution:

As stated earlier, the use of median values mitigates the effect of outliers on the valuation conclusion. In this instance, the P/Es for CenturyLink and Charter Communications are clearly outliers. Therefore, the median trailing P/E for the group, 15.03, is more appropriate than the mean trailing P/E of 24.55 for use as the benchmark value of the P/E. Note that when a group includes an odd number of companies, as here, the median value will be the middle value when the values are ranked (in either ascending or descending order). When the group includes an even number of companies, the median value will be the average of the two middle values.

2. State whether Verizon is relatively fairly valued, relatively overvalued, or relatively undervalued, assuming no differences in fundamentals among the peer group companies. Justify your answer.

Solution:

If you assume no differences in fundamentals among the peer group companies, Verizon appears to be fairly valued because its P/E is identical to the median P/E of 15.03.

3. Identify the stocks in this group of telecommunication companies that appear to be relatively undervalued when the median trailing P/E is used as a benchmark. Explain what further analysis might be appropriate to confirm your answer.

Solution:

AT&T, China Telecom, and CenturyLink appear to be undervalued relative to their peers because their trailing P/Es are lower than the median P/E. Verizon appears to be relatively fairly valued because its P/E equals the median P/E. Charter Communications, Comcast Corporation, and Windstream appear to be overvalued.

To confirm this valuation conclusion, you should look at other metrics. One issue for this particular industry is that earnings may differ significantly from cash flow. These companies invest considerable amounts of money to build out their networks—whether it be landlines or increasing bandwidth capacity for mobile users. Because telecommunication service providers are frequently required to take large noncash charges on their infrastructure, reported earnings are typically very volatile and frequently much lower than cash flow.

A metric that appears to address the impact of earnings growth on P/E is the P/E-to-growth (PEG) ratio. The **PEG ratio** is calculated as the stock's P/E divided by the expected earnings growth rate (in percentage terms). The ratio, in effect, is a calculation of a stock's P/E per percentage point of expected growth. Stocks with lower PEG ratios are more attractive than stocks with higher PEG ratios, all else being equal. Some consider that a PEG ratio less than 1 is an indicator of an attractive value level. The PEG ratio is useful but must be used with care for several reasons:

- The PEG ratio assumes a linear relationship between P/E and growth. The model for P/E in terms of the DDM shows that, in theory, the relationship is not linear.
- The PEG ratio does not factor in differences in risk, an important determinant of P/E.
- The PEG ratio does not account for differences in the duration of growth. For example, dividing P/Es by short-term (five-year) growth forecasts may not capture differences in long-term growth prospects.

The way in which fundamentals can add insight to comparables is illustrated in Example 11.

EXAMPLE 11

A Peer-Group Comparison Modified by Fundamentals

Continuing with the valuation of telecommunication service providers, you gather information on selected fundamentals related to risk (beta), profitability (five-year earnings growth forecast), and valuation (trailing and forward P/Es). Analysts may also use other measures of risk in comparables work. These data are reported in Exhibit 6. The use of forward P/Es recognizes that differences in trailing P/Es could be the result of transitory effects on earnings.

Exhibit 6: Valuation Data for Telecommunication Services Companies (as of 11 September 2013)

Company	Trailing P/E	Forward P/E	Five-Year EPS Growth Forecast	Forward PEG Ratio	Beta
AT&T	13.20	9.36	1.83%	5.11	0.56
Comcast Corporation	16.23	12.92	11.29	1.14	1.09
CenturyLink	NMF	8.89	8.52	1.04	0.81
China Telecom	13.14	10.31	6.90	1.49	0.81
Charter Communications	70.67	30.32	45.30	0.67	1.24
Verizon	15.03	11.99	2.51	4.78	0.50
Windstream Holdings	19.01	16.29	3.19	5.11	0.45
Mean	24.55	14.30	11.30	2.76	0.78
Median	15.03	11.99	6.90	1.49	0.78

Notes: NMF = not meaningful. The trailing P/E for CenturyLink is a negative number, which would result in a P/E that is not meaningful.

Source: www.finviz.com.

Based on the data in Exhibit 6, answer the following questions:

1. In Example 10, Part 3, AT&T, China Telecom, and CenturyLink were identified as possibly relatively undervalued compared with the peer group as a whole, and Verizon was identified as relatively fairly valued. What does the additional information relating to profitability and risk suggest about the relative valuation of the stocks in Exhibit 6?

Solution:

Among the three companies identified as underpriced (based on their low forward P/Es), CenturyLink has the highest five-year EPS growth forecast and the lowest PEG ratio. AT&T and China Telecom have lower growth rates and higher PEG ratios than CenturyLink. Among the other companies in Exhibit 6, Comcast and Charter Communications had the highest EPS growth forecasts and the third lowest and lowest PEG ratios. The three stocks with the lowest trailing P/Es (AT&T, CenturyLink, and China Telecom) also had the lowest forward P/Es.

The two stocks with the highest growth forecasts, Comcast and Charter Communications, also had the highest betas, which is consistent with studies that have shown that growth stocks tend to have higher beta values than those of value stocks. Based on the high trailing and forward P/Es, it appears that investors in Charter Communications have high expectations concerning the company's future earnings potential. However, the high beta value is likely reflective of the uncertainty surrounding the earnings forecast and the possibility that actual future earnings may be less than expected.

Some analysts consider a PEG ratio below 1 to be a signal of undervaluation. However, one limitation of the PEG ratio is that it does not account for the overall growth rate of an industry or the economy as a whole. Hence, it is typically a good idea for an investor to compare a stock's PEG ratio to an average or median PEG ratio for the industry, as well as the entire market, to get an accurate sense of how fairly valued a stock is. The PEG ratio of CenturyLink is not below 1, but it is significantly lower than the PEG ratios for the other telecommunication companies—further indicating that this company is relatively undervalued.

2. AT&T has a consensus year-ahead EPS forecast of $3.63. Suppose the median P/E of 11.99 for the peer group is subjectively adjusted upward to 13.00 to reflect AT&T's superior profitability and below-average risk. Estimate AT&T's intrinsic value.

Solution:

$3.63 × 13.0 = $47.19 is an estimate of intrinsic value.

3. AT&T's current market price is $33.98. State whether AT&T appears to be fairly valued, overvalued, or undervalued when compared with the intrinsic value estimated in the answer to Part 2.

Solution:

Because the estimated intrinsic value of $47.19 is greater than the current market price of $33.98, AT&T appears to be undervalued by the market on an absolute basis.

In Problem 2 of the Example 11, a peer median P/E of 11.99 was subjectively adjusted upward to 13.00. Depending on the context, the justification for using the specific value of 13.00 as the relevant benchmark rather than some other value could be raised. To avoid that issue, one way to express the analysis and results would be as follows: Given its modest growth and lower risk, AT&T should trade at a premium to the median P/E (11.99) of its peer group. Of course, this is a bullish outlook for AT&T because its forward P/E is only 9.36.

Analysts frequently compare a stock's multiple with the median or mean value of the multiple for larger sets of assets than a company's peer group. The next sections examine comparisons with these larger groups.

Industry and Sector Multiples

Median or mean P/Es for industries and for economic sectors are frequently used in relative valuations. Although median P/Es have the advantage that they are insensitive to outliers, some databases report only mean values of multiples for industries.

The mechanics of using industry multiples are identical to those used for peer-group comparisons. Taking account of relevant fundamental information, we compare a stock's multiple with the median or mean multiple for the company's industry.

Using industry and sector data can help an analyst explore whether the peer-group comparison assets are themselves appropriately priced. Comparisons with broader segments of the economy can potentially provide insight about whether the relative valuation based on comparables accurately reflects intrinsic value. For example, Value Line reports a relative P/E that is calculated as the stock's current P/E divided by the median P/E of all issues under Value Line review. The less closely matched the stock is to the comparison assets, the more dissimilarities are likely to be present to complicate the analyst's interpretation of the data. Arguably, however, the larger the number of comparison assets, the more likely that mispricings of individual assets cancel out. In some cases, we may be able to draw inferences about an industry or sector overall. For example, during the 1998–2000 internet bubble, comparisons of an individual internet stock's value with the overall market would have been more likely to point to overvaluation than comparisons of relative valuation only among internet stocks.

Overall Market Multiple

Although the logic of the comparables approach suggests the use of industry and peer companies as comparison assets, equity market indexes also have been used as comparison assets. The mechanics of using the method of comparables do not change in such an approach, although the user should be cognizant of any size differences between the subject stock and the stocks in the selected index.

The question of whether the overall market is fairly priced has captured analyst interest throughout the entire history of investing. We mentioned one approach to market valuation (using a DDM) in an earlier reading.

Example 12 shows a valuation comparison to the broad equity market on the basis of P/E.

EXAMPLE 12

Valuation Relative to the Market

You are analyzing three large-cap US stock issues with approximately equal earnings growth prospects and risk. As one step in your analysis, you have decided to check valuations relative to the S&P 500 Index. Exhibit 7 provides the data.

Exhibit 7: Comparison with an Index Multiple (Prices and EPS in US Dollars; as of 28 June 2019)

Measure	Stock A	Stock B	Stock C	S&P 500
Current price	23	50	80	2,941.76
P/E	15.2	30.0	15.2	21.8
Five-year average P/E (as a % of S&P 500 P/E)	80	120	105	

Source: www.us.spindices.com for S&P 500 data.

Based only on the data in Exhibit 7, address the following:

1. Explain which stock appears relatively undervalued when compared with the S&P 500.

Solution:

Stock C appears to be undervalued when compared to the S&P 500. Stock A and Stock C are both trading at a P/E of 15.2 relative to trailing earnings, versus a P/E of 21.8 for the S&P 500. But the last row of Exhibit 7 indicates that Stock A has historically traded at a P/E reflecting a 20% discount to the S&P 500 (which, based on the current level of the S&P 500, would imply a P/E of $0.8 \times 21.8 = 17.4$). In contrast, Stock C has usually traded at a premium to the S&P 500 P/E but now trades at a discount to it. Stock B is trading at a high P/E, even higher than its historical relationship to the S&P 500's P/E ($1.2 \times 21.8 = 26.2$).

2. State the assumption underlying the use of five-year average P/E comparisons.

Solution:

Using historical relative-value information in investment decisions relies on an assumption of stable underlying economic relationships (that is, that the past is relevant for the future).

Because many equity indexes are market-capitalization weighted, financial databases often report the average market P/E with the individual P/Es weighted by the company's market capitalization. As a consequence, the largest constituent stocks heavily influence the calculated P/E. If P/Es differ systematically by market capitalization, however, differences in a company's P/E multiple from the index's multiple may be explained by that effect. Therefore, particularly for stocks in the middle-cap range, the analyst should favor using the median P/E for the index as the benchmark value of the multiple.

As with other comparison assets, the analyst may be interested in whether the equity index itself is efficiently priced. A common comparison is the index's P/E in relation to historical values. Siegel (2014) noted that recent P/Es were more than twice as high as the average P/E for US stocks over a long time period. Potential justifications for a higher-than-average P/E include lower-than-average interest rates and/or higher-than-average expected growth rates. An alternative hypothesis in a situation (historical high P/Es) is that the market as a whole is overvalued or, alternatively, that earnings are abnormally low.

The time frame for comparing average multiples is important. For example, at the end of the fourth quarter of 2008, the P/E for the S&P 500 was 60.70. That value is much higher than the 15.8 historical average since 1935. From 2006 through 2018, the highest quarterly P/E was 122.4 (30 June 2009) and the lowest was 13.0 (30 September 2011), and the quarterly P/E ranged between 18.9 and 24.1 over the five years ending in 2018. The use of past data relies on the key assumption that the past (sometimes the distant past) is relevant for the future.

We end this section with an introduction to valuation of the equity market itself on the basis of P/E. A well-known comparison is the earnings yield (the E/P) on a group of stocks and the interest yield on a bond. The so-called Fed model, based on a paper written by three analysts at the US Federal Reserve, predicts the return on the S&P 500 on the basis of the relationship between forecasted earnings yields and yields on bonds (Lander, Orphanides, and Douvogiannis 1997). Example 13 illustrates the Fed model.

EXAMPLE 13

The Fed Model

One of the main drivers of P/E for the market as a whole is the level of interest rates. The inverse relationship between value and interest rates can be seen from the expression of P/E in terms of fundamentals, because the risk-free rate is one component of the required rate of return that is inversely related to value. The Fed model relates the earnings yield on the S&P 500 to the yield to maturity on 10-year US Treasury bonds. As we have defined it, the earnings yield (E/P) is the inverse of the P/E; the Fed model uses expected earnings for the next 12 months in calculating the ratio.

Based on the premise that the two yields should be closely linked, on average, the trading rule based on the Fed model considers the stock market to be overvalued when the market's current earnings yield is less than the 10-year Treasury bond (T-bond) yield. The intuition is that when risk-free T-bonds offer a yield that is higher than that of stocks—which are a riskier investment—stocks are an unattractive investment.

According to the model, the justified or fair value P/E for the S&P 500 is the reciprocal of the 10-year T-bond yield. As of 28 December 2018, according to the model, with a 10-year T-bond yielding 2.72%, the justified P/E on the S&P 500 was 1/0.0272 = 36.8. The trailing P/E based for 31 December 2018 was 18.9.

We previously presented an expression for the justified P/E in terms of the Gordon growth model. That expression indicates that the expected growth rate in dividends or earnings is a variable that enters into the intrinsic value of a stock (or an index of stocks). A concern in considering the Fed model is that this variable is lacking in the model. Please note that the earnings yield is, in fact, the expected rate of return on a no-growth stock (under the assumption that price equals value). With the PVGO (present value of growth opportunities) and setting price equal to value, we obtain $P_0 = E_1/r + \text{PVGO}$. Setting the present value of growth opportunities equal to zero and rearranging, we obtain $r = E_1/P_0$. Example 14 presents a valuation model for the equity market that incorporates the expected growth rate in earnings.

EXAMPLE 14

The Yardeni Model

Yardeni (2000) developed a model that incorporates the expected growth rate in earnings—a variable that is missing in the Fed model. This model is presented as one example of more-complex models than the Fed model. Yardeni's model is

$$\text{CEY} = \text{CBY} - b \times \text{LTEG} + \text{Residual},$$

where CEY is the current earnings yield on the market index, CBY is the current Moody's Investors Service A rated corporate bond yield, and LTEG is the consensus five-year earnings growth rate forecast for the market index. The coefficient b measures the weight the market gives to five-year earnings projections. (Recall that the expression for P/E in terms of the Gordon growth model is based on the long-term sustainable growth rate and that five-year forecasts of growth may not be sustainable.) Although CBY incorporates a default risk premium relative to T-bonds, it does not incorporate an equity risk premium per se. For example, in the bond yield plus risk premium model for the cost of equity, an analyst typically adds 300–400 basis points to a corporate bond yield.

Yardeni found that, prior to publication of the model in 2000, the coefficient b had averaged 0.10. In recent years, he has reported valuations based on growth weights of 0.10, 0.20, and 0.25. Noting that CEY is E/P and taking the inverse of both sides of this equation, Yardeni obtained the following expression for the justified P/E on the market:

$$\frac{P}{E} = \frac{1}{\text{CBY} - b \times \text{LTEG}}.$$

Consistent with valuation theory, in Yardeni's model, higher current corporate bond yields imply a lower justified P/E and higher expected long-term growth results in a higher justified P/E.

Critics of the Fed model point out that it ignores the equity risk premium (Stimes and Wilcox 2011). The model also inadequately reflects the effects of inflation and incorrectly incorporates the differential effects of inflation on earnings and interest payments (e.g., Siegel 2014). Some empirical evidence has shown that prediction of future returns based on simple P/E outperforms prediction based on the Fed model's differential with bond yields (for the US market, see Arnott and Asness 2003; for nine other markets, see Aubert and Giot 2007).

Another drawback to the Fed model is that the relationship between interest rates and earnings yields is not a linear one. This drawback is most noticeable at low interest rates; Example 13 provided an example of this limitation of the model. Furthermore, small changes in interest rates and/or corporate profits can significantly alter the justified P/E predicted by the model. Overall, an analyst should look to the Fed model only as one tool for calibrating the overall value of the stock market and should avoid overreliance on the model as a predictive method, particularly in periods of low inflation and low interest rates.

Own Historical P/E

As an alternative to comparing a stock's valuation with that of other stocks, one traditional approach uses past values of the stock's own P/E as a basis for comparison. Underlying this approach is the idea that a stock's P/E may regress to historical average levels.

An analyst can obtain a benchmark value in a variety of ways with this approach. Value Line reports as a "P/E median" a rounded average of four middle values of a stock's average annual P/E for the previous 10 years. The five-year average trailing P/E is another reasonable metric. In general, trailing P/Es are more commonly used than forward P/Es in such computations. In addition to "higher" and "lower" comparisons with this benchmark, justified price based on this approach may be calculated as follows:

$$\text{Justified price} = (\text{Benchmark value of own historical P/Es}) \times (\text{Most recent EPS}). \quad (3)$$

Normalized EPS replaces most recent EPS in this equation when EPS is negative and whenever otherwise appropriate.

Example 15 illustrates the use of past values of the stock's own P/E as a basis for reaching a valuation conclusion.

EXAMPLE 15

Valuation Relative to Own Historical P/Es

As of June 2019, you are valuing Honda Motor Company, among the market leaders in Japan's auto manufacturing industry. You are applying the method of comparables using Honda's five-year average P/E as the benchmark value of the multiple. Exhibit 8 presents the data.

Exhibit 8: Historical P/Es for Honda Motor Company

2018	2017	2016	2015	2014	Mean	Median
6.9	10.0	10.9	10.8	9.7	9.7	10.0

Sources: The Value Line Investment Survey for average annual P/Es; calculations for mean and median P/Es.

1. State a benchmark value for Honda's P/E.

Solution:

From Exhibit 8, the benchmark value based on the median P/E value is 10.0 and based on the mean P/E value is 9.7.

2. Given forecasted EPS for fiscal year 2019 (ended 31 December) of ¥381.93, calculate and interpret a justified price for Honda.

Solution:

The calculation is 10.0 × ¥381.93 = ¥3,819 when the median-based benchmark P/E is used and 9.7 × ¥381.93 = ¥3,704 when the mean-based benchmark P/E is used.

3. Compare the justified price with the stock's recent price of ¥2,837.

Solution:

The stock's recent price is 26.2% (calculated as 2,817/3,819 – 1) less than the justified price of the stock based on median historical P/E but 23.9% (calculated as 2,817/3,704 – 1) less than the justified price of the stock based on mean historical P/E. The stock may be undervalued, and misvaluation, if present, appears significant.

In using historical P/Es for comparisons, analysts should be alert to the impact on P/E levels of changes in a company's business mix and leverage over time. If the company's business has changed substantially within the time period being examined, the method based on a company's own past P/Es is prone to error. Shifts in the use of financial leverage may also impair comparability based on average own past P/E.

Changes in the interest rate environment and economic fundamentals over different time periods can be another limitation to using an average past value of P/E for a stock as a benchmark. A specific caution is that inflation can distort the economic meaning of reported earnings. Consequently, if the inflationary environments reflected in current P/E and average own past P/E are different, a comparison between the two P/Es may be misleading. Changes in a company's ability to pass through cost inflation to higher prices over time may also affect the reliability of such comparisons, as illustrated in Example 16 in the next section.

P/Es in Cross-Country Comparisons

When comparing the P/Es of companies in different countries, the analyst should be aware of the following effects that may influence the comparison:

- The effect on EPS of differences in accounting standards: Comparisons (without analyst adjustments) among companies preparing financial statements based on different accounting standards may be distorted. Such distortions may occur when, for example, the accounting standards differ as to permissible recognition of revenues, expenses, or gains.
- The effect on market-wide benchmarks of differences in their macroeconomic contexts: Differences in macroeconomic contexts may distort comparisons of benchmark P/E levels among companies operating in different markets.

A specific case of the second bullet point is differences in inflation rates and in the ability of companies to pass through inflation in their costs in the form of higher prices to their customers. For two companies with the same pass-through ability, the company operating in the environment with higher inflation will have a lower justified P/E; if the inflation rates are equal but pass-through rates differ, the justified P/E should be lower for the company with the lower pass-through rate. Example 16 provides analysis in support of these conclusions.

EXAMPLE 16

An Analysis of P/Es and Inflation

Assume a company with no real earnings growth, such that its earnings growth can result only from inflation, will pay out all its earnings as dividends. Based on the Gordon (constant growth) DDM, the value of a share is

$$P_0 = \frac{E_0(1+I)}{r-I},$$

where

P_0 = current price, which is substituted for the intrinsic value, V_0, for purposes of analyzing a justified P/E

E_0 = current EPS, which is substituted for current dividends per share, D_0, because the assumption in this example is that all earnings are paid out as dividends

I = rate of inflation, which is substituted for expected growth, g, because of the assumption in this example that the company's only growth is from inflation

r = required return

Suppose the company has the ability to pass on some or all inflation to its customers, and let λ represent the percentage of inflation in costs that the company can pass through to earnings. The company's earnings growth may then be expressed as λI, and the equation becomes

$$P_0 = \frac{E_0(1 + \lambda I)}{r - \lambda I} = \frac{E_1}{r - \lambda I}.$$

Now, introduce a real rate of return, defined here as r minus I and represented as ρ. The value of a share and the justified forward P/E can now be expressed, respectively, as follows:

$$P_0 = \frac{E_1}{\rho + (1 - \lambda)I},$$

and

$$\frac{P_0}{E_1} = \frac{1}{\rho + (1 - \lambda)I}.$$

(Note that the denominator of this equation is derived from the previous equation as follows: $r - \lambda I = r - I + I - I\lambda = (r - I) + (1 - \lambda)I = \rho + (1 - \lambda)I$.

If a company can pass through all inflation, such that $\lambda = 1$ (100%), then the P/E is equal to $1/\rho$. But if the company can pass through no inflation, such that $\lambda = 0$, then the P/E is equal to $1/(\rho + I)$—that is, $1/r$.

You are analyzing two companies, Company M and Company P. The real rate of return required on the shares of Company M and Company P is 3% per year. Using the analytic framework provided, address the following:

1. Suppose both Company M and Company P can pass through 75% of cost increases. Cost inflation is 6% for Company M but only 2% for Company P.

   A. Estimate the justified P/E for each company.

   B. Interpret your answer to Part A.

Solution:

A. For Company M, $\frac{1}{0.03 + (1 - 0.75)0.06} = 22.2.$

For Company P, $\frac{1}{0.03 + (1 - 0.75)0.02} = 28.6.$

B. With less than 100% cost pass-through, the justified P/E is inversely related to the inflation rate.

2. Suppose both Company M and Company P face 6% a year inflation. Company M can pass through 90% of cost increases, but Company P can pass through only 70%.

   A. Estimate the justified P/E for each company.

   B. Interpret your answer to Part A.

Solution:

A. For Company M, $\frac{1}{0.03 + (1 - 0.90)0.06} = 27.8.$

For Company P, $\frac{1}{0.03 + (1 - 0.70)0.06} = 20.8.$

B. For equal inflation rates, the company with the higher pass-through rate has a higher justified P/E.

Note that this example follows the analysis of Solnik and McLeavey (2004, pp. 289–290).

Example 16 illustrates that with less than 100% cost pass-through, the justified P/E is inversely related to the inflation rate (with complete cost pass-through, the justified P/E should not be affected by inflation). The higher the inflation rate, the greater the impact of incomplete cost pass-through on P/E. From Example 16, one can also infer that the higher the inflation rate, the more serious the effect on justified P/E of a pass-through rate that is less than 100%.

Using P/Es to Obtain Terminal Value in Multistage Dividend Discount Models

In using a DDM to value a stock, whether applying a multistage model or modeling within a spreadsheet (forecasting specific cash flows individually up to some horizon), estimation of the terminal value of the stock is important. The key condition that must be satisfied is that terminal value reflects earnings growth that the company can sustain in the long run. Analysts frequently use price multiples—in particular, P/Es and P/Bs—to estimate terminal value. We can call such multiples **terminal price multiples**. Choices for the terminal multiple, with a terminal P/E multiple used as the example, include the following two types:

Terminal price multiple based on fundamentals: As illustrated earlier, analysts can restate the Gordon growth model as a multiple by, for example, dividing both sides of the model by EPS. For terminal P/E multiples, dividing both sides of the Gordon growth model by EPS at time n, where n is the point in time at which the final stage begins (i.e., E_n), gives a trailing terminal price multiple; dividing both sides by EPS at time $n + 1$ (i.e., E_{n+1}) gives a leading terminal price multiple. Of course, an analyst can use the Gordon growth model to estimate terminal value and need not go through the process of deriving a terminal price multiple and then multiplying by the same value of the fundamental to estimate terminal value. Because of their familiarity, however, multiples may be useful in communicating an estimate of terminal value.

Terminal price multiple based on comparables: Analysts have used various choices for the benchmark value, including:

- median industry P/E,
- average industry P/E, and
- average of own past P/Es.

Having selected a terminal multiple, the expression for terminal value when using a terminal P/E multiple is

$$V_n = \text{Benchmark value of trailing terminal P/E} \times E_n$$

or

$$V_n = \text{Benchmark value of forward terminal P/E} \times E_{n+1},$$

where V_n = Terminal value at time n.

The use of a comparables approach has the strength that it is entirely grounded in market data. In contrast, the Gordon growth model calls for specific estimates (the required rate of return, the dividend payout ratio, and the expected mature growth rate), and the model's output is very sensitive to changes in those estimates. A possible disadvantage to the comparables approach is that when the benchmark value reflects mispricing (over- or undervaluation), so will the estimate of terminal value. Example 17 illustrates the use of P/Es and the Gordon growth model to estimate terminal value.

EXAMPLE 17

Using P/Es and the Gordon Growth Model to Value the Mature Growth Phase

As an energy analyst, you are valuing the stock of an oil exploration company. You have projected earnings and dividends three years out (to $t = 3$), and you have gathered the following data and estimates:

- Required rate of return = 0.10.
- Average dividend payout rate for mature companies in the market = 0.45.
- Industry average ROE = 0.13.
- E_3 = \$3.00.
- Industry average P/E = 14.3.

On the basis of this information, carry out the following:

1. Calculate terminal value based on comparables, using your estimated industry average P/E as the benchmark.

Solution:

V_n = Benchmark value of P/E × E_n = 14.3 × \$3.00 = \$42.90.

2. Contrast your answer in Part 1 to an estimate of terminal value using the Gordon growth model.

Solution:

Recall that the Gordon growth model expresses intrinsic value, V, as the present value of dividends divided by the required rate of return, r, minus the growth rate, g: $V_0 = D_0(1 + g)/(r - g)$. Here we are estimating terminal value, so the relevant expression is $V_n = D_n(1 + g)/(r - g)$. You would estimate that the dividend at $t = 3$ will equal earnings in Year 3 of \$3.00 times the average payout ratio of 0.45, or D_n = \$3.00 × 0.45 = \$1.35. Recall also the sustainable growth rate expression—that is, $g = b \times \text{ROE}$, where b is the retention rate and equivalent to 1 minus the dividend payout ratio. In this example, $b = (1 - 0.45) = 0.55$, and you can use ROE = 0.13 (the industry average). Therefore, $g = b \times \text{ROE} = 0.55 \times 0.13 = 0.0715$. Given the required rate of return of 0.10, you obtain the estimate V_n = (\$1.35)(1 + 0.0715)/(0.10 − 0.0715) = \$50.76. In this example, therefore, the Gordon growth model estimate of terminal value is 18.3% higher than the estimate based on comparables calculated in Part 1 (i.e., 0.1832 = \$50.76/\$42.90 − 1).

PRICE/BOOK VALUE

5

- ☐ calculate and interpret a justified price multiple
- ☐ describe rationales for and possible drawbacks to using alternative price multiples and dividend yield in valuation
- ☐ calculate and interpret alternative price multiples and dividend yield
- ☐ describe fundamental factors that influence alternative price multiples and dividend yield
- ☐ calculate and interpret the justified price-to-earnings ratio (P/E), price-to-book ratio (P/B), and price-to-sales ratio (P/S) for a stock, based on forecasted fundamentals
- ☐ evaluate a stock by the method of comparables and explain the importance of fundamentals in using the method of comparables
- ☐ evaluate whether a stock is overvalued, fairly valued, or undervalued based on comparisons of multiples

The ratio of market price per share to book value per share (P/B), like P/E, has a long history of use in valuation practice. According to the 2012 BofA Merrill Lynch Institutional Factor Survey, 53% of respondents considered P/B when making investment decisions.

In the P/E multiple, the measure of value (EPS) in the denominator is a flow variable relating to the income statement. In contrast, the measure of value in the P/B's denominator (book value per share) is a stock or level variable coming from the balance sheet. (*Book* refers to the fact that the measurement of value comes from accounting records or books, in contrast to market value.) Intuitively, therefore, we note that book value per share attempts to represent, on a per-share basis, the investment that common shareholders have made in the company. To define book value per share more precisely, we first find **shareholders' equity** (total assets minus total liabilities). Because our purpose is to value common stock (as opposed to valuing the company as a whole), we subtract from shareholders' equity any value attributable to preferred stock to obtain common shareholders' equity, or the **book value of equity** (often called simply book value). Dividing book value by the number of common stock shares outstanding, we obtain **book value per share**, the denominator in P/B.

In the remainder of this section, we present the reasons analysts have offered for using P/B and possible drawbacks to its use. We then illustrate the calculation of P/B and discuss the fundamental factors that drive P/B. We end the section by showing the use of P/B based on the method of comparables.

Analysts have offered several rationales for the use of P/B; some specifically compare P/B with P/E:

- Because book value is a cumulative balance sheet amount, book value is generally positive even when EPS is zero or negative. An analyst can generally use P/B when EPS is zero or negative, whereas P/E based on a zero or negative EPS is not meaningful.
- Because book value per share is more stable than EPS, P/B may be more meaningful than P/E when EPS is abnormally high or low or is highly variable.
- As a measure of net asset value per share, book value per share has been viewed as appropriate for valuing companies composed chiefly of liquid assets, such as finance, investment, insurance, and banking institutions

(Wild, Bernstein, and Subramanyam 2001, p. 233). For such companies, book values of assets may approximate market values. When information on individual corporate assets is available, analysts may adjust reported book values to market values where they differ.

- Book value has also been used in the valuation of companies that are not expected to continue as a going concern (Martin 1998, p. 22).
- Differences in P/Bs may be related to differences in long-run average returns, according to empirical research (Bodie, Kane, and Marcus 2008).

Possible drawbacks of P/Bs in practice include the following:

- Assets in addition to those recognized in financial statements may be critical operating factors. For example, in many service companies, **human capital**—the value of skills and knowledge possessed by the workforce—is more important than physical capital as an operating factor, but it is not reflected as an asset on the balance sheet. Similarly, the good reputation that a company develops by consistently providing high-quality goods and services is not reflected as an asset on the balance sheet.
- P/B may be misleading as a valuation indicator when the levels of assets used by the companies under examination differ significantly. Such differences may reflect differences in business models.
- Accounting effects on book value may compromise how useful book value is as a measure of the shareholders' investment in the company. In general, intangible assets that are generated internally (as opposed to being acquired) are not shown as assets on a company's balance sheet. For example, companies account for advertising and marketing as expenses, so the value of internally generated brands, which are created and maintained by advertising and marketing activities, do not appear as assets on a company's balance sheet under IFRS or US GAAP. Similarly, when accounting standards require that research and development (R&D) expenditures be treated as expenses, the value of internally developed patents does not appear as assets. Certain R&D expenditures can be capitalized, although rules vary among accounting standards. Accounting effects such as these may impair the comparability of P/B among companies and countries unless appropriate analyst adjustments are made.
- Book value reflects the reported value of assets and liabilities. Some assets and liabilities, such as some financial instruments, may be reported at fair value as of the balance sheet date; other assets, such as property, plant, and equipment, are generally reported at historical cost, net of accumulated depreciation, amortization, depletion, and/or impairment. It is important to examine the notes to the financial statements to identify how assets and liabilities are measured and reported. For assets measured at net historical cost, inflation and technological change can eventually result in significant divergence between the book value and the market value of assets. As a result, book value per share often does not accurately reflect the value of shareholders' investments. When comparing companies, significant differences in the average age of assets may lessen the comparability of P/Bs.
- Share repurchases or issuances may distort historical comparisons.

As an example of the effects of share repurchases, consider Colgate-Palmolive Company. As of 13 September 2013, Colgate-Palmolive's trailing P/E and P/B were, respectively, 24.84 and 36.01. Five years earlier, Colgate-Palmolive's trailing P/E and P/B were 23.55 and 15.94. In other words, the company's P/E widened by 5.5% (= 24.84/23.55 – 1) while its P/B widened by 125.9% (= 36.01/15.94 – 1). The majority of the difference in changes in these two multiples can be attributed to the substantial amount of shares that Colgate-Palmolive repurchased over those five years, as reflected by book value (i.e., total common equity) declining from $2.48 billion as of 30 June 2008 to $1.53 billion as of 30 June 2013. Because of those share repurchases, Colgate-Palmolive's book value declined at an annual rate of 9.2%. In summary, when a company repurchases shares at a price higher than the current book value per share, it lowers the overall book value per share for the company. All else being equal, the effect is to make the stock appear more expensive if the current P/B is compared to its historical values.

Example 18 illustrates another potential limitation to using P/B in valuation.

EXAMPLE 18

Differences in Business Models Reflected in Differences in P/Bs

The US banking industry has a wide range of P/Bs. Much of these differences in P/Bs can be attributed to differences in company-specific business models. Exhibit 9 presents P/Bs for three major US banks as of 31 December 2018.

Exhibit 9: P/Bs for Selected US Banks

Entity	P/B
Citigroup, Inc.	0.69
Wells Fargo & Company	1.21
US Bancorp	1.63

Source: S&P Capital IQ

Citigroup's low P/B versus its peers is a reflection of the "one-stop shopping" business model it and some other mega-banks pursued in the 1990s. Citigroup suffered huge losses during the global financial crisis and had to be rescued in November 2008 by the US government.

Wells Fargo derives most of its revenue from loans and service fees. Its business model focuses on cross-selling multiple products, and in 2012 it was responsible for originating close to a third of all US home loans. Wells Fargo is also predominantly a domestic business, whereas other large banks are much more exposed to overseas markets.

US Bancorp's relatively risk-averse business model is focused on consumer and business banking as well as trusts and payment processing. Compared with other mega-banks, US Bancorp has a much smaller presence in investment banking and capital markets. Another reason for the bank's relatively high P/B was its acquisition activity, which has helped it grow its business considerably.

Determining Book Value

In this section, we illustrate how to calculate book value and how to adjust book value to improve the comparability of P/Bs among companies. To compute book value per share, we need to refer to the business's balance sheet, which has a shareholders' (or stockholders') equity section. The computation of book value is as follows:

- (Shareholders' equity) – (Total value of equity claims that are senior to common stock) = Common shareholders' equity.

- (Common shareholders' equity)/(Number of common stock shares outstanding) = Book value per share.

Possible claims senior to the claims of common stock, which would be subtracted from shareholders' equity, include the value of preferred stock and the dividends in arrears on preferred stock. Example 19 illustrates the calculation.

EXAMPLE 19

Computing Book Value per Share

Headquartered in Toronto, Canada, the Toronto-Dominion Bank and its subsidiaries are collectively known as TD Bank Group (TD). With operations organized into four segments (Canadian Personal and Commercial Banking, US Personal and Commercial Banking, Wholesale Banking, and Wealth and Insurance), in 2018 TD provided financial products and services to approximately 26 million customers. Exhibit 10 presents data from the equity section of TD's consolidated balance sheets for the years 2016–2018. TD's fiscal years end on 31 October.

Exhibit 10: Equity Data for TD Bank Group (Millions of Canadian Dollars)

	31 October 2018	31 October 2017	31 October 2016
Equity			
Common shares	CAD21,221	CAD20,931	CAD20,711
Millions of shares issued and outstanding:			
2018: 1,830.4			
2017: 1,842.5			
2016: 1,857.6			
Preferred shares	5,000	4,750	4,400
Millions of shares issued and outstanding:			
2018: 200.0			
2017: 190.0			
2016: 176.0			
Treasury shares—common	(151)	(183)	(36)
Millions of shares held:			
2018: 2.1			
2017: 2.9			
2016: 0.4			
Treasury shares—preferred	(1)	—	(1)
2018: nil			
2017: nil			
2016: nil			
Contributed surplus	193	214	203
Retained earnings	46,145	40,489	35,452
Accumulated and other comprehensive income	6,639	8,006	11,834
	79,047	74,207	72,564

	31 October 2018	31 October 2017	31 October 2016
Non-controlling interests in subsidiaries	993	983	1,650
Total equity	CAD80,040	CAD75,190	CAD74,214

Source: TD Bank Group 2018 annual report.

1. Using the data in Exhibit 10, calculate book value per share for 2016, 2017, and 2018.

Solution:

Because preferred shareholders have a claim on income and assets that is senior to that of the common shareholders, total equity must be adjusted by the value of outstanding and repurchased preferred shares. The divisor is the number of common shares outstanding.

2018: Book value per share = (80,040 – 5,000)/1,830.4 = CAD41.00.

2017: Book value per share = (75,190 – 4,750)/1,842.5 = CAD38.23.

2016: Book value per share = (74,214 – 4,400)/1,857.6 = CAD37.58.

2. Given a closing price of CAD73.03 on 31 October 2018, calculate TD's 2018 P/B.

Solution:

P/B = CAD73.03/CAD41.00 = 1.78.

Example 19 illustrated the calculation of book value per share without any adjustments. Adjusting P/B has two purposes: (1) to make the book value per share more accurately reflect the value of shareholders' investment and (2) to make P/B more useful for making comparisons among different stocks. Some adjustments are as follows:

- Some services and analysts report a **tangible book value per share**. Computing tangible book value per share involves subtracting reported intangible assets on the balance sheet from common shareholders' equity. The analyst should be familiar with the calculation. From the viewpoint of financial theory, however, the general exclusion of all intangibles may not be warranted. In the case of individual intangible assets, such as patents, which can be separated from the entity and sold, exclusion may not be justified. Exclusion may be appropriate, however, for goodwill from acquisitions, particularly for comparative purposes. **Goodwill** represents the excess of the purchase price of an acquisition beyond the fair value of acquired tangible assets and specifically identifiable intangible assets. Many analysts believe that goodwill does not represent an asset because it is not separable and may reflect overpayment for an acquisition.
- Certain adjustments may be appropriate for enhancing comparability. For example, one company may use FIFO whereas a peer company uses LIFO, which in an inflationary environment will generally understate inventory values. To accurately assess the relative valuation of the two companies, the analyst should restate the book value of the company using LIFO to what it would be based on FIFO. For a more complete discussion of adjustments to balance sheet amounts, refer to readings on financial statement analysis.

- For book value per share to most accurately reflect current values, the balance sheet should be adjusted for significant off-balance-sheet assets and liabilities. An example of an off-balance-sheet liability is a guarantee to pay a debt of another company in the event of that company's default. US accounting standards require companies to disclose off-balance-sheet liabilities.

Example 20 illustrates adjustments an analyst might make to a financial firm's P/B to obtain an accurate firm value.

EXAMPLE 20

Adjusting Book Value (Historical Example)

Edward Stavos is a junior analyst at a major US pension fund. Stavos is researching Barclays PLC for his fund's Credit Services Portfolio and is preparing background information prior to an upcoming meeting with the company. Headquartered in London, United Kingdom, Barclays is a major global financial services provider engaged in personal banking, credit cards, corporate and investment banking, and wealth and investment management with an extensive international presence in Europe, the Americas, Africa, and Asia.

Stavos is particularly interested in Barclays' P/B and how adjusting asset and liability accounts to their current fair value impacts the ratio. He gathers the condensed 2012 balance sheet (as of 31 December) and footnote data from Barclay's website as shown in Exhibit 11.

Exhibit 11: Barclays PLC 2012 Condensed Consolidated Balance Sheet and Footnote Data (£ in Millions)

	2012
Assets	
Cash and balances at central banks	£86,175
Items in the course of collection from other banks	1,456
Trading portfolio assets	145,030
Financial assets designated at fair value	46,061
Derivative financial instruments	469,146
Available for sale investments	75,109
Loans and advances to banks	40,489
Loans and advances to customers	425,729
Reverse repurchase agreements and other similar secured lending	176,956
Prepayments, accrued income, and other assets	4,360
Investments in associates and joint ventures	570
Property, plant, and equipment	5,754
Goodwill and intangible assets	7,915
Current tax assets	252
Deferred tax assets	3,016
Retirement benefit assets	2,303
Total assets	£1,490,321
Liabilities	

	2012
Deposits from banks	77,010
Items in the course of collection due to other banks	1,573
Customer accounts	385,707
Repurchase agreements and other similar secured borrowing	217,342
Trading portfolio liabilities	44,794
Financial liabilities designated at fair value	78,280
Derivative financial instruments	462,468
Debt securities in issue	119,581
Subordinated liabilities	24,018
Accruals, deferred income, and other liabilities	12,232
Provisions	2,766
Current tax liabilities	621
Deferred tax liabilities	719
Retirement benefit liabilities	253
Total liabilities	1,427,364
Shareholders' equity	
Shareholders' equity excluding non-controlling interests	53,586
Non-controlling interests	9,371
Total shareholders' equity	62,957
Total liabilities and shareholders' equity	£1,490,321

Excerpt from Footnotes to the Barclays Financial Statements: Financial Assets and Liabilities at Carrying Amount and Fair Value

	2012	
	Carrying amount	Fair value
Financial assets		
Loans and advances to banks	£40,489	£40,489
Loans and advances to customers:		
—Home loans	174,988	164,608
—Credit cards, unsecured and other retail lending	66,414	65,357
—Corporate loans	184,327	178,492
Reverse repurchase agreements and other similar secured lending	176,956	176,895
	£643,174	£625,841
Financial liabilities		
Deposits from banks	77,010	77,023
Customer accounts:		
—Current and demand accounts	127,819	127,819
—Savings accounts	99,875	99,875
—Other time deposits	158,013	158,008

	2012	
	Carrying amount	Fair value
Debt securities in issue	119,581	119,725
Repurchase agreements and other similar secured borrowing	217,342	217,342
Subordinated liabilities	24,018	23,467
	£823,658	£823,259

Source: Barclays' 2012 annual report.

The 31 December 2012 share price for Barclays was £2.4239, and the diluted weighted average number of shares was 12,614 million. Stavos computes book value per share initially by dividing total shareholders' equity by the share count and arrives at a book value per share of £4.9910 (£62,957/12,614) and a P/B of 0.49 (£2.4239/£4.9910).

Stavos then computes tangible book value per share as £4.3636 (calculated as £62,957 minus £7,915 of goodwill and intangible assets, which is then divided by 12,614 shares). The P/B based on tangible book value per share is 0.56 (£2.4239/£4.3636).

Stavos then turns to the footnotes to examine the fair value data. He notes the fair value of financial assets is £17,333 million less than their carrying amount (£643,174 – £625,841) and the fair value of financial liabilities is £399 million less than their carrying amount (£823,658 – £823,259). Including these adjustments to tangible book value results in an adjusted book value per share of £3.0211 [(£62,957 – £7,915 - £17,333 + £399)/12,614]. Stavos' adjusted P/B is 0.80 (£2.4239/£3.0211).

Stavos is concerned about the wide range in his computed P/Bs. He knows that if quoted prices are not available for financial assets and liabilities, IAS 39 allows for the use of valuation models to estimate fair value. He decides to question management regarding the use of models to value assets, liabilities, and derivatives and the sensitivity of these accounts to changes in interest rates and currency values.

An analyst should also be aware of differences in accounting standards related to how assets and liabilities are valued in financial statements. Accounting standards currently require companies to report some assets and liabilities at fair value and others at historical cost (with some adjustments).

Financial assets, such as investments in marketable securities, are usually reported at fair value. Investments classified as "held to maturity" and reported on a historical cost basis are an exception. (Instead of the term "held-to-maturity," IFRS refer to this category of investments as financial assets measured at amortized cost.) Some financial liabilities also are reported at fair value.

Nonfinancial assets, such as land and equipment, are generally reported at their historical acquisition costs, and in the case of equipment, the assets are depreciated over their useful lives. The value of these assets may have increased over time, however, or the value may have decreased more than is reflected in the accumulated depreciation. When the reported amount of an asset—that is, its carrying value—exceeds its recoverable amount, both international accounting standards (IFRS) and US accounting standards (GAAP) require companies to reduce the reported amount of the asset and show the reduction as an impairment loss (the two sets of standards differ in the measurement of impairment losses). US GAAP, however, prohibit subsequent reversal of impairment losses, whereas IFRS permit subsequent reversals. In addition, as mentioned above, IFRS allow companies to measure fixed assets using either the historical cost model or a revaluation model, under which the assets are reported at their current value. When assets are reported at fair value, P/Bs become more comparable among companies; for this reason, P/Bs are considered to be more comparable for companies with significant amounts of financial assets.

Valuation Based on Forecasted Fundamentals

We can use forecasts of a company's fundamentals to estimate a stock's justified P/B. For example, assuming the Gordon growth model and using the expression $g = b \times \text{ROE}$ for the sustainable growth rate, the expression for the justified P/B based on the most recent book value (B_0) is

$$\frac{P_0}{B_0} = \frac{\text{ROE} - g}{r - g}. \quad (4)$$

For example, if a business's ROE is 12%, its required rate of return is 10%, and its expected growth rate is 7%, then its justified P/B based on fundamentals is (0.12 – 0.07)/(0.10 – 0.07) = 1.67.

DERIVING THE JUSTIFIED P/B EXPRESSION

According to the Gordon growth model, $V_0 = E_1 \times (1 - b)/(r - g)$. Defining ROE as E_1/B_0 so that $E_1 = B_0 \times \text{ROE}$ and substituting for E_1 into the prior expression, we have $V_0 = B_0 \times \text{ROE} \times (1 - b)/(r - g)$, giving $V_0/B_0 = \text{ROE} \times (1 - b)/(r - g)$. The sustainable growth rate expression is $g = b \times \text{ROE}$. Substituting $b = g/\text{ROE}$ into the expression just given for V_0/B_0, we have $V_0/B_0 = (\text{ROE} - g)/(r - g)$. Because justified price is intrinsic value, V_0, we obtain Equation 4.

Equation 4 states that the justified P/B is an increasing function of ROE, all else equal. Because the numerator and denominator are differences of, respectively, ROE and r from the same quantity, g, what determines the justified P/B in Equation 4 is ROE in relation to the required rate of return, r. The larger ROE is in relation to r, the higher is the justified P/B based on fundamentals. This relationship can be seen clearly if we set g equal to 0 (the no-growth case): $P_0/B_0 = \text{ROE}/r$.

A practical insight from Equation 4 is that we cannot conclude whether a particular value of the P/B reflects undervaluation without taking into account the business's profitability. Equation 4 also suggests that if we are evaluating two stocks with the same P/B, the one with the higher ROE is relatively undervalued, all else equal. These relationships have been confirmed through cross-sectional regression analyses (Harris and Marston 1994; Fairfield, 1994).

Further insight into P/B comes from the residual income model, which is discussed in detail in another reading. The expression for the justified P/B based on the residual income valuation is

$$\frac{P_0}{B_0} = 1 + \frac{\text{Present value of expected future residual earnings}}{B_0}. \quad (5)$$

Equation 5, which makes no special assumptions about growth, states the following:

- If the present value of expected future residual earnings is zero—for example, if the business just earns its required return on investment in every period—the justified P/B is 1.
- If the present value of expected future residual earnings is positive (negative), the justified P/B is greater than (less than) 1.

JUSTIFIED P/B EXPRESSION BASED ON RESIDUAL INCOME

Noting that (ROE – r) × B_0 would define a level residual income stream, we can show that Equation 4 is consistent with Equation 5 (a general expression) as follows. In $P_0/B_0 = (\text{ROE} - g)/(r - g)$, we can successively rewrite the numerator $(\text{ROE} - g) + r - r = (r - g) + (\text{ROE} - r)$, so $P_0/B_0 = [(r - g) + (\text{ROE} - r)]/(r - g) = 1 + (\text{ROE} - r)/(r - g)$, which can be written $P_0/B_0 = 1 + [(\text{ROE} - r)/(r - g)] \times B_0/B_0 = 1 + [(\text{ROE} - r) \times B_0/(r - g)]/B_0$; the second term in the final expression is the present value of residual income divided by B_0 as in Equation 5.

Valuation Based on Comparables

To use the method of comparables for valuing stocks using a P/B, we follow the steps given earlier. In contrast to EPS, however, analysts' forecasts of book value are not aggregated and widely disseminated by financial data vendors; in practice, most analysts use trailing book value in calculating P/Bs. Evaluation of relative P/Bs should consider differences in ROE, risk, and expected earnings growth. The use of P/Bs in the method of comparables is illustrated in Example 21.

EXAMPLE 21

P/B Comparables Approach (Historical Example)

1. You are working on a project to value an independent securities brokerage firm. You know the industry had a significant decline in valuations during the 2007–09 financial crisis. You decide to perform a time series analysis on three firms: E*TRADE Financial Corp. (ETFC), the Charles Schwab Corporation (SCHW), and TD Ameritrade Holding Corp. (AMTD). Exhibit 12 presents information on these firms.

Exhibit 12: Price-to-Book Comparables

	Price-to-Book Value Ratio								
Entity	2006	2007	2008	2009	2010	2011	2012	As of 19 July 2013	Mean
ETFC	2.37	2.38	0.68	0.88	0.84	0.74	0.54	0.65	1.14
Forecasted growth in book value: 1.5%									
Forecasted growth in revenues: –1.0%									
Beta: 1.65									
SCHW	4.23	6.69	6.14	3.54	3.15	2.50	1.96	2.31	3.81
Forecasted growth in book value: 10.5%									
Forecasted growth in revenues: 5.0%									
Beta: 1.20									
AMTD	6.96	4.85	3.33	2.60	2.68	2.44	2.20	2.53	3.45
Forecasted growth in book value: 9.0%									

Price-to-Book Value Ratio									
Entity	2006	2007	2008	2009	2010	2011	2012	As of 19 July 2013	Mean
Forecasted growth in revenues: 3.5%									
Beta: 1.10									

Source: The Value Line Investment Survey. The price-to-book value ratio is based on the average of the annual high and low prices and end-of-year book value.

Based only on the information in Exhibit 12, discuss the relative valuation of ETFC relative to the other two companies.

Solution:

ETFC is currently selling at a P/B that is less than 30% of the P/B for either SCHW or AMTD. It is also selling at a P/B that is less than 60% of its average P/B for the time period noted in the exhibit. The likely explanation for ETFC's low P/B is that its growth forecasts for book value and revenues are lower and its beta is higher than those for SCHW and AMTD. In deciding whether ETFC is overvalued or undervalued, an analyst would likely decide how his or her growth forecast and the uncertainty surrounding that forecast compare to the market consensus.

PRICE/SALES

6

- ☐ calculate and interpret a justified price multiple
- ☐ describe rationales for and possible drawbacks to using alternative price multiples and dividend yield in valuation
- ☐ calculate and interpret alternative price multiples and dividend yield
- ☐ describe fundamental factors that influence alternative price multiples and dividend yield
- ☐ calculate and interpret the justified price-to-earnings ratio (P/E), price-to-book ratio (P/B), and price-to-sales ratio (P/S) for a stock, based on forecasted fundamentals
- ☐ evaluate a stock by the method of comparables and explain the importance of fundamentals in using the method of comparables
- ☐ evaluate whether a stock is overvalued, fairly valued, or undervalued based on comparisons of multiples

Certain types of privately held companies, including investment management companies and many types of companies in partnership form, have long been valued by a multiple of annual revenues. In recent decades, the ratio of price to sales has become well known as a valuation indicator for the equity of publicly traded companies as well. Based on US data, O'Shaughnessy (2005) characterized P/S as the best ratio for selecting undervalued stocks.

According to the 2012 BofA *Merrill Lynch Institutional Factor Survey*, about 30% of respondents consistently used P/S in their investment process. Analysts have offered the following rationales for using P/S:

- Sales are generally less subject to distortion or manipulation than are other fundamentals, such as EPS or book value. For example, through discretionary accounting decisions about expenses, company managers can distort EPS as a reflection of economic performance. In contrast, total sales, as the top line in the income statement, is prior to any expenses.
- Sales are positive even when EPS is negative. Therefore, analysts can use P/S when EPS is negative, whereas the P/E based on a zero or negative EPS is not meaningful.
- Because sales are generally more stable than EPS, which reflects operating and financial leverage, P/S is generally more stable than P/E. P/S may be more meaningful than P/E when EPS is abnormally high or low.
- P/S has been viewed as appropriate for valuing the stocks of mature, cyclical, and zero-income companies (Martin 1998).
- Differences in P/S multiples may be related to differences in long-run average returns, according to empirical research (Nathan, Sivakumar and Vijayakumar, 2001; O'Shaughnessy, 2005).

Possible drawbacks of using P/S in practice include the following:

- A business may show high growth in sales even when it is not operating profitably as judged by earnings and cash flow from operations. To have value as a going concern, a business must ultimately generate earnings and cash.
- Share price reflects the effect of debt financing on profitability and risk. In the P/S multiple, however, price is compared with sales, which is a prefinancing income measure—a logical mismatch. For this reason, some experts use a ratio of enterprise value to sales because enterprise value incorporates the value of debt.
- P/S does not reflect differences in cost structures among different companies.
- Although P/S is relatively robust with respect to manipulation, revenue recognition practices have the potential to distort P/S.

Despite the contrasts between P/S to P/E, the ratios have a relationship with which analysts should be familiar. The fact that (Sales) × (Net profit margin) = Net income means that (P/E) × (Net profit margin) = P/S. For two stocks with the same positive P/E, the stock with the higher P/S has a higher (actual or forecasted) net profit margin, calculated as the ratio of P/S to P/E.

Determining Sales

P/S is calculated as price per share divided by annual net sales per share (net sales is total sales minus returns and customer discounts). Analysts usually use annual sales from the company's most recent fiscal year in the calculation, as illustrated in Example 22. Because valuation is forward looking in principle, the analyst may also develop and use P/S multiples based on forecasts of next year's sales.

EXAMPLE 22

Calculating P/S

1. Stora Enso Oyj (Helsinki Stock Exchange: STERV) is an integrated paper, packaging, and forest products company headquartered in Finland. In its fiscal year ended 31 December 2018, Stora Enso reported net sales of €10,486 million and had 788.4 million shares outstanding. Calculate the P/S for Stora Enso based on a closing price of €10.34 on 28 June 2019.

Solution:

Sales per share = €10,486 million/788.6 million shares = €13.30. So, P/S = €10.34/€13.30 = 0.778.

Although the determination of sales is more straightforward than the determination of earnings, the analyst should evaluate a company's revenue recognition practices—in particular those tending to speed up the recognition of revenues—before relying on the P/S multiple. An analyst using a P/S approach who does not also assess the quality of accounting for sales may place too high a value on the company's shares. Example 23 illustrates the problem.

Valuation Based on Forecasted Fundamentals

Like other multiples, P/S can be linked to DCF models. In terms of the Gordon growth model, we can state P/S as

$$\frac{P_0}{S_1} = \frac{\left(\frac{E_1}{S_1}\right)(1-b)}{r-g}. \tag{6}$$

where E_1/S_1 is the business's forward-looking profit margin (the equation can be obtained from the Gordon Growth model $P_0=D_1/(r-g)$, by substituting $D_1=E_1(1-b)$ into the numerator and then dividing both sides by S_1). Equation 6 states that the justified P/S is an increasing function of the profit margin and earnings growth rate, and the intuition behind Equation 6 generalizes to more-complex DCF models.

EXAMPLE 23

Revenue Recognition Practices (1)

Analysts label stock markets "bubbles" when market prices appear to lose contact with intrinsic values. To many analysts, the run-up in the prices of internet stocks in the US market in the 1998–2000 period represented a bubble. During that period, many analysts adopted P/S as a metric for valuing the many internet stocks that had negative earnings and cash flow. Perhaps at least partly as a result of this practice, some internet companies engaged in questionable revenue recognition practices to justify their high valuations. To increase sales, some companies engaged in bartering website advertising with other internet companies. For example, InternetRevenue.com might barter $1,000,000 worth of banner advertising with RevenueIsUs.com. Each could then show $1,000,000 of revenue and $1,000,000 of expenses. Although neither had any net income or cash flow, each company's revenue growth and market valuation was enhanced (at least temporarily). In addition, the value placed on the advertising was frequently questionable.

As a result of these and other questionable activities, the US SEC issued a stern warning to companies and formalized revenue recognition practices for barter in Staff Accounting Bulletin No. 101. Similarly, international accounting standard setters issued Standing Interpretations Committee Interpretation 31 to define revenue recognition principles for barter transactions involving advertising services. The analyst should review footnote disclosures to assess whether a company may be recognizing revenue prematurely or otherwise aggressively.

Example 24 illustrates another classic instance in which an analyst should look behind the accounting numbers.

EXAMPLE 24

Revenue Recognition Practices (2)

1. Sales on a **bill-and-hold basis** involve selling products but not delivering those products until a later date. Sales on this basis have the effect of accelerating the recognition of those sales into an earlier reporting period. In its form 10-K filed 30 September 2008, Diebold, a provider of bank security systems and ATMs, provided the following note:

   Revenues

   Bill and Hold—The largest of the revenue recognition adjustments relates to the Company's previous long-standing method of accounting for bill and hold transactions under Staff Accounting Bulletin 104, Revenue Recognition in Financial Statements (SAB 104), in its North America and International businesses. On January 15, 2008, the Company announced that it had concluded its discussions with the OCA in regard to its practice of recognizing certain revenue on a bill and hold basis in its North America business segment. As a result of those discussions, the Company determined that its previous, long-standing method of accounting for bill and hold transactions was in error, representing a misapplication of GAAP. To correct for this error, the Company announced it would discontinue the use of bill and hold as a method of revenue recognition in its North America and International businesses and restate its financial statements for this change.

   The Company completed an analysis of transactions and recorded adjusting journal entries related to revenue and costs recognized previously under a bill and hold basis that is now recognized upon customer acceptance of products at a customer location. Within the North America business segment, when the Company is contractually responsible for installation, customer acceptance will be upon completion of the installation of all of the items at a job site and the Company's demonstration that the items are in operable condition. Where items are contractually only delivered to a customer, revenue recognition of these items will continue upon shipment or delivery to a customer location depending on the terms in the contract. Within the International business segment, customer acceptance is upon either delivery or completion of the installation depending on the terms in the contract with the customer. The Company restated for transactions affecting both product revenue for hardware sales and service revenue for installation and other services that had been previously recognized on a bill and hold basis.

Other Revenue Adjustments—The Company also adjusted for other specific revenue transactions in both its North America and International businesses related to transactions largely where the Company recognized revenue in incorrect periods. The majority of these adjustments were related to misapplication of GAAP related to revenue recognition requirements as defined within SAB 104. Generally, the Company recorded adjustments for transactions when the Company previously recognized revenue prior to title and/or risk of loss transferring to the customer.

In 2010, Diebold agreed to pay $25 million to settle Securities and Exchange Commission charges that it manipulated its earnings from at least 2002 through 2007. During that period, the company misstated the company's reported pre-tax earnings by at least $127 million.

According to the SEC, Diebold's financial management received reports, sometimes on a daily basis, comparing the company's actual earnings to analyst earnings forecasts. Diebold's management would prepare "opportunity lists" of ways to close the gap between the company's actual financial results and analyst forecasts. Many of the methods were fraudulent accounting transactions designed to improperly recognize revenue or otherwise inflate Diebold's financial performance. Among the fraudulent practices identified by the SEC were the following: improper use of bill and hold accounting, recognition of revenue on a lease agreement subject to a side buy-back agreement, manipulating reserves and accruals, improperly delaying and capitalizing expenses, and writing up the value of used inventory.

Example 25 briefly summarizes another example of aggressive revenue recognition practices.

EXAMPLE 25

Revenue Recognition Practices (3)

Groupon is a deal-of-the-day website that features discounted gift certificates usable at local or national companies. Before going public in November 2011, Groupon amended its registration statement eight times. One SEC-mandated restatement forced it to change an auditor-sanctioned method of reporting revenue, reducing sales by more than 50%. Essentially, Groupon had initially counted the gross amount its members paid for coupons or certificates as revenue, without deducting the share (typically half or more) that it sends to local merchants. The SEC also demanded Groupon remove from its offering document a non-GAAP metric it had invented called "adjusted consolidated segment operating income." This measure was considered misleading because it ignored marketing expenses, which are one of the major risks of Groupon's business model.

Even when a company discloses its revenue recognition practices, the analyst cannot always determine precisely by how much sales may be overstated. If a company is engaging in questionable revenue recognition practices and the amount being manipulated is unknown, the analyst might do well to suggest avoiding investment in that company's securities. At the very least, the analyst should be skeptical and assign the company a higher risk premium than otherwise, which would result in a lower justified P/S.

Valuation Based on Forecasted Fundamentals

Like other multiples, P/S can be linked to DCF models. In terms of the Gordon growth model, we can state P/S as

$$\frac{P_0}{S_0} = \frac{(E_0/S_0)\ (1-b)\,(1+g)}{r-g}, \tag{7}$$

where E_0/S_0 is the business's profit margin (the equation can be obtained from the Gordon growth model, $P_0 = D_0(1 + g)/(r - g)$, by substituting $D_0 = E_0(1 - b)$ into the numerator and then dividing both sides by S_0). Although the profit margin is stated in terms of trailing sales and earnings, the analyst may use a long-term forecasted profit margin in Equation 7. Equation 7 states that the justified P/S is an increasing function of the profit margin and earnings growth rate, and the intuition behind Equation 7 generalizes to more-complex DCF models.

Profit margin is a determinant of the justified P/S not only directly but also through its effect on g. We can illustrate this concept by restating the equation for the sustainable growth rate [g = (Retention rate, b) × ROE], as follows:

$$g = b \times \text{PM}_0 \times \frac{\text{Sales}}{\text{Total assets}} \times \frac{\text{Total assets}}{\text{Shareholders' equity}},$$

where PM_0 is profit margin and the last three terms come from the DuPont analysis of ROE. An increase (decrease) in the profit margin produces a higher (lower) sustainable growth rate as long as sales do not decrease (increase) proportionately. Example 26 illustrates the use of justified P/S and how to apply it in valuation.

EXAMPLE 26

Justified P/S Based on Forecasted Fundamentals

As a health care analyst, you are valuing the stocks of three medical equipment manufacturers, including the Swedish company Getinge AB (GETI) in March 2019. Based on an average of estimates obtained from capital asset pricing model (CAPM) and bond yield plus risk premium approaches, you estimate that GETI's required rate of return is 9%. You have gathered the following data from GETI's annual reports (amounts in millions of Swedish krona, or SEK):

	2009	2010	2011	2012	2013	2014	2015	2016	2017	2018
Net sales	22,816	22,712	21,854	24,248	25,287	26,669	30,235	29,756	22,496	24,172
Growth rates (geometric)										
2009–2018	0.6%									
2014–2018	−2.4%									
Year / Year		−0.5%	−3.8%	11.0%	4.3%	5.5%	13.4%	−1.6%	−24.4%	7.5%
Net profit	1,914	2,280	2,537	2,531	2,285	1,433	1,390	1,188	1,376	−967
Growth rates (geometric)										
2009–2018	NMF									
2014–2018	NMF									
Year / Year		19.1%	11.3%	−0.2%	−9.7%	−37.3%	−3.0%	−14.5%	15.8%	−170.3%
Net profit margin	8.4%	10.0%	11.6%	10.4%	9.0%	5.4%	4.6%	4.0%	6.1%	−4.0%
Averages										
2009–2018	6.6%									
2014–2018	3.2%									
Dividend payout ratio	0.3%	34.0%	35.3%	39.2%	43.3%	69.3%	49.7%	57.7%	36.0%	−43.8%
Averages										

	2009	2010	2011	2012	2013	2014	2015	2016	2017	2018
2009–2018	32.1%									
2014–2018	33.8%									

Sales growth and profitability have been quite variable in recent years, particularly in 2017 and 2018, making it difficult to extrapolate future trends. Based on further research on the company and its industry, you make the following long-term forecasts:

Profit margin = 9.0%

Dividend payout ratio = 35.0%

Earnings growth rate = 7.0%

1. Based on these data, calculate GETI's justified P/S.

Solution:

From Equation 6, GETI's justified P/S is calculated as follows:

$$\frac{P_0}{S_1} = \frac{(E_1/S_1)(1-b)}{r-g} = \frac{0.09 \times 0.35}{0.09 - 0.07} = 1.575$$

2. Given a forecast of GETI's sales per share (in Swedish krona) for 2019 of SEK94.3, estimate the intrinsic value of GETI stock.

Solution:

An estimate of the intrinsic value of GETI stock is 1.575 × SEK94.3 = SEK148.52.

3. Given a market price for GETI of SEK133.70 on 26 August 2019 and your answer to Part 2, determine whether GETI stock appears to be fairly valued, overvalued, or undervalued.

Solution:

GETI stock appears to be undervalued because its current market value of SEK133.70 is less than its estimated intrinsic value of SEK148.52.

Valuation Based on Comparables

Using P/S in the method of comparables to value stocks follows the steps given in Section 3.1.5. As mentioned earlier, P/Ss are usually reported on the basis of trailing sales. Analysts may also base relative valuations on P/S multiples calculated on forecasted sales. In doing so, analysts may make their own sales forecasts or may use forecasts supplied by data vendors. In valuing stocks using the method of comparables, analysts should also gather information on profit margins, expected earnings growth, and risk. As always, the quality of accounting also merits investigation. Example 27 illustrates the use of P/S in the comparables approach.

EXAMPLE 27

P/S Comparables Approach

Continuing with the project to value Getinge AB, you have compiled the information on GETI and peer companies Cantel Medical Corporation (CMD) and New Genomics (NEO) given in Exhibit 13.

Exhibit 13: P/S Comparables (as of 26 October 2019)

Measure	GETI	CMD	NEO
Price/Sales (TTM)	1.54	3.96	8.79
Profit Margin (TTM)	−2.49%	6.95%	14.53%
Quarterly Revenue Growth (YoYy)	9.50%	5.20%	1.50%
Total Debt/Equity (mrq)	58.43	35.58	28.50
Enterprise Value/Revenue (TTM)	1.88	4.14	8.23

Source: Yahoo! Finance.

Use the data in Exhibit 13 to address the following:

1. Based on the P/S but referring to no other information, assess GETI's relative valuation.

Solution:

Because the P/S for GETI, 1.54, is the lowest of the three P/S multiples, if no other information is referenced, GETI appears to be relatively undervalued.

2. State whether GETI is more closely comparable to CMD or to NEO. Justify your answer.

Solution:

On the basis of the information given, GETI appears to be more closely matched to CMD than to NEO. NEO's P/S is significantly higher than the P/S for GETI and CMD. The profit margin and revenue growth are key fundamentals in the P/S approach, and NEO's higher P/S reflects its high profit margin. GETI's funding (Total debt/Equity) is higher than that of CMD and NEO, and its Enterprise value/Revenue is low and much closer to CMD's ratio than to that of NEO. Overall, GETI's valuation seems to be more like that of CMD than that of NEO. GETI's low P/S is consistent with its other relative-valuation metrics in Exhibit 13.

7 PRICE/CASH FLOW

- ☐ calculate and interpret a justified price multiple
- ☐ describe rationales for and possible drawbacks to using alternative price multiples and dividend yield in valuation
- ☐ calculate and interpret alternative price multiples and dividend yield

- ☐ describe fundamental factors that influence alternative price multiples and dividend yield
- ☐ calculate and interpret the justified price-to-earnings ratio (P/E), price-to-book ratio (P/B), and price-to-sales ratio (P/S) for a stock, based on forecasted fundamentals
- ☐ evaluate a stock by the method of comparables and explain the importance of fundamentals in using the method of comparables
- ☐ evaluate whether a stock is overvalued, fairly valued, or undervalued based on comparisons of multiples

Price to cash flow is a widely reported valuation indicator. According to the 2012 BofA Merrill Lynch Institutional Factor Survey, price to free cash flow trailed only P/E, beta, enterprise value/EBITDA, ROE, size, and P/B in popularity as a valuation factor and was used as a valuation metric by approximately half of the institutions surveyed.

In this section, we present price to cash flow based on alternative major cash flow concepts. Note that "price to cash flow" is used to refer to the ratio of share price to any one of these definitions of cash flow whereas "P/CF" is reserved for the ratio of price to the earnings-plus-noncash-charges definition of cash flow, explained later. Because of the wide variety of cash flow concepts in use, the analyst should be especially careful to understand (and communicate) the exact definition of "cash flow" that is the basis for the analysis.

Analysts have offered the following rationales for the use of price to cash flow:

- Cash flow is less subject to manipulation by management than earnings.
- Because cash flow is generally more stable than earnings, price to cash flow is generally more stable than P/E.
- Using price to cash flow rather than P/E addresses the issue of differences in accounting conservatism between companies (differences in the quality of earnings).
- Differences in price to cash flow may be related to differences in long-run average returns, according to empirical research (O'Shaughnessy 2005).

Possible drawbacks to the use of price to cash flow include the following:

- When cash flow from operations is defined as EPS plus noncash charges, items affecting actual cash flow from operations, such as noncash revenue and net changes in working capital, are ignored. So, for example, aggressive recognition of revenue (front-end loading) would not be accurately captured in the earnings-plus-noncash-charges definition because the measure would not reflect the divergence between revenues as reported and actual cash collections related to that revenue.
- Theory views free cash flow to equity (FCFE) rather than cash flow as the appropriate variable for price-based valuation multiples. We can use P/FCFE, but FCFE does have the possible drawback of being more volatile than cash flow for many businesses. FCFE is also more frequently negative than cash flow.
- As analysts' use of cash flow has increased over time, some companies have increased their use of accounting methods that enhance cash flow measures. Operating cash flow, for example, can be enhanced by securitizing accounts receivable to speed up a company's operating cash inflow or by outsourcing the payment of accounts payable to slow down the company's operating cash outflow (while the outsource company continues to make timely payments

and provides financing to cover any timing differences). Mulford and Comiskey (2005) described a number of opportunistic accounting choices that companies can make to increase their reported operating cash flow.

- Operating cash flow from the statement of cash flows under IFRS may not be comparable to operating cash flow under US GAAP because IFRS allow more flexibility in classification of interest paid, interest received, and dividends received. Under US GAAP, all three of these items are classified in operating cash flow, but under IFRS, companies have the option to classify them as operating or investing (for interest and dividends received) and as operating or financing (for interest paid).

One approximation of cash flow in practical use is EPS plus per-share depreciation, amortization, and depletion. This simple approximation is used in Example 28 to highlight issues of interest to the analyst in valuation.

EXAMPLE 28

Accounting Methods and Cash Flow

1. Consider two hypothetical companies, Company A and Company B, that have constant cash revenues and cash expenses (as well as a constant number of shares outstanding) in 2018, 2019, and 2020. In addition, both companies incur total depreciation of $15.00 per share during the three-year period, and both use the same depreciation method for tax purposes. The two companies use different depreciation methods, however, for financial reporting. Company A spreads the depreciation expense evenly over the three years (straight-line depreciation, or SLD). Because its revenues, expenses, and depreciation are constant over the period, Company A's EPS is also constant. In this example, Company A's EPS is assumed to be $10 each year, as shown in Column 1 in Exhibit 14.

   Company B is identical to Company A except that it uses accelerated depreciation. Company B's depreciation is 150% of SLD in 2018 and declines to 50% of SLD in 2020, as shown in Column 5.

Exhibit 14: Earnings Growth Rates and Cash Flow (All Amounts per Share)

	Company A			Company B		
Year	Earnings (1)	Depreciation (2)	Cash Flow (3)	Earnings (4)	Depreciation (5)	Cash Flow (6)
2018	$10.00	$5.00	$15.00	$7.50	$7.50	$15.00
2019	10.00	5.00	15.00	10.00	5.00	15.00
2020	10.00	5.00	15.00	12.50	2.50	15.00
Total		$15.00			$15.00	

Because of the different depreciation methods used by Company A and Company B for financial reporting purposes, Company A's EPS (Column 1) is flat at $10.00 whereas Company B's EPS (Column 4) shows 29% compound growth: $(\$12.50/\$7.50)^{1/2} - 1.00 = 0.29$. Thus, Company B appears to have positive earnings momentum. Analysts comparing Companies A and B might be misled by using the EPS numbers as reported instead of putting

EPS on a comparable basis. For both companies, however, cash flow per share is level at $15.

Depreciation may be the simplest noncash charge to understand; write-offs and other noncash charges may offer more latitude for the management of earnings.

Determining Cash Flow

In practice, analysts and data vendors often use simple *approximations* of cash flow from operations in calculating cash flow for price-to-cash-flow analysis. For many companies, depreciation and amortization are the major noncash charges regularly added to net income in the process of calculating cash flow from operations by the add-back method, so the approximation focuses on them. A representative approximation specifies cash flow per share as EPS plus per-share depreciation, amortization, and depletion. We call this estimation the "earnings-plus-noncash-charges" definition and in this section use the acronym CF for it. Keep in mind, however, that this definition is only one commonly used in calculating price to cash flow, not a technically accurate definition from an accounting perspective. We will also describe more technically accurate cash flow concepts: cash flow from operations, free cash flow to equity, and EBITDA (an estimate of pre-interest, pretax operating cash flow).

Most frequently, trailing price to cash flow is reported. A trailing price to cash flow is calculated as the current market price divided by the sum of the most recent four quarters' cash flow per share. A fiscal year definition is also possible, as in the case of EPS.

Example 29 illustrates the calculation of P/CF with cash flow defined as earnings plus noncash charges.

EXAMPLE 29

Calculating Price to Cash Flow with Cash Flow Defined as Earnings plus Noncash Charges

1. In 2018, Koninklijke Philips Electronics N.V. (PHIA) reported net income from continuing operations of €1,310 million, equal to EPS of €1.41. The company's depreciation and amortization was €1,089 million, or €1.17 per share. An AEX price for PHIA as of 29 March 2019 was €36.31. Calculate the P/CF for PHIA.

Solution:

CF (defined as EPS plus per-share depreciation, amortization, and depletion) is €1.41 + €1.17 = €2.58 per share. Thus, P/CF = €36.31/€2.58 = 14.1.

Rather than use an approximate EPS-plus-noncash-charges concept of cash flow, analysts can use cash flow from operations (CFO) in a price multiple. CFO is found in the statement of cash flows. Similar to the adjustments to normalize earnings, adjustments to CFO for components not expected to persist into future time periods may also be appropriate. In addition, adjustments to CFO may be required when comparing companies that use different accounting standards. For example, as noted above, under IFRS, companies have flexibility in classifying interest payments, interest receipts, and dividend receipts across operating, investing, and financing. US GAAP require companies to classify interest payments, interest receipts, and dividend receipts as operating cash flows.

As an alternative to CF and CFO, the analyst can relate price to FCFE, the cash flow concept with the strongest link to valuation theory. Because the amounts of capital expenditures in proportion to CFO generally differ among companies being compared, the analyst may find that rankings by price to cash flow from operations (P/CFO) and by P/CF will differ from rankings by P/FCFE. Period-by-period FCFE may be more volatile than CFO (or CF), however, so a trailing P/FCFE is not necessarily more informative in a valuation. For example, consider two similar businesses with the same CFO and capital expenditures over a two-year period. If the first company times its capital expenditures to fall toward the beginning of the period and the second times its capital expenditures to fall toward the end of the period, the P/FCFEs for the two stocks may differ sharply without representing a meaningful economic difference. The analyst could, however, appropriately use the FCFE discounted cash flow model value, which incorporates all expected future free cash flows to equity. This concern can be addressed, at least in part, by using price to average free cash flow, as in Hackel, Livnat, and Rai (1994).

Another cash flow concept used in multiples is EBITDA (earnings before interest, taxes, depreciation, and amortization). To forecast EBITDA, analysts usually start with their projections of EBIT and simply add depreciation and amortization to arrive at an estimate for EBITDA. In calculating EBITDA from historical numbers, one can start with earnings from continuing operations, excluding nonrecurring items. To that earnings number, interest, taxes, depreciation, and amortization are added.

In practice, both EV/EBITDA and P/EBITDA have been used by analysts as valuation metrics. EV/EBITDA has been the preferred metric, however, because its numerator includes the value of debt; therefore, it is the more appropriate method because EBITDA is pre-interest and is thus a flow to both debt and equity. EV/EBITDA is discussed in detail in a later section.

Valuation Based on Forecasted Fundamentals

The relationship between the justified price to cash flow and fundamentals follows from the familiar mathematics of the present value model. The justified price to cash flow, all else being equal, is inversely related to the stock's required rate of return and positively related to the growth rate(s) of expected future cash flows (however defined). We can find a justified price to cash flow based on fundamentals by finding the value of a stock using the most suitable DCF model and dividing that number by cash flow (based on our chosen definition of cash flow). Example 30 illustrates the process.

EXAMPLE 30

Justified Price to Cash Flow Based on Forecasted Fundamentals

As a consumer staples analyst, you are working on the valuation of Colgate-Palmolive (CL), a global consumer products supplier. As a first estimate of value, you are applying an FCFE model under the assumption of a stable long-term growth rate in FCFE:

$$V_0 = \frac{(1+g)\text{FCFE}_0}{r-g},$$

where g is the expected growth rate of FCFE. You estimate trailing FCFE at \$2.66 per share and trailing CF (based on the earnings-plus-noncash-charges definition) at \$3.26. Your other estimates are a 7.4% required rate of return and a 3.2% expected growth rate of FCFE.

1. What is the intrinsic value of CL according to a constant growth FCFE model?

Solution:

Calculate intrinsic value as (1.032 × \$2.66)/(0.074 – 0.032) = \$65.36.

2. What is the justified P/CF based on forecasted fundamentals?

Solution:

Calculate a justified P/CF based on forecasted fundamentals as \$65.36/\$3.26 = 20.05.

3. What is the justified P/FCFE based on forecasted fundamentals?

Solution:

The justified P/FCFE is \$65.36/\$2.66 = 24.57.

Valuation Based on Comparables

The method of comparables for valuing stocks based on price to cash flow follows the steps given previously and illustrated for P/E, P/B, and P/S. Example 31 is a simple exercise in the comparables method based on price-to-cash-flow measures.

EXAMPLE 31

Price to Cash Flow and Comparables

1. Exhibit 15 provides information on P/CF, P/FCFE, and selected fundamentals as of 16 April 2020 for two hypothetical companies. Using the information in Exhibit 15, compare the valuations of the two companies.

Exhibit 15: Comparison of Two Companies (All Amounts per Share)

Company	Current Price (£)	Trailing CF per Share (£)	P/CF	Trailing FCFE per Share (£)	P/FCFE	Consensus Five-Year CF Growth Forecast (%)	Beta
Company A	17.98	1.84	9.8	0.29	62	13.4	1.50
Company B	15.65	1.37	11.4	–0.99	NMF	10.6	1.50

Company A is selling at a P/CF (9.8) approximately 14% smaller than the P/CF of Company B (11.4). Based on that comparison, we expect that, all else equal, investors would anticipate a higher growth rate for Company B. Contrary to that expectation, however, the consensus five-year earnings growth forecast for Company A is 280 basis points higher than it is for Company B. As of the date of the comparison, Company A appears to be relatively undervalued compared with Company B, as judged by P/CF and expected growth. The information in Exhibit 15 on FCFE supports the proposition that Company A may be relatively undervalued. The positive FCFE for Company A indicates that operating cash flows and new debt borrowing are more than sufficient to cover capital expenditures. Negative FCFE for Company B suggests the need for external funding of growth.

8 PRICE/DIVIDENDS AND DIVIDEND YIELD

- [ ] calculate and interpret a justified price multiple
- [ ] describe rationales for and possible drawbacks to using alternative price multiples and dividend yield in valuation
- [ ] calculate and interpret alternative price multiples and dividend yield
- [ ] describe fundamental factors that influence alternative price multiples and dividend yield
- [ ] calculate and interpret the justified price-to-earnings ratio (P/E), price-to-book ratio (P/B), and price-to-sales ratio (P/S) for a stock, based on forecasted fundamentals
- [ ] evaluate a stock by the method of comparables and explain the importance of fundamentals in using the method of comparables
- [ ] evaluate whether a stock is overvalued, fairly valued, or undervalued based on comparisons of multiples

The total return on an equity investment has a capital appreciation component and a dividend yield component. Dividend yield data are frequently reported to provide investors with an estimate of the dividend yield component in total return. Dividend yield is also used as a valuation indicator. Although the 2012 BofA Merrill Lynch Institutional Factor Survey did not survey this metric, in its surveys from 1989 to 2006 slightly more than one-quarter of respondents on average reported using dividend yield as a factor in the investment process.

Analysts have offered the following rationales for using dividend yields in valuation:

- Dividend yield is a component of total return.
- Dividends are a less risky component of total return than capital appreciation.

Possible drawbacks of using dividend yields include the following:

- Dividend yield is only one component of total return; not using all information related to expected return is suboptimal.
- Investors may trade off future earnings growth to receive higher current dividends. That is, holding return on equity constant, dividends paid now displace earnings in all future periods (a concept known as the **dividend displacement of earnings**). Arnott and Asness (2003) and Zhou and Ruland (2006), however, showed that caution must be exercised in assuming that dividends displace future earnings in practice, because dividend payout may be correlated with future profitability.
- The argument about the relative safety of dividends presupposes that market prices reflect in a biased way differences in the relative risk of the components of return.

Calculation of Dividend Yield

This reading so far has presented multiples with market price (or market capitalization) in the numerator. P/Ds have sometimes appeared in valuation, particularly with respect to indexes. Many stocks, however, do not pay dividends, and P/D is undefined with zero in the denominator. For such non-dividend-paying stocks, dividend yield (D/P) *is* defined: It is equal to zero. For practical purposes, then, dividend yield is the preferred way to present this multiple.

Trailing dividend yield is generally calculated by using the dividend rate divided by the current market price per share. The annualized amount of the most recent dividend is known as the **dividend rate**. For companies paying quarterly dividends, the dividend rate is calculated as four times the most recent quarterly per-share dividend. (Some data sources use the dividends in the last four quarters as the dividend rate for purposes of a trailing dividend yield.) For companies that pay semiannual dividends comprising an interim dividend that typically differs in magnitude from the final dividend, the dividend rate is usually calculated as the most recent annual per-share dividend.

The dividend rate indicates the annual amount of dividends per share under the assumption of no increase or decrease over the year. The analyst's forecast of leading dividends could be higher or lower and is the basis of the leading dividend yield. The **leading dividend yield** is calculated as forecasted dividends per share over the next year divided by the current market price per share. Example 32 illustrates the calculation of dividend yield.

EXAMPLE 32

Calculating Dividend Yield

Exhibit 16 gives quarterly dividend data for Canadian telecommunications company BCE Inc. (BCE) and semiannual dividend data for the ADRs of BT Group (BT), formerly British Telecom.

Exhibit 16: Dividends Paid per Share for BCE Inc. and for BT Group ADRs

Period	BCE ($)	BT ADR ($)
4Q:2016	0.51	
1Q:2017	0.54	0.685
2Q:2017	0.53	
3Q:2017	0.57	0.339
Total	2.15	1.024
4Q:2017	0.56	
1Q:2018	0.60	0.675
2Q:2018	0.58	
3Q:2018	0.58	0.301
Total	2.32	0.976

Source: Value Line.

1. Given a price per share for BCE of $39.53 during 4Q:2018, calculate this company's trailing dividend yield.

Solution:

The dividend rate for BCE is $0.58 × 4 = $2.32. The dividend yield is $2.32/$39.53 = 0.0587, or 5.87%.

2. Given a price per ADR for BT of \$15.20 during 4Q:2018, calculate the trailing dividend yield for the ADRs.

Solution:

Because BT pays semiannual dividends that differ in magnitude between the interim and final dividends, the dividend rate for BT's ADR is the total dividend in the most recent year, \$0.976. The dividend yield is \$0.976/\$15.20 = 0.0642, or 6.52%.

Valuation Based on Forecasted Fundamentals

The relationship of dividend yield to fundamentals can be illustrated in the context of the Gordon growth model. From that model, we obtain the expression

$$\frac{D_0}{P_0} = \frac{r-g}{1+g}. \tag{8}$$

Equation 8 shows that dividend yield is negatively related to the expected rate of growth in dividends and positively related to the stock's required rate of return. The first point implies that the selection of stocks with relatively high dividend yields is consistent with an orientation to a value rather than growth investment style.

Valuation Based on Comparables

Using dividend yield with comparables is similar to the process that has been illustrated for other multiples. An analyst compares a company with its peers to determine whether it is attractively priced, considering its dividend yield and risk. The analyst should examine whether differences in expected growth explain the differences in dividend yield. Another consideration used by some investors is the security of the dividend (the probability that it will be reduced or eliminated). A useful metric in assessing the safety of the dividend is the payout ratio: A high payout relative to other companies operating in the same industry may indicate a less secure dividend because the dividend is less well covered by earnings. Balance sheet metrics are equally important in assessing the safety of the dividend, and relevant ratios to consider include the interest coverage ratio and the ratio of net debt to EBITDA. Example 33 illustrates use of the dividend yield in the method of comparables.

EXAMPLE 33

Dividend Yield Comparables

1. William Leiderman is a portfolio manager for a US pension fund's domestic equity portfolio. The portfolio is exempt from taxes, so any differences in the taxation of dividends and capital gains are not relevant. Leiderman's client requires high current income. Leiderman is considering the purchase

of utility stocks for the fund in August 2019. In the course of his review, he considers the four large-cap US electric utilities shown in Exhibit 17.

Exhibit 17: Using Dividend Yield to Compare Stocks

Company	Consensus Earnings Growth Forecast (%)	Beta	Dividend Yield (%)	Payout Ratio (%)
Duke Energy	7.20	0.18	4.24	89
NiSource Inc.	4.63	0.22	2.70	NMF
Portland General Electric Co.	5.20	0.24	2.76	59
PPL Corp.	0.60	0.55	5.37	63

Sources: www.finviz.com and Yahoo! Finance.

All of the securities exhibit similar low market risk; they each have a beta substantially less than 1.00. The dividend payout ratio for NiSource is not meaningful due to a negative EPS. Duke Energy's dividend payout ratio of 89%, the highest of the group, also suggests that its dividend may be subject to greater risk. Leiderman notes that PPL Corp.'s relatively low payout ratio means that the dividend is well supported; however, the expected low earnings growth rate is a negative factor. Summing Portland General Electric's dividend yield and expected earnings growth rate, Leiderman estimates Portland General Electric's expected total return is about 7.96%; because the total return estimate is relatively attractive and because Portland General Electric does not appear to have any strong negatives, Leiderman decides to focus his further analysis on Portland General Electric.

ENTERPRISE VALUE/EBITDA

9

- ☐ explain alternative definitions of cash flow used in price and enterprise value (EV) multiples and describe limitations of each definition
- ☐ calculate and interpret EV multiples and evaluate the use of EV/EBITDA
- ☐ evaluate whether a stock is overvalued, fairly valued, or undervalued based on comparisons of multiples

Enterprise value multiples are multiples that relate the enterprise value of a company to some measure of value (typically, a pre-interest income measure). Perhaps the most frequently advanced argument for using enterprise value multiples rather than price multiples in valuation is that enterprise value multiples are relatively less sensitive to the effects of financial leverage than price multiples when one is comparing companies that use differing amounts of leverage. Enterprise value multiples, in defining the numerator as they do, take a control perspective (discussed in more detail later). Thus, even where leverage differences are not an issue, enterprise value multiples may complement the perspective of price multiples. Indeed, although some analysts strictly favor one type of multiple, other analysts report both price and enterprise value multiples.

Enterprise Value/EBITDA

Enterprise value to EBITDA is by far the most widely used enterprise value multiple.

Earlier, EBITDA was introduced as an estimate of pre-interest, pretax operating cash flow. Because EBITDA is a flow to both debt and equity, as noted, defining an EBITDA multiple by using a measure of total company value in the numerator, such as EV, is appropriate. Recall that **enterprise value** is total company value (the market value of debt, common equity, and preferred equity) minus the value of cash and short-term investments. Thus, EV/EBITDA is a valuation indicator for the overall company rather than solely its common stock. If, however, the analyst can assume that the business's debt and preferred stock (if any) are efficiently priced, the analyst can use EV/EBITDA to draw an inference about the valuation of common equity. Such an inference is often reasonable.

Analysts have offered the following rationales for using EV/EBITDA:

- EV/EBITDA is usually more appropriate than P/E alone for comparing companies with different financial leverage (debt), because EBITDA is a pre-interest earnings figure, in contrast to EPS, which is postinterest.
- By adding back depreciation and amortization, EBITDA controls for differences in depreciation and amortization among businesses, in contrast to net income, which is postdepreciation and postamortization. For this reason, EV/EBITDA is frequently used in the valuation of capital-intensive businesses (for example, cable companies and steel companies). Such businesses typically have substantial depreciation and amortization expenses.
- EBITDA is frequently positive when EPS is negative.

Possible drawbacks to using EV/EBITDA include the following (Moody's 2000; Grant and Parker 2001):

- EBITDA will overestimate cash flow from operations if working capital is growing. EBITDA also ignores the effects of differences in revenue recognition policy on cash flow from operations.
- Free cash flow to the firm (FCFF), which directly reflects the amount of the company's required capital expenditures, has a stronger link to valuation theory than does EBITDA. Only if depreciation expenses match capital expenditures do we expect EBITDA to reflect differences in businesses' capital programs. This qualification to EBITDA comparisons may be particularly meaningful for the capital-intensive businesses to which EV/EBITDA is often applied.

Determining Enterprise Value

We illustrated the calculation of EBITDA previously. As discussed, analysts commonly define enterprise value as follows:

Market value of common equity (Number of shares outstanding × Price per share)

Plus: Market value of preferred stock (if any) and any minority interest (unless included elsewhere)

Plus: Market value of debt

Less: Cash and investments (specifically, cash, cash equivalents, and short-term investments)

Equals: Enterprise value.

Cash and investments (sometimes termed **nonearning assets**) are subtracted because EV is designed to measure the net price an acquirer would pay for the company as a whole. The acquirer must buy out current equity and debt providers but then receives access to the cash and investments, which lower the net cost of the acquisition. (For example, cash and investments can be used to pay off debt or loans used to finance the purchase.) The same logic explains the use of market values: In repurchasing debt, an acquirer has to pay market prices. Some debt, however, may be private and does not trade; some debt may be publicly traded but may trade infrequently. When analysts do not have market values, they often use book values obtained from the balance sheet. Alternatively, they may use so-called matrix price estimates of debt market values in such cases; where they are available, they may be more accurate. Matrix price estimates are based on characteristics of the debt issue and information on how the marketplace prices those characteristics. Example 34 illustrates the calculation of EV/EBITDA.

EXAMPLE 34

Calculating EV/EBITDA

1. Colgate-Palmolive (CL) provides a variety of household products. Exhibit 18 presents the company's consolidated balance sheet as of 31 December 2018.

Exhibit 18: Colgate-Palmolive Condensed Consolidated Balance Sheet (in Millions except Par Values; Unaudited)

Assets	
Current assets:	
Cash and cash equivalents	$726
Accounts receivable, net	1,400
Inventories	1,250
Other current assets	417
Total current assets	3,793
Property and equipment, net	3,881
Goodwill and other intangible assets, net	4,167
Other non-current assets	320
Total assets	$12,161

Liabilities and Shareholders' Equity	
Current liabilities:	
Accounts payable	$1,222
Accrued income taxes	411
Other accruals	1,696
Current portion of long-term debt	0
Notes and loans payable	12

Liabilities and Shareholders' Equity	
Total current liabilities	3,341
Long-term debt	6,354
Other non-current liabilities	2,269
Total liabilities	$11,964
Shareholders' equity:	
Preference stock	—
Common stock outstanding—863 million shares	1,466
Additional paid-in capital	2,204
Accumulated comprehensive income (loss)	(4,191)
Retained earnings	21,615
Treasury stock—common shares at cost	(21,196)
Noncontrolling interests	299
Total shareholders' equity	197
Total liabilities and shareholders' equity	$12,161

Source: Company financial report.

This financial statement is audited because US companies are required to have audits only for their annual financial statements. Quarterly statements are labeled as unaudited.

From CL's financial statements, the income statement and statement of cash flows for the year ended 31 December 2018 provided the following items (in millions):

Item	Source	Year Ended 31 December 2018
Net income	Income statement	$2,400
Interest expense (net of interest income)	Income statement	143
Income tax provision	Income statement	906
Depreciation and amortization	Statement of cash flows	511

The company's share price as of 15 February 2019 was $66.48. Based on the above information, calculate EV/EBITDA.

Solution:

- For EV, we first calculate the total value of CL's equity: 863 million shares outstanding times $66.48 price per share equals $57,372 million market capitalization.

  CL has only one class of common stock, no preferred shares, but has **minority interest**. For companies that have multiple classes of common stock, market capitalization includes the total value of all classes of common stock. Similarly, for companies that have preferred stock and/or minority interest, the market value of preferred stock and the amount of minority interest are added to market capitalization.

EV also includes the value of long-term debt obligations. Per CL's balance sheet, this is the sum of long-term debt ($6,354 million), the current portion of long-term debt ($0 million), and other non-current liabilities ($2,269 million), or $8,623 million. Typically, the book value of long-term debt is used in EV. If, however, the market value of the debt is readily available and materially different from the book value, the market value should be used.

EV excludes cash, cash equivalents, and short-term investments. Per CL's balance sheet, the total of cash and cash equivalents is $726 million.

So, CL's EV is $57,372 million + $8,623 million +$299 million − $720 million = $65,568 million.

- For EBITDA, we use the trailing 12-month (TTM) data, which are shown in the table above for the year ending 31 December 2018. The EBITDA calculation is

EBITDA = Net income + Interest + Income taxes + Depreciation and amortization.

EBITDA = $2,400 + $143 + $906 + $511 = $3,960 million.

CL does not have preferred equity. Companies that do have preferred equity typically present in their financial statement net income available to common shareholders. In those cases, the EBITDA calculation uses net income available to *both* preferred and common equity holders.

For CL, we conclude that EV/EBITDA = ($65,568 million)/($3,960 million) = 16.6.

Valuation Based on Forecasted Fundamentals

As with other multiples, intuition about the fundamental drivers of enterprise value to EBITDA can help when applying the method of comparables. All else being equal, the justified EV/EBITDA based on fundamentals should be positively related to the expected growth rate in free cash flow to the firm, positively related to expected profitability as measured by return on invested capital, and negatively related to the business's weighted average cost of capital. **Return on invested capital** (ROIC) is calculated as operating profit after tax divided by invested capital. In analyzing ratios such as EV/EBITDA, ROIC is the relevant measure of profitability because EBITDA flows to all providers of capital.

Valuation Based on Comparables

All else equal, a lower EV/EBITDA value relative to peers indicates that a company is relatively undervalued. An analyst's recommendations, however, are usually not completely determined by relative EV/EBITDA; from an analyst's perspective, EV/EBITDA is simply one piece of information to consider.

Example 35 presents a comparison of enterprise value multiples for four peer companies. The example includes a measure of total firm value—**total invested capital** (TIC), sometimes also known as the **market value of invested capital**—that is an alternative to enterprise value. Similar to EV, TIC includes the market value of equity and debt but does not deduct cash and investments.

EXAMPLE 35

Comparable Enterprise Value Multiples

Exhibit 19 presents EV multiples on 27 August 2019 for four companies in the household products industry: Colgate-Palmolive (CL), Kimberly Clark Corp. (KMB), Clorox Co. (CLX), and Church & Dwight Co. (CHD).

Exhibit 19: Enterprise Value Multiples for Industry Peers (Amounts in $ Millions, Except Where Indicated Otherwise)

Measure	CL	KMB	CLX	CHD
Price	$72.60	$140.25	$156.96	$79.15
Times: Shares outstanding (millions)	860	344	127	247
Equals: Equity market cap	62.44	48.25	19.93	19.55
Plus: Debt (most recent quarter)	7.33	8.46	2.69	2.38
Plus: Preferred stock	—	—	—	—
Equals: Market value of TIC	69.77	56.71	22.62	21.93
Less: Cash	0.93	0.53	0.11	0.10
Equals: Enterprise value (EV)	$68.84	$56.18	$22.51	$21.83
EBITDA (TTM)	$4.07	$3.81	$1.28	$0.97
TIC/EBITDA	17.1	14.9	17.7	22.6
EV/EBITDA	16.9	14.7	17.6	22.5
Profit margin (TTM)	14.8%	9.8%	13.2%	5.0%
Quarterly revenue growth (year over year)	–0.5%	–0.2%	–3.8%	13.8%

Sources: Yahoo! Finance; authors' calculations.

1. Exhibit 19 provides two alternative enterprise value multiples, TIC/EBITDA and EV/EBITDA. The ranking of the companies' multiples is identical by both multiples. In general, what could cause the rankings to vary?

Solution:

The difference between TIC and EV is that EV excludes cash, cash equivalents, and marketable securities. So, a material variation among companies in cash, cash equivalents, or marketable securities relative to EBITDA could cause the rankings to vary.

2. Each EBITDA multiple incorporates a comparison with enterprise value. How do these multiples differ from price-to-cash-flow multiples?

Solution:

These multiples differ from price-to-cash-flow multiples in that the numerator is a measure of firm value rather than share price, to match the denominator, which is a pre-interest measure of earnings. These multiples thus provide a more appropriate comparison than price to cash flow when companies have significantly different capital structures.

3. Based solely on the information in Exhibit 19, how does the valuation of CL compare with that of the other three companies?

Solution:

Based on its lower TIC/EBITDA and EV/EBITDA multiples of 17.1 and 16.9, respectively, CL appears undervalued relative to CLX and CHD and overvalued relative to KMB. These valuation ratios may be warranted given differences in profitability and growth rates. Compared with CHD, CL has a similar profit margin and lower revenue growth, which may explain CL's lower valuation multiples. Compared with KMB, the enterprise value multiples of CL are higher, which is consistent with CL being more profitable than KMB (profit margin of 14.8% versus 9.8%).

OTHER ENTERPRISE VALUE MULTIPLES 10

- ☐ explain alternative definitions of cash flow used in price and enterprise value (EV) multiples and describe limitations of each definition
- ☐ calculate and interpret EV multiples and evaluate the use of EV/EBITDA
- ☐ evaluate whether a stock is overvalued, fairly valued, or undervalued based on comparisons of multiples

Although EV/EBITDA is the most widely known and used enterprise value multiple, other enterprise value multiples are used together with or in place of EV/EBITDA—either in a broad range of applications or for valuations in a specific industry. EV/FCFF is an example of a broadly used multiple; an example of a special-purpose multiple is EV/EBITDAR (where R stands for rent expense), which is favored by airline industry analysts. Here we review the most common such multiples (except EV/sales, which is covered in the next section). In each case, a valuation metric could be formulated in terms of TIC rather than EV.

Major alternatives to using EBITDA in the denominator of enterprise value multiples include FCFF (free cash flow to the firm), EBITA (earnings before interest, taxes, and amortization), and EBIT (earnings before interest and taxes). Exhibit 20 summarizes the components of each of these measurements and how they relate to net income. Note that, in practice, analysts typically forecast EBITDA by forecasting EBIT and adding depreciation and amortization.

Exhibit 20: Alternative Denominators in Enterprise Value Multiples

Free Cash Flow to the Firm =	Net Income	plus Interest Expense	minus Tax Savings on Interest	plus Depreciation	plus Amortization	less Investment in Working Capital	less Investment in Fixed Capital
EBITDA =	Net Income	plus Interest Expense	plus Taxes	plus Depreciation	plus Amortization		

EBITA =	Net Income	plus Interest Expense	plus Taxes	plus Amortization
EBIT =	Net Income	plus Interest Expense	plus Taxes	

Note that the calculation of all the measures given in Exhibit 20 add interest back to net income, which reflects that these measures are flows relevant to all providers of both debt and equity capital. As one moves down the rows of Exhibit 20, the measures incorporate increasingly less precise information about a company's tax position and its capital investments, although each measure has a rationale. For example, EBITA may be chosen in cases in which amortization (associated with intangibles) but not depreciation (associated with tangibles) is a major expense for companies being compared. EBIT may be chosen where neither depreciation nor amortization is a major item.

In addition to enterprise value multiples based on financial measures, in some industries or sectors, the analyst may find it appropriate to examine enterprise value multiples based on a nonfinancial measurement that is specific to that industry or sector. For example, for satellite and cable TV broadcasters, an analyst might usefully examine EV to subscribers. For a resource-based company, a multiple based on reserves of the resource may be appropriate.

Regardless of the specific denominator used in an enterprise value multiple, the concept remains the same—namely, to relate the market value of the total company to some fundamental financial or nonfinancial measure of the company's value.

Enterprise Value to Sales

Enterprise value to sales is a major alternative to the price-to-sales ratio. The P/S multiple has the conceptual weakness that it fails to recognize that for a debt-financed company, not all sales belong to a company's equity investors. Some of the proceeds from the company's sales will be used to pay interest and principal to the providers of the company's debt capital. For example, a P/S for a company with little or no debt would not be comparable to a P/S for a company that is largely financed with debt. EV/S would be the basis for a valid comparison in such a case. In summary, EV/S is an alternative sales-based ratio that is particularly useful when comparing companies with diverse capital structures. Example 36 illustrates the calculation of EV/S multiples.

EXAMPLE 36

Calculating Enterprise Value to Sales

1. As described in Example 22, Stora Enso Oyj (Helsinki Stock Exchange: STERV) reported net sales of €10,486 million for 2018. Based on 788.6 million shares outstanding and a stock price of €10.34 on 28 June 2019, the total market value of the company's equity was €8,154 million. The company reported non-current debt of €2,970 million and cash of €1,130 million. Assume that the market value of the company's debt is equal to the amount reported. Calculate the company's EV/S.

Solution:

Enterprise value = €8,145 million + €2,970 million – €1,130 million = €9,994 million. So, EV/S = €9,994 million/€10,486 million = 0.953.

Price and Enterprise Value Multiples in a Comparable Analysis: Some Illustrative Data

In previous sections, we explained the major price and enterprise value multiples. Analysts using multiples and a benchmark based on closely similar companies should be aware of the range of values for multiples for peer companies and should track the fundamentals that may explain differences. For the sake of illustration, Exhibit 21 shows the median value of various multiples by GICS economic sector, the median dividend payout ratio, and median values of selected fundamentals:

- ROE and its determinants (net profit margin, asset turnover, and financial leverage)
- The compound average growth rate in operating margin for the three years ending with FY2007 (shown in the last column under "3-Year CAGR Operating Margin")

Exhibit 21 is based on the S&P 1500 Composite Index for US equities, consisting of the S&P 500, the S&P MidCap 400 Index, and the S&P SmallCap 600 Index. GICS was described earlier.

At the level of aggregation shown in Exhibit 21, the data are, arguably, most relevant to relative sector valuation. For the purposes of valuing individual companies, analysts would most likely use more narrowly defined industry or sector classification.

INTERNATIONAL CONSIDERATIONS WHEN USING MULTIPLES 11

☐ explain sources of differences in cross-border valuation comparisons

Clearly, to perform a relative-value analysis, an analyst must use comparable companies and underlying financial data prepared by applying comparable methods. Therefore, using relative-valuation methods in an international setting is difficult. Comparing companies across borders frequently involves differences in accounting methods, cultural differences, economic differences, and resulting differences in risk and growth opportunities. P/Es for individual companies in the same industry but in different countries have been found to vary widely. Furthermore, P/Es of different national markets often vary substantially at any single point in time.

Although international accounting standards are converging, significant differences still exist across borders, sometimes making comparisons difficult. Even when harmonization of accounting principles is achieved, the need to adjust accounting data for comparability will remain. As we showed earlier, even within a single country's accounting standards, differences between companies result from accounting choices (e.g., FIFO versus average cost for inventory valuation). Prior to 2008, the US SEC required non-US companies whose securities trade in US markets to provide a reconciliation between their earnings from home-country accounting principles to US GAAP. This requirement not only assisted the analyst in making necessary adjustments but also provided some insight into appropriate adjustments for other companies not required to provide this data. In December 2007, however, the SEC eliminated the reconciliation requirement for non-US companies that use IFRS. Research analyzing reconciliations by EU companies with US listings shows that most of those companies reported net income under IFRS that was higher than they would have reported under

Exhibit 21: Fundamental and Valuation Statistics by GICS Economic Sector: Median Values from S&P 1500, FY2007

	Valuation Statistics							Fundamental Statistics					
GICS Sector (count)	Trailing P/E	P/B	P/S	P/CF	Dividend Yield (%)	EV/ EBITDA	EV/S	Net Profit Margin (%)	Asset Turnover	Financial Leverage	ROE (%)	Dividend Payout Ratio (%)	3-Year CAGR Operating Margin (%)
Energy (85)	14.406	2.531	2.186	8.622	0.4	7.733	2.64	13.942	0.573	2.103	19.688	4.024	12.035
Materials (85)	15.343	2.254	0.888	9.588	1.4	7.686	1.095	5.568	0.995	2.465	15.728	17.874	4.157
Industrials (207)	17.275	2.578	1.045	11.642	1.0	8.979	1.209	6.089	1.139	2.143	15.262	16.066	5.337
Consumer Discretionary (279)	15.417	2.254	0.789	9.986	0.7	7.634	0.928	4.777	1.383	2.12	13.289	0	−2.682
Consumer Staples (80)	19.522	3.048	1.122	13.379	1.4	10.66	1.237	5.306	1.351	2.208	17.264	23.133	−0.88
Health Care (167)	23.027	3.088	2.061	15.762	0	11.623	2.274	6.637	0.83	1.854	12.399	0	−1.708
Financials (257)	14.648	1.559	1.888	11.186	3.1	9.482	4.017	13.113	0.113	5.848	10.348	41.691	−4.124
Information Technology (252)	20.205	2.444	2.162	45.073	0	11.594	1.811	7.929	0.743	1.587	10.444	0	1.524
Telecommunication Services (13)	19.585	2.485	1.527	5.266	0.8	6.681	2.345	7.109	0.471	2.367	5.43	6.862	−2.421
Utilities (75)	16.682	1.784	1.151	8.405	3.1	9.056	1.903	7.21	0.439	3.52	11.853	52.738	0.361
Overall (1,500)	17.148	2.246	1.398	11.328	0.8	9.108	1.626	7.318	0.839	2.227	12.701	8.051	0.181

Source: Standard & Poor's Research Insight.

US GAAP and lower shareholders' equity than they would have under US GAAP, with a result that more of the sample companies reported higher ROE under IFRS than under US GAAP.

In a study of companies filing such reconciliations to US GAAP, Harris and Muller (1999) classified common differences into seven categories, as shown in Exhibit 22.

Exhibit 22: Reconciliation of IFRS to US GAAP: Average Adjustment

Category	Earnings	Equity
Differences in the treatment of goodwill	Minus	Plus
Deferred income taxes	Plus	Plus
Foreign exchange adjustments	Plus	Minus
Research and development costs	Minus	Minus
Pension expense	Minus	Plus
Tangible asset revaluations	Plus	Minus
Other	Minus	Minus

In a more recent study of reconciliation data, Henry, Lin, and Yang (2009) found that among 20 categories of reconciliations, the most frequently occurring adjustments are in the pension category (including post-retirement benefits) and the largest value of adjustments are in the goodwill category.

Although the SEC's decision to eliminate the requirement for reconciliation has eliminated an important resource for analysts, accounting research can provide some insight into areas where differences between IFRS and US GAAP have commonly arisen. Going forward, analysts must be aware of differences between standards and make adjustments when disclosures provide sufficient data to do so.

International accounting differences affect the comparability of all price multiples. Of the price multiples we examined, P/CFO and P/FCFE will generally be least affected by accounting differences. P/B, P/E, and multiples based on such concepts as EBITDA, which start from accounting earnings, will generally be the most affected.

MOMENTUM VALUATION INDICATORS 12

☐ describe momentum indicators and their use in valuation

The valuation indicators we call momentum indicators relate either price or a fundamental, such as earnings, to the time series of their own past values or, in some cases, to the fundamental's expected value. One style of growth investing uses positive momentum in various senses as a selection criterion, and practitioners sometimes refer to such strategies as "growth/momentum investment strategies." Momentum indicators based on price, such as the relative-strength indicator we will discuss here, have also been referred to as **technical indicators**. According to the BofA Merrill Lynch Institutional Factor Survey, various momentum indicators were used by many institutional investors. In this section, we review three representative momentum indicators: earnings surprise, standardized unexpected earnings, and relative strength.

To define standardized unexpected earnings, we define **unexpected earnings** (also called **earnings surprise**) as the difference between reported earnings and expected earnings:

$UE_t = \text{EPS}_t - E(\text{EPS}_t)$,

where UE_t is the unexpected earnings for quarter t, EPS_t is the reported EPS for quarter t, and $E(\text{EPS}_t)$ is the expected EPS for the quarter.

For example, a stock with reported quarterly earnings of $1.05 and expected earnings of $1.00 would have a positive earnings surprise of $0.05. Often, the percentage earnings surprise (i.e., earnings surprise divided by expected EPS) is reported by data providers; in this example, the percentage earning surprise would be $0.05/$1.00 = 0.05, or 5%. When used directly as a valuation indicator, earnings surprise is generally scaled by a measure reflecting the variability or range in analysts' EPS estimates. The principle is that the less disagreement among analysts' forecasts, the more meaningful the EPS forecast error of a given size in relation to the mean. A way to accomplish such scaling is to divide unexpected earnings by the standard deviation of analysts' earnings forecasts, which we refer to as the **scaled earnings surprise**. Example 37 illustrates the calculation of such a scaled earnings surprise.

EXAMPLE 37

Calculating Scaled Earnings Surprise by Using Analysts' Forecasts

1. During the third quarter of 2019, the mean consensus earnings forecast for BP plc for the fiscal year ending December 2019 was $3.26. Of the 11 estimates, the low forecast was $2.76, the high forecast was $3.74, and the standard deviation was $0.29. If actual reported earnings for 2019 come in equal to the high forecast, what would be the measure of the earnings surprise for BP scaled to reflect the dispersion in analysts' forecasts?

Solution:

In this case, scaled earnings surprise would be ($3.74 – $3.26)/$0.29 = $0.48/$0.29 = 1.66.

The rationale behind using earnings surprise is the thesis that positive surprises may be associated with persistent positive abnormal returns, or alpha. The same rationale lies behind a momentum indicator that is closely related to earnings surprise but more highly researched—namely, **standardized unexpected earnings** (SUE). The SUE measure is defined as

$$\text{SUE}_t = \frac{\text{EPS}_t - E(\text{EPS}_t)}{\sigma[\text{EPS}_t - E(\text{EPS}_t)]},$$

where

EPS_t = Actual EPS for time t

$E(\text{EPS}_t)$ = Expected EPS for time t

$\sigma[\text{EPS}_t - E(\text{EPS}_t)]$ = Standard deviation of $[\text{EPS}_t - E(\text{EPS}_t)]$ over some historical time period

In words, the numerator is the unexpected earnings at time t and the denominator is the standard deviation of past unexpected earnings over some period prior to time t—for example, the 20 quarters prior to t, as in Latané and Jones (1979), the article that introduced the SUE concept (for a summary of the research on SUE, see Brown 1997). In SUE, the magnitude of unexpected earnings is scaled by a measure of the size of historical forecast errors or surprises. The principle is that the smaller (larger) the historical size of forecast errors, the more (less) meaningful a given size of EPS forecast error.

Suppose that for a stock with a $0.05 earnings surprise, the standard deviation of past surprises is $0.20. The $0.05 surprise is relatively small compared with past forecast errors, which would be reflected in a SUE score of $0.05/$0.20 = 0.25. If the standard error of past surprises were smaller—say, $0.07—the SUE score would be $0.05/$0.07 = 0.71. Example 38 applies analysis of SUE to two companies.

EXAMPLE 38

Unexpected Earnings (Historical Example)

Exhibit 23 and Exhibit 24 provide information about the earnings surprise history for two companies: Exxon Mobil Corporation and Volkswagen AG (VW).

Exhibit 23: Earnings Surprise History for Exxon Mobil Corporation (in US$)

Quarter Ending	EPS Release Date	Mean Consensus EPS Forecast	Actual EPS	% Surprise	Std. Dev.	SUE Score
Sep 2013	31 Oct 2013	1.77	1.79	0.88	0.1250	0.16
Jun 2013	1 Aug 2013	1.90	1.55	−18.39	0.0997	−3.51
Mar 2013	25 Apr 2013	2.05	2.12	3.59	0.0745	0.94
Dec 2012	1 Feb 2013	2.00	2.20	10.20	0.0463	4.32

Exhibit 24: Earnings Surprise History for Volkswagen AG (in Euros)

Quarter Ending	EPS Release Date	Mean Consensus EPS Forecast	Actual EPS	% Surprise	Std. Dev.	SUE Score
Sep 2013	30 Oct 2013	4.53	3.79	−16.37	0.2846	−2.60
Jun 2013	30 Jul 2013	5.10	5.86	14.99	0.3858	1.97
Mar 2013	24 Apr 2013	4.15	4.24	2.17	1.1250	0.08
Dec 2012	22 Feb 2013	5.56	3.54	−36.33	0.5658	−3.57

Source: Thomson Surprise Report.

1. Explain how Exxon's SUE score of 0.16 for the quarter ending September 2013 is calculated.

Solution:

The amount of Exxon's unexpected earnings (i.e., its earnings surprise) for the quarter ending September 2013 was $1.79 – $1.77 = $0.02. Dividing by the standard deviation of $0.1250 gives a SUE score of 0.16.

2. Based on these exhibits, for which company were the consensus forecasts less accurate over the past four quarters?

Solution:

The answer depends on whether accuracy is measured by the percentage surprise or by the SUE score. If accuracy is measured by the percentage surprise, then VW's consensus forecasts were less accurate: Percentage surprise varied from −36.33% to +14.99% for VW versus −18.39% to +10.20% for Exxon. Using SUE, Exxon's consensus forecasts were less accurate: SUE varied from −3.51 to +4.32 for Exxon versus −3.57 to +1.13 for VW. The reason for these differing results is that the standard deviation of the earnings estimates is relatively smaller for Exxon than it is for VW.

3. Was the consensus forecast more accurate for Exxon or VW for the quarter ending March 2013?

Solution:

For the quarter ending March 2013, the consensus forecast was more accurate for VW than Exxon. Both the percentage surprise and SUE were lower for VW in this quarter.

Another set of indicators, **relative-strength indicators**, compares a stock's performance during a particular period either with its own past performance or with the performance of some group of stocks. The simplest relative-strength indicator that compares a stock's performance during a period with its past performance is the stock's compound rate of return over some specified time horizon, such as six months or one year. This indicator has also been referred to as **price momentum** in the academic literature. Despite its simplicity, this measure has been used in numerous studies. The rationale behind its use is the thesis that patterns of persistence or reversal exist in stock returns that may be shown empirically to depend on the investor's time horizon (Lee and Swaminathan 2000).

Other definitions of relative strength relate a stock's return over a recent period to its return over a longer period that includes the more recent period. For example, a classic study of technical momentum indicators (Brock, Lakonishok, and LeBaron 1992) examined trading strategies based on two technical rules—namely, a moving-average oscillator and a trading-range break (i.e., resistance and support levels)—in which buy and sell signals are determined by the relationship between a short period's moving average and a longer period's moving average (and bands around those averages). The reader should keep in mind that research on patterns of historical stock returns is notoriously vulnerable to data snooping and hindsight biases. Furthermore, investing strategies based purely on technical momentum indicators are viewed as inherently self-destructing, in that "once a useful technical rule (or price pattern) is discovered, it ought to be invalidated when the mass of traders attempts to exploit it" (Bodie, Kane, and Marcus 2008, p. 377). Yet, the possibility of discovering a profitable trading rule and exploiting it prior to mass use continues to motivate research.

A simple relative-strength indicator of the second type (i.e., the stock's performance relative to the performance of some group of stocks) is the stock's performance divided by the performance of an equity index. If the value of this ratio increases, the stock price increases relative to the index and displays positive relative strength. Often, the relative-strength indicator is scaled to 1.0 at the beginning of the study period. If the stock goes up at a higher (lower) rate than the index, then relative strength will be above (below) 1.0. Relative strength in this sense is often calculated for industries and individual stocks. Example 39 explores this indicator.

EXAMPLE 39

Relative Strength in Relation to an Equity Index

Exhibit 25 shows the values of the S&P 500 and three exchange-traded funds (ETFs) for the end of each of 18 months from March 2018 through August 2019. The ETFs are for long-term US Treasury securities, for the STOXX Europe 50 Index, and for emerging markets. SPDRs and iShares are families of exchange-traded funds managed by State Street Global Advisors and by Blackrock, Inc.

Exhibit 25: A Relative-Strength Comparison

First Day of	S&P 500 Index	iShares 20+ Year Treasury Bond ETF (TLT)	SPDR STOXX Europe 50 ETF (FEU)	iShares Emerging Markets ETF (EEM)
Mar-18	2,640.87	121.90	34.64	48.28
Apr-18	2,648.05	119.10	35.36	46.92
May-18	2,705.27	121.22	34.29	45.69
Jun-18	2,718.37	121.72	33.43	43.33
Jul-18	2,816.29	119.70	34.94	44.86
Aug-18	2,901.52	121.00	33.53	43.17
Sep-18	2,913.98	117.27	33.60	42.92
Oct-18	2,711.74	113.58	31.51	39.16
Nov-18	2,760.17	115.33	31.61	41.08
Dec-18	2,506.85	121.51	29.89	39.06
Jan-19	2,704.10	121.97	31.38	43.10
Feb-19	2,784.49	120.02	32.61	42.44
Mar-19	2,834.40	126.44	33.09	42.92
Apr-19	2,945.83	123.65	34.14	43.93
May-19	2,752.06	131.83	32.71	40.71
Jun-19	2,941.76	132.81	34.17	42.91
Jul-19	2,980.38	132.89	33.22	41.77
Aug-19	2,923.65	144.04	32.47	39.70

To produce the information for Exhibit 26, we divided each ETF value by the S&P 500 value for the same month and then scaled those results so that the value of the relative-strength indicator (RSTR) for March 2018 would equal 1.0. To illustrate, on 1 March 2018, the value of TLT divided by the S&P 500 was 121.90/2,640.87 = 0.04616. The RSTR for TLT on that date, by design, is then 0.04616/0.04616 = 1.0. In April, the value of TLT divided by the S&P 500 was 119.10/2,648.05 = 0.04498, which we scaled by the April number. The RSTR for 1 April 2018 for TLT is 0.04498/0.04616 = 0.9744, shown in Exhibit 26 as 0.974.

Exhibit 26: Relative-Strength Indicators

First Day of	RSTR iShares 20+ Year Treasury Bond ETF (TLT)	RSTR SPDR STOXX Europe 50 ETF (FEU)	RSTR iShares Emerging Markets ETF (EEM)
Mar-18	1.000	1.000	1.000
Apr-18	0.974	1.018	0.969

First Day of	RSTR iShares 20+ Year Treasury Bond ETF (TLT)	RSTR SPDR STOXX Europe 50 ETF (FEU)	RSTR iShares Emerging Markets ETF (EEM)
May-18	0.971	0.966	0.924
Jun-18	0.970	0.938	0.872
Jul-18	0.921	0.946	0.871
Aug-18	0.903	0.881	0.814
Sep-18	0.872	0.879	0.806
Oct-18	0.907	0.886	0.790
Nov-18	0.905	0.873	0.814
Dec-18	1.050	0.909	0.852
Jan-19	0.977	0.885	0.872
Feb-19	0.934	0.893	0.834
Mar-19	0.966	0.890	0.828
Apr-19	0.909	0.884	0.816
May-19	1.038	0.906	0.809
Jun-19	0.978	0.886	0.798
Jul-19	0.966	0.850	0.767
Aug-19	1.067	0.847	0.743

On the basis of Exhibit 25 and Exhibit 26, address the following:

1. State the relative strength of long-term US Treasury securities, the STOXX Europe 50 Index, and emerging market stocks over the entire time period March 2018 through August 2019. Interpret the relative strength for each sector over that period.

Solution:

The relative-strength indicator for long-term US Treasuries is 1.067. This number represents 1.067 – 1.000 = 0.067, or 6.7% overperformance relative to the S&P 500 over the time period. The relative-strength indicator for the STOXX Europe 50 Index is 0.847. This number represents 0.847 – 1.000 = –0.153, or 15.3% underperformance relative to the S&P 500 over the time period. The relative-strength indicator for the emerging market ETF is 0.743, indicating that it underperformed the S&P 500 by 25.7% over the time frame.

2. Discuss the relative performance of the STOXX Europe 50 Index ETF and the emerging market ETF in the month of December 2018.

Solution:

The December 2018 performance is found by comparing the RSTR at 1 December 2018 and 1 January 2019. The December 2019 RSTR for the STOXX Europe 50 Index ends at 0.885, which is 2.7% lower than its value for the prior month (0.909). The emerging market RSTR, at 0.872, is higher than the prior month value of 0.852 by 2.3%. In December 2018, the emerging market ETF outperformed the STOXX Europe 50 Index ETF. The relative performance for that one month differs from the relative performance over the entire period, during which the STOXX Europe 50 Index significantly outperformed the emerging market ETF.

Overall, momentum indicators have a substantial following among professional investors. Some view momentum indicators as signals that should prompt an analyst to consider whether a stock price is moving successively *farther from* or successively *closer to* the fundamental valuations derived from models and multiples. In other words, an analyst might be correct about the intrinsic value of a firm, and the momentum indicators might provide a clue about when the market price will converge with that intrinsic value. The use of such indicators continues to be a subject of active research in industry and in business schools.

13 VALUATION INDICATORS: ISSUES IN PRACTICE

☐ explain the use of the arithmetic mean, the harmonic mean, the weighted harmonic mean, and the median to describe the central tendency of a group of multiples

All the valuation indicators discussed are quantitative aids but not necessarily solutions to the problem of security selection. In this section, we discuss some issues that arise in practice when averages are used to establish benchmark multiples and then illustrate the use of multiple valuation indicators.

Averaging Multiples: The Harmonic Mean

The harmonic mean and the weighted harmonic mean are often applied to average a group of price multiples.

Consider a hypothetical portfolio that contains two stocks. For simplicity, assume the portfolio owns 100% of the shares of each stock. One stock has a market capitalization of €715 million and earnings of €71.5 million, giving it a P/E of 10. The other stock has a market capitalization of €585 million and earnings of €29.25 million, for a P/E of 20. Note that the P/E for the portfolio is calculated directly by aggregating the companies' market capitalizations and earnings: (€715 + €585)/(€71.50 + €29.25) = €1,300/€100.75 = 12.90. The question that will be addressed is, What calculation of portfolio P/E, based on the individual stock P/Es, best reflects the value of 12.90?

If the ratio of an individual holding is represented by X_i, the expression for the simple **harmonic mean** of the ratio is

$$X_H = \frac{n}{\sum_{i=1}^{n}(1/X_i)}, \tag{9}$$

which is the reciprocal of the arithmetic mean of the reciprocals.

The expression for the **weighted harmonic mean** is

$$X_{WH} = \frac{1}{\sum_{i=1}^{n}(w_i/X_i)}, \tag{10}$$

where the w_i are portfolio value weights (summing to 1) and $X_i > 0$ for $i = 1, 2, \ldots, n$.

Exhibit 27 displays the calculation of the hypothetical portfolio's simple arithmetic mean P/E, weighted mean P/E, (simple) harmonic mean P/E, and weighted harmonic mean P/E.

Exhibit 27: Alternative Mean P/Es

	Market Cap							
Security	**(€ Millions)**	**Percent**	**Earnings (€ Millions)**	**Stock P/E**	**(1)**	**(2)**	**(3)**	**(4)**
Stock 1	715	55	71.50	10	0.5 × 10	0.55 × 10	0.5 × 0.1	0.55 × 0.1
Stock 2	585	45	29.25	20	0.5 × 20	0.45 × 20	0.5 × 0.05	0.45 × 0.05
					15	14.5	0.075	0.0775
Arithmetic mean P/E (1)					**15**			
Weighted mean P/E (2)						**14.5**		
Harmonic mean P/E (3)							1/0.075 = **13.33**	
Weighted harmonic mean P/E (4)								1/0.0775 = **12.90**

The weighted harmonic mean P/E precisely corresponds to the portfolio P/E value of 12.90. This example explains why index fund vendors frequently use the weighted harmonic mean to calculate the "average" P/E or average value of other price multiples for indexes. In some applications, an analyst might not want or be able to incorporate the market value weight information needed to calculate the weighted harmonic mean. In such cases, the simple harmonic mean can still be calculated.

Note that the simple harmonic mean P/E is smaller than the arithmetic mean and closer to the directly calculated value of 12.90 in this example. The harmonic mean inherently gives less weight to higher P/Es and more weight to lower P/Es. In general, unless all the observations in a data set have the same value, the harmonic mean is less than the arithmetic mean.

As explained and illustrated earlier, using the median rather than the arithmetic mean to derive an average multiple mitigates the effect of outliers. The harmonic mean is sometimes also used to reduce the impact of large outliers—which are typically the major concern in using the arithmetic mean multiple—but not the impact of small outliers (i.e., those close to zero). The harmonic mean tends to mitigate the impact of large outliers. The harmonic mean may aggravate the impact of small outliers, but such outliers are bounded by zero on the downside.

We can use the group of telecommunications companies examined earlier (see Exhibit 5) to illustrate differences between the arithmetic mean and the harmonic mean. This group includes two large outliers for P/E: CenturyLink, with a P/E that is not meaningful, and Charter Communications, with a P/E of 70.67. Exhibit 28 shows mean values excluding CenturyLink and excluding both CenturyLink and Charter Communications (two outliers).

Exhibit 28: Arithmetic versus Harmonic Mean

Company	Trailing P/E (without CenturyLink)	Trailing P/E (No Outliers)
AT&T	13.20	13.20
Comcast Corporation	16.23	16.23
CenturyLink	NMF	
China Telecom	13.14	13.14
Charter Communications Corp.	70.67	

Company	Trailing P/E (without CenturyLink)	Trailing P/E (No Outliers)
Verizon Communications	15.03	15.03
Windstream Holdings	24.55	24.55
Arithmetic mean	25.30	16.43
Median	15.23	15.03
Harmonic mean	17.70	15.39

Note that for the entire group, the arithmetic mean (25.30) is far higher than the median (15.23) because of the high P/E of Charter Communications (CenturyLink was not included). The harmonic mean (17.70) is much closer to the median and more plausible as representing central tendency. Once the outliers are eliminated, the values for the arithmetic mean (16.43), median (15.03), and harmonic mean (15.39) are more tightly grouped. The lower value for the harmonic mean reflects the fact that this approach mitigates the effect of the relatively high P/E for Charter Communications.

This example illustrates the importance for the analyst of understanding how an average has been calculated, particularly when the analyst is reviewing information prepared by another analyst, and the usefulness of examining several summary statistics.

Using Multiple Valuation Indicators

Because each carefully selected and calculated price multiple, momentum indicator, or fundamental may supply some piece of the puzzle of stock valuation, many investors and analysts use more than one valuation indicator (in addition to other criteria) in stock valuation and selection. Example 40 illustrates the use of multiple indicators.

EXAMPLE 40

Multiple Indicators in Stock Valuation

Analysts may use more valuation indicators than they describe in their company reports. The two following excerpts, adapted from past equity analyst reports, illustrate the use of multiple ratios in communicating views about a stock's value. In the first excerpt, from a report on Aussie Beverage Ltd. (ABEV), the analyst has used a discounted cash flow valuation as the preferred methodology but notes that the stock is also attractive when a price-to-earnings ratio (PER in the report) is used. In the second excerpt, from a report on Südliche Logistik (SLOG), an analyst evaluates the stock price (then trading at 42.80) by using two multiples, price to earnings (P/E) and EV/EBITDA, in relation to revised forecasts.

Aussie Beverage

Our DCF for ABEV is A$0.82ps, which represents a 44% prem. to the current price. Whilst the DCF valuation is our preferred methodology, we recognise that ABEV also looks attractive on different metrics.

Applying a mid-cycle PER multiple of 10.5 × (30% disc to mkt) to FY08 EPS of 7.6cps, we derive a valuation of A$0.80. Importantly, were the stock to reach our target of A$0.75ps in 12mths, ABEV would be trading on a fwd PER of 9.1×, which we do not view as demanding. At current levels, the stock is also offering an attractive dividend yield of 5.7% (fully franked). [*Note*: "Fully franked" is a concept specific to the Australian market and refers to tax treatment of the dividend.]

Südliche Logistik

Based on our slightly increased estimates, the shares are valued at a P/E and EV/EBITDA 2012 of 12.4x and 9x, slightly below the valuation of peer companies. Given its stronger profit growth, SLOG could command a premium. We raise our target price from EUR52 to EUR53, implying a 24% upside. Buy.

In selecting stocks, institutional investors surveyed in the BofA Merrill Lynch Institutional Factor Surveys from 1989 to 2012 used an average of 9.3 factors in selecting stocks (does not include 2008–2010 due to a lack of sufficient responses). The survey factors included not only price multiples, momentum indicators, and the DDM but also the fundamentals ROE, debt to equity, projected five-year EPS growth, EPS variability, EPS estimate dispersion, size, beta, foreign exposure, low price, and neglect. Exhibit 29 lists the factors classified by percentage of investors indicating that they use that factor in making investment decisions, out of 137 responders in 2012.

Exhibit 29: Frequency of Investor Usage of Factors in Making Investment Decisions

High (•) >50%; Med (♦) >30% <50%; Low (○) <30%

Factor	Frequency
P/E	•
Beta	•
EV/EBITDA	•
ROE	•
Size	•
P/B	•
P/FCF	♦
Share Repurchase	♦
Earnings Estimate Revision	♦
Margins	♦
Relative Strength	♦
EPS Momentum	♦
D/E	♦
EPS Variability	♦
DDM/DCF	♦
PEG Ratio	♦
Long-Term Price Trend	♦
P/CF	♦
Analyst Neglect	♦
Dividend Growth	♦
Projected 5-Year EPS Growth	♦
Mean Reversion	♦
Normalized P/E	♦
P/S	♦
Net Debt/EBITDA	○
EPS Surprise	○
ROC	○

High (•) >50%; Med (♦) >30% <50%; Low (○) <30%	
Factor	**Frequency**
ROA	○
EPS Estimate Dispersion	○
Analyst Rating Revisions	○
Foreign Exposure	○
Long-Term Price Trend w/ Short-Term Reversal	○
Trading Volume	○
Price Target	○
Ownership	○
Short-Term Price Trend	○
EV/Sales	○
Low Price	○
Altman Z-Score	○
Equity Duration	○

Source: 2012 BofA Merrill Lynch Institutional Factor Survey.

An issue concerning the use of ratios in an investing strategy is look-ahead bias. **Look-ahead bias** is the use of information that was not contemporaneously available in computing a quantity. Investment analysts often use historical data to back test an investment strategy that involves stock selection based on price multiples or other factors. When back testing, an analyst should be aware that time lags in the reporting of financial results create the potential for look-ahead bias in such research. For example, as of early January 2019, most companies had not reported EPS for the last quarter of 2018, so at that time, a company's trailing P/E would be based on EPS for the first, second, and third quarters of 2018 and the last quarter of 2017. Any investment strategy based on a trailing P/E that used actual EPS for the last quarter of 2018 could be implemented only after the data became available. Thus, if an analysis assumed that an investment was made in early January 2019 based on full-year 2018 data, the analysis would involve look-ahead bias. To avoid this bias, an analyst would calculate the trailing P/E based on the most recent four quarters of EPS then being reported. The same principle applies to other multiples calculated on a trailing basis.

The application of a set of criteria to reduce an investment universe to a smaller set of investments is called **screening**. Stock screens often include not only criteria based on the valuation measures that featured in our discussion but also on fundamental criteria that may explain differences in such measures. Computerized stock screening is an efficient way to narrow a search for investments and is a part of many stock selection disciplines. The limitations to many commercial databases and screening tools usually include lack of control by the user of the calculation of important inputs (such as EPS); the absence of qualitative factors in most databases is another important limitation. Example 41 illustrates the use of a screen in stock selection.

EXAMPLE 41

Using Screens to Find Stocks for a Portfolio

Janet Larsen manages an institutional portfolio and is currently looking for new stocks to add to the portfolio. Larsen has a commercial database with information on US stocks. She has designed several screens to select stocks with low P/Es and low P/B multiples. Because Larsen is aware that screening for low

P/E and low P/B multiples may identify stocks with low expected growth, she also wants stocks that have a PEG ratio less than 1.0. She decides to screen for stocks with a dividend yield of at least 3.0% and a total market capitalization over $10 billion. Exhibit 30 shows the number of stocks that successively met each of the five criteria as of 17 July 2019 (so, the number of stocks that met all five criteria is 10).

Exhibit 30: Stock Screen

Criterion	Stocks Meeting Each Criterion Successively
P/E < 20.0	2,096
P/B < 2.0	1,384
PEG ratio < 1.0	89
Dividend yield ≥ 3.0%	23
Market capitalization over $10 billion	10

Other information:

- The screening database indicates that the trailing P/E was 22.3, P/B was 3.5, and the dividend yield was 1.9% for the S&P 500 as of the date of the screen.
- The "S&P U.S. Style Indices Methodology" (June 2019) indicates that the style indexes measure growth and value by the following six factors, which S&P standardizes and uses to compute growth and value scores for each company:

  Three Growth Factors

  Three-year change in EPS over price per share

  Three-year sales per-share growth rate

  Momentum (12-month percentage price change)

  Three Value Factors

  Book value-to-price ratio

  Earnings-to-price ratio

  Sales-to-price ratio

- In February of 2019, the S&P Dow Jones US Index Committee raised the market cap guidelines used when selecting companies for the S&P 500, S&P MidCap 400 and S&P SmallCap 600. The new guidelines are as follows:

  S&P 500: Over $8.2 billion

  S&P MidCap 400: $2.4 billion to $8.2 billion

  S&P SmallCap 600: $600 million to $2.4 billion

Using the information supplied, answer the following questions:

1. What type of valuation indicators does Larsen *not* include in her stock screen?

Solution:

Larsen has not included momentum indicators in the screen.

2. Characterize the overall orientation of Larsen as to investment style.

Solution:

Larsen can be characterized as a large-cap value investor, based on the specified market capitalization. Although her screen does include a PEG ratio, it excludes explicit growth rate criteria, such as those used by S&P, and it excludes momentum indicators usually associated with a growth orientation, such as positive earnings surprise. Larsen also uses a cutoff for P/B that is less than the average P/B for the S&P 500. Note that her criteria for multiples are all "less than" criteria.

3. State two limitations of Larsen's stock screen.

Solution:

Larsen does not include any profitability criteria or risk measurements. These omissions are a limitation because a stock's expected low profitability or high risk may explain its low P/E. Another limitation of her screen is that the computations of the value indicators in a commercial database may not reflect the appropriate adjustments to inputs. The absence of qualitative criteria is also a possible limitation.

Investors also apply all the metrics that we have illustrated in terms of individual stocks to industries and economic sectors. For example, average price multiples and momentum indicators can be used in sector rotation strategies to determine relatively under- or overvalued sectors. A sector rotation strategy is an investment strategy that overweights economic sectors that are anticipated to outperform or lead the overall market.

SUMMARY

We have defined and explained the most important valuation indicators in professional use and illustrated their application to a variety of valuation problems.

- Price multiples are ratios of a stock's price to some measure of value per share.
- Price multiples are most frequently applied to valuation in the method of comparables. This method involves using a price multiple to evaluate whether an asset is relatively undervalued, fairly valued, or overvalued in relation to a benchmark value of the multiple.
- The benchmark value of the multiple may be the multiple of a similar company or the median or average value of the multiple for a peer group of companies, an industry, an economic sector, an equity index, or the company's own median or average past values of the multiple.
- The economic rationale for the method of comparables is the law of one price.

- Price multiples may also be applied to valuation in the method based on forecasted fundamentals. Discounted cash flow (DCF) models provide the basis and rationale for this method. Fundamentals also interest analysts who use the method of comparables because differences between a price multiple and its benchmark value may be explained by differences in fundamentals.
- The key idea behind the use of price-to-earnings ratios (P/Es) is that earning power is a chief driver of investment value and earnings per share (EPS) is probably the primary focus of security analysts' attention. The EPS figure, however, is frequently subject to distortion, often volatile, and sometimes negative.
- The two alternative definitions of P/E are trailing P/E, based on the most recent four quarters of EPS, and forward P/E, based on next year's expected earnings.
- Analysts address the problem of cyclicality by normalizing EPS—that is, calculating the level of EPS that the business could achieve currently under mid-cyclical conditions (normalized EPS).
- Two methods to normalize EPS are the method of historical average EPS (calculated over the most recent full cycle) and the method of average return on equity (EPS = average ROE multiplied by current book value per share).
- Earnings yield (E/P) is the reciprocal of the P/E. When stocks have zero or negative EPS, a ranking by earnings yield is meaningful whereas a ranking by P/E is not.
- Historical trailing P/Es should be calculated with EPS lagged a sufficient amount of time to avoid look-ahead bias. The same principle applies to other multiples calculated on a trailing basis.
- The fundamental drivers of P/E are the expected earnings growth rate and the required rate of return. The justified P/E based on fundamentals bears a positive relationship to the first factor and an inverse relationship to the second factor.
- The PEG (P/E-to-growth) ratio is a tool to incorporate the impact of earnings growth on P/E. The PEG ratio is calculated as the ratio of the P/E to the consensus growth forecast. Stocks with low PEG ratios are, all else equal, more attractive than stocks with high PEG ratios.
- We can estimate terminal value in multistage DCF models by using price multiples based on comparables. The expression for terminal value, V_n, is (using P/E as the example)

$$V_n = \text{Benchmark value of trailing P/E} \times E_n$$

or

$$V_n = \text{Benchmark value of forward P/E} \times E_{n+1}.$$

- Book value per share is intended to represent, on a per-share basis, the investment that common shareholders have in the company. Inflation, technological change, and accounting distortions, however, may impair the use of book value for this purpose.
- Book value is calculated as common shareholders' equity divided by the number of shares outstanding. Analysts adjust book value to accurately reflect the value of the shareholders' investment and to make P/B (the price-to-book ratio) more useful for comparing different stocks.

- The fundamental drivers of P/B are ROE and the required rate of return. The justified P/B based on fundamentals bears a positive relationship to the first factor and an inverse relationship to the second factor.
- An important rationale for using the price-to-sales ratio (P/S) is that sales, as the top line in an income statement, are generally less subject to distortion or manipulation than other fundamentals, such as EPS or book value. Sales are also more stable than earnings and are never negative.
- P/S fails to take into account differences in cost structure between businesses, may not properly reflect the situation of companies losing money, and may be subject to manipulation through revenue recognition practices.
- The fundamental drivers of P/S are profit margin, growth rate, and the required rate of return. The justified P/S based on fundamentals bears a positive relationship to the first two factors and an inverse relationship to the third factor.
- Enterprise value (EV) is total company value (the market value of debt, common equity, and preferred equity) minus the value of cash and investments.
- The ratio of EV to total sales is conceptually preferable to P/S because EV/S facilitates comparisons among companies with varying capital structures.
- A key idea behind the use of price to cash flow is that cash flow is less subject to manipulation than are earnings. Price-to-cash-flow multiples are often more stable than P/Es. Some common approximations to cash flow from operations have limitations, however, because they ignore items that may be subject to manipulation.
- The major cash flow (and related) concepts used in multiples are earnings plus noncash charges (CF), cash flow from operations (CFO), free cash flow to equity (FCFE), and earnings before interest, taxes, depreciation, and amortization (EBITDA).
- In calculating price to cash flow, the earnings-plus-noncash-charges concept is traditionally used, although FCFE has the strongest link to financial theory.
- CF and EBITDA are not strictly cash flow numbers because they do not account for noncash revenue and net changes in working capital.
- The fundamental drivers of price to cash flow, however defined, are the expected growth rate of future cash flow and the required rate of return. The justified price to cash flow based on fundamentals bears a positive relationship to the first factor and an inverse relationship to the second.
- EV/EBITDA is preferred to P/EBITDA because EBITDA, as a pre-interest number, is a flow to all providers of capital.
- EV/EBITDA may be more appropriate than P/E for comparing companies with different amounts of financial leverage (debt).
- EV/EBITDA is frequently used in the valuation of capital-intensive businesses.
- The fundamental drivers of EV/EBITDA are the expected growth rate in free cash flow to the firm, profitability, and the weighted average cost of capital. The justified EV/EBITDA based on fundamentals bears a positive relationship to the first two factors and an inverse relationship to the third.
- Dividend yield has been used as a valuation indicator because it is a component of total return and is less risky than capital appreciation.
- Trailing dividend yield is calculated as four times the most recent quarterly per-share dividend divided by the current market price.

- The fundamental drivers of dividend yield are the expected growth rate in dividends and the required rate of return.
- Comparing companies across borders frequently involves dealing with differences in accounting standards, cultural differences, economic differences, and resulting differences in risk and growth opportunities.
- Momentum indicators relate either price or a fundamental to the time series of the price's or fundamental's own past values (in some cases, to their expected values).
- Momentum valuation indicators include earnings surprise, standardized unexpected earnings (SUE), and relative strength.
- Unexpected earnings (or earnings surprise) equals the difference between reported earnings and expected earnings.
- SUE is unexpected earnings divided by the standard deviation in past unexpected earnings.
- Relative-strength indicators allow comparison of a stock's performance during a period either with its own past performance (first type) or with the performance of some group of stocks (second type). The rationale for using relative strength is the thesis that patterns of persistence or reversal in returns exist.
- Screening is the application of a set of criteria to reduce an investment universe to a smaller set of investments and is a part of many stock selection disciplines. In general, limitations of such screens include the lack of control in vendor-provided data of the calculation of important inputs and the absence of qualitative factors.

REFERENCES

Arnott, Robert D. and Clifford S. Asness. 2003. "Surprise! Higher Dividends = Higher Earnings Growth." *Financial Analysts Journal* 59 (1): 70–87. 10.2469/faj.v59.n1.2504

Aubert, Samuel and Pierre Giot. 2007. "An International Test of the Fed Model." *Journal of Asset Management* 8 (2): 86–100. 10.1057/palgrave.jam.2250063

Bodie, Zvi, Alex Kane, and Alan J. Marcus. 2008. *Investments*. 7th ed.New York: McGraw-Hill.

Brock, William, Joseph Lakonishok, and Blake LeBaron. 1992. "Simple Technical Trading Rules and the Stochastic Properties of Stock Returns." *Journal of Finance* 47 (5): 1731–64. 10.1111/j.1540-6261.1992.tb04681.x

Brown, Lawrence D. 1997. "Earnings Surprise Research: Synthesis and Perspectives." *Financial Analysts Journal* 53 (2): 13–20. 10.2469/faj.v53.n2.2067

Chan, L. K. C. and J. Lakonishok. 2004. "Value and Growth Investing: Review and Update." *Financial Analysts Journal* 60 (1): 71–86. 10.2469/faj.v60.n1.2593

Damodaran, Aswath. 2012. *Investment Valuation: Tools and Techniques for Determining the Value of Any Asset*. 3rd ed.Hoboken, NJ: John Wiley & Co.

Fairfield, Patricia M. 1994. "P/E, P/B and the Present Value of Future Dividends." *Financial Analysts Journal* 50 (4): 23–31. 10.2469/faj.v50.n4.23

Fama, Eugene F. and Kenneth R. French. 1992. "The Cross-Section of Expected Stock Returns." *Journal of Finance* 47 (2): 427–65. 10.1111/j.1540-6261.1992.tb04398.x

Graham, Benjamin and David L. Dodd. 1934. *Security Analysis*. McGraw-Hill Professional Publishing.

Grant, Julia and Larry Parker. 2001. "EBITDA!" *Research in Accounting Regulation* 15:205–11.

Hackel, Kenneth S., Joshua Livnat, and Atul Rai. 1994. "The Free Cash Flow/Small-Cap Anomaly." *Financial Analysts Journal* 50 (5): 33–42. 10.2469/faj.v50.n5.33

Harris, Mary and Karl A. Muller. 1999. "The Market Valuation of IAS versus U.S. GAAP Accounting Measures Using Form 20-F Reconciliations." *Journal of Accounting and Economics* 26 (1–3): 285–312. 10.1016/S0165-4101(99)00003-8

Harris, Robert S. and Felicia C. Marston. 1994. "Value versus Growth Stocks: Book-to-Market, Growth, and Beta." *Financial Analysts Journal* 50 (5): 18–24. 10.2469/faj.v50.n5.18

Henry, E., S. Lin, and Y. Yang. 2009. "The European–U.S. GAAP Gap: Amount, Type, Homogeneity, and Value Relevance of IFRS to U.S. GAAP Form 20-F Reconciliations." *Accounting Horizons* 23 (2): 121–50. 10.2308/acch.2009.23.2.121

Kisor, Manown and Volkert S. Whitbeck. 1963. "A New Tool in Investment Decision-Making." *Financial Analysts Journal* 19 (3): 55–62. 10.2469/faj.v19.n3.55

Lakonishok, J., A. Shleifer, and R. W. Vishny. 1994. "Contrarian Investment, Extrapolation and Risk." *Journal of Finance* 49 (5): 1541–78. 10.1111/j.1540-6261.1994.tb04772.x

Lander, Joel, Athanasios Orphanides, and Martha Douvogiannis. 1997. "Earnings Forecasts and the Predictability of Stock Returns: Evidence from Trading the S&P." *Journal of Portfolio Management* 23 (4): 24–35. 10.3905/jpm.1997.409620

Latané, Henry A. and Charles P. Jones. 1979. "Standardized Unexpected Earnings—1971–77." *Journal of Finance* 34 (3): 717–24.

Lee, Charles M.C. and Bhaskaran Swaminathan. 2000. "Price Momentum and Trading Volume." *Journal of Finance* 55 (5): 2017–69. 10.1111/0022-1082.00280

Malkiel, Burton and John Cragg. 1970. "Expectations and the Structure of Share Prices." *American Economic Review* 60 (4): 601–17.

Martin, Thomas A. 1998. "Traditional Equity Valuation Methods." In *Equity Research and Valuation Techniques*. Charlottesville, VA: AIMR. 10.2469/cp.v1998.n2.5

Mulford, Charles W. and Eugene E. Comiskey. 2005. *Creative Cash Flow Reporting: Uncovering Sustainable Financial Performance*. Hoboken, NJ: John Wiley & Sons.

Nathan, Siva, Kumar Sivakumar, and Jayaraman Vijayakumar. 2001. "Returns to Trading Strategies Based on Price-to-Earnings and Price-to-Sales Ratios." *Journal of Investing* 10 (2): 17–28. 10.3905/joi.2001.319458

O'Shaughnessy, James P. 2005. *What Works on Wall Street: A Guide to the Best-Performing Investment Strategies of All Time*. 3rd ed.New York: McGraw-Hill Professional Publishing.

Pinto, Jerald, Thomas Robinson, and John Stowe. 2018. "Equity Valuation: A Survey of Professional Practice." *Review of Financial Economics* 37:219–33. 10.1002/rfe.1040

Siegel, Jeremy. 2014. *Stocks for the Long Run*. 5th ed.New York: McGraw-Hill.

Solnik, Bruno and Dennis McLeavey. 2004. *International Investments*. 5th ed.Boston: Pearson Addison-Wesley.

Stimes, Peter C. and Stephen E. Wilcox. 2011. "Equity Market Valuation." Chap. 11 in *Investments: Principles of Portfolio and Equity Analysis*. Hoboken, NJ: John Wiley & Sons.

Wild, John J., Leopold A. Bernstein, and K. R. Subramanyam. 2001. *Financial Statement Analysis*. 7th ed.New York: McGraw-Hill Irwin.

Yardeni, Edward. 2000. *"How to Value Earnings Growth." Topical Study #49*. Deutsche Banc Alex Brown.

Zhou, Ping and William Ruland. 2006. "Dividend Payout and Future Earnings Growth." *Financial Analysts Journal* 62 (3): 58–69. 10.2469/faj.v62.n3.4157

PRACTICE PROBLEMS

The following information relates to questions 1-3

As of February 2020, you are researching Jonash International, a hypothetical company subject to cyclical demand for its services. Jonash shares closed at $57.98 on 2 February 2019. You believe the 2015–18 period reasonably captures average profitability:

Measure	2019	2018	2017	2016	2015
EPS	E$3.03	$1.45	$0.23	$2.13	$2.55
BV per share	E$19.20	$16.21	$14.52	$13.17	$11.84
ROE	E16.0%	8.9%	1.6%	16.3%	21.8%

1. Define normalized EPS.
2. Calculate a normalized EPS for Jonash based on the method of historical average EPS, and then calculate the P/E based on normalized EPS.
3. Calculate a normalized EPS for Jonash based on the method of average ROE and the P/E based on normalized EPS.

The following information relates to questions 4-5

An analyst plans to use P/E and the method of comparables as a basis for recommending purchasing shares of one of two peer-group companies in the business of manufacturing personal digital assistants. Neither company has been profitable to date, and neither is expected to have positive EPS over the next year. Data on the companies' prices, trailing EPS, and expected growth rates in sales (five-year compounded rates) are given in the following table:

Company	Price	Trailing EPS	P/E	Expected Growth (Sales)
Hand	$22	–$2.20	NMF	45%
Somersault	$10	–$1.25	NMF	40%

Unfortunately, because the earnings for both companies have been negative, their P/Es are not meaningful. On the basis of this information, address the following:

4. Discuss how the analyst might make a relative valuation in this case.
5. State which stock the analyst should recommend.

The following information relates to questions 6-7

May Stewart, CFA, a retail analyst, is performing a P/E-based comparison of two hypothetical jewelry stores as of early 2020. She has the following data for Hallwhite Stores (HS) and Ruffany (RUF).

- HS is priced at $44. RUF is priced at $22.50.
- HS has a simple capital structure, earned $2.00 per share (basic and diluted) in 2019, and is expected to earn $2.20 (basic and diluted) in 2020.
- RUF has a complex capital structure as a result of its outstanding stock options. Moreover, it had several unusual items that reduced its basic EPS in 2019 to $0.50 (versus the $0.75 that it earned in 2018).
- For 2020, Stewart expects RUF to achieve net income of $30 million. RUF has 30 million shares outstanding and options outstanding for an additional 3,333,333 shares.

6. Which P/E (trailing or forward) should Stewart use to compare the two companies' valuation?

7. Which of the two stocks is relatively more attractive when valued on the basis of P/Es (assuming that all other factors are approximately the same for both stocks)?

The following information relates to questions 8-9

You are researching the valuation of the stock of a company in the food-processing industry. Suppose you intend to use the mean value of the forward P/Es for the food-processing industry stocks as the benchmark value of the multiple. This mean P/E is 18.0. The forward or expected EPS for the next year for the stock you are studying is $2.00. You calculate 18.0 × $2.00 = $36, which you take to be the intrinsic value of the stock based only on the information given here. Comparing $36 with the stock's current market price of $30, you conclude the stock is undervalued.

8. Give two reasons why your conclusion that the stock is undervalued may be in error.

9. What additional information about the stock and the peer group would support your original conclusion?

The following information relates to questions 10-16

Mark Cannan is updating research reports on two well-established consumer companies before first quarter 2021 earnings reports are released. His supervisor, Sharolyn Ritter, has asked Cannan to use market-based valuations when updating the reports.

Delite Beverage is a manufacturer and distributor of soft drinks and recently acquired a major water bottling company in order to offer a broader product line. The acquisition will have a significant impact on Delite's future results.

You Fix It is a US retail distributor of products for home improvement, primarily for those consumers who choose to do the work themselves. The home improvement industry is cyclical; the industry was adversely affected by the recent downturn in the economy, the level of foreclosures, and slow home sales. Although sales and earnings at You Fix It weakened, same store sales are beginning to improve as consumers undertake more home improvement projects. Poor performing stores were closed, resulting in significant restructuring charges in 2020.

Before approving Cannan's work, Ritter wants to discuss the calculations and choices of ratios used in the valuation of Delite and You Fix It. The data used by Cannan in his analysis are summarized in Exhibit 1.

Exhibit 1: Select Financial Data for Delite Beverage and You Fix It

	Delite Beverage	You Fix It
2020 earnings per share (EPS)	\$3.44	\$1.77
2021 estimated EPS	\$3.50	\$1.99
Book value per share end of year	\$62.05	\$11.64
Current share price	\$65.50	\$37.23
Sales (billions)	\$32.13	\$67.44
Free cash flow per share	\$2.68	\$0.21
Shares outstanding end of year	2,322,034,000	1,638,821,000

Cannan advises Ritter that he is considering three different approaches to value the shares of You Fix It:

Approach 1 Price-to-book ratio (P/B)

Approach 2 Price-to-earnings ratio (P/E) using trailing earnings

Approach 3 Price-to-earnings ratio using normalized earnings

Cannan tells Ritter that he calculated the price-to-sales ratio (P/S) for You Fix It but chose not to use it in the valuation of the shares. Cannan states to Ritter that it is more appropriate to use the P/E than the P/S because

Reason 1 Earnings are more stable than sales.

Reason 2 Earnings are less easily manipulated than sales.

Reason 3 The P/E reflects financial leverage, whereas the P/S does not.

Cannan also informs Ritter that he did not use a price-to-cash-flow multiple in valuing the shares of Delite or You Fix It. The reason is that he could not identify a cash flow measure that would both account for working capital and noncash revenues and be after interest expense and thus not be mismatched with share price. Ritter advises Cannan that such a cash flow measure does exist.

Ritter provides Cannan with financial data on three close competitors as well as the overall beverage sector, which includes other competitors, in Exhibit 2. She asks Cannan to determine, based on the P/E-to-growth (PEG) ratio, whether Delite shares are overvalued, fairly valued, or undervalued.

Exhibit 2: Beverage Sector Data

	Forward P/E	Earnings Growth
Delite	—	12.41%
Fresh Iced Tea Company	16.59	9.52%
Nonutter Soda	15.64	11.94%
Tasty Root Beer	44.10	20%
Beverage sector average	16.40	10.80%

After providing Ritter his answer, Cannan is concerned about the inclusion of Tasty Root Beer in the comparables analysis. Specifically, Cannan says to Ritter: "I feel we should mitigate the effect of large outliers but not the impact of small outliers (i.e., those close to zero) when calculating the beverage sector P/E. What measure of central tendency would you suggest we use to address this concern?"

Ritter requests that Cannan incorporate their discussion points before submitting the reports for final approval.

10. Based on the information in Exhibit 1, the *mostappropriate* price-to-earnings ratio to use in the valuation of Delite is *closest* to:

    A. 18.71.

    B. 19.04.

    C. 24.44.

11. Based on the information in Exhibit 1, the price-to-sales ratio for You Fix It is *closest* to:

    A. 0.28.

    B. 0.55.

    C. 0.90.

12. Which valuation approach would be *most* appropriate in valuing shares of You Fix It?

    A. Approach 1

    B. Approach 2

    C. Approach 3

13. Cannan's preference to use the P/E over the P/S is *best* supported by:

    A. Reason 1.

    B. Reason 2.

    C. Reason 3.

14. The cash flow measure that Ritter would *most likely* recommend to address Cannan's concern is:

    A. free cash flow to equity.

    B. earnings plus noncash charges.

C. earnings before interest, tax, depreciation, and amortization.

15. Based on the information in Exhibits 1 and 2, Cannan would most likely conclude that Delite's shares are:

A. overvalued.

B. undervalued.

C. fairly valued.

16. The measure of central tendency that Ritter will *most likely* recommend is the:

A. median.

B. harmonic mean.

C. arithmetic mean.

The following information relates to questions 17-22

Andrea Risso is a junior analyst with AquistareFianco, an independent equity research firm. Risso's supervisor asks her to update, as of 1 January 2020, a quarterly research report for Centralino S.p.A., a telecommunications company headquartered in Italy. On that date, Centralino's common share price is €50 and its preferred shares trade for €5.25 per share.

Risso gathers information on Centralino. Exhibit 1 presents earnings and dividend data, and Exhibit 2 presents balance sheet data. Net sales were €3.182 billion in 2019. Risso estimates a required return of 15% for Centralino and forecasts growth in dividends of 6% into perpetuity.

Exhibit 1: Earnings and Dividends for Centralino, 2016–2020

	2016	2017	2018	2019	2020(E)
Earnings per share (EPS, €)	4.93	5.25	4.46	5.64	6.00
Dividends per share (DPS, €)	2.45	2.60	2.60	2.75	2.91
Return on equity (ROE)	13.01%	13.71%	11.58%	14.21%	14.96%

Note: The data for 2016–2019 are actual and for 2020 are estimated.

Exhibit 2: Summary Balance Sheet for Centralino, Year Ended 31 December 2019

Assets (€ millions)		Liabilities and Shareholders' Equity (€ millions)	
Cash and cash equivalents	102	Current liabilities	259
Accounts receivable	305	Long-term debt	367
Inventory	333	**Total liabilities**	626
Total current assets	740	Preferred shares	80

Assets (€ millions)		Liabilities and Shareholders' Equity (€ millions)	
Property and equipment, net	913	Common shares	826
Total assets	1,653	Retained earnings	121
		Total shareholders' equity	1,027
		Total liabilities and shareholders' equity	1,653

Notes: The market value of long-term debt is equal to its book value. Shares outstanding are 41.94 million common shares and 16.00 million preferred shares.

Exhibit 3 presents forward price-to-earnings ratios (P/Es) for Centralino's peer group. Risso assumes no differences in fundamentals among the peer-group companies.

Exhibit 3: Peer Group Forward P/Es

Company	Forward P/E
Brinaregalo	5.9
Camporio	8.3
Esperto	3.0
Fornodissione	15.0
Radoresto	4.6

Risso also wants to calculate normalized EPS using the average return on equity method. She determines that the 2016–19 time period in Exhibit 1 represents a full business cycle for Centralino.

17. Based on Exhibit 1, the trailing P/E for Centralino as of 1 January 2020, ignoring any business-cycle influence, is *closest to*:

    A. 8.3.

    B. 8.9.

    C. 9.9.

18. Based on Exhibit 1 and Risso's estimates of return and dividend growth, Centralino's justified forward P/E based on the Gordon growth dividend discount model is *closest* to:

    A. 5.4.

    B. 5.7.

    C. 8.3.

19. Based on Exhibit 2, the price-to-book multiple for Centralino is *closest* to:

    A. 2.0.

    B. 2.2.

    C. 2.5.

20. Based on Exhibit 2, the multiple of enterprise value to sales for Centralino as of

31 December 2019 is *closest* to:

A. 0.67.

B. 0.74.

C. 0.77.

21. Based on Exhibit 1 and using the harmonic mean of the peer group forward P/Es shown in Exhibit 3 as a valuation indicator, the common shares of Centralino are:

A. undervalued.

B. fairly valued.

C. overvalued.

22. Based on Exhibits 1 and 2, the normalized earnings per share for Centralino as calculated by Risso should be *closest* to:

A. €2.94.

B. €3.21.

C. €5.07.

The following information relates to questions 23-29

Cátia Pinho is a supervisor in the equity research division of Suite Securities. Pinho asks Flávia Silveira, a junior analyst, to complete an analysis of Adesivo S.A., Enviado S.A., and Gesticular S.A.

Pinho directs Silveira to use a valuation metric that would allow for a meaningful ranking of relative value of the three companies' shares. Exhibit 1 provides selected financial information for the three companies.

Exhibit 1: Selected Financial Information for Adesivo, Enviado, and Gesticular (Brazilian Real, BRL)

	Adesivo	Enviado	Gesticular
Stock's current price	14.72	72.20	132.16
Diluted EPS (last four quarters)	0.81	2.92	−0.05
Diluted EPS (next four quarters)	0.91	3.10	2.85
Dividend rate (annualized most recent dividend)	0.44	1.24	0.00

Silveira reviews underlying trailing EPS for Adesivo. Adesivo has basic trailing EPS of BRL0.84. Silveira finds the following note in Adesivo's financial statements:

"On a per share basis, Adesivo incurred in the last four quarters

i. from a lawsuit, a nonrecurring gain of BRL0.04; and

ii. from factory integration, a nonrecurring cost of BRL0.03 and a recurring cost of BRL0.01 in increased depreciation."

Silveira notes that Adesivo is forecasted to pay semiannual dividends of BRL0.24 next year. Silveira estimates five-year earnings growth rates for the three companies, which are presented in Exhibit 2.

Exhibit 2: Earnings Growth Rate Estimates over Five Years

Company	Earnings Growth Rate Estimate (%)
Adesivo	16.67
Enviado	21.91
Gesticular	32.33

Pinho asks Silveira about the possible use of the price-to-sales ratio (P/S) in assessing the relative value of the three companies. Silveira tells Pinho:

Statement 1 The P/S is not affected by revenue recognition practices.

Statement 2 The P/S is less subject to distortion from expense accounting than is the P/E.

Pinho asks Silveira about using the Fed and Yardeni models to assess the value of the equity market. Silveira states:

Statement 3 The Fed model concludes that the market is undervalued when the market's current earnings yield is greater than the 10-year Treasury bond yield.

Statement 4 The Yardeni model includes the consensus five-year earnings growth rate forecast for the market index.

Silveira also analyzes the three companies using the enterprising value (EV)-to-EBITDA multiple. Silveira notes that the EBITDA for Gesticular for the most recent year is BRL560 million and gathers other selected information on Gesticular, which is presented in Exhibit 4.

Exhibit 3: Selected Information on Gesticular at Year End (BRL Millions)

Market Value of Debt	Market Value of Common Equity	Market Value of Preferred Equity	Cash	Short-Term Investments
1,733	6,766	275	581	495

Pinho asks Silveira about the use of momentum indicators in assessing the shares of the three companies. Silveira states:

Statement 5 Relative-strength indicators compare an equity's performance during a period with the performance of some group of equities or its own past performance.

Statement 6 In the calculation of standardized unexpected earnings (SUE), the magnitude of unexpected earnings is typically scaled by the standard deviation of analysts' earnings forecasts.

23. Based on Pinho's directive and the data from the last four quarters presented in Exhibit 1, the valuation metric that Silveira should use is the:
    - **A.** price-to-earnings ratio (P/E).
    - **B.** production-to-demand ratio (P/D).
    - **C.** earnings-to-price ratio (E/P).

24. Based on Exhibit 1 and the note to Adesivo's financial statements, the trailing P/E for Adesivo using underlying EPS is *closest* to:
    - **A.** 17.7.
    - **B.** 18.2.
    - **C.** 18.4.

25. Based on Exhibits 1 and 2, which company's shares are the most attractively priced based on the five-year forward P/E-to-growth (PEG) ratio?
    - **A.** Adesivo
    - **B.** Enviado
    - **C.** Gesticular

26. Which of Silveira's statements concerning the use of the P/S is correct?
    - **A.** Statement 1 only
    - **B.** Statement 2 only
    - **C.** Both Statement 1 and Statement 2

27. Which of Silveira's statements concerning the Fed and Yardeni models is correct?
    - **A.** Statement 3 only
    - **B.** Statement 4 only
    - **C.** Both Statement 3 and Statement 4

28. Based on Exhibit 4, Gesticular's EV/EBITDA multiple is *closest* to:
    - **A.** 11.4.
    - **B.** 13.7.
    - **C.** 14.6.

29. Which of Silveira's statements concerning momentum indicators is correct?
    - **A.** Statement 5 only
    - **B.** Statement 6 only
    - **C.** Both Statement 5 and Statement 6

The following information relates to questions 30-31

Christie Johnson, CFA, has been assigned to analyze Sundanci. Johnson assumes that Sundanci's earnings and dividends will grow at a constant rate of 13%. Exhibits 1 and 2 provide financial statements for the most recent two years (2020 and 2021) and other information for Sundanci.

Exhibit 1: Sundanci Actual 2020 and 2021 Financial Statements for Fiscal Years Ending 31 May (in Millions except Per-Share Data)

Income Statement	2020	2021
Revenue	$474	$598
Depreciation	20	23
Other operating costs	368	460
Income before taxes	86	115
Taxes	26	35
Net income	60	80
Dividends	18	24
Earnings per share	$0.714	$0.952
Dividends per share	$0.214	$0.286
Common shares outstanding	84.0	84.0
Balance Sheet	**2020**	**2021**
Current assets	$201	$326
Net property, plant, and equipment	474	489
Total assets	675	815
Current liabilities	57	141
Long-term debt	0	0
Total liabilities	57	141
Shareholders' equity	618	674
Total liabilities and equity	675	815
Other Information		
Capital expenditures	34	38

Exhibit 2: Selected Financial Information	
Required rate of return	14%
Growth rate of industry	13%
Industry P/E	26

30. Based on information in Exhibits 1 and 2 and on Johnson's assumptions for Sundanci, calculate justified trailing and forward P/Es for this company.

31. Identify, within the context of the constant dividend growth model, how *each* of the following fundamental factors would affect the P/E:

    i. The risk (beta) of Sundanci increases substantially.

    ii. The estimated growth rate of Sundanci's earnings and dividends increases.

    iii. The equity risk premium increases.

    Note: A change in a fundamental factor is assumed to happen in isolation; interactive effects between factors are ignored. That is, every other item of the company is unchanged.

---

32. Suppose an analyst uses an equity index as a comparison asset in valuing a stock. In making a decision to recommend purchase of an individual stock, which price multiple(s) would cause concern about the impact of potential overvaluation of the equity index?

The following information relates to questions 33-34

Tom Smithfield is valuing the stock of a food-processing business. He feels confident explicitly projecting earnings and dividends to three years (to $t = 3$). Other information and estimates are as follows:

- Required rate of return = 0.09.
- Average dividend payout rate for mature companies in the market = 0.45.
- Industry average ROE = 0.10.
- E_3 = \$3.00.
- Industry average P/E = 12.

On the basis of this information, answer the following questions:

33. Compute terminal value (V_3) based on comparables.

34. Contrast your answer in Part A to an estimate of terminal value based on the Gordon growth model.

---

35. Discuss three types of stocks or investment situations for which an analyst could

appropriately use P/B in valuation.

The following information relates to questions 36-37

Aratatech is a multinational distributor of semiconductor chips and related products to businesses. Its leading competitor around the world is Trymye Electronics. Aratatech has a current market price of $10.00, 20 million shares outstanding, annual sales of $1 billion, and a 5% profit margin. Trymye has a market price of $20.00, 30 million shares outstanding, annual sales of $1.6 billion, and a profit margin of 4.9%. Based on the information given, answer the following questions:

36. Which of the two companies has a more attractive valuation based on P/S?

37. Identify and explain one advantage of P/S over P/E as a valuation tool.

The following information relates to questions 38-41

GN Growing AG (GG) is currently selling for €240, with TTM EPS and dividends per share of €1.5 and €0.9, respectively. The company's trailing P/E is 16.0, P/B is 3.2. P/Sales based on forecast sales, is 1.5. ROE is 20%, and for the profit margin on sales is 10.0%. The Treasury bond rate is 4.9%, the equity risk premium is 5.5%, and GG's beta is 1.2.

38. What is GG's required rate of return, based on the capital asset pricing model (CAPM)?

39. Assume that the dividend and earnings growth rates are 8%. What trailing P/E and P/B multiples would be justified in light of the required rate of return in Part A and current values of the dividend payout ratio and ROE ?

40. Calculate the justified P/Sales ratio based on the forward-looking margin of 10% and current values of dividend payout.

41. Given that the assumptions and constant growth model are appropriate, state and justify whether GG, based on fundamentals, appears to be fairly valued, overvalued, or undervalued.

42. Define the major alternative cash flow concepts, and state one limitation of each.

43. Data for two hypothetical companies in the pharmaceutical industry, DriveMed and MAT Technology, are given in the following table. For both companies, expenditures on fixed capital and working capital during the previous year reflect anticipated average expenditures over the foreseeable horizon.

Measure	DriveMed	MAT Technology
Current price	$46.00	$78.00
Trailing CF per share	$3.60	$6.00
P/CF	12.8	13.0

Measure	DriveMed	MAT Technology
Trailing FCFE per share	$1.00	$5.00
P/FCFE	46.0	15.6
Consensus five-year growth forecast	15%	20%
Beta	1.25	1.25

On the basis of the information supplied, discuss the valuation of MAT Technology relative to DriveMed. Justify your conclusion.

The following information relates to questions 44-46

Jorge Zaldys, CFA, is researching the relative valuation of two companies in the aerospace/defense industry, NCI Heavy Industries (NCI) and Relay Group International (RGI). He has gathered relevant information on the companies in the following table.

EBITDA Comparisons (in € Millions except Per-Share and Share-Count Data)

Company	RGI	NCI
Price per share	150	100
Shares outstanding	5 million	2 million
Market value of debt	50	100
Book value of debt	52	112
Cash and investments	5	2
Net income	49.5	12
Net income from continuing operations	49.5	8
Interest expense	3	5
Depreciation and amortization	8	4
Taxes	2	3

Using the information in the table, answer the following questions:

44. Calculate P/EBITDA for NCI and RGI.

45. Calculate EV/EBITDA for NCI and RGI.

46. Which company should Zaldys recommend as relatively undervalued? Justify the selection.

The following information relates to questions 47-48

Wilhelm Müller, CFA, has organized the selected data on four food companies that appear below (TTM stands for trailing 12-month):

Measure	Hoppelli Foods	Telli Foods	Drisket Co.	Whiteline Foods
Stock price	€25.70	€11.77	€23.65	€24.61
Shares outstanding (thousands)	138,923	220,662	108,170	103,803
Market cap (€ millions)	3,570	2,597	2,558	2,555
Enterprise value (€ millions)	3,779	4,056	3,846	4,258
Sales (€ millions)	4,124	10,751	17,388	6,354
Operating income (€ millions)	285	135	186	396
Operating profit margin	6.91%	1.26%	1.07%	6.23%
Net income (€ millions)	182	88	122	252
TTM EPS	€1.30	€0.40	€1.14	€2.43
Return on equity	19.20%	4.10%	6.40%	23.00%
Net profit margin	4.41%	0.82%	0.70%	3.97%

On the basis of the data given, answer the following questions:

47. Calculate the trailing P/E and EV/sales for each company.

48. Explain, on the basis of fundamentals, why these stocks have different EV/S multiples.

49. John Jones, CFA, is head of the research department at Peninsular Research. Peninsular has a client who has inquired about the valuation method best suited for comparing companies in an industry with the following characteristics:

- Principal competitors within the industry are located in the United States, France, Japan, and Brazil.
- The industry is currently operating at a cyclical low, with many companies reporting losses.

Jones recommends that the client consider the following valuation ratios:

1. P/E
2. P/B
3. EV/S

Determine which *one* of the three valuation ratios is most appropriate for comparing companies in this industry. Support your answer with *one* reason that makes that ratio superior to either of the other two ratios in this case.

The following information relates to questions 50-51

Your value-oriented investment management firm recently hired a new analyst, Bob Westard, because of his expertise in the life sciences and biotechnology areas. At the firm's weekly meeting, during which each analyst proposes a stock idea for inclusion in the firm's approved list, Westard recommends Hitech Clothing International (HCI). He bases his recommendation on two considerations.

First, HCI has pending patent applications but a P/E that he judges to be low in light of the potential earnings from the patented products. Second, HCI has had high relative strength versus the S&P 500 over the past month.

50. Explain the difference between Westard's two approaches—that is, the use of price multiples and the relative-strength approach.

51. State which, if any, of the bases for Westard's recommendation is consistent with the investment orientation of your firm.

The following information relates to questions 52-53

Kirstin Kruse, a portfolio manager, has an important client who wants to alter the composition of her equity portfolio, which is currently a diversified portfolio of 60 global common stocks. Because of concerns about the economy and based on the thesis that the consumer staples sector will be less hurt than others in a recession, the client wants to add stocks trading in the United States (including ADRs) from the consumer staples sector. In addition, the client wants the stocks to meet the following criteria:

- Stocks must be considered large cap (i.e., have a large market capitalization).
- Stocks must have a dividend yield of at least 4.0%.
- Stocks must have a forward P/E no greater than 15.

The following table shows how many stocks satisfied each screen, which was run in June 2019.

Screen	Number Satisfying
Consumer staples sector	424
Large cap	361
Dividend yield of at least 4.0%	887
P/E less than 15	5,409
All four screens	3

The stocks meeting all four screens were Altria Group, Inc.; British American Tobacco PLC (the company's ADR); and Kraft Heinz Co.

52. Critique the construction of the screen.

53. Do these criteria identify appropriate additions to this client's portfolio?

SOLUTIONS

1. Normalized EPS is the level of earnings per share that the company could currently achieve under mid-cyclical conditions.

2. Averaging EPS over the 2015–18 period, we find that ($2.55 + $2.13 + $0.23 + $1.45)/4 = $1.59. According to the method of historical average EPS, Jonash's normalized EPS is $1.59. The P/E based on this estimate is $57.98/$1.59 = 36.5.

3. Averaging ROE over the 2015–18 period, we find that (0.218 + 0.163 + 0.016 + 0.089)/4 = 0.1215. For current BV per share, you would use the estimated value of $19.20 for year end 2019. According to the method of average ROE, 0.1215 × $19.20 = $2.33 is the normalized EPS. The P/E based on this estimate is $57.98/$2.33 = 24.9.

4. The analyst can rank the two stocks by earnings yield (E/P). Whether EPS is positive or negative, a lower E/P reflects a richer (higher) valuation and a ranking from high to low E/P has a meaningful interpretation.

   In some cases, an analyst might handle negative EPS by using normalized EPS in its place. Neither business, however, has a history of profitability. When year-ahead EPS is expected to be positive, forward P/E is positive. Thus, the use of forward P/Es sometimes addresses the problem of trailing negative EPS. Forward P/E is not meaningful in this case, however, because next year's earnings are expected to be negative.

5. Hand has an E/P of –0.100, and Somersault has an E/P of –0.125. A higher earnings yield has an interpretation that is similar to that of a lower P/E, so Hand appears to be relatively undervalued. The difference in earnings yield cannot be explained by differences in sales growth forecasts. In fact, Hand has a higher expected sales growth rate than Somersault. Therefore, the analyst should recommend Hand.

6. Because investing looks to the future, analysts often favor forward P/E when earnings forecasts are available, as they are here. A specific reason to use forward P/Es is the fact given that RUF had some unusual items affecting EPS for 2020. The data to make appropriate adjustments to RUF's 2020 EPS are not given. In summary, Stewart should use forward P/Es.

7. Because RUF has a complex capital structure, the P/Es of the two companies must be compared on the basis of diluted EPS.

   For HS, forward P/E = $44/2.20 = 20.

   For RUF, forward P/E per diluted share

   = $22.50/($30,000,000/33,333,333) = $22.50/$0.90 = 25.

   Therefore, HS has the more attractive valuation at present.

   The problem illustrates some of the considerations that should be taken into account in using P/Es and the method of comparables.

8. Your conclusion may be in error because of the following:

   - The peer-group stocks themselves may be overvalued; that is, the mean P/E of 18.0 may be too high in terms of intrinsic value. If so, using 18.0 as a multiplier of the stock's expected EPS will lead to an estimate of stock value in excess of intrinsic value.

- The stock's fundamentals may differ from those of the mean food-processing industry stock. For example, if the stock's expected growth rate is lower than the mean industry growth rate and its risk is higher than the mean, the stock may deserve a lower P/E than the industry mean.

In addition, mean P/E may be influenced by outliers.

9. The following additional evidence would support the original conclusion:
   - Evidence that stocks in the industry are, at least on average, fairly valued (that stock prices reflect fundamentals)
   - Evidence that no significant differences exist in the fundamental drivers of P/E for the stock being compared and the average industry stock

10. A is correct. The forward P/E should be used given the recent significant acquisition of the water bottling company. Since a major change such as an acquisition or divestiture can affect results, the forward P/E, also known as the leading P/E or prospective P/E, is the most appropriate P/E to use for Delite. Earnings estimates for 2021 should incorporate the performance of the water bottling company. The forward P/E is calculated as the current price divided by the projected earnings per share, or $65.50/$3.50 = 18.71.

11. C is correct. The price-to-sales ratio is calculated as price per share divided by annual net sales per share.

    Price per share = $37.23.

    Annual net sales per share = $67.44 billion/1.638821 billion shares = $41.15.

    Price-to-sales ratio (P/S) = $37.23/$41.15 = 0.90.

12. C is correct. You Fix It is in the cyclical home improvement industry. The use of normalized earnings should address the problem of cyclicality in You Fix It earnings by estimating the level of earnings per share that the company could achieve currently under mid-cyclical conditions.

13. C is correct. The price to sales ratio (P/S) fails to consider differences in cost structures. Also, while share price reflects the effect of debt financing on profitability and risk, sales is a pre-financing income measure and does not incorporate the impact of debt in the firm's capital structure. Earnings reflect operating and financial leverage, and thus the price-to-earnings ratio (P/E) incorporates the impact of debt in the firm's capital structure.

14. A is correct. Free cash flow to equity (FCFE) is defined as cash flow available to shareholders after deducting all operating expenses, interest and debt payments, and investments in working and fixed capital. Cannan's requirement that the cash flows include interest expense, working capital, and noncash revenue is satisfied by FCFE.

15. C is correct. The P/E-to-growth (PEG) ratio is calculated by dividing a stock's P/E by the expected earnings growth rate, expressed as a percentage. To calculate Delite's PEG ratio, first calculate the P/E: $65.50/$3.50 = 18.71. In this case, the forward earnings should be used given the recent acquisition of the water bottling company. Next, calculate Delite's PEG ratio: 18.71/12.41 = 1.51.

    Comparing Delite's PEG ratio of 1.51 with the PEG ratios of 1.74 (16.59/9.52) for Fresh Iced Tea and 1.31 (15.64/11.94) for Nonutter Soda and with the beverage sector average of 1.52 (16.40/10.80), it appears that Delite's shares are fairly valued. This is determined by the fact that Delite's PEG ratio is in the middle of the range of PEG ratios and very close to the sector average. Therefore, the shares appear to be fairly valued.

16. B is correct. The harmonic mean is sometimes used to reduce the impact of large outliers—which are typically the major concern in using the arithmetic mean multiple—but not the impact of small outliers (i.e., those close to zero). The harmonic mean may aggravate the impact of small outliers, but such outliers are bounded by zero on the downside.

17. B is correct. The trailing P/E is calculated as follows:

    Stock's current price/Most recent four quarters' EPS =

    €50/€5.64 = 8.9.

18. A is correct. The justified forward P/E is calculated as follows:

$$\frac{P_0}{E_1} = \frac{D_1/E_1}{r-g}$$

$$= \frac{(2.91/6.00)}{(0.15-0.06)} = 5.4.$$

19. B is correct. Price to book is calculated as the current market price per share divided by book value per share. Book value per share is common shareholders' equity divided by the number of common shares outstanding. Common shareholders' equity is calculated as total shareholders' equity minus the value of preferred stock.

    Thus,

    Common shareholders' equity = €1,027 – €80 = €947 million.

    Book value per share = €947 million/41.94 million = €22.58.

    Price-to-book ratio (P/B) for Centralino = €50/€22.58 = 2.2.

20. C is correct. Enterprise value (EV) is calculated as follows:

    EV = Market value of common equity + Market value of preferred stock + Market value of debt – Cash, cash equivalents, and short-term investments

    = (€50 × 41.94 million) + (€5.25 × 16.00 million) + €367 million – €102 million

    = €2,446 million (or €2.446 billion).

    So, EV/sales = €2.446 billion/€3.182 billion = 0.77.

21. C is correct. The harmonic mean is calculated as follows:

$$x_H = \frac{n}{\sum_{i=1}^{n}\left(\frac{1}{x_i}\right)} = \frac{5}{\left(\frac{1}{5.9}\right)+\left(\frac{1}{8.3}\right)+\left(\frac{1}{3.0}\right)+\left(\frac{1}{15.0}\right)+\left(\frac{1}{4.6}\right)} = 5.5.$$

    The forward P/E for Centralino is €50/€6.00 = 8.3. Because Centralino's forward P/E is higher than the harmonic mean of the peer group, the shares of Centralino appear relatively overvalued.

22. A is correct. Based on the method of average ROE, normalized EPS are calculated as the average ROE from the most recent full business cycle multiplied by current book value per share. The most recent business cycle was 2011–2014,

and the average ROE over that period was

$$\frac{0.1301 + 0.1371 + 0.1158 + 0.1421}{4} = 0.131.$$

The book value of (common) equity, or simply book value, is the value of shareholders' equity less any value attributable to the preferred stock: €1,027 million – €80 million = €947 million.

Current book value per share (BVPS) is calculated as €947 million/41.94 million = €22.58.

So, normalized EPS is calculated as

Average ROE × BVPS = 0.131 × €22.58 = €2.96.

23. C is correct. The E/P based on trailing earnings would offer the most meaningful ranking of the shares. Using E/P places Gesticular's negative EPS in the numerator rather than the denominator, leading to a more meaningful ranking.

24. C is correct. The EPS figure that Silveira should use is diluted trailing EPS of BRL0.81, adjusted as follows:

    1. Subtract the BRL0.04 nonrecurring legal gain.

    2. Add BRL0.03 for the nonrecurring factory integration charge.

    No adjustment needs to be made for the BRL0.01 charge related to depreciation because it is a recurring charge.

    Therefore, underlying trailing EPS = BRL0.81 – BRL0.04 + BRL0.03 = BRL0.80 and trailing P/E using underlying trailing EPS = BRL14.72/BRL0.80 = 18.4.

25. A is correct. The forward PEG ratios for the three companies are calculated as follows:

    Forward P/E = Stock's current price/Forecasted EPS.

    Forward PEG ratio

    = Forward P/E ÷ Expected earnings growth rate (in percentage terms).

    Adesivo forward P/E = BRL14.72/BRL0.91 = 16.18.

    Adesivo forward PEG ratio = 16.18/16.67 = 0.97.

    Enviado forward P/E = BRL72.20/BRL3.10 = 23.29.

    Enviado forward PEG ratio = 23.29/21.91 = 1.06.

    Gesticular forward P/E = BRL132.16/BRL2.85 = 46.37.

    Gesticular forward PEG ratio = 46.37/32.33 = 1.43.

    Adesivo has the lowest forward PEG ratio, 0.97, indicating that it is the most undervalued of the three equities based on the forward PEG ratio.

26. B is correct. Statement 2 is correct because sales, as the top line of the income statement, are less subject to accounting distortion or manipulation than are other fundamentals, such as earnings. Statement 1 is incorrect because sales figures can be distorted by revenue recognition practices, in particular those tending to speed up the recognition of revenues.

27. C is correct. The Fed model considers the equity market to be undervalued when the market's current earnings yield is greater than the 10-year Treasury bond

yield. The Yardeni model incorporates the consensus five-year earnings growth rate forecast for the market index, a variable missing in the Fed model.

28. B is correct. The EV for Gesticular is calculated as follows:

$$\text{EV} = \text{Market value of debt} + \text{Market value of common equity} + \text{Market value of preferred equity} - \text{Cash and short-term investments.}$$

$$\text{EV} = \text{BRL1,733 million} + \text{BRL6,766 million} + \text{BRL275 million} - \text{BRL581 million} - \text{BRL495 million}$$

$$= \text{BRL7,698 million.}$$

$$\text{EV/EBITDA} = \text{BRL7,698 million/BRL560 million} = 13.7.$$

29. A is correct. Relative-strength indicators compare an equity's performance with the performance of a group of equities or with its own past performance. SUE is unexpected earnings scaled by the standard deviation in past unexpected earnings (not the standard deviation of analysts' earnings forecasts, which is used in the calculation of the scaled earnings surprise).

30. The formula for calculating the justified forward P/E for a stable-growth company is the payout ratio divided by the difference between the required rate of return and the growth rate of dividends. If the P/E is being calculated on trailing earnings (Year 0), the payout ratio is increased by 1 plus the growth rate. According to the 2020 income statement, the payout ratio is 18/60 = 0.30; the 2021 income statement gives the same number (24/80 = 0.30). Thus, we can find the following:
P/E based on trailing earnings:

$$\text{P/E} = [\text{Payout ratio} \times (1 + g)] / (r - g)$$
$$= (0.30 \times 1.13) / (0.14 - 0.13) = 33.9.$$

P/E based on next year's earnings:

$$\text{P/E} = \text{Payout ratio} / (r - g)$$
$$= 0.30 / (0.14 - 0.13) = 30.$$

31.

Fundamental Factor	Effect on P/E	Explanation (Not Required in Question)
The risk (beta) of Sundanci increases substantially.	Decrease	P/E is a decreasing function of risk; that is, as risk increases, P/E decreases. Increases in the risk of Sundanci stock would be expected to lower its P/E.
The estimated growth rate of Sundanci's earnings and dividends increases.	Increase	P/E is an increasing function of the growth rate of the company; that is, the higher the expected growth, the higher the P/E. Sundanci would command a higher P/E if the market price were to incorporate expectations of a higher growth rate.
The equity risk premium increases.	Decrease	P/E is a decreasing function of the equity risk premium. An increased equity risk premium increases the required rate of return, which lowers the price of a stock relative to its earnings. A higher equity risk premium would be expected to lower Sundanci's P/E.

32. In principle, the use of any price multiple for valuation is subject to the concern stated. If the stock market is overvalued, an asset that appears to be fairly or even undervalued in relation to an equity index may also be overvalued.

33. V_n = Benchmark value of P/E × E_n = 12 × \$3.00 = \$36.0.

34. In the expression for the sustainable growth rate, $g = b \times \text{ROE}$, you can use (1 − 0.45) = 0.55 = b and ROE = 0.10 (the industry average), obtaining 0.55 × 0.10 = 0.055. Given the required rate of return of 0.09, you obtain the estimate \$3.00(0.45)(1.055)/(0.09 − 0.055) = \$40.69. In this case, the estimate of terminal value obtained from the Gordon growth model is higher than the estimate based on multiples. The two estimates may differ for a number of reasons, including the sensitivity of the Gordon growth model to the values of the inputs.

35. Although the measurement of book value has a number of widely recognized shortcomings, P/B may still be applied fruitfully in several circumstances:

    - The company is not expected to continue as a going concern. When a company is likely to be liquidated (so ongoing earnings and cash flow are not relevant), the value of its assets less its liabilities is of utmost importance. Naturally, the analyst must establish the fair value of these assets.
    - The company is composed mainly of liquid assets, which is the case for finance, investment, insurance, and banking institutions.
    - The company's EPS is highly variable or negative.

36. Aratatech: P/S = (\$10 price per share)/[(\$1 billion sales)/(20 million shares)] = \$10/(\$1,000,000,000/20,000,000) = 0.2.

    Trymye: P/S = (\$20 price per share)/[(\$1.6 billion sales)/(30 million shares)] = \$20/(\$1,600,000,000/30,000,000) = 0.375.

    Aratatech has a more attractive valuation than Trymye based on its lower P/S but a comparable profit margin.

37. One advantage of P/S over P/E is that companies' accounting decisions typically have a much greater impact on reported earnings than they are likely to have on reported sales. Although companies are able to make a number of legitimate

business and accounting decisions that affect earnings, their discretion over reported sales (revenue recognition) is limited. Another advantage is that sales are almost always positive, so using P/S eliminates issues that arise when EPS is zero or negative.

38. Based on the CAPM, the required rate of return is 4.9% + 1.2 × 5.5% = 11.5%.

39. The dividend payout ratio is €0.9/€1.50 = 0.6. The justified values for the trailing P/E and P/BV ratios should be

$$\frac{P_0}{E_0} = \frac{(1-b)\times(1+g)}{r-g} = \frac{0.6\times(1+0.08)}{0.115-0.08} = 18.5$$

$$\frac{P_0}{B_0} = \frac{ROE-g}{r-g} = \frac{0.20-0.08}{0.115-0.08} = 3.4$$

40. The justified P/S ratio based on assumed profit margin of 10% should be

$$\frac{P_0}{S_1} = \frac{\left(\frac{E_1}{S_1}\right)(1-b)}{r-g} = \frac{0.10\times0.6}{0.115-0.08} = 1.7$$

41. The justified trailing P/E is higher than the trailing P/E (18.5 versus 16), the justified trailing P/B is higher than the actual trailing P/B (3.4 versus 3.2). The justified P/S based on forward looking margin assumptions is higher than the actual P/S based of forecast sales (1.7 versus 1.5). Therefore, based on these three measures, GG appears to be slightly undervalued.

42. The major concepts are as follows:

   - EPS plus per-share depreciation, amortization, and depletion (CF)

     Limitation: Ignores changes in working capital and noncash revenue; not a free cash flow concept.
   - Cash flow from operations (CFO)

     Limitation: Not a free cash flow concept, so not directly linked to theory.
   - Free cash flow to equity (FCFE)

     Limitation: Often more variable and more frequently negative than other cash flow concepts.
   - Earnings before interest, taxes, depreciation, and amortization (EBITDA)

     Limitation: Ignores changes in working capital and noncash revenue; not a free cash flow concept. Relative to its use in P/EBITDA, EBITDA is mismatched with the numerator because it is a pre-interest concept.

43. MAT Technology is relatively undervalued compared with DriveMed on the basis of P/FCFE. MAT Technology's P/FCFE multiple is 34% the size of DriveMed's FCFE multiple (15.6/46 = 0.34, or 34%). The only comparison slightly in DriveMed's favor, or approximately equal for both companies, is the comparison based on P/CF (i.e., 12.8 for DriveMed versus 13.0 for MAT Technology). However, FCFE is more strongly grounded in valuation theory than P/CF. Because DriveMed's and MAT Technology's expenditures for fixed capital and working capital during the previous year reflected anticipated average expenditures over the foreseeable horizon, you would have additional confidence in the P/FCFE comparison.

44. EBITDA = Net income (from continuing operations) + Interest expense + Taxes

+ Depreciation + Amortization.

EBITDA for RGI = €49.5 million + €3 million + €2 million + €8 million = €62.5 million.

Per-share EBITDA = (€62.5 million)/(5 million shares) = €12.5.

P/EBITDA for RGI = €150/€12.5 = 12.

EBITDA for NCI = €8 million + €5 million + €3 million + €4 million = €20 million.

Per-share EBITDA = (€20 million)/(2 million shares) = €10.

P/EBITDA for NCI = €100/€10 = 10.

45. For RGI:

Market value of equity = €150 × 5 million = €750 million.

Market value of debt = €50 million.

Total market value = €750 million + €50 million = €800 million.

EV = €800 million − €5 million (cash and investments) = €795 million.

Now, Zaldys would divide EV by total (as opposed to per-share) EBITDA:

EV/EBITDA for RGI = (€795 million)/(€62.5 million) = 12.72.

For NCI:

Market value of equity = €100 × 2 million = €200 million.

Market value of debt = €100 million.

Total market value = €200 million + €100 million = €300 million.

EV = €300 million − €2 million (cash and investments) = €298 million.

Now, Zaldys would divide EV by total (as opposed to per-share) EBITDA:

EV/EBITDA for NCI = (€298 million)/(€20 million) = 14.9.

46. Zaldys should select RGI as relatively undervalued.

First, it is correct that NCI *appears* to be relatively undervalued based on P/EBITDA, because NCI has a lower P/EBITDA multiple:

- P/EBITDA = €150/€12.5 = 12 for RGI.
- P/EBITDA = €100/€10 = 10 for NCI.

RGI is relatively undervalued on the basis of EV/EBITDA; however, because RGI has the lower EV/EBITDA multiple,

- EV/EBITDA = (€795 million)/(€62.5 million) = 12.72 for RGI.
- EV/EBITDA = (€298 million)/(€20 million) = 14.9 for NCI.

EBITDA is a pre-interest flow; therefore, it is a flow to both debt and equity and the EV/EBITDA multiple is more appropriate than the P/EBITDA multiple. Zaldys would rely on EV/EBITDA to reach his decision if the two ratios conflicted. Note that P/EBITDA does not take into account differences in the use of financial leverage. Substantial differences in leverage exist in this case (NCI uses much more debt), so the preference for using EV/EBITDA rather than P/EBITDA is supported.

47. The P/Es are as follows:

Hoppelli	25.70/1.30 = 19.8.
Telli	11.77/0.40 = 29.4.
Drisket	23.65/1.14 = 20.7.
Whiteline	24.61/2.43 = 10.1.

The EV/S multiples for each company are as follows:

Hoppelli	3,779/4,124 = 0.916.
Telli	4,056/10,751 = 0.377.
Drisket	3,846/17,388 = 0.221.
Whiteline	4,258/6,354 = 0.670.

48. The data for the problem include measures of profitability, such as operating profit margin, ROE, and net profit margin. Because EV includes the market values of both debt and equity, logically the ranking based on EV/S should be compared with a pre-interest measure of profitability—namely, operating profit margin. The ranking of the stocks by EV/S from highest to lowest and the companies' operating margins are shown below:

Company	EV/S	Operating Profit Margin (%)
Hoppelli	0.916	6.91
Whiteline	0.670	6.23
Telli	0.377	1.26
Drisket	0.221	1.07

The differences in EV/S appear to be explained, at least in part, by differences in cost structure as measured by operating profit margin.

49. For companies in the industry described, EV/S would be superior to either of the other two ratios. Among other considerations, EV/S is:

- more useful than P/E in valuing companies with negative earnings;
- better than either P/E or P/B for comparing companies in different countries that are likely to use different accounting standards (a consequence of the multinational nature of the industry);
- less subject to manipulation than earnings (i.e., through aggressive accounting decisions by management, who may be more motivated to manage earnings when a company is in a cyclical low, rather than in a high, and thus likely to report losses).

50. Relative strength is based strictly on price movement (a technical indicator). As used by Westard, the comparison is between the returns on HCI and the returns on the S&P 500. In contrast, the price multiple approaches are based on the relationship of current price not to past prices but to some measure of value, such as EPS, book value, sales, or cash flow.

51. Only the reference to the P/E in relationship to the pending patent applications in Westard's recommendation is consistent with the company's value orientation. High relative strength would be relevant for a portfolio managed with a growth/momentum investment style.

52. As a rule, a screen that includes a maximum P/E should include criteria requiring

positive earnings; otherwise, the screen could select companies with negative P/Es. The screen may be too narrowly focused on value measures. It did not include criteria related to expected growth, required rate of return, risk, or financial strength.

53. The screen results in a very concentrated portfolio. The screen selected only three companies, including two tobacco companies, which typically pay high dividends. Owning these three stocks would provide little diversification.

LEARNING MODULE

5

Residual Income Valuation

by Jerald E. Pinto, PhD, CFA, Elaine Henry, PhD, CFA, Thomas R. Robinson, PhD, CFA, CAIA, and John D. Stowe, PhD, CFA.

Jerald E. Pinto, PhD, CFA, is at CFA Institute (USA). Elaine Henry, PhD, CFA, is at Stevens Institute of Technology (USA). Thomas R. Robinson, PhD, CFA, CAIA, Robinson Global Investment Management LLC, (USA). John D. Stowe, PhD, CFA, is at Ohio University (USA).

LEARNING OUTCOMES

Mastery	*The candidate should be able to:*
☐	calculate and interpret residual income, economic value added, and market value added
☐	describe the uses of residual income models
☐	calculate the intrinsic value of a common stock using the residual income model and compare value recognition in residual income and other present value models
☐	explain fundamental determinants of residual income
☐	explain the relation between residual income valuation and the justified price-to-book ratio based on forecasted fundamentals
☐	calculate and interpret the intrinsic value of a common stock using single-stage (constant-growth) and multistage residual income models
☐	calculate the implied growth rate in residual income, given the market price-to-book ratio and an estimate of the required rate of return on equity
☐	explain continuing residual income and justify an estimate of continuing residual income at the forecast horizon, given company and industry prospects
☐	compare residual income models to dividend discount and free cash flow models
☐	explain strengths and weaknesses of residual income models and justify the selection of a residual income model to value a company's common stock
☐	describe accounting issues in applying residual income models

1 INTRODUCTION

- [ ] calculate and interpret residual income, economic value added, and market value added
- [ ] describe the uses of residual income models

Residual income models of equity value have become widely recognized tools in both investment practice and research. Conceptually, residual income is net income less a charge (deduction) for common shareholders' opportunity cost in generating net income. It is the residual or remaining income after considering the costs of all of a company's capital. The appeal of residual income models stems from a shortcoming of traditional accounting. Specifically, although a company's income statement includes a charge for the cost of debt capital in the form of interest expense, it does not include a charge for the cost of equity capital. A company can have positive net income but may still not be adding value for shareholders if it does not earn more than its cost of equity capital. Residual income models explicitly recognize the costs of all the capital used in generating income.

As an economic concept, residual income has a long history, dating back to Alfred Marshall in the late 1800s (Alfred Marshall, 1890). As far back as the 1920s, General Motors used the concept in evaluating business segments. More recently, residual income has received renewed attention and interest, sometimes under names such as economic profit, abnormal earnings, or economic value added. Although residual income concepts have been used in a variety of contexts, including the measurement of internal corporate performance, we will focus on the residual income model for estimating the intrinsic value of common stock. Among the questions we will study to help us apply residual income models are the following:

- How is residual income measured, and how can an analyst use residual income in valuation?
- How does residual income relate to fundamentals, such as return on equity and earnings growth rates?
- How is residual income linked to other valuation methods, such as a price-multiple approach?
- What accounting-based challenges arise in applying residual income valuation?

The following section develops the concept of residual income, introduces the use of residual income in valuation, and briefly presents alternative measures used in practice. The subsequent sections present the residual income model and illustrate its use in valuing common stock, show practical applications, and describe the relative strengths and weaknesses of residual income valuation compared with other valuation methods. The last section addresses accounting issues in the use of residual income valuation. We then conclude with a summary.

Residual Income

Traditional financial statements, particularly the income statement, are prepared to reflect earnings available to owners. As a result, the income statement shows net income after deducting an expense for the cost of debt capital (i.e., interest expense). The income statement does not, however, deduct dividends or other charges for equity capital. Thus, traditional financial statements essentially let the owners decide whether earnings cover their opportunity costs. Conversely, the economic concept of residual income explicitly deducts the estimated cost of equity capital, the finance concept that measures shareholders' opportunity costs. The cost of equity is the marginal cost of equity, also referred to as the required rate of return on equity. The cost of equity is a marginal cost because it represents the cost of additional equity, whether generated internally or by selling more equity interests. Example 1 illustrates, in a stylized setting, the calculation and interpretation of residual income. To simplify this introduction, we assume that net income accurately reflects clean surplus accounting, a condition that income (earnings) reflects all changes in the book value of equity other than ownership transactions. This concept will be explained later. Our discussions also assume that companies' financing consists only of common equity and debt. In the case of a company that also has preferred stock financing, the residual income calculation would reflect the deduction of preferred stock dividends from net income.

EXAMPLE 1

Calculation of Residual Income

Axis Manufacturing Company, Inc. (AXCI), a very small company in terms of market capitalization, has total assets of €2 million financed 50% with debt and 50% with equity capital. The cost of debt is 7% before taxes; this example assumes that interest is tax deductible, so the after-tax cost of debt is 4.9%. Note that in countries where corporate interest is not tax deductible, the after-tax cost of debt equals the pretax cost of debt. The cost of equity capital is 12%. The company has earnings before interest and taxes (EBIT) of €200,000 and a tax rate of 30%. Net income for AXCI can be determined as follows:

EBIT	€200,000
Less: Interest Expense	€70,000
Pretax Income	€130,000
Less: Income Tax Expense	€39,000
Net Income	€91,000

With earnings of €91,000, AXCI is clearly profitable in an accounting sense. But was the company's profitability adequate return for its owners? Unfortunately, it was not. To incorporate the cost of equity capital, compute residual income. One approach to calculating residual income is to deduct an **equity charge** (the estimated cost of equity capital in money terms) from net income. Compute the equity charge as follows:

Equity charge = Equity capital × Cost of equity capital

= €1,000,000 × 12%

= €120,000.

As stated, residual income is equal to net income minus the equity charge:

Net Income	€91,000
Less: Equity Charge	€120,000
Residual Income	(€29,000)

AXCI did not earn enough to cover the cost of equity capital. As a result, it has negative residual income. Although AXCI is profitable in an accounting sense, it is not profitable in an economic sense.

In Example 1, residual income is calculated based on net income and a charge for the cost of equity capital. Analysts will also encounter another approach to calculating residual income that yields the same results under certain assumptions. In this second approach, which takes the perspective of all providers of capital (both debt and equity), a **capital charge** (the company's total cost of capital in money terms) is subtracted from the company's after-tax operating profit. In the case of AXCI in Example 1, the capital charge is €169,000:

Equity charge	0.12 × €1,000,000 =	€120,000
Debt charge	0.07(1 – 0.30) × €1,000,000 =	€49,000
Total capital charge		€169,000

The company's net operating profit after taxes (NOPAT) is €140,000 (€200,000 – 30% taxes). The capital charge of €169,000 is higher than the after-tax operating profit of €140,000 by €29,000, the same figure obtained in Example 1.

As the following table illustrates, both approaches yield the same results in this case because of two assumptions. First, this example assumes that the marginal cost of debt equals the current cost of debt—that is, the cost used to determine net income. Specifically, in this instance, the after-tax interest expense incorporated in net income [€49,000 = €70,000 × (1 – 30%)] is equal to the after-tax cost of debt incorporated into the capital charge. Second, this example assumes that the weights used to calculate the capital charge are derived from the book value of debt and equity. Specifically, it uses the weights of 50% debt and 50% equity.

Approach 1		Reconciliation	Approach 2	
Net income	€91,000	Plus the after-tax interest expense of €49,000	Net operating profit after tax	€140,000
Less: Equity charge	€120,000	Plus the after-tax capital charge for debt of €49,000	Less: Capital charge	€169,000
Residual income	(€29,000)		Residual income	(€29,000)

That the company is not profitable in an economic sense can also be seen by comparing the company's cost of capital with its return on capital. Specifically, the company's capital charge is greater than its after-tax return on total assets or capital. The after-tax net operating return on total assets or capital is calculated as profits divided by total assets (or total capital). In this example, the after-tax net operating return on total assets is 7% (€140,000/€2,000,000), which is 1.45 percentage points less than the company's effective capital charge of 8.45% (€169,000/€2,000,000). The amount of after-tax net operating profits as a percentage of total assets or capital has been called **return on invested capital** (ROIC). Residual income can also be calculated as (ROIC – Effective capital charge) × Beginning capital.

The Use of Residual Income in Equity Valuation

A company that is generating more income than its cost of obtaining capital—that is, one with positive residual income—is creating value. Conversely, a company that is not generating enough income to cover its cost of capital—that is, a company with negative residual income—is destroying value. Thus, all else equal, higher (lower) residual income should be associated with higher (lower) valuations.

To illustrate the effect of residual income on equity valuation using the case of AXCI presented in Example 1, assume the following:

- Initially, AXCI equity is selling for book value or €1 million with 100,000 shares outstanding. Thus, AXCI's book value per share and initial share price are both €10.

- Earnings per share (EPS) is €0.91 (€91,000/100,000 shares).
- Earnings will continue at the current level indefinitely.
- All net income is distributed as dividends.

Because AXCI is not earning its cost of equity, as shown in Example 1, the company's share price should fall. Given the information, AXCI is destroying €29,000 of value per year, which equals €0.29 per share (€29,000/100,000 shares). Discounted at 12% cost of equity, the present value of the perpetuity is €2.42 (€0.29/12%). The current share price minus the present value of the value being destroyed equals €7.58 (€10 – €2.42).

Another way to look at these data is to note that the earnings yield (E/P) for a no-growth company is an estimate of the expected rate of return. Therefore, when price reaches the point at which E/P equals the required rate of return on equity, an investment in the stock is expected to just cover the stock's required rate of return. With EPS of €0.91, the earnings yield is exactly 12% (AXCI's cost of equity) when its share price is €7.58333 (i.e., €0.91/€7.58333 = 12%). At a share price of €7.58333, the total market value of AXCI's equity is €758,333. When a company has negative residual income, shares are expected to sell at a discount to book value. In this example, AXCI's price-to-book ratio (P/B) at this level of discount from book value would be 0.7583. In contrast, if AXCI were earning positive residual income, then its shares should sell at a premium to book value. In summary, higher residual income is expected to be associated with higher market prices (and higher P/Bs), all else being equal.

Residual income (RI) models have been used to value both individual stocks and stock indexes such as the Dow Jones Industrial Average (see Fleck, Craig, Bodenstab, Harris, and Huh 2001; and Lee, Myers, and Swaminathan 1999). Recall that **impairment** in an accounting context means downward adjustment, and **goodwill** is an intangible asset that may appear on a company's balance sheet as a result of its purchase of another company.

Residual income and residual income models have been referred to by a variety of names. Residual income has sometimes been called **economic profit** because it estimates the company's profit after deducting the cost of all capital: debt and equity. In forecasting future residual income, the term **abnormal earnings** is also used. Under the assumption that in the long term the company is expected to earn its cost of capital (from all sources), any earnings in excess of the cost of capital can be termed abnormal earnings. The residual income model has also been called the **discounted abnormal earnings model** and the **Edwards–Bell–Ohlson model** after the names of researchers in the field. Our focus is on a general residual income model that analysts can apply using publicly available data and nonproprietary accounting adjustments. A number of commercial implementations of the approach, however, are also very well known. Before returning to the general residual income model we briefly discuss one such commercial implementation and the related concept of market value added.

Commercial Implementations

One example of several competing commercial implementations of the residual income concept is **economic value added** (EVA, an acronym trademarked by Stern Stewart & Co. and generally associated with a specific set of adjustments proposed by Stern Stewart & Co.). EVA aims to produce a value that is a good approximation of economic profit (see Stewart 1991 and Peterson and Peterson 1996). The previous section illustrated a calculation of residual income starting from net operating profit after taxes, and EVA takes the same broad approach. Specifically, economic value added is computed as

$$\text{EVA} = \text{NOPAT} - (\text{C\%} \times \text{TC}), \quad (1)$$

where NOPAT is the company's net operating profit after taxes, C% is the cost of capital, and TC is total capital. In this model, both NOPAT and TC are determined under generally accepted accounting principles and adjusted for a number of items. Some of the more common adjustments include the following:

- Research and development (R&D) expenses are capitalized and amortized rather than expensed (i.e., R&D expense, net of estimated amortization, is added back to earnings to compute NOPAT).
- In the case of strategic investments that are not expected to generate an immediate return, a charge for capital is suspended until a later date.
- Deferred taxes are eliminated such that only cash taxes are treated as an expense.
- Any inventory LIFO (last in, first out) reserve is added back to capital, and any increase in the LIFO reserve is added in when calculating NOPAT.
- Operating leases are treated as capital leases, and non-recurring items are adjusted.

Because of the adjustments made in calculating EVA, a different numerical result will be obtained, in general, than that resulting from the use of the simple computation presented in Example 1. In practice, general (nonbranded) residual income valuation also considers the effect of accounting methods on reported results. Analysts' adjustments to reported accounting results in estimating residual income, however, will generally reflect some differences from the set specified for EVA. A later section will explore accounting considerations in more detail.

Over time, a company must generate economic profit for its market value to increase. A concept related to economic profit (and EVA) is market value added (MVA):

$$\begin{aligned} \text{MVA} = &\ \text{Market value of the company} \\ &- \text{Accounting book value of total capital} \end{aligned} \tag{2}$$

A company that generates positive economic profit should have a market value in excess of the accounting book value of its capital.

Research on the ability of value-added concepts to explain equity value and stock returns has reached mixed conclusions. Peterson and Peterson (1996) found that value-added measures are slightly more highly correlated with stock returns than traditional measures, such as return on assets and return on equity. Bernstein and Pigler (1997) and Bernstein, Bayer, and Pigler (1998) found that value-added measures are no better at predicting stock performance than are such measures as earnings growth.

A variety of commercial models related to the residual income concept have been marketed by other major accounting and consulting firms. Interestingly, the application focus of these models is not, in general, equity valuation. Rather, these implementations of the residual income concept are marketed primarily for measuring internal corporate performance and determining executive compensation.

THE RESIDUAL INCOME MODEL

2

- ☐ calculate the intrinsic value of a common stock using the residual income model and compare value recognition in residual income and other present value models
- ☐ explain fundamental determinants of residual income
- ☐ explain the relation between residual income valuation and the justified price-to-book ratio based on forecasted fundamentals

In the previous section, we discussed the concept of residual income and briefly introduced the relationship of residual income to equity value. In the long term, companies that earn more than the cost of capital should sell for more than book value, and companies that earn less than the cost of capital should sell for less than book value. The **residual income model** of valuation analyzes the intrinsic value of equity as the sum of two components:

- the current book value of equity, and
- the present value of expected future residual income.

Note that when the change is made from valuing total shareholders' equity to directly valuing an individual common share, earnings per share rather than net income is used. According to the residual income model, the intrinsic value of common stock can be expressed as follows:

$$V_0 = B_0 + \sum_{t=1}^{\infty} \frac{\mathrm{RI}_t}{(1+r)^t} = B_0 + \sum_{t=1}^{\infty} \frac{E_t - rB_{t-1}}{(1+r)^t} \quad (3)$$

where

V_0 = value of a share of stock today (t = 0)

B_0 = current per-share book value of equity

B_t = expected per-share book value of equity at any time t

r = required rate of return on equity investment (cost of equity)

E_t = expected EPS for period t

RI_t = expected per-share residual income, equal to $E_t - rB_{t-1}$

The per-share residual income in period t, RI_t, is the EPS for the period, E_t, minus the per-share equity charge for the period, which is the required rate of return on equity multiplied by the book value per share at the beginning of the period, or rB_{t-1}. Whenever earnings per share exceed the per-share cost of equity, per-share residual income is positive; and whenever earnings are less, per-share residual income is negative. Example 2 illustrates the calculation of per-share residual income.

EXAMPLE 2

Per-Share Residual Income Forecasts

1. David Smith is evaluating the expected residual income as of the end of January 2019 of the Canadian Railway Company (CNR). Using an adjusted beta of 1.02 relative to the TSX 300 Index, a 10-year government bond yield of

1.75%, and an estimated equity risk premium of 7.5%, Smith uses the capital asset pricing model (CAPM) to estimate CNR's required rate of return, *r*, at 9.40% [1.75% + (1.02 × 7.5%)]. Smith obtains the following (in Canadian dollars, CAD) as of the close on 1 February 2019:

Current market price	109.12
Book value per share as of 31 December 2018	24.32
Consensus annual earnings estimates	
FY 2019 (ending December)	6.23
FY 2020	6.96
Annualized dividend per share forecast	
FY 2019	2.15
FY 2020	2.32

What is the forecast residual income for fiscal years ended December 2019 and December 2020?

Solution:

Forecasted residual income and calculations are shown in Exhibit 1.

Exhibit 1: Canadian National Railway Company (all data in CAD)

Year	2019		2020	
Forecasting book value per share				
Beginning book value (B_{t-1})		24.32		28.40
Earnings per share forecast (E_t)	6.23		6.96	
Less dividend forecast (D_t)	2.15		2.31	
Add Change in retained earnings ($E_t - D_t$)		4.08		4.65
Forecast ending book value per share ($B_{t-1} + E_t - D_t$)		28.40		33.05
Calculating the equity charge				
Beginning book value per share	24.32		28.40	
Multiply cost of equity	× 0.094		× 0.094	
Per-share equity charge ($r \times B_{t-1}$)		2.29		2.67
Estimating per share residual income				
EPS forecast	6.23		6.96	
Less equity charge	2.29		2.67	
Per-share residual income		3.94		4.29

The use of Equation 3, the expression for the estimated intrinsic value of common stock, is illustrated in Example 3.

EXAMPLE 3

Using the Residual Income Model (1)

Bugg Properties' expected EPS is \$2.00, \$2.50, and \$4.00 for the next three years. Analysts expect that Bugg will pay dividends of \$1.00, \$1.25, and \$12.25 for the three years. The last dividend is anticipated to be a liquidating dividend; analysts expect Bugg will cease operations after Year 3. Bugg's current book value is \$6.00 per share, and its required rate of return on equity is 10%.

1. Calculate per-share book value and residual income for the next three years.

Solution:

The book value and residual income for the next three years are shown in Exhibit 2.

Exhibit 2

Year	1	2	3
Beginning book value per share (B_{t-1})	\$6.00	\$7.00	\$8.25
Net income per share (EPS)	2.00	2.50	4.00
Less dividends per share (D)	1.00	1.25	12.25
Change in retained earnings ($EPS - D$)	1.00	1.25	−8.25
Ending book value per share (B_{t-1} + EPS − D)	\$7.00	\$8.25	\$0.00
Net income per share (EPS)	2.00	2.50	4.000
Less per-share equity charge (rB_{t-1})	0.60	0.70	0.825
Residual income (EPS − Equity charge)	\$1.40	\$1.80	\$3.175

2. Estimate the stock's value using the residual income model given in Equation 3

$$V_0 = B_0 + \sum_{t=1}^{\infty} \frac{E_t - rB_{t-1}}{(1+r)^t}$$

Solution:

The value using the residual income model is

$$V_0 = 6.00 + \frac{1.40}{(1.10)} + \frac{1.80}{(1.10)^2} + \frac{3.175}{(1.10)^3}$$
$$= 6.00 + 1.2727 + 1.4876 + 2.3854$$
$$= \$11.15$$

3. Confirm your valuation estimate in Part 2 using the discounted dividend approach (i.e., estimating the value of a share as the present value of expected future dividends).

Solution:

The value using a discounted dividend approach is

$$V_0 = \frac{1.00}{(1.10)} + \frac{1.25}{(1.10)^2} + \frac{12.25}{(1.10)^3}$$
$$= 0.9091 + 1.0331 + 9.2036$$
$$= \$11.15$$

Example 3 illustrates two important points about residual income models. First, the RI model is fundamentally similar to other valuation models, such as the dividend discount model (DDM), and given consistent assumptions will yield equivalent results. Second, recognition of value typically occurs earlier in RI models than in the DDM. In Example 3, the RI model attributes \$6.00 of the \$11.15 total value to the beginning of the *first* period. In contrast, the DDM attributes \$9.2036 of the \$11.15 total value to the present value of the *final* period. The rest of this section develops the most familiar general expression for the RI model and illustrates the model's application.

The General Residual Income Model

The residual income model has a clear relationship to other valuation models, such as the DDM. In fact, the residual income model given in Equation 3 can be derived from the DDM. The general expression for the DDM is

$$V_0 = \frac{D_1}{(1+r)^1} + \frac{D_2}{(1+r)^2} + \frac{D_3}{(1+r)^3} + \ldots$$

The **clean surplus relation** states the relationship among earnings, dividends, and book value as follows:

$$B_t = B_{t-1} + E_t - D_t$$

In other words, the ending book value of equity equals the beginning book value plus earnings minus dividends, apart from ownership transactions. The condition that income (earnings) reflects all changes in the book value of equity other than ownership transactions is known as clean surplus accounting. By rearranging the clean surplus relation, the dividend for each period can be viewed as the net income minus the earnings retained for the period, or net income minus the increase in book value:

$$D_t = E_t - (B_t - B_{t-1}) = E_t + B_{t-1} - B_t$$

Substituting $E_t + B_{t-1} - B_t$ for D_t in the expression for V_0 results in:

$$V_0 = \frac{E_1 + B_0 - B_1}{(1+r)^1} + \frac{E_2 + B_1 - B_2}{(1+r)^2} + \frac{E_3 + B_2 - B_3}{(1+r)^3} + \ldots$$

This equation can be rewritten as follows:

$$V_0 = B_0 + \frac{E_1 - rB_0}{(1+r)^1} + \frac{E_2 - rB_1}{(1+r)^2} + \frac{E_3 - rB_2}{(1+r)^3} + \ldots$$

Expressed with summation notation, the following equation restates the residual income model given in Equation 3:

$$V_0 = B_0 + \sum_{t=1}^{\infty} \frac{\text{RI}_t}{(1+r)^t} = B_0 + \sum_{t=1}^{\infty} \frac{E_t - rB_{t-1}}{(1+r)^t}$$

According to the expression, the value of a stock equals its book value per share plus the present value of expected future per-share residual income. Note that when the present value of expected future per-share residual income is positive (negative), intrinsic value, V_0, is greater (smaller) than book value per share, B_0.

The residual income model used in practice today has its origins largely in the academic work of Ohlson (1995) and Feltham and Ohlson (1995) along with the earlier work of Edwards and Bell (1961), although in the United States this method has been used to value small businesses in tax cases since the 1920s. In tax valuation, the approach is known as the **excess earnings method** (Hitchner 2017 and US IRS Revenue Ruling 68-609). The general expression for the residual income model based on this work (Hirst and Hopkins 2000) can also be stated as:

$$V_0 = B_0 + \sum_{t=1}^{\infty} \frac{(\text{ROE}_t - r)B_{t-1}}{(1+r)^t} \quad (4)$$

Equation 4 is equivalent to the expressions for V_0 given earlier because in any year, t, $RI_t = (ROE_t - r)B_{t-1}$. Other than the required rate of return on common stock, the inputs to the residual income model come from accounting data. Note that return on equity (ROE) in this context uses beginning book value of equity in the denominator, whereas in financial statement analysis ROE is frequently calculated using the average book value of equity in the denominator. Example 4 illustrates the estimation of value using Equation 4.

EXAMPLE 4

Using the Residual Income Model (2)

1. To recap the data from Example 3, Bugg Properties has expected earnings per share of \$2.00, \$2.50, and \$4.00 and expected dividends per share of \$1.00, \$1.25, and \$12.25 for the next three years. Analysts expect that the last dividend will be a liquidating dividend and that Bugg will cease operating after Year 3. Bugg's current book value per share is \$6.00, and its estimated required rate of return on equity is 10%.

   Using this data, estimate the value of Bugg Properties' stock using a residual income model of the form:

$$V_0 = B_0 + \sum_{t=1}^{\infty} \frac{(\text{ROE}_t - r)\, B_{t-1}}{(1+r)^t}$$

Solution:

To value the stock, forecast residual income. Exhibit 3 illustrates the calculation of residual income. (Note that Exhibit 3 arrives at the same estimates of residual income as Exhibit 2 in Example 3.)

Exhibit 3

Year	1	2	3
Earnings per share	\$2.00	\$2.50	\$4.00
Divided by beginning book value per share	÷ 6.00	÷ 7.00	÷ 8.25
ROE	0.3333	0.3571	0.4848
Less required rate of return on equity	– 0.1000	– 0.1000	– 0.1000
Abnormal rate of return (ROE – r)	0.2333	0.2571	0.3848
Multiply by beginning book value per share	× 6.00	× 7.00	× 8.25
Residual income (ROE – r) × Beginning BV	\$1.400	\$1.800	\$3.175

Estimate the stock value as follows:

$$V_0 = 6.00 + \frac{1.40}{(1.10)} + \frac{1.80}{(1.10)^2} + \frac{3.175}{(1.10)^3}$$
$$= 6.00 + 1.2727 + 1.4876 + 2.3854$$
$$= \$11.15$$

Note that the value is identical to the estimate obtained using Equation 3, as illustrated in Example 3, because the assumptions are the same and Equation 3 andEquation 4 are equivalent expressions:

$$V_0 = \underset{\text{Equation 3}}{B_0 + \sum_{t=1}^{\infty} \frac{E_t - rB_{t-1}}{(1+r)^t}} = \underset{\text{Equation 4}}{B_0 + \sum_{t=1}^{\infty} \frac{(ROE_t - r)B_{t-1}}{(1+r)^t}}$$

Example 4 showed that residual income value can be estimated using current book value, forecasts of earnings, forecasts of book value, and an estimate of the required rate of return on equity. The forecasts of earnings and book value translate into ROE forecasts.

EXAMPLE 5

Valuing a Company Using the General Residual Income Model

1. Robert Sumargo, an equity analyst, is considering the valuation of Alphabet Inc. Class C shares (GOOG), in mid 2019 when a recent closing price is \$1,037.39. (Alphabet Inc. is the parent company of Google.) Sumargo notes that in general, Alphabet had a fairly high ROE during the past 10 years and that consensus analyst forecasts for EPS for the next two fiscal years reflect a fairly high expected ROE percentage. He expects that a high ROE may not be sustainable in the future. Sumargo usually takes a present value approach to valuation. As of the date of the valuation, Alphabet does not pay dividends; although a discounted dividend valuation is possible, Sumargo does not feel confident about predicting the date of a dividend initiation. He decides to apply the residual income model to value Alphabet and uses the following data and assumptions:

   - According to the CAPM, Alphabet has a required rate of return of approximately 8.2%.
   - Alphabet's book value per share on 31 December 2018 was \$255.40.
   - ROE is expected to be 20.2% for 2019. Because of competitive pressures, Sumargo expects Google's ROE to decline in the following years and incorporates an assumed decline of 0.5% each year until it reaches the CAPM required rate of return. In 2043, the ROE will be 8.2%, and residual income that year and after will be zero.
   - Google does not currently pay a dividend. Sumargo does not expect the company to pay a dividend in the foreseeable future, so all earnings will be reinvested. In addition, Sumargo expects that share repurchases will approximately offset new share issuances.

   Compute the value of Google using the residual income model (Equation 4).

Solution:

Book value per share is initially \$255.40. Based on a ROE forecast of 20.2% in the first year, the forecast EPS would be \$51.59. Because no dividends are paid and the clean surplus relation is assumed to hold, book value at the end of the period is forecast to be \$306.99 (\$255.40 + \$51.59). For 2019, residual income is measured as projected EPS of \$51.59 minus an equity charge of \$20.94, or \$30.65. This amount is equivalent to the beginning book value per share of \$255.40 multiplied by the difference between ROE of 20.2% and r of 8.2% [i.e., \$255.40 × (0.20.2 – 0.082) = \$30.65]. The present value of \$30.65 at 8.2% for one year is \$28.33. This process is continued year by year as presented in Exhibit 4. The value of Alphabet using this residual income model would be the present value of each year's residual income plus the current book value per share. Because residual income is zero starting in 2043, no forecast is required beyond that period. The estimated value under this model is $972.25, as shown in Exhibit 4.

Exhibit 4: Valuation of Alphabet Using the Residual Income Model

Year	Projected Income EPS	Projected Dividend per Share	Book Value per Share	Forecast ROE (Based on Beginning Book Value)	Cost of Equity	Equity Charge	Residual Income (RI)	PV of BV and RI
	[Plus]	[Minus]	255.40					255.40
2019	$51.59	$0.00	$306.99	20.20%	8.20%	$20.94	$30.65	28.33
2020	60.48	0.00	367.47	19.70%	8.20%	25.17	35.30	30.16
2021	70.55	0.00	438.02	19.20%	8.20%	30.13	40.42	31.91
2022	81.91	0.00	519.93	18.70%	8.20%	35.92	45.99	33.56
2023	94.63	0.00	614.56	18.20%	8.20%	42.63	51.99	35.06
2024	108.78	0.00	723.34	17.70%	8.20%	50.39	58.38	36.39
2025	124.41	0.00	847.75	17.20%	8.20%	59.31	65.10	37.50
2026	141.57	0.00	989.32	16.70%	8.20%	69.52	72.06	38.36
2027	160.27	0.00	1,149.60	16.20%	8.20%	81.12	79.15	38.94
2028	180.49	0.00	1,330.08	15.70%	8.20%	94.27	86.22	39.20
2029	202.17	0.00	1,532.25	15.20%	8.20%	109.07	93.11	39.13
2030	225.24	0.00	1,757.50	14.70%	8.20%	125.64	99.60	38.68
2031	249.56	0.00	2,007.06	14.20%	8.20%	144.11	105.45	37.85
2032	274.97	0.00	2,282.03	13.70%	8.20%	164.58	110.39	36.62
2033	301.23	0.00	2,583.25	13.20%	8.20%	187.13	114.10	34.99
2034	328.07	0.00	2,911.33	12.70%	8.20%	211.83	116.25	32.94
2035	355.18	0.00	3,266.51	12.20%	8.20%	238.73	116.45	30.50
2036	382.18	0.00	3,648.69	11.70%	8.20%	267.85	114.33	27.67
2037	408.65	0.00	4,057.35	11.20%	8.20%	299.19	109.46	24.49
2038	434.14	0.00	4,491.48	10.70%	8.20%	332.70	101.43	20.97
2039	458.13	0.00	4,949.61	10.20%	8.20%	368.30	89.83	17.17
2040	480.11	0.00	5,429.73	9.70%	8.20%	405.87	74.24	13.11
2041	499.53	0.00	5,929.26	9.20%	8.20%	445.24	54.30	8.86
2042	515.85	0.00	6,445.11	8.70%	8.20%	486.20	29.65	4.47
Total								972.25

Note: PV is present value and BV is book value. This table was created in Excel, so numbers may differ from what will be obtained using a calculator, because of rounding.

Example 5 refers to the assumption of clean surplus accounting. The residual income model, as stated earlier, assumes clean surplus accounting. The clean surplus accounting assumption is illustrated in Exhibit 4, for example, in which ending book value per share is computed as beginning book value plus net income minus dividends. Under International Financial Reporting Standards (IFRS) and US generally accepted accounting principles (US GAAP), several items of income and expense occurring during a period, such as changes in the market value of certain securities, bypass the income statement and affect a company's book value of equity directly. Items that bypass the income statement (dirty surplus items) are referred to as **other comprehensive income** (the relationship is Comprehensive income = Net income + Other comprehensive income). Strictly speaking, residual income models involve all items of income and expense (income under clean surplus accounting). If an analyst can reliably estimate material differences from clean surplus accounting expected in the future, an adjustment to net income may be appropriate. We explore violations of the clean surplus accounting assumption in more detail later.

Fundamental Determinants of Residual Income

In general, the residual income model makes no assumptions about future earnings and dividend growth. If constant earnings and dividend growth are assumed, a version of the residual income model that usefully illustrates the fundamental drivers of residual income can be derived. The following expression is used for justified P/B based on forecasted fundamentals, assuming the Gordon (constant growth) DDM and the sustainable growth rate equation, $g = b \times \text{ROE}$:

$$\frac{P_0}{B_0} = \frac{\text{ROE} - g}{r - g},$$

which is mathematically equivalent to

$$\frac{P_0}{B_0} = 1 + \frac{\text{ROE} - r}{r - g}.$$

The justified price is the stock's intrinsic value ($P_0 = V_0$). Therefore, using the previous equation and remembering that residual income is earnings less the cost of equity, or ($\text{ROE} \times B_0$) – ($r \times B_0$), a stock's intrinsic value under the residual income model, assuming constant growth, can be expressed as:

$$V_0 = B_0 + \frac{\text{ROE} - r}{r - g} B_0 \tag{5}$$

Under this model, the estimated value of a share is the book value per share (B_0) plus the present value [$(\text{ROE} - r)B_0/(r - g)$] of the expected stream of residual income. In the case of a company for which ROE exactly equals the cost of equity, the intrinsic value is equal to the book value per share. Equation 5 is considered a single-stage (or constant-growth) residual income model.

In an idealized world, where the book value of equity represents the fair value of net assets and clean surplus accounting prevails, the term B_0 reflects the value of assets owned by the company less its liabilities. The second term, $(\text{ROE} - r)B_0/(r - g)$, represents additional value expected because of the company's ability to generate returns in excess of its cost of equity; the second term is the present value of the company's expected economic profits. However, both IFRS and US GAAP allow companies to exclude some liabilities from their balance sheets, and neither set of rules reflects the fair value of many corporate assets. Internationally, however, a move toward fair value accounting is occurring, particularly for financial assets. Further, controversies, such as the failure of Enron Corporation in the United States, have highlighted the importance of identifying off-balance-sheet financing techniques.

The residual income model is most closely related to the P/B. A stock's justified P/B is directly related to expected future residual income. Another closely related concept is **Tobin's *q***, the ratio of the market value of debt and equity to the replacement cost of total assets:

$$\text{Tobin's } q = \frac{\text{Market value of debt and equity}}{\text{Replacement cost of total assets}}$$

Although similar to P/B, Tobin's q also has some obvious differences. The numerator includes the market value of total capital (debt as well as equity). The denominator uses total assets rather than equity. Further, assets are valued at replacement cost rather than at historical accounting cost; replacement costs take into account the effects of inflation. All else equal, Tobin's q is expected to be higher the greater the productivity of a company's assets (note that Tobin theorized that q would average to 1 for all companies because the economic rents or profits earned by assets would average to zero). One difficulty in computing Tobin's q is the lack of information on the replacement cost of assets. If available, market values of assets or replacement costs can be more useful in a valuation than historical costs.

SINGLE-STAGE AND MULTISTAGE RESIDUAL INCOME VALUATION 3

- ☐ calculate and interpret the intrinsic value of a common stock using single-stage (constant-growth) and multistage residual income models
- ☐ calculate the implied growth rate in residual income, given the market price-to-book ratio and an estimate of the required rate of return on equity
- ☐ explain continuing residual income and justify an estimate of continuing residual income at the forecast horizon, given company and industry prospects
- ☐ compare residual income models to dividend discount and free cash flow models
- ☐ explain strengths and weaknesses of residual income models and justify the selection of a residual income model to value a company's common stock

The single-stage (constant-growth) residual income model assumes that a company has a constant return on equity and constant earnings growth rate through time. This model was given in Equation 5:

$$V_0 = B_0 + \frac{\text{ROE} - r}{r - g} B_0$$

EXAMPLE 6

Single-Stage Residual Income Model (1)

1. Joseph Yoh is evaluating a purchase of Koninklijke Philips N.V. Current book value per share is €13.22, and the current price per share is €35.40. Yoh expects the long-term ROE to be 12% and long-term growth to be 6.75%. Assuming a cost of equity of 8.5%, what is the intrinsic value of Canon stock calculated using a single-stage residual income model?

Solution:

Using Equation 5:

$$V_0 = 13.22 + \frac{0.12 - 0.085}{0.085 - 0.675} \times 13.22$$
$$V_0 = €39.66$$

Similar to the Gordon growth DDM, the single-stage RI model can be used to assess the market expectations of residual income growth—that is, an implied growth rate—by inputting the current price into the model and solving for g.

EXAMPLE 7

Single-Stage Residual Income Model (2)

Joseph Yoh is curious about the market-perceived growth rate, given that he is comfortable with his other inputs. By using the current price per share of €35.40 for Philips, Yoh solves the following equation for g:

$$35.40 = 13.22 + \frac{0.12 - 0.085}{0.085 - g} \times 13.22$$

He finds an implied growth rate of 6.41%.

In Example 6 and Example 7, the company was valued at almost 2.7× its book value because its ROE exceeded its cost of equity. If ROE was equal to the cost of equity, the company would be valued at book value. If ROE was lower than the cost of equity, the company would have negative residual income and be valued at less than book value. (When a company has no prospect of being able to cover its cost of capital, a liquidation of the company and redeployment of assets may be appropriate.)

In many applications, a drawback to the single-stage model is that it assumes the excess ROE above the cost of equity will persist indefinitely. More likely, a company's ROE will revert to a mean value of ROE over time, and at some point, the company's residual income will be zero. If a company or industry has an abnormally high ROE, other companies will enter the marketplace, thus increasing competition and lowering returns for all companies. Similarly, if an industry has a low ROE, companies will exit the industry (through bankruptcy or otherwise) and ROE will tend to rise over time. As with the single-stage DDM, the single-stage residual income model also assumes a constant growth rate through time. In light of these considerations, the residual income model has been adapted in practice to handle declining residual income. For example, Lee and Swaminathan (1999) and Lee, Myers, and Swaminathan (1999) used a residual income model to value the Dow 30 by assuming that ROE fades (reverts) to the industry mean over time. Lee and Swaminathan found that the residual income model had more ability than traditional price multiples to predict future returns. Fortunately, other models are available that enable analysts to relax the assumption of indefinite persistence of excess returns. The following section describes a multistage residual income model.

Multistage Residual Income Valuation

As with other valuation approaches, such as DDM and free cash flow, a multistage residual income approach can be used to forecast residual income for a certain time horizon and then estimate a terminal value based on continuing residual income at the end of that time horizon. **Continuing residual income** is residual income after the forecast horizon. As with other valuation models, the forecast horizon for the initial stage should be based on the ability to explicitly forecast inputs in the model. Because ROE has been found to revert to mean levels over time and may decline to the cost of equity in a competitive environment, residual income approaches often model ROE fading toward the cost of equity. As ROE approaches the cost of equity, residual income approaches zero. An ROE equal to the cost of equity would result in residual income of zero.

In residual income valuation, the current book value often captures a large portion of total value and the terminal value may not be a large component of total value because book value is larger than the periodic residual income and because ROE may fade over time toward the cost of equity. This contrasts with other multistage approaches (DDM and DCF), in which the present value of the terminal value is frequently a significant portion of total value.

Analysts make a variety of assumptions concerning continuing residual income. Frequently, one of the following assumptions is made:

- residual income continues indefinitely at a positive level;
- residual income is zero from the terminal year forward;
- residual income declines to zero as ROE reverts to the cost of equity through time; or
- residual income reflects the reversion of ROE to some mean level.

The following examples illustrate several of these assumptions.

One finite-horizon model of residual income valuation assumes that at the end of time horizon T, a certain premium over book value ($P_T - B_T$) exists for the company, in which case, current value equals the following (Bauman, 1999):

$$V_0 = B_0 + \sum_{t=1}^{T} \frac{(E_t - rB_{t-1})}{(1+r)^t} + \frac{P_T - B_T}{(1+r)^T} \quad (6)$$

Alternatively,

$$V_0 = B_0 + \sum_{t=1}^{T} \frac{(\text{ROE}_t - r)B_{t-1}}{(1+r)^t} + \frac{P_T - B_T}{(1+r)^T} \quad (7)$$

The last component in both specifications represents the premium over book value at the end of the forecast horizon. The longer the forecast period, the greater the chance that the company's residual income will converge to zero. For long forecast periods, this last term may be treated as zero. For shorter forecast periods, a forecast of the premium should be calculated.

EXAMPLE 8

Multistage Residual Income Model (1)

Diana Rosato, CFA, is considering an investment in Zenlandia Chemical Company, a fictitious manufacturer of specialty chemicals. Rosato obtained the following facts and estimates as of August 2020:

- Current price equals ZL$95.6.
- Cost of equity equals 12%.
- Zenlandia Chemical's ROE has ranged from 18% to 22.9% during the period 2015–2019. The only time ROE was below 20% during that period was in 2016.
- In 2019, the company paid a cash dividend of ZL$2.9995.
- Book value per share was ZL$28.8517 at the end of 2019.
- Rosato's forecasts of EPS are ZL$7.162 for 2020 and ZL$8.356 for 2021. She expects dividends of ZL$2.9995 for 2020 and ZL$3.2995 for 2021.

- Rosato expects Zenlandia Chemical's ROE to be 25% from 2022 through 2026 and then decline to 20% through 2039.
- For the period after 2021, Rosato assumes an earnings retention ratio of 60%.
- Rosato assumes that after 2039, ROE will be 12% and residual income will be zero; therefore, the terminal value would be zero. Rosato's residual income model is shown in Exhibit 5.

Exhibit 5: Zenlandia Chemical

Year	Book Value (ZL$)	Projected Income (ZL$)	Dividend per Share (ZL$)	Forecasted ROE (Beg. Equity, %)	COE (%)	COE (ZL$)	Residual Income (ZL$)	Present Value of Residual Income (ZL$)
2019	28.8517							28.85
2020	33.0142	7.1620	2.9995	24.82	12.00	3.4622	3.6998	3.30
2021	38.0707	8.3560	3.2995	25.31	12.00	3.9617	4.3943	3.50
2022	43.7813	9.5177	3.8071	25.00	12.00	4.5685	4.9492	3.52
2023	50.3485	10.9453	4.3781	25.00	12.00	5.2538	5.6916	3.62
2024	57.9008	12.5871	5.0349	25.00	12.00	6.0418	6.5453	3.71
2025	66.5859	14.4752	5.7901	25.00	12.00	6.9481	7.5271	3.81
2026	76.5738	16.6465	6.6586	25.00	12.00	7.9903	8.6562	3.92
2027	85.7626	15.3148	6.1259	20.00	12.00	9.1889	6.1259	2.47
2028	96.0541	17.1525	6.8610	20.00	12.00	10.2915	6.8610	2.47
2029	107.5806	19.2108	7.6843	20.00	12.00	11.5265	7.6843	2.47
2030	120.4903	21.5161	8.6065	20.00	12.00	12.9097	8.6065	2.47
2031	134.9492	24.0981	9.6392	20.00	12.00	14.4588	9.6392	2.47
2032	151.1431	26.9898	10.7959	20.00	12.00	16.1939	10.7959	2.47
2033	169.2802	30.2286	12.0914	20.00	12.00	18.1372	12.0914	2.47
2034	189.5938	33.8560	13.5424	20.00	12.00	20.3136	13.5424	2.47
2035	212.3451	37.9188	15.1675	20.00	12.00	22.7513	15.1675	2.47
2036	237.8265	42.4690	16.9876	20.00	12.00	25.4814	16.9876	2.47
2037	266.3657	47.5653	19.0261	20.00	12.00	28.5392	19.0261	2.47
2038	298.3296	53.2731	21.3093	20.00	12.00	31.9639	21.3093	2.47
2039	334.1291	59.6659	23.8664	20.00	12.00	35.7996	23.8664	2.47
							Present value ZL$	86.41

Terminal Premium = 0.00

The market price of ZL$95.6 exceeds the estimated value of ZL$86.41. The market price reflects higher forecasts of residual income during the period to 2039, a higher terminal premium than Rosato forecasts, and/or a lower cost of equity. If Rosato is confident in her forecasts she may conclude that the company is overvalued in the current marketplace.

Lee and Swaminathan (1999) and Lee, Myers, and Swaminathan (1999) have presented a residual income model based on explicit forecasts of residual income for three years. Thereafter, ROE is forecast to fade to the industry mean value of ROE. The terminal value at the end of the forecast horizon (T) is estimated as the terminal-year residual income discounted in perpetuity. Lee and Swaminathan stated that this assumes any growth in earnings after T is value neutral. Exhibit 6 presents sector ROE data from CSIMarket. In forecasting a fading ROE, the analyst should also consider any trends in industry ROE.

Exhibit 6: US Sector ROEs

Sectors	ROE (%)
Basic Materials	11.14
Consumer Goods	19.96
Consumer Non-cyclicals	26.59
Energy	8.81
Financial	12.76
Healthcare	19.95
Industrial Goods	23.16
Retail	23.37
Technology	28.97
Transportation	21.49
Utilities	8.18

Source: Based on data from CSIMarket on 5 August 2019.

EXAMPLE 9

Multistage Residual Income Model (2)

Rosato's supervisor questions her assumption that Zenlandia Chemical will have no premium at the end of her forecast period. Rosato assesses the effect of a terminal value based on a perpetuity of Year 2039 residual income. She computes the following terminal value:

TV = ZL\$23.8664/0.12 = ZL\$198.8867

The present value of this terminal value is as follows:

PV = ZL\$198.8867/$(1.12)^{20}$ = ZL\$20.6179

Adding ZL\$20.6179 to the previous value of ZL\$86.41 (for which the terminal value was zero) yields a total value of ZL\$107.03. Because the current market price of ZL\$95.6 is less than ZL\$107.03, market participants expect a continuing residual income that is lower than her new assumptions and/or are forecasting a lower interim ROE. If Rosato agrees with her supervisor and is confident in her new forecasts, she may now conclude that the company is undervalued.

Another multistage model assumes that ROE fades over time to the cost of equity. In this approach, ROE can be explicitly forecast each period until reaching the cost of equity. The forecast would then end and the terminal value would be zero.

Dechow, Hutton, and Sloan (1999) presented an analysis of a residual income model in which residual income fades over time:

$$V_0 = B_0 + \sum_{t=1}^{T-1}\frac{(E_t - rB_{t-1})}{(1+r)^t} + \frac{E_T - rB_{T-1}}{(1+r-\omega)(1+r)^{T-1}} \quad (8)$$

This model adds a persistence factor, ω, which is between zero and one. A persistence factor of one implies that residual income will not fade at all; rather it will continue at the same level indefinitely (i.e., in perpetuity). A persistence factor of zero implies that residual income will not continue after the initial forecast horizon. The higher the value of the persistence factor, the higher the stream of residual income in the final stage, and the higher the valuation, all else being equal. Dechow et al. found that in a large sample of company data from 1976 to 1995, the persistence factor equaled 0.62, which was interpreted by Bauman (1999) as equivalent to residual income decaying at an average rate of 38% a year. The persistence factor considers the long-run mean-reverting nature of ROE, assuming that in time ROE regresses toward r and that resulting residual income fades toward zero. Clearly, the persistence factor varies from company to company. For example, a company with a strong market leadership position would have a lower expected rate of decay (Bauman 1999). Dechow et al. provided insight into some characteristics, listed in Exhibit 7, that can indicate a lower or higher level of persistence.

Exhibit 7: Final-Stage Residual Income Persistence

Lower Residual Income Persistence	Higher Residual Income Persistence
Extreme accounting rates of return (ROE)	Low dividend payout
Extreme levels of special items (e.g., non-recurring items)	High historical persistence in the industry
Extreme levels of accounting accruals	

Example 10 illustrates the assumption that continuing residual income will decline to zero as ROE approaches the required rate of return on equity.

EXAMPLE 10

Multistage Residual Income Model (3)

Rosato extends her analysis to consider the possibility that ROE will slowly decay toward r in 2040 and beyond, rather than using a perpetuity of Year 2037 residual income. Rosato estimates a persistence parameter of 0.60. The present value of the terminal value is determined as

$$\frac{E_T - rB_{T-1}}{(1 + r - \omega)(1 + r)^{T-1}},$$

with T equal to 20 and 2037 residual income equal to 23.8664, in which the 1.12 growth factor reflects a 12% growth rate calculated as the retention ratio multiplied by ROE, or (0.60)(20%) = 0.12.

$$\frac{23.8664}{(1 + 0.12 - 0.60)(1.12)^{19}} = 5.33$$

Total value is ZL$86.26, calculated by adding the present value of the terminal value, ZL$5.33, to ZL$83.93 (the sum of the PV of residual income in the first 19 years). Rosato concludes that if Zenlandia Chemical's residual income does not persist at a stable level past 2039 and deteriorates through time, the shares are modestly overvalued at a price of ZL$95.6.

In the previous example, the company's terminal residual value was estimated based on the residual income in the final year of stage 1 and on future growth or decay functions. As shown in Equations 6 and 7, the terminal residual value of the firm is

$P_T - B_T$, the terminal price minus the terminal book value. The terminal price could be based on any valuation model, such as a DDM, a price–earnings multiple, or a price–book multiple. Example 11 uses a two-stage residual income model in which the terminal price per share is based on a P/B.

EXAMPLE 11

Two-Stage Residual Income Model

Andreea Popescu is using the two-stage residual income model to value the shares of URS Holdings. For her analysis, she assumes the following:

- Beginning book value per share is €15.00.
- Cost of equity equals 7.95%.
- EPS will be 25% of beginning book value for the next six years.
- Cash dividends will be 30% of EPS each year.
- At the end of six years, market price per share will be 1.80× book value per share.

1. Calculate per-share book value and residual income for the next three years.

Solution:

Exhibit 8 shows the book values, net income, dividends, and residual income.

Exhibit 8: Residual Income for URS Holdings

Year	Beginning Book Value	Net Income	Dividends	Ending Book Value	Residual Income	Present Value of Residual Income
1	15.000	3.750	1.125	17.625	2.558	2.369
2	17.625	4.406	1.322	20.709	3.005	2.579
3	20.709	5.177	1.553	24.334	3.531	2.807
4	24.334	6.083	1.825	28.592	4.149	3.055
5	28.592	7.148	2.144	33.595	4.875	3.325
6	33.595	8.399	2.520	39.475	5.728	3.620
			Sum of PV of Residual Income			17.755

Each year, net income is 25% of beginning book value, dividends are 30% of net income, ending book value is beginning book value plus net income minus dividends, and residual income is net income minus 7.95% of beginning book value.

2. Estimate the stock's value using the residual income model given in Equation 6:

$$V_0 = B_0 + \sum_{t=1}^{T} \frac{(E_t - rB_{t-1})}{(1+r)^t} + \frac{P_T - B_T}{(1+r)^T}$$

Solution:

In Exhibit 8, the present values of residual income are found by discounting at the 7.95% cost of equity. Using the logic in Equation 6, the value per share is:

Current book value per share		15.000
Present value of 6 years' residual income		17.755
Terminal value $[P_T - B_T = (1.8 \times B_T) - B_T]$	31.580	
Present value of terminal value (at 7.95%)		19.956
Value per share		€52.711

3. Confirm your valuation estimate in Part 2 using the discounted dividend approach (i.e., estimating the value of a share as the present value of expected future dividends and terminal price).

Solution:

The value using a discounted dividend approach is

$$V_0 = \sum_{t=1}^{T} \frac{D_t}{(1+r)^t} + \frac{P_T}{(1+r)^T}$$

Exhibit 9: DDM Valuation of URS Holdings

Year	Dividends	PV of Dividends
1	1.125	1.042
2	1.322	1.134
3	1.553	1.235
4	1.825	1.344
5	2.144	1.463
6	2.520	1.592
Sum of PVs of six years' dividends		7.810
Terminal price = $1.8 \times B_T$	71.054	
PV of terminal price (@7.95%)		44.901
Value per share using DDM		€52.711

4 RELATIONSHIP TO OTHER APPROACHES

- ☐ compare residual income models to dividend discount and free cash flow models
- ☐ explain strengths and weaknesses of residual income models and justify the selection of a residual income model to value a company's common stock

Before addressing accounting issues in using the residual income model, we briefly summarize the relationship of the residual income model to other valuation models.

Valuation models based on discounting dividends or on discounting free cash flows are as theoretically sound as the residual income model. Unlike the residual income model, however, the discounted dividend and free cash flow models forecast future cash flows and find the value of stock by discounting them back to the present using the required return. Recall that the required return is the cost of equity for both the DDM and the free cash flows to equity (FCFE) model. For the free cash flow to the firm (FCFF) model, the required return is the overall weighted average cost of capital. The RI model approaches this process differently. It starts with a value based on the balance sheet, the book value of equity, and adjusts this value by adding the present values of expected future residual income. Thus, in theory, the recognition of value is different, but the total present value, whether using expected dividends, expected free cash flow, or book value plus expected residual income, should be consistent (Shrieves and Wachowicz, 2001).

Example 12 again illustrates the important point that the recognition of value in residual income models typically occurs earlier than in dividend discount models. In other words, residual income models tend to assign a relatively small portion of a security's total present value to the earnings that occur in later years. Note also that this example makes use of the fact that the present value of a perpetuity in the amount of X can be calculated as X/r.

EXAMPLE 12

Valuing a Perpetuity with the Residual Income Model

Assume the following data:

- A company will earn \$1.00 per share forever.
- The company pays out all earnings as dividends.
- Book value per share is \$6.00.
- The required rate of return on equity (or the percent cost of equity) is 10%.

1. Calculate the value of this stock using the DDM.

Solution:

Because the dividend, D, is a perpetuity, the present value of D can be calculated as D/r.

$$V_0 = D/r = \$1.00/0.10 = \$10.00 \text{ per share}$$

2. Calculate the level amount of per-share residual income that will be earned each year.

Solution:

Because each year all net income is paid out as dividends, book value per share will be constant at \$6.00. Therefore, with a required rate of return on equity of 10%, for all future years, per-share residual income will be as follows:

$$\text{RI}_t = E_t - rB_{t-1} = \$1.00 - 0.10(\$6.00) = \$1.00 - \$0.60 = \$0.40$$

3. Calculate the value of the stock using a RI model.

Solution:

Using a residual income model, the estimated value equals the current book value per share plus the present value of future expected residual income (which in this example can be valued as a perpetuity):

V_0 = Book value + PV of expected future per-share residual income

= \$6.00 + \$0.40/0.10

= \$6.00 + \$4.00

= \$10.00

4. Create a table summarizing the year-by-year valuation using the DDM and the RI model.

Solution:

Exhibit 10 summarizes the year-by-year valuation using the DDM and the RI models.

Exhibit 10: Value Recognition in the DDM and the RI Model

Dividend Discount Model			Residual Income Model	
Year	D_t	PV of D_t	B_0 or RI_t	PV of B_0 or RI_t
0			\$6.00	\$6.000
1	\$1.00	\$0.909	0.40	0.364
2	1.00	0.826	0.40	0.331
3	1.00	0.751	0.40	0.301
4	1.00	0.683	0.40	0.273
5	1.00	0.621	0.40	0.248
6	1.00	0.564	0.40	0.226
7	1.00	0.513	0.40	0.205
8	1.00	0.467	0.40	0.187
⋮	⋮	⋮	⋮	⋮
Total		\$10.00		\$10.00

In the RI model, most of the stock's total value is attributed to the earlier periods. Specifically, the current book value of \$6.00 represents 60% of the stock's total present value of \$10.

In contrast, in the DDM, value is derived from the receipt of dividends, and typically, a smaller proportion of value is attributed to the earlier periods. Less than \$1.00 of the total \$10 derives from the first year's dividend, and collectively, the first five years' dividends (\$0.909 + \$0.826 + \$0.751 + \$0.683 + \$0.621 = \$3.79) contribute only about 38% of the total present value of \$10.

As shown earlier and illustrated again in Example 11, the dividend discount and residual income models are in theory mutually consistent. Because of the real-world uncertainty in forecasting distant cash flows, however, the earlier recognition of value in a residual income approach relative to other present value approaches is a practical advantage. In the dividend discount and free cash flow models, a stock's value is often modeled as the sum of the present value of individually forecasted dividends or free cash flows up to some terminal point plus the present value of the expected terminal value of the stock. In practice, a large fraction of a stock's total present value, in either the discounted dividend or free cash flow models, is represented by the present value of the expected terminal value. Substantial uncertainty, however, often surrounds the terminal value. In contrast, residual income valuations typically are less sensitive to terminal value estimates. (In some residual income valuation contexts, the terminal value may actually be set equal to zero.) The derivation of value from the earlier portion of a forecast horizon is one reason residual income valuation can be a useful analytical tool.

Strengths and Weaknesses of the Residual Income Model

Now that the implementation of the residual income model has been illustrated with several examples, a summary of the strengths and weaknesses of the residual income approach follows:

The strengths of residual income models include the following:

- Terminal values do not make up a large portion of the total present value, relative to other models.
- RI models use readily available accounting data.
- The models can be readily applied to companies that do not pay dividends or to companies that do not have positive expected near-term free cash flows.
- The models can be used when cash flows are unpredictable.
- The models have an appealing focus on economic profitability.

The potential weaknesses of residual income models include the following:

- The models are based on accounting data that can be subject to manipulation by management.
- Accounting data used as inputs may require significant adjustments.
- The models require either that the clean surplus relation (explained later) holds or that the analyst makes appropriate adjustments when the clean surplus relation does not hold.
- The residual income model's use of accounting income assumes that the cost of debt capital is reflected appropriately by interest expense.

Broad Guidelines for Using a Residual Income Model

The above list of potential weaknesses helps explain the following section's focus on accounting considerations. In light of its strengths and weaknesses, the following are broad guidelines for using a residual income model in common stock valuation.

A residual income model is most appropriate when:

- a company does not pay dividends, or its dividends are not predictable;
- a company's expected free cash flows are negative within the analyst's comfortable forecast horizon; or
- great uncertainty exists in forecasting terminal values using an alternative present value approach.

Residual income models are least appropriate when:

- significant departures from clean surplus accounting exist, or
- significant determinants of residual income, such as book value and ROE, are not predictable.

Because various valuation models can be derived from the same underlying theoretical model, when fully consistent assumptions are used to forecast earnings, cash flow, dividends, book value, and residual income through a full set of pro forma (projected) financial statements, and the same required rate of return on equity is used as the discount rate, the same estimate of value should result when using each model. Practically speaking, however, it may not be possible to forecast each of these items with the same degree of certainty. For example, if a company has near-term negative free cash flow and forecasts for the terminal value are uncertain, a residual income model may be more appropriate. But a company with positive, predictable cash flow that does not pay a dividend would be well suited for a discounted free cash flow valuation (Penman and Sougiannis 1998; Penman 2001; Lundholm and O'Keefe 2001a; and Lundholm and O'Keefe 2001b).

Residual income models, just like the discounted dividend and free cash flow models, can also be used to establish justified market multiples, such as P/E or P/B. For example, the value can be determined by using a residual income model and dividing by earnings to arrive at a justified P/E.

A residual income model can also be used in conjunction with other models to assess the consistency of results. If a wide variation of estimated value is found and each model appears appropriate, the inconsistency may lie with the assumptions used in the models. The analyst would need to perform additional work to determine whether the assumptions are mutually consistent and which model is most appropriate for the subject company.

5 ACCOUNTING AND INTERNATIONAL CONSIDERATIONS

☐ describe accounting issues in applying residual income models

To most accurately apply the residual income model in practice, the analyst may need to adjust book value of common equity for off-balance-sheet items and adjust reported net income to obtain **comprehensive income** (all changes in equity other than contributions by, and distributions to, owners). In this section, we will discuss issues relating to these tasks.

Bauman (1999) has noted that the strength of the residual income model is that the two components (book value and future earnings) of the model have a balancing effect on each other, provided that the clean surplus relationship is followed:

> All other things held constant, companies making aggressive (conservative) accounting choices will report higher (lower) book values and lower (higher) future earnings. In the model, the present value of differences in future income is exactly offset by the initial differences in book value. (Bauman 1999, page 31)

Unfortunately, this argument has several problems in practice because the clean surplus relationship does not prevail, and analysts often use past earnings to predict future earnings. IFRS and US GAAP permit a variety of items to bypass the income statement and be reported directly in stockholders' equity. Further, off-balance-sheet liabilities or nonoperating and non-recurring items of income may obscure a company's financial performance. The analyst must thus be aware of such items when evaluating the book value of equity and return on equity to be used as inputs into a residual income model.

With regard to the possibility that aggressive accounting choices will lead to lower reported future earnings, consider an example in which a company chooses to capitalize an expenditure in the current year rather than expense it. Doing so overstates current-year earnings as well as current book value. If an analyst uses current earnings (or ROE) naively in predicting future residual earnings, the RI model will overestimate the company's value. Take, for example, a company with $1,000,000 of book value and $200,000 of earnings before taxes, after expensing an expenditure of $50,000. Ignoring taxes, this company has a ROE of 20%. If the company capitalized the expenditure rather than expensing it immediately, it would have a ROE of 23.81% ($250,000/$1,050,000). Although at some time in the future this capitalized item will likely be amortized or written off, thus reducing realized future earnings, analysts' expectations often rely on historical data. If capitalization of expenditures persists over time for a company whose size is stable, ROE can decline because net income will normalize over the long term, but book value will be overstated. For a growing company, for which the expenditure in question is increasing, ROE can continue at high levels over time. In practice, because the RI model uses primarily accounting data as inputs, the model can be sensitive to accounting choices, and aggressive accounting methods (e.g., accelerating revenues or deferring expenses) can result in valuation errors. The analyst must, therefore, be particularly careful in analyzing a company's reported data for use in a residual income model.

Two principal drivers of residual earnings are ROE and book value. Analysts must understand how to use historical reported accounting data for these items to the extent they use historical data in forecasting future ROE and book value. Elsewhere we have explained the DuPont analysis of ROE, which can be used as a tool in forecasting, and discussed the calculation of book value. We extend these discussions below with specific application to residual income valuation, particularly in addressing the following accounting considerations:

- violations of the clean surplus relationship;
- balance sheet adjustments for fair value;
- intangible assets;
- non-recurring items;
- aggressive accounting practices; and
- international considerations.

In any valuation, close attention must be paid to the accounting practices of the company being valued. The following sections address the aforementioned issues with respect to how they specifically affect residual income valuation.

Violations of the Clean Surplus Relationship

One potential accounting issue in applying a residual income model is a violation of the clean surplus accounting assumption. Violations of this assumption occur when accounting standards permit charges directly to stockholders' equity, bypassing the income statement. An example is the case of changes in the market value of "available-for-sale" investments under US GAAP and "equity instruments measured at fair value through other comprehensive income" under IFRS. Under both IFRS (IFRS 9 Financial Instruments, paragraph 5.7.5) and US GAAP (ASC 320-10-35-1), these categories of investments are shown on the balance sheet at market value. Any unrealized change in their market value, however, is reflected in other comprehensive income rather than as income on the income statement.

As stated earlier, comprehensive income is defined as all changes in equity during a period other than contributions by, and distributions to, owners. Comprehensive income includes net income reported on the income statement and *other comprehensive income*, which is the result of other events and transactions that result in a change to equity but are not reported on the income statement. Items that commonly bypass the income statement include

- unrealized changes in the fair value of some financial instruments, as already discussed;
- foreign currency translation adjustments;
- certain pension adjustments;
- a portion of gains and losses on certain hedging instruments;
- changes in revaluation surplus related to property, plant, and equipment or intangible assets (applicable under IFRS but not under US GAAP); and
- for certain categories of liabilities, a change in fair value attributable to changes in the liability's credit risk (applicable under IFRS but not under US GAAP).

Under both international and US standards, such items as fair value changes for some financial instruments and foreign currency translation adjustments bypass the income statement. In addition, under IFRS, which unlike US GAAP permits revaluation of fixed assets (IAS 16, paragraph 39–42), some changes in the fair value of fixed assets also bypass the income statement and directly affect equity.

In all of these cases in which items bypass the income statement, the book value of equity is stated accurately because it includes "accumulated other comprehensive income," but net income is not stated properly from the perspective of residual income valuation. The analyst should be most concerned with the effect of these items on forecasts of net income and ROE, which has net income in the numerator, and hence residual income. Note that for best results, historical ROE should be calculated at the aggregate level (e.g., as net income divided by shareholders' equity, rather than as earnings per share divided by book value per share), because such actions as share issuance and share repurchases can distort ROE calculated on a per-share basis. Because some items (including those listed earlier) bypass the income statement, they are excluded from historical ROE data. As noted by Frankel and Lee (1999), bias will be introduced into the valuation only if the present expected value of the clean surplus violations does not net to zero. In other words, reductions in income from some periods may be offset by increases from other periods. The analyst must examine the equity section of the balance sheet and the related statements of shareholders' equity and comprehensive income carefully for items that have bypassed the income statement. The analyst can then assess whether amounts are likely to be offsetting and can assess the effect on future ROE.

EXAMPLE 13

Evaluating Clean Surplus Violations

1. Excerpts from two companies' statements of changes in stockholders' equity are shown in Exhibit 11 and Exhibit 12. The first statement, prepared under IFRS as of 31 December 2018, is for Nokia Corporation, a provider of network equipment, software, and services to telecom network companies. The second statement, prepared under US GAAP as of 31 December 2018, is for SAP AG, which is headquartered in Germany and is a worldwide provider of enterprise application software, including enterprise resource planning, customer relationship management, and supply chain management software.

Exhibit 12: SAP AG and Subsidiaries Statement of Changes in Shareholders' Equity (€ millions)

	Equity Attributable to Owners of Parent							
	Issued Capital	Share Premium	Retained Earnings	Other Components of Equity	Treasury Shares	Total	Non-controlling interests	Total Equity
1 January 2018	1,229	570	24,987	347	−1,591	25,542	31	25,573
Profit after tax			4,083			4,083	6	4,088
Other comprehensive income			11	887		898		898
Comprehensive income			**4,093**	**887**	**0**	**4,980**	**6**	**4,986**
Share-based payments		−40				−40		−40
Dividends			−1,671			−1,671	−13	−1,684
Reissuance of treasury shares under share-based payments		13			11	24		24
Shares to be issued			7			7		7
Hyperinflation			−8			−8		−8
Changes in non-controlling interests						0	19	19
Other changes			−2			−2	3	1
12/31/2018	**1,229**	**543**	**27,407**	**1,234**	**−1,580**	**28,832**	**45**	**28,877**

Source: www.sap.com.

For Nokia, items that have bypassed the income statement in 2018 are those in the columns labeled "Share issue premium," "Translation differences," "Fair value and other reserves," and "Reserve for invested unrestricted equity." For SAP, the amounts that bypassed the income statement in 2018 are "Share premium" and "Other components of equity."

To illustrate the issues in interpreting these items, consider the columns "Translation differences" (Nokia) and "Other components of equity" (SAP). The amounts in these columns reflect currency translation adjustments to equity that have bypassed the income statement. For Nokia, the adjustment for the year 2018 was €341 million. Because this is a positive adjustment to stockholders' equity, this item would have increased income if it had been reported on the income statement. For SAP, the "Other components of eq-

Exhibit 11: Nokia Corporation Statement of Changes in Shareholders' Equity (€ millions except number of shares)

	Number of Shares Outstanding	Share Capital	Share Issue Premium	Treasury Shares	Translation Differences	Fair Value and Other Reserves	Reserve for Invested Unrestricted Equity	(Accumulated Deficit)/ Retained Earnings	Attributable to Equity Holders of the Parent	Non-controlling Interests	Total Equity
As of 1 January 2018	5,579,517	246	447	–1,480	–932	842	15,616	1,345	16,084	80	16,164
Re-measurements and defined benefit pension plans, net of tax						293			293		293
Translation differences					402				402		402
Net investment hedges, net of tax					–61	3			–58		–58
Cash flow hedges, net of tax						–43			–43		–43
Financial assets at fair value through other comprehensive income, net of tax						–38			–38		–38
Other increase, net						6			5	1	6
Loss for the year									–340	5	–335
Total comprehensive income for the year					**341**	**221**			**221**	**6**	**227**
Share-based payment			68						68		68

	Number of Shares Outstanding	Share Capital	Share Issue Premium	Treasury Shares	Translation Differences	Fair Value and Other Reserves	Reserve for Invested Unrestricted Equity	(Accumu-lated Deficit)/ Retained Earnings	Attributable to Equity Holders of the Parent	Non-con-trolling Interests	Total Equity
Excess tax benefit on share-based payment	13,221		6						6		6
Settlement of performance and restricted shares			–85	72			–11		–24		–24
Cancellation of treasury shares	424			1,000				–1,000			
Stock options exercised							1		1		1
Dividends								–1,063	–1,063	–5	–1,068
Acquisitions of non-controlling interests								–1	–1	1	0
Other movements					–1			–2	–3		–3
Total other equity movements		**0**	**–11**	**1,072**	**–1**	**0**	**–10**	**–2,066**	**–1,016**	**-4**	**-1020**
As of December 31, 2018	**5,593,162**	**246**	**436**	**–408**	**–592**	**1,063**	**15,606**	**–1,062**	**15,289**	**82**	**15371**

*Source:*www.nokia.com.

uity" adjustment (which includes translation adjustment for the year 2018) was €887 million. Again, because this is a positive adjustment to stockholders' equity, this item would have increased income if it had been reported on the income statement. If the analyst expects this trend of positive translation adjustments to continue and has used historical data as the basis for initial estimates of ROE to be used in residual income valuation, an upward adjustment in that estimated future ROE might be warranted. It is possible, however, that future exchange rate movements will reverse this trend.

The examples we have explored used the actual beginning equity and a forecasted level of ROE (return on beginning equity) to compute the forecasted net income. Because equity includes accumulated other comprehensive income (AOCI), the assumptions about future other comprehensive income (OCI) will affect forecasted net income and thus residual income. To illustrate, Exhibit 13 shows a hypothetical company's financials for a single previous year, labeled year $t - 1$, followed by three different forecasts for the following two years. In year $t - 1$, the company reports net income of \$120, which is a 12% return on beginning equity of \$1,000. The company paid no dividends, so ending retained earnings equal \$120. In year $t - 1$, the company also reports OCI of –\$100, a loss, so the ending amount shown in AOCI is –\$100. (Companies typically label this line item "accumulated other comprehensive income (loss)," indicating that the amount is an accumulated loss when given in parentheses.) All three forecasts in Exhibit 13 assume that ROE will be 12% and use this assumption to forecast net income for year t and $t + 1$ by using the expression 0.12 × Beginning book value. Each forecast, however, incorporates different assumptions about future OCI. Forecast A assumes that the company will have no OCI in year t or year $t + 1$, so the amount of AOCI does not change. Forecast B assumes that the company will continue to have the same amount of OCI in year t and year $t + 1$ as it had in the prior year, so the amount of AOCI becomes more negative each year. Forecast C assumes that the company's OCI will reverse in year t, so at the end of year t, AOCI will be zero. As shown, because the forecasts use the assumed ROE to compute forecasted net income, the forecasts for net income and residual income in year $t + 1$ vary significantly.

Because this example assumes all earnings are retained, a forecast of 12% ROE also implies that net income and residual income will grow at 12%. Only the year t to year $t + 1$ under Forecast A, which assumes no future OCI, correctly reflects that relationship. Specifically, in Forecast A, both net income and residual income increase by 12% from year t to year $t + 1$. Net income grows from \$122.40 to \$137.09, an increase of 12% [(\$137.09/\$122.40) – 1]; and residual income grows from \$20.40 to \$22.85, an increase of 12% [(\$22.85/\$20.40) – 1]. In contrast to Forecast A, neither Forecast B nor Forecast C correctly reflects the relationship between ROE and growth in income (net and residual). Growth in residual income from year t to year $t + 1$ was 2.2% under Forecast B and 21.8% under Forecast C.

If, alternatively, the forecasts of future ROE and the residual income computation had incorporated total comprehensive income (net income plus OCI), the results of the residual income computation would have differed significantly. For example, suppose that in Forecast B, which assumes the company will continue to have the same amount of OCI, the estimated future ROE was 2.0%, using total comprehensive income [(\$120 – \$100)/\$1,000 = \$20/\$1,000]. If the residual income computation had then also used forecasted total comprehensive income at time t, the amount of residual income would be negative. Specifically, for time t, forecast comprehensive income would be \$22.40 (net income plus other comprehensive income), the equity charge would be \$102 (required return of 10% multiplied by beginning equity of \$1,020), and residual income would be –\$79.60 (comprehensive income of \$22.40 minus equity charge of \$102). Clearly, residual income on this basis significantly falls short of the positive \$20.40 when the violation of clean surplus is ignored. As this example demonstrates,

Exhibit 13: Hypothetical Company Alternative Forecasts with Different Assumptions about Comprehensive Income

	Actual	Forecast A		Forecast B		Forecast C	
Year	**$t - 1$**	**t**	**$t + 1$**	**t**	**$t + 1$**	**t**	**$t + 1$**
Beginning Balance Sheet							
Assets	$1,000.00	$1,020.00	$1,142.40	$1,020.00	$1,042.40	$1,020.00	$1,242.40
Liabilities	—	—	—	—	—	—	—
Common stock	1,000.00	1,000.00	1,000.00	1,000.00	1,000.00	1,000.00	1,000.00
Retained earnings	—	120.00	242.40	120.00	242.40	120.00	242.40
AOCI	—	(100.00)	(100.00)	(100.00)	(200.00)	(100.00)	—
Total equity	1,000.00	1,020.00	1,142.40	1,020.00	1,042.40	1,020.00	1,242.40
Total liabilities and total equity	$1,000.00	$1,020.00	$1,142.40	$1,020.00	$1,042.40	$1,020.00	$1,242.40
Net income	120.00	122.40	137.09	122.40	125.09	122.40	149.09
Dividends	—	—	—	—	—	—	—
Other comprehensive income	(100.00)	—	—	(100.00)	(100.00)	100.00	—
Ending Balance Sheet							
Assets	$1,020.00	$1,142.40	$1,279.49	$1,042.40	$1,067.49	$1,242.40	$1,391.49
Liabilities	—	—	—	—	—	—	—
Common stock	1,000.00	1,000.00	1,000.00	1,000.00	1,000.00	1,000.00	1,000.00
Retained earnings	120.00	242.40	379.49	242.40	367.49	242.40	391.49
AOCI	(100.00)	(100.00)	(100.00)	(200.00)	(300.00)	—	—
Total equity	$1,020.00	$1,142.40	$1,279.49	$1,042.40	$1,067.49	$1,242.40	$1,391.49
Total liabilities and total equity	$1,020.00	$1,142.40	$1,279.49	$1,042.40	$1,067.49	$1,242.40	$1,391.49
Residual income calculation based on beginning total equity							
Net income	120.00	122.40	137.09	122.40	125.09	122.40	149.09
Equity charge at 10%	100.00	102.00	114.24	102.00	104.24	102.00	124.24
Residual income	$20.00	$20.40	$22.85	$20.40	$20.85	$20.40	$24.85

using an ROE forecast or a net income forecast that ignores violations of clean surplus accounting will distort estimates of residual income. Unless the present value of such distortions net to zero, using those forecasts will also distort valuations.

What are the implications for implementing a residual-income-based valuation? If future OCI is expected to be significant relative to net income and if the year-to-year amounts of OCI are not expected to net to zero, the analyst should attempt to incorporate these items so that residual income forecasts are closer to what they would be if the clean surplus relation held. Specifically, when possible, the analyst should incorporate explicit assumptions about future amounts of OCI.

Example 14 illustrates, by reference to the DDM value, the error that results when OCI is omitted from residual income calculations (assuming an analyst has a basis for forecasting future amounts of OCI). The example also shows that the growth rate in residual income generally does not equal the growth rate of net income or dividends.

EXAMPLE 14

Incorporating Adjustments in the Residual Income Model

Exhibit 14 gives per-share forecasts for Mannistore, Inc., a hypothetical company operating a chain of retail stores. The company's cost of equity capital is 10%.

Exhibit 14: Forecasts for Mannistore, Inc.

	Year				
Variable	**1**	**2**	**3**	**4**	**5**
Shareholders' equity$_{t-1}$	\$8.58	\$10.32	\$11.51	\$14.68	\$17.86
Plus net income	2.00	2.48	3.46	3.47	4.56
Less dividends	0.26	0.29	0.29	0.29	0.38
Less other comprehensive income	0.00	1.00	0.00	0.00	0.00
Equals shareholders' equity$_t$	\$10.32	\$11.51	\$14.68	\$17.86	\$22.04

1. Assuming the forecasted terminal price of Mannistore's shares at the end of Year 5 (time t = 5) is \$68.40, estimate the value per share of Mannistore using the DDM.

Solution:

The estimated value using the DDM is

$$V_0 = \frac{\$0.26}{(1.10)^1} + \frac{\$0.29}{(1.10)^2} + \frac{\$0.29}{(1.10)^3} + \frac{\$0.29}{(1.10)^4} + \frac{\$0.38}{(1.10)^5} + \frac{\$68.40}{(1.10)^5} = \$43.59$$

2. Given that the forecast terminal price of Mannistore's shares at the end of Year 5 (time t = 5) is \$68.40, estimate the value of a share of Mannistore using the RI model and calculate residual income based on:

   A. net income without adjustment, and

   B. net income plus other comprehensive income.

Solution:

A. Calculating residual income as net income (NI) minus the equity charge, which is beginning shareholders' equity (SE) multiplied by the cost of equity capital (r), gives the following for years 1 through 5:

	Year				
	1	**2**	**3**	**4**	**5**
$RI = NI - (SE_{t-1} \times r)$	1.14	1.45	2.30	2.00	2.77

So, the estimated value using the RI model (using Equation 6), with residual income calculated based on net income, is

$$V_0 = \$8.58 + \frac{\$1.14}{(1.10)^1} + \frac{\$1.45}{(1.10)^2} + \frac{\$2.30}{(1.10)^3} + \frac{\$2.00}{(1.10)^4} + \frac{\$2.77}{(1.10)^5} + \frac{\$68.40 - \$22.04}{(1.10)^5}$$

$$V_0 = \$8.58 + 35.84 = \$44.42$$

B. Calculating residual income as net income adjusted for OCI (NI + OCI) minus the equity charge, which equals beginning shareholders' equity (SE) multiplied by the cost of equity capital (r), gives the following for years 1 through 5:

	Year				
	1	**2**	**3**	**4**	**5**
$RI = (NI + OCI) - (SE_{t-1} \times r)$	\$1.14	\$0.45	\$2.30	\$2.00	\$2.77

So, the estimated value using the RI model, with residual income based on net income adjusted for OCI, is

$$V_0 = \$8.58 + \frac{\$1.14}{(1.10)^1} + \frac{\$.45}{(1.10)^2} + \frac{\$2.30}{(1.10)^3} + \frac{\$2.00}{(1.10)^4} + \frac{\$2.77}{(1.10)^5} + \frac{\$68.40 - \$22.04}{(1.10)^5}$$

$$V_0 = \$8.58 + 35.01 = \$43.59$$

3. Interpret your answers to Parts 2A and 2B.

Solution:

The first calculation (2A) incorrectly omits an adjustment for a violation of the clean surplus relation. The second calculation (2B) includes an adjustment and yields the correct value estimate, which is consistent with the DDM estimate.

4. Assume that a forecast of the terminal price of Mannistore's shares at the end of Year 5 (time $t = 5$) is not available. Instead, an estimate of terminal price based on the Gordon growth model is appropriate. You estimate that the growth in net income and dividends from $t = 5$ to $t = 6$ will be 8%.

Predict residual income for Year 6, and based on that 8% growth estimate, determine the growth rate in forecasted residual income from $t = 5$ to $t = 6$.

Solution:

Given the estimated 8% growth in net income and dividends in Year 6, the estimated Year 6 net income is $4.92 ($4.56 × 1.08), and the estimated amount of Year 6 dividends is $0.42 ($0.38 × 1.08).

Residual income will then equal $2.72 (which is net income of $4.92 minus the equity charge of beginning book value of $22.04 multiplied by the cost of capital of 10%). So, the growth rate in residual income is negative at approximately −2% ($2.72/$2.77 − 1).

Lacking a basis for explicit assumptions about future amounts of OCI, the analyst should nonetheless be aware of the potential effect of OCI on residual income and adjust ROE accordingly. Finally, as noted earlier, the analyst may decide that an alternative valuation model is more appropriate.

6 ACCOUNTING CONSIDERATIONS: OTHER

☐ describe accounting issues in applying residual income models

To have a reliable measure of book value of equity, an analyst should identify and scrutinize significant off-balance-sheet assets and liabilities. Additionally, reported assets and liabilities should be adjusted to fair value when possible. Off-balance-sheet assets and liabilities may become apparent through an examination of the financial statement footnotes. Probably the most common example is the use of operating leases. Operating leases do not affect the amount of equity (because leases involve off-balance-sheet assets that offset the off-balance-sheet liabilities) but can affect an assessment of future earnings for the residual income component of value. Other assets and liabilities may be stated at values other than fair value. For example, inventory may be stated at LIFO and require adjustment to restate to current value. (LIFO is not permitted under IFRS.) The following are some common items to review for balance sheet adjustments. Note, however, that this list is not comprehensive:

- inventory;
- deferred tax assets and liabilities;
- operating leases;
- reserves and allowances (for example, bad debts); and
- intangible assets.

Additionally, the analyst should examine the financial statements and footnotes for items unique to the subject company.

Intangible Assets

Intangible assets can have a significant effect on book value. In the case of specifically identifiable intangibles that can be separated from the entity (e.g., sold), it is generally appropriate to include these in determining book value of equity. If these assets have a finite useful life, they will be amortized over time as an expense. Intangible assets, however, require special consideration because they are often not recognized as an asset unless they are obtained in an acquisition. For example, advertising expenditures can create a highly valuable brand, which is clearly an intangible asset. Advertising expenditures, however, are shown as an expense, and the value of a brand would not appear as an asset on the financial statements unless the company owning the brand was acquired.

To demonstrate this, consider a simplified example involving two companies, Alpha and Beta, with the following summary financial information (all amounts in thousands, except per-share data):

	Alpha (€)	Beta (€)
Cash	1,600	100
Property, plant, and equipment	3,400	900
Total assets	5,000	1,000
Equity	5,000	1,000
Net income	600	150

Each company pays out all net income as dividends (no growth), and the clean surplus relation holds. Alpha has a 12% ROE and Beta has a 15% ROE, both expected to continue indefinitely. Each has a 10% required rate of return. The fair market value of each company's property, plant, and equipment is the same as its book value. What is the value of each company in a residual income framework?

Using total book value rather than per-share data, the value of Alpha would be €6,000, determined as follows (note that result would be the same if calculated on a per-share basis):

$$V_0 = B_0 + \frac{\text{ROE} - r}{r - g} B_0 = 5,000 + \frac{0.12 - 0.10}{0.10 - 0.00} 5,000 = 6,000$$

Similarly, the value of Beta would be €1,500:

$$V_0 = B_0 + \frac{\text{ROE} - r}{r - g} B_0 = 1,000 + \frac{0.15 - 0.10}{0.10 - 0.00} 1,000 = 1,500$$

The value of the companies on a combined basis would be €7,500. Note that both companies are valued more highly than the book value of equity because they have ROE in excess of the required rate of return. Absent an acquisition transaction, the financial statements of Alpha and Beta do not reflect this value. If either is acquired, however, an acquirer would allocate the purchase price to the acquired assets, with any excess of the purchase price above the acquired assets shown as goodwill.

Suppose Alpha acquires Beta by paying Beta's former shareholders €1,500 in cash. Alpha has just paid €500 in excess of the value of Beta's total reported assets of €1,000. Assume that Beta's property, plant and equipment is already shown at its fair market value of €1,000, and that the €500 is considered to be the fair value of a license owned by Beta, say an exclusive right to provide a service. Assume further that the original cost of obtaining the license was an immaterial application fee, which does not appear on Beta's balance sheet, and that the license covers a period of 10 years. Because the entire purchase price of €1,500 is allocated to identifiable assets, no goodwill is recognized. Alpha's balance sheet immediately after the acquisition would be as follows:

	Alpha (€)
Cash	200
Property, plant, and equipment	4,300
License	500
Total assets	5,000
Equity	5,000

Note that the total book value of Alpha's equity did not change, because the acquisition was made for cash and thus did not require Alpha to issue any new shares. Also note that, for example, cash of €200 is calculated as €1,600 (cash of Alpha) + €100 (cash of Beta) – €1,500 (purchase price of Beta).

Under the assumption that the license is amortized over a 10-year period, the combined company's expected net income would be €700 (€600 + €150 – €50 amortization). If this net income number is used to derive expected ROE, the expected ROE would be 14%. Under a residual income model, with no adjustment for amortization, the value of the combined company would be

$$V_0 = B_0 + \frac{\text{ROE} - r}{r - g} B_0 = 5,000 + \frac{0.14 - 0.10}{0.10 - 0.00} 5,000 = 7,000$$

Why would the combined company be worth less than the two separate companies? If the assumption is made that a fair price was paid to Beta's former shareholders, the combined value should not be lower. The lower value using the residual income model results from a reduction in ROE as a result of the amortization of the intangible license asset. If this asset were not amortized (or if the amortization expense were added back before computing ROE), net income would be €750 and ROE would be 15%. The value of the combined entity would be

$$V_0 = B_0 + \frac{\text{ROE} - r}{r - g} B_0 = 5,000 + \frac{0.15 - 0.10}{0.10 - 0.00} 5,000 = 7,500$$

This amount, €7,500, is the same as the sum of the values of the companies on a separate basis.

Would the answer be different if the acquiring company used newly issued stock rather than cash in the acquisition? The form of currency used to pay for the transaction should not affect the total value. If Alpha used €1,500 of newly issued stock to acquire Beta, its balance sheet would be as follows:

	Alpha (€)
Cash	1,700
Property, plant, and equipment	4,300
License	500
Total assets	6,500
Equity	6,500

Projected earnings, excluding the amortization of the license, would be €750, and projected ROE would be 11.538%. Value under the residual income model would be

$$V_0 = B_0 + \frac{\text{ROE} - r}{r - g} B_0 = 6,500 + \frac{0.11538 - 0.10}{0.10 - 0.00} 6,500 = 7,500$$

The overall value remains unchanged. The book value of equity is higher but offset by the effect on ROE. Once again, this example assumes that the buyer paid a fair value for the acquisition. If an acquirer overpays for an acquisition, the overpayment should become evident in a reduction in future residual income.

Research and development (R&D) costs provide another example of an intangible asset that must be given careful consideration. Under US GAAP, R&D is generally expensed to the income statement directly (except in certain cases such as ASC 985-20-25, which permits the capitalization of R&D expenses related to software development after product feasibility has been established). Also, under IFRS, some R&D costs can be capitalized and amortized over time. R&D expenditures are reflected in a company's ROE, and hence residual income, over the long term. If a company engages in unproductive R&D expenditures, these will lower residual income through the expenditures made. If a company engages in productive R&D expenditures, these should result in higher revenues to offset the expenditures over time. In summary, on a continuing basis for a mature company, ROE should reflect the productivity of R&D expenditures without requiring an adjustment.

As explained in Lundholm and Sloan (2007), including and subsequently amortizing an asset that was omitted from a company's reported assets has no effect on valuation under a residual income model. Such an adjustment would increase the estimated equity value by adding the asset to book value at time zero but decrease the estimated value by an equivalent amount, which would include a) the present value of the asset when amortized in the future and b) the present value of a periodic capital charge based on the amount of the asset multiplied by the cost of equity. Expensing R&D, however, results in an immediately lower ROE vis-à-vis capitalizing R&D. But expensing R&D will result in a slightly higher ROE relative to capitalizing R&D in future years because this capitalized R&D is amortized. Because ROE is used in a number of expressions derived from the residual income model and may also be used in forecasting net income, the analyst should carefully consider a company's R&D expenditures and their effect on long-term ROE.

Non-recurring Items

In applying a residual income model, it is important to develop a forecast of future residual income based on recurring items. Companies often report non-recurring charges as part of earnings, which can lead to overestimates and underestimates of future residual earnings if no adjustments are made. No adjustments to book value are necessary for these items, however, because non-recurring gains and losses are reflected in the value of assets in place. Hirst and Hopkins (2000) noted that non-recurring items sometimes result from accounting rules and at other times result from "strategic" management decisions. Regardless, they highlighted the importance of examining the financial statement notes and other sources for items that may warrant adjustment in determining recurring earnings, such as

- unusual items;
- extraordinary items (applicable under US GAAP but not under IFRS);
- restructuring charges;
- discontinued operations; and
- accounting changes.

In some cases, management may record restructuring or unusual charges in every period. In these cases, the item may be considered an ordinary operating expense and may not require adjustment.

Companies sometimes inappropriately classify non-operating gains as a reduction in operating expenses (such as selling, general, and administrative expenses). If material, this inappropriate classification can usually be uncovered by a careful reading of financial statement footnotes and press releases. Analysts should consider whether these items are likely to continue and contribute to residual income in time. More likely, they should be removed from operating earnings when forecasting residual income.

Other Aggressive Accounting Practices

Companies may engage in accounting practices that result in the overstatement of assets (book value) and/or overstatement of earnings. We discussed some of these practices in the preceding sections. Other activities that a company may engage in include accelerating revenues to the current period or deferring expenses to a later period (Schilit and Perler 2010). Both activities simultaneously increase earnings and book value. For example, a company might ship unordered goods to customers at year-end, recording revenues and a receivable. As another example, a company could capitalize rather than expense a cash payment, resulting in lower expenses and an increase in assets.

Conversely, companies have also been criticized for the use of "cookie jar" reserves (reserves saved for future use), in which excess losses or expenses are recorded in an *earlier* period (for example, in conjunction with an acquisition or restructuring) and then used to reduce expenses and increase income in future periods. The analyst should carefully examine the use of reserves when assessing residual earnings. Overall, the analyst must evaluate a company's accounting policies carefully and consider the integrity of management when assessing the inputs in a residual income model.

International Considerations

Accounting standards differ internationally. These differences result in different measures of book value and earnings internationally and suggest that valuation models based on accrual accounting data might not perform as well as other present value models in international contexts. It is interesting to note, however, that Frankel and Lee (1999) found that the residual income model works well in valuing companies on an international basis. Using a simple residual income model without any of the adjustments discussed here, they found that their residual income valuation model accounted for 70% of the cross-sectional variation of stock prices among 20 countries. Frankel and Lee concluded that there are three primary considerations in applying a residual income model internationally:

- the availability of reliable earnings forecasts;
- systematic violations of the clean surplus assumption; and
- "poor quality" accounting rules that result in delayed recognition of value changes.

Analysts should expect the model to work best in situations in which earnings forecasts are available, clean surplus violations are limited, and accounting rules do not result in delayed recognition. Because Frankel and Lee found good explanatory power for a residual income model using unadjusted accounting data, one expects that if adjustments are made to the reported data to correct for clean surplus and other violations, international comparisons should result in comparable valuations. For circumstances in which clean surplus violations exist, accounting choices result in delayed recognition, or accounting disclosures do not permit adjustment, the residual income model would not be appropriate and the analyst should consider a model less dependent on accounting data, such as a FCFE model.

It should be noted, however, that IFRS is increasingly becoming widely used. As of 2019, according to AICPA (an accociation representing the accounting profession), approximately 120 nations and reporting jurisdictions permit or require IFRS for domestic listed companies, although approximately 90 countries have fully conformed with IFRS as promulgated by the IASB and include a statement acknowledging such conformity in audit reports. Furthermore, standard setters in numerous countries continue to work toward convergence between IFRS and home-country GAAP. In time, concerns about the use of different accounting standards should become less severe. Nonetheless, even within a single set of accounting standards, companies make choices and estimates that can affect valuation.

SUMMARY

We have discussed the use of residual income models in valuation. Residual income is an appealing economic concept because it attempts to measure economic profit, which are profits after accounting for all opportunity costs of capital.

- Residual income is calculated as net income minus a deduction for the cost of equity capital. The deduction, called the equity charge, is equal to equity capital multiplied by the required rate of return on equity (the cost of equity capital in percent).
- Economic value added (EVA) is a commercial implementation of the residual income concept. EVA = NOPAT − (C% × TC), where NOPAT is net operating profit after taxes, C% is the percent cost of capital, and TC is total capital.
- Residual income models (including commercial implementations) are used not only for equity valuation but also to measure internal corporate performance and for determining executive compensation.
- We can forecast per-share residual income as forecasted earnings per share minus the required rate of return on equity multiplied by beginning book value per share. Alternatively, per-share residual income can be forecasted as beginning book value per share multiplied by the difference between forecasted ROE and the required rate of return on equity.
- In the residual income model, the intrinsic value of a share of common stock is the sum of book value per share and the present value of expected future per-share residual income. In the residual income model, the equivalent mathematical expressions for intrinsic value of a common stock are

$$V_0 = B_0 + \sum_{t=1}^{\infty}\frac{\text{RI}_t}{(1+r)^t} = B_0 + \sum_{t=1}^{\infty}\frac{E_t - rB_{t-1}}{(1+r)^t}$$

$$= B_0 + \sum_{t=1}^{\infty}\frac{(\text{ROE}_t - r)B_{t-1}}{(1+r)^t}$$

where

V_0 = value of a share of stock today (t = 0)

B_0 = current per-share book value of equity

B_t = expected per-share book value of equity at any time t

r = required rate of return on equity (cost of equity)

E_t = expected earnings per share for period t

RI_t = expected per-share residual income, equal to $E_t - rB_{t-1}$ or to (ROE − r) × B_{t-1}

ROE_T = return on equity

- In the two-stage model with continuing residual income in stage two, the intrinsic value of a share of stock is

$$V_0 = B_0 + \sum_{t=1}^{T}\frac{\text{RI}_t}{(1+r)^t} + \frac{P_T - B_T}{(1+r)^T} = B_0 + \sum_{t=1}^{T}\frac{(E_t - rB_{t-1})}{(1+r)^t} + \frac{P_T - B_T}{(1+r)^T}$$

$$V_0 = B_0 + \sum_{t=1}^{T}\frac{(\text{ROE}_t - r)B_{t-1}}{(1+r)^t} + \frac{P_T - B_T}{(1+r)^T}$$

where

P_T = expected per share price at terminal time T

B_T = expected per share book value at terminal time T

- In most cases, value is recognized earlier in the residual income model compared with other present value models of stock value, such as the dividend discount model.
- Strengths of the residual income model include the following:
  - Terminal values do not make up a large portion of the value relative to other models.
  - The models use readily available accounting data.
  - The models can be used in the absence of dividends and near-term positive free cash flows.
  - The models can be used when cash flows are unpredictable.
- Weaknesses of the residual income model include the following:
  - The models are based on accounting data that can be subject to manipulation by management.
  - Accounting data used as inputs may require significant adjustments.
  - The models require that the clean surplus relation holds, or that the analyst makes appropriate adjustments when the clean surplus relation does not hold.
- The residual income model is most appropriate in the following cases:
  - A company is not paying dividends or if it exhibits an unpredictable dividend pattern.
  - A company has negative free cash flow many years out but is expected to generate positive cash flow at some point in the future.
  - A great deal of uncertainty exists in forecasting terminal values.
- The fundamental determinants or drivers of residual income are book value of equity and return on equity.
- Residual income valuation is most closely related to P/B. When the present value of expected future residual income is positive (negative), the justified P/B based on fundamentals is greater than (less than) one.
- When fully consistent assumptions are used to forecast earnings, cash flow, dividends, book value, and residual income through a full set of pro forma (projected) financial statements, and the same required rate of return on equity is used as the discount rate, the same estimate of value should result from a residual income, dividend discount, or free cash flow valuation. In practice, however, analysts may find one model easier to apply and possibly arrive at different valuations using the different models.
- Continuing residual income is residual income after the forecast horizon. Frequently, one of the following assumptions concerning continuing residual income is made:
  - Residual income continues indefinitely at a positive level. (One variation of this assumption is that residual income continues indefinitely at the rate of inflation, meaning it is constant in real terms.)
  - Residual income is zero from the terminal year forward.
  - Residual income declines to zero as ROE reverts to the cost of equity over time.
  - Residual income declines to some mean level.

- The residual income model assumes the clean surplus relation of $B_t = B_{t-1} + E_t - D_t$. In other terms, the ending book value of equity equals the beginning book value plus earnings minus dividends, apart from ownership transactions.
- In practice, to apply the residual income model most accurately, the analyst may need to do the following:
  - adjust book value of common equity for:
    - off-balance-sheet items;
    - discrepancies from fair value; or
    - the amortization of certain intangible assets.
  - adjust reported net income to reflect clean surplus accounting.
  - adjust reported net income for non-recurring items misclassified as recurring items.

REFERENCES

Schilit and Perler. 2010. *Financial Shenanigans*. 3rd ed., McGraw-Hill.

Bauman, Mark P. 1999. "Importance of Reported Book Value in Equity Valuation." *Journal of Financial Statement Analysis* 4, vol. , no. 2:31–40.

Bernstein, Richard, Kari Bayer, and Carmen Pigler. 1998. "An Analysis of EVA® Part II." *Quantitative Viewpoint*. Merrill Lynch. 3 February.

Bernstein, Richard and Carmen Pigler. 1997. "An Analysis of EVA®." *Quantitative Viewpoint*. Merrill Lynch. 19 December.

Dechow, Patricia M., Amy P. Hutton, and Richard G. Sloan. 1999. "An Empirical Assessment of the Residual Income Valuation Model." *Journal of Accounting and Economics* 26, vol. , no. 1-3:1–34. 10.1016/S0165-4101(98)00049-4

Feltham, Gerald A. and James A. Ohlson. 1995. "Valuation and Clean Surplus Accounting for Operating and Financial Activities." *Contemporary Accounting Research* 11, vol. , no. 4:689–731. 10.1111/j.1911-3846.1995.tb00462.x

Fleck, Shelby A., Scott D. Craig, Michael Bodenstab, Trevor Harris, and Elmer Huh. 2001. *Technology: Electronics Manufacturing Services*. Industry Overview; Morgan Stanley Dean Witter. 28 March.

Frankel, Richard M. and Charles M.C. Lee. 1999. "Accounting Diversity and International Valuation." Working Paper, May.

Hirst, D. Eric and Patrick E. Hopkins. 2000. *Earnings: Measurement, Disclosure, and the Impact on Equity Valuation*. Charlottesville, VA: Research Foundation of AIMR and Blackwell Series in Finance.

Hitchner, James R. 2017. *Financial Valuation: Applications and Models*, 4th edition. Hoboken, NJ: John Wiley & Sons.

Lee, Charles M.C., James Myers, and Bhaskaran Swaminathan. 1999. "What is the Intrinsic Value of the Dow?" *Journal of Finance* 54, vol. , no. 5:1693–1741. 10.1111/0022-1082.00164

Lee, Charles M.C. and Bhaskaran Swaminathan. 1999. "Valuing the Dow: A Bottom-Up Approach." *Financial Analysts Journal* 55, vol. , no. 5:4–23. 10.2469/faj.v55.n5.2295

Lundholm, Russell J. and Terrence B. O'Keefe. 2001a. "Reconciling Value Estimates from the Discounted Cash Flow Model and the Residual Income Model." *Contemporary Accounting Research* 18, vol. , no. 2:311–335. 10.1506/W13B-K4BT-455N-TTR2

Lundholm, Russell J. and Terrence B. O'Keefe. 2001b. "On Comparing Residual Income and Discounted Cash Flow Models of Equity Valuation: A Response to Penman 2001." *Contemporary Accounting Research* 18, vol. , no. 4:693–696. 10.1506/Y51R-C3YF-MT0T-BWE2

Lundholm, Russell J. and Richard G. Sloan. 2007. *Equity Valuation and Analysis with eVal*, 2nd edition. McGraw-Hill Irwin. New York.

Ohlson, James A. 1995. "Earnings, Book Values, and Dividends in Equity Valuation." *Contemporary Accounting Research* 11, vol. , no. 4:661–687. 10.1111/j.1911-3846.1995.tb00461.x

Penman, Stephen H. 2001. "On Comparing Cash Flow and Accrual Accounting Models for Use in Equity Valuation: A Response to Lundholm and O'Keefe." *Contemporary Accounting Research* 18, vol. , no. 4:681–692. 10.1506/DT0R-JNEG-QL60-7CBP

Penman, Stephen H. and Theodore Sougiannis. 1998. "A Comparison of Dividend, Cash Flow and Earnings Approaches to Equity Valuation." *Contemporary Accounting Research* 15, vol. , no. 3:343–383. 10.1111/j.1911-3846.1998.tb00564.x

Peterson, Pamela P. and David R. Peterson. 1996. *Company Performance and Measures of Value Added*. Charlottesville, VA: The Research Foundation of the ICFA.

Shrieves, Ronald E. and John M. Wachowicz. 2001. "Free Cash Flow (FCF), Economic Value Added (EVA™), and Net Present Value (NPV): A Reconciliation of Variations of Discounted-Cash-Flow (DCF) Valuation." *Engineering Economist* 46, vol. , no. 1:33–52. 10.1080/00137910108967561

Stewart, G. Bennett. 1991. *The Quest for Value*. New York: HarperCollins.

PRACTICE PROBLEMS

1. Based on the following information, determine whether Vertically Integrated Manufacturing (VIM) earned any residual income for its shareholders:

   - VIM had total assets of $3,000,000, financed with twice as much debt capital as equity capital.
   - VIM's pretax cost of debt is 6% and cost of equity capital is 10%.
   - VIM had EBIT of $300,000 and was taxed at a rate of 40%.

   Calculate residual income by using the method based on deducting an equity charge.

2. Because New Market Products (NMP) markets consumer staples, it is able to make use of considerable debt in its capital structure; specifically, 90% of the company's total assets of $450,000,000 are financed with debt capital. Its cost of debt is 8% before taxes, and its cost of equity capital is 12%. NMP achieved a pretax income of $5.1 million in 2006 and had a tax rate of 40%. What was NMP's residual income?

3. In 2020, Smithson–Williams Industries (SWI) achieved an operating profit after taxes of €10 million on total assets of €100 million. Half of its assets were financed with debt with a pretax cost of 9%. Its cost of equity capital is 12%, and its tax rate is 40%. Did SWI achieve a positive residual income?

The following information relates to questions 4-6

Calculate the economic value added or residual income, as requested, for each of the following:

4. NOPAT = $100
   Beginning book value of debt = $200
   Beginning book value of equity = $300
   Weighted average cost of capital (WACC) = 11%
   Calculate EVA.

5. Net income = €5.00
   Dividends = €1.00
   Beginning book value of equity = €30.00
   Required rate of return on equity = 11%
   Calculate residual income.

6. Return on equity = 18%
   Required rate of return on equity = 12%
   Beginning book value of equity = €30.00
   Calculate residual income.

The following information relates to questions 7-8

Jim Martin is using economic value added and market value added to measure the performance of Sundanci. Martin uses the fiscal year 2020 information below for his analysis.

- Adjusted net operating profit after taxes is $100 million.
- Total capital is $700 million (no debt).
- Closing stock price is $26.
- Total shares outstanding is 84 million.
- The cost of equity is 14%.

Calculate the following for Sundanci. Show your work.

7. EVA for fiscal year 2020.

8. MVA as of fiscal year-end 2020.

The following information relates to questions 9-16

Mangoba Nkomo, CFA, a senior equity analyst with Robertson-Butler Investments, South Africa, has been assigned a recent graduate, Manga Mahlangu, to assist in valuations. Mahlangu is interested in pursuing a career in equity analysis. In their first meeting, Nkomo and Mahlangu discuss the concept of residual income and its commercial applications. Nkomo asks Mahlangu to determine the market value added for a hypothetical South African firm using the data provided in Exhibit 1.

Exhibit 1: Hypothetical Firm Data (amounts in South African rand)

Current share price	R25.43
Book value per share	R20.00
Total shares outstanding	30 million
Cost of equity	13%
Market value of debt	R55 million
Accounting book value of total capital	R650 million
Intrinsic share value of equity derived from residual income model	R22.00

Nkomo also shares his valuation report of the hypothetical firm with Mahlangu. Nkomo's report concludes that the intrinsic value of the hypothetical firm, based on the residual income model, is R22.00 per share. To assess Mahlangu's knowledge of residual income valuation, Nkomo asks Mahlangu two questions about the hypothetical firm:

Question 1 What conclusion can we make about future residual earnings given the current book value per share and my estimate of intrinsic value per share?

Question 2 Suppose you estimated the intrinsic value of a firm's shares using a constant growth residual income model, and you found that your estimate of intrinsic value equaled the book value per share. What would that finding imply about that firm's return on equity?

Satisfied with Mahlangu's response, Nkomo requests that Mahlangu use the single-stage residual income model to determine the intrinsic value of the equity of Jackson Breweries, a brewery and bottling company, using data provided in Exhibit 2.

Exhibit 2: Jackson Breweries Data (amounts in South African rand)

Constant long-term growth rate	9.5%
Constant long-term ROE	13%
Current market price per share	R150.70
Book value per share	R55.81
Cost of equity	11%

Nkomo also wants to update an earlier valuation of Amersheen, a food retailer. The valuation report, completed at the end of 2020, concluded an intrinsic value per share of R11.00 for Amersheen. The share price at that time was R8.25. Nkomo points out to Mahlangu that in late 2020, Amersheen announced a significant restructuring charge, estimated at R2 million, that would be reported as part of operating earnings in Amersheen's 2020 annual income statement. Nkomo asks Mahlangu the following question about the restructuring charge:

Question 3 What was the correct way to treat the estimated R2 million restructuring charge in my 2020 valuation report?

Satisfied with Mahlangu's response, Nkomo mentions to Mahlangu that Amersheen recently (near the end of 2021) completed the acquisition of a chain of convenience stores. Nkomo requests that Mahlangu complete, as of the beginning of 2022, an updated valuation of Amersheen under two scenarios:

Scenario 1 Estimate the value of Amersheen shares using a multistage residual income model with the data provided in Exhibit 3. Under Scenario 1, expected ROE in 2025 is 26%, but it is assumed that the firm's ROE will slowly decline towards the cost of equity thereafter.

Scenario 2 Estimate the value of Amersheen shares using a multistage residual income model with the data provided in Exhibit 3, but assume that at the end of 2024, share price is expected to equal book value per share.

Scenario 3

Exhibit 3: Amersheen Data (amounts in South African rand)

Long-term growth rate starting in 2025	9.0%
Expected ROE in 2025	26%

Current market price per share	R16.55
Book value per share, beginning of 2022	R7.60
Cost of equity	10%
Persistence factor	0.70

	2022	2023	2024
Expected earnings per share	R3.28	R3.15	R2.90
Expected dividend per share	R2.46	R2.36	R2.06

9. Based on the information in Exhibit 1, the market value added of the hypothetical firm is *closest* to:

   A. R65 million.

   B. R113 million.

   C. R168 million.

10. The *most* appropriate response to Nkomo's Question 1 would be that the present value of future residual earnings is expected to be:

    A. zero.

    B. positive.

    C. negative.

11. The *most* appropriate response to Nkomo's Question 2 would be that the firm's return on equity is:

    A. equal to the firm's cost of equity.

    B. lower than the firm's cost of equity.

    C. higher than the firm's cost of equity.

12. Based on the information in Exhibit 2, the intrinsic value per share of the equity of Jackson Breweries is *closest* to:

    A. R97.67.

    B. R130.22.

    C. R186.03.

13. If Nkomo's 2020 year-end estimate of Amersheen shares' intrinsic value was accurate, then Amersheen's shares were *most likely*:

    A. overvalued.

    B. undervalued.

    C. fairly valued.

14. The *most* appropriate treatment of the estimated restructuring charge, in re-

sponse to Nkomo's Question 3, would be:

A. an upward adjustment to book value.

B. an upward adjustment to the cost of equity.

C. to exclude it from the estimate of net income.

15. Under Scenario 1, the intrinsic value per share of the equity of Amersheen is *closest* to:

A. R13.29.

B. R15.57.

C. R16.31.

16. Under Scenario 2, the intrinsic value per share of the equity of Amersheen is *closest* to:

A. R13.29.

B. R15.57.

C. R16.31.

The following information relates to questions 17-26

Elena Castovan is a junior analyst with Contralith Capital, a long-only equity investment manager. She has been asked to value three stocks on Contralith's watch list: Portous, Inc. (PTU), SSX Financial (SSX), and Tantechi Ltd. (TTCI).

During their weekly meeting, Castovan and her supervisor, Ariana Beckworth, discuss characteristics of residual income models. Castovan tells Beckworth the following.

Statement 1 The present value of the terminal value in RI models is often a larger portion of the total intrinsic value than it is in other DCF valuation models.

Statement 2 The RI model's use of accounting income assumes that the cost of debt capital is appropriately reflected by interest expense.

Statement 3 RI models cannot be readily applied to companies that do not have positive expected near-term free cash flows.

Beckworth asks Castovan why an RI model may be more appropriate for valuing PTU than the dividend discount model or a free cash flow model. Castovan tells Beckworth that, over her five-year forecast horizon, she expects PTU to perform the following actions.

Reason 1 Pay dividends that are unpredictable

Reason 2 Generatepositiveand fairly predictable free cash flows

Reason 3 Report significant amounts of other comprehensive income

At the conclusion of their meeting, Beckworth asks Castovan to value SSX using RI models. Selected financial information on SSX is presented in Exhibit 1.

Exhibit 1: SSX Financial (SSX) Selected Financial Data

Total assets (millions)	€4,000.00
Capital structure	60% debt/40% equity
EBIT (millions)	€700.00
Tax rate	35.00%
Return on equity (ROE)	23.37%
Pretax cost of debt[a]	5.20%
Cost of equity	15.00%
Market price per share	€48.80
Price-to-book ratio	2.10

[a] *Interest expense is tax-deductible.*

Castovan's final assignment is to determine the intrinsic value of TTCI using both a single-stage and a multistage RI model. Selected data and assumptions for TTCI are presented in Exhibit 2.

Exhibit 2: Tantechi Ltd. (TTCI) Selected Financial Data and Assumptions

Book value per share	€45.25
Market price per share	€126.05
Constant long-term ROE	12.00%
Constant long-term earnings growth rate	4.50%
Cost of equity	8.70%

For the multistage model, Castovan forecasts TTCI's ROE to be higher than its long-term ROE for the first three years. Forecasted earnings per share and dividends per share for TTCI are presented in Exhibit 3. Starting in Year 4, Castovan forecasts TTCI's ROE to revert to the constant long-term ROE of 12% annually. The terminal value is based on an assumption that residual income per share will be constant from Year 3 into perpetuity.

Exhibit 3: Tantechi Ltd. (TTCI) Forecasts of Earnings and Dividends

	Year 1	Year 2	Year 3
Earnings per share (€)	7.82	8.17	8.54
Dividends per share (€)	1.46	1.53	1.59

Beckworth questions Castovan's assumption regarding the implied persistence factor used in the multistage RI valuation. She tells Castovan that she believes that a persistence factor of 0.10 is appropriate for TTCI.

17. Which of Castovan's statements regarding residual income models is correct?

    A. Statement 1

    B. Statement 2

    C. Statement 3

18. Which of Castovan's reasons *best* justifies the use of a residual income model to value PTU?

    A. Reason 1

    B. Reason 2

    C. Reason 3

19. The forecasted item described in Reason 3 will *most likely* affect:

    A. earnings per share.

    B. dividends per share.

    C. book value per share.

20. Based on Exhibit 1, residual income for SSX is *closest* to:

    A. €40.9 million.

    B. €90.2 million.

    C. €133.9 million.

21. Based on Exhibit 1 and the single-stage residual income model, the implied growth rate of earnings for SSX is *closest* to:

    A. 5.8%.

    B. 7.4%.

    C. 11.0%.

22. Based on the single-stage RI model and Exhibit 2, Castovan should conclude that TTCI is:

    A. undervalued.

    B. fairly valued.

    C. overvalued.

23. Based on Exhibit 2, the justified price-to-book ratio for TTCI is *closest* to:

    A. 1.79.

    B. 2.27.

    C. 2.79.

24. Based on Exhibits 2 and 3 and the multistage RI model, Castovan should estimate

the intrinsic value of TTCI to be *closest* to:

A. €54.88.

B. €83.01.

C. €85.71.

25. The persistence factor suggested by Beckworth will lead to a multistage value estimate of TTCI's shares that is:

A. less than Castovan's multistage value estimate.

B. equal to Castovan's multistage value estimate.

C. greater than Castovan's multistage value estimate.

26. The *best* justification for Castovan to use Beckworth's suggested persistence factor is that TTCI has:

A. a low dividend payout.

B. extreme accounting rates of return.

C. a strong market leadership position.

---

27. Use the following information to estimate the intrinsic value of VIM's common stock using the residual income model:

- VIM had total assets of $3,000,000, financed with twice as much debt capital as equity capital.
- VIM's pretax cost of debt is 6% and cost of equity capital is 10%.
- VIM had EBIT of $300,000 and was taxed at a rate of 40%. EBIT is expected to continue at $300,000 indefinitely.
- VIM's book value per share is $20.
- VIM has 50,000 shares of common stock outstanding.

28. Palmetto Steel, Inc. (PSI) maintains a dividend payout ratio of 80% because of its limited opportunities for expansion. Its return on equity is 15%. The required rate of return on PSI equity is 12%, and its long-term growth rate is 3%. Compute the justified P/B based on forecasted fundamentals, consistent with the residual income model and a constant growth rate assumption.

The following information relates to questions 29-30

Protected Steel Corporation (PSC) has a book value of $6 per share. PSC is expected to earn $0.60 per share forever and pays out all of its earnings as dividends. The required rate of return on PSC's equity is 12%. Calculate the value of the stock using the following:

29. Dividend discount model.

30. Residual income model.

The following information relates to questions 31-32

Notable Books (NB) is a family controlled company that dominates the retail book market. NB has book value of $10 per share, is expected to earn $2.00 per share forever, and pays out all of its earnings as dividends. Its required return on equity is 12.5%. Value the stock of NB using the following:

31. Dividend discount model.

32. Residual income model.

The following information relates to questions 33-35

Simonson Investment Trust International (SITI) is expected to earn $4.00, $5.00, and $8.00 per share for the next three years. SITI will pay annual dividends of $2.00, $2.50, and $20.50 in each of these years. The last dividend includes a liquidating payment to shareholders at the end of Year 3 when the trust terminates. SITI's book value is $8 per share and its required return on equity is 10%.

33. What is the current value per share of SITI according to the dividend discount model?

34. Calculate per-share book value and residual income for SITI for each of the next three years and use those results to find the stock's value using the residual income model.

35. Calculate return on equity and use it as an input to the residual income model to calculate SITI's value.

---

36. Foodsco Incorporated (FI), a leading distributor of food products and materials to restaurants and other institutions, has a remarkably steady track record in terms of both return on equity and growth. At year-end 2017, FI had a book value of $30 per share. For the foreseeable future, the company is expected to achieve a ROE of 15% (on trailing book value) and to pay out one-third of its earnings in dividends. The required return is 12%. Forecast FI's residual income for the year ending 31 December 2022.

The following information relates to questions 37-39

Thales S.A. (Paris: HO.PA) has a current stock price of €98.73. It also has book value per share of €26.83. and a P/B of 3.68. Assume that the single-stage growth model is appropriate for valuing the company. Thales S.A.'s adjusted beta is 0.68, the risk-free rate is 4.46%, and the equity risk premium is 5.50%.

37. If the growth rate is 5.50% and the ROE is 20%, what is the justified P/B for

Thales?

38. If the growth rate is 5.50%, what ROE is required to yield Thales S.A.'s current P/B?

39. If the ROE is 20%, what growth rate is required for Thales to have its current P/B?

---

40. Retail fund manager Seymour Simms is considering the purchase of shares in upstart retailer Hottest Topic Stores (HTR). The current book value of HTS is \$20 per share, and its market price is \$35. Simms expects long-term ROE to be 18%, long-term growth to be 10%, and cost of equity to be 14%. What conclusion would you expect Simms to arrive at if he uses a single-stage residual income model to value these shares?

41. Dayton Manufactured Homes (DMH) builds prefabricated homes and mobile homes. Favorable demographics and the likelihood of slow, steady increases in market share should enable DMH to maintain its ROE of 15% and growth rate of 10% through time. DMH has a book value of \$30 per share and the required rate of return on its equity is 12%. Compute the value of its equity using the single-stage residual income model.

42. Use the following inputs and the finite horizon form of the residual income model to compute the value of Southern Trust Bank (STB) shares as of 31 December 2020:

    - ROE will continue at 15% for the next five years (and 10% thereafter) with all earnings reinvested (no dividends paid).
    - Cost of equity equals 10%.
    - B_0 = \$10 per share (at year-end 2020).
    - Premium over book value at the end of five years will be 20%.

The following information relates to questions 43-46

Shunichi Kobayashi is valuing Procter & Gamble Company (NYSE: PG). Kobayashi has made the following assumptions:

- Book value per share is estimated at \$21.30 on 31 March 2019.
- EPS will be 18% of the beginning book value per share for the next eight years.
- Cash dividends paid will be 70% of EPS.
- At the end of the eight-year period, the market price per share will be four times the book value per share.
- The beta for PG is 0.50, the risk-free rate is 2.0%, and the equity risk premium is 6.2%.

The current market price of PG is \$107.50, which indicates a current P/B of 5.05.

43. Prepare a table that shows the beginning and ending book values, net income, and cash dividends annually for the eight-year period.

44. Estimate the residual income and the present value of residual income for the

eight years.

45. Estimate the value per share of PG stock using the residual income model.

46. Estimate the value per share of PG stock using the dividend discount model. How does this value compare with the estimate from the residual income model?

---

47. Consider the following information about Industrias Gómez.

- Current book value per share is €20.00.
- Expected earnings per share for the next five years are €1.50, €2.50, €3.50, €4.50, and €5.50.
- Dividends per share are projected to be €1.00 for the first three years and €2.00 for the last two years.
- The terminal share price (at the end of Year 5) is expected to be 14× trailing earnings.
- The required rate of return on equity is 9%.
- Estimate the residual income each year, the terminal residual value, and the value per share of Industrias Gómez shares using the residual income model.
- Estimate the value per share of Industrias Gómez shares using the dividend discount model.

48. Lendex Electronics (LE) had a great deal of turnover of top management for several years and was not followed by analysts during this period of turmoil. Because the company's performance has been improving steadily for the past three years, technology analyst Stephanie Kent recently reinitiated coverage of LE. A meeting with management confirms Kent's positive impression of LE's operations and strategic plan. Kent decides LE merits further analysis.

Careful examination of LE's financial statements revealed that the company had negative other comprehensive income from changes in the value of available-for-sale securities in each of the past five years. How, if at all, should this observation about LE's other comprehensive income affect the figures that Kent uses for the company's ROE and book value for those years?

SOLUTIONS

1. Yes, VIM earned a positive residual income of $8,000.

EBIT	$300,000	
Interest	120,000	($2,000,000 × 6%)
Pretax income	$180,000	
Tax expense	72,000	
Net income	$108,000	

Equity charge = Equity capital × Required return on equity

= (1/3)($3,000,000) × 0.10

= $1,000,000 × 0.10 = $100,000

Residual income = Net income – Equity charge

= $108,000 – $100,000 = $8,000

2. In this problem (unlike Problems 1 and 2), interest expense has already been deducted in arriving at NMP's pretax income of $5.1 million.

Therefore,

Net income = Pretax income × (1 – Tax rate)
= $5.1 million × (1 – 0.4)
= $5.1 × 0.6 = $3.06 million

Equity charge = Total equity × Cost of equity capital
= (0.1 × $450 million) × 12%
= $45 million × 0.12 = $5,400,000

Residual income = Net income – Equity charge
= $3,0600,000 - $5,400,000 = –$2,340,000

NMP had negative residual income of –$2,340,000.

3. To achieve a positive residual income, a company's net operating profit after taxes as a percentage of its total assets can be compared with its weighted average cost of capital. For SWI,

NOPAT/Assets = €10 million/€100 million = 10%

WACC = Percent of debt × After-tax cost of debt + Percent of equity × Cost of equity

= (0.5)(0.09)(0.6) + (0.5)(0.12)

= (0.5)(0.054) + (0.5)(0.12) = 0.027 + 0.06 = 0.087

= 8.7%

Therefore, SWI's residual income was positive. Specifically, residual income equals €1.3 million [(0.10 – 0.087) × €100 million].

4. $$\begin{aligned} \text{EVA} &= \text{NOPAT} - \text{WACC} \times \text{Beginning book value of assets} \\ &= \$100 - (11\%) \times (\$200 + \$300) = \$100 - (11\%)(\$500) = \$45 \end{aligned}$$

5. $$\begin{aligned} \text{RI}_t &= E_t - rB_{t-1} \\ &= €5.00 - (11\%)(€30.00) = €5.00 - €3.30 = €1.70 \end{aligned}$$

6. $$\begin{aligned} \text{RI}_t &= (\text{ROE}_t - r) \times B_{t-1} \\ &= (18\% - 12\%) \times (€30) = €1.80 \end{aligned}$$

7. Economic value added = Net operating profit after taxes – (Cost of capital × Total capital) = $100 million – (14% × $700 million) = $2 million. In the absence of information that would be required to calculate the weighted average cost of debt and equity, and given that Sundanci has no long-term debt, the only capital cost used is the required rate of return on equity of 14%.

8. Market value added = Market value of capital – Total capital = $26 stock price × 84 million shares – $700 million = $1,484,000,000.

   Market value added per share = $1,484,000,000 / 84 million shares= $17.67 per share.

9. C is correct. Market value added equals the market value of firm minus total accounting book value of total capital.

   Market value added = Market value of company – Accounting book value of total capital

   Market value of firm = Market value of debt + Market value of equity

   Market value of firm = R55 million + (30,000,000 × R25.43)

   Market value of firm = R55 million + R762.9 million = R817.9 million

   Market value added = R817.9 million – R650 million = R167.9 million, or approximately R168 million.

10. B is correct. The intrinsic value of R22.00 is greater than the current book value of R20.00. The residual income model states that the intrinsic value of a stock is its book value per share plus the present value of expected (future) per share residual income. The higher intrinsic value per share, relative to book value per share, indicates that the present value of expected per share residual income is positive.

11. A is correct because the intrinsic value is the book value per share, B_0,plus the expected residual income stream, or $B_0 + [(\text{ROE} - r)B_0/(r - g)]$. If ROE equals the cost of equity (r), then $V_0 = B_0$. This implies that ROE is equal to the cost of the equity, and therefore there is no residual income contribution to the intrinsic value. As a result, intrinsic value would be equal to book value.

12. B is correct. With a single-stage residual income (RI) model, the intrinsic value, $V_{0,}$ is calculated assuming a constant return on equity (ROE) and a constant earnings growth (g).

    $$V_0 = B_0 + B_0\frac{(\text{ROE} - r)}{(r - g)}$$

    $$V_0 = \text{R}55.81 + \text{R}55.81\frac{(0.13 - 0.11)}{(0.11 - 0.095)}$$

    $$V_0 = \text{R}130.22$$

13. B is correct. The share price of R8.25 was lower than the intrinsic value of R11.00. Shares are considered undervalued when the current share price is less than intrinsic value per share.

14. C is correct. The restructuring charge is a non-recurring item and not indicative of future earnings. In applying a residual income model, it is important to develop a forecast of future residual income based on recurring items. Using the net income reported in Amersheen's 2020 net income statement to model subsequent future earnings, without adjustment for the restructuring charge, would understate the firm's future earnings. By upward adjusting the firm's net income, by adding back the R2 million restructuring charge to reflect the fact that the charge is non-recurring, future earnings will be more accurately forecasted.

15. C is correct. The multistage residual income model results in an intrinsic value of R16.31.

    This variation of the multistage residual income model, in which residual income fades over time, is:

$$V_0 = B_0 + \sum_{t=1}^{T-1} \frac{(E_t - rB_{t-1})}{(1+r)^t} + \frac{(E_T - rB_{T-1})}{(1 + r - \omega)(1+r)^{T-1}}$$

    where ω is the persistence factor.

    The first step is to calculate residual income per share for years 2022–2025:

	2022	2023	2024	2025
Beginning book value per share	R7.60 (given)	R7.60 + R3.28 – R2.46 = R8.42	R8.42 + R3.15 – R2.36 = R9.21	R9.21 + 2.90 – R2.06 = R10.05
ROE	R3.28/R7.60 = 0.4316	R3.15/R8.42 = 0.3741	R2.90/R9.21 = 0.3149	26% (given)
Retention rate	1 – (R2.46/R3.28) = 0.25	1 – (R2.36/R3.15) = 0.2508	1 – (R2.06/R2.90) = 0.2897	N/A
Growth rate	0.4316 × 0.25 =0.1079	0.3741 × 0.2508 = 0.0938	0.3149 × 0.2897 = 0.0912	9% (given)
Equity charge per share	R7.60 × 0.10 = R0.76	R8.42 × 0.10 = R0.842	R9.21 × 0.10 = R0.921	R10.05 × 0.10 = R1.005
Residual income per share	R3.28 – R0.76 = R2.52	R3.15 – R0.842 = R2.31	R2.90 – 0.921 = R1.98	[0.26 × R10.05] – R1.005 = R1.608

    ROE = Earnings/Book value

    Growth rate = ROE × Retention rate

    Retention rate = 1 – (Dividends/Earnings)

    Book value$_t$ = Book value$_{t-1}$ + Earnings$_{t-1}$ – Dividends$_{t-1}$

    Residual income per share = EPS – Equity charge per share

    Equity charge per share = Book value per share$_t$ × Cost of equity

    Using the residual income per share for 2015 of R1.608, the second step is to calculate the present value of the terminal value:

$$\text{PV of Terminal Value} = \frac{\text{R}1.608}{(1 + 0.10 - 0.70)(1.10)^3} = \text{R}3.0203$$

    Then, intrinsic value per share is:

$$V_0 = \text{R}7.60 + \frac{\text{R}2.52}{(1.10)} + \frac{\text{R}2.31}{(1.10)^2} + \frac{\text{R}1.98}{(1.10)^3} + \text{R}3.0203 = \text{R}16.31$$

16. A is correct. The multistage residual income model results in an intrinsic value of R13.29. The multistage residual income model, is:

$$V_0 = B_0 + \sum_{t=1}^{T} \frac{(E_t - rB_{t-1})}{(1+r)^t} + \frac{(P_T - B_T)}{(1+r)^T}$$

The first step is to calculate residual income per share for years 2022–2024:

	2022	2023	2024
Beginning book value per share	R7.60 (given)	R7.60 + R3.28 – R2.46 = R8.42	R8.42 + R3.15 – R2.36 = R9.21
ROE	R3.28/R7.60 = 0.4316	R3.15/R8.42 = 0.3741	R2.90/R9.21 = 0.3149
Retention rate	1 – (R2.46/R3.28) = 0.25	1 – (R2.36/R3.15) = 0.2508	1 – (R2.06/R2.90) = 0.2897
Growth rate	0.4316 × 0.25=0.1079	0.3741 × 0.2508 = 0.0938	0.3149 × 0.2897= 0.0912
Equity charge per share	R7.60 × 0.10 = R0.76	R8.42 × 0.10 = R0.842	R9.21 × 0.10 = R0.921
Residual income per share	R3.28 – R0.76 = R2.52	R3.15 – R0.842 = R2.31	R2.90 – 0.921= R1.98

ROE = Earnings/Book value

Growth rate = ROE × Retention rate

Retention rate = 1 – (Dividends/Earnings)

Book value$_t$ = Book value$_{t-1}$ + Earnings$_{t-1}$ – Dividends$_{t-1}$

Residual income per share = EPS – Equity charge per share

Equity charge per share = Book value per share$_t$ × Cost of equity

Under Scenario 2, at the end of 2024, it is assumed that share price will be equal to book value per share. This results in the second term in the equation above, the present value of the terminal value, being equal to zero.

Then, intrinsic value per share is:

$$V_0 = \text{R}7.60 + \frac{\text{R}2.52}{(1.10)} + \frac{\text{R}2.31}{(1.10)^2} + \frac{\text{R}1.98}{(1.10)^3} = \text{R}13.29$$

17. B is correct. The residual income model's use of accounting income assumes that the cost of debt capital is reflected appropriately by interest expense.

18. A is correct. Dividend payments are forecasted to be unpredictable over Castovan's five-year forecast horizon. A residual income model is appropriate when a company does not pay dividends or when its dividends are not predictable, which is the case for PTU.

19. C is correct. Other comprehensive income bypasses the income statement and goes directly to the statement of stockholders' equity (which is a violation of the clean surplus relationship). Therefore, book value per share for PTU will be affected by forecasted OCI.

20. C is correct. The residual income can be calculated using net income and the equity charge or using net operating profit after taxes and the total capital charge.

Residual income = Net income – Equity charge

Calculation of Net Income (values in millions):

EBIT	€700.0	
Less Interest expense	€124.8	(= €4,000 × 0.60 × 0.052)
Pretax income	€575.2	
Less Income tax expense	€201.3	(= €575.20 × 0.35)
Net income	€373.9	

Equity charge = Total assets × Equity weighting × Cost of equity

Equity charge = €4,000 million × 0.40 × 0.15 = €240 million

Therefore, residual income = €373.9 million – €240 million = €133.9 million. Alternatively, residual income can be calculated from NOPAT as follows.

Residual income = NOPAT – Total capital charge

NOPAT = EBIT × (1 – Tax rate)

NOPAT = €700 million × (1 – 0.35) = €455 million

The total capital charge is as follows.

Equity charge = Total assets × Equity weighting × Cost of equity

= €4,000 million × 0.40 × 0.15

= €240 million

Debt charge = Total assets × Debt weighting × Pretax cost of debt × (1 – Tax rate)

= €4,000 million × 0.60 × 0.052(1 – 0.35)

= €81.1 million

Total capital charge = €240 million + €81.1 million

= €321.1 million

Therefore, residual income = €455 million – €321.1 million = €133.9 million.

21. B is correct. The implied growth rate of earnings from the single-stage RI model is calculated by solving for g in the following equation:

$$V_0 = B_0 + \left(\frac{\text{ROE} - r}{r - g}\right) B_0$$

Book value per share can be calculated using the given price-to-book ratio and market price per share as follows.

Book value per share (B_0) = Market price per share/Price-to-book ratio

= €48.80/2.10 = €23.24

Then, solve for the implied growth rate.

$$€48.80 = €23.24 + \left(\frac{0.2337 - 0.15}{0.15 - g}\right) €23.24$$

g = 7.4%

22. C is correct. Using the single-stage RI model, the intrinsic value of TTCI is calculated as

$$V_0 = B_0 + \left(\frac{\text{ROE} - r}{r - g}\right) B_0$$

$$= €45.25 + \left(\frac{0.12 - 0.087}{0.087 - 0.045}\right) €45.25$$

$$= €80.80$$

The intrinsic value of €80.80 is less than the market price of €126.05, so Castovan should conclude that the stock is overvalued.

23. A is correct. The justified price-to-book ratio is calculated as

$$\frac{P}{B} = 1 + \left(\frac{\text{ROE} - r}{r - g}\right)$$
$$= 1 + \left(\frac{0.12 - 0.087}{0.087 - 0.045}\right) = 1.79$$

24. C is correct. Residual income per share for the next three years is calculated as follows.

	Year 1	Year 2	Year 3
Beginning book value per share	45.25	51.61	58.25
Earnings per share	7.82	8.17	8.54
Less dividends per share	1.46	1.53	1.59
Change in retained earnings	6.36	6.64	6.95
Ending book value per share	51.61	58.25	65.20
Earnings per share	7.82	8.17	8.54
Less per share equity charge*	3.94	4.49	5.07
Residual income	3.88	3.68	3.47

** Per share equity charge = Beginning book value per share × Cost of equity*
Year 1 per share equity charge = 45.25 × 0.087 = 3.94
Year 2 per share equity charge = 51.61 × 0.087 = 4.49
Year 3 per share equity charge = 58.25 × 0.087 = 5.07

Because Castovan forecasts that residual income per share will be constant into perpetuity, equal to Year 3 residual income per share, the present value of the terminal value is calculated using a persistence factor of 1.

$$\text{Present value of terminal value} = \frac{8.54 - (0.087 \times 58.25)}{(1 + 0.087 - 1)(1 + 0.087)^2}$$
$$= \frac{3.47}{(0.087)(1.087)^2}$$
$$= 33.78$$

So, the intrinsic value of TTCI is then calculated as follows.

$$V_0 = €45.25 + \frac{3.88}{1.087} + \frac{3.68}{1.087^2} + 33.78 = €85.71$$

25. A is correct. In Castovan's multistage valuation, she assumes that TTCI's residual income will remain constant in perpetuity after Year 3. This perpetuity assumption implies a persistence factor of 1 in the calculation of the terminal value. A persistence factor of 0.10 indicates that TTCI's residual income is forecasted to decline at an average rate of 90% per year. This assumption would lead to a lower valuation than Castovan's multistage value estimate, which assumes that residual income will remain constant in perpetuity after Year 3.

26. B is correct. Beckworth's suggested persistence factor for TTCI is 0.10, which is quite low. Companies with extreme accounting rates of return typically have low persistence factors. Companies with strong market leadership positions and low dividend payouts are likely to have high persistence factors.

27. According to the residual income model, the intrinsic value of a share of common stock equals book value per share plus the present value of expected future per-share residual income. Book value per share was given as $20. If we note that debt is $2,000,000 [(2/3)($3,000,000)] so that interest is $120,000 ($2,000,000 × 6%), VIM's residual income is $8,000, which is calculated (as in Problem 1) as

follows:

Residual income = Net income – Equity charge

= [(EBIT – Interest)(1 – Tax rate)] – [(Equity capital)(Required return on equity)]

= [($300,000 – $120,000)(1 – 0.40)] – [($1,000,000)(0.10)]

= $108,000 – $100,000

= $8,000

Therefore, residual income per share is $0.16 per share ($8,000/50,000 shares). Because EBIT is expected to continue at the current level indefinitely, the expected per-share residual income of $0.16 is treated as a perpetuity. The present value of $0.16 is discounted at the required return on equity of 10%, so the present value of the residual income is $1.60 ($0.16/0.10).

Intrinsic value = Book value per share + PV of expected future income per-share residual income

= $20 + $1.60 = $21.60

28. With $g = b \times \text{ROE} = (1 - 0.80)\ (0.15) = (0.20)\ (0.15) = 0.03$,

$P/B = (\text{ROE} - g)/(r - g)$

$= (0.15 - 0.03)/(0.12 - 0.03)$

$= 0.12/0.09 = 1.33$

or

$P/B = 1 + (\text{ROE} - r)/(r - g)$

$= 1 + (0.15 - 0.12)/(0.12 - 0.03)$

$= 1.33$

29. Because the dividend is a perpetuity, the no-growth form of the DDM is applied as follows:

$V_0 = D/r$

$= \$0.60/0.12 = \$5$ per share

30. According to the residual income model, V_0 = Book value per share + Present value of expected future per-share residual income.
Residual income is calculated as:

$\text{RI}_t = E - rB_{t-1}$

$= \$0.60 - (0.12)(\$6) = -\$0.12$

Present value of perpetual stream of residual income is calculated as:

$\text{RI}_t/r = -\$0.12/0.12 = -\$1.00$

The value is calculated as:

$V_0 = \$6.00 - \$1.00 = \$5.00$ per share

31. According to the DDM, $V_0 = D/r$ for a no-growth company.

$V_0 = \$2.00/0.125 = \$16$ per share

32. Under the residual income model, $V_0 = B_0$ + Present value of expected future per-share residual income.
Residual income is calculated as:

$$\text{RI}_t = E - rB_{t-1}$$
$$= \$2 - (0.125)(\$10) = \$0.75$$

Present value of stream of residual income is calculated as:

$\text{RI}_t/r = 0.75/0.125 = \$6$

The value is calculated as:

$V_0 = \$10 + \$6 = \$16$ per share

33. V_0 = Present value of the future dividends
$= \$2/1.10 + \$2.50/(1.1)^2 + \$20.50/(1.1)^3$
$= \$1.818 + \$2.066 + \$15.402 = \$19.286$

34. The book values and residual incomes for the next three years are as follows:

Year	1	2	3
Beginning book value	\$ 8.00	\$10.00	\$12.50
Retained earnings (Net income – Dividends)	2.00	2.50	(12.50)
Ending book value	\$10.00	\$12.50	\$ 0.00
Net income	\$ 4.00	\$ 5.00	\$ 8.00
Less equity charge (r × Book value)	0.80	1.00	1.25
Residual income	\$ 3.20	\$ 4.00	\$ 6.75

Under the residual income model,

$V_0 = B_0$ + Present value of expected future per-share residual income

$V_0 = \$8.00 + \$3.20/1.1 + \$4.00/(1.1)^2 + \$6.75/(1.1)^3$

$V_0 = 8.00 + \$2.909 + \$3.306 + \$5.071 = \$19.286$

35.

Year	1	2	3
Net income (NI)	\$4.00	\$5.00	\$8.00
Beginning book value (BV)	8.00	10.00	12.50
Return on equity (ROE) = NI/BV	50%	50%	64%

Year	1	2	3
ROE − r	40%	40%	54%
Residual income (ROE − r) × BV	\$3.20	\$4.00	\$6.75

Under the residual income model,

$V_0 = B_0$ + Present value of expected future per-share residual income

$V_0 = \$8.00 + \$3.20/1.1 + \$4.00/(1.1)^2 + \$6.75/(1.1)^3$

$V_0 = 8.00 + \$2.909 + \$3.306 + \$5.071 = \$19.286$

36.

Year	2018	2019	2022
Beginning book value	\$30.00	\$33.00	\$43.92
Net income = ROE × Book value	4.50	4.95	6.59
Dividends = payout × Net income	1.50	1.65	2.20
Equity charge (r × Book value)	3.60	3.96	5.27
Residual income = Net income − Equity charge	0.90	0.99	1.32
Ending book value	\$33.00	\$36.30	\$48.32

The table shows that residual income in Year 2018 is \$0.90, which equals Beginning book value × (ROE − r) = \$30 × (0.15 − 0.12). The Year 2019 column shows that residual income grew by 10% to \$0.99, which follows from the fact that growth in residual income relates directly to the growth in net income as this example is configured. When both net income and dividends are a function of book value and return on equity is constant, then growth, g, can be predicted from (ROE)(1 − Dividend payout ratio). In this case, g = 0.15 × (1 − 0.333) = 0.10 or 10%. Net income and residual income will grow by 10% annually.

Therefore, residual income in Year 2022 = (Residual income in Year 2018) × $(1.1)^4$ = 0.90 × 1.4641 = \$1.32.

37. The justified P/B can be found with the following formula:

$$\frac{P_0}{B_0} = 1 + \frac{\text{ROE} - r}{r - g}$$

ROE is 20%, g is 5.5%, and r is 8.2% [$R_F + \beta_i[E(R_M) - RF]$ = 4.46% + (0.68)(5.5%)]. Substituting in the values gives a justified P/B of

$$\frac{P_0}{B_0} = 1 + \frac{0.20 - 0.082}{0.082 - 0.055} = 5.37$$

The assumed parameters give a justified P/B of 5.37, slightly above the current P/B of 3.68.

38. To find the ROE that would result in a P/B of 3.68, we substitute 3.68, r, and g into the following equation:

$$\frac{P_0}{B_0} = 1 + \frac{\text{ROE} - r}{r - g}$$

This yields

$$3.68 = 1 + \frac{ROE - 0.082}{0.082 - 0.055}$$

Solving for ROE requires several steps to finally derive a ROE of 0.15435 or 15.4%. This value of ROE is consistent with a P/B of 3.68.

39. To find the growth rate that would result with a P/B of 3.68, use the expression given in Part B, but solve for g instead of ROE:

$$\frac{P_0}{B_0} = 1 + \frac{\text{ROE} - r}{r - g}$$

Substituting in the values gives:

$$3.68 = 1 + \frac{0.20 - 0.082}{0.082 - g}$$

The growth rate g is 0.03797, or 3.8%. If we assume that the single-stage growth model is applicable to Thales, the current P/B and current market price can be justified with values for ROE or g that are quite a bit lower than the starting values of 20% and 5.5%, respectively.

40.
$$\begin{aligned} V_0 &= B_0 + (\text{ROE} - r) B_0 / (r - g) \\ &= \$20 + (0.18 - 0.14)(\$20) / (0.14 - 0.10) \\ &= \$20 + \$20 = \$40 \end{aligned}$$

Given that the current market price is \$35 and the estimated value is \$40, Simms will probably conclude that the shares are somewhat undervalued.

41.
$$\begin{aligned} V_0 &= B_0 + (\text{ROE} - r) B_0 / (r - g) \\ &= \$30 + (0.15 - 0.12)(\$30) / (0.12 - 0.10) \\ &= \$30 + \$45 = \$75 \text{ per share} \end{aligned}$$

42.

Year	Net Income (Projected)	Ending Book Value	ROE (%)	Equity Charge (in Currency)	Residual Income	PV of RI
2020		$10.00				
2021	$1.50	11.50	15	$1.00	$0.50	$0.45
2022	1.73	13.23	15	1.15	0.58	0.48
2023	1.99	15.22	15	1.32	0.67	0.50
2024	2.29	17.51	15	1.52	0.77	0.53
2025	2.63	20.14	15	1.75	0.88	0.55
						$2.51

Using the finite horizon form of residual income valuation,

$$V_0 = B_0 + \text{Sum of discounted RIs} + \text{Premium (also discounted to present)}$$

$$= \$10 + \$2.51 + (0.20)(20.14)/(1.10)^5$$

$$= \$10 + \$2.51 + \$2.50 = \$15.01$$

43. Columns (a) through (d) in the table show calculations for beginning book value, net income, dividends, and ending book value.

	(a)	(b)	(c)	(d)	(e)	(f)
Year	Beginning Book Value	Net Income	Dividends	Ending Book Value	Residual Income	PV of RI
1	$21.300	$3.834	$2.684	$22.450	$2.748	$2.614
2	22.450	4.041	2.829	23.663	2.896	2.622
3	23.663	4.259	2.981	24.940	3.052	2.629
4	24.940	4.489	3.142	26.287	3.217	2.637
5	26.287	4.732	3.312	27.707	3.391	2.644
6	27.707	4.987	3.491	29.203	3.574	2.652
7	29.203	5.256	3.680	30.780	3.767	2.659
8	30.780	5.540	3.878	32.442	3.971	2.667
Total						$21.125

For each year, net income is 18% of beginning book value. Dividends are 70% of net income. The ending book value equals the beginning book value plus net income minus dividends.

44. Column (e) of the table in Part A shows Residual income, which equals Net income – Cost of equity (%) × Beginning book value.

To find the cost of equity, use the CAPM:

$$r = R_F + \beta_i[E(R_M) - R_F] = 2\% + (0.50)(6.2\%) = 5.1\%$$

For Year 1 in the table,

$$\text{Residual income} = \text{RI}_t = E - rB_{t-1}$$
$$= 3.834 - (5.1\%)(21.30)$$
$$= 3.834 - 1.086 = \$2.748$$

This same calculation is repeated for Years 2 through 8.

Column (f) of the table gives the present value of the calculated residual income, discounted at 5.1%.

45. To find the stock value with the residual income method, use this equation:

$$V_0 = B_0 + \sum_{t=1}^{T} \frac{(E_t - rB_{t-1})}{(1+r)^t} + \frac{P_T - B_T}{(1+r)^T}$$

- In this equation, B_0 is the current book value per share of $21.30.
- The second term, the sum of the present values of the eight years' residual income is shown in the table, $21.125.
- To estimate the final term, the present value of the excess of the terminal stock price over the terminal book value, use the assumption that the terminal stock price is assumed to be 4.0× the terminal book value. So, by assumption, the terminal stock price is $129.767 [$P_T = 4.0(32.442)$]. $P_T - B_T$ is $97.325 (129.767 – 32.442), and the present value of this amount discounted at 5.1% for eight years is $65.374.
- Summing the relevant terms gives a stock price of $107.799 ($V_0 = 21.30 + 21.125 + 65.374$).

46. The appropriate DDM expression expresses the value of the stock as the sum of

the present value of the dividends plus the present value of the terminal value:

$$V_0 = \sum_{t=1}^{T} \frac{D_t}{(1+r)^t} + \frac{P_T}{(1+r)^T}$$

Discounting the dividends from the table shown in the solution to Part A above at 5.10% gives:

Year	Dividend	PV of Dividend
1	$2.684	2.554
2	2.829	2.561
3	2.981	2.568
4	3.142	2.575
5	3.312	2.583
6	3.491	2.590
7	3.680	2.598
8	3.878	2.605
All		$20.634

- The present value of the eight dividends is $20.634. The estimated terminal stock price, calculated in the solution to Part C above is $129.767, which equals $87.165 discounted at 5.1% for eight years.
- The value for the stock, the present value of the dividends plus the present value of the terminal stock price, is V_0 = 20.634 + 87.165 = $107.799.
- The stock values estimated with the residual income model and the dividend discount model are identical. Because they are based on similar financial assumptions, this equivalency is expected. Even though the two models differ in their timing of the recognition of value, their final results are the same.

47.

A. The value found with the residual income model is:

Year	Beginning BV	Net Income	Dividends	Ending BV	Residual Income	PV of Residual Income
1	20.00	1.50	1.00	20.50	−0.300	−0.275
2	20.50	2.50	1.00	22.00	0.655	0.551
3	22.00	3.50	1.00	24.50	1.520	1.174
4	24.50	4.50	2.00	27.00	2.295	1.626
5	27.00	5.50	2.00	30.50	3.070	1.995
			Sum PVRI			5.071
			Terminal $P_T - B_T$		46.500	
			PV of $P_T - B_T$			30.222
			B_0			20.000
			Total value:			€55.293

Residual income each year is Net income – 0.09 × (Beginning BV). The PV of residual income is found by discounting at 9%. The terminal price is 14 × EPS in Year 5, or 14 × 5.50 = €77.00. The terminal residual value is $P_T - B_T$ = 77.00 – 30.50 = €46.50. Discounted at 9%, the PV of €46.50 is €30.222. The value per share is B_0 + PV of residual income + PV of terminal residual value, which is €55.293.

B. The value found with the dividend discount model is as follows:

Year	Dividend or Price	PV of Dividend or Price
1	1.00	0.917
2	1.00	0.842
3	1.00	0.772
4	2.00	1.417
5	2.00	1.300
5	77.00	50.045
	Total PV	€55.293

The values per share found with the DDM and the residual income model are an identical €55.293.

48. When such items as changes in the value of available-for-sale securities bypass the income statement, they are generally assumed to be nonoperating items that will fluctuate from year to year, although averaging to zero in a period of years. The evidence suggests, however, that changes in the value of available-for-sale securities are not averaging to zero but are persistently negative. Furthermore, these losses are bypassing the income statement. It appears that the company is either making an inaccurate assumption or misleading investors in one way or another. Accordingly, Kent might adjust LE's income downward by the amount of loss for other comprehensive income for each of those years. ROE would then decline commensurately. LE's book value would *not* be misstated because the decline in the value of these securities was already recognized and appears in the shareholders' equity account "Accumulated Other Comprehensive Income."

LEARNING MODULE

6

Private Company Valuation

LEARNING OUTCOMES

Mastery	The candidate should be able to:
☐	contrast important public and private company features for valuation purposes
☐	describe uses of private business valuation and explain key areas of focus for financial analysts
☐	explain cash flow estimation issues related to private companies and adjustments required to estimate normalized earnings
☐	explain factors that require adjustment when estimating the discount rate for private companies
☐	compare models used to estimate the required rate of return to private company equity (for example, the CAPM, the expanded CAPM, and the build-up approach)
☐	explain and evaluate the effects on private company valuations of discounts and premiums based on control and marketability
☐	explain the income, market, and asset-based approaches to private company valuation and factors relevant to the selection of each approach
☐	calculate the value of a private company using income-based methods
☐	calculate the value of a private company using market-based methods and describe the advantages and disadvantages of each method

INTRODUCTION

1

Until now we have focused on the valuation of publicly held companies with periodic audited financial statements and an observable market-based share price. Private companies are those whose shares are not listed on public markets ranging from sole proprietorships to multigenerational family businesses to formerly public companies that have been taken private in management buyouts or other transactions. Many large, successful companies exist that have remained private since inception, such as the Tata Group in India, IKEA and ALDI in Europe, and Cargill and Bechtel in the United States.

The process of valuing private companies based on discounted cash flows or relative value based on multiples is the same as for public companies. However, the lack of market pricing, audited financial statements in some cases, concentrated control, and other issues unique to privately held firms require adjustments to the valuation process. In what follows, we identify and address these differences, introduce principles of private company valuation, and demonstrate their application using several examples. These principles apply to firms of different sizes, life-cycle stages, and ownership structures, as well as other private markets such as real estate and infrastructure.

OVERVIEW

- In contrast to public companies, private companies which choose not to or cannot access public equity markets range widely in size, stage of development, and quality of financial disclosure and often involve illiquid, concentrated ownership directly held by the company's management or private equity investors.
- Private company valuations are conducted to facilitate transactions, ensure compliance with financial or tax reporting, or resolve legal disputes. Key areas of focus include cash flow and earnings issues, discount rate or required rate of return adjustments, and valuation discounts or premiums.
- Cash flow and earnings adjustments for private companies aim to identify and address financial statement inconsistencies to ensure their relevance as a baseline for forecasting future earnings.
- Discount rates representing a private company's cost of capital or cost of equity are usually adjusted for company-specific factors including size and lack of public market access. The limited applicability of CAPM to private company rates of return results in the use of an expanded CAPM or a build-up approach which adds risk premia to the risk-free rate.
- Adjustments to private company value involve the application of a control premium, or a lack of control and marketability discount based upon the circumstances of specific private companies and their shareholders.
- Valuation approaches for private companies are conceptually similar to those used for public companies and include an income approach based upon discounted cash flows, a market approach based upon price multiples of firms with similar features, and an asset-based approach which seeks to estimate the value of underlying assets less liabilities.
- The process of valuing a mature private firm using an income- or market-based approach often involves using comparable public companies to estimate a company's cost of capital or price multiples.

PUBLIC VS. PRIVATE COMPANY VALUATION

2

☐ contrast important public and private company features for valuation purposes

Public company valuation is usually conducted based on standard issuer disclosures and a share price which represents the collective expectations of market participants regarding firm value. Analysts typically rely on audited financial statements as a basis to project future cash flows, taking the perspective of an outside investor with a non-controlling stake in the company. The intrinsic value from the valuation process is compared to the market price to assess whether a company's stock is over- or undervalued.

Features which distinguish private company investments that are broadly relevant for the valuation process are summarized in Exhibit 1.

Exhibit 1: Public Versus Private Company Features

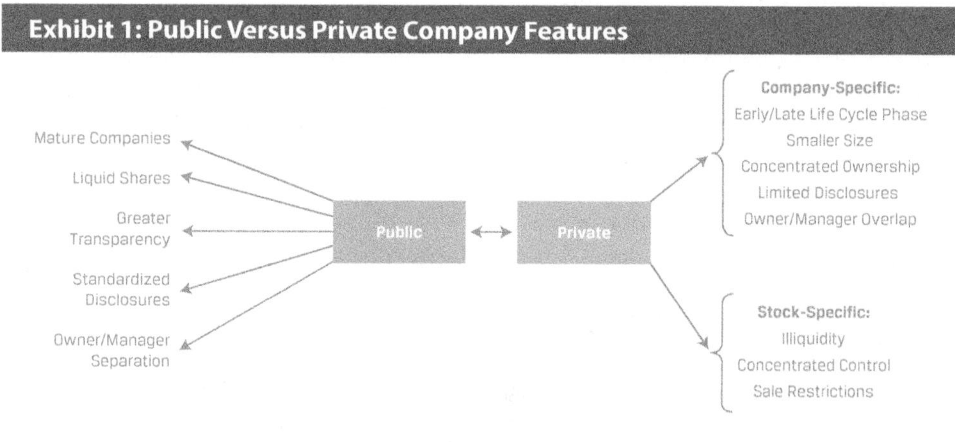

These characteristics include company-specific factors including its life-cycle stage, size, and the characteristics and goals of management. Private company ownership stakes also differ significantly from common shares in publicly traded companies due to their lack of liquidity, concentration of ownership control which may impact some shareholders differently than others, and share sale restrictions, all of which affect company valuation.

Public stock exchanges usually impose company listing requirements including a minimum number of shareholders or float, a minimum asset or net worth size, as well as positive net income and reporting requirements which increase transparency. Private companies in contrast often involve small companies at an early stage of development with minimal capital, assets, or employees, but may also involve large, stable, going concerns or failed companies in the process of liquidation. Family ownership or other forms of concentrated control (i.e., through private equity or different share classes) can make public companies take on private firm characteristics.

Private firms in an industry tend to be smaller than public firms as gauged by income, asset size, or other measures. The valuation of smaller firms often warrants the use of a higher required rate of return due to greater income variability and risk resulting from fewer and less-diversified lines of business and customers; less well developed marketing, sales, and distribution; or in some cases limited growth prospects because of reduced access to capital.

In contrast to that of most public companies, the senior management of many private firms often has a controlling ownership interest in the company. This feature of private companies greatly reduces the principal-agent problem which may arise when owners and managers are separate. The alignment of private company ownership and management allows more direct control over strategic decisions than for public companies. For example, private equity firms often acquire underperforming public companies to restructure, divest, or acquire lines of business while under private ownership and control with the goal of selling the reorganized firm at a higher price to another private buyer or the public via an IPO. Private company managers can take a longer-term perspective in strategic decision making without pressure from external investors seeking short-term gains on publicly traded shares. As many private companies are family owned, family dynamics often play a role as well.

FAMILY OWNERSHIP OF PRIVATE COMPANIES

Family owned and operated businesses dominate the private company landscape in many developed and developing economies.

For example, the small and medium-sized enterprises in the German-speaking countries of Germany, Austria, and Switzerland known as the *Mittelstand* are predominantly family owned and managed. In Germany, they comprise over 90% of total companies, employ approximately 58% of the workforce, and generate over a third of all domestic sales of goods and services. Many *Mittelstand* companies are globally competitive, export-oriented producers of niche products in the capital goods and electronics sectors.

In developing markets where the legal, institutional, and financial infrastructure is often less well established, family companies often benefit from pooled resources from family and friends as well as earnings reinvestment, a greater reliance on trust and personal business relationships, and in some cases a culture in which family members are often more likely to continue operating businesses than to transition solely to an investor role.

As family firms in both developed and emerging markets are passed from one generation to the next, private company valuation often plays an important role as business owners consider turning over control to non-family managers while retaining ownership, accessing external capital, or selling a minority stake or the entire business.

In addition to the company-specific factors just discussed, the ownership features of private company stock frequently differ markedly from those of public companies. Stock-specific factors include the illiquidity of private company shares which is a primary feature affecting company valuation. The limited number of existing and potential buyers reduces the value of the shares in private companies versus otherwise similar public companies.

Other stock-specific factors include the fact that private companies typically have fewer shareholders, with control often concentrated with one or among very few investors. Concentrated control may lead to corporate actions which benefit some shareholders at the expense of others. For example, above-market executive compensation or transactions with entities related to a controlling shareholder group at above-market prices can transfer value away from the corporation's non-controlling shareholders. Note that the "concentration of control" factor may also be viewed as "company specific." Shareholder agreements that restrict the ability to sell shares may also reduce the marketability of equity interests.

The stock-specific factors just listed are generally a negative for private company valuation. However, company-specific factors may be positive or negative. For example, an early-stage private company controlled by a founder may have far greater growth potential than many public companies, while a private firm in an established industry which is smaller than public rivals may be at a competitive disadvantage. The range of private company features is such that the spectrum of risk and return requirements is wider than for public companies. Valuation assumptions and estimates applied to private companies often diverge more than for public firms based upon the purpose of the valuation and the analyst's perspective as well as the amount and quality of financial information available.

KNOWLEDGE CHECK

1. Thunder Corporation is a small household products company privately held by its original shareholders, none of whom are employed by the company. Thunder's senior management has managed operations for the past decade and expects to remain in that capacity after any sale. The company has no access to public debt markets. The least likely source of differences in valuing Thunder compared with valuing a publicly traded company is:

   A. access to public debt markets.

   B. principal-agent issues.

   C. company size.

   Solution:

   B is correct. Thunder's size and lack of access to public debt markets are potential factors affecting its valuation compared with a public company. Given the separation of ownership and control at Thunder similar to that at public companies, however, principal-agent issues are not a distinguishing factor in its valuation.

2. Sun and Moon Ltd. is owned and managed by five general partners. Two of the partners each own 35% stakes in the company, while the other three general partners each own 10% stakes in the company. Once per year, a private valuation expert values each partner's stake in the business. Which factor reflects why there could be a difference in the value (on a per share basis) across the different partners' stakes?

   A. Concentrated ownership

   B. Owner/manager overlap

   C. Concentrated control

   Solution:

   C is correct. The two partners with 35% stakes will have a higher probability of creating a control position of Sun and Moon by coordinating their ownership stakes with each other, thus creating a 70% stake and effective control of the company. The 10% shareholders must coordinate across at least two of their fellow shareholders to create a control position. While the coordination of general partners can create majority control, the size of each partner's stake does not represent concentrated ownership, so A is not correct. B is not correct because each partner is involved in managing the company, so the owner/manager overlap should not affect the valuation of each partner's stake.

3. Privacy Group and PT Corp. are two very similar businesses in terms of size and business models, and both are majority family-owned companies with significant family influence in the management of the companies. The only

major difference is that PT Corp. has publicly traded stock while Privacy Group has no public shareholders. Which factor is likely to account for any significant difference in the valuation of these two firms?

A. Owner/manager agency problems

B. Illiquidity of shares

C. Concentrated control

Solution:

B is correct. PT's stock is publicly traded, thus its shareholders benefit from the liquidity of the shares while Privacy's shareholders are hurt by the lack of a liquid market for their shares. Both companies are majority family-owned and managed, thus any agency problems are likely not severe, and concentration of control is not materially different.

3 PRIVATE COMPANY VALUATION USES AND AREAS OF FOCUS

☐ describe uses of private business valuation and explain key areas of focus for financial analysts

Uses of Private Company Valuation

Private business or equity valuations are typically conducted to facilitate a potential transfer of ownership or incremental financing, as well as for compliance and litigation purposes as summarized in Exhibit 2.

Exhibit 2: Purposes of Private Company Valuation

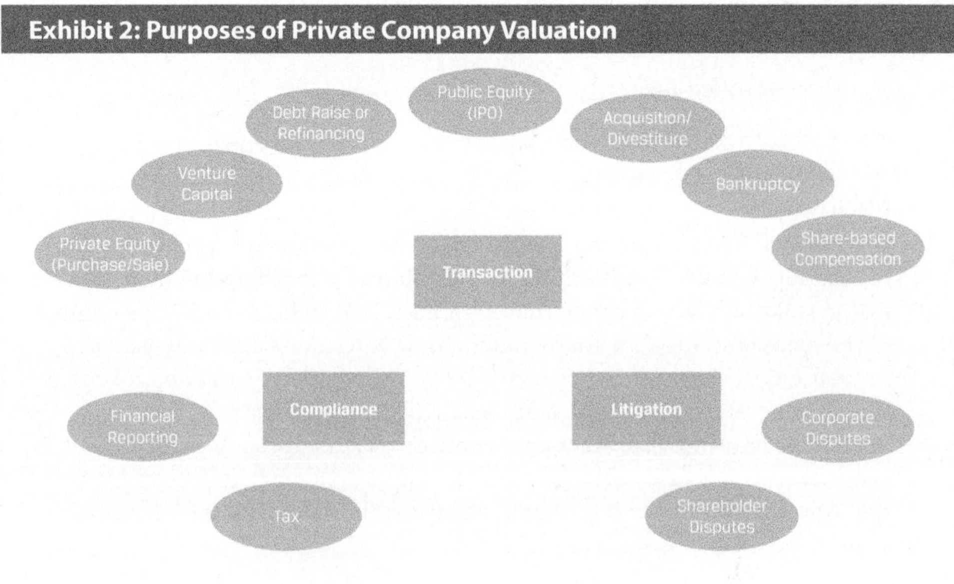

Transaction-related valuations encompass events affecting the ownership or financing of a business and represent a primary area of private company valuation. These transactions include the following:

- *Venture capital financing (early stage).* Early-stage or venture capital (VC) firms often seek equity investors through multiple rounds of financing tied to the achievement of key company developments or milestones. When future cash flows are highly uncertain, less formal valuations are often used as a basis for negotiation between the company and prospective investors.
- *Private equity financing (growth or buyout stage).* These are typically growth or buyout transactions. Growth equity funds target companies with potential for scalable and renewed growth. Unlike buyout funds, they usually take a minority stake with the intention of rapidly growing the business. But—as with buyout funds—the goal is to exit at a higher valuation. Unlike VC or growth equity, which both involve minority-stake investments in early-stage or growing companies, leveraged buyout firms acquire majority control and seek to create value through more efficient business practices and optimizing the balance sheet.
- *Debt financing.* Private company issuers and lenders may perform a valuation to determine a firm's ability to repay existing debt from current operating cash flows, or its capacity to assume additional debt to restructure the company, expand, or purchase another company.
- *Initial public offering (IPO).* Prospective primary market investors, the issuer, and their investment banking advisors typically prepare valuations as part of the IPO process when a private company approaches the public equity market. IPOs are often conducted under the following circumstances:
- An early-stage firm expands beyond private founder and VC financing to attract public equity investment.
- A new public company is created from the divestiture or spin-off of a division or line of business from an existing public company.
- A firm which was previously held by the public returns to public markets following a restructuring phase under private ownership.
- *Acquisitions and divestitures.* The purchase or sale of a stand-alone company or an existing company division or line of business is a common strategy for development-stage or mature companies. Acquisition-related valuations may be performed by the management of the target and/or buyer as well as investment banking advisors typically involved in larger transactions.
- *Bankruptcy.* Firms operating under bankruptcy protection may use company- and asset-based valuations to determine whether a company is more valuable as a going concern or in liquidation. For viable going concerns operating in bankruptcy, valuation insights may be critical to the restructuring of an overleveraged capital structure.
- *Share-based incentive compensation.* Share-based payments can be viewed as transactions between a company and its employees. These transactions often have accounting and tax implications for the issuer and the employee. Share-based payments include stock option grants, restricted stock grants, and transactions involving an employee stock ownership plan in the United States and equivalent structures elsewhere. For private companies, stock option grants will frequently require valuations.

Compliance-related valuations support actions required by law or regulation and include financial reporting and tax reporting.

- *Financial reporting.* Investment firms require ongoing valuations for performance reporting and measurement purposes, as do (public or private) companies that have acquired another company for the purposes of impairment testing. Components or divisions of public companies are also valued using private company valuation techniques.
- *Tax reporting.* Tax-related reasons for private company valuations include corporate and individual tax reporting. For example, activities such as corporate restructurings, transfer pricing, and property tax matters may require valuations. An individual's tax requirements, such as those arising from estate and gift taxation in some jurisdictions, may generate a need for private company valuations.
- *Litigation.* Legal proceedings requiring valuations include those related to damages, lost profits, shareholder disputes, and divorce. Litigation may affect public or private companies or may be between shareholders with no effect at the corporate level.

Each of the three major practice areas (transactions, compliance, and litigation) for private company valuation requires specialized knowledge and skills, leading many valuation professionals to focus their efforts in one of these areas. Transactions, for example, often involve investment bankers, while compliance valuations usually require detailed knowledge of relevant accounting or tax rules. Litigation-related valuations require effective presentations in a legal setting.

Different definitions or standards of value exist depending upon the context of a valuation and key elements pertaining to the private company. For example, a firm's fair market value for financial or tax reporting purposes may differ from its investment value to a potential acquiror willing to pay a premium given the possible synergies of a business combination.

Private Company Valuation Areas of Focus

Three key areas related to private company valuation warrant the particular attention of analysts, regardless of the purpose of the valuation or the analyst's perspective in conducting the valuation as shown in Exhibit 3.

Exhibit 3: Areas of Focus for Private Company Valuation

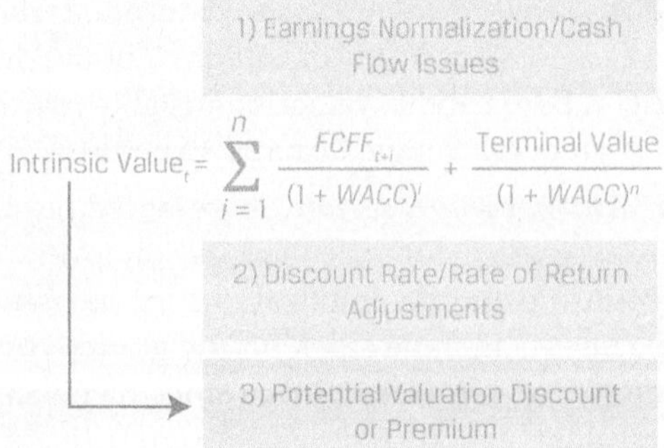

$$FCFF = EBITDA(1 - t) + Depreciation(t) - \Delta LT\ Assets - \Delta Working\ Capital$$

Analysts using the familiar enterprise-based free cash flow to the firm (FCFF) discounted cash flow valuation approach to public companies must consider three important adjustments when valuing a private company:

1 *Cash Flow and Earnings Adjustments:* Periodic financial statements prepared according to generally accepted accounting principles are equally accessible to all analysts for public companies. However, in the case of private companies, analysts must first identify and adjust key balance sheet and income statement items to address private versus public company differences to estimate a company's normalized earnings. These adjustments affect the *numerator* of a valuation calculation.

2 *Discount Rate and Rate of Return Adjustments:* Shareholder rates of return used to discount future cash flows or earnings are a second key area of focus for private versus public companies. In addition, due to the lack of observable market prices for debt and equity, the assumptions associated with the CAPM for public companies often do not apply to private companies and require estimation and adjustment. These changes affect the *denominator* used to discount normalized cash flows and earnings.

3 *Valuation Discount or Premium:* Once private company-specific adjustments are made to both the numerator in terms of cash flow and the denominator or discount rate when valuing a firm, stock-specific considerations related to either the benefit of greater control or the drawback of illiquidity and a minority interest in a business with lesser control must be factored into a company's valuation.

These three areas of attention distinguishing private company valuations from public company valuations will be addressed in detail in the following sections.

KNOWLEDGE CHECK

1. Jun Nakatami is interviewing for a position with a firm focused on a variety of private business valuation areas. Jun is trying to assess which practice area conducts valuations of share-based payments to its employees. Which practice area is most likely the one in which share-based payments are valued?

   A. Transaction

   B. Compliance

   C. Litigation

   Solution:

   A is correct. Share-based payments to employees reflect a transaction involving issuance of securities to its employees. Issuers of such securities need to know the value at which to reflect these transactions.

2. Mohammad al Mollabi serves as an analyst covering publicly traded consumer discretionary stocks and has been asked to analyze the value of a privately held consumer discretionary company. What types of adjustments (compared to public company valuations) will al Mollabi most likely need to make in valuing the private company?

   A. Only cash flow adjustments

   B. Only discount rate adjustments

C. Both cash flow and discount rate adjustments

Solution:

C is correct. To value a private company, both cash flows (i.e., the numerator of the valuation) and discount rate (i.e., the denominator of the valuation) must be adjusted.

3. Aliya Chandra is a senior executive at a family-owned firm whose compensation includes personal use of company assets. For an analyst conducting a discounted cash flow valuation of the family firm, this would:

   A. primarily affect the denominator of the valuation calculation.

   B. primarily affect the numerator of the valuation calculation.

   C. primarily affect the valuation discount or premium.

   Solution:

   B is correct. As Chandra's personal use of company assets affects the company's income statement, this will primarily affect the numerator of the valuation calculation.

4 EARNINGS NORMALIZATION AND CASH FLOW ESTIMATION

☐ explain cash flow estimation issues related to private companies and adjustments required to estimate normalized earnings

In general, private companies tend to have less historical financial information available, use different and often less stringent accounting standards, and often combine personal and business expenses or compensation given the overlap between ownership and management.

For example, private companies may have their financial statements reviewed rather than audited. **Reviewed financial statements** involve an opinion letter with representations and limited assurances by the reviewing accountant and a less thorough review than for audited financials. **Compiled financial statements** are the most basic approach and are unaccompanied by an auditor's opinion letter. While an audit represents the highest level of assurance, reviewed or compiled statements usually require adjustment.

Analysts seek to identify and address any inconsistencies in financial statements that detract from their relevance as a baseline for forecasting future earnings under new ownership. In such cases, the earnings should be adjusted to a basis relevant for forecasting future results. As a first step in the valuation process, an investment analyst seeking to determine the potential value of a company must accurately assess the earnings and cash flow capacity of a private business as if it were acquired and run efficiently.

Earnings Normalization Issues for Private Companies

Private company valuations may require significant adjustments to estimate a firm's earnings potential. While the term **normalized earnings** is generally used among analysts to address cyclicality, seasonality, or one-time revenue or expense items, in the context of private company valuation it is often used to describe specific adjustments for non-recurring, non-economic items as well as for ongoing anomalies which prevent direct comparisons to publicly owned entities. For example, goodwill impairment is one of the most frequent financial reporting valuations that a securities analyst might encounter. As described earlier in the curriculum, goodwill impairment is an earnings charge that companies record on their income statements after they identify evidence that the asset associated with the goodwill can no longer demonstrate the financial results expected from it at the time of its purchase. Other common adjustments are shown in Exhibit 4.

Exhibit 4: Selected Earnings Adjustments for Private Companies

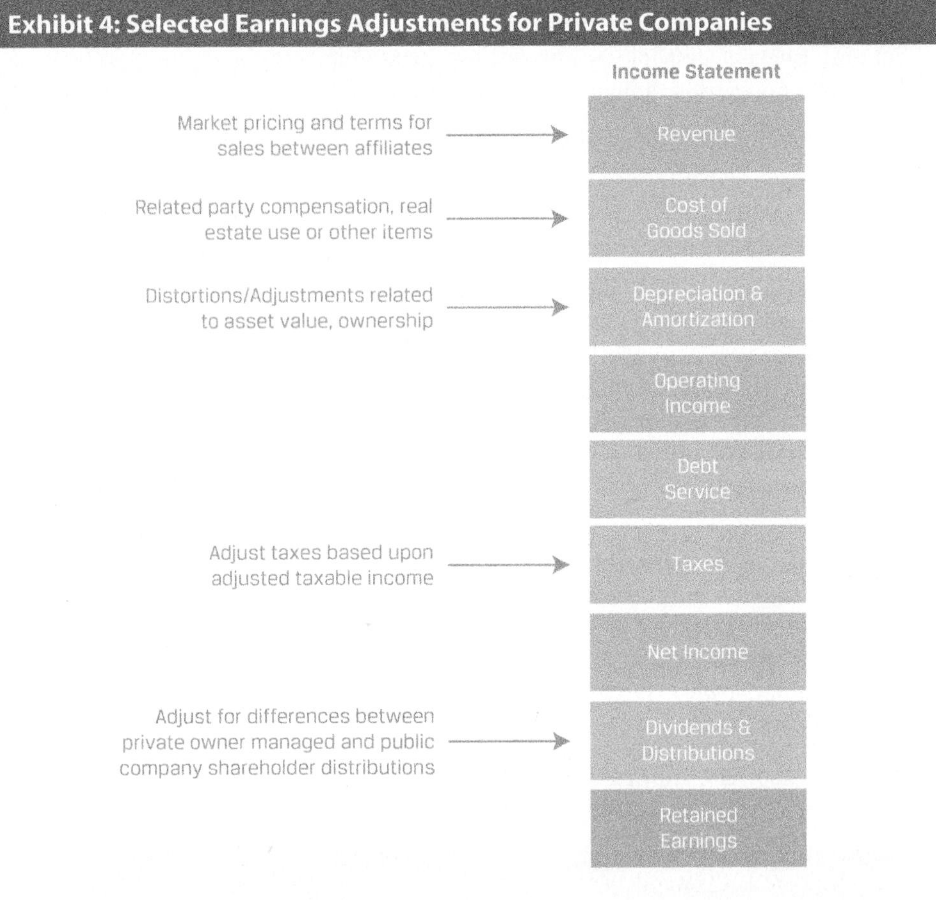

In the case of private companies, it is important to distinguish between one-time events and ongoing distortions. For example, a company owner may either contribute assets such as real estate or other property to a private firm or take a one-time distribution which reduces its assets and income. Ongoing distortions requiring adjustment often result from revenues or expenses which may be considered **related-party transactions**. A related party transaction is one between parties which share economic or other interests, while an **arm's length transaction** is one between independent parties acting in their own self-interest which occur and are recorded at or near fair market value. Private company transactions which may not take place at fair market value include the following:

- Transactions which occur between a private company and its controlling owners and are often related to compensation or non-operating assets

- Transactions occurring between related private entities controlled by controlling shareholders which include tangible goods, services, financing and/or use of intangible property such as licenses or cost sharing

Example 1 illustrates a case where a prospective buyer of a private company seeks to adjust for transactions between an owner and a private business.

EXAMPLE 1

Normalizing Earnings for Fyt for Life, Inc.

Cheryl Xin is the sole shareholder and CEO of Fyt for Life, Inc. (FLI), which produces and distributes a line of outdoor fitness products tailored to a young, active customer base. Dev Khan is a private equity analyst evaluating the purchase of FLI. Khan notes the following facts affecting the most recent fiscal year's results:

- Xin's compensation for the year was SGD 1.5 million. Khan's compensation consultant believes a normalized compensation expense of SGD 500,000 for a CEO of a company like FLI is appropriate. Compensation is included in selling, general, and administrative (SG&A) expenses.
- Certain corporate assets including ranch property and a condominium are in Khan's view not required for the company's core operations. Fiscal year expenses associated with the ranch and condominium were SGD 400,000, including SGD 300,000 of such operating expenses as property upkeep, property taxes, and insurance reflected in SG&A expenses, and depreciation expense of SGD 100,000. All other asset balances (including cash) are believed to be at normal levels required to support current operations.
- FLI's debt balance of SGD 2,000,000 (interest rate of 7.5%) was lower than what might be considered an optimal level of debt expected for the company. As reported interest expense did not reflect an optimal charge, Khan believes the use of an earnings figure that excludes interest expense altogether, specifically operating income after taxes, will facilitate the assessment of FLI.

Khan uses the reported income statement to derive reported operating income after taxes as follows:

FLI Operating Income after Taxes

As of 31 December (in SGD)	As Reported
Revenues	50,000,000
Cost of goods sold	30,000,000
Gross profit	20,000,000
SG&A expenses	5,000,000
EBITDA	15,000,000
Depreciation and amortization	1,000,000
Earnings before interest and taxes	14,000,000
Pro forma taxes (at 17%)	2,380,000
Operating income after taxes	11,620,000

1. Identify the adjustments Khan should make to reported financials to estimate normalized operating income after taxes.

   Solution:

   First, SG&A expenses should be reduced by SGD 1,500,000 – SGD 500,000 = SGD 1,000,000 to reflect the expected salary expense under professional management at a market rate of compensation. Second, the ranch and condominium are non-operating assets, so expense items should be adjusted to reflect their removal (e.g., through a sale). Two related income statement lines are affected: SG&A expenses should be reduced by SGD 300,000, and depreciation and amortization reduced by SGD 100,000.

2. Based on your answer to 1, construct a pro forma statement of normalized operating income after taxes for FLI.

   Solution:

   The pro forma statement of after-tax normalized operating income is as follows:

FLI Normalized Operating Income after Taxes

As of 31 December (in SGD)	As Adjusted
Revenues	50,000,000
Cost of goods sold	30,000,000
Gross profit	20,000,000
SG&A expenses	3,700,000
EBITDA	16,300,000
Depreciation and amortization	900,000
Earnings before interest and taxes	15,400,000
Pro forma taxes (at 17%)	2,618,000
Operating income after taxes	12,782,000

In Example 1, above-market compensation reduces the company's taxable income and income tax expense. Excessive employee benefits are an additional area for review and for possible adjustment. For example, personal expenses, personal use assets, and excess entertainment expenses may be included as expenses of the private company and require reconciliation. Personal residences, aircraft, and luxury or excessive use of corporate vehicles for personal use may also require an adjustment. Life insurance and loans to shareholders would also merit review, if present.

For private companies with limited profits or reported losses, expenses may on the other hand be understated with the reported income of the entity overstated. Active owner managers may not take compensation commensurate with market levels required by an employee for similar activities.

If more than one shareholder or separate private companies with the same owner(s) are involved, analysts must consider distortions and adjustments which involve a transfer of value from one shareholder or group of shareholders to another as well as transfers between related private companies which are not reflected in financial statements. For example, above-market compensation or expenses can result in a controlling shareholder receiving a disproportionately high return versus other shareholders. A private company purchasing inventory, using assets, or receiving services at a recorded cost below fair market value from another private company with the same controlling shareholder(s) will appear more profitable than it would be if owned by a separate third party.

Real estate used by the private company is a common area for consideration. When a private company owns real estate, some analysts separate the real estate from the operating company. This separation consists of removing any revenues and expenses associated with the real estate from the income statement. If the company is using owned property in its business operations, adding a market rental charge for the use of the real estate to the expenses of the company would produce a more accurate estimate of the earnings of the business operations. Adjusting reported earnings to include a provision for third-party real estate costs would produce a value of the business operations excluding the owned real estate. Because the real estate is still owned by the entity, its value would represent a non-operating asset of the entity. These adjustments for the financial impact of owned real estate can be appropriate because the business operations and real estate have different risk levels and growth expectations. Example 2 illustrates how the use and ownership of real estate may require adjustment in the financial statements of private companies.

EXAMPLE 2

Chandra Consolidated and the Use of Real Estate

Chandra Consolidated is a family-owned private firm consisting of two primary companies: an established commercial real estate business (Chandra Holdings) and a recently founded luxury retail business (Chandra Shops). Chandra Holdings owns several office buildings in major business centers across India. Given growing demand for luxury goods among urban white-collar workers and seeing an opportunity to better utilize building capacity less suited for corporate leases, the Chandra family established Chandra Shops, a separate business which operates luxury retail stores which utilize ground floor space in its office buildings.

While Chandra Shops directly covers the cost of operating expenses other than rent, the separate units of Chandra Consolidated have no formal agreement and no payments occur between the two units related to the retail space use.

1. Describe how an analyst should approach normalizing the earnings of the two Chandra companies regarding the use of retail space.

   Solution:

   The payment of operating expenses other than rent only in the case of Chandra Shops significantly understates the true opportunity cost of retail space usage. That is, Chandra Shops does not report a rental expense in its income statement, nor does Chandra Holdings recognize rental revenue from its retail space.

   An analyst considering a normalization of Chandra Shops' earnings should assess the market cost of comparable retail leases in major business centers and add a market rental charge as a periodic expense to Chandra Shops' income statement. This market rental charge should be reported as rental income on Chandra Holdings' income statement.

2. The Chandra family is considering the sale of a minority interest of its recently founded venture to a business partner with more experience in the

luxury retail sector. What effect might the normalization of earnings have on the valuation of Chandra Shops?

Solution:

The underreporting of rental costs by Chandra Shops results in lower normalized earnings and a lower valuation than one conducted using Chandra Holdings' financial statements, while Chandra Holdings has higher normalized earnings and a higher valuation once adjustments are made. For Chandra to properly value each business unit, the company needs to normalize the retail company's costs and the real estate company's revenues to reflect a proper amount of rental transfer for the use of the space.

As Example 2 demonstrates, analysts must also consider the effect of transactions between related entities when conducting private company valuations as is true for some public companies as well. In addition to these adjustments to private company valuation, it is important to note that adjustments applicable to both private and public companies such as inventory accounting methods, depreciation assumptions, and capitalization versus expensing of various costs among others must also be considered in valuing private companies.

Cash Flow Estimation Issues for Private Companies

In addition to earnings normalization, cash flow estimation is an important element of the valuation process. Two distinct forms of cash flow relevant for company valuation were introduced earlier in the curriculum:

- FCFF: Cash flow at the enterprise level available to debt and equity investors
- Free cash flow to equity (FCFE): Cash flow available to shareholders only and is used to directly value equity

Specific challenges associated with private company cash flow valuation include the nature of the interest being valued, potentially acute uncertainties regarding future operations, and managerial involvement in forecasting.

In contrast to a public company valuation from a non-controlling shareholder perspective, the equity interest appraised and the intended use of the appraisal for a private firm are key in determining the appropriate definition of value for a specific valuation. Assumptions included in cash flow estimates may differ if a small minority equity interest is appraised rather than the total equity of a business.

Cash flow projections for a mature business are typically based upon a range of growth and profitability assumptions. However, uncertainty regarding a potentially wide range of future cash flow possibilities creates challenges for this valuation approach. For example, a privately held company may face outcomes over a forecast period which include an IPO, acquisition, continued private operation, or bankruptcy. An early-stage company may face proof of concept or approval milestones in creating a successful product. In these cases, a valuation based upon scenario analysis as introduced in earlier lessons and shown in Example 3 is a common approach.

EXAMPLE 3

Scenario Analysis to Value Nano Beta S.r.L.

Nano Beta is a private Italian biotech firm formed to develop nanoparticles used to overcome limitations of conventional cancer treatment methods and drug resistance. Nano Beta is seeking regulatory approval from the European Medicines Agency (EMA) for its novel immunotherapy approach for which it expects preliminary approval a year from now and final approval in two years. A VC analyst seeking to estimate Nano Beta's value today has created the following decision tree based upon expectations for EMA approval and applicability of the prospective treatment.

Scenario Analysis for Nano Beta S.r.L. EMA Approval Process

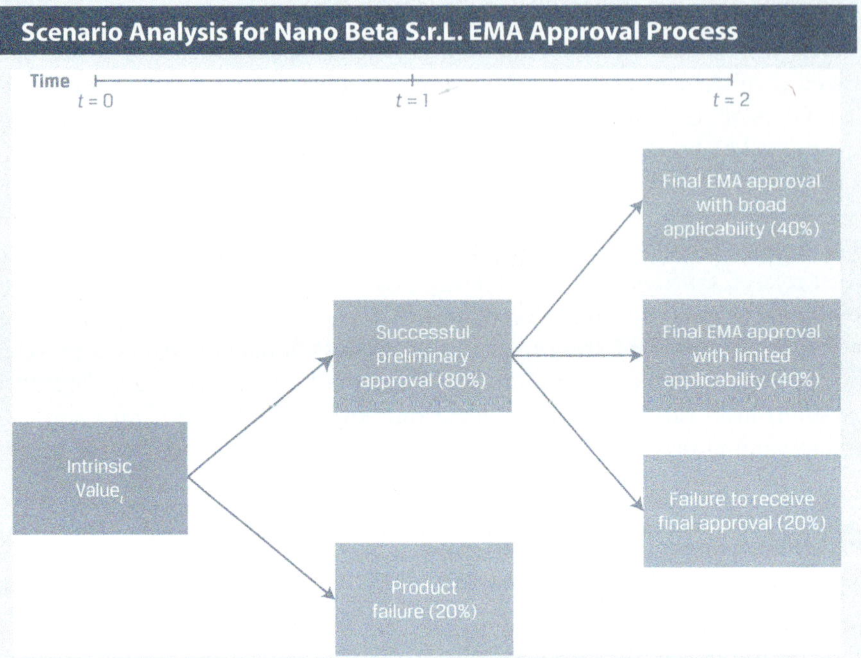

The company is assumed to have zero value if the product is not approved. Assuming a weighted average cost of capital (WACC) of 15% and constant growth under a discounted cash flow approach, the analyst has established two possible scenarios:

Broad applicability: Nano Beta is able to apply this new therapy to several pervasive forms of cancer. Annual FCFF is expected to be EUR 200 million with perpetual constant growth (g) of 5%.

Limited applicability: Due to the therapy's limited efficacy, Nano Beta is only able to apply its therapy on a limited basis to a few rare cancer types. Annual FCFF is expected to be EUR 50 million with 2% constant growth.

Solve for future firm value (at time t = 2) assuming that FCFF grows at a constant rate in perpetuity under each scenario as follows:

$$\text{Firm value}_t = \frac{\text{FCFF}_{t+1}}{\text{WACC} - g}, \text{ with FCFF}_{t+1} = \text{FCFF}_t(1+\text{g})$$

$$\text{Broad applicability: Firm value}_t = \text{EUR 2.1 billlion} = \frac{\text{EUR 200 million}(1 + 0.05)}{0.15 - 0.05}$$

$$\text{Limited applicability: Firm value}_t = \text{EUR } 392,307,692 = \frac{\text{EUR 50 million}(1 + 0.02)}{0.15 - 0.02}$$

We can calculate the future (probability-weighted) firm value in two years' time to be EUR 797,538,462 by first calculating the probability of successful approval for both broad and limited applicability to be 0.32 (= 0.80 × 0.40) and then solving for future firm value as follows:

Future firm value: (0.32 × EUR 2.1billion) + (0.32 × EUR 392,307,692)

Discount the future firm value at the WACC to estimate firm value today:

$$\text{Firm value}_t = \text{EUR } 603,053,657 = \frac{\text{EUR } 797,538,462}{(1 + 0.15)^2}$$

The value of the product line based on the probabilities associated with the two approval scenarios is EUR 603 million. An important component of the two scenarios is not simply the differences in operating income assumptions, but also the difference in growth rate assumptions between the two scenarios.

Private company managers generally have much more information about their business than outside analysts. Management may develop cash flow forecasts to be used in a valuation with appraiser input, or appraisers may develop their own forecasts consulting management as needed. An analyst should be aware of potential managerial biases that possibly overstate values in the case of goodwill impairment testing or understate values in the case of incentive stock option grants. Analysts should also consider whether projections adequately capture future capital needs.

KNOWLEDGE CHECK

1. In Example 1, Cheryl Xin received SGD 1.5 million as compensation from her position as CEO of FLI. Assume that instead, Xin takes no compensation and instead receives SGD 1.5 million as a dividend. Which of the following best describes how FLI's earnings would have to be normalized in this case if reported figures remain the same?

   A. Because the dividend and compensation amounts are equivalent, there would be no need to normalize FLI's earnings.

   B. FLI's earnings would be normalized lower to reflect the omission of a proper CEO compensation expense, thus FLI's earnings would be reduced after this adjustment.

   C. FLI's earnings would be normalized to be higher because of an excessive dividend paid to Xin.

   Solution:

   B is correct. As discussed in Example 1, a proper amount for CEO compensation would be SGD 500,000, and the normalized income statement should take this as a deduction. Thus, normalized earnings would be lower after the adjustment.

2. Suppose that in Example 1, FLI's products are manufactured in a building owned by Xin's family. FLI reports no expense related to the use of this asset on its income statements. Which statement best reflects how Khan should use this information to normalize FLI's earnings?

   A. Khan does not need to normalize FLI's earnings as the asset is not owned by FLI.

   B. Khan does not need to normalize FLI's earnings, but only needs to restate FLI's balance sheet to reflect the value of the building.

   C. Khan needs to incorporate an appropriate expense, such as a market-determined rental rate, to reflect the use of the building space in FLI's operations, thus reducing FLI's income on a normalized basis.

   Solution:

   C is correct. The use of the building for manufacturing should involve a rental expense at fair market value as would be the case if it were an arm's length transaction. The higher expense would reduce FLI's normalized earnings.

3. Revisiting Example 3, Nano Beta researchers now believe that while preliminary EMA approval is less likely, the immunotherapy treatment is considered more likely to achieve broader applicability if approved. The VC analyst decides to amend the probability of preliminary approval from 80% to 60%, with an increase from 40% to 60% likelihood of broad applicability at t=2 and a decrease from 40% to 20% probability of limited applicability. Which response best reflects the change in Nano Beta's estimated value versus the original scenario?

   A. No change in value

   B. Increase of EUR 4.2 million in estimated value

   C. Increase of EUR 258 million in estimated value

   Solution:

   B is correct. While the values at t=2 remain the same as in Example 3, the probability of broad applicability rises to 36% (= 60% × 60%) from 32%, and limited applicability falls to a 12% likelihood (= 60% × 20%) from 32% in the original example. We can calculate the future (probability-weighted) firm value in two years' time to be EUR 803,076,923 as follows:

   Future Firm Value: (0.36 × EUR 2.1billion) + (0.12 × EUR 392,307,692)

   Discount the future firm value at the WACC to estimate firm value today:

$$\text{Firm Value}_t = \text{EUR } 607{,}241{,}530 = \frac{\text{EUR } 803{,}076{,}923}{(1 + 0.15)^2}$$

   This results in a EUR 4.2 million greater value than in the previous example.

5 PRIVATE COMPANY DISCOUNT RATES AND REQUIRED RATES OF RETURN

- ☐ explain factors that require adjustment when estimating the discount rate for private companies
- ☐ compare models used to estimate the required rate of return to private company equity (for example, the CAPM, the expanded CAPM, and the build-up approach)

Earlier lessons on valuing public companies used market prices for debt and equity in WACC calculations as well as required rates of return to shareholders based upon the CAPM as follows:

WACC: Cost of capital is estimated by weighting the expected cost of debt and equity by the proportion of each used in a company's capital target structure:

$$r_{\text{WACC}} = w_d r_d + w_e r_e \quad (1)$$

where w_d and w_e represent the respective debt and equity weights as a percentage of total market value of capital, and r_d and r_e represent the respective costs of debt and equity. Recall that debt cost r_d is an after-tax rate given the deductibility of interest expense against taxable income.

$$R_d = r(1 - t) \quad (2)$$

CAPM: Cost of equity is estimated by adding a company-specific risk premium determined by the systematic risk (β) of the firm's shares as compared to overall equity market returns (r_m) to the risk-free rate r_f:

$$r_e = r_f + \beta(r_m - r_f) \quad (3)$$

In addition to the lack of observable market prices for equity and debt, assumptions underlying these approaches are often violated for private companies. In this case, betas for comparable public companies are often used once adjusted to match the leverage of the private company as shown later.

Factors Affecting Private Company Discount Rates

Several factors make estimating a rate at which to discount a private company's expected future cash flows challenging.

- *Application of size premiums to discount rates.* In assessing private company valuations, size premiums are frequently used, resulting in a small size discount in private company valuations. This practice is less prevalent in the valuation of public companies. In some cases, size premium estimates based on public company data for the smallest market cap segments are a result of financial and/or operating distress that may be irrelevant to the company being valued.
- *Relative debt availability and cost of debt.* Another valuation challenge involves correctly estimating a private company's debt capacity. In calculating a WACC for a valuation based on FCFF, analysts should note that a private company may have less access to debt financing than a similar public company. Reduced debt access may lead a private company to rely more on equity financing, which would tend to increase its WACC. Furthermore, a smaller private company could face greater operating risk and a higher cost of debt.
- *Discount rates in an acquisition context.* Earlier lessons suggested that the cost of capital used to evaluate an acquisition should be based on the target company's capital structure and the riskiness of the target company's cash flows—the buyer's cost of capital is irrelevant. When larger, more mature companies acquire smaller, riskier target companies, the buyer would be expected to have a lower cost of capital than the target. However, use of the buyer's lower cost of capital (resulting in a higher valuation) from the seller's perspective would imply that the buyer would be paying the seller for possible value it brings to a transaction due to its lower capital costs.
- *Discount rate adjustment for projection risk.* A relative lack of information concerning a private company's operations or business model compared with that of a similar public company introduces greater uncertainty into projections that may lead to a higher required rate of return. A second area of focus may involve less private company management experience in forecasting future financial performance used by analysts. Projections may reflect excessive optimism or pessimism. Adjustments to a discount rate due to projection risk or lack of managerial forecasting experience would typically be highly judgmental.

Required Rate of Return Models

Analysts often question whether the CAPM is appropriate for developing required rate of return on equity estimates for private companies. For example, small companies with little prospect of going public or being acquired by a public company may be viewed as not comparable to the public companies for which market-based beta estimates are available. Also, while beta measures non-diversifiable risk only and assumes that investors have well-diversified portfolios, buyers and sellers of private firms often violate this assumption and should arguably be subject to a higher risk premium than suggested by beta. These issues are often addressed by modifying the CAPM assumptions used. Exhibit 5 summarizes the alternatives to CAPM for private company equity.

Exhibit 5: Alternatives to the CAPM for Private Company Valuation

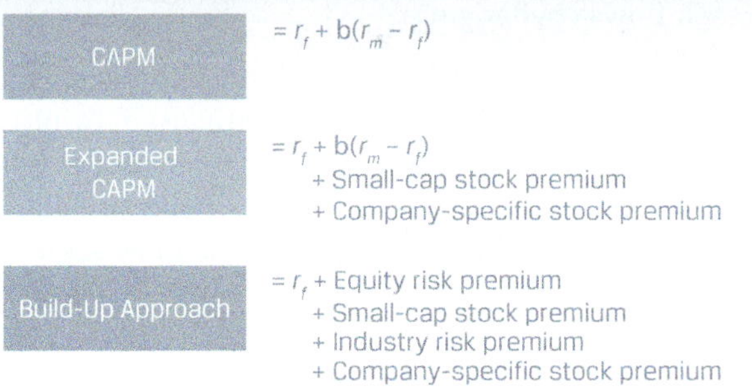

- *Expanded CAPM.* The **expanded CAPM** is an adaptation of the CAPM that adds to the single premium based upon beta to take small size and company-specific risk into account shown here as additions to the cost of equity. Estimation of company-specific risk is a relatively subjective element of the valuation process which is conducted based upon industry and company analysis as well as the consideration of comparable public companies often referred to as **guideline public companies**.
- *Elements of the build-up approach.* The build-up approach involves a required rate of return established as a set of premia added to the risk-free rate. The added premia are typically based on factors such as size and company risk. Analysts often use a build-up approach when comparable public companies are unavailable or of questionable comparability. Unlike the expanded CAPM, this approach excludes the application of beta to the equity risk premium. The build-up model implicitly assumes a beta of one, while an industry risk adjustment (premium or discount) is often used instead. This approach is outlined in Example 4.

EXAMPLE 4

Calculating FLI's Discount Rate

Dev Khan is considering which discount rate to use to value FLI. While CEO Xin explored various sources of debt financing to operate FLI with a lower overall cost of capital, FLI operated with little debt. Analysis of public companies in FLI's industry indicated several guideline public companies for possible use in estimating a discount rate for FLI.

Khan agreed on the following estimates:

- Risk-free rate: Estimated at 3.8%.
- Equity risk premium: A 5% equity risk premium was deemed appropriate.
- Beta: Estimated at 1.1 based on publicly traded comparable companies.
- Small stock premium: FLI's smaller size and less diversified operations suggest greater risk relative to public comparable companies, resulting in a 3% small stock premium included in the equity return calculation.
- Company-specific risk premium: Beyond Xin's key role at the company, no other unusual elements were considered to create additional risk. A 1% company-specific risk adjustment was included.
- Industry risk premium (build-up method only): An industry risk premium of zero was assumed, as no industry-related factors were considered to materially affect the overall required return on equity estimate.
- Pre-tax cost of debt: Estimated at 7.5%.
- Ratio of debt to total capital for comparable companies: Estimated at 20%.
- Optimal ratio of debt to total capital: Estimated at 10% based on discussions with various sources of financing. FLI would not be able to reach the industry capital structure based on its smaller size versus public comparables and the greater risk of its operations as a standalone company.
- Actual ratio of debt to total capital: For FLI, the actual ratio was 2%.
- Combined corporate tax rate: Estimated at 17%.

Answer the following questions based upon the information provided:

1. Calculate FLI's required return on equity using the CAPM.

Solution:

Using Equation 3 to solve for the CAPM with a risk-free rate r_f of 3.8%, a market risk premium r_m of 5% and beta of 1.1:

$r_e = r_f + \beta(r_m - r_f)$

$= 3.8\% + 1.1(5\%)$

$= 9.30\%.$

2. Calculate FLI's required return on equity using the expanded CAPM.

Solution:

Using the expanded CAPM which adds risk premia to Equation 3 as follows:

$r_e = r_f + \beta(r_m - r_f)$

+ Small stock premium

+ Company-specific risk adjustment

The required rate of return is 13.3% as shown in the following tabular format.

FLI Expanded CAPM: Required Rate of Return on Equity

Risk-free rate (r_f)	**3.8%**
Plus: CAPM Equity risk premium ($\beta(r_m - r_f)$)	5.5%*
Plus: Small stock premium	3.0%
Plus: Company-specific risk adjustment	1.0%
Indicated required return on equity	13.3%

* *1.1 beta × 5.0% equity risk premium = 5.5%.*

3. Calculate FLI's required return on equity using the build-up method.

Solution:

The build-up method is the sum of risk premia in excess of the risk-free rate r_f:

$r_e = r_f$

+ Equity risk premium

+ Small stock premium

+ Industry risk premium

+ Company-specific risk adjustment

Note the absence of a beta adjustment. The fact that beta (1.1) is close to one suggests any possible industry risk adjustment would be small in magnitude.

FLI Build-Up Method: Required Rate of Return on Equity

Risk-free rate (r_f)	3.8%
Plus: Equity risk premium ($r_m - r_f$)	5.0%
Plus: Small stock premium	3.0%
Plus: Industry risk premium	0.0%
Plus: Company-specific risk adjustment	1.0%
Indicated return on equity	12.8%

4. Discuss the selection of capital structure weights in determining the WACC for FLI.

Solution:

For valuation concerning the possible sale of FLI, it is appropriate to assume optimal capital structure weights in calculating WACC as an acquirer would be able and motivated to establish the optimum. FLI's current capital structure involves less debt than is optimal, and therefore the company's WACC is currently higher than it needs to be. Note, however, that the weight on debt of similar large public companies may be higher than what is optimal for FLI. Large public companies would be expected to have greater access to public debt markets. Also, FLI's small size increases its risk relative to larger public companies. These two factors tend to increase FLI's cost of debt relative to a large public comparable and lead to a lower optimal weight of debt compared with such a company.

5. Calculate the WACC for FLI using the current capital structure and a 13% cost of equity.

Solution:

Use the WACC calculation in Equation 1 based on FLI's existing capital structure as follows:

$$r_{WACC} = w_d r_d + w_e r_e$$

where

$$r_d = r(1 - t)$$

FLI WACC: Current Capital Structure

Pre-tax cost of debt r	7.5%	
$(1 - t)$	0.83	
After-tax cost of debt r_d	6.225%	
Weight w_d	× 0.02	
Weighted cost of debt $r_d \times w_d$		0.1%
Cost of equity r_e	13.0%	
Weight w_e	× 0.98	
Weighted cost of equity $r_e \times w_e$		12.7%
WACC r_{WACC}		12.9%

6. Calculate the WACC for FLI based on the optimal capital structure and a 13% cost of equity.

Solution:

Use the WACC calculation in Equation 1 based on FLI's optimal capital structure as follows:

$$r_{WACC} = w_d r_d + w_e r_e$$

where

$$r_d = r(1 - t)$$

FLI's cost of capital using the optimal capital structure involves a higher proportion of debt financing, resulting in a lower WACC as follows:

FLI WACC: Optimal Capital Structure

Pre-tax cost of debt r	7.5%	
Tax rate complement $(1 - t)$	0.83	
After-tax cost of debt r_d	6.225%	
Weight w_d	× 0.10	
Weighted cost of debt $r_d \times w_d$		0.62%
Cost of equity r_e	13.0%	
Weight w_e	× 0.90	
Weighted cost of equity $r_e \times w_e$		11.7%
WACC r_{WACC}		12.3%

Note: Rounded figures are used.

KNOWLEDGE CHECK

Example 4 illustrates the calculation of cost of capital estimates for FLI, a summary of which is shown in the following table:

Calculated variable	Model	Result
Required return on equity	CAPM	9.3%
Required return on equity	Expanded CAPM	13.3%
Required return on equity	Build-up approach	12.8%
Cost of equity r_e		13.0%
WACC	Using FLI actual debt ratio	12.9%
WACC	Using FLI optimal debt ratio	12.3%

Dev Khan shows these results to a partner at the private equity firm and is asked to explain the sources of specific differences in the results. The following questions reflect the partner's queries.

1. Which factor most accurately reflects the main significant difference in the required return on equity from the expanded CAPM versus the required return on equity from the CAPM?

   A. Size premium

   B. Company-specific premium

   C. Industry risk premium

   Solution:

   A is correct. The size premium of 3% reflects the majority of the difference between the 13.3% associated with the expanded CAPM and the 9.3% associated with the CAPM. B is incorrect as the company-specific premium only accounts for 1% of the difference. Industry risk premiums do not factor into either the CAPM or the expanded CAPM, so C is incorrect.

2. The partner points out that there are more factors included in the build-up approach as compared to the expanded CAPM, so asks Khan as to why the required return on equity from the build-up approach is lower than the result from the expanded CAPM. Which of the following most correctly states how Khan should respond?

   A. The industry risk premium is the only additional factor included in the build-up approach and was assumed to be negative for FLI.

   B. The equity risk premium in the build-up approach uses a lower assumed market return than the equity risk premium in the expanded CAPM.

   C. The industry risk premium is the only additional factor included in the build-up approach, and this was assumed as zero for FLI's industry. However, the equity risk premium in the build-up approach is lower for stocks with a beta greater than 1.0.

   Solution:

   C is correct. There are two important distinctions between the build-up approach and the expanded CAPM. First, the inclusion of an industry risk premium is an extra factor, but this was assumed as zero in the example. The second significant difference is that the build-up approach does not utilize a beta to adjust the equity risk premium. In the FLI example, beta was 1.1 in the expanded CAPM, which added an extra 0.5% to the result for the expanded CAPM. A is incorrect as the industry risk premium was assumed to be zero, and B is incorrect as there is no difference between the market return assumptions in the two models.

3. The partner notes that the WACC using an optimal capital structure is lower than the WACC using FLI's existing capital structure. Which statement best describes the acquisition complication that this difference creates for the private equity firm?

   A. FLI's existing capital structure consists of more debt than is optimal, and so its cost of debt is currently higher than it should be. As a result, the acquisition will need to include a plan to pay off some of FLI's existing debt.

   B. If the private equity firm calculates an acquisition price for FLI from the lower WACC, it will pay a higher price. As a result, value is transferred from the private equity buyer to FLI for a change to the company's capital structure after the acquisition.

   C. The higher WACC is an outcome of higher projection risk due to non-optimal capital structure. The private equity buyer had to adjust the cost of capital higher to reflect this added risk.

Solution:

B is correct. The buyer may need to base its acquisition price on future changes, resulting in a more efficiently run business. In doing so, it pays the seller for changes to the company not made by the seller, but instead those which the buyer expects to make after the transaction. A incorrectly states that FLI's debt ratio was above the optimal capital structure. C incorrectly refers to projection risk as the source of the higher WACC.

VALUATION DISCOUNTS AND PREMIUMS 6

☐ explain and evaluate the effects on private company valuations of discounts and premiums based on control and marketability

In contrast to public company valuations which are usually based upon an expected exchange of liquid shares between non-controlling buyers and sellers, private company valuations may involve an adjustment for more or less control as well as the limited ability to exchange private shares. These relationships are summarized in Exhibit 6.

Exhibit 6: Valuation Discounts and Premiums for Private Companies

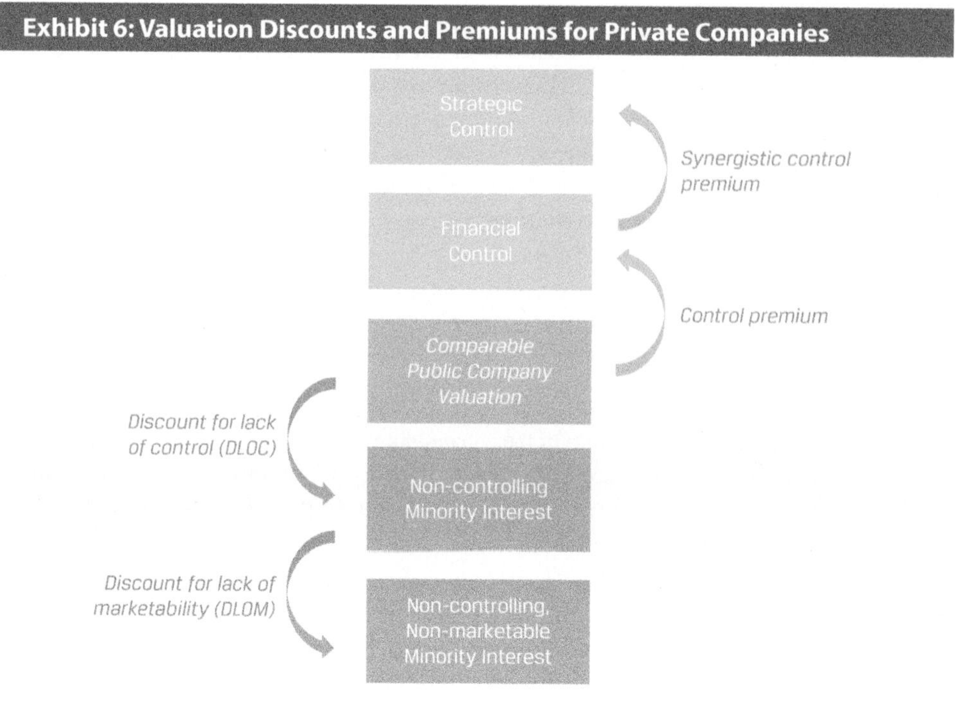

The highest possible value indication for an entity would be its investment value to a so-called **strategic buyer** able to capitalize on synergies. This value reflects a buyer who intends to use their controlling stake to take action to increase firm revenue and/or decrease costs beyond current expectations in order to increase the company's value. The highest bidder for a private firm is typically an investor who not only sees the greatest potential for synergies but is also able and willing to assume the execution risk associated with their realization.

A **financial buyer** on the other hand may be willing to pay a premium for a controlling interest for a private firm but is either unable to identify any synergies from a controlling interest, may be unable or unwilling to take advantage of them due to a lack of operational or management expertise, or has limited risk appetite. Financial buyers include investors who seek a synergistic buyer or partner or may be an existing minority shareholder who may otherwise benefit from control under current operations.

A non-controlling equity interest that is readily marketable is generally equivalent to the price at which publicly traded companies trade in the market.

Two forms of valuation discount, namely a discount due to lack of control as well as a reduction to value due to the lack of marketability, are covered in detail in the following sections. The application of valuation premiums and discounts is fact specific and highly dependent upon whether the valuation is part of a competitive bidding process. As a result, estimates may vary dramatically. Variations in estimated discounts and premiums may relate to the challenging comparability of the data used to quantify discounts. Discounts may also vary based on interpretation of the importance of the size of shareholding and distribution of shares, the relationship of parties, laws affecting minority shareholder rights, investors' alignment with the controlling shareholder, and other factors.

The timing of a potential liquidity event is one key consideration. An interest in a private company that is pursuing either an IPO or a strategic sale might be valued with relatively modest valuation discounts. An equity interest in a private company that has not paid dividends and has no prospect for a liquidity event would likely require much higher valuation discounts.

Lack of Control Discounts

A **discount for lack of control** (DLOC) involves a deduction from the pro rata share of 100% of the value of an equity interest to reflect the absence of some or all powers of control. A lack of control may be disadvantageous to an investor because of the inability to select directors, officers, and management that control an entity's operations. Without control, an investor is unable to distribute cash, buy and sell assets, obtain financing, or influence other company actions which could affect the investment's value, the timing of distributions, and ultimate return to the investor.

Although an investor may lack control, the effect on value is uncertain. In some cases, the existence of disproportionate returns supports the application of a lack of control discount. Disproportionate returns result when controlling shareholders increase their returns through above-market compensation and other actions that reduce the returns available to minority shareholders. While private companies pursuing an IPO or strategic sale of the entity are less likely to have a controlling group which takes actions that reduce an entity's earnings, in some cases pre-IPO investors retain a concentration of control versus common shareholders.

Data available for estimating a lack of control discount are limited and interpretations can vary markedly. For interests in operating companies, control premium data from public company acquisitions are often used. The same factors used for a control premium are often considered when estimating a lack of control discount as shown below and in Example 5:

$$\text{DLOC} = 1 - [1/(1 + \text{Control premium})] \tag{4}$$

EXAMPLE 5

Everfloat Limited Control Premium

1. Andrea Miceli is analyzing the value of a non-controlling minority interest in Everfloat Ltd., a private UK company for which shares have not recently traded. Miceli estimates Everfloat's unadjusted value to be GBP 1.65 billion and uses data from similar public companies to estimate a control premium of 15%. What is Everfloat's DLOC and adjusted value?

   Solution:

   We may solve for Everfloat's DLOC using Equation 4:

   $$\text{DLOC} = 1 - [1/(1 + \text{Control premium})]$$

   For a 15% control premium, the DLOC is 1 – (1/1.15) = 0.130, or 13.0%. Everfloat's adjusted value is GBP1.65 billion × (1-0.13) = GBP1.4355 billion.

The decision of whether to apply a DLOC depends upon the perspective taken when conducting a private valuation. Valuation indications from discounted cash flows are generally agreed to be a controlling interest value if the cash flows and discount rate are estimated on a controlling interest basis. If control cash flows are not used and/or the discount rate does not reflect an optimal capital structure, the resulting value is generally considered to already reflect a lack of control.

Lack of Marketability Discounts

A **discount for lack of marketability** (DLOM) is a deduction from an ownership interest's value to reflect the relative absence (compared with publicly traded companies) of a liquid market for a company's shares.

Lack of marketability discounts are frequently applied in the valuation of non-controlling equity interests in private companies. Although a DLOM differs from a DLOC, they are often linked; that is, if a valuation is on a non-controlling interest basis, a lack of marketability discount is typically appropriate. Key variables affecting a marketability discount include prospects for liquidity such as market conditions, restrictions on transferability, limitations on the pool of potential buyers, and ownership concentration. At a minimum, an illiquid investment involves an opportunity cost associated with the inability to redeploy investment funds.

Restricted stock transactions and IPOs are two types of data used to quantify DLOMs, and option pricing models are also sometimes used to develop marketability discount estimates. All these approaches are subject to differences in interpretation.

Restricted stock is generally identical to freely traded stock of a public company except for the trading restrictions. Unlike interests in private companies, restricted stock transactions typically involve shares that will soon be freely tradable. The sale of blocks of restricted stock that exceed public trading activity in the stock may be the most comparable data for quantifying a lack of marketability discount. A private sale of such a block may reflect a valuation discount related to the price risk associated with the holding.

The relationship of stock sales prior to IPOs is another source of marketability discounts. For many early-stage or high-growth companies approaching an IPO, an increase in value may result from lower risk and uncertainty as a company progresses in its development. The lower risk of realizing predicted cash flows or a narrowing of the ranges of possible future cash flows may lead to a reduction in the implied marketability discount.

Option-based approaches seek to quantify DLOMs using the right to sell shares as captured by a put option premium. This premium is used to quantify the ability to sell at a given price. As a first step, an at-the-money put option is priced. The put option premium as a percentage of the stock value provides an estimate of the DLOM as shown in Example 6.

EXAMPLE 6

Everfloat Limited DLOM Estimate Using a Put Option

In seeking to estimate a DLOM for Everfloat Ltd., Andrea Miceli determines that Shipline PLC (a non-dividend-paying stock) represents the closest comparable public company to the valuation target. Shipline's current share price is GBP 50 and Miceli assumes a six-month time horizon.

Given the current risk-free rate of 5.0%, Miceli calculates the value of a six-month at-the-money put option with a strike at the six-month forward price of GBP 51.27 ($=50e^{(0.5\times0.05)}$). Using a Black–Scholes model and observing implied volatility of 60% for Shipline, she solves for a put option premium of GBP 8.40.

The estimated DLOM for Everfloat is GBP 8.40 / GBP 50, or 16.8%.

One advantage of the put option analysis is the ability to directly address perceived risk of the private company through the volatility estimate. The volatility estimate may better capture the risks of the stock compared with restricted stock or IPO transactions in which volatility may be one of many variables influencing the level of discount. Volatility estimates may be based on either historical or implied volatilities of public companies or the volatility estimates embedded in the prices of publicly traded options. Put options provide only price protection for the life of the option. They do not, however, provide liquidity for the asset holding, raising a concern on the use of this form of DLOM estimate. Put options also allow the holder of the underlying security to benefit from potential price increases in share value and therefore do not exactly model lack of marketability.

In addition to control and marketability discounts, a variety of other potential valuation discounts exist that may require consideration. These include key person discounts, portfolio discounts (discounts for non-homogeneous assets), and possible discounts for non-voting shares.

If both lack of control and lack of marketability discounts are applied, this occurs in sequence and the total discount is multiplicative rather than additive as shown in the following equation and in Example 7.

$$\text{Total Discount} = [1 - (1 - \text{DLOC})\times(1 - \text{DLOM})] \quad (5)$$

EXAMPLE 7

Everfloat Limited Total Discount Estimate

1. As Miceli has determined that the Everfloat DLOC is 13% and the DLOM using option pricing is 16.8%, calculate the total value discount for Everfloat.

   Solution:

   Using Equation 5, we may solve for a total discount of 27.6% as follows:

   $$\text{Total Discount} = [1 - (1 - 0.13)\times(1 - 0.168)] = 0.276$$

Valuation discounts or premiums follow discrete steps, first moving from a controlling to a non-controlling ownership basis, and then from a marketable to a non-marketable basis to establish the valuation discount to be applied.

KNOWLEDGE CHECK

1. The management of Starbeam LLC, a private company owned solely by its managers, is seeking to raise funds by selling an equity stake in the company while maintaining control. A private valuation expert recently estimated Starbeam's company value based on its current status as a 100% management-owned company. Which type(s) of premiums and/or discounts would most likely be applied to the recent valuation in valuing the proposed equity stake?

   A. Control premium and DLOM

   B. DLOC

   C. DLOC and DLOM

   Solution:

   B is correct. The recent valuation would have reflected a control premium because of management's controlling position and a DLOM because Starbeam is a private company, thus A would only be correct for the recent valuation, rather than the valuation of the proposed stake. C would not be correct because the DLOM would already have been applied in estimating the recent valuation. Thus, the proposed, non-controlling stake would only need a DLOC.

2. During the process of seeking out a buyer for a non-controlling stake, Starbeam's management is approached by a well-known public markets investor

who commonly buys controlling stakes in well-managed private companies. This investor allows the management to stay in place. If this investor bids on a controlling stake in Starbeam, should the offer price include a premium over the recent valuation and, if so, what type of premium?

A. Yes, financial control premium

B. Yes, synergistic control premium

C. No control premium over the recent valuation is needed.

Solution:

A is correct. Answer choice C seems reasonable because the recent valuation reflected management's controlling position. However, for the investor to entice management to give up control, a premium over the recent valuation must be offered associated only with financial control. As the investor is a financial buyer, there would most likely not be synergies on which to base a control premium.

3. Starbeam eventually sells a non-controlling stake in its business. Suppose a typical control premium is 30% and a typical DLOM is 20%. Which of the following would be closest to the total discount for the non-controlling stake in Starbeam compared to publicly traded comparables?

A. 44.0%

B. 43.1%

C. 38.5%

Solution:

C is correct. The total discount is 1 – (1-DLOC)×(1-DLOM). The DLOC is equal to 23.1% [1 – (1/1.30)], not 30%. So, the solution is 1 – (1-0.231)×(1-0.2).

7 PRIVATE COMPANY VALUATION APPROACHES

☐ explain the income, market, and asset-based approaches to private company valuation and factors relevant to the selection of each approach

Valuation approaches for private companies are conceptually similar to those used for public companies, although the labels used and details of their application may differ based upon the availability and reliability of information, an analyst's confidence in the data, as well as a company's stage in its life cycle and industry, among other factors. Three primary approaches exist:

- The **income approach** corresponds to the discounted cash flow approach to valuation introduced earlier for public companies. This includes variations such as the **capitalized cash flow method**, which assumes constant cash flow growth, and the **excess earnings method**, which is conceptually the same as the residual income approach.

- The **market approach** values a company based on a ratio of a market-based price to a key monetary variable (or multiple) as compared to companies with similar features to gauge relative value. As in the case of the method of comparables, pricing multiples may be based on share price or multiples based on enterprise value.
- The **asset-based approach** values a private company based on the values of its underlying assets less the value of any related liabilities.

The income approach corresponds to what public equity analysts call discounted cash flow models or present value models. Along with asset-based models, discounted cash flow models are classified as absolute valuation models. In contrast, analysts use a relative valuation model when they apply a market-based approach in evaluating price and enterprise multiples relative to the value of a comparable company. These approaches and how they differ for private companies are the subject of the following sections.

Income-Based Approaches

Free Cash Flow Valuation Approach

Free cash flow valuation for private and public companies follows a substantially similar process. Recall from earlier lessons that FCFF is a flexible measure which may be applied to different capital structures and is appropriate for controlling investors with influence over earnings distribution and debt policies.

By using the WACC as the relevant discount rate, FCFF models estimating a company's intrinsic value (IV_t) incorporate the cost of both debt and equity:

$$IV_t = \sum_{i=1}^{n} \frac{\text{FCFF}_{t+i}}{(1+\text{WACC})^i} + \frac{E(S_{t+n})}{(1+\text{WACC})^n} \tag{6}$$

FCFF valuation combines periodic cash flow projections for n years discounted at WACC, with a discounted terminal value estimate ($E(S_{t+n})$) representing firm value at the end of the initial n year period.

As is the case for public companies, terminal value estimates for private firms may be interpreted as either an expected sale price at the end of a finite holding period, or a point beyond which individual cash flow estimates are less certain and a perpetuity is used with a constant growth rate of g. Three basic approaches to establishing a terminal value for private companies are shown in Exhibit 7:

Exhibit 7: Terminal Value Approaches

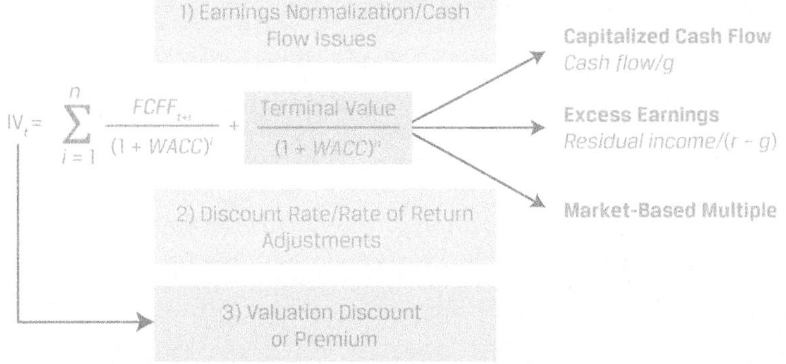

1) Earnings Normalization/Cash Flow Issues

$$IV_t = \sum_{i=1}^{n} \frac{FCFF_{t+i}}{(1+WACC)^i} + \frac{\text{Terminal Value}}{(1+WACC)^n}$$

2) Discount Rate/Rate of Return Adjustments

3) Valuation Discount or Premium

Capitalized Cash Flow
Cash flow/g

Excess Earnings
Residual income/(r − g)

Market-Based Multiple

Private companies may involve limited financial data or projections, significant intangible assets, or an uncertain growth trajectory given their early stage in the company life cycle. In the following sections, we address how and when these approaches are applied and, in some cases, adjusted to accommodate these company characteristics.

Capitalized Cash Flow Method

The capitalized cash flow method (CCM) estimates value based on a company's projected performance as a growing perpetuity under the assumption of stable growth. While less frequently used for the valuation of public companies, larger private companies, or in the context of acquisitions or financial reporting, a CCM may be particularly appropriate in valuing a private company for which no projections are available and/or market pricing evidence from similar public companies or transactions is limited.

While the CCM is often used to derive a terminal value as shown in Exhibit 7, in its most basic form using expected FCFF as a cash flow measure as shown in an earlier example, the capitalized cash flow (CCF) calculation is calculated as a perpetuity discounted by the WACC minus the constant cash flow growth rate (g):

$$Firm\ Value_t = \frac{FCFF_{t+1}}{WACC - g} \quad (7)$$

The expected FCFF ($FCFF_{t+1}$) may be estimated using the company's expected after-tax EBIT and the firm's **reinvestment rate**, or the rate of investment in working capital and long-term assets which combined are analogous to the retention ratio introduced in earlier lessons which is necessary to maintain operations and support assumed growth. We may solve for the reinvestment rate as follows:

$$\text{Revinvestment rate} = \text{RIR} = \frac{g}{\text{WACC}} \quad (8)$$

Solve for firm value in Equation 7 using projected EBIT as follows:

$$\text{Firm Value}_t = \frac{\text{EBIT}_{t+1}(1-t)(1-\text{RIR})}{\text{WACC} - g} \quad (9)$$

In order to solve for the company's intrinsic equity value (IV_t), we must subtract the estimated market value of debt from firm value. Note that the use of a constant WACC assumes the capital structure will remain unchanged.

Analysts must estimate the market value of private debt when traded market values are unavailable. If debt represents a small fraction of overall financing and operations are stable, the face value of debt may be an acceptable estimate. In instances where a private company has significant leverage, the company faces changing financial conditions, and/or significant volatility is expected in its performance, the company's debt may be valued at a significant premium or discount from face value. Debt maturities and terms should also be considered, particularly if significant maturities occur during the life of the investment. In these cases, an analyst may estimate market value based on public debt with similar characteristics such as debt type, tenor, credit quality, and industry.

FCFE, introduced earlier in the curriculum, excludes payments to debtholders and uses the cost of equity (r_e) rather than the WACC to directly value equity:

$$IV_t = \frac{\text{FCFE}_{t+1}}{r_e - g} \quad (10)$$

The denominator in Equation 10 is often referred to as the **capitalization rate**. Firm equity value is estimated by dividing forecasted cash flow by the capitalization rate as shown in Example 8.

EXAMPLE 8

Vinuvia Limitada's CCF

Alicia Carrenza is a private equity general partner assessing a potential purchase of Vinuvia Limitada, a successful privately held Brazilian wine distributor. Carrenza arrives at the following estimates based upon limited company disclosures and market information:

- Vinuvia Limitada's most recent cash flow statement showed FCFF of BRL 15,000,000 and FCFE of BRL 14,500,000.
- Carrenza estimates a 15% required return to equity and a 10% cost of debt based upon estimates from public companies. Vinuvia has BRL 50,000,000 in total assets and is 90% financed by equity and 10% by debt. Vinuvia's tax rate is 34%.
- Carrenza expects operations to remain stable and forecasts constant FCFF growth of 5% in the future.

Answer the following questions based upon the information provided:

1. Calculate Vinuvia's equity value using CCF on a FCFF basis.

Solution:

Solve for CCF on an FCFF basis using Equation 7:

$$\text{Firm Value}_t = \frac{\text{FCFF}_{t+1}}{\text{WACC} - g}$$

Calculate inputs as follows:

$\text{FCFF}_{t+1} =$ BRL 15,750,000 (=BRL 15,000,000 × 1.05)

WACC = 14.2% ($r_{WACC} = w_d r_d + w_e r_e$; $=0.1\times(1\text{-}0.34)\times10\% + 0.9\times15\%$)

Solve for Firm Value$_t$ using g = 5% as BRL 171,943,231. Subtract Vinuvia's debt of BRL 5,000,000 (=0.1 × BRL 50,000,000) to get equity value of BRL 166,943,231, using book value given the small size of Vinuvia's debt and its stable operations.

2. Determine how Carrenza's CCF estimate changes if the expected growth rate is 2% instead.

Solution:

Solve for CCF on an FCFF basis using Equation 7 as in Question 1 with g = 2%:

$$\text{Firm Value}_t = \frac{\text{BRL}15,750,000}{0.142 - 0.02}$$

to derive an estimated Vinuvia equity value of BRL 120,822,368. The 3% reduction in future expected growth therefore reduces estimated equity value by over 25%.

As Example 8 shows, valuations are highly sensitive to assumed parameters such as growth rates. For companies where an analyst has sufficient information to forecast cash flows for several periods or expects cash flow to grow at different rates in the future, free cash flow valuation using a series of discrete cash flow projections as well as multistage growth assumptions where applicable is theoretically preferable to the CCM. However, a basic CCM can also be helpful in assessing discount rate or growth assumptions embedded in value indications from other approaches.

Excess Earnings Method

In a business valuation context, the excess earnings method (EEM) involves estimating the earnings remaining after deducting amounts that reflect the required returns to working capital and fixed assets (i.e., the tangible assets) and is outlined in Exhibit 8.

Exhibit 8: Excess Earnings Method

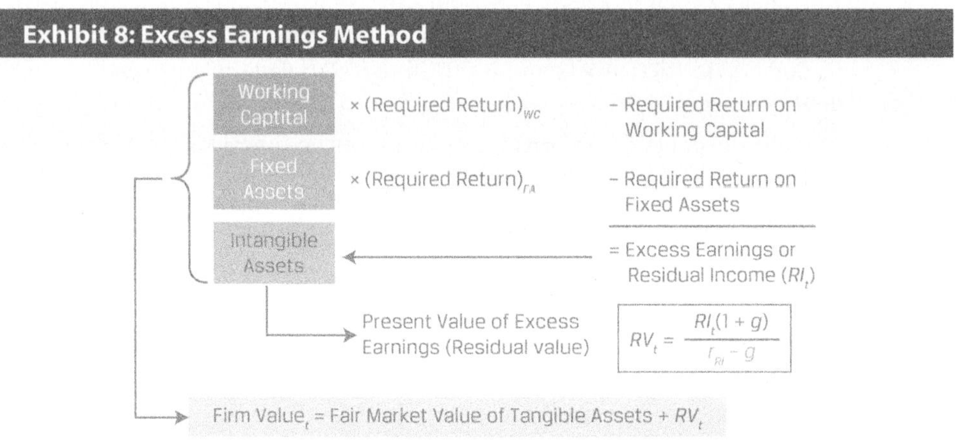

As a first step, estimate a company's normalized earnings using the adjustments shown earlier. Second, determine the fair market value of tangible assets, including working capital and fixed assets, as well as respective required rates of return. Working capital is the lowest risk and most liquid asset with the lowest required rate of return (r_{WC}), while fixed assets typically involve a higher rate of return (r_{FA}). Intangible assets, given their limited liquidity, potentially unique value to a specific company, and high risk, often require the highest return (r_{RI}). Third, deduct required return on tangible assets from normalized earnings to solve for excess earnings (residual income or RI_t).

$$RI_t = \text{Normalized Income} - (\text{Working Capital} \times r_{WC}) - (\text{Fixed Assets} \times r_{FA}) \quad (11)$$

The residual income introduced in earlier Equity lessons is capitalized using a similar growing perpetuity formula to CCM to solve for the present value of intangible assets (residual value or RV_t), where g represents the residual income growth rate.

$$RV_t = \frac{RIt(1+g)}{r_{RI}-g} \quad (12)$$

Firm value is the sum of the value of tangible assets and the residual value of excess earnings from intangible assets.

The EEM approach has generally been used to value intangible assets and very small businesses when other market approach methods are not feasible. Consider the EEM valuation presented in Example 9.

EXAMPLE 9

Digigraf GmbH – EEM

Digigraf GmbH is a small, privately held digital media firm with several patents seeking a new round of early-stage financing and intends to apply the EEM to value the business. The company's most recent financial statements indicate EUR 1,000,000 in total assets, consisting of working capital (EUR 200,000) and fixed assets (EUR 800,000), respectively, which are close to their fair market value. Following several adjustments, normalized earnings for the most recent year were EUR 120,000.

Steps in estimating Digigraf's firm value using an EEM approach are as follows:

1. *Develop discount rates for working capital (r_{WC}) and fixed assets (r_{FA}).* Based upon an assessment of the opportunity cost of working capital ais well as fixed assets, the required returns on working capital and fixed assets are estimated to be 5% and 11%, respectively.
2. *Calculate residual income (RI_t) by deducting required returns on assets from normalized income.* We can solve for RI_t using Equation 11:

RI_t = EUR 22,000

= EUR 120,000 – (EUR 200,000 × 5%) – (EUR 800,000 × 11%)

This residual income must reflect the value associated with intangible assets.

3. *Estimate a residual income discount rate and growth rate in order to value the intangible assets.* This estimate typically represents all intangible assets (including customer relationships, technology, trade names, and the assembled work force, among others). Here we assume the discount rate r_{RI} is 12% and the residual income growth rate g is 3%.
4. *Value intangible assets using the growing perpetuity in Equation 12.* Given the residual income of EUR 22,000, a growth rate of 3%, and an intangible asset discount rate of 12%, we solve for the present value of intangible assets as follows:

$$= \frac{\text{EUR}22,000 \times (1.03)}{0.12 - 0.03}$$

RV_t = EUR 251,778

EUR 22,000 is the normalized income for the most recent year, which is increased by its assumed 3% growth rate to forecast next year's residual income.

5. *Firm value is the sum of working capital, fixed assets, and intangible assets.* The EEM estimate for Digigraf GmbH is

EUR 1,251,778 = EUR 200,000 + EUR 800,000 + EUR 251,778.

The EEM is used only rarely in pricing entire private businesses, and then only for small ones. Some view the specific return requirements for working capital, tangible assets, and the residual income associated with intangible assets as not readily measurable and relatively subjective in nature. That said, for financial reporting purposes, the concept of residual income is an important element of intangible asset valuations and has wide acceptance.

Market-Based Approaches

Earlier lessons on the market-based relative value approach to public equity valuation used a company's equity market price or its enterprise value (EV) to establish a ratio or multiple to measure value. The market approach uses direct comparisons to public companies and acquired enterprises to estimate the fair value of an equity interest in a private company.

Because the market approach relies on data generated in actual market transactions, it is the most frequently used approach, and considered by many to be conceptually preferable to the income- and asset-based approaches for private company valuation. In addition to the approaches' used for compliance and litigation purposes, analysts often incorporate the market approach when triangulating among different approaches to arrive at an appropriate transaction value. The primary assumption of the market approach is that transactions providing pricing evidence are reasonably comparable to the those of the private company being evaluated.

There are three major variations of the market approach:

- The **guideline public company method** (GPCM) establishes a value estimate based on observed multiples from trading activity in the shares of public companies viewed as comparable to the subject private company.
- The **guideline transactions method** (GTM) establishes a value estimate based on pricing multiples derived from the acquisition of control of entire public or private companies.
- The **prior transaction method** considers actual transactions in the stock of the subject private company.

GPCM

Analysts frequently use multiples from comparable public companies to value private firms. These comparable companies are selected to match the relative risk and growth prospects of the private company as closely as possible using market information from publicly traded companies. For example, it is important to consider not only firms from the same industry but also firms of similar size, leverage, and stage in the company life cycle when choosing comparables.

The multiples used in public and private company valuation analysis may differ in the financial metrics used in the valuation process. Price-based multiples such as the price/earnings ratio are frequently cited in the valuation of public companies, while metrics such as EV which take the value of the entire firm into consideration are more common in private company valuation, as they offer greater flexibility to accommodate changes to the capital structure over the valuation period.

Another important adjustment to consider when comparing private companies to comparable public companies is differences in leverage. When using beta measures for purposes of comparison based on multiples, it is important to adjust for these differences by "unlevering" observed public company beta and "relevering" beta to match the capital structure of the private company. First, we "unlever" beta as follows.

$$\beta_{unlevered} = \frac{\beta_{levered}}{\left[1 + (1 - t) \times \left(\frac{\text{Debt}}{\text{Equity}}\right)\right]} \quad (13)$$

where both the tax rate t and the ratio of debt (Debt/Equity) reflect those of the public company in question. We then apply the unlevered beta to the tax rate and debt ratio of the private company to derive a levered beta:

$$\beta^*_{levered} = \beta_{unlevered}\left[1 + (1 - t^*) \times \left(\frac{\text{Debt}}{\text{Equity}}\right)^*\right] \quad (14)$$

where the tax rate t^* and the ratio of debt (Debt/Equity)* reflect those of the private company being evaluated as demonstrated in Example 10.

EXAMPLE 10

Valuing Quik Chip S.A. Using Guideline Public Companies

Quik Chip S.A. operates a chain of 50 quick-service restaurants throughout Europe. The process of estimating a value for Quik Chip may begin by assessing multiples and other fundamental financial variables from a set of guideline public companies operating in the quick-service restaurant industry globally. The guideline companies were limited to those expected to be similar in EV to Quik Chip. The data gathered are shown in the following table:

Comparables	P/E	EV/EBITDA	EV/EBIT	EV/Sales	Beta	Debt/Equity	Tax rate
Company A	21.6	13.6	18.5	3.7	1.3	61%	25%
Company B	21.6	12.5	17.5	1.7	1.2	47%	19%
Company C	24.3	8.8	15.0	1.5	1.2	56%	20%
Company D	17.7	11.8	15.7	2.2	1.1	33%	24%
Company E	18.4	10.8	16.1	1.0	1.0	22%	25%
Company F	29.1	11.8	16.5	1.8	1.3	54%	18%
Company G	29.9	11.2	21.5	1.5	1.5	67%	20%
Company H	16.6	9.6	14.0	0.8	0.9	28%	21%
Company I	24.2	18.8	20.7	3.6	1.4	82%	22%
Mean	**22.6**	**12.1**	**17.3**	**2.0**	**1.21**	**50.0%**	**21.6%**
Median	**21.6**	**11.8**	**16.5**	**1.7**	**1.2**	**53.8%**	**21.0%**
Low	**16.6**	**8.8**	**14.0**	**0.8**	**0.9**	**22.0%**	**18.0%**
High	**29.9**	**18.8**	**21.5**	**3.7**	**1.5**	**81.8%**	**25.0%**

The summary data from this table may be used as one tool for estimating the value of Quik Chip. For example, if the valuation analyst believes that Quik Chip is well represented by the average company from this comparable set, one or more of the four multiples may be used as part of a market-based valuation.

Alternatively, if capital structure (i.e., leverage) is different from public comparables, an income-based valuation may require a beta estimate, and public company data estimates may be used to estimate beta. Furthermore, the debt ratio and tax rate information from public companies can be used to unlever the beta estimates from the public companies.

Answer the following questions based upon the information provided:

1. If Quik Chip has a debt-to-equity ratio of 25% and a tax rate of 18%, what is a reasonable beta estimate for Quik Chip?

   Solution

   A valuation analyst starts with the 1.21 average beta from comparable companies. This beta can then be unlevered using the average Debt/Equity ratio and tax rate from guideline companies as shown in Equation 13.

$$\beta_{unlevered} = \frac{\beta_{levered}}{\left[1 + (1 - t) \times \left(\frac{\text{Debt}}{\text{Equity}}\right)\right]}$$

$\beta_{\text{unlevered}} = 1.21/[1+(1-0.216)\times0.50]$

$= 0.8693$

Then, re-lever the unlevered beta from the guideline companies to estimate a levered beta for Quik Chip using Equation 14.

$$\beta^*_{levered} = \beta_{unlevered}\left[1 + (1 - t^*) \times \left(\frac{\text{Debt}}{\text{Equity}}\right)^*\right]$$

$\beta^*_{levered} = 0.8693\times[1+ (1-0.18)\times0.25]$

$= 0.8693$

2. Assuming Quik Chip has sales of EUR 250,000,000 and EBIT of EUR 35,000,000, establish a range for Quik Chip's EV using peer multiples.

Solution:

Use mean peer multiples for EV/EBIT (17.3) and EV/Sales (2.0), respectively, calculate Quik Chip's implied EV for each:

$EV_{EV/EBIT}$ = EUR 605,500,000 (= 17.3 × EUR 35,000,000)

$EV_{EV/Sales}$ = EUR 500,000,000 (= 2.0 × EUR 250,000,000)

Note that Quik Chip's estimated EV is higher using an EBIT-based as opposed to a sales-based multiple, as the company is more profitable on an EBIT/Sales basis at 14% (=EUR 35,000,000 / EUR 250,000,000) for Quik Chip versus 11.6% (dividing EV/Sales of 2.0 by EV/EBIT of 17.3) for its public peers.

When a private company under analysis conducts business in more than one sector or industry, it may be necessary to create a composite profile from more than one group of comparable companies. Composite profiles are most often derived by weighting multiples using a percentage of sales or net income, which includes sales margin, leverage, and tax effects. Use of a composite profile is of particular importance when the risk or growth levels of these activities vary significantly across segments within the private company as shown in Example 11.

EXAMPLE 11

Establishing a Composite Multiple for Everfloat Limited

Example 5 introduced Everfloat Ltd., a privately held company based in the United Kingdom. Andrea Miceli seeks to estimate the value of Everfloat's EV using a market approach. While the company is well-known as a traditional marine navigation equipment provider, Everfloat has focused on diversification efforts over the last decade, with this business line now comprising just 70% of revenue. The company now has a growing logistics equipment business facilitating ground transportation as well as alternative energy technology for marine applications. In particular, Everfloat is pursuing electrification solutions as the shipping industry seeks to diversify away from fossil fuels, an effort which produces revenues, but is not yet profitable. The following table summarizes Everfloat's current business lines.

Everfloat Limited Financial Data (GBP millions)

Lines of Business	Revenue	Assets	EBITDA
Marine Navigation	700	1560	187.5
Logistics Services	250	400	75
Energy Solutions	50	40	-12.5
Total	**1,000**	**2,000**	**250**

Miceli identifies a group of publicly traded comparable companies for each of Everfloat's three business lines. As marine navigation is the dominant component of Everfloat's business metrics, these comparables will receive the largest weighting in the valuation.

Miceli focuses her analysis based on two market multiples: EV to sales (EV/Sales) and EV to EBITDA (EV/EBITDA). She identifies public companies of similar size and stage of development that operate primarily in each of Everfloat's business lines, gathers multiples for each, and summarizes the data by calculating the average multiple for each segment. Public peers in Logistics Services and Marine Navigation exhibit similar EV/EBITDA multiples, while publicly traded firms in Energy Solutions businesses similar to Everfloat trade at significantly higher EV/EBITDA multiples. EV/Sales shows a similar pattern, although EV/Sales multiples are significantly higher for Marine Navigation as compared to Logistics Services.

Everfloat Limited Comparable Multiples

Lines of Business	EV/Sales	EV/EBITDA
Marine Navigation	2.8	8.2
Logistics Services	1.1	8.1
Energy Solutions	8.0	20.0

Answer the following questions based upon the information provided:

1. Calculate a single EV/Sales multiple to value Everfloat.

Solution:

Weight peer multiples by Everfloat sales to derive composite EV/Sales of 2.6:

Composite EV/Sales = 2.6

$= (700/1{,}000)\times 2.8 + (250/1{,}000)\times 1.1 + (50/1{,}000)\times 8.0$

2. Calculate a single EV/EBITDA multiple to value Everfloat.

Solution:

Given Everfloat's negative Energy Solutions EBITDA, we weight peer multiples by the proportion of Everfloat's EBITDA as follows:

Composite EV/EBITDA = 7.6

$= (187.5/250)\times 8.2 + (75/250)\times 8.1 + (-12.5/250)\times 20.0$

An alternative would be to value Energy Solutions using Sales multiples and other divisions using EBITDA multiples.

The primary advantage of this method is the potentially large pool of guideline companies and the significant descriptive, financial, and trading information available to the analyst/appraiser. Disadvantages include possible issues regarding comparability and subjectivity in the risk and growth adjustments to the pricing multiple.

Control premiums may be used in valuing a controlling interest in a company. The trading of interests in public companies typically reflect small blocks without control of the entity. Given this information, many but not all believe the resulting pricing multiples do not reflect control of the entity.

A control premium adjustment may be appropriate depending on the specific facts. Historically, control premiums have been estimated based on transactions in which public companies were acquired. Several factors require careful consideration in estimating a control premium.

- *Type of transaction.* Some transaction databases classify acquisitions as either financial or strategic transactions as defined earlier. Compared with financial transactions, control premiums for an acquisition by a strategic buyer are typically larger because of the expected synergies.
- *Industry factors.* Industry sectors with acquisition activity are considered to be "in play" at a valuation date; that is, pricing of public companies in the sector may reflect some part of a possible control premium in the share prices. Control premiums measured at a different time may reflect a different industry environment from that of the valuation date.
- *Form of consideration.* Transactions involving the exchange of significant amounts of stock (as opposed to cash) may be less relevant as a basis of measuring a control premium since acquiring company management may execute such transactions when they believe their shares to be overvalued in the public market.

Multiples resulting from applying a control premium to pricing multiples from publicly traded companies should be assessed for reasonableness.

Guideline Transactions and Prior Transaction Methods

The GTM is conceptually similar to the GPCM. Unlike the GPCM, the GTM uses pricing multiples derived from acquisitions of public or private companies. Transaction data available on publicly reported acquisitions are compiled from public filings made by parties to the transaction with the regulatory bodies, such as the Financial Conduct Authority in the United Kingdom or the Securities and Exchange Commission in the United States. Data on transactions not subject to public disclosure may be available from certain transaction databases. Because information may be limited and is generally not readily confirmed, many appraisers challenge the reliability of this data. All other things equal, transaction multiples would be the most relevant evidence for valuation of a controlling interest in a private company. Several factors must be considered in assessing transaction-based pricing multiples.

- *Synergies.* The pricing of strategic acquisitions may include payment for anticipated synergies such as cost saving from consolidating corporate functions and/or revenue growth from cross-selling opportunities and include a control premium, while guideline transaction multiples do not. The relevance of payments for synergies to the case at hand merits consideration.
- *Contingent consideration.* **Contingent consideration** represents potential future payments to the seller that are contingent on the achievement of certain milestones. Obtaining a regulatory approval for a specific business activity or merger or achieving a targeted level of EBITDA are examples of contingencies. Contingent consideration may be included in the structure of acquisition. The inclusion of contingent consideration in the purchase price

paid for an enterprise often reflects uncertainty regarding the entity's future financial performance. For example, a prospective acquiror of Nano Beta in the earlier example might offer contingent consideration based upon EMA approval.

- *Non-cash consideration*. Acquisitions may include stock in the consideration. The cash equivalent value of a large block of stock may create uncertainty regarding the transaction price.
- *Availability of transactions*. Meaningful transactions for a specific private company may be limited. The relevance of pricing indications from a historical transaction may be challenged given any significant changes to the company, industry, or economy over the period.
- *Changes between transaction date and valuation date*. Unlike the GPCM, which develops pricing multiples based on stock prices at or near the valuation date, the GTM relies on pricing evidence from past acquisitions of control of firms. In many industries, transactions are limited and transactions several months or more from a valuation date may be the only transaction evidence available. Changes in market conditions could result in different risk and growth expectations, requiring an adjustment to the pricing multiple.
- Differences in company size, country, tax status, and leverage may also be relevant.

KNOWLEDGE CHECK

1. In Example 8, Vinuvia, a privately held Brazilian wine distributor, was estimated to have equity value of approximately BRL 167 million using the CCM. Vinuvia's FCFF was BRL 15 million, and the valuation assumed WACC of 15% and a perpetual growth rate of FCFF of 5%. Which statement is most accurate about the underlying assumption of Vinuvia's reinvestment rate?

   A. Vinuvia's assumed reinvestment rate is 33.33%.

   B. Vinuvia's assumed reinvestment rate is 66.67%.

   C. Vinuvia's reinvestment rate is not known based on the example.

   Solution:

   A is correct. Equation 8 shows that the assumed reinvestment rate in the CCM can be calculated by dividing the assumed perpetual growth rate of FCFF by the assumed WACC. In this case, reinvestment is equal to 33.33% (5%/15%).

2. In Example 9, Digigraf GmbH, a privately held company, was valued at approximately EUR 1,252,000 using the EEM approach. In checking the valuation, an analyst discovers that each of the discount rates for working capital, fixed assets, and intangible assets were incorrectly entered into the model. The correct estimates of discount rates are 4% for working capital, 10% for fixed assets, and 11% for intangible assets. Which of the following is closest to the corrected estimate of Digigraf's EEM value?

   A. EUR 1,283,000

   B. EUR 1,366,000

C. EUR 1,412,000

Solution:

C is correct. The discount rate mistakes on working capital and fixed assets require an updated calculation of residual income of EUR 32,000,000 (=120,000 – (200,000 x 4%) – (800,000 x 10%)). Next, the residual value calculation is updated as EUR 412,000 (=(32,000 x 1.03) / (11% - 3%)). Finally, the EEM value is the sum of residual value of EUR 412,000, working capital of EUR 200,000, and fixed assets of EUR 800,000.

3. In Example 10, a set of guideline public companies were identified as potential comparables for Quik Chip, a private quick-service restaurant chain company. The comparables were specifically chosen to be similar to Quik Chip with respect to industry and firm size. Which characteristic is least useful for choosing guideline public companies?

A. Similar debt ratio

B. Similar growth prospects

C. Similar risk

Solution:

A is correct. Private companies may have less access to debt than their public comparables and would therefore tend to have lower debt ratios. Similar growth prospects and similar risk are both useful characteristics in selection of guideline public companies.

8 PRIVATE COMPANY VALUATION: INCOME-BASED APPROACH

☐ calculate the value of a private company using income-based methods

In earlier sections, we addressed issues specific to the valuation of private companies including required adjustments to the numerator of the valuation model such as normalization of income and cash flow, and changes to the denominator including modifications to the required rate of return. Once the firm value or equity value is established based on these appropriately adjusted parameters, a premium or discount due to control and marketability factors may be applied based upon both the perspective and objectives of the evaluator. For example, an evaluator seeking to control a company in a competitive bid situation may offer to pay a premium

We now turn our attention to the process of conducting a private company valuation using the income approach and incorporating these adjustments, which is summarized in Exhibit 9.

Exhibit 9: Private Company Valuation Process: Income Approach

1) Estimate top-down FCFF from company information

$$FCFF = EBIT(1 - Tax\ Rate) + Depreciation(Tax\ Rate) - \Delta LT\ Assets - \Delta Working\ Capital$$

2) Calculate WACC from public comparables

Solve for Unlevered Equity Beta of Public Comparables

Calculate Estimate Target Company Levered Beta

Solve for WACC Using Observed/Estimated Debt Cost and Tax Rate

3) Estimate growth rate g based on company profile

4) Solve for enterprise value (EV) using DCF model

$$EV_t = \sum_{i=1}^{n} \frac{FCFF_{t+i}}{(1 + WACC)^i} + \frac{FCFF_{t+n+1}/(WACC - g)}{(1 + WACC)^n}$$

5) Add premium/discount for liquidity or control factors

This process is illustrated in the following case based upon Example 4.

EXAMPLE 12

FLI Valuation Using the Income Approach

Recall from Example 1 that Dev Khan, a private equity analyst, was asked to develop a valuation estimate of FLI from the perspective of a non-controlling shareholder. Khan takes the following steps in this process:

- Estimate WACC using comparable public companies and the CAPM, an expanded CAPM, or a build-up approach
- Develop a base-year estimate of FCFF
- Estimate EV from forecasted FCFF and an expected terminal value
- Apply appropriate discounts/premiums to complete the valuation

Step 1. Estimate WACC

Recall from Example 4 that Dev Khan calculated discount rates for FLI's business as summarized in the following table:

Calculated variable	Approach	Result
Required return on equity	CAPM	9.3%
Required return on equity	Expanded CAPM	13.3%
Required return on equity	Build-up approach	12.8%
WACC	Using FLI actual debt ratio	12.8%
WACC	Using FLI optimal debt ratio	12.3%

While the expanded CAPM method suggested a required return on equity of 13.3%, the build-up approach gave an estimate of 12.8%. Khan decides to combine these results for a 13.0% required return on equity as part of the WACC calculation. Finally, Khan chooses an average of differing assumptions about FLI's future debt ratios to arrive at a WACC estimate of 12.55%.

Step 2. Develop a base-year estimate of FCFF

In Example 1, FLI's operating income was normalized to account for overstated expenses related to CEO compensation and use of real estate assets. FLI's EBIT was adjusted upward from its reported level of SGD 14 million to a normalized amount of SGD 15.4 million as summarized in the following table.

FLI's Normalized Operating Income after Taxes

As of 31 December (in SGD)	As Adjusted
Revenues	50,000,000
Cost of goods sold	30,000,000
Gross profit	20,000,000
SG&A expenses	3,700,000
EBITDA	16,300,000
Depreciation and amortization	900,000
Earnings before interest and taxes	15,400,000

Using FLI's tax rate of 17% and additional information that FLI had capital expenditures of SGD 1,200,000 and increased working capital by SGD 500,000 over the period, Khan solves for a base-year FCFF of SGD 11,982,000:

$$\text{FCFF} = \text{EBITDA}(1 - \text{Tax rate}) + \text{Depreciation}(\text{Tax rate}) - \Delta\text{LT Assets} - \Delta\text{Working Capital}$$

$$\text{SGD } 11{,}982{,}000$$
$$= 16{,}300{,}000 \times (1 - 0.17) + 900{,}000 \times 0.17 - 1{,}200{,}000 - 500{,}000$$

Step 3. Estimate EV using an FCFF forecast and expected terminal value

Khan has sufficient confidence to forecast five years of revenue based upon expected industry trends, with an optimistic case of 8% FCFF growth for the next five years, a base case of 5%, and a downside estimate of 2% growth over the period. The terminal value is calculated using an expected perpetual growth rate of 3%. For example, in the downside case, Year 5 FCFF may be calculated as follows:

$$\text{FCFF(Downside)}_5 = \text{SGD } 13{,}229{,}096 = \text{FCFF}_0(1{+}0.02)^5$$

Using this result, terminal value for the downside case may be solved for as SGD 141,295,059 as follows:

$$\text{Terminal Value (Downside)} = \text{FCFF(Downside)}_5 \times (1{+}0.02)/(0.1255{-}0.03)$$

$$= \text{SGD } 13{,}493{,}678/(0.0955)$$

$$= \text{SGD } 141{,}295{,}059$$

These results for all three scenarios may be summarized as follows:

FLI FCFF and Terminal Value Forecasts (SGD millions)

Year	Downside	Base	Optimistic
Base year	11.982	11.982	11.982
Year 1	12.222	12.581	12.941
Year 2	12.466	13.210	13.976
Year 3	12.715	13.871	15.094
Year 4	12.970	14.564	16.301
Year 5	13.229	15.292	17.605
Terminal Value	142.680	164.934	189.881

We discount these annual cash flows at the WACC of 12.55% using the Excel NPV function (=(*rate,value1,value2*, ...)) to arrive at the following results:

FLI Enterprise and Equity Value Estimates (SGD millions)

Case	Downside	Base	Optimistic
EV	124.027	140.202	158.161
Equity value	121.527	137.702	155.661

Since FLI has a small amount of debt outstanding at a market value of SGD 2.5 million, an equity valuation must deduct the debt amount from the EV estimate:

Equity value = EV – Debt value

Equity value estimates in each scenario reflect a deduction of SGD 2.5 million.

Step 4. Apply appropriate discounts/premiums to complete the valuation

The equity value estimates presented in Step 3 may be viewed as the outcomes of valuing a marketable position as discussed earlier. To account for FLI's privately held company status, the value estimates should be discounted for lack of marketability and/or control. Khan used an option-based approach to assess the size of the DLOM and concluded that a 18% DLOM would be appropriate for FLI. While Xin owns a controlling stake in FLI, Khan did not see a rationale to view the current value of her controlling interest as including a control premium, so he assumed no DLOC. The following table shows Khan's estimated value range for FLI after discounting for lack of marketability.

FLI Non-Marketable Equity Value Estimates (SGD millions)

Case	Downside	Base	Optimistic
Equity value less DLOM	99.653	112.916	127.642

KNOWLEDGE CHECK

Macro Associates is a privately held business owned jointly by two general partners. Over the past year, the partners have had significant disagreements about Macro's strategy. The partners agreed to seek a dissolution of the partnership in which one partner will sell their ownership stake to the other based upon an independent valuation conducted by Clinical Valuations. Clinical's partner on this engagement has decided to value Macro using an income approach. During the process of gathering and synthesizing information necessary to conduct the valuation, several issues have arisen for which Clinical's analyst must draw appropriate conclusions in order to arrive at a valid estimate of Macro's value.

Issue 1: The selling partner has received above-market compensation for several years for performing the role of Chief Operating Officer. The buying partner serves as CEO and her compensation has been similar to that of a set of benchmark private company CEOs.

Issue 2: Macro lacks comparable public companies from which to base a beta estimate. The analyst is concerned that it will be difficult to estimate a valid required return on equity without a comparable public company beta.

Issue 3: Given the lack of similar comparable public companies, the analyst is deciding between the CCM and the EEM to estimate the terminal value.

1. Which of the following actions reflect what the analyst should do in preparing Macro's base-year FCFF?

   A. Normalize Macro's compensation cost such that the company's EBIT is lower than shown in its reviewed financial statements.

   B. Normalize Macro's compensation cost such that the company's EBIT is higher than shown in its reviewed financial statements.

   C. Use the EBIT as reported in the reviewed financial statements.

   Solution:

   B is correct. Given that the selling partner has received above-market compensation, the reviewed income statement costs are overstated. As such, costs will be normalized lower, resulting in higher income used to create Macro's base-year FCFF.

2. The analyst decides to rely on the build-up method to estimate Macro's required return on equity. Which statement provides the most accurate reflection as to why this choice of method addresses the issue of the lack of public comparable companies from which to estimate beta?

   A. The build-up method uses a standard equity-risk premium without adjusting it by a beta estimate.

   B. The build-up method assumes a beta of zero.

C. The build-up method assumes a company-specific risk premium and this alleviates the need for a beta.

Solution:

A is correct. The build-up method begins with the risk-free rate, then adds an equity risk premium without an adjustment for beta. This omission effectively assumes a beta of one. This approach differs from using the CAPM or expanded CAPM in which beta estimates are necessary. B is incorrect because the build-up method assumes beta of one, not zero. C is incorrect because the company-specific risk premium does not rely on comparable public companies and this premium is included in both the build-up and expanded CAPM methods.

3. Suppose the analyst chooses the CCM to estimate Macro's terminal value instead of using the EEM. Which statement best describes the advantage of the CCM over excess earnings?

   A. The CCM does not rely on comparable public company data.

   B. The CCM will be more effective at estimating the value of Macro's intangible assets.

   C. The CCM allows for the use of only one discount rate while the EEM requires multiple discount rates to be estimated.

Solution:

C is correct. The CCM uses the following equation:

$$\text{Firm Value}_t = \frac{\text{FCFF}_{t+1}}{\text{WACC} - g}$$

Thus, WACC is the only discount rate. The EEM requires separate discount rates for working capital, tangible assets, and residual income. A is not correct because neither the CCF nor the EEM requires public company comparables. B is incorrect, because this is a correct statement about the EEM, not the CCF method.

PRIVATE COMPANY VALUATION: MARKET-BASED APPROACH

9

☐ calculate the value of a private company using market-based methods and describe the advantages and disadvantages of each method

Analysts often seek to estimate private company values based on observed market-based multiples using the shares of comparable public companies, rather than the income-based valuation approach in the prior section. While in some cases these multiples are adjusted to reflect differences in relative risk and growth prospects, in others more than one group of comparable companies is used to mirror the business profile of a private firm operating in more than one line of business.

We apply this technique in conducting a private company valuation using a market approach as summarized in Exhibit 10.

Exhibit 10: Private Company Valuation Process: Market Approach

1) Choose public comparables and weight to match private company

2) Gather and summarize multiples from comparable public companies

Enterprise Value-Based Ratio (EV_i) to:

EBITDA	EBITA	EBIT	FCFF	Sales

3) Estimate private company enterprise value from multiples

For an EV/Sales multiple, weight the respective multiples by the percentage of private company business line sales to estimate enterprise value:

$$EV_t = \sum_{w=1}^{n} w_i \left(\frac{EV_i}{Sales_i} (\text{Private Company Sales})_i \right); \quad w_i = \frac{\textit{Business Line Sales}}{\textit{Total Sales}}$$

4) Discount estimated value for illiquidity or minority ownership

---

We return to the case of Everfloat from Examples 5 and 11.

EXAMPLE 13

Everfloat Ltd. Valuation Using the Market Approach

Example 5 introduced Everfloat Ltd., a privately held company based in the United Kingdom. Andrea Miceli seeks to estimate the value of Everfloat's EV from a non-controlling, minority interest shareholder perspective using a market approach. To employ this process, she must follow these steps:

- Identify Everfloat's lines of business and compile a set of publicly traded comparable companies from each respective segment.
- Select and calculate appropriate composite market multiples.
- Calculate a range of value estimates for Everfloat, noting that these estimated values are reflective of public, not private, company valuations.
- Apply appropriate discounts and/or premiums to reflect appropriate adjustments for control and marketability.

Step 1. Identify comparable public companies across business lines

In Example 11, Miceli identified comparable companies in Everfloat's three business lines. The following table summarizes Everfloat's revenues, EBITDA, and assets as a percentage of the total.

Everfloat Limited Financial Data (% of total)

Lines of Business	Revenue	Assets	EBITDA
Marine Navigation	70%	78%	75%
Logistics Services	25%	20%	30%
Energy Solutions	5%	2%	-5%

Step 2. Gather and summarize multiples from comparable public companies

The following table from Example 11 summarizes public company multiples in each of Everfloat's three business lines as well as a composite multiple for each category based on respective sales or EBITDA weights.

Everfloat Limited Public Comparable Multiples

Lines of Business	EV/Sales	EV/EBITDA
Marine Navigation	2.8	8.2
Logistics Services	1.1	8.1
Energy Solutions	8.0	20.0
Composite	**2.635**	**7.58**

Step 3. Use multiples to derive initial estimate of value

To arrive at an initial estimate of Everfloat's EV, Miceli must multiply the respective peer industry multiples by Everfloat's fundamental variables associated with each multiple.

Recall from Example 11 that Miceli weighted each business line based on Everfloat's revenues to compute a composite EV/Sales multiple of 2.635.

$$\text{Composite EV/Sales} = (700/1{,}000)\times 2.8 + (250/1{,}000)\times 1.1 + (50/1{,}000)\times 8.0 = 2.635$$

Miceli derives a preliminary value estimate for Everfloat by simply multiplying this composite by Everfloat's total revenues of GBP 1 billion to find an initial estimated EV based on EV/Sales of GBP 2.635 billion:

$$\text{EV}_{EV/Sales} = \text{GBP } 2{,}635{,}000{,}000 = 2.635 \times \text{GBP } 1{,}000{,}000{,}000$$

Note that this estimate is based upon public company comparables and requires further adjustment.

As an alternative approach, Miceli could simply multiply the individual EV/Sales segment multiples by Everfloat's respective revenue for each business line as shown in the following table:

Everfloat Valuation by Segment Based on EV/Sales

Lines of Business	Revenue (GBP million)	EV/Sales	Stand-Alone Value (GBP million)
Marine Navigation	700	2.8	1,960
Logistics Services	250	1.1	275
Energy Solutions	50	8.0	400

Note that while the sum of the resulting values by segment in the far right column gives us the same GBP 2.635 billion result, each of the three terms may be interpreted as an initial public company value estimate of the three different divisions. For example, ignoring any adjustments for synergies among the segments or to a prospective controlling buyer, this implies Everfloat's Energy Solutions business would be worth GBP 400 million as a stand-alone entity.

A similar approach using the EV/EBITDA multiple by segment poses a challenge for the Energy Solutions business since it implies negative value for the segment. Instead of assuming that the division's losses are associated with a poorly run business, an analyst may take the view that the segment is at an early stage in its life cycle. In aggregate we may follow the same process using EV/EBITDA multiples and Everfloat's EBITDA of GBP 250 million to derive a value estimate based on EV/EBITDA of GBP 1.895 billion:

$$EV_{EV/EBITDA} = \text{GBP } 1{,}895{,}000{,}000 = 7.58 \times \text{GBP } 250{,}000{,}000$$

Step 4. Apply appropriate discounts/premiums to complete the valuation

Using the public company equivalent derived in Step 3, Miceli must adjust Everfloat's value to reflect a non-controlling and non-marketable shareholder's perspective. Miceli estimated 13% as a DLOC and 16.8% as a DLOM, resulting in a total discount of 27.6% in Example 7. As a final step, Miceli must adjust each of her valuation estimates for this discount as follows.

$$EV_{\text{EV/Sales}} = \text{GBP } 1{,}907{,}740{,}000 = \text{GBP } 2{,}635{,}000{,}000 \times (1 - 27.6\%)$$

$$EV_{\text{EV/EBITDA}} = \text{GBP } 1{,}371{,}980{,}000 = \text{GBP } 1{,}895{,}000{,}000 \times (1 - 27.6\%)$$

Miceli may derive a single valuation estimate by simply averaging the two market-based results to arrive at GBP 1,639,860,000 (=(GBP 1,907,740,000 + GBP 1,371,980,000)/2) or expand the approach by considering additional multiples in the valuation.

KNOWLEDGE CHECK

Andrea Miceli continues her valuation of Everfloat using the market approach. Her manager has questioned the applicability of the different multiples to value the company, especially since the composite multiples she has created include implications for the values of each division within Everfloat.

1. Based on the EV/Sales multiples shown in Example 13 and the Sales by division information from Example 11 in Section 6, which of the Everfloat divisions is the least valuable?

   A. Marine Navigation

   B. Logistics Services

   C. Energy Solutions

   Solution:

   B is correct. The Logistics Services comparable EV/Sales multiple is 1.1, and Everfloat's sales in this division is GBP 250 million, so this division's contribution to the overall value of Everfloat is GBP 275 million (250 million × 1.1). By contrast, the Marine Navigation division is worth GBP 1,960 million (700 million × 2.8), and the Energy Solutions division is worth GBP 400 million (50 million × 8.0).

2. Miceli is concerned with the composite EV/EBITDA multiple in valuing Everfloat at GBP 1,895 million shown in Example 13. Which statement is the most valid concern about using this multiple?

   A. Since Everfloat's Energy Solutions business has negative EBITDA, the use of a composite EV/EBITDA multiple implies that this division has negative value.

   B. The value estimate for Everfloat is considerably lower when using EV/EBITDA rather than EV/Sales.

   C. Logistics Services shows a higher proportion of EBITDA as a percentage of Everfloat's total EBITDA.

   Solution:

   A is correct. A negative value of an Everfloat unit implies that it would have to pay another party to buy that unit. As a result, using a multiple for a company that exhibits a negative fundamental variable (such as the EBITDA of the Energy Solutions division) poses a problem for using that multiple in practice. Both B and C are factual statements, but neither should be a concern. When using multiple valuation methods, results will often differ. The statement in C simply reflects that Logistics Services has higher profitability than the other Everfloat divisions.

3. Miceli's original approach in Example 11 in Section 6 was to create a composite multiple from comparables in each line of business. Miceli now discovers that most public companies she identified within the marine equipment industry have similar divisional revenue and EBITDA proportions to Everfloat. How should this information change Miceli's choice of comparable companies?

   A. This new information should not change Miceli's choice of public company comparables.

   B. This new information should cause Miceli to seek out a new set of public marine navigation comparables to replace the current set.

   C. This new information should cause Miceli to use only the companies listed as marine equipment comparables.

   Solution:

   C is correct. Because the marine equipment comparables consists of companies with similar business line mixes as Everfloat, these should be viewed as appropriate public company comparables. Thus, comparables from the other two lines of business are not necessary. Choice B implies that there are different marine equipment companies with navigation as their only line of business, but these companies would have likely already been identified in the prior search for marine shipping companies.

PRACTICE PROBLEMS

The following information relates to questions 1-5

Ulrich Schwalke has been recently hired as an analyst at a private equity firm that specializes in buying and restructuring private companies to be taken public within five years. Given his background with valuing public firms, this role will provide him his first experiences in valuing private companies.

Before starting his new position, Schwalke meets with a former classmate who works as an associate focused on private company valuations in order to resolve legal disputes. During the meeting, Schwalke's classmate mentions that private business valuation often requires normalizing certain expense items on a company's income statement before taking next steps.

On his first assignment, Schwalke is asked to estimate a WACC for a potential private target company. The partner has commented that the private target has a far lower debt ratio than would be considered optimal.

Schwalke's firm recently announced plans to buy one of the private companies that Schwalke has valued. Schwalke spent considerable time assessing the validity of different control premiums in analyzing a possible offer price.

1. Which valuation feature will Schwalke find different in valuing private companies versus public companies?

   A. Using FCFF to value companies

   B. Using market multiples to value companies

   C. Assessing discounts to account for illiquidity

2. During Schwalke's meeting with his former classmate, they discuss how their approaches to private company valuation vary given the different uses of their analysis. Which of the following best characterizes how Schwalke's approach differs from that of his former classmate?

   A. Schwalke usually incorporates a DLOM.

   B. Schwalke usually adjusts the investment value as a minority interest.

   C. Schwalke's approach usually considers a synergistic control premium.

3. Which of the following statements best describes the meaning of "normalizing earnings" in the context of private business valuation?

   A. Adjustments to revenues and/or costs necessary to allow comparison of private company financial results to comparable public companies

   B. Adjustments to offset the cyclicality of revenues and/or costs for private companies

   C. Adjustments that allow comparisons due to the lack of marketability for private companies

4. Which statement best describes a possible bias in the WACC of the private target with a suboptimal debt ratio?

   A. Private companies are likely to have WACC estimates below their optimal WACC because of a lower weight on debt.

   B. Private companies are likely to have WACC estimates above their optimal WACC because of a higher weight on equity.

   C. Private companies are likely to have WACC estimates above their optimal WACC because of a higher weight on debt.

5. Schwalke learns that his firm intends to combine the new target company with an existing portfolio company prior to taking it public. Should Schwalke apply a financial or synergistic control premium, and how does this level of control premium compare to the other?

   A. Financial; higher

   B. Financial; lower

   C. Synergistic; higher

The following information relates to questions 6-10

Ulrich Schwalke continues his work in valuing private companies, taking specific interest in transactions involving public companies buying private company targets. As he has seen in his work, private company discount rates are often biased because private firms typically have less access to debt capital.

While Schwalke has experience using CAPM for public companies, he has rarely used it for private firms, instead relying on the expanded CAPM or a build-up approach to estimate required return on equity. When using the expanded CAPM for a private company, JNK Corporation, Schwalke gathered beta estimates from publicly traded comparable companies. On a recent engagement, he found the average beta from public comparables of 1.20. The average debt ratio of the public comparables exceeded that of JNK, while tax rates were equal between the public comparables and JNK.

Continuing in his role, Schwalke completed many private company valuations for entire businesses. As a result, certain methods of calculating terminal values seemed to be more useful for his work than other methods.

Schwalke had initially struggled with applying discounts in private company valuation but became more comfortable with different estimation methods. In particular, he finds an option-based approach to quantifying the lack of marketability quite useful. In his recent work on valuing JNK, he estimated the value of three put options with three months until expiration on the most similar public comparable company to JNK. The public comparable was trading at a stock price of EUR 29.70. The three-month risk-free rate is 4%. The put option valuation results are summarized as follows:

JNK Put Option Exercise Prices and Values	
Exercise price	**Put option value**
EUR 25	EUR 1.25
EUR 30	EUR 3.75
EUR 35	EUR 6.95

6. Which statement best reflects how discount rate biases may affect offer prices in transactions involving public company buyers and private company targets?

   A. Public company buyers pay offer prices for private firms that reflect improvements the buyer will make after a successful acquisition.

   B. Public company buyers pay offer prices for private firms that reflect the higher discount rates that apply to private companies.

   C. Public company buyers pay offer prices for private companies that do not reflect any control premium.

7. Which statement best explains why the CAPM may be inappropriate for estimating required return on equity for private firms?

   A. The CAPM was only designed for publicly traded stocks.

   B. The CAPM does not utilize a company-specific risk premium.

   C. The CAPM assumes investors are well diversified.

8. Which statement is most correct regarding Schwalke's estimation of JNK's beta?

   A. Schwalke estimates JNK's beta to be less than 1.20.

   B. Schwalke estimates JNK's beta to be 1.20.

   C. Schwalke estimates JNK's beta to be greater than 1.20.

9. Which terminal value estimation method is least useful for Schwalke?

   A. CCM

   B. EEM

   C. Market multiple method

10. Which amount most closely estimates the DLOM for JNK?

    A. 12.4%

    B. 12.6%

    C. 12.5%

The following information relates to questions 11-15

Schwalke is currently valuing LPE, a private furniture manufacturing company based in France. The company is owned entirely by the Lapiere family, with several family members employed as senior company managers. Jean Lapiere is the current CEO and owns 25% of LPE stock. LPE's most recent income statement as part of its reviewed financial statements is as follows:

As of 31 December (in EUR)	As Reported
Revenues	30,000,000
Cost of goods sold	18,000,000
Gross profit	12,000,000
SG&A expenses	8,000,000
EBITDA	4,000,000
Depreciation and amortization	2,400,000
Earnings before interest and taxes	1,600,000
Pro forma taxes (at 25%)	400,000
Operating income after taxes	1,200,000

As Schwalke reviews compensation expenses, he learns that Jean Lapiere's annual compensation is EUR 300,000 and that CEOs of similarly sized consumer durable goods companies earn EUR 600,000 on average.

To estimate LPE's required return on equity, Schwalke gathers betas from public furniture manufacturing companies, and after making appropriate adjustments, estimates LPE's beta at 0.80. He uses an equity risk premium of 6%, a small-cap stock premium of 2%, a company-specific stock premium of 1.5%, and an industry risk premium of 1%.

After making other normalizing assumptions to LPE's income statement and deducting the change in long-term assets of EUR 600,000 (equal to EUR 3,000,000 in capital expenditures less EUR 2,400,000 in depreciation), Schwalke estimates FCFF for the base year to be EUR 600,000. He decides to use the CCM in his income approach to valuing LPE with a WACC of 8% and perpetual growth of 4%.

Given the availability of similar publicly traded furniture manufacturing companies, Schwalke also uses a market approach to value LPE. He finds an average EV/Sales multiple of 0.60 from these public comparable companies. Schwalke notes that LPE's debt is currently EUR 6 million.

Jean Lapiere is seeking an estimate of the value of his LPE ownership stake. In the course of discussing the ownership structure, Schwalke concludes that none of the family members, including Jean, has a controlling interest in the company. Schwalke estimates discounts for lack of control and lack of marketability as 20% and 15%, respectively.

11. Which amount is closest to LPE's normalized EBITDA after considering Jean Lapiere's compensation?

    A. EUR 3.7 million

    B. EUR 4.0 million

    C. EUR 4.3 million

12. Which amount most accurately reflects the difference between Schwalke's esti-

mates of LPE's required return on equity using the build-up approach versus the expanded CAPM?

A. 1.0% (build-up > expanded CAPM).

B. 1.2% (build-up > expanded CAPM).

C. 2.2% (build-up > expanded CAPM).

13. Which of the following is closest to the proper calculation of LPE's EV using the CCM?

A. EUR 15 million

B. EUR 30 million

C. EUR 15.6 million

14. Which of the following is closest to the proper calculation of LPE's equity value using the EV/Sales multiple?

A. EUR 18 million

B. EUR 12 million

C. EUR 24 million

15. Which of the following is closest to the size of the total discount taken in calculating the value of Jean Lapiere's equity stake?

A. 35.0%

B. 32.0%

C. 29.2%

SOLUTIONS

1. C is correct. An issue with private versus public company valuations is the need to adjust the valuation downward to account for a lack of liquidity. A and B are both incorrect because FCFF and multiples are used in both private and public company valuations.

2. C is correct. As Schwalke's firm specializes in buying and restructuring private companies to be taken public, as a strategic buyer it will consider a control premium. Choices A and B are inconsistent with his firm's strategy of controlling and restructuring companies over a five-year period.

3. A is correct. Private companies, especially when a controlling owner also serves as a senior manager, may engage in economic transactions such as non-market-based market compensation that distorts earnings versus comparable public companies. Cyclicality is a factor that may need to be adjusted in public companies as well, while lack of marketability should not affect earnings.

4. B is correct. Recall the formula for WACC:

   $$r_{WACC} = w_d r_d + w_e r_e$$

   First, a higher equity weight implies a lower debt weight, as these proportions combined must equal one. Also, $r_e > r_d$, as equity is riskier than debt. Therefore, as w_d falls, the WACC increases, approaching r_e as the debt ratio approaches zero. A suboptimal debt ratio translates to a higher than optimal WACC. A is incorrect because a lower debt ratio does not reduce WACC. C is incorrect because a higher debt weight likely lowers the WACC.

5. C is correct. As Schwalke's firm seeks to realize synergies from the business combination of the target and existing portfolio company, it is likely to consider a synergistic premium which exceeds that of a financial buyer.

6. A is correct. Acquisition offer prices often reflect the improvements that a public company buyer will make to the private firm, such as reducing expenses. B is incorrect as this statement contradicts the statement in A. C is incorrect as the public company buyer is likely to pay a premium to successfully gain control of the private company.

7. C is correct. Private company owners are rarely well diversified, as much of their wealth is tied up in their company. CAPM assumes that investors are only exposed to market risk, not the total risk of a company. B is incorrect, as the CAPM includes a company-specific risk component measured by beta multiplied by the equity risk premium. A is incorrect, as the CAPM can measure the expected return of any financial asset, not just traded stocks.

8. A is correct. Observed beta estimates from public companies are levered betas. The levered beta must be adjusted to remove the effects of the debt on firm risk by applying the following unlevered beta equation.

   $$\beta_{unlevered} = \frac{\beta_{levered}}{\left[1 + (1 - t) \times \left(\frac{\text{Debt}}{\text{Equity}}\right)\right]}$$

   The larger the public company debt ratio, the lower the unlevered beta result. The unlevered beta is re-levered using JNK's debt ratio using the following levered beta equation.

$$\beta^*_{levered} = \beta_{unlevered}\left[1 + (1 - t^*) \times \left(\frac{\text{Debt}}{\text{Equity}}\right)^*\right]$$

As JNK's debt ratio is below that of the public companies, the resulting levered beta will not be as high as the levered beta for the public companies.

9. B is correct. Because Schwalke's work involves valuing entire businesses, the EEM is likely to be the least useful due to its reliance on multiple discount rates. The EEM is more commonly used to value a company's intangible assets, while the CCF and market multiple methods are more useful in valuing entire businesses.

10. B is correct. The put option approach involves an at-the-money option based on the prevailing forward price. Given the current price of EUR 29.70, the three-month forward price using a 4% risk-free rate is EUR 30 ($=29.70e^{(0.25\times0.04)}$), so the put option with exercise price of EUR 30 should be used. Dividing the 3.75 option value by the EUR 29.70 stock price equals 12.6%.

11. A is correct. Jean Lapiere receives EUR 0.3 million less as LPE's CEO than what he should expect in an arms-length contract. LPE's normalized EBITDA should therefore be EUR 0.3 million below its reported EUR 4.0 million.

12. C is correct. The build-up method is the sum of the equity risk premium (6%), small-cap stock premium (2%), company-specific premium (1.5%), and industry risk premium (1%), or 10.5%.

    The expanded CAPM reflects the sum of the beta-adjusted equity risk premium (0.8×6%), the small-cap stock premium (2%), and the company-specific premium (1.5%), or 8.3%.

13. C is correct. The CCM uses the following formula:

$$\text{Firm Value}_t = \frac{\text{FCFF}_{t+1}}{\text{WACC} - g}$$

    Recall that the FCFF at time t+1 must equal the base year FCFF multiplied by one plus the growth rate.

$$\text{Firm Value}_t = \frac{600{,}000 \times 1.04}{0.08 - 0.04} = 15{,}600{,}000$$

14. B is correct. Applying the EV/Sales multiple of 0.60 to LPE's base year sales of EUR 30 million results in an EV of EUR 18 million. To calculate equity value from EV, we deduct the debt of EUR 6 million to arrive at an equity value of EUR 12 million.

15. B is correct. The total discount equals 1 – (1 – 0.20)×(1 – 0.15) or 32.0%.

Glossary

Abnormal earnings See *residual income.*

Abnormal return The amount by which a security's actual return differs from its expected return, given the security's risk and the market's return.

Absolute convergence The idea that developing countries, regardless of their particular characteristics, will eventually catch up with the developed countries and match them in per capita output.

Absolute valuation model A model that specifies an asset's intrinsic value.

Absolute version of PPP An extension of the law of one price whereby the prices of goods and services will not differ internationally once exchange rates are considered.

Accounting estimates Estimates used in calculating the value of assets or liabilities and in the amount of revenue and expense to allocate to a period. Examples of accounting estimates include, among others, the useful lives of depreciable assets, the salvage value of depreciable assets, product returns, warranty costs, and the amount of uncollectible receivables.

Accuracy The percentage of correctly predicted classes out of total predictions. It is an overall performance metric in classification problems.

Acquisition When one company, the acquirer, purchases from the seller most or all of another company's (the target) shares to gain control of either an entire company, a segment of another company, or a specific group of assets in exchange for cash, stock, or the assumption of liabilities, alone or in combination. Once an acquisition is complete, the acquirer and target merge into a single entity and consolidate management, operations, and resources.

Activation function A functional part of a neural network's node that transforms the total net input received into the final output of the node. The activation function operates like a light dimmer switch that decreases or increases the strength of the input.

Active factor risk The contribution to active risk squared resulting from the portfolio's different-than-benchmark exposures relative to factors specified in the risk model.

Active return The return on a portfolio minus the return on the portfolio's benchmark.

Active risk The standard deviation of active returns.

Active risk squared The variance of active returns; active risk raised to the second power.

Active share A measure of how similar a portfolio is to its benchmark. A manager who precisely replicates the benchmark will have an active share of zero; a manager with no holdings in common with the benchmark will have an active share of one.

Active specific risk The contribution to active risk squared resulting from the portfolio's active weights on individual assets as those weights interact with assets' residual risk.

Activist short selling A hedge fund strategy in which the manager takes a short position in a given security and then publicly presents his/her research backing the short thesis.

Adjustable rate Interest rate for a mortgage or other loan that combines a fixed-rate period with a variable-rate period, which fluctuates based on market reference rates.

Adjusted funds from operations Funds from operations adjusted to remove any non-cash rent reported under straight-line rent accounting and to subtract maintenance-type capital expenditures and leasing costs, including leasing agents' commissions and tenants' improvement allowances.

Adjusted present value As an approach to valuing a company, the sum of the value of the company, assuming no use of debt, and the net present value of any effects of debt on company value.

Adjusted R^2 Goodness-of-fit measure that adjusts the coefficient of determination, R^2, for the number of independent variables in the model.

Advanced set An arrangement in which the reference interest rate is set at the time the money is deposited.

Advanced settled An arrangement in which a forward rate agreement (FRA) expires and settles at the same time, at the FRA expiration date.

Agglomerative clustering A bottom-up hierarchical clustering method that begins with each observation being treated as its own cluster. The algorithm finds the two closest clusters, based on some measure of distance (similarity), and combines them into one new larger cluster. This process is repeated iteratively until all observations are clumped into a single large cluster.

Akaike's information criterion (AIC) A statistic used to compare sets of independent variables for explaining a dependent variable. It is preferred for finding the model that is best suited for prediction.

Allowance for loan losses A balance sheet account; it is a contra asset account to loans.

Alpha The return on an asset in excess of the asset's required rate of return. Sometimes referred to as an *abnormal return.*

American Depositary Receipt A negotiable certificate issued by a depositary bank that represents ownership in a non-US company's deposited equity (i.e., equity held in custody by the depositary bank in the company's home market).

Analysis of variance (ANOVA) A table that presents the sums of squares, degrees of freedom, mean squares, and F-statistic for a regression model.

Application programming interface (API) A set of well-defined methods of communication between various software components and typically used for accessing external data.

Appraisals Professional estimates of current market value for a real estate property.

Arbitrage (1) The simultaneous purchase of an undervalued asset or portfolio and sale of an overvalued but equivalent asset or portfolio in order to obtain a riskless profit on the price differential. Taking advantage of a market inefficiency in a risk-free manner. (2) The condition in a financial market in which equivalent assets or combinations of assets sell for two different prices, creating an opportunity to profit at no risk with no commitment of money. In a well-functioning financial market, few arbitrage opportunities are possible. (3) A risk-free operation that earns an expected positive net profit but requires no net investment of money.

Arbitrage opportunity An opportunity to conduct an arbitrage; an opportunity to earn an expected positive net profit without risk and with no net investment of money.

Arbitrage portfolio The portfolio that exploits an arbitrage opportunity.

Arbitrage-free models Term structure models that project future interest rate paths that emanate from the existing term structure. Resulting prices are based on a no-arbitrage condition.

Arbitrage-free valuation An approach to valuation that determines security values consistent with the absence of any opportunity to earn riskless profits without any net investment of money.

Arm's-length transaction Both buyer and seller act independently without any preexisting relationship that may sway their decision making.

Asset-based approach Approach that values a private company based on the values of the underlying assets of the entity less the value of any related liabilities.

Asset-based valuation An approach to valuing natural resource companies that estimates company value on the basis of the market value of the natural resources the company controls.

At market contract When a forward contract is established, the forward price is negotiated so that the market value of the forward contract on the initiation date is zero.

Authorized participants (APs) A special group of institutional investors who are authorized by the ETF issuer to participate in the creation/redemption process. APs are large broker/dealers, often market makers.

Autocorrelations The correlations of a time series with its own past values.

Autoregressive model (AR) A time series regressed on its own past values in which the independent variable is a lagged value of the dependent variable.

Back-testing The process that approximates the real-life investment process, using historical data, to assess whether an investment strategy would have produced desirable results.

Backward propagation The process of adjusting weights in a neural network, to reduce total error of the network, by moving backward through the network's layers.

Backwardation A downward-sloping, or inverted, forward curve in a futures market.

Bag-of-words (BOW) A collection of a distinct set of tokens from all the texts in a sample dataset. BOW does not capture the position or sequence of words present in the text.

Balance sheet restructuring Altering the composition of the balance sheet by either shifting the asset composition, changing the capital structure, or both.

Bankruptcy Legal proceedings, which vary by jurisdiction, allowing a firm whose liabilities exceed its assets to restructure existing debt obligations or liquidate assets in an orderly manner.

Barbell portfolio Fixed-income portfolio that combines short and long maturities.

Base error Model error due to randomness in the data.

Basic earnings per share (EPS) Net earnings available to common shareholders (i.e., net income minus preferred dividends) divided by the weighted average number of common shares outstanding during the period.

Basis The difference between the spot price and the futures price. As the maturity date of the futures contract nears, the basis converges toward zero.

Basis trade A trade based on the pricing of credit in the bond market versus the price of the same credit in the CDS market. To execute a basis trade, go long the "underpriced" credit and short the "overpriced" credit. A profit is realized as the implied credit prices converge.

Bearish flattening Term structure shift in which short-term bond yields rise more than long-term bond yields, resulting in a flatter yield curve.

Benchmark value of the multiple In using the method of comparables, the value of a price multiple for the comparison asset; when we have comparison assets (a group), the mean or median value of the multiple for the group of assets.

Bias error Describes the degree to which a model fits the training data. Algorithms with erroneous assumptions produce high bias error with poor approximation, causing underfitting and high in-sample error.

Bill-and-hold basis Sales on a bill-and-hold basis involve selling products but not delivering those products until a later date.

Blockage factor An illiquidity discount that occurs when an investor sells a large amount of stock relative to its trading volume (assuming it is not large enough to constitute a controlling ownership).

Bond indenture A legal document between a bond issuer and investors that governs each party's rights and responsibilities.

Bond risk premium The expected excess return of a default-free long-term bond less that of an equivalent short-term bond.

Bond yield plus risk premium (BYPRP) approach An estimate of the cost of common equity that is produced by summing the before-tax cost of debt and a risk premium that captures the additional yield on a company's stock relative to its bonds.

Bonus issue of shares A type of dividend in which a company distributes additional shares of its common stock to shareholders instead of cash.

Book value Shareholders' equity (total assets minus total liabilities) minus the value of preferred stock; common shareholders' equity.

Book value of equity Shareholders' equity (total assets minus total liabilities) minus the value of preferred stock; common shareholders' equity.

Book value per share The amount of book value (also called carrying value) of common equity per share of common stock, calculated by dividing the book value of shareholders' equity by the number of shares of common stock outstanding.

Bootstrap aggregating (or bagging) A technique whereby the original training dataset is used to generate n new training datasets or bags of data. Each new bag of data is generated by random sampling with replacement from the initial training set.

Bootstrapping The use of a forward substitution process to determine zero-coupon rates by using the par yields and solving for the zero-coupon rates one by one, from the shortest to longest maturities.

Breakup value The value derived using a sum-of-the-parts valuation.

Breusch–Godfrey (BG) test A test used to detect autocorrelated residuals up to a predesignated order of the lagged residuals.

Breusch–Pagan (BP) test A test for the presence of heteroskedasticity in a regression.

Bullet portfolio A fixed-income portfolio concentrated in a single maturity.

Bullish flattening Term structure change in which the yield curve flattens in response to a greater decline in long-term rates than short-term rates.

Bullish steepening Term structure change in which short-term rates fall by more than long-term yields, resulting in a steeper term structure.

Buy-side analysts Analysts who work for investment management firms, trusts, bank trust departments, and similar institutions.

Buyback A transaction in which a company buys back its own shares. Unlike stock dividends and stock splits, share repurchases use corporate cash.

Callable bond A bond containing an embedded call option that gives the issuer the right to buy the bond back from the investor at specified prices on predetermined dates.

Canceled shares Shares that were issued, subsequently repurchased by the company, and then retired (cannot be reissued).

Capital asset pricing model (CAPM) An equation describing the expected return on any asset (or portfolio) as a linear function of its beta relative to the market portfolio.

Capital charge The company's total cost of capital in money terms.

Capital deepening An increase in the capital-to-labor ratio.

Capitalization rate The rate used to discount expected NOI, which combines the required rate of return on similar properties with an implied constant growth rate.

Capitalized cash flow method In the context of private company valuation, a valuation model based on an assumption of a constant growth rate of free cash flow to the firm or a constant growth rate of free cash flow to equity. Also called *capitalized cash flow model.*

Capped floater Floating-rate bond with a cap provision that prevents the coupon rate from increasing above a specified maximum rate. It protects the issuer against rising interest rates.

Carry arbitrage model A no-arbitrage approach in which the underlying instrument is either bought or sold along with an opposite position in a forward contract.

Carry benefits Benefits that arise from owning certain underlyings; for example, dividends, foreign interest, and bond coupon payments.

Carry costs Costs that arise from owning certain underlyings. They are generally a function of the physical characteristics of the underlying asset and also the interest forgone on the funds tied up in the asset.

Cash available for distribution See *adjusted funds from operations.*

Cash settlement A procedure used in certain derivative transactions that specifies that the long and short parties settle the derivative's difference in value between them by making a cash payment.

Catalyst An event or piece of information that causes the marketplace to re-evaluate the prospects of a company.

CDS spread A periodic premium paid by the buyer to the seller that serves as a return over a market reference rate required to protect against credit risk.

Ceiling analysis A systematic process of evaluating different components in the pipeline of model building. It helps to understand what part of the pipeline can potentially improve in performance by further tuning.

Centroid The center of a cluster formed using the *k*-means clustering algorithm.

Chain rule of forecasting A forecasting process in which the next period's value as predicted by the forecasting equation is substituted into the right-hand side of the equation to give a predicted value two periods ahead.

Cheapest-to-deliver The debt instrument that can be purchased and delivered at the lowest cost yet has the same seniority as the reference obligation.

Classification and regression tree A supervised machine learning technique that can be applied to predict either a categorical target variable, producing a classification tree, or a continuous target variable, producing a regression tree. CART is commonly applied to binary classification or regression.

Clean surplus relation The relationship between earnings, dividends, and book value in which ending book value is equal to the beginning book value plus earnings less dividends, apart from ownership transactions.

Closed DB plan A DB plan that is not accepting new enrollees.

Club convergence The idea that only rich and middle-income countries sharing a set of favorable attributes (i.e., are members of the "club") will converge to the income level of the richest countries.

Cluster A subset of observations from a dataset such that all the observations within the same cluster are deemed "similar."

Clustering The sorting of observations into groups (clusters) such that observations in the same cluster are more similar to each other than they are to observations in other clusters.

Cobb–Douglas production function A function of the form $Y = K^{\alpha} L^{1-\alpha}$ relating output (Y) to labor (L) and capital (K) inputs.

Coefficient of determination A measure of how well data points fit a linear statistical model, indicated in percentage terms from 0 to 100%. Also known as *R-squared* (R^2).

Cointegrated Describes two time series that have a long-term financial or economic relationship such that they do not diverge from each other without bound in the long run.

Collateral return The component of the total return on a commodity futures position attributable to the yield for the bonds or cash used to maintain the futures position. Also called *collateral yield.*

Collection frequency (CF) The number of times a given word appears in the whole corpus (i.e., collection of sentences) divided by the total number of words in the corpus.

Commodity swap A type of swap involving the exchange of payments over multiple dates as determined by specified reference prices or indexes relating to commodities.

Company fundamental factors Factors related to the company's internal performance, such as factors relating to earnings growth, earnings variability, earnings momentum, and financial leverage.

Company share-related factors Valuation measures and other factors related to share price or the trading characteristics of the shares, such as earnings yield, dividend yield, and book-to-market value.

Comparables Assets used as benchmarks when applying the method of comparables to value an asset. Also called *comps*, *guideline assets*, or *guideline companies*.

Compiled financial statements Financial statements that are not accompanied by an auditor's opinion letter.

Complexity A term referring to the number of features, parameters, or branches in a model and to whether the model is linear or non-linear (non-linear is more complex).

Composite variable A variable that combines two or more variables that are statistically strongly related to each other.

Comprehensive income All changes in equity other than contributions by, and distributions to, owners; income under clean surplus accounting; includes all changes in equity during a period except those resulting from investments by owners and distributions to owners. Comprehensive income equals net income plus other comprehensive income.

Comps Assets used as benchmarks when applying the method of comparables to value an asset.

Concentrated ownership Ownership structure consisting of an individual shareholder or a group (controlling shareholders) with the ability to exercise control over the corporation.

Conditional convergence The idea that convergence of per capita income is conditional on the countries having the same savings rate, population growth rate, and production function.

Conditional heteroskedasticity A condition in which the variance of residuals of a regression are correlated with the value of the independent variables.

Conditional VaR (CVaR) The weighted average of all loss outcomes in the statistical (i.e., return) distribution that exceed the VaR loss. Thus, CVaR is a more comprehensive measure of tail loss than VaR is. Sometimes referred to as the *expected tail loss* or *expected shortfall*.

Confirmation bias A type of cognitive bias that makes individuals view information that confirms beliefs they already hold as more salient.

Confusion matrix A grid used for error analysis in classification problems, it presents values for four evaluation metrics including true positive (TP), false positive (FP), true negative (TN), and false negative (FN).

Conglomerate discount When an issuer is trading at a valuation lower than the sum of its parts, which is generally the result of diseconomies of scale or scope or the result of the capital markets having overlooked the business and its prospects.

Constant dividend payout ratio policy A policy in which a constant percentage of net income is paid out in dividends.

Constant returns to scale The condition that if all inputs into the production process are increased by a given percentage, then output rises by that same percentage.

Contango Refers to spot price below forward price in a futures market.

Contingent consideration Potential future payments to the seller that are contingent on the achievement of certain agreed-on occurrences.

Continuing earnings Earnings excluding nonrecurring components. Also referred to as *core earnings*, *persistent earnings*, or *underlying earnings*.

Continuing residual income Residual income after the forecast horizon.

Continuing value The analyst's estimate of a stock's value at a particular point in the future.

Contraction risk The risk of earlier repayment of a mortgage-backed security than expected.

Control premium An increment or premium to value associated with a controlling ownership interest in a company.

Convergence The property by which as expiration approaches, the price of a newly created forward or futures contract will approach the price of a spot transaction. At expiration, a forward or futures contract is equivalent to a spot transaction in the underlying.

Conversion period The period over which a convertible bond may be exchanged for equity at a predetermined price.

Conversion price Predetermined share price at which convertible debt may be fully exchanged for common shares during the conversion period.

Conversion rate (or ratio) For a convertible bond, the number of shares of common stock that a bondholder receives from converting the bond into shares.

Conversion value The current contingency feature value derived by comparing a convertible bond's price with its value if a bondholder were to exchange bonds for shares.

Convertible bond A bond that gives the bondholder the right to exchange the bond for a specified number of common shares in the issuing company.

Convexity The second order, usually a positive change in the price of a bond for a given change in yield, which can be negative for a callable bond such as a high-yield bond.

Core earnings Earnings excluding nonrecurring components. Also referred to as *continuing earnings*, *persistent earnings*, or *underlying earnings*.

Core real estate Real estate investments in well-developed, stable-income-producing commercial and residential properties.

Corpus A collection of text data in any form, including list, matrix, or data table forms.

Cost of carry model A model that relates the forward price of an asset to the spot price by considering the cost of carry (also referred to as future-spot parity model).

Cost of debt The required return on debt financing for a company, such as when it issues a bond, takes out a bank loan, or leases an asset through a finance lease.

Cost of equity The return required by equity investors to compensate for both the time value of money and the risk. Also referred to as the required rate of return on common stock or the required return on equity.

Cost restructuring Actions to reduce costs by improving operational efficiency and profitability, often to raise margins to a historical level or to those of comparable industry peers.

Country risk premium (CRP) The additional return required by investors to compensate for the risk associated with investing in a foreign country relative to the investor's domestic market.

Country risk rating (CRR) The rating of a country based on many risk factors, including economic prosperity, political risk, and ESG risk.

Covariance stationary Describes a time series when its expected value and variance are constant and finite in all periods and when its covariance with itself for a fixed number of periods in the past or future is constant and finite in all periods.

Covered bonds A senior debt obligation of a financial institution that gives recourse to the originator/issuer and a predetermined underlying collateral pool.

Covered interest rate parity The relationship among the spot exchange rate, the forward exchange rate, and the interest rates in two currencies that ensures that the return on a hedged (i.e., covered) foreign risk-free investment is the same as the return on a domestic risk-free investment. Also called *interest rate parity*.

Cox-Ingersoll-Ross model A general equilibrium term structure model that assumes interest rates are mean reverting and interest rate volatility is directly related to the level of interest rates.

Creation basket The list of securities (and share amounts) the authorized participant (AP) must deliver to the ETF manager in exchange for ETF shares. The creation basket is published each business day.

Creation units Large blocks of ETF shares transacted between the authorized participant (AP) and the ETF manager that are usually but not always equal to 50,000 shares of the ETF.

Creation/redemption The process in which ETF shares are created or redeemed by authorized participants transacting with the ETF issuer.

Credit correlation The correlation of credit (or default) risks of the underlying single-name CDS contained in an index CDS.

Credit curve The credit spreads for a range of maturities of a company's debt.

Credit default swap A derivative contract between two parties in which the buyer makes a series of cash payments to the seller and receives a promise of compensation for credit losses resulting from the default.

Credit derivative A derivative instrument in which the underlying is a measure of the credit quality of a borrower.

Credit event An occurrence that triggers the settlement of a CDS contract, including failure to make a debt payment, debt restructuring, or a bankruptcy filing.

Credit protection buyer One party to a credit default swap; the buyer makes a series of cash payments to the seller and receives a promise of compensation for credit losses resulting from the default.

Credit protection seller One party to a credit default swap; the seller makes a promise to pay compensation for credit losses resulting from the default.

Credit risk The expected economic loss under a potential borrower default over the life of the contract.

Credit spread The compensation for the risk of default in a debt security, typically measured by the yield-to-maturity difference between a bond and a comparable government benchmark security.

Credit valuation adjustment The value of the credit risk of a bond in present value terms.

Cross-sectional momentum A managed futures trend following strategy implemented with a cross-section of assets (within an asset class) by going long those that are rising in price the most and by shorting those that are falling the most. This approach generally results in holding a net zero (market-neutral) position and works well when a market's out- or underperformance is a reliable predictor of its future performance.

Cross-validation A technique for estimating out-of-sample error directly by determining the error in validation samples.

Cumulative preferred stock Preferred stock that requires that the dividends be paid in full to preferred stock owners for any missed dividends prior to any payment of dividends to common stock owners.

Current exchange rate For accounting purposes, the spot exchange rate on the balance sheet date.

Current rate method Approach to translating foreign currency financial statements for consolidation in which all assets and liabilities are translated at the current exchange rate. The current rate method is the prevalent method of translation.

Curvature One of the three factors (the other two are level and steepness) that empirically explain most of the changes in the shape of the yield curve. A shock to the curvature factor affects mid-maturity interest rates, resulting in the term structure becoming either more or less hump-shaped.

Curve trade Buying a CDS of one maturity and selling a CDS on the same reference entity with a different maturity.

Customer concentration risk The risk associated with sales dependent on a few customers.

Cyclical businesses Businesses with high sensitivity to business- or industry-cycle influences.

Data preparation (cleansing) The process of examining, identifying, and mitigating (i.e., cleansing) errors in raw data.

Data snooping The subconscious or conscious manipulation of data in a way that produces a statistically significant result (i.e., the p-value is sufficiently small or the t-statistic sufficiently large to indicate statistical significance), such as by running multiple simulations and naively accepting the best result. Also known as p-hacking.

Data wrangling (preprocessing) This task performs transformations and critical processing steps on cleansed data to make the data ready for ML model training (i.e., preprocessing), and includes dealing with outliers, extracting useful variables from existing data points, and scaling the data.

Debt service coverage ratio A key indicator of credit performance equal to the ratio of net operating income to debt service.

Dedicated short-selling A hedge fund strategy in which the manager takes short-only positions in equities deemed to be expensively priced versus their deteriorating fundamental situations. Short exposures may vary only in terms of portfolio sizing by, at times, holding higher levels of cash.

Deep learning An area of artificial intelligence in which a system uses neural networks to perform multistage, non-linear data processing to identify patterns. Also called *deep learning nets*.

Deep neural networks Neural networks with many hidden layers—at least 2 but potentially more than 20—that have proven successful across a wide range of artificial intelligence applications.

Default risk See *credit risk*.

Delta The sensitivity of the derivative price to a small change in the value of the underlying asset.

Dendrogram A type of tree diagram used for visualizing a hierarchical cluster analysis; it highlights the hierarchical relationships among the clusters.

Depository Trust and Clearinghouse Corporation A US-headquartered entity providing post-trade clearing, settlement, and information services.

Depreciable base Total construction or original acquisition cost plus any property improvements less the cost of land written down over the estimated useful life, as in the case of a company's fixed assets.

Diluted earnings per share (Diluted EPS) Net income, minus preferred dividends, divided by the weighted average number of common shares outstanding considering all dilutive securities (e.g., convertible debt and options); the EPS that would result if all dilutive securities were converted into common shares.

Dilution An increase in the number of shares outstanding from share issuance that decreases the percentage of shares owned by existing shareholders.

Dimension reduction A set of techniques for reducing the number of features in a dataset while retaining variation across observations to preserve the information contained in that variation.

Diminishing marginal productivity When each additional unit of an input, keeping the other inputs unchanged, increases output by a smaller increment.

Direct capitalization method Valuation approach that estimates the value of an income-producing property using a discounted cash flow approach based on a single year's net operating income.

Discount To reduce the value of a future payment in allowance for how far away it is in time; to calculate the present value of some future amount. Also, the amount by which an instrument is priced below its face (par) value.

Discount factor The price equivalent of a zero rate. Also may be stated as the present value of a currency unit on a future date.

Discount for lack of control An amount or percentage deducted from the pro rata share of 100% of the value of an equity interest in a business to reflect the absence of some or all of the powers of control.

Discount for lack of marketability An amount of percentage deducted from the value of an ownership interest to reflect the relative absence of marketability.

Discount function Discount factors for the range of all possible maturities. The spot curve can be derived from the discount function and vice versa.

Discounted abnormal earnings model A model of stock valuation that views intrinsic value of stock as the sum of book value per share plus the present value of the stock's expected future residual income per share.

Discounted cash flow method A valuation method involving a series of income projections discounted to the present with a terminal value.

Discounted cash flow model A model of intrinsic value that views the value of an asset as the present value of the asset's expected future cash flows.

Dispersed ownership Ownership structure consisting of many shareholders, none of which has the ability to individually exercise control over the corporation.

Divestiture When a seller sells a company, segment of a company, or group of assets to an acquirer. Once complete, control of the target is transferred to the acquirer.

Dividend coverage ratio The ratio of net income to dividends.

Dividend discount model (DDM) The model of the value of stock that is the present value of all future dividends, discounted at the required return on equity.

Dividend displacement of earnings The concept that dividends paid now displace earnings in all future periods.

Dividend imputation tax system A taxation system that effectively assures corporate profits distributed as dividends are taxed just once and at the shareholder's tax rate.

Dividend index point A measure of the quantity of dividends attributable to a particular index.

Dividend payout ratio The ratio of cash dividends paid to earnings for a period.

Dividend policy The strategy a company follows with regard to the amount and timing of dividend payments.

Dividend rate The annualized amount of the most recent dividend.

Dividend recapitalization A change in the mix of debt and equity outstanding for an existing corporate issuer which increases leverage via debt-financed dividends or share repurchases to benefit existing shareholders.

Dividend yield Annual dividends per share divided by share price.

Dividends Distributions of profits and/or net assets from a corporation to its shareholders. While often in cash, dividends can be also be paid in stock or assets, such as property.

Divisive clustering A top-down hierarchical clustering method that starts with all observations belonging to a single large cluster. The observations are then divided into two clusters based on some measure of distance (similarity). The algorithm then progressively partitions the intermediate clusters into smaller ones until each cluster contains only one observation.

Document frequency (DF) The number of documents (texts) that contain a particular token divided by the total number of documents. It is the simplest feature selection method and often performs well when many thousands of tokens are present.

Document term matrix (DTM) A matrix where each row belongs to a document (or text file), and each column represents a token (or term). The number of rows is equal to the number of documents (or text files) in a sample text dataset. The number of columns is equal to the number of tokens from the BOW built using all the documents in the sample dataset. The cells typically contain the counts of the number of times a token is present in each document.

Dominance An arbitrage opportunity when a financial asset with a risk-free payoff in the future must have a positive price today.

Double taxation system Corporate earnings are taxed twice when paid out as dividends. First, corporate pretax earnings are taxed regardless of whether they will be distributed as dividends or retained at the corporate level. Second, dividends are taxed again at the individual shareholder level.

Downstream A transaction between two related companies, an investor company (or a parent company) and an associate company (or a subsidiary) such that the investor company records a profit on its income statement. An example is a sale of inventory by the investor company to the associate or by a parent to a subsidiary company.

Dual-class shares Shares that grant one share class superior or even sole voting rights, whereas the other share class has inferior or no voting rights.

Due diligence Investigation and analysis in support of an investment action, decision, or recommendation.

Dummy variable An independent variable that takes a value of either 1 or 0, depending on a specified condition. Also known as an *indicator variable*.

Duration The first-order, linear change in a bond's price for a given yield change in yield, which is a negative or inverse relationship.

Durbin–Watson (DW) test A test for the presence of first-order serial correlation.

Dutch disease A situation in which currency appreciation driven by strong export demand for resources makes other segments of the economy (particularly manufacturing) globally uncompetitive.

Earnings surprise The difference between reported EPS and expected EPS. Also referred to as *unexpected earnings*.

Earnings yield EPS divided by price; the reciprocal of the P/E.

Economic profit Equal to accounting profit less the implicit opportunity costs not included in total accounting costs; the difference between total revenue (TR) and total cost (TC). Also called *abnormal profit* or *supernormal profit*.

Economic sectors Large industry groupings.

Economic value added (EVA®) A commercial implementation of the residual income concept; the computation of EVA® is the net operating profit after taxes minus the cost of capital, where these inputs are adjusted for a number of items.

Edwards–Bell–Ohlson model A model of stock valuation that views intrinsic value of stock as the sum of book value per share plus the present value of the stock's expected future residual income per share.

Effective convexity An interest rate risk statistic that measures the non-linear/second-order effect of changes in the benchmark yield curve on a bond's price.

Effective duration The sensitivity of the bond's price to an instantaneous parallel shift in a benchmark yield curve—for example, the government par curve.

Effective gross income Gross rent plus other income minus deductions for vacancies or concessions.

Eigenvalue A measure that gives the proportion of total variance in the initial dataset that is explained by each eigenvector.

Eigenvector A vector that defines new mutually uncorrelated composite variables that are linear combinations of the original features.

Embedded options Contingency provisions found in a bond's indenture representing rights that enable their holders to take advantage of interest rate movements. They can be exercised by the issuer, by the bondholder, or automatically depending on the course of interest rates.

Ensemble learning A technique of combining the predictions from a collection of models to achieve a more accurate prediction.

Ensemble method The method of combining multiple learning algorithms, as in ensemble learning.

Enterprise value A measure of a company's total market value from which the value of cash and short-term investments have been subtracted.

Enterprise value multiple A valuation multiple that relates the total market value of all sources of a company's capital (net of cash) to a measure of fundamental value for the entire company (such as a pre-interest earnings measure).

Equity charge The estimated cost of equity capital in money terms.

Equity dividend rate Equityholder return that considers the first-year return on equity on an income-producing property involving the before-tax cash flow divided by the property purchase price less the mortgage loan outstanding.

Equity investment A company purchasing another company's equity but less than 50% of its shares. The two companies maintain their independence, but the investor company has investment exposure to the investee and, in some cases depending on the size of the investment, can have representation on the investee's board of directors to influence operations.

Equity REITs REITs that primarily own and operate properties and distribute dividends to shareholders.

Equity swap A swap transaction in which at least one cash flow is tied to the return to an equity portfolio position, often an equity index.

Error autocorrelations The autocorrelations of the error term.

ESG integration The inclusion of ESG considerations within financial analysis and investment decisions. This may be done in various ways, tailored to the investment style and approach of the fund manager.

***Ex ante* tracking error** A measure of the degree to which the performance of a given investment portfolio might be expected to deviate from its benchmark; also known as *relative VaR*.

***Ex ante* version of PPP** The hypothesis that expected changes in the spot exchange rate are equal to expected differences in national inflation rates. An extension of relative purchasing power parity to expected future changes in the exchange rate.

Ex-dividend Trading ex-dividend refers to shares that no longer carry the right to the next dividend payment.

Ex-dividend date The first date that a share trades without (i.e., "ex") the right to receive the declared dividend for the period.

Excess earnings method Income approach that estimates the value of all intangible assets of the business by capitalizing future earnings in excess of the estimated return requirements associated with working capital and fixed assets.

Excess tax benefit The amount by which the tax deduction associated with a share-based award exceeds the cumulative share-based compensation expense recognized in accordance with US GAAP or IFRS. Excess tax benefits occur when the value of a share-based award at settlement exceeds the value at the grant date.

Exercise value The value of an option if it were exercised. Also sometimes called *intrinsic value*.

Expanded CAPM An adaptation of the CAPM that adds to the CAPM a premium for small size and company-specific risk.

Expectations approach A procedure for obtaining the value of an option derived from discounting at the risk-free rate its expected future payoff based on risk neutral probabilities.

Expected exposure The projected amount of money an investor could lose if an event of default occurs, before factoring in possible recovery.

Expected shortfall The average loss conditional on exceeding the VaR cutoff; sometimes referred to as *conditional VaR* or *expected tail loss*.

Expected tail loss See *conditional VaR*.

Exploratory data analysis (EDA) The preliminary step in data exploration, where graphs, charts, and other visualizations (heat maps and word clouds) as well as quantitative methods (descriptive statistics and central tendency measures) are used to observe and summarize data.

Exposure to foreign exchange risk The risk of a change in value of an asset or liability denominated in a foreign currency due to a change in exchange rates.

Extendible bond Bond with an embedded option that gives the bondholder the right to keep the bond for a number of years after maturity, possibly with a different coupon.

Extension risk The risk of later repayment of a mortgage-backed security than expected.

Extra dividend A dividend paid by a company that does not pay dividends on a regular schedule, or a dividend that supplements regular cash dividends with an extra payment.

F1 score The harmonic mean of precision and recall. F1 score is a more appropriate overall performance metric (than accuracy) when there is unequal class distribution in the dataset and it is necessary to measure the equilibrium of precision and recall.

Factor A common or underlying element with which several variables are correlated.

Factor betas An asset's sensitivity to a particular factor; a measure of the response of return to each unit of increase in a factor, holding all other factors constant.

Factor portfolio See *pure factor portfolio*.

Factor price The expected return in excess of the risk-free rate for a portfolio with a sensitivity of 1 to one factor and a sensitivity of 0 to all other factors.

Factor risk premium The expected return in excess of the risk-free rate for a portfolio with a sensitivity of 1 to one factor and a sensitivity of 0 to all other factors. Also called *factor price*.

Factor risk premiums The expected return in excess of the risk-free rate for a portfolio with a sensitivity of 1 to one factor and a sensitivity of 0 to all other factors. Also called factor price.

Failure to pay When a borrower does not make a scheduled payment of principal or interest on any outstanding obligations after a grace period.

Fair market value The price, expressed in terms of cash equivalents, at which a property (asset) would change hands between a hypothetical willing and able buyer and a hypothetical willing and able seller, acting at "arm's length" in an open and unrestricted market, when neither is under compulsion to buy or sell and when both have reasonable knowledge of the relevant facts. Fair market value is most often used in a tax reporting context in the United States.

Fair value A market-based measure of an investment based on observable or derived assumptions to determine a price that market participants would use to exchange an asset or liability in an orderly transaction at a specific time.

Fama–French models Factor models that explain the drivers of returns related to three, four, or five factors.

Feature engineering A process of creating new features by changing or transforming existing features.

Feature selection A process whereby only pertinent features from the dataset are selected for model training. Selecting fewer features decreases model complexity and training time.

Features The independent variables (X's) in a labeled dataset.

Finance (or capital) lease A lease that is viewed as a financing arrangement.

Financial buyer An owner seeking to earn investment returns from an existing company without identifying or capitalizing on synergies from a controlling interest.

Financial leverage The use of debt in the capital structure. Measured using ratios such as operating income to operating income less interest expense, total assets to total equity, or debt to equity.

First-differencing A transformation that subtracts the value of the time series in period $t - 1$ from its value in period t.

First-order serial correlation The correlation of residuals with residuals adjacent in time.

Fitting curve A curve which shows in- and out-of-sample error rates (E_{in} and E_{out}) on the y-axis plotted against model complexity on the x-axis.

Fixed price tender offer Offer made by a company to repurchase a specific number of shares at a fixed price that is typically at a premium to the current market price.

Fixed-rate perpetual preferred stock Non-convertible, non-callable preferred stock with a specified dividend rate that has a claim on earnings senior to the claim of common stock, and no maturity date.

Flight to quality During times of market stress, investors sell higher-risk asset classes such as stocks and commodities in favor of default-risk-free government bonds.

Float Amounts collected as premium and not yet paid out as benefits.

Floored floater Floating-rate bond with a floor provision that prevents the coupon rate from decreasing below a specified minimum rate. It protects the investor against declining interest rates.

Flotation cost Fees charged to companies by investment bankers and other costs associated with raising new capital.

Forced conversion For a convertible bond, when the issuer calls the bond and forces bondholders to convert their bonds into shares, which typically happens when the underlying share price increases above the conversion price.

Foreign currency transactions Transactions that are denominated in a currency other than a company's functional currency.

Forward curve The term structure of forward rates for loans made on a specific initiation date.

Forward dividend yield A dividend yield based on the anticipated dividend during the next 12 months.

Forward P/E A P/E calculated on the basis of a forecast of EPS; a stock's current price divided by next year's expected earnings.

Forward price Represents the price agreed upon in a forward contract to be exchanged at the contract's maturity date, T. This price is shown in equations as $F_0(T)$.

Forward pricing model The model that describes the valuation of forward contracts.

Forward propagation The process of adjusting weights in a neural network, to reduce total error of the network, by moving forward through the network's layers.

Forward rate An interest rate determined today for a loan that will be initiated in a future period.

Forward rate agreement An over-the-counter forward contract in which the underlying is an interest rate on a deposit. A forward rate agreement (FRA) calls for one party to make a fixed interest payment and the other to make an interest payment at a rate to be determined at contract expiration.

Forward rate model The forward pricing model expressed in terms of spot and forward interest rates.

Forward rate parity The proposition that the forward exchange rate is an unbiased predictor of the future spot exchange rate.

Forward value The monetary value of an existing forward contract.

Forward-looking estimates Estimates based on current and expectations. Also referred to as ex ante estimates.

Franchising A situation where an owner of an asset and associated intellectual property divests the asset and licenses intellectual property to a third-party operator (franchisee) in exchange for royalties. Franchisees operate under the constraints of a franchise agreement.

Franking credit A tax credit received by shareholders for the taxes that a corporation paid on its distributed earnings.

Free cash flow to equity The cash flow available to a company's common shareholders after all operating expenses, interest, and principal payments have been made and necessary investments in working and fixed capital have been made.

Free cash flow to equity model A model of stock valuation that views a stock's intrinsic value as the present value of expected future free cash flows to equity.

Free cash flow to the firm The cash flow available to the company's suppliers of capital after all operating expenses (including taxes) have been paid and necessary investments in working and fixed capital have been made.

Free cash flow to the firm model A model of stock valuation that views the value of a firm as the present value of expected future free cash flows to the firm.

Frequency analysis The process of quantifying how important tokens are in a sentence and in the corpus as a whole. It helps in filtering unnecessary tokens (or features).

Frozen DB plan A DB plan that is no longer accruing benefits for employee service.

Fulcrum securities Partially-in-the-money claims (not expected to be repaid in full) whose holders end up owning the reorganized company in a corporate reorganization situation.

Functional currency The currency of the primary economic environment in which an entity operates.

Fund of funds Funds that hold a portfolio of hedge funds; also called *funds of hedge funds*.

Fundamental factor models A multifactor model in which the factors are attributes of stocks or companies that are important in explaining cross-sectional differences in stock prices.

Fundamentals Economic characteristics of a business, such as profitability, financial strength, and risk.

Funded status The present value of the DB obligation less the fair value of plan assets (if any).

Funds available for distribution See *adjusted funds from operations*.

Funds from operations Net income (computed in accordance with generally accepted accounting principles) *plus* (1) gains and losses from sales of properties and (2) depreciation and amortization.

Futures price The pre-agreed price at which a futures contract buyer (seller) agrees to pay (receive) for the underlying at the maturity date of the futures contract.

Futures value The monetary value of an existing futures contract.

FX carry trade An investment strategy that involves taking long positions in high-yield currencies and short positions in low-yield currencies.

Gamma A numerical measure of how sensitive an option's delta (the sensitivity of the derivative's price) is to a change in the value of the underlying.

General linear *F*-test A test statistic used to assess the goodness of fit for an entire regression model, so it tests all independent variables in the model.

Generalize When a model retains its explanatory power when predicting out-of-sample (i.e., using new data).

Global CAPM (GCAPM) A single-factor model with a global index representing the single factor.

Going-concern assumption The assumption that the business will maintain its business activities into the foreseeable future.

Going-concern value A business's value under a going-concern assumption.

Going-in cap rate The capitalization rate based on the first year of ownership used to discount the initial annual cash flow from a real estate property.

Goodwill An intangible asset that represents the excess of the purchase price of an acquired company over the value of the net identifiable assets acquired.

Gordon growth model A DDM that assumes dividends grow at a constant rate into the future.

Green bond Bonds in which the proceeds are designated by issuers to fund a specific project or portfolio of projects that have environmental or climate benefits.

Greenmail The purchase of the accumulated shares of a hostile investor by a company that is targeted for takeover by that investor, usually at a substantial premium over market price.

Greenwashing The risk that a green bond's proceeds are not actually used for a beneficial environmental or climate-related project.

Grid search A method of systematically training a model by using various combinations of hyperparameter values, cross validating each model, and determining which combination of hyperparameter values ensures the best model performance.

Gross domestic product The market value of all final goods and services produced within the economy during a given period (output definition) or, equivalently, the aggregate income earned by all households, all companies, and the government within the economy during a given period (income definition).

Gross potential rental income Equal to the current market rent of a property at full occupancy.

Gross rent The average lease or rental price realized per square foot multiplied by the total rentable space.

Ground truth The known outcome (i.e., target variable) of each observation in a labelled dataset.

Growth accounting equation The production function written in the form of growth rates. For the basic Cobb–Douglas production function, it states that the growth rate of output equals the rate of technological change plus α multiplied by the growth rate of capital plus $(1 - \alpha)$ multiplied by the growth rate of labor.

Guideline assets Assets used as benchmarks when applying the method of comparables to value an asset.

Guideline companies Assets used as benchmarks when applying the method of comparables to value an asset.

Guideline public companies Public-company comparables for the company being valued.

Guideline public company method A variation of the market approach; establishes a value estimate based on the observed multiples from trading activity in the shares of public companies viewed as reasonably comparable to the subject private company.

Guideline transactions method A variation of the market approach; establishes a value estimate based on pricing multiples derived from the acquisition of control of entire public or private companies that were acquired.

Hard-catalyst event-driven approach An event-driven approach in which investments are made in reaction to an already announced corporate event (mergers and acquisitions, bankruptcies, share issuances, buybacks, capital restructurings, re-organizations, accounting changes) in which security prices related to the event have yet to fully converge.

Harmonic mean A type of weighted mean computed as the reciprocal of the arithmetic average of the reciprocals.

Hazard rate The probability that an event will occur, given that it has not already occurred.

Hedonic index A real estate index that is not based on repeat sales of the same property but, rather, that controls for differences in property characteristics, such as size, age, quality of construction, and location, for the properties sold in each period.

Heteroskedastic When the variance of the residuals differs across observations in a regression.

Heteroskedasticity Non-constant variance across all observations.

Hierarchical clustering An iterative unsupervised learning procedure used for building a hierarchy of clusters.

High-leverage point An observation of an independent variable that has an extreme value and is potentially influential.

Historical exchange rates For accounting purposes, the exchange rates that existed when the assets and liabilities were initially recorded.

Historical scenario analysis A technique for exploring the performance and risk of investment strategies in different structural regimes.

Historical simulation A simulation method that uses past return data and a random number generator that picks observations from the historical series to simulate an asset's future returns.

Historical simulation method The application of historical price changes to the current portfolio.

Historical stress testing The process that tests how investment strategies would perform under some of the most negative (i.e., adverse) combinations of events and scenarios.

Holding period return The single-period internal rate of return for a real estate property that includes property income and the change in property value over the period.

Holdout samples Data samples that are not used to train a model.

Homoskedasticity Constant variance across all observations.

Horizontal ownership Companies with mutual business interests (e.g., key customers or suppliers) that have cross-holding share arrangements with each other.

Household formation An economic statistic which tracks the establishment of new residences as a group of people (or household) decide to live together, which increases housing demand.

Ho–Lee model The first arbitrage-free term structure model. The model is calibrated to market data and uses a binomial lattice approach to generate a distribution of possible future interest rates.

Human capital The present value of an individual's future expected labor income.

Hyperparameter A parameter whose value must be set by the researcher before learning begins.

I-spreads Shortened form of "interpolated spreads" and a reference to a linearly interpolated yield.

Illiquidity discount A reduction or discount to value that reflects the lack of depth of trading or liquidity in that asset's market.

Impairment Diminishment in value as a result of carrying (book) value exceeding fair value and/or recoverable value.

Impairment of capital rule A legal restriction that dividends cannot exceed retained earnings.

Implied volatility The volatility that option traders use to price an option, implied by the price of the option and a particular option-pricing model.

In-sample forecast errors The residuals from a fitted time-series model within the sample period used to fit the model.

iNAVs "Indicated" net asset values are intraday "fair value" estimates of an ETF share based on its creation basket.

Income approach A valuation approach that values an asset as the present discounted value of the income expected from it. In the context of real estate, this approach estimates the value of a property based on an expected rate of return. The estimated value is the present value of the expected future income from the property, including proceeds from resale at the end of a typical investment holding period.

Incremental borrowing rate (IBR) The rate of interest that the lessee would have to pay to borrow using a collateralized loan over the same term as a lease.

Incremental VaR (IVaR) A measure of the incremental effect of an asset on the VaR of a portfolio by measuring the difference between the portfolio's VaR while including a specified asset and the portfolio's VaR with that asset eliminated.

Indenture A written contract between a lender and borrower that specifies the terms of the loan, such as interest rate, interest payment schedule, or maturity.

Independent board directors Directors with no material relationship with the company with regard to employment, ownership, or remuneration.

Index CDS A type of credit default swap that involves a combination of borrowers.

Indexed rents Contractually agreed periodic rent changes based on an observed market variable, such as the consumer price index.

Industry risk premium (IP) The additional return that is required to bear industry -specific risk.

Industry shocks Unexpected changes to an industry from regulations or the legal environment, technology, or changes in the growth rate of the industry.

Industry structure An industry's underlying economic and technical characteristics.

Influential observation An observation in a statistical analysis whose inclusion may significantly alter regression results.

Information gain A metric which quantifies the amount of information that the feature holds about the response. Information gain can be regarded as a form of non-linear correlation between Y and X.

Information ratio The ratio of mean active return to standard deviation (active return).

Insiders Corporate managers and board directors who are also shareholders of a company.

Intangible assets Assets without a physical form, such as patents and trademarks.

Inter-temporal rate of substitution The ratio of the marginal utility of consumption *s* periods in the future (the numerator) to the marginal utility of consumption today (the denominator).

Interaction term A term that combines two or more independent variables and represents their joint influence on the dependent variable.

Intercept dummy An indicator variable that allows a single regression model to estimate two lines of best fit, each with differing intercepts, depending on whether the dummy takes a value of 1 or 0.

Interest rate risk The risk that interest rates will rise and therefore the market value of current portfolio holdings will fall so that their current yields to maturity then match comparable instruments in the marketplace.

Interlocking directorates Corporate structure in which individuals serve on the board of directors of multiple corporations.

International CAPM (ICAPM) A two-factor model with a global index and a wealth-weighted currency index.

International Fisher effect The proposition that nominal interest rate differentials across currencies are determined by expected inflation differentials.

Intrinsic value See *exercise value.*

Inverse price ratio The reciprocal of a price multiple—for example, in the case of a P/E, the "earnings yield" E/P (where P is share price and E is earnings per share).

Investment value The value to a specific buyer, taking account of potential synergies based on the investor's requirements and expectations.

ISDA Master Agreement A standard or "master" agreement published by the International Swaps and Derivatives Association. The master agreement establishes the terms for each party involved in the transaction.

Joint test of hypotheses The test of hypotheses that specify values for two or more independent variables in the hypotheses.

Joint venture Two or more companies form and control a new, separate company to achieve a business objective. Each participant contributes assets, employees, know-how, or other resources to the joint venture company. The participants maintain their independence otherwise and continue to do business apart from the joint venture, but they share in the joint venture's profits or losses.

Justified (fundamental) P/E The price-to-earnings ratio that is fair, warranted, or justified on the basis of forecasted fundamentals.

Justified price multiple The estimated fair value of the price multiple, usually based on forecasted fundamentals or comparables.

***K*-fold cross-validation** A technique in which data (excluding test sample and fresh data) are shuffled randomly and then are divided into k equal sub-samples, with $k - 1$ samples used as training samples and one sample, the kth, used as a validation sample.

***K*-means** A clustering algorithm that repeatedly partitions observations into a fixed number, k, of non-overlapping clusters.

***K*-nearest neighbor** A supervised learning technique that classifies a new observation by finding similarities ("nearness") between this new observation and the existing data.

Kalotay–Williams–Fabozzi (KWF) model An arbitrage-free term structure model that describes the dynamics of the log of the short rate and assumes constant drift, no mean reversion, and constant volatility.

Key rate durations Sensitivity of a bond's price to changes in specific maturities on the benchmark yield curve. Also called *partial durations.*

***k*th-order autocorrelation** The correlation between observations in a time series separated by k periods.

Labeled dataset A dataset that contains matched sets of observed inputs or features (X's) and the associated output or target (Y).

Labor force Everyone of working age (ages 16 to 64) who either is employed or is available for work but not working.

Labor force participation rate The percentage of the working age population that is in the labor force.

Labor productivity The quantity of real GDP produced by an hour of labor. More generally, output per unit of labor input.

Labor productivity growth accounting equation States that potential GDP growth equals the growth rate of the labor input plus the growth rate of labor productivity.

Lack of marketability discount An extra return to investors to compensate for lack of a public market or lack of marketability.

LASSO Least absolute shrinkage and selection operator is a type of penalized regression which involves minimizing the sum of the absolute values of the regression coefficients. LASSO can also be used for regularization in neural networks.

Law of one price A principle that states that if two investments have the same or equivalent future cash flows regardless of what will happen in the future, then these two investments should have the same current price.

Leading dividend yield Forecasted dividends per share over the next year divided by current stock price.

Leading P/E A P/E calculated on the basis of a forecast of EPS; a stock's current price divided by next year's expected earnings.

Learning curve A curve that plots the accuracy rate (= 1 – error rate) in the validation or test samples (i.e., out-of-sample) against the amount of data in the training sample, which is thus useful for describing under- and overfitting as a function of bias and variance errors.

Learning rate A parameter that affects the magnitude of adjustments in the weights in a neural network.

Lessee Tenant or property user that enters a lease with a property owner or lessor.

Lessor Property owner or manager that leases a property to a tenant or property user.

Level One of the three factors (the other two are steepness and curvature) that empirically explain most yield curve shape changes. A shock to the level factor changes the yield for all maturities by an almost identical amount.

Leverage A measure for identifying a potentially influential high-leverage point.

Leveraged buyout (LBO) A transaction in which a private acquiror uses equity and a high proportion of debt to acquire a public or private company in order to make changes to increase value over an investment period.

Libor–OIS spread The difference between Libor and the overnight indexed swap rate.

Life settlement The sale of a life insurance contract to a third party. The valuation of a life settlement typically requires detailed biometric analysis of the individual policyholder and an understanding of actuarial analysis.

Likelihood ratio (LR) test A method to assess the fit of logistic regression models that is based on the log-likelihood metric that describes the model's fit to the data.

Linear classifier A binary classifier that makes its classification decision based on a linear combination of the features of each data point.

Linear trend A trend in which the dependent variable changes at a constant rate with time.

Liquidating dividend A dividend that is a return of capital rather than a distribution from earnings or retained earnings.

Liquidation value The value of a company if the company were dissolved and its assets sold individually.

Liquidity preference theory A term structure theory that asserts liquidity premiums exist to compensate investors for the added interest rate risk they face when lending long term.

Liquidity premium The compensation for liquidity risk that increases in proportion to the investment's illiquidity.

Loan-to-value ratio A primary measure of leverage involving the ratio of mortgage principal outstanding to the property's current value.

Local currency The currency of the country where a company is located.

Local expectations theory A term structure theory that contends the return for all bonds over short periods is the risk-free rate.

Log odds The natural log of the odds of an event or characteristic happening. Also known as the *logit function*.

Log-linear model With reference to time-series models, a model in which the growth rate of the time series as a function of time is constant.

Logistic regression (logit) A regression in which the dependent variable uses a logistic transformation of the event probability.

Logistic transformation The log of the probability of an occurrence of an event or characteristic divided by the probability of the event or characteristic not occurring.

Long/short credit trade A credit protection seller with respect to one entity combined with a credit protection buyer with respect to another entity.

Look-ahead bias The bias created by using information that was unknown or unavailable in the time periods over which backtesting is conducted. Survivorship bias is a type of look-ahead bias.

Lookback period The time period used to gather a historical data set.

Loss given default The amount that will be lost if a default occurs.

Loss to lease The difference between rental rates on existing leases and current market rents.

Macroeconomic factor model A multifactor model in which the factors are surprises in macroeconomic variables that significantly explain equity returns.

Macroeconomic factors Factors related to the economy, such as the inflation rate, industrial production, or economic sector membership.

Majority shareholders Shareholders that own more than 50% of a corporation's shares.

Majority-vote classifier A classifier that assigns to a new data point the predicted label with the most votes (i.e., occurrences).

Marginal VaR (MVaR) A measure of the effect of a small change in a position size on portfolio VaR.

Market approach Valuation approach that values an asset based on pricing multiples from sales of assets viewed as similar to the subject asset.

Market condition A performance condition that is related to the market price (or value) of the entity's equity instruments such as attaining a specified share price or a specified target based on the market price (or value) of the entity's equity instruments relative to an index of market prices of other companies.

Market conditions Interest rates, inflation rates, and other economic characteristics that comprise the macroeconomic environment.

Market conversion premium per share For a convertible bond, the difference between the market conversion price and the underlying share price, which allows investors to identify the premium or discount payable when buying a convertible bond rather than the underlying common stock.

Market conversion premium ratio For a convertible bond, the market conversion premium per share expressed as a percentage of the current market price of the shares.

Market efficiency A finance perspective on capital markets that deals with the relationship of price to intrinsic value. The traditional efficient markets formulation asserts that an asset's price is the best available estimate of its intrinsic value. The rational efficient markets formulation asserts that investors should expect to be rewarded for the costs of information gathering and analysis by higher gross returns.

Market model A regression model with the return on a stock as the dependent variable and the returns on a market index as the independent variable.

Market value of invested capital The market value of debt and equity.

Mature growth rate The earnings growth rate in a company's mature phase; an earnings growth rate that can be sustained long term.

Maximum drawdown The worst cumulative loss ever sustained by an asset or portfolio. More specifically, maximum drawdown is the difference between an asset's or a portfolio's maximum cumulative return and its subsequent lowest cumulative return.

Maximum likelihood estimation (MLE) A method that estimates values for the intercept and slope coefficients in a logistic regression that make the data in the regression sample most likely.

Mean reversion The tendency of a time series to fall when its level is above its mean and rise when its level is below its mean; a mean-reverting time series tends to return to its long-term mean.

Metadata Data that describes and gives information about other data.

Method based on forecasted fundamentals An approach to using price multiples that relates a price multiple to forecasts of fundamentals through a discounted cash flow model.

Method of comparables An approach to valuation that involves using a price multiple to evaluate whether an asset is relatively fairly valued, relatively undervalued, or relatively overvalued when compared to a benchmark value of the multiple.

Minority interest The proportion of the ownership of a subsidiary not held by the parent (controlling) company.

Minority shareholders Particular shareholders or a block of shareholders holding a small proportion of a company's outstanding shares, resulting in a limited ability to exercise control in voting activities.

Mispricing Any departure of the market price of an asset from the asset's estimated intrinsic value.

Mixed-use development Commercial real estate properties that combine more than one tenant type and economic use.

Model specification The set of independent variables included in a model and the model's functional form.

Molodovsky effect The observation that P/Es tend to be high on depressed EPS at the bottom of a business cycle and tend to be low on unusually high EPS at the top of a business cycle.

Momentum indicators Valuation indicators that relate either price or a fundamental (such as earnings) to the time series of their own past values (or in some cases to their expected value).

Monetary assets and liabilities Assets and liabilities with value equal to the amount of currency contracted for, a fixed amount of currency. Examples are cash, accounts receivable, accounts payable, bonds payable, and mortgages payable. Inventory is not a monetary asset. Most liabilities are monetary.

Monetary/non-monetary method Approach to translating foreign currency financial statements for consolidation in which monetary assets and liabilities are translated at the current exchange rate. Non-monetary assets and liabilities are translated at historical exchange rates (the exchange rates that existed when the assets and liabilities were acquired).

Monetizing Unwinding a position to either capture a gain or realize a loss.

Monte Carlo simulation A technique that uses the inverse transformation method for converting a randomly generated uniformly distributed number into a simulated value of a random variable of a desired distribution. Each key decision variable in a Monte Carlo simulation requires an assumed statistical distribution; this assumption facilitates incorporating non-normality, fat tails, and tail dependence as well as solving high-dimensionality problems.

Multi-class trading An equity market-neutral strategy that capitalizes on misalignment in prices and involves buying and selling different classes of shares of the same company, such as voting and non-voting shares.

Multi-manager fund Can be of two types—one is a multi-strategy fund in which teams of portfolio managers trade and invest in multiple different strategies within the same fund; the second type is a fund of hedge funds (or fund-of-funds) in which the manager allocates capital to separate, underlying hedge funds that themselves run a range of different strategies.

Multi-strategy fund A fund in which teams of portfolio managers trade and invest in multiple different strategies within the same fund.

Multicollinearity When two or more independent variables are highly correlated with one another or are approximately linearly related.

Multiple linear regression Modeling and estimation method that uses two or more independent variables to describe the variation of the dependent variable. Also referred to as *multiple regression*.

Mutual information Measures how much information is contributed by a token to a class of texts. MI will be 0 if the token's distribution in all text classes is the same. MI approaches 1 as the token in any one class tends to occur more often in only that particular class of text.

N-grams A representation of word sequences. The length of a sequence varies from 1 to n. When one word is used, it is a unigram; a two-word sequence is a bigram; and a 3-word sequence is a trigram; and so on.

***n*-Period moving average** The average of the current and immediately prior $n - 1$ values of a time series.

Naked credit default swap A position where the owner of the CDS does not have a position in the underlying credit.

Name entity recognition An algorithm that analyzes individual tokens and their surrounding semantics while referring to its dictionary to tag an object class to the token.

Negative serial correlation A situation in which residuals are negatively related to other residuals.

Nested models Models in which one regression model has a subset of the independent variables of another regression model.

Net asset balance sheet exposure When assets translated at the current exchange rate are greater in amount than liabilities translated at the current exchange rate. Assets exposed to translation gains or losses exceed the exposed liabilities.

Net asset value per share Net asset value divided by the number of shares outstanding.

Net liability balance sheet exposure When liabilities translated at the current exchange rate are greater assets translated at the current exchange rate. Liabilities exposed to translation gains or losses exceed the exposed assets.

Net operating income A commonly used measure of income-producing property returns prior to the inclusion of financing costs or income taxes.

Network externalities The impact that users of a good, a service, or a technology have on other users of that product; it can be positive (e.g., a critical mass of users makes a product more useful) or negative (e.g., congestion makes the product less useful).

Neural networks A type of computer program design based on how the human brain learns and processes information.

No-arbitrage approach A procedure for obtaining the value of an option based on the creation of a portfolio that replicates the payoffs of the option and deriving the option value from the value of the replicating portfolio.

No-growth company A company without positive expected net present value projects.

No-growth value per share The value per share of a no-growth company, equal to the expected level amount of earnings divided by the stock's required rate of return.

Non-cash rent An amount equal to the difference between the average contractual rent over a lease term (the straight-line rent) and the cash rent actually paid during a period. This figure is one of the deductions made from FFO to calculate AFFO.

Non-convergence trap A situation in which a country remains relatively poor, or even falls further behind, because it fails to implement necessary institutional reforms and/or adopt leading technologies.

Non-monetary assets and liabilities Assets and liabilities that are not monetary assets and liabilities. Non-monetary assets include inventory, fixed assets, and intangibles, and non-monetary liabilities include deferred revenue.

Non-renewable resources Finite resources that are depleted once they are consumed; oil and coal are examples.

Nonearning assets Cash and investments (specifically cash, cash equivalents, and short-term investments).

Normal EPS The EPS that a business could achieve currently under mid-cyclical conditions. Also called *normalized EPS*.

Normal Q-Q plot A visual used to compare the distribution of the residuals from a regression to a theoretical normal distribution.

Normalized earnings The expected level of mid-cycle earnings for a company in the absence of any unusual or temporary factors that affect profitability (either positively or negatively).

Normalized EPS The EPS that a business could achieve currently under mid-cyclical conditions. Also called *normal EPS*.

Normalized P/E P/E based on normalized EPS data.

Notional amount The amount of protection being purchased in a CDS.

NTM P/E Next 12-month P/E: current market price divided by an estimated next 12-month EPS.

Off-the-run Seasoned government bonds that are often less liquid.

Offshoring Refers to relocating operations from one country to another, mainly to reduce costs through lower labor costs or to achieve economies of scale through centralization, but still maintaining operations within the corporation.

Omitted variable bias Bias resulting from the omission of an important independent variable from a regression model.

On-the-run Most recently issued, and liquid, government bonds.

One hot encoding The process by which categorical variables are converted into binary form (0 or 1) for machine reading. It is one of the most common methods for handling categorical features in text data.

One-sided durations Effective durations when interest rates go up or down, which are better at capturing the interest rate sensitivity of bonds with embedded options that do not react symmetrically to positive and negative changes in interest rates of the same magnitude.

One-tier board Board structure consisting of a single board of directors, composed of executive (internal) and non-executive (external) directors.

Opportunistic real estate Real estate investments primarily in commercial and/or residential properties involving major redevelopment, repurposing of assets, taking on large vacancies, or speculating on significant improvement in market conditions.

Opportunity cost Reflects the foregone opportunity of investing in a different asset. It is typically denoted by the risk-free rate of interest, r.

Option-adjusted spread Or OAS for a bond is its Z-spread adjusted for the value of an embedded option.

Orderly liquidation value The estimated gross amount of money that could be realized from the liquidation sale of an asset or assets, given a reasonable amount of time to find a purchaser or purchasers.

Other comprehensive income Changes to equity that bypass (are not reported in) the income statement; the difference between comprehensive income and net income.

Other post-employment benefits (OPEB) DB post-employment benefit plans other than plans that pay cash retirement benefits (e.g., retiree medical care benefit plans).

Out-of-sample forecast errors The differences between actual and predicted values of time series outside the sample period used to fit the model.

Outlier An observation that has an extreme value of the dependent variable and is potentially influential.

Outsourcing Shifting internal business services to a subcontractor that can offer services at lower costs by scaling to serve many clients.

Overage rent Contractual sale-based rental adjustments that result in higher rent if a tenant's sales exceed a pre-agreed minimum target.

Overfitting When a machine learning model learns the input and target dataset too precisely, making the system more likely to discover false relationships or unsubstantiated patterns that will lead to prediction errors.

Overfunded plan A DB plan with a positive funded status; the present value of the DB obligation is less than the fair value of plan assets.

Overnight indexed swap (OIS) rate An interest rate swap in which the periodic floating rate of the swap equals the geometric average of a daily unsecured overnight rate (or overnight index rate).

Pairs trading An equity market-neutral strategy that capitalizes on the misalignment in prices of pairs of similar under- and overvalued equities. The expectation is the differential valuations or trading relationships will revert to their long-term mean values or their fundamentally-correct trading relationships, with the long position rising and the short position declining in value.

Par curve A hypothetical yield curve for coupon-paying Treasury securities that assumes all securities are priced at par.

Par swap A swap in which the fixed rate is set so that no money is exchanged at contract initiation.

Parametric method A method of estimating VaR that uses the historical mean, standard deviation, and correlation of security price movements to estimate the portfolio VaR. Generally assumes a normal distribution but can be adapted to non-normal distributions with the addition of skewness and kurtosis. Sometimes called the *variance–covariance method* or the *analytical method*.

Partial regression coefficient Coefficient that describes the effect of a one-unit change in the independent variable on the dependent variable, holding all other independent variables constant. Also known as *partial slope coefficient*.

Parts of speech An algorithm that uses language structure and dictionaries to tag every token in the text with a corresponding part of speech (i.e., noun, verb, adjective, proper noun, etc.).

Payout amount The loss given default times the notional.

Payout policy The principles by which a company distributes cash to common shareholders by means of cash dividends and/or share repurchases.

Payouts Cash dividends and the value of shares repurchased in any given year.

PEG ratio The P/E-to-growth ratio, calculated as the stock's P/E divided by the expected earnings growth rate.

Penalized regression A regression that includes a constraint such that the regression coefficients are chosen to minimize the sum of squared residuals *plus* a penalty term that increases in size with the number of included features.

Pension obligation The present value, without deducting any plan assets, of expected future payments required to settle the obligation resulting from employee service in the current and prior periods.

Perfect capital markets Markets in which, by assumption, there are no taxes, no transaction costs, and no bankruptcy costs and in which all investors have equal ("symmetric") information.

Performance condition A vesting condition comprising a service condition and the meeting of a specified performance target during the service period. A performance target is typically defined as an accounting measure or a market condition.

Performance shares Shares used in a share-based compensation arrangement that have performance-based vesting conditions.

Perpetuity A perpetual annuity, or a set of never-ending level sequential cash flows, with the first cash flow occurring one period from now.

Persistent earnings Earnings excluding nonrecurring components. Also referred to as *core earnings, continuing earnings,* or *underlying earnings.*

Physical settlement Involves actual delivery of the debt instrument in exchange for a payment by the credit protection seller of the notional amount of the contract.

Point-in-time data Data consisting of the exact information available to market participants as of a given point in time. Point-in-time data is used to address look-ahead bias.

Portfolio balance approach A theory of exchange rate determination that emphasizes the portfolio investment decisions of global investors and the requirement that global investors willingly hold all outstanding securities denominated in each currency at prevailing prices and exchange rates.

Positive serial correlation A situation in which residuals are positively related to other residuals.

Potential GDP The maximum amount of output an economy can sustainably produce without inducing an increase in the inflation rate. The output level that corresponds to full employment with consistent wage and price expectations.

Precision In error analysis for classification problems it is ratio of correctly predicted positive classes to all predicted positive classes. Precision is useful in situations where the cost of false positives (FP), or Type I error, is high.

Preferred habitat theory A term structure theory that contends that investors have maturity preferences and require yield incentives before they will buy bonds outside of their preferred maturities.

Premium leg The series of payments the credit protection buyer promises to make to the credit protection seller.

Premiums Amounts paid by the purchaser of insurance products.

Prepayment risk The risk that the some or all of a mortgage-backed security's principal is repaid at a different speed than expected, either in the form of contraction risk (or earlier repayment than expected) or extension risk (later repayment).

Present value model A model of intrinsic value that views the value of an asset as the present value of the asset's expected future cash flows.

Present value of growth opportunities The difference between the actual value per share and the no-growth value per share. Also called *value of growth.*

Presentation currency The currency in which financial statement amounts are presented.

Price momentum A valuation indicator based on past price movement.

Price multiples The ratio of a stock's market price to some measure of value per share.

Price-to-earnings ratio (P/E) The ratio of share price to earnings per share.

Priced risk Risk for which investors demand compensation for bearing (e.g., equity risk, company-specific factors, macroeconomic factors).

Principal components analysis (PCA) An unsupervised ML technique used to transform highly correlated features of data into a few main, uncorrelated composite variables.

Principle of no arbitrage In well-functioning markets, prices will adjust until there are no arbitrage opportunities.

Prior transaction method A variation of the market approach; considers actual transactions in the stock of the subject private company.

Private market value The value derived using a sum-of-the-parts valuation.

Pro forma financial statements Financial statements that include the effect of a corporate restructuring.

Probability of default The likelihood that a borrower defaults or fails to meet its obligation to make full and timely payments of principal and interest.

Probability of survival The probability that a bond issuer will meet its contractual obligations on schedule.

Projection error The vertical (perpendicular) distance between a data point and a given principal component.

Property classes A relative ranking of properties based on a combination of features such as location, property age, local income levels, recent property appreciation, and relative condition.

Property maintenance allowance Expenses incurred to maintain a property's current level of income generation.

Prospective P/E A P/E calculated on the basis of a forecast of EPS; a stock's current price divided by next year's expected earnings.

Protection leg The contingent payment that the credit protection seller may have to make to the credit protection buyer.

Protection period Period during which a bond's issuer cannot call the bond.

Provision for loan losses An income statement expense account that increases the amount of the allowance for loan losses.

Pruning A regularization technique used in CART to reduce the size of the classification or regression tree—by pruning, or removing, sections of the tree that provide little classifying power.

Purchasing power gain A gain in value caused by changes in price levels. Monetary liabilities experience purchasing power gains during periods of inflation.

Purchasing power loss A loss in value caused by changes in price levels. Monetary assets experience purchasing power loss during periods of inflation.

Purchasing power parity (PPP) The idea that exchange rates move to equalize the purchasing power of different currencies.

Pure expectations theory A term structure theory that contends the forward rate is an unbiased predictor of the future spot rate. Also called the *unbiased expectations theory.*

Pure factor portfolio A portfolio with sensitivity of 1 to the factor in question and a sensitivity of 0 to all other factors.

Putable bond Bond that includes an embedded put option, which gives the bondholder the right to put back the bonds to the issuer prior to maturity, typically when interest rates have risen and higher-yielding bonds are available.

Qualitative dependent variable A dependent variable that is discrete (binary). Also known as a *categorical dependent variable.*

Quality of earnings analysis The investigation of issues relating to the accuracy of reported accounting results as reflections of economic performance. Quality of earnings analysis is broadly understood to include not only earnings management but also balance sheet management.

Quantitative market-neutral An approach to building market-neutral portfolios in which large numbers of securities are traded and positions are adjusted on a daily or even an hourly basis using algorithm-based models.

Random forest classifier A collection of a large number of decision trees trained via a bagging method.

Random walk A time series in which the value of the series in one period is the value of the series in the previous period plus an unpredictable random error.

Rate implicit in the lease (RIIL) The discount rate that equates the present value of the lease payment with the fair value of the leased asset, considering also the lessor's direct costs and the present value of the leased asset's residual value.

Rational efficient markets formulation See *market efficiency.*

Readme files Text files provided with raw data that contain information related to a data file. They are useful for understanding the data and how they can be interpreted correctly.

Real estate cycle Phases of recovery, expansion, oversupply, and recession that combine short-term adjustments in lease rates and occupancy in response to changing market conditions.

Real estate investment trusts Investment vehicles that directly own and operate real estate properties or debt investments and distribute dividends and other income to shareholders.

Real estate operating companies Corporate issuers whose primary activity is in the construction, development, operation, and servicing of real estate.

Real interest rate parity The proposition that real interest rates will converge to the same level across different markets.

Real options Refers to the right but not the obligation to take future action. The existence of such options may affect the value of a real estate investment.

Rebalance return A return from rebalancing the component weights of an index.

Recall Also known as *sensitivity,* in error analysis for classification problems it is the ratio of correctly predicted positive classes to all actual positive classes. Recall is useful in situations where the cost of false negatives (FN), or Type II error, is high.

Recency bias The behavioral tendency to place more relevance on recent events.

Reconstitution When dealers recombine appropriate individual zero-coupon securities and reproduce an underlying coupon Treasury.

Recovery rate The percentage of the loss recovered.

Redemption basket The list of securities (and share amounts) the authorized participant (AP) receives when it redeems ETF shares back to the ETF manager. The redemption basket is published each business day.

Reference entity The borrower (debt issuer) covered by a single-name CDS.

Reference obligation A particular debt instrument issued by the borrower that is the designated instrument being covered.

Regime The governing set of relationships (between variables) that stem from technological, political, legal, and regulatory environments. Changes in such environments or policy stances can be described as changes in regime.

Regular expression (regex) A series of texts that contains characters in a particular order. Regex is used to search for patterns of interest in a given text.

Regularization A term that describes methods for reducing statistical variability in high-dimensional data estimation problems.

Reinforcement learning Machine learning in which a computer learns from interacting with itself or data generated by the same algorithm.

Reinvestment rate A company's rate of investment in working capital and long-term assets necessary to maintain operations and support assumed growth.

Related-party transactions A business transaction between parties which share economic or other interests and may not take place at fair market value.

Relative valuation models A model that specifies an asset's value relative to the value of another asset.

Relative value volatility arbitrage A volatility trading strategy that aims to source and buy cheap volatility and sell more expensive volatility while netting out the time decay aspects normally associated with options portfolios.

Relative VaR The minimum portfolio loss expected to occur over a given time period at a specific confidence level based on a portfolio containing active positions minus benchmark holdings.

Relative version of PPP The hypothesis that changes in (nominal) exchange rates over time are equal to national inflation rate differentials.

Relative-strength indicators Valuation indicators that compare a stock's performance during a period either to its own past performance or to the performance of some group of stocks.

Renewable resources Resources that can be replenished, such as a forest.

Rental price of capital The cost per unit of time to rent a unit of capital.

Reorganization A court-supervised restructuring process available in some jurisdictions for companies facing insolvency from burdensome debt levels. A bankruptcy court assumes control of the company and oversees an orderly negotiation process between the company and its creditors for asset sales, conversion of debt to equity, refinancing, and so on.

Repeat sales index A real estate price index that relies on multiple sales of the same property.

Replacement cost Estimate of expenses associated with purchasing land and building a new property on a site with the same features and economic use as a property being appraised.

Required rate of return on equity The minimum rate of return required by an investor to invest in an asset, given the asset's riskiness. Also known as the required return on equity.

Residual autocorrelations The sample autocorrelations of the residuals.

Residual income Earnings for a given period, minus a deduction for common shareholders' opportunity cost in generating the earnings. Also called *economic profit* or *abnormal earnings.*

Residual income model (RIM) A model of stock valuation that views intrinsic value of stock as the sum of book value per share plus the present value of the stock's expected future residual income per share. Also called *discounted abnormal earnings model* or *Edwards–Bell–Ohlson model.*

Restricted model A regression model with a subset of the complete set of independent variables.

Restricted stock A share with selling or other restrictions, commonly used in share-based compensation arrangements with employees.

Restricted stock units (RSUs) An instrument used in share-based compensation plans that represents the right to receive a common share upon vesting. RSUs are not tradeable, nor do they have voting rights or participate in dividends.

Restructuring Reorganizing the capital structure of a firm.

Return on invested capital A measure of the profitability of a company relative to the amount of capital invested by the equity- and debtholders.

Reverse carry arbitrage A strategy involving the short sale of the underlying and an offsetting opposite position in the derivative.

Reverse stock split A reduction in the number of shares outstanding with a corresponding increase in share price but no change to the company's underlying fundamentals.

Reverse stress testing A risk management approach in which the user identifies key risk exposures in the portfolio and subjects those exposures to extreme market movements.

Reviewed financial statements A type of non-audited financial statements; typically provide an opinion letter with representations and assurances by the reviewing accountant that are less than those in audited financial statements.

Rho The change in a given derivative instrument for a given small change in the risk-free interest rate, holding everything else constant. Rho measures the sensitivity of the option to the risk-free interest rate.

Risk budgeting The establishment of objectives for individuals, groups, or divisions of an organization that takes into account the allocation of an acceptable level of risk.

Risk decomposition The process of converting a set of holdings in a portfolio into a set of exposures to risk factors.

Risk factors Variables or characteristics with which individual asset returns are correlated. Sometimes referred to simply as *factors.*

Risk parity A portfolio allocation scheme that weights stocks or factors based on an equal risk contribution.

Risk-based models Models of the return on equity that identify risk factors or drivers and sensitivities of the return to these factors.

Risk-free rate The minimum rate of return expected on a security that has no default risk.

Robust standard errors Method for correcting residuals for conditional heteroskedasticity. Also known as *heteroskedasticity-consistent standard errors* or *White-corrected standard errors.*

Roll When an investor moves its investment position from an older series to the most current series.

Roll return The component of the return on a commodity futures contract attributable to rolling long futures positions forward through time. Also called *roll yield.*

Rolling down the yield curve A maturity trading strategy that involves buying bonds with a maturity longer than the intended investment horizon. Also called *riding the yield curve.*

Rolling windows A backtesting method that uses a rolling-window (or walk-forward) framework, rebalances the portfolio after each period, and then tracks performance over time. As new information arrives each period, the investment manager optimizes (revises and tunes) the model and readjusts stock positions.

Rollover risk The likelihood that a property owner will lose an existing tenant and forgo income until a new one is found.

Root mean squared error (RMSE) The square root of the average squared forecast error; used to compare the out-of-sample forecasting performance of forecasting models.

Sale-leaseback A situation in which a company sells the building it owns and occupies to a real estate investor and the company then signs a long-term lease with the buyer to continue to occupy the building. At the end of the lease, use of the property reverts to the landlord.

Sales comparison approach Real estate valuation approach that considers the price at which similar or comparable properties (comparables) are purchased and sold in the current market; also referred to as the *market approach.*

Sales risk The uncertainty regarding the price and number of units sold of a company's products.

Scaled earnings surprise Unexpected earnings divided by the standard deviation of analysts' earnings forecasts.

Scaling The process of adjusting the range of a feature by shifting and changing the scale of the data. Two of the most common ways of scaling are normalization and standardization.

Scatterplot matrix A visualization technique that shows the scatterplots between different sets of variables, often with the histogram for each variable on the diagonal. Also referred to as a *pairs plot.*

Schwarz's Bayesian information criterion (BIC or SBC) A statistic used to compare sets of independent variables for explaining a dependent variable. It is preferred for finding the model with the best goodness of fit.

Scree plots A plot that shows the proportion of total variance in the data explained by each principal component.

Screening The application of a set of criteria to reduce a set of potential investments to a smaller set having certain desired characteristics.

Seasonality A characteristic of a time series in which the data experience regular and predictable periodic changes; for example, fan sales are highest during the summer months.

Secured overnight financing rate (SOFR) A daily volume-weighted index of rates on qualified cash borrowings collateralized by US Treasuries that is expected to replace Libor as a floating reference rate for swaps.

Security selection risk See *active specific risk.*

Segmented markets theory A term structure theory that contends yields are solely a function of the supply and demand for funds of a particular maturity.

Sell-side analysts Analysts who work at brokerages.

Sensitivity analysis A form of analysis used to determine the impact of a change in one or more key variables affecting investment returns or valuation.

Sentence length The number of characters, including spaces, in a sentence.

Serial correlation A condition found most often in time series in which residuals are correlated across observations. Also known as *autocorrelation.*

Serial-correlation consistent standard errors Method for correcting serial correlation. Also known as *serial correlation and heteroskedasticity adjusted standard errors, Newey–West standard errors,* and *robust standard errors.*

Service condition A vesting condition that requires the employee to complete a period of service provision to the employer. A service condition does not require a performance target to be met.

Settled in arrears An arrangement in which the interest payment is made (i.e., settlement occurs) at the maturity of the underlying instrument.

Settlement The closing date at which the counterparties of a derivative contract exchange payment for the underlying as required by the contract.

Shadow banking Lending by financial institutions that are not regulated as banks.

Shaping risk The sensitivity of a bond's price to the changing shape of the yield curve.

Share repurchase A transaction in which a company buys back its own shares. Unlike stock dividends and stock splits, share repurchases use corporate cash.

Shareholder activism A range of actions by a corporation's shareholders that are intended to result in some change in the corporation, typically a change in the board of directors, management, or business strategy.

Shareholders' equity Assets less liabilities; the residual interest in the assets after subtracting the liabilities.

Short biased These strategies use quantitative, technical, and fundamental analysis to short overvalued equity securities with limited or no long-side exposures.

Simulation A technique for exploring how a target variable (e.g. portfolio returns) would perform in a hypothetical environment specified by the user, rather than a historical setting.

Single-manager fund A fund in which one portfolio manager or team of portfolio managers invests in one strategy or style.

Single-name CDS Credit default swap on one specific borrower.

Sinking fund bond A bond that requires the issuer to set aside funds over time to retire the bond issue, thus reducing credit risk.

Size premium (SP) Additional return compensation for bearing the additional risk associated with smaller companies.

Slope dummy An indicator variable that allows a single regression model to estimate two lines of best fit, each with differing slopes, depending on whether the dummy takes a value of 1 or 0.

Soft margin classification An adaptation in the support vector machine algorithm which adds a penalty to the objective function for observations in the training set that are misclassified.

Soft-catalyst event-driven approach An event-driven approach in which investments are made proactively in anticipation of a corporate event (mergers and acquisitions, bankruptcies, share issuances, buybacks, capital restructurings, re-organizations, accounting changes) that has yet to occur.

Sovereign yield spread The spread between the yield on a foreign country's sovereign bond and a similar-maturity domestic sovereign bond.

Special dividend A dividend paid by a company that does not pay dividends on a regular schedule, or a dividend that supplements regular cash dividends with an extra payment.

Specific-company risk premium (SCRP) Additional return required by investors for bearing non-diversifiable company-specific risk.

Spin off When a company separates a distinct part of its business into a new, independent company. The term is used to describe both the transaction and the separated component, while the company that conducts the transaction and formerly owned the spin off is known as the parent.

Split-rate tax system In reference to corporate taxes, a split-rate system taxes earnings to be distributed as dividends at a different rate than earnings to be retained. Corporate profits distributed as dividends are taxed at a lower rate than those retained in the business.

Spot curve Yields-to-maturity on a series of default-risk-free zero-coupon bonds.

Spot price The current price of an asset or security. For commodities, the current price to deliver a physical commodity to a specific location or purchase and transport it away from a designated location.

Spot rate The interest rate that is determined today for a risk-free, single-unit payment at a specified future date.

Spot yield curve The term structure of spot rates for loans made today.

Stabilized NOI Normalized or expected long-term level of net operating income level used to value real estate properties.

Stable dividend policy A policy in which regular dividends are paid that reflect long-run expected earnings. In contrast to a constant dividend payout ratio policy, a stable dividend policy does not reflect short-term volatility in earnings.

Standardized beta With reference to fundamental factor models, the value of the attribute for an asset minus the average value of the attribute across all stocks, divided by the standard deviation of the attribute across all stocks.

Standardized unexpected earnings Unexpected earnings per share divided by the standard deviation of unexpected earnings per share over a specified prior time period.

Statistical factor model A multifactor model in which statistical methods are applied to a set of historical returns to determine portfolios that best explain either historical return covariances or variances.

Steady-state rate of growth The constant growth rate of output (or output per capita) that can or will be sustained indefinitely once it is reached. Key ratios, such as the capital–output ratio, are constant on the steady-state growth path.

Steepness The difference between long-term and short-term yields that constitutes one of the three factors (the other two are level and curvature) that empirically explain most of the changes in the shape of the yield curve.

Step-up clauses Pre-specified contractual future rent increases.

Stock dividend A type of dividend in which a company distributes additional shares of its common stock to shareholders instead of cash.

Stop-loss limit Constraint used in risk management that requires a reduction in the size of a portfolio, or its complete liquidation, when a loss of a particular size occurs in a specified period.

Straight bond An underlying option-free bond with a specified issuer, issue date, maturity date, principal amount and repayment structure, coupon rate and payment structure, and currency denomination.

Straight debt Debt with no embedded options.

Straight voting A shareholder voting process in which shareholders receive one vote for each share owned.

Straight-line rent The average annual rent under a multi-year lease agreement that contains contractual increases in rent during the life of the lease.

Straight-line rent adjustment See *non-cash rent*.

Stranded assets A resource that is no longer economically valuable owing to changes in demand, regulations, or availability of substitutes—for example, a newly discovered oil well that will not be brought into production.

Strategic buyer An investor seeking to capitalize on synergies by extending the value creation process initiated by a GP, combining a business with another portfolio company, or taking other actions to increase firm value.

Stress tests A risk management technique that assesses the portfolio's response to extreme market movements.

Stripping A dealer's ability to separate a bond's individual cash flows and trade them as zero-coupon securities.

Stub trading An equity market-neutral strategy that capitalizes on misalignment in prices and entails buying and selling stock of a parent company and its subsidiaries, typically weighted by the percentage ownership of the parent company in the subsidiaries.

Studentized deleted residual A deleted residual divided by its estimated standard deviation.

Studentized residuals t-distributed statistics that are used to detect outliers.

Subject property A real estate property that is being appraised.

Succession event A change of corporate structure of the reference entity, such as through a merger, a divestiture, a spinoff, or any similar action, in which ultimate responsibility for the debt in question is unclear.

Sum-of-the-parts valuation A valuation approach that considers the value of a firm's business segments if they are sold separately.

Summation operator A functional part of a neural network's node that multiplies each input value received by a weight and sums the weighted values to form the total net input, which is then passed to the activation function.

Supernormal growth Above-average or abnormally high growth rate in earnings per share.

Supervised learning A type of machine learning in which the system attempts to learn to model relationships based on labeled training data.

Support vector machine A linear classifier that determines the hyperplane that optimally separates the observations into two sets of data points.

Survivorship bias Relates to the inclusion of only current investment funds in a database. As such, the returns of funds that are no longer available in the marketplace (have been liquidated) are excluded from the database. Also see *backfill bias*.

Sustainable growth rate The rate of dividend (and earnings) growth that can be sustained over time for a given level of return on equity, keeping the capital structure constant and without issuing additional common stock.

Swap curve The term structure of swap rates.

Swap rate The fixed rate to be paid by the fixed-rate payer specified in a swap contract.

Swap rate curve The term structure of swap rates.

Swap spread The difference between the fixed rate on an interest rate swap and the rate on a Treasury note with equivalent maturity; it reflects the general level of credit risk in the market.

Synergies The combination of two companies being more valuable than the sum of the parts. Generally, synergies take the form of lower costs ("cost synergies") or increased revenues ("revenue synergies") through combinations that generate lower costs or higher revenues, respectively.

Systematic risk Risk that affects the entire market or economy; it cannot be avoided and is inherent in the overall market. Systematic risk is also known as *non-diversifiable* or *market risk*.

Tail risk The possibility of extreme losses.

Takeover premium The amount by which the per-share takeover price exceeds the unaffected price expressed as a percentage of the unaffected price. It reflects the amount shareholders require to relinquish their control of the company to the acquirer.

Tangible assets Identifiable, physical assets such as property, plant, and equipment.

Tangible book value per share Common shareholders' equity minus intangible assets reported on the balance sheet, divided by the number of shares outstanding.

Target In machine learning, the dependent variable (Y) in a labeled dataset; the company in a merger or acquisition that is being acquired.

Target capital structure Management's desired proportions of debt and equity financing, usually stated on a book value basis or indirectly using a financial leverage metric, such as net or gross debt to EBITDA or credit rating.

Target payout ratio A strategic corporate goal representing the long-term proportion of earnings that the company intends to distribute to shareholders as dividends.

Taxable REIT subsidiaries Subsidiaries that pay income taxes on earnings from non-REIT-qualifying activities, such as merchant development or third-party property management.

Technical indicators Momentum indicators based on price.

TED spread A measure of perceived credit risk determined as the difference between Libor and the T-bill yield of matching maturity.

Temporal method A variation of the monetary/non-monetary translation method that requires not only monetary assets and liabilities, but also non-monetary assets and liabilities that are measured at their current value on the balance sheet date to be translated at the current exchange rate. Assets and liabilities are translated at rates consistent with the timing of their measurement value. This method is typically used when the functional currency is other than the local currency.

Term frequency (TF) Ratio of the number of times a given token occurs in all the texts in the dataset to the total number of tokens in the dataset.

Term premium The additional return required by lenders to invest in a bond to maturity net of the expected return from continually reinvesting at the short-term rate over that same time horizon.

Terminal cap rate Capitalization rate for a real estate property used to discount a final projected NOI that typically incorporates a constant future growth rate.

Terminal price multiples The price multiple for a stock assumed to hold at a stated future time.

Terminal share price The share price at a particular point in the future.

Terminal value of the stock The analyst's estimate of a stock's value at a particular point in the future. Also called *continuing value of the stock*.

Test sample A data sample that is used to test a model's ability to predict well on new data.

Theta The change in a derivative instrument for a given small change in calendar time, holding everything else constant. Specifically, the theta calculation assumes nothing changes except calendar time. Theta also reflects the rate at which an option's time value decays.

Time series A set of observations on a variable's outcomes in different time periods.

Time-series momentum A managed futures trend following strategy in which managers go long assets that are rising in price and go short assets that are falling in price. The manager trades on an absolute basis, so be net long or net short depending on the current price trend of an asset. This approach works best when an asset's own past returns are a good predictor of its future returns.

Tobin's *q* The ratio of the market value of debt and equity to the replacement cost of total assets.

Token The equivalent of a word (or sometimes a character).

Tokenization The process of representing ownership rights to physical assets on a blockchain or distributed ledger.

Total factor productivity (TFP) A multiplicative scale factor that reflects the general level of productivity or technology in the economy. Changes in total factor productivity generate proportional changes in output for any input combination.

Total invested capital The sum of market value of common equity, book value of preferred equity, and face value of debt.

Tracking error The standard deviation of the differences between a portfolio's returns and its benchmark's returns; a synonym of active risk.

Tracking risk The standard deviation of the differences between a portfolio's returns and its benchmarks returns. Also called *tracking error*.

Trailing dividend yield The reciprocal of current market price divided by the most recent annualized dividend.

Trailing P/E A stock's current market price divided by the most recent four quarters of EPS (or the most recent two semi-annual periods for companies that report interim data semi-annually). Also called *current P/E*.

Training sample A data sample that is used to train a model.

Tranche CDS A type of credit default swap that covers a combination of borrowers but only up to pre-specified levels of losses.

Transaction exposure The risk of a change in value between the transaction date and the settlement date of an asset of liability denominated in a foreign currency.

Treasury shares/stock Shares that were issued and subsequently repurchased by the company.

Trend A long-term pattern of movement in a particular direction.

Triangular arbitrage An arbitrage transaction involving three currencies that attempts to exploit inconsistencies among pairwise exchange rates.

Trimming Also called truncation, it is the process of removing extreme values and outliers from a dataset.

Two-tier board Board structure consisting of a supervisory board that oversees a management board.

Unbiased expectations theory A term structure theory that contends the forward rate is an unbiased predictor of the future spot rate. Also called the *pure expectations theory*.

Unconditional heteroskedasticity When heteroskedasticity of the error variance is not correlated with the regression's independent variables.

Uncovered interest rate parity The proposition that the expected return on an uncovered (i.e., unhedged) foreign currency (risk-free) investment should equal the return on a comparable domestic currency investment.

Underfunded plan A DB plan with a negative funded status; the present value of the DB obligation is greater than the fair value of plan assets.

Underlying earnings Earnings excluding nonrecurring components. Also referred to as *continuing earnings*, *core earnings*, or *persistent earnings*.

Unexpected earnings The difference between reported EPS and expected EPS. Also referred to as an *earnings surprise*.

Unfunded Post-employment plans for which the sponsor has not set aside assets to pay benefits. Benefits for unfunded plans are paid from company cash

Unit root A time series that is not covariance stationary is said to have a unit root.

Units of comparison Measure used to compare the current market value of real estate properties, such as purchase price per square meter or square foot of leasable area or total area.

Unrestricted model A regression model with the complete set of independent variables.

Unsupervised learning A type of machine learning in which the system tries to learn the structure of unlabeled data.

Upfront payment The difference between the credit spread and the standard rate paid by the protection buyer if the standard rate is insufficient to compensate the protection seller. Also called *upfront premium*.

Upfront premium See *upfront payment*.

Upstream A transaction between two related companies, an investor company (or a parent company) and an associate company (or a subsidiary company) such that the associate company records a profit on its income statement. An example is a sale of inventory by the associate to the investor company or by a subsidiary to a parent company.

Validation sample A data sample that is used to validate and tune a model.

Valuation The process of determining the value of an asset or service either on the basis of variables perceived to be related to future investment returns or on the basis of comparisons with closely similar assets.

Value additivity An arbitrage opportunity when the value of the whole equals the sum of the values of the parts.

Value at risk (VaR) The minimum loss that would be expected a certain percentage of the time over a certain period of time given the assumed market conditions.

Value of growth The difference between the actual value per share and the no-growth value per share.

Variance error Describes how much a model's results change in response to new data from validation and test samples. Unstable models pick up noise and produce high variance error, causing overfitting and high out-of-sample error.

Variance inflation factor (VIF) A statistic that quantifies the degree of multicollinearity in a model.

Vasicek model A partial equilibrium term structure model that assumes interest rates are mean reverting and interest rate volatility is constant.

Vega A measure of the sensitivity of an option's price to changes in the underlying's volatility.

Vertical ownership Ownership structure in which a company or group that has a controlling interest in two or more holding companies, which in turn have controlling interests in various operating companies.

Vesting The process of an employee becoming unconditionally entitled to, and an employer becoming obligated to pay, compensation.

Visibility The extent to which a company's operations are predictable with substantial confidence.

Voting caps Legal restrictions on the voting rights of large share positions.

Web spidering (scraping or crawling) programs Programs that extract raw content from a source, typically web pages.

Weighted average cost of capital (WACC) The expected cost of debt and equity weighted by the proportion of each used in a company's capital structure.

Weighted harmonic mean See *harmonic mean*.

Winsorization The process of replacing extreme values and outliers in a dataset with the maximum (for large value outliers) and minimum (for small value outliers) values of data points that are not outliers.

Write-down A reduction in the value of an asset as stated in the balance sheet.

Yield curve factor model A model or a description of yield curve movements that can be considered realistic when compared with historical data.

Zero A bond that does not pay a coupon but is priced at a discount and pays its full face value at maturity.

Zero-coupon bonds Bonds that do not pay interest during their life. They are issued at a discount to par value and redeemed at par. Also called pure discount bond.